THE ARCHAEOLOGY
OF MEDIEVAL NOVGOROD
IN CONTEXT

STUDIES IN CENTRE/PERIPHERY RELATIONS

THE ARCHAEOLOGY OF MEDIEVAL NOVGOROD

SERIES PREFACE

Novgorod is one of the most intensively and continuously studied urban sites in northern Europe. Systematic excavations began in 1932 and have continued almost every year since then. The excellent preservation of organic and inorganic material in its anaerobic soils, including the structural remains of streets, properties and buildings, has made it possible to study entire quarters of the town as well as the activities of its inhabitants. With deposits up to 8 m deep in places and with well-dated sequences from the early to mid 10th century, its importance to the study of both medieval Russia and the development of Europe cannot be over emphasized. In addition, excavations have recovered many examples of the organic remains normally lost to archaeologists, including a stunning collection of birch bark letters, unique written documents of the medieval period, which now number over a thousand separate inscriptions. Because of this the site has received attention from scholars with a wide range of specialisms from differing fields including medieval archaeology, history, architecture, botany, zoology and linguistics.

This publication series presents some of the recent results obtained from international, multidisciplinary projects supported by various European universities and institutions into the origins and development of the medieval town and its hinterland. With the support of EU funding via INTAS (the International Association for the Promotion of Scientific Collaboration between the EU and former Soviet Union countries), a number of projects were initiated which have used the Novgorod area as a test bed for wider issues concerning urban origins, town-hinterland relationships, environmental analyses, trade connections, accurate chronologies, innovative artefact studies, and the development of accounting systems and the spread of written language.

These publications are the outcome of collaborative projects that have their origins in the mid 1990s when funding was obtained from INTAS to set up an international collaboration into aspects of medieval towns and their hinterlands in NW Russia. Most of the field work took place from 1993 to 2004 in and around Novgorod, but includes material from other key sites in the area such as Ryurik Gorodishche, Staraya Russa, Pskov and sites, such as Minino, in the Byeloozero region on the northern margin of the territory of Novgorod (a territory that comprised the city's own medieval state, known as Novgorod Lands, which at its height covered an area larger than modern day France).

The volumes in this series cover some of the topics currently being investigated by the Novgorod Archaeological Research Centre with the support of INTAS-funded projects and focus on the following aspects of medieval Novgorod and its region:

- The pottery from medieval Novgorod and its region (published 2006)
- Wood use in medieval Novgorod (published 2007)
- Animals and archaeology in northern medieval Russia: zooarchaeological studies in Novgorod, Gorodishche and Minino (forthcoming)
- The archaeology of Novgorod in its wider context: a study of the town, its hinterland and its territory (this volume)

The first two volumes contain papers on key materials, namely pottery and wooden artefacts. Whilst elsewhere throughout Europe pottery tends to take the lion's share of attention and wood less so, partially due to its lack of survival, in Novgorod this position is reversed. Wood survives in abundance and what's more it was used prolifically for artefacts, fuel, buildings, fences, and even streets, making it the key means of dating site levels by extensive use of dendrochronology. As pottery has never been relied on for dating purposes, its typological and scientific study has lagged behind ceramic studies in Western Europe. For this reason the pottery volume in this series has attempted to set out some preliminary findings as well as discussing differences in methodology, sampling and analysis.

It is the intention that the third volume in this series on zooarchaeological aspects of recent work in Novgorod and the Novgorod Lands will follow on from those on pottery and wood to raise issues to do with recording, sample selection, methodology, and the integration of animal studies into the social and economic context (for example the fur trade and butchery practices), as well as discussing the differences and similarities in the material from the town, its hinterland and its wider territory.

Turning to this particular volume, it was the intention from its inception that this work would include papers by both Russian and non-Russian specialists on aspects of the environmental and technological context of the relationship between urban centre and rural hinterland. This was always going to be a tall order with so much data in most areas, yet little systematic study of key materials such as pollen, animal bones, plant remains, insects, leather, and pottery. Inevitably there were essential matters to deal with first, such as sampling strategies and methodologies, something which is widely acknowledged in many of the papers contained in this volume. In this sense, this collection of papers is best viewed as a starting point for attempting to put Novgorod into a wider context. It does certainly not claim to be definitive, far from it. But if it serves to begin and extend discussion of these issues and brings some of the enormous wealth of evidence to a wider audience, then it will have succeeded.

As to the structure of this volume, it begins by examining the environmental context for the settlement pattern that developed from the 9th to 15th centuries and examining the role that various natural resources had in contributing to that pattern. After a general paper on the natural environment based on a recent palynological study commissioned as part of this project, it presents data from three study areas (the first in the Byeloozero area to the NE of Novgorod; the second in the immediate hinterland of Novgorod and the third within Novgorod itself). It will consider what, where and how certain natural resources were exploited during the medieval period in these areas. Where possible, it will also attempt to explain the processes by which these resources were produced as commodities (via craft production, centralised workshops, household production, specialised settlements, etc) and place the evidence from the three other volumes on ceramics, wood use and zooarchaeology into a wider context, concentrating on the exploitation, manufacture and consumption of these and other materials.

Mark Brisbane
Bournemouth

THE ARCHAEOLOGY OF MEDIEVAL NOVGOROD IN CONTEXT

Studies in centre/periphery relations

Edited by

Mark A. Brisbane, Nikolaj A. Makarov
and Evgenij N. Nosov

*With Russian translations
by Katharine Judelson*

OXBOW BOOKS

Published by
Oxbow Books, Oxford, UK

ISBN 978-1-84217-278-0

Front cover: 'Novgorod Marketplace', a painting by Appolinarii M. Vasnetsov (1856–1933). Reproduced by kind permission of The State Tretyakov Gallery (Moscow) and The Novgorod State Museum.

This book is available direct from

Oxbow Books, Oxford, UK
(Tel: 01865 241249 Fax: 01865 794449)

and

The David Brown Books Company
PO Box 511, Oakville, CT 06779, USA
(Phone: 860-945-9329; Fax: 860-945-9468)

or from our website

www.oxbowbooks.com

A CIP record for this book is available from the British Library

Library of Congress Cataloging-in-Publication Data

The archaeology of medieval Novgorod in context : studies in centre/periphery relations / edited by Mark A. Brisbane, Nikolaj A. Makarov and Evgen. N. Nosov ; with Russian translations by Katharine Judelson.
   pages : illustrations ; cm. + 1 CD-ROM -- (Archaeology of medieval Novgorod ; v. 4)
  Includes an accompanying CD with supporting data.
  Includes bibliographical references and index.
  ISBN 978-1-84217-278-0
1. Velikii Novgorod (Russia)--Antiquities. 2. Excavations (Archaeology)--Russia (Federation)--Velikii Novgorod. 3. Cities and towns, Medieval--Russia. 4. Manufacturing industries--Russia (Federation)--Velikii Novgorod. 5. Palynology--Russia (Federation)--Velikii Novgorod. I. Brisbane, Mark. II. Makarov, N. A. (Nikolai Andreevich) III. Nosov, E. N. IV. Judelson, Katherine. V. Series: Archaeology of medieval Novgorod ; v. 4.
  DK651.N506A74 2012
  947'.22--dc23
                          2011050182

Printed in Great Britain by
Short Run Press, Exeter

CONTENTS

CONTENTS

CONTENTS

CD-ROM (INSIDE BACK COVER)
Index to CD-ROM

Ch. 2 Spiridonova & Aleshinskaya:
Pollen diagrams for all profiles studied
Micro-photographs of pollen grains
Notes on present day vegetation in the Lake Ilmen area

Ch. 5 Zaitseva:
Table of results from analyses of copper alloy objects

Ch. 7 Zakharov:
List of references to unpublished archives used in this chapter

Ch. 8 Yeremeyev:
Details of the nine areas in the Lake Ilmen area considered within the chapter

Ch. 16 Reilly:
Photographs and identifications of insect remains
Species list for all samples from Troitsky XI, XII and XIII, Novgorod

Ch. 17 Monk & Johnston:
Plant remains tables
List of samples analysed
List of taxa found with common names

Ch. 18 Alsleben:
Supporting tables: plant species from sites studied

LIST OF ILLUSTRATIONS

LIST OF ILLUSTRATIONS

LIST OF ILLUSTRATIONS

LIST OF TABLES

EDITORS' PREFACE

The material in this volume, which is the fruit of collaborative research involving Russian and western European archaeologists in the framework of projects funded by INTAS, and initiated and co-ordinated by Mark Brisbane, has made it possible to bring together studies of medieval urbanization and the settlement of rural territories. It addresses specific questions raised by research aimed at piecing together economic activity and production in both towns and a range of rural settlements. Collectively the papers shed light on many aspects of the medieval economy and the cultural landscape of the northern part of Eastern Europe, which had not previously been the object of close study. In addition, they attempt to achieve a more profound and integrated interpretation of Novgorod's economic base and its utilization of resources from the centre and margins of its territory, in the development of its economy and general prosperity.

None of this study would have been possible without the dedicated research and investigation undertaken by the Novgorod Archaeological Research Centre, supported by the Novgorod State Museum, the Dept of Archaeology of Moscow State University, the Institute of Archaeology (Moscow), and the Institute for the History of Material Culture (St Petersburg). Their achievements in conducting large-scale, open-area excavations continuously since the late 1940s, as well as an excavation pedigree stretching back to 1932, has extended the rich data base for this site to such an extent that they can justifiably claim to have created one of the largest archives and collections on a medieval European city and its hinterland. Through various INTAS-supported projects (Brisbane 2001) it has been possible to bring together specialists from other parts of Europe to work collaboratively on this material.

After an introductory chapter which attempts to sketch out the historical and geographical context of the Novgorod Lands, the volume moves on to a paper by Spiridonova and Aleshinskaya presenting readers with the results of their palaeo-botanical research carried out in two historically significant micro-regions: (a) the area around Lake Ilmen near the fortified settlement of Ryurik Gorodishche and (b) the area around Lake Kubenskoye, where the Minino settlements have been identified and excavated. This palynological research has made it possible to piece together a detailed picture of the landscape in the two areas, at the time when settlements were being founded, and has also shown that subsequent changes in the vegetation and natural environment were determined to a significant extent by the impact of human activity. Comparisons of ranges of palynological materials from similar periods show that the emergence of an agrarian landscape around Lake Ilmen began 200 years earlier than it did in the area around Lake Kubenskoye. The results also show that the banks of the River Volkhov near the place where it emerges from Lake Ilmen,

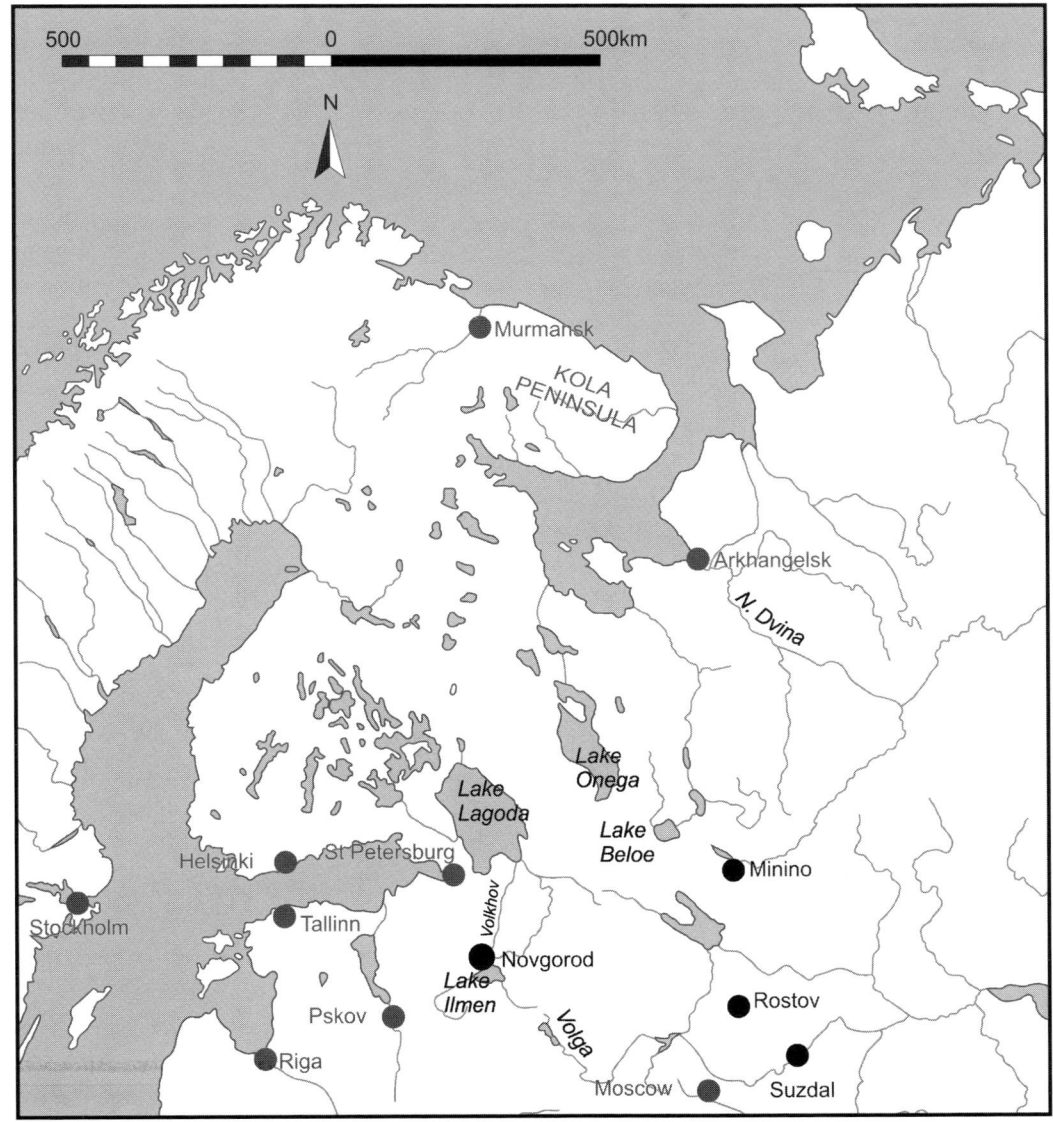

Figure 1 *Map showing the location of Novgorod, Lake Ilmen, Minino on Lake Kubenskoye in the Byeloozero region and other places for location purposes. Drawn by John Hodgson and Mark Dover.*

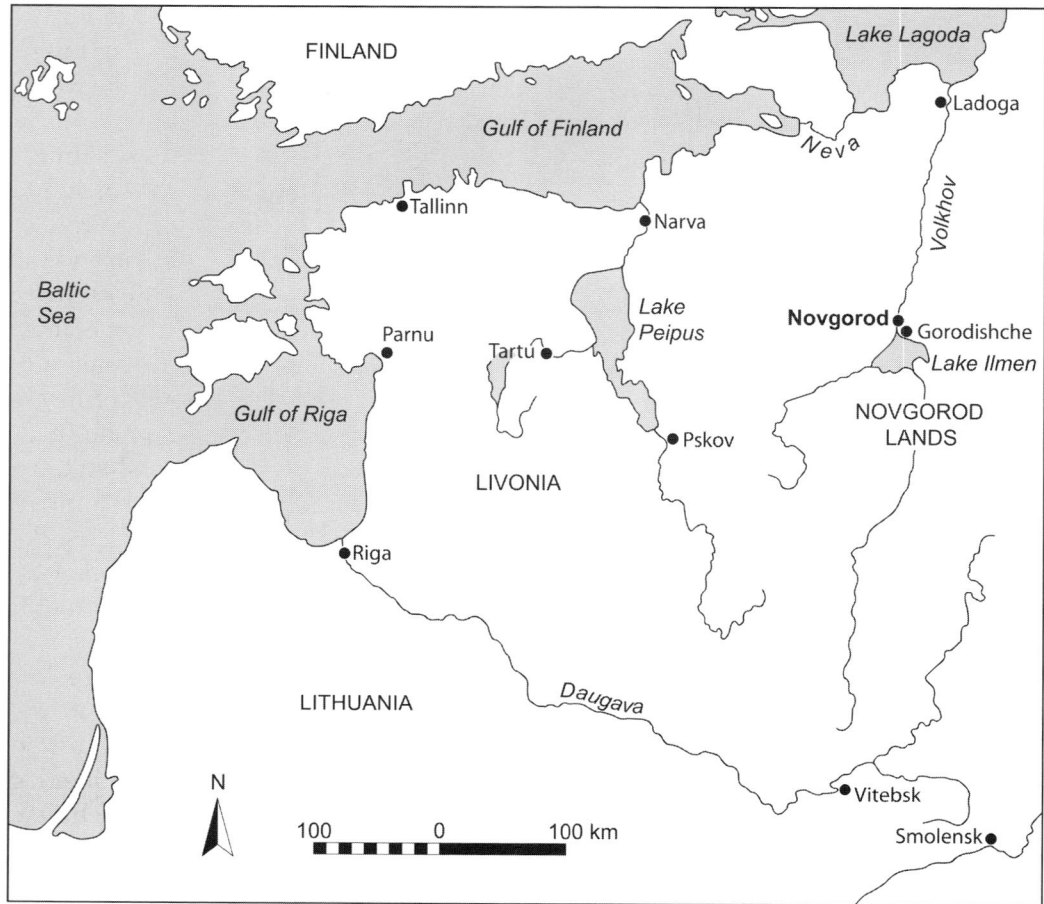

Figure 2 *Map showing the location of Novgorod and Gorodishche. Drawn by John Hodgson.*

constituted a semi-open landscape, in which woods alternated with meadows, in contrast to the wooded landscape around Lake Kubenskoye.

Five chapters are devoted to the archaeological materials from the Minino Archaeological Complex on the shores of Lake Kubenskoye, which was investigated by a team of archaeologists led by Makarov. This area can be seen as a model of a rural micro-region in the northern margins of medieval Russia. Strictly speaking, this area lies just beyond the confines of the Novgorod Lands, but as has been demonstrated by the artefacts found there, the settlements around Lake Kubenskoye were closely linked both economically and culturally with North-Western Russia in the 11th and early-12th centuries. The extremely thorough study of the medieval settlements and burial grounds in the Minino micro-region makes it possible to piece together a detailed picture of the economy, culture, commodity exchange and palaeo-environmental aspects of the colonization of that region. These sites are of key importance for the interpretation of relations between centre and periphery, and the influence of towns and international trade on the economy and culture of remote rural areas in the North of Russia (see various papers in Makarov 2007 and 2009).

Four chapters are devoted to Ryurik Gorodishche and the area around Lake Ilmen, which formed the original nucleus of the Novgorod Lands and were later to constitute the nearest resource base for the enormous medieval city of Novgorod. The role of Ryurik Gorodishche, as the earliest urban centre in the vicinity of Lake Ilmen, and the precursor of Novgorod, has been convincingly expounded by Nosov (1990). Features of medieval settlement in the area around Lake Ilmen, the culture of the early medieval settlements and the way in which agriculture was developed in this area have already been examined in detail (Nosov 1991: 5–37; 1992: 5–65). The chapter by Yeremeyev published here attempts to create a comprehensive map of Early Slavonic sites near Lake Ilmen, and to analyse the natural conditions encountered by the inhabitants of those settlements. The research also endeavours to identify separate rural micro-regions and to single out the main historical-geographical patterns underlying the settlement of that territory at the end of the first millennium AD. The chapter by Khvoshchinskaya examines jewellery production at Ryurik Gorodishche and other settlements near Lake Ilmen. The author demonstrates that although jewellery was being made in other settlements as well, the main centre for its manufacture was Ryurik Gorodishche, where craftsmen were making jewellery of both Slavonic and Scandinavian types and setting standards for a new material culture in the area around Lake Ilmen from the late 8th century onwards. The chapter by Toropov examines for the first time the evidence of iron production in the settlements around Lake Ilmen, which are important for any evaluation of the economic potential of the environs of Novgorod in the 10th to 13th centuries.

Six chapters are devoted to palaeo-environmental materials and the remains of production from Novgorod, which shed light on the consumption and economic activity of its citizens. Research into the leather articles, remains of textiles, household articles made of wood and metal slags found in the city enables us to appreciate Novgorod as a centre of craft production and consumption, which required a wide range of raw materials and resources to be able to produce such an enormous amount of craft articles. Clarification of the specific origins of various raw materials and completed craft articles, which made their way to Novgorod, is an interesting research subject, on which work has so far only just begun.

The final seven chapters are integrative papers which look at various materials. The first of these by Alsleben concerns plant remains, specifically domesticated cereals from Novgorod's hinterland and from the sites around Minino. This paper should be compared to the study from Novgorod by Monk and Johnston who have made tremendous inroads into the abundant material from the town. There is also a group of papers on the zooarchaeological remains summarised by Maltby (for a full account of this material see Volume 3 in this series), the fur trade by Makarov and the leather-

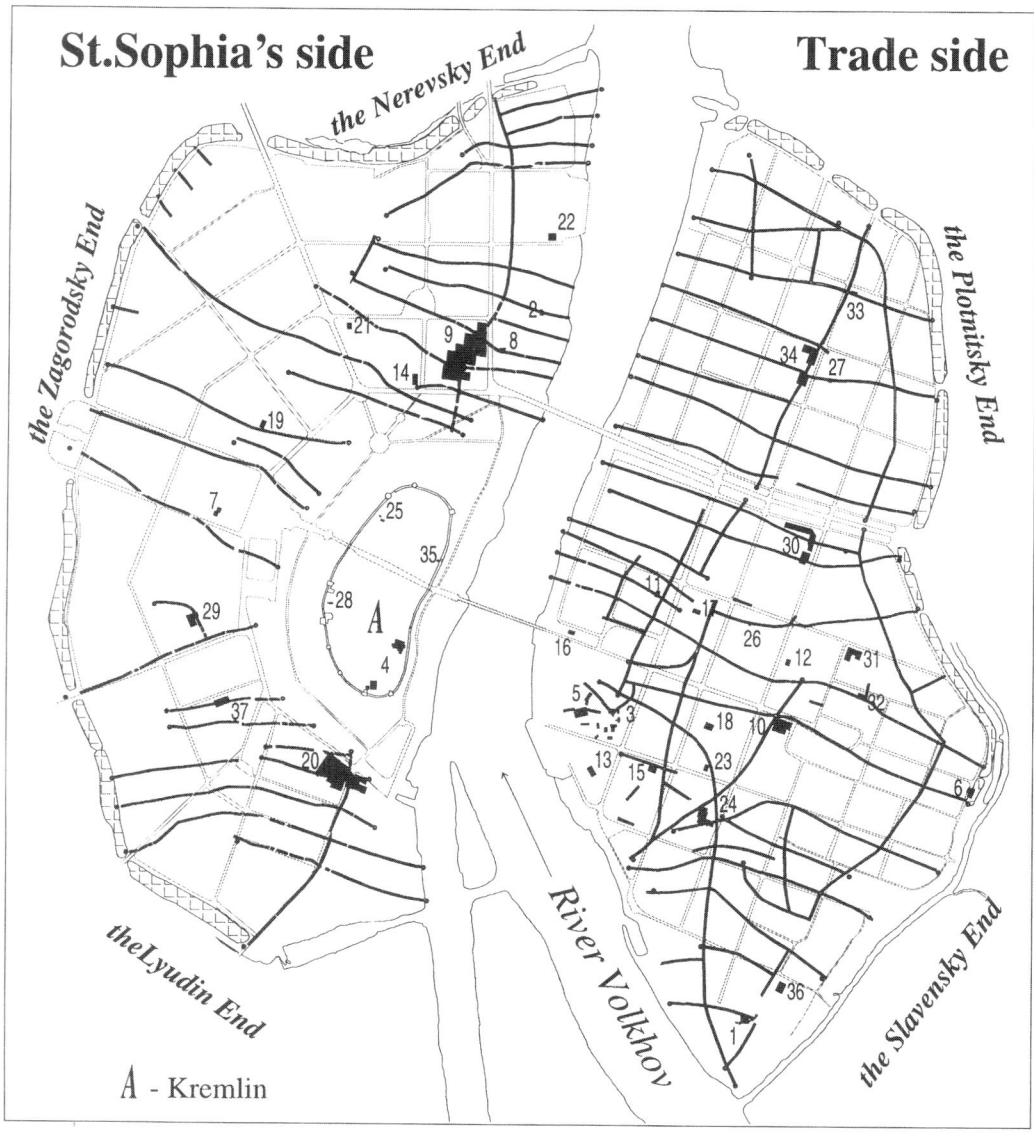

The sites are numbered in the order they were excavated and are as follows: 1 - on Slavensky Hill.
2 - on Borkovaya Street. 3 + 5 - in Yaroslav's Court. 4, 25, 28 + 35 - in the Kremlin.
6 - on the eastern rampart. 7 - on Chudintsevaya Street. 8 - on Kholopya Street. 9 - Nerevsky.
10 - Ilyinsky. 11 - Buyany. 12 - Slavensky. 13 - Gotsky. 14 - Tikhvinsky. 15 - Mikhailovsky.
16 - Torgovy. 17 - Rogatitsky. 18 - Kirovsky. 19 - Lyudogoshchinsky. 20 - Troitsky.
21 - Kosmodemyansky. 22 - Dmitrievsky. 23 - Duboshin. 24 - Nutny. 26 - on Bolshevikov Street.
27 - Molotkovsky. 29 - Mikhailo-Arkhangelsky. 30 - Fedorovsky. 31 - Ipatevsky. 32 - Lukinsky.
33 - Konyukhov. 34 - Andreevsky. 36 - Polsolsky. 37 - Dobrynin.

Figure 3 *Plan of Novgorod showing the five Ends (Districts), the ramparts (cross-hatched), the street layout (known medieval streets in black and modern grid pattern dotted), and the location of excavations undertaken from 1932 to 2001. Based on plans supplied by the Novgorod State Museum. North is to the top.*

working industry by Kurbatov, which taken together offer some significant insights into the way in which animals were exploited during this period. There can be little doubt of the importance of the fur trade to the economic success of Novgorod, but these studies show a wider context for a range of economically vital animal products and attempt to move towards a holistic study of these resources.

There follows two papers on pottery and specialisation. The first of these by Brorsson examines some of the local and foreign influences in the ceramic tradition of NW Russia in this period, while the second by Orton is a fresh look at the concept of specialisation applied to the rather conservative styles of medieval Novgorodian pottery. The final chapter by Rybina presents the evidence for craft production contained within the famous birch-bark documents of Novgorod. These stunning documents now total over 1000 individual finds from excavations within the city and are an invaluable source of information on this and many other topics.

EDITORS' ACKNOWLEDGEMENTS

The studies published in this book were funded as part of three projects co-ordinated by Bournemouth University and funded by INTAS from 1993–1996 (INTAS 93-463), 1997–2000 (INTAS 96-099), and 2001–2004 (INTAS 2000-154). The fieldwork was also assisted by grants from the Societies of Antiquaries of London, UCL Institute of Archaeology Grants Sub-Committee, the School of Conservation Sciences of Bournemouth University, and from the Russian side by several grants from the Russian Humanitarian Scientific Fund. All of the Russian texts in this volume were translated by Katharine Judelson, to whom the editors owe a special debt of gratitude for her commitment to these projects over many years. In total she translated 14 contributions (Chapters 2–10, 14–15, 20–21 and 24). We would also like to thank Mike Allen for his advice and assistance with Chapter Two, Sue Vaughan for compiling the index, and the anonymous referees for their comments and advice during the final stages of the preparation of this volume. Finally, we would like to acknowledge and thank Clare Litt, Julie Gardner and Julie Blackmore of Oxbow Books and Mark Dover of Bournemouth University for their assistance.

Mark Brisbane would also like to acknowledge and thank his family (Tye, Alice and Anna) who lived with these Novgorodian projects and publications for over 20 years, putting up with fatherly absences and neglected familial duties far more than they should have. Their support was much appreciated and I am greatly indebted to all three of them. I would also like to thank a corps of devoted supporters, especially Mark Maltby, Mick Monk, Jon Hather, Sheila Hamilton-Dyer, Lyuba Holden and Clive Orton, and my two co-editors, Nikolaj Makarov and Evgenij Nosov, for their long-term commitment to these adventures. Finally, to all my friends in Novgorod, I owe you a huge debt of gratitude for all your kindness and support over many, many years.

CONTRIBUTORS

A. S. Aleshinskaya
Institute of Archaeology,
Russian Academy of Science,
117036, Dm.Ulianova, 19,
Moscow, 117036, Russia.
asalesh@mail.ru

A. Alsleben
Academy of Science and Literature (Mainz),
Stiftung Schleswig-Holsteinische
Landesmuseen, Archäologisches
   Landesmuseum,
Schloss Gottorf, D – 24837,
Schleswig, Germany.
alsleben@schloss-gottorf.de

M. A. Brisbane
School of Conservation Sciences,
Bournemouth University,
Fern Barrow,
Poole, Dorset BH12 5BB, UK.
mbrisbane@bmth.ac.uk

T. Brorsson
Ceramic Studies,
Vadensjövägen 150,
261 91 Landskrona, Sweden.
torbjorn.brorsson@ceramicstudies.se

N. V. Eniosova
Dept. of Archaeology,
Faculty of History,
Moscow State University,
Leninskje Gory, GSP-I, 119991,
Moscow, Russia.
eniosova@inbox.ru

D. Jeffrey
℅ The University of Arizona
Materials Science & Engineering
Mines Building, P.O. Box 210012
Tucson, AZ 85721-0012 USA

P. Johnston
Eachtra Archaeological Projects,
The Forge, Innishannon,
Co. Cork, Ireland.
penny@eachtra.ie

N. V. Khvoshchinskaya
Institute for the History of Material Culture,
Russian Academy of Sciences.
Dvortzovaya nab., 18,
St. Petersburg, 191186, Russia.
vesti@archeo.ru

E. K. Kublo
Novgorod State Museum,
The Kremlin,
173007 Novgorod, Russia.
nold@novsu.ac.ru

A. V. Kurbatov
Institute for the History of Material Culture,
Russian Academy of Sciences.
Dvortzovaya nab., 18,
St. Petersburg, 191186, Russia.
admin@archeo.ru

N. A. Makarov
Institute of Archaeology of the Russian
   Academy of Sciences,
117036,
Dm.Ulianova, 19, Moscow, Russia.
nmakarov1@yandex.ru

M. Maltby
School of Conservation Sciences,
Bournemouth University,
Fern Barrow,
Poole, Dorset BH12 5BB, UK.
mmaltby@bmth.ac.uk

M. Martinon-Torres
University College London,
Institute of Archaeology,
31–34 Gordon Square,
London WC1H 0PY, UK.

M. L. Mokrushin
Archaeological Research Centre (Ancient
   Monuments of the North)
(Drevnosti Severa),
Vologda,160001,
Cheluskintsev,12, Russia.
drsever@vologda.ru

CONTRIBUTORS

M. Monk
Dept of Archaeology,
University College Cork,
Cork, Ireland.
MMonk@archaeology.ucc.ie

E. N. Nosov
Institute for the History of Material Culture,
Russian Academy of Sciences.
Dvortzovaya nab., 18,
St. Petersburg, 191186, Russia.
nosov.evg@gmail.com

C. Orton
University College London,
Institute of Archaeology,
31–34 Gordon Square,
London WC1H 0PY, UK.
tcfa002@ucl.ac.uk

Th. Rehren
University College London,
Institute of Archaeology,
31–34 Gordon Square,
London WC1H 0PY, UK.
th.rehren@ucl.ac.uk

E. Reilly
15 Brook House,
Riverview,
Richmond Road,
Dublin 3, Ireland.
eireilly@tcd.ie

E. A. Rybina
Dept of Archaeology,
Moscow State University,
Vorobjevy gory, 117234
Moscow, Russia.
ear42@list.ru

D. I. Solovyov
Novgorod Archaeological Research Centre,
Ilina st., 26, Znamenskoe podvorie
Novgorod, 173000, Russia.

L. N. Solovyova
Institute of Archaeology of the Russian
  Academy of Sciences,
117036, Dm.Ulianova, 19,
Moscow, Russia.
lidia77-77@mail.ru

E. A. Spiridonova
Institute of Archaeology of the Russian
Academy
  of Sciences, 117036,
Dm.Ulianova, 19, Moscow, Russia.
asalesh@mail.ru

D. Sully
University College London,
Institute of Archaeology,
31–34 Gordon Square,
London WC1H 0PY, UK.
d.sully@ucl.ac.uk

S. E. Toropov
Novgorod State Museum and Historical
  Reserve,
The Kremlin, Novgorod, Russia.
s_toropov@mail.ru

I. I. Yeremeyev
Institute for the History of Material Culture,
  Russian Academy of Sciences.
Dvortzovaya nab., 18, St. Petersburg, 191186,
Russia. admin@archeo.ru

I. E. Zaitseva
Institute of Archaeology of the Russian
Academy
  of Sciences, 117036,
Dm.Ulianova, 19, Moscow, Russia.
izaitseva@yandex.ru

S. D. Zakharov
Institute of Archaeology of the Russian
  Academy of Sciences,
 117036,
Dm.Ulianova, 19, Moscow, Russia.
zsdbook@yandex.ru

TIMELINE

All dates are AD

mid-8th century	earliest archaeological deposits from Staraya Ladoga
mid-9th century	earliest archaeological deposits from Ryurik Gorodishche
859 (or 862)	traditional date for the foundation of Novgorod (different chronicle versions give different dates)
circa 910 to 930	earliest dated archaeological deposits at Novgorod
988	traditional date of conversion of Rus to Christianity
1034	Pskov annexed by Novgorod
1044	First reference in the chronicles to the building of the Kremlin on the west bank of the River Volkhov
1071	Battle of Mansikert; defeat of Byzantine army leads to most of Asia Minor falling to the Seljuk Turks
By 1180	German trading enclave established in Novgorod
1204	Fall of Constantinople to the Fourth Crusade
From 1237	Tartar-Mongol invasions begins; Novgorod remains independent, but pays heavy tribute
1251–1480	Golden-Horde (Tartar) period
late 13th century	Pskov becomes independent of Novgorod
1453	Fall of Constantinople to the Ottoman Turks
1478	Novgorod incorporated by Moscow under Ivan III
1480	end of Mongol rule in Russia
1494	Hanseatic Kontor in Novgorod is closed by Ivan III
1510	Pskov incorporated by Moscow
1570	Novgorod depopulated under Ivan IV

DEDICATION

The origins and development of this twenty-year collaboration owes a great debt of gratitude to two men, Peter J. Ucko and Alexander S. Khoroshev.

Following the World Archaeological Congress held in Southampton in 1986, a programme of archaeological collaboration was developed and agreed between the Department of Archaeology, University of Southampton, and the Institute for the History of Material Culture of the Russian Academy of Sciences, St. Petersburg (at that time known as the Leningrad Branch of the Institute of Archaeology, Academy of Sciences of the USSR). Two people were crucial to this initiative, namely Professor Peter Ucko (then Head of the Department of Archaeology at Southampton) and Professor Vadim Masson (then Director of the Institute in Leningrad), whose personal friendship and shared commitment to establishing concrete work programmes led to the creation of a formal agreement, supported initially by the British Academy, in 1988.

This agreement initiated several Anglo-Soviet collaborative projects, including two concerned with Palaeolithic and Bronze Age research. A third project involved the study of the origin and development of early medieval towns in North-West Russia, and their comparison with towns in Western Europe, especially Britain. At the head of this project were Mark Brisbane (at that time employed by Southampton City Council's Museums Service) and Evgenij Nosov (from the then Institute of Archaeology, Leningrad). After initial exchange visits in 1989 and 1990, it was decided that the main area to focus this work should be Novgorod and its hinterland including the site of Ryurik Gorodishche.

One of the first tangible outputs of the collaboration was the publication in England in 1992 of a monograph, *The Archaeology of Novgorod, Russia. Recent results from the Town and its Hinterland,* for the Society for Medieval Archaeology. From 1994 onwards, through the International Association for the Promotion of Co-operation with Scientists from the New Independent States of the Former Soviet Union (INTAS), a number of grants were received for various programmes of investigations into Novgorod, its hinterland and its more distant territory. This funding also brought together colleagues from Ireland, Germany, Sweden and Denmark, as well as other institutions in both the UK and Russia, making it a truly international, scientific collaboration. New materials were studied and analyzed, and reports and publications were prepared.

Throughout this time, Peter's interest in the Novgorod project continued to grow and when he went to the Institute of Archaeology in London as its Director he encouraged his staff, such as Clive Orton, Jon Hather and Thilo Rehren, to participate. In later years Peter became more associated perhaps with his high profile links with Chinese archaeology, but it should be remembered that his initiatives in Russian archaeology, while it was still Soviet archaeology in the late 1980s, were equally trailblazing and significant. We are immensely indebted to him for all his encouragement, friendship and, occasionally challenging, advice.

From the very beginning of this collaboration, an extremely active and supportive role was played by Alexander Stepanovich Khoroshev, Director of the Novgorod Archaeological Research Centre and Professor at Moscow (Lomonosov) State University. He took part in all our joint projects and was a prolific contributor to the publications from the start. His organizational support and encouragement over more than 15 years helped to ensure that the collaboration was a success and this included his active support for analyses, some of which, it must be said, were not always seen as essential by some of his colleagues at the time. For instance, his advocacy, persistence and energy to ensure the creation of a Faunal Remains Reference Collection at the Novgorod Archaeological Research Centre were crucial to the success of this aspect of the project. Just as important and much appreciated were his constant courtesy and concern for foreign visitors, specialists and students alike, and his sincere desire and efforts to make all visitors feel part of the Novgorod scene.

Alexander (or Sasha as he was known to all) first took part in the excavations of Novgorod in 1962 as a student and from then on most of his academic research was closely connected with this rather special place. He became the Director of many excavations in different parts of the town, but will be most remembered for his beloved site of Troitsky, where he was the head of excavations for many years. Along with Academician Valentin Yanin and Museum Director Nikolai Grinyov, he was instrumental in the creation of the Novgorod Archaeological Research Centre in 1992.

This volume is gratefully and respectfully
dedicated to the memory of

Alexander Stepanovich Khoroshev (14 May 1941–15 Sept 2007)
Peter John Ucko (27 July 1938–14 June 2007)

Peter Ucko, right, with Vadim Masson in St Petersburg.

Alexander S. Khoroshev at the Novgorod Archaeological Research Centre.

MEDIEVAL NOVGOROD IN ITS WIDER CONTEXT

M. A. Brisbane, N. A. Makarov and E. N. Nosov

BACKGROUND

As is well known, the depth and extent of the preservation of Novgorod's waterlogged habitation levels from the 10th to 15th centuries is a unique phenomenon in the urban archaeology of Europe. It is therefore not surprising that modern excavations, which began in 1932, have taken place annually since, only being interrupted during World War II. It is only natural that the rich materials obtained from these excavations should have attracted the attention of scholars from far and wide, who have devoted dozens of monographs and articles to Novgorod (see for instance the comprehensive Novgorod bibliographies compiled by Gaidukov 1992; 2006; 2007).

However, the city did not exist in isolation. It was linked to its environs by thousands of different threads and could not have survived without that hinterland. From those rural areas food for people, fodder for livestock, raw materials for various types of production, building materials and manufactured items all flowed into Novgorod. The city in its turn supplied the rural population with diverse items, some fashioned by its craftsmen and others imported from further afield.

For many years scholars' attention has been largely focused on the study of the eye-catching materials discovered within the city. Rather surprisingly, analyses of the relationship between town and country and comparisons between various kinds of rural settlements against the background of the city's culture had not been undertaken. For example, until work on the INTAS projects began in the mid-1990s, inadequate attention had been paid to faunal assemblages, plant macrofossils, pollen and other data that can monitor local and regional environmental conditions, agriculture and the economy. These analyses, and in particular, comparisons between the city and its wider territory, represent key tasks for today's scholars engaged in the study of Novgorod and were to become one of the main foci of the INTAS projects represented by the reports and papers contained within this volume.

There were two main types of rural territories linked with the city. First, those in its immediate vicinity, notably the area adjacent to Lake Ilmen and in particular the area known as Poozerie (see Figure 1.1), a narrow strip of fertile land to the north-west of the lake, which had been densely populated since at least the late 7th or early 8th century. Some of the numerous settlements in Poozerie have been excavated and their materials analysed (Nosov 1992; 2001). It was the population of this area which we know supplied Novgorod with foodstuffs. A late medieval example of this can be

Figure 1.1 *Map showing location of Novgorod and Ryurik Gorodishche with the area of early medieval settlement known as Poozerie along the north-west edge of Lake Ilmen. Drawn by John Hodgson.*

seen in the land registers of the Shelon *pyatina* (a former administrative subdivision) of Novgorod dating from 1498 to 1503, where we see that eight cabbages, 80 turnips, 20 brooms and two bundles of green vegetables were sent regularly each week from the village of Rakoma in Poozerie to the governors employed by the Grand Prince at Ryurik Gorodishche (the former seat of the Prince). The same range of products would also be sent to the *dvoretskii* or chamberlain in charge of the palace household and to the *tiun* or judge. Furthermore, the chamberlain could also count on some sheep and a pile of firewood 80 m long to see him through the winter. It is clear that similar deliveries must have been made earlier as well, but we do not have any information of this from written sources. Other rural settlements around the shores of Lake Ilmen would also have had similar close links to the city of Novgorod.

Secondly, there were the rural territories that lay at some distance from the city and which together comprised the so-called Novgorod Lands (Figure 1.2). These lands made up a huge territory controlled and exploited by Novgorod, although it would be wrong to see this as a unified political entity (see for instance Halperin 1999). At their greatest extent from the 12th to 15th century, they stretched from the Baltic to the Urals and covered an area approximately the size of present day France, Belgium and the Netherlands combined.

The evolution and structure of rural settlements further away from Novgorod and the other main centres of northern and north-eastern Russia differed in certain

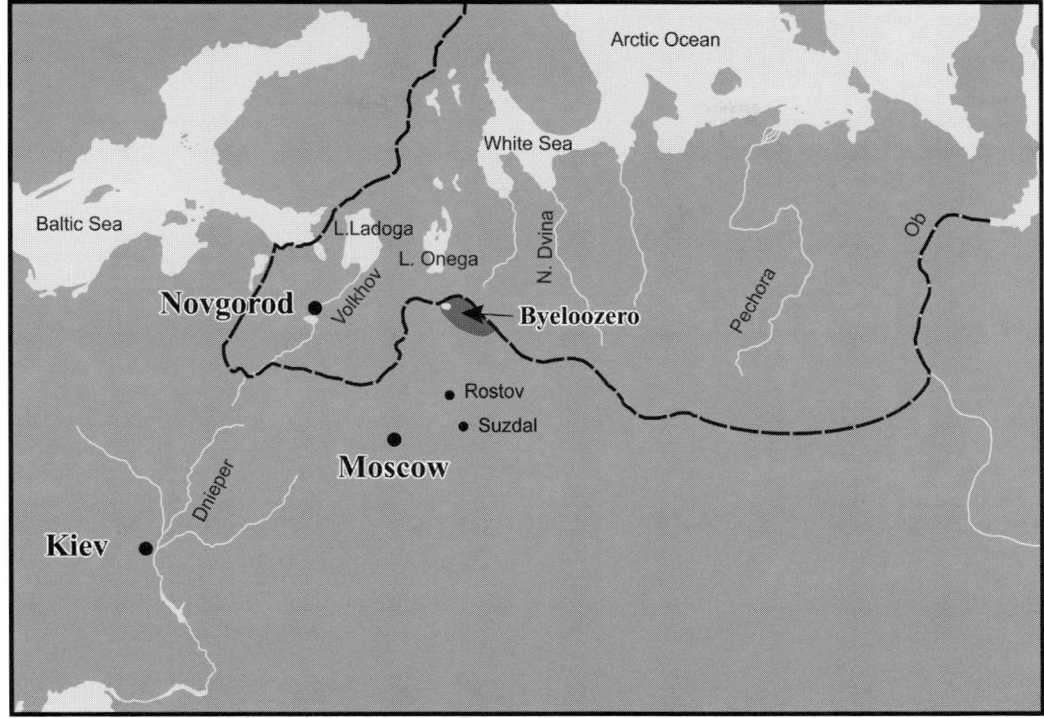

Figure 1.2 Map of Novgorod Land around AD 1400. After Yanin 1990, 74. Redrawn by Mark Dover.

respects from those in the immediate vicinity of the city. These differences can be observed in relation to their economic development, the role of crafts, agriculture, trade, hunting, fishing and various other activities. Nevertheless, the wide-ranging and detailed study of medieval sites such as the settlements at Minino on Lake Kubenskoye in the Byeloozero region, together with the analysis of materials from Novgorod's immediate environs and Novgorod itself, help us to understand the historical and cultural processes at work within the northern part of the medieval Russian state at various stages of its history.

Many of the papers in this volume have been produced as part of a project that aimed to draw out some of the details that contribute to an understanding of first, the relationships between the centre, its hinterland and its periphery, and second the various types of activities that took place in each of these locations.

THE STUDY OF NOVGOROD AND NOVGOROD LAND

Medieval Novgorod was the centre of an enormous territory with a complex economy, whose prosperity and political might were made possible by the city's control over far-flung lands in the northern part of European Russia, which stretched from the Gulf of Finland to the Northern Urals. It is impossible to uncover the history of the emergence of Novgorod without investigating its rural hinterland, which provided the foundation for the city's development and the formation and expansion of the Novgorod Lands, the natural resources at the disposal of the Novgorod population, and the actual methods for the exploitation of those resources, which made wealth creation possible.

Archaeological discoveries in Novgorod have lent powerful momentum to the study of the historical geography of these Novgorod Lands and the way they were administered, to research into aspects of the medieval colonization of north-western Russia, and into rural patterns of settlement in its various regions.

During the last 15 years or so, archaeological investigations in and around Novgorod have increased interest in the environmental context of Novgorod's development and the key rural regions of northern Russia. As research in these directions has advanced, it has emerged that the interconnections between medieval Novgorod, the rural territories of the Novgorod Lands and the natural resources of the North as factors in the growth of the medieval economy and of the prosperity of the Novgorod *boyars* were both complicated and far-reaching. The task of this volume has not been to provide a comprehensive picture of Novgorod as the organizing force behind the economy of the North, nor was it intended to produce a definitive account of agricultural and craft production and the circulation of these products by the population of the territories under Novgorod's control. Rather its main aim is to acquaint the reader with some of the important results of recent archaeological and palaeo-environmental research, which are beginning to provide new insights into certain aspects of these topics.

The growth and structure of Novgorod Land

The general geographical extent of the Novgorod Lands in the 12th–13th centuries was established in the studies by Nasonov and Kuza on the basis of information provided in the chronicles and legal documents. These include agreements concluded between the *veche* (popular assembly) of Novgorod and its princes, the earliest of which dates from 1264 (Nasonov 1951, 69–117; Kuza 1975, 144–201). It has long been established by scholars that the enormous Novgorod Lands included the main area nearer to Novgorod itself with a system of rural parishes (*pogost*) – administrative centres responsible for tax collection – and *volost*s, which were separate administrative units on the fringes of the Novgorod Lands that enjoyed special legal status, but who nevertheless paid tribute, mostly in furs, to Novgorod.

Initially, the nucleus of the Novgorod Lands had been relatively modest in size and was confined mainly to the territory around Lake Ilmen and along the River Volkhov. As suggested by Yanin, it was not until the middle of the 10th century that territory around the floodplains of the River Luga and the River Msta (which flows into Lake Ilmen), areas that contained large clusters of medieval settlements, came under Novgorod's control. He dates their incorporation into the Novgorod Lands to the year 947, when, according to the chronicles, Princess Olga "gave orders for *pogost*s and tax collection" to be introduced along the Msta and Luga Rivers (Yanin 2004, 129). The outline of the earliest core of the Novgorod Lands in the area around Lake Ilmen and the gradual expansion of the Novgorod domain into the Ilmen Basin and the upper reaches of the Volga in the 10th and 11th centuries has been examined in detail by Nosov (Nosov 1992, 15–35; Nosov *et al.* 2005, 5–7). He and his team have identified a high concentration of medieval settlements in Poozerie (an area adjacent to Lake Ilmen, SW of Novgorod), which reflects the special role of that territory during the rise of Northern Russia in the medieval period.

However, written sources on the territorial expansion of the Novgorod Lands and their administrative structures in the 11th–13th centuries are extremely meagre. This is why the discovery of birch-bark documents within the Novgorod excavations is so significant in the archaeological study of medieval Russia, for their texts not only contain the names of geographical locations but also the names of *volost*s and centres of population in various parts of the Ilmen Basin and the upper reaches of the Volga (Rybina 1993, 344–347; Yanin 2001, 66–67; 2004, 110–113). For instance, some of the birch-bark documents contain lists of payments and interest in connection with money-lending coming in from the regions bordering on the Rivers Luga and Shelon and Lake Seliger (BBD No. 526, second third of the 11th century), payments received from the Shidovitskii parish in the valley of the River Tvertsa and the village of Lama on the River Volchina, a tributary of the Mologa (BBD No. 789, last quarter of the 11th century), payments from the village of Ezsk on the River Mologa and the *volost* of Volchina (BBD No. 902, late 11th or early 12th century), the distribution of land possessions beyond the River Msta (BBD No. 724, 1160s), the inhabitants of the Imovolozhe and Zhabna *pogost*s and the village of Mlevo on the River Msta (BD No. 885, mid-12th century).

In addition to the birch-bark documents, wooden cylindrical seals have been discovered in Novgorod bearing inscriptions containing the names of rural parishes of the 11th–12th centuries in the basin of the Onega and Northern Dvina Rivers, on the far north-eastern fringe of the Novgorod Lands (Yanin 1982, 138–157; 2001, 68–82; 2004, 101–110). Also on cylinders dating from the 11th and first quarter of the 12th century, we find the names "Tikhmega" (the parish of Tikhmanga on Lake Lacha in the basin of the Onega River), "Vaga" and "Ust-Vaga" (taxation districts on the River Vaga, a southern tributary of the Northern Dvina), and "Emtsa" (a taxation district on the river Emtsa, a southern tributary of the Northern Dvina river) (Yanin 2004, 101–110; Makarov 2003, 149–163).

Yanin has convincingly argued that these wooden cylinders were locks from sacks, in which furs were brought to Novgorod (Yanin 2007, 204). These had been collected as tribute in the northern regions, such as Zavolochie. Inscriptions on the cylinders designated the taxation district, in which the valuable furs had been collected. Birch-bark documents and wooden cylinders of the 11th and 12th centuries bearing names of taxation districts and *pogost*s are therefore vitally important, not only for providing a detailed picture of medieval settlement patterns and administrative arrangements, but also as convincing evidence of the presence of a Novgorod administration within extensive areas of the North. They confirm that Novgorod had, indeed, been receiving "resources from the periphery", i.e. tribute and payments from the upper reaches of the Volga, the valleys of the Luga and Msta rivers and *pogost*s in Zavolochie.

Rivals to Novgorod: the growth of Rostov-Suzdal

Novgorod was not the only centre endeavouring to spread its power and influence within the northern expanses of north-eastern Europe at this time. Its rivals in the colonization of the North were the urban centres of the Rostov-Suzdal Lands, which lay to the east of Novgorod and its territory. These had extended their influence from the Volga-Klyazma interfluve to as far as the east bank of the Volga, the River Sheksna, the lake known as Byeloe Ozero (literally White Lake), the Northern Dvina river and to its southern tributary, the Vaga (Nasonov 1951, 188–197; Kuchkin 1984, 55–104). The outposts of the colonisation outwards from the Rostov-Suzdal Lands were the town of Byeloozero, the fortress of Gleden built in 1178, the town of Velikii Ustyug founded in 1212, and the settlements near the source of the Northern Dvina. Byeloozero, on the south shore of Byeloe Ozero, is mentioned in the chronicles and is one of the earliest Russian towns in the area with settlement evidence dating from the second half of the 10th century (Makarov *et al.* 2001).

Northern boundary disputes between Rostov-Suzdal possessions and those of Novgorod were accompanied by fierce armed conflicts, which were first mentioned in the chronicles in the year 1169, when Novgorod forces defeated tribute collectors from Suzdal and seized what they had collected from territories under the jurisdiction of the Suzdal princes. The military rivalry between Novgorod and the Vladimir-Suzdal princes in the late-12th and early-13th centuries has been examined by historians, who have made exhaustive searches of the written sources, which unfortunately are far from extensive (Nasonov 1951, 188–197; Kuchkin 1984, 89–103). An important supplement to the chronicles is provided by Novgorod birch-bark document No. 724 sent from the North to Novgorod. This contains a report from a certain Sava, leader of Novgorod tribute-collectors, which tells of his own unsuccessful attempt to collect furs but that "our man Andrei" (a representative of Andrei Yurievich Bogolyubskii, Prince of Vladimir) had obtained the tribute (Yanin 1993, 114–119). With reference to archaeological materials, it can be assumed that the beginning of the rivalry in the North between Novgorod and the rulers of Rostov and Suzdal dates from the 10th century, when men from Novgorod made their way as far as Byeloe Ozero and the Sheksna river from the West, and settlers from Rostov came up from the South, moving up the Sheksna river (Makarov 1989; 1997, 166–168). The fact that there existed lands under the jurisdiction of Novgorod on the one hand, and under that of Rostov and Suzdal on the other, on the 'wrong' side of the demarcation line in the valley of the River Sukhon and in the basin of the Vaga reflects the complicated nature of this long struggle, the details of which do not find their way into the pages of the chronicles.

Colonisation of the North

Extensive archaeological surveys of rural areas in this northern region of north-eastern Europe in the close vicinity of medieval towns that formed the central core of large administrative units, but on the margins of the Novgorod and Rostov-Suzdal Lands, were embarked upon in the 1970s and then expanded in the 1990s. These surveys shed light on the nature of the cultural landscape and settlement patterns at the end of the first and beginning of the second millennium AD. This era is characterized by the emergence of a new network of settlements, which was not linked with the territorial units of the earlier period, extending over enormous expanses of land from the upper reaches of the River Dnieper and the River Volga to the area round Lake Ladoga and the Northern Dvina (Makarov *et al.* 2001, 217–226). The rapid growth in the number of rural settlements and the expansion of settled territories in these largely flat, wooded landscapes (where during previous millennia the concentration of people and exploitation of material resources had been extremely low) constituted a phenomenon of crucial importance in the medieval history of Eastern Europe in this period (probably no less significant than the beginning of urbanisation). The dynamics and intensity of colonization differed considerably from region to region, when new territories were being settled in the Russian north. Compact groups of rural settlements began taking shape usually near the water resources of large lakes and the valleys of large rivers interspersed by sparsely populated areas in the watersheds of river systems. Spore and pollen research shows that the emergence of new settlements was accompanied by the partial felling of forests, the laying out of fields, and the appearance of new agricultural crops. Despite specific features of rural colonization in all the different areas, it is clear that it began earlier in the north-west of Russia and developed more intensively there than in the north-east.

In view of the fact that the study of medieval settlement patterns in rural areas took the form of a number of separate regional projects and did not encompass the whole of the northern part of European Russia, it is impossible at the present time to piece together a general map of the main centres of rural settlement. In the north-west of Russia the territories that have been studied in the most detail are those around Lake Ilmen and along the River Volkhov. A small area of land stretching along the north-west shore of Lake Ilmen, which came to be known as (Ilmenskoye) Poozerie, is regarded by Nosov as one of the key areas of the wooded zone in eastern Europe. It is here that an extremely high concentration of rural settlements dating from the 9th and 10th centuries has been recorded. As the most recent research has shown, the first medieval settlements in this territory took shape no later than the 8th century (Nosov 1991, 5–37; 1992, 5–65; Nosov *et al.* 2005, 122–154). The emergence of compact groups of medieval settlements in two other central parts of the Novgorod Lands, in the middle reaches of the Msta river and along the Luga river, evidently relates to a slightly later period, namely the 9th and 10th centuries (Nosov 1992, 23–25; Konetskii and Nosov 1995, 29–54; Platonova *et al.* 2007). At the end of the first millennium AD, centres with a high concentration of settlements also emerged in the central part of the future Rostov-Suzdal Lands, that is, in the Volga-Klyazma interfluve near Lake Nero (near the town of Rostov) and Lake Pleshcheevo, and in the Opolie region near Suzdal (Leontiev 1996, 19–66; Makarov *et al.* 2005, 196–215). At that time there also existed large and stable clusters of settlements in the Mologa-Suda interfluve (Bashenkin 1995, 3–28). However, in large areas of the North there are only isolated traces of 9th/10th-century settlements or none at all. Colonization was pursued on a significantly wider scale in the 11th and 12th centuries, predominantly in an easterly and north-easterly direction. During this period the network of rural settlements in areas already long settled became denser and more compact (Makarov *et al.* 2005, 196–215), while in the margins of the Novgorod and Rostov-Suzdal Lands newly populated rural areas were emerging.

For an understanding of the history of the colonization of the northern margins of medieval Russia, the results of many years' research into the settlements on the shores of the Byeloe Ozero and Lake Kubenskoye are highly relevant. Scholars have attempted to identify and map all the settlements in those areas dating from the 11th to the 13th century. In the basin of the first of those two lakes (a large expanse of water, from which rises the River Sheksna, one of the eastern tributaries of the Volga), some 170 large medieval villages have been identified within an area of approximately 9,000 km^2. Most of these settlements were not large and they occupied low terraces near large rivers and lakes and they tended to be grouped together in clusters. The network of 9th- and 10th-century settlements around Byeloe Ozero was sparse: the real growth in their number began in the 11th century and accelerated in the early 12th and 13th century. Some settlements were situated at portages linking the water systems of the Volga, the Northern Dvina and Onega rivers and Lake Onega. It was not until the 14th century that watershed areas began to be settled. In the second half of the 13th century the network of settlements underwent a major transformation reflected in the partial abandonment of settlements, which had come into being in the 10th to 13th centuries, and a spread of colonization to higher ground within the watersheds (Makarov *et al.* 2001). Colonization developed in a similar way in the area around Lake Kubenskoye to the east of Byeloe Ozero, in which the River Sukhon rises. Around that lake, which has a total area of approximately 370 km^2, 16 settlements dating from the 10th to the 13th centuries have been identified: most of which were small and situated near the mouths of rivers flowing into the lake (Makarov 2007, 43–62). The system of settlements which took shape in that period on the shores of Byeloe Ozero and Lake Kubenskoye provided convenient links for the major urban centres of both north-western and north-eastern Russia, providing access to the main products and resources of the North. Although the territories around Byeloe Ozero and Lake Kubenskoye were part of the Rostov-Suzdal Lands, a large proportion of the artefact collections dating from the 10th to 13th centuries are objects of a north-western type, reflecting their close cultural and commercial links with Novgorod and the Baltic region (see also Makarov 2009).

When scholars turned their attention to archaeological materials, which were being collected from excavations of northern Russian settlements, and which characterized the culture, production and consumption to be found in rural settlements, they were obliged to reconsider many stereotypes in the assessment of rural society in medieval Russia of the 10th–13th centuries, which had taken shape in historical writing. Archaeological sources testify to high levels of prosperity in rural society, to its involvement in commerce and to the complex organization underlying the economy of rural settlements, in which trades and crafts played an important part. In addition, they showed that a large proportion of the household articles and jewellery found in the towns was also accessible to the rural population. Equally surprising were finds of high-status articles and imports, which are common from many rural sites, although the variety and abundance of such articles can vary considerably from one settlement to another. Researchers are aware that they will soon have at their disposal increasing amounts of such material, demonstrating that the cultural and economic differences between the towns and villages of medieval northern Russia did not run nearly as deep as has been believed up till now. It is worth stressing again how these findings run counter to existing historical explanations and narratives.

CONCLUSIONS

It can thus be seen that the growth of Novgorod and the consolidation of its role as an economic and political centre in the 10th to 13th centuries took place at a time when rural areas were being colonized on a wide scale. The power of the Novgorod elite made itself felt through large parts of the North and an extensive exchange of commodities between Novgorod and rural settlements was taking place, as is testified by finds of numerous imports and articles made by urban craftsmen in the rural settlements. In order to shed light on the actual connection between the advance of Novgorod, the colonization of rural areas and the emergence of mechanisms for incorporating the agricultural products and resources from the northern areas of eastern Europe into the broader system of international trade, new forms of data were required. These needed to characterize the following: the palaeo-environment of medieval settlements; the settlement of rural areas in both the central and peripheral parts of the Novgorod Lands; the economy and patterns of consumption in medieval settlements; and the resources and raw materials used by the actual inhabitants of Novgorod. Studies of a wide range of materials presented in this volume include articles that collectively shed light on all of these topics.

– 2 –

RESULTS OF PALYNOLOGICAL INVESTIGATIONS OF THE ARCHAEOLOGICAL SITES IN THE LAKE ILMEN AND LAKE KUBENSKOYE STUDY AREAS

E. A. Spiridonova and A. S. Aleshinskaya

INTRODUCTION

Palynological analysis is a sensitive indicator of change in natural conditions and as a result it is of importance for establishing the detailed climatic stratigraphy essential for archaeological research. In archaeology, spore and pollen analysis is applied fairly widely for the resolution of various palaeo-geographical questions. The methods used for this research vary widely and they are directed towards re-establishing the palaeo-phytocenotic conditions of the past and also identifying synchronic levels and establishing possible correlations. Higher plants produce an enormous amount of pollen grains, which, when they fall, may be buried and fossilised, thus being incorporated into deposits providing sporo-pollen spectra of a specific age.

The selection of samples is the key to the level of interpretation the palynologist can provide. The reliability and degree of detail in the results finally obtained depend upon the accuracy and completeness of the sample suite. The more frequent the samples from the archaeological sequences, the more complete and uninterrupted the picture of the changes in plant communities it will be possible to obtain.

The report below is provided as a narrative from the two main study areas (Lake Kubenskoye in Byeloozero and Lake Ilmen near Novgorod) and covers ten main pollen profiles, eight of which were taken from within archaeological excavations. From the Lake Kubenskoye area (Byeloozero), these include four sections from the Minino (henceforth referred to as sections M3, M4, M6 and M7), and two from Vladishevo (sections V1 and V2), while from the Lake Ilmen area these include four sections from the excavations at Ryurik Gorodishche (sections RG1, RG2, RG3 and RG4). Full correlation of these cores is provided in Table 2.2. Please note that all ten pollen diagrams used in this study are included on the accompanying CD, but only selected examples are included in the text (Figures 2.1 to 2.5).

METHODS

Pollen separation methods used were those devised by Grichuk (1950) with amendments. Samples were boiled in a 10% HCl solution and then, after it had been washed in distilled water, this process was repeated in a 10% KOH solution. The residue was washed again in water and centrifuged in a potassium iodide and cadmium iodide solution with a specific weight of approximately 2.2–2.3 and the material obtained placed in a test-tube with glycerine. The identification of pollen and spores, the calculation of grains and the micro-photography of micro-fossils were carried out using a light microscope Olympus CX-41 with a magnification of ×400. Calculations included all pollen grains and spores, and due attention was paid to the morphological development of the shapes and their state of preservation. For the micro-photographs and identifications, please see the accompanying CD.

All the microfossils encountered were sorted into three groups: tree and shrub species, grasses and herbaceous plants, and spores. The composition of these groups was calculated in relation to the total number of all the species encountered. The percentage of the pollen content of the tree species was calculated in relation to the total of the arboreal pollen, that of the grass and herbaceous plants in relation to the total of the grass and herbaceous plants and that of the spores in relation to the total of sporophytes. In the diagrams the general composition of the spectrum at Ryurik Gorodishche is shown using symbols, while the other components of the spectrum are indicated with shading.

PALYNOLOGICAL STUDIES

In the Vologda Region (Byeloozero), palynology was used at two sites: Minino and Vladyshnevo situated on the western shore of Lake Kubenskoye. Four sections were studied at the archaeological site of the Minino settlement, three of which had been selected in trenches (Sections M3, M6 and M7) and one natural section through deposits of marshy soils near the settlement (Section M4). At the Vladyshnevo settlement one section was studied within the settlement (Section V1) and also one natural section (Section V2). As a result of the research carried out and the comparison of the data obtained, 20 palynological zones were identified which characterize the stages in the development of the vegetation in the environs of the settlements during the medieval period.

In the Novgorod Region where Lake Ilmen is located, Ryurik Gorodishche was studied using palynology where four sections from the archaeological excavation were selected for this purpose. Each consecutive section (from the top down) is a continuation of the preceding one and taken together they yield information on the habitation levels starting from the 8th/9th centuries up to the 13th century. The exception in this respect is Section RG3, which was sunk in the middle part of the trench parallel to Section RG2. In so far as the deposits in Section RG3 are represented by a layer of sediments from the east slope of the rampart which gradually comes to meet the formations which fill the moat, they are of no interest for any reconstruction of the palaeo-landscape and are not included in Table 2.2.

In the light of all the results obtained from analysis, 32 palynological zones were identified (see Table 2.2) and these help to characterize the development of the vegetation in the Ryurik Gorodishche area between the 8th and the 13th century.

CHANGE IN THE VEGETATION IN THE ENVIRONS OF RYURIK GORODISHCHE AROUND LAKE ILMEN

The territory of the Novgorod region, in geo-botanical terms, forms part of the southern taiga and sub-taiga sub-province of the East European Province, which is part of the European-Siberian dark coniferous sub-region of the Euro-Asiatic region. The border between these sub-provinces is along a line which passes through Novgorod, Borovichi and the Rybinsk Reservoir. Palynological analysis was undertaken of archaeological deposits at Ryurik Gorodishche (hereafter Gorodishche), which is situated in the sub-taiga province and lies 2 kilometres south of Novgorod on an elevation, which stretches from South-west to North-east. In the West the elevation is bordered by the River Volkhov, in the South by Spasovskii Stream, while in the North and East it gradually slopes downwards to become part of the Volkhovets flood-plain (Nosov 1990). During Spring and early Summer the whole flood-plain of the Volkhov and its tributaries is inundated, transforming the elevated areas into islands. In ancient times the Gorodishche elevation and the low ground that surrounded it formed an island at the river head of the Volkhovets and the Volkhov (Nosov 1990). This geographical location was particularly important at the time of the floods.

The relief of this locality is varied to a rare degree, but in places it has been rendered smooth by denudation processes. The glaciated landscape includes moraine and lacustrine glacial deposits and a typical feature is the predominance of a low poorly drained relief. The hills contain a mosaic of soils and vegegetion, with variable local groundwater conditions (*Atlas of the Novgorod Region,* 1982). The territory round Lake Ilmen benefits from a typical moderate continental climate, with 220–225 days above freezing (for further information on 19th and 20th century climate in the area, see Barysheva 1966).

The present-day vegetation groups are closely associated with the different elements of the relief and different soils. On lacustrine glacial clays and loams the most typical tree-cover consists of spruce woods with mountain sorrel. On the sands and sandy loams of similar origin spruce woods with *Hylcommium, Dicranum* and *Rhytidicidelphus* appear. On the outcrops of moraine clays and loams mixed spruce woods are found. In this forest broad-leaved trees are also found. In the undergrowth rowan, honeysuckle and rosehips are to be found. On the fluvio-glacial and glacial sands what grow most frequently of all are pine forests with cowberries and heather and in the wetter places on the edge of marshes, sedge and sphagnum pine woods appear. The role of the boreal elements and their proportion in the different types of sub-taiga pine forests vary considerably. The largest group is that of nemoral species, which form the basis of the plant communities. Sub-taiga broad-leaved-and-pine forests have been seriously damaged by human activity: in places they have been cut down altogether and the cleared land has then been used for agriculture.

Full details of the modern vegetation can be found on the accompanying CD.

Pollen Results (see pollen diagrams Figures 2.1, 2.2 and 2.3)

The most detailed information about the nature of the plant cover and the landscape of the people living near Gorodishche has been obtained relating to the very earliest stages of habitation at the site (i.e. 8th–10th centuries), which has been successfully studied using palynological analysis. Pollen analysis makes it possible not only to clarify the nature of the natural habitat during a particular period of time, but also to trace the pattern of changes in palaeo-landscapes over time, to identify the evolution of archaeological cultures and to compare them (both at multi-level sites and at those a good distance from each other, as for example the settlements in the Vologda region on the one hand and Gorodishche on the other). Four main sequences (RG1, RG2, RG3 and RG4) were analysed from Gorodishche (Table 2.2) and the results are presented in Figures 2.1 to 2.3, as well as in the accompanying CD.

The nature of the plant cover of the Lake Ilmen region took shape over a long historical period, and the area has been settled by human beings since ancient times. In this chapter the earliest stage studied in the settlement relating to the medieval period was the 8th century, during which time the natural environment was changing, although the range of climatic fluctuations was insignificant and came to no more than 1° C in the summer period (Klimanov *et al.* 1995). The level of Lake Ilmen was quite high and only the elevated features in the territory could have protruded above the water. At that time no more than 60% of the surrounding landscapes were covered with woods. The forest stand was made up of pines, spruces and broad-leaved species, such as lime, oak and, less frequently, elm. Hazel and guelder-rose bushes were constant features of the landscape and in the damper inhabited areas grey alder and willows grew. This meant that spruces, pines, lime and oak were the main forest-forming species to be found in the primary forest. With regard to meadow vegetation, broad-leaved boreal species predominated forming flood-plain meadow, woodland and marsh communities.

In general the character of the landscape was semi-open until the Gorodishche settlement appeared: after that the proportion of tree species sometimes sank to as little as 49%. Yet it might be noted that the natural conditions were always defined by the humidification of the soils. Among the meadow plants encountered an important role was that played by various kinds of water-loving forbs represented by *Filipendula ulmaria,* by various kinds of *Ranunculus sp., Rumex sp.,* Iridaceae, Apiaceae, Caryophyllaceae and also that of the constantly present *Typha.*

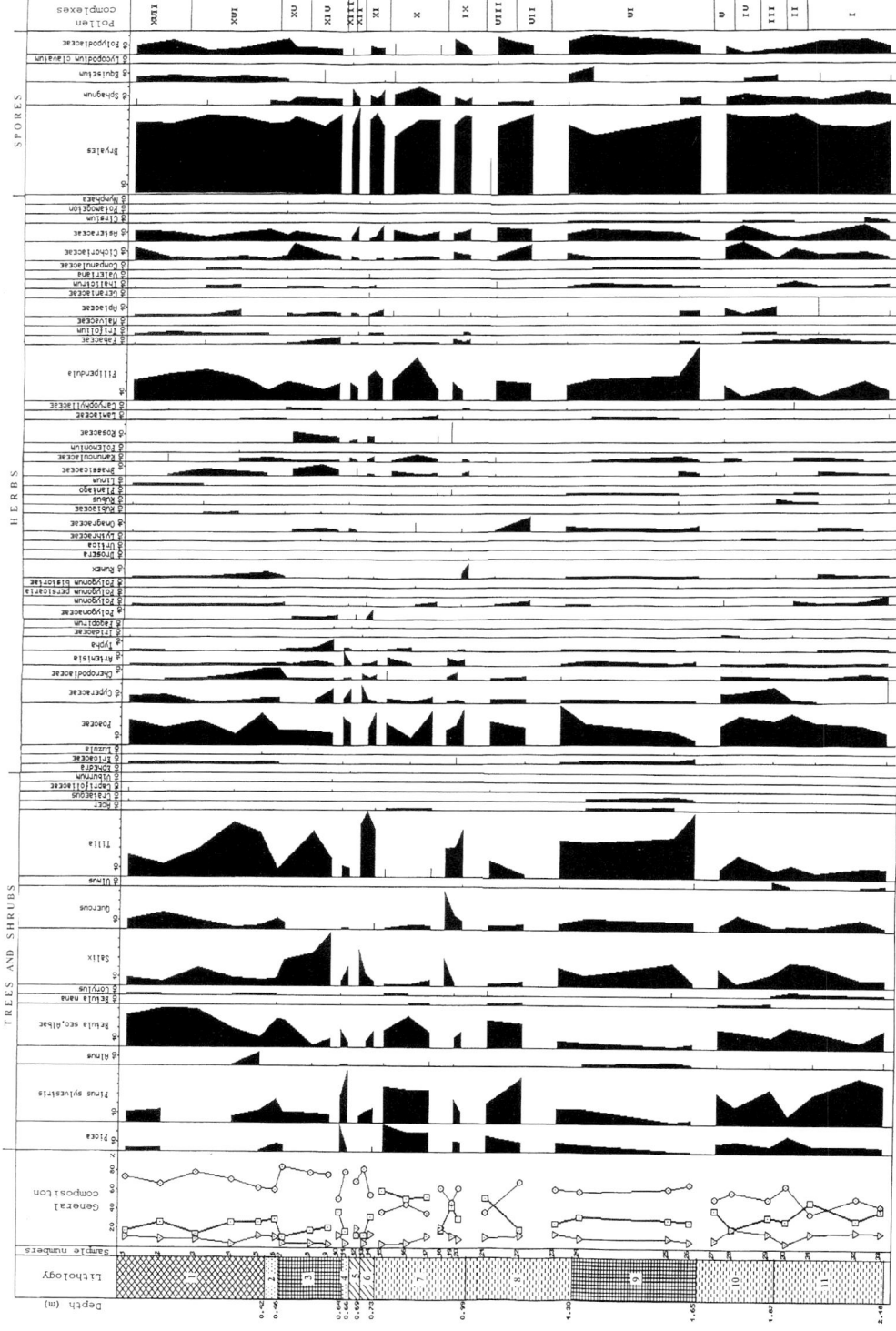

Figure 2.1 Pollen diagram of Section 4 from Ryurik Gorodishche.

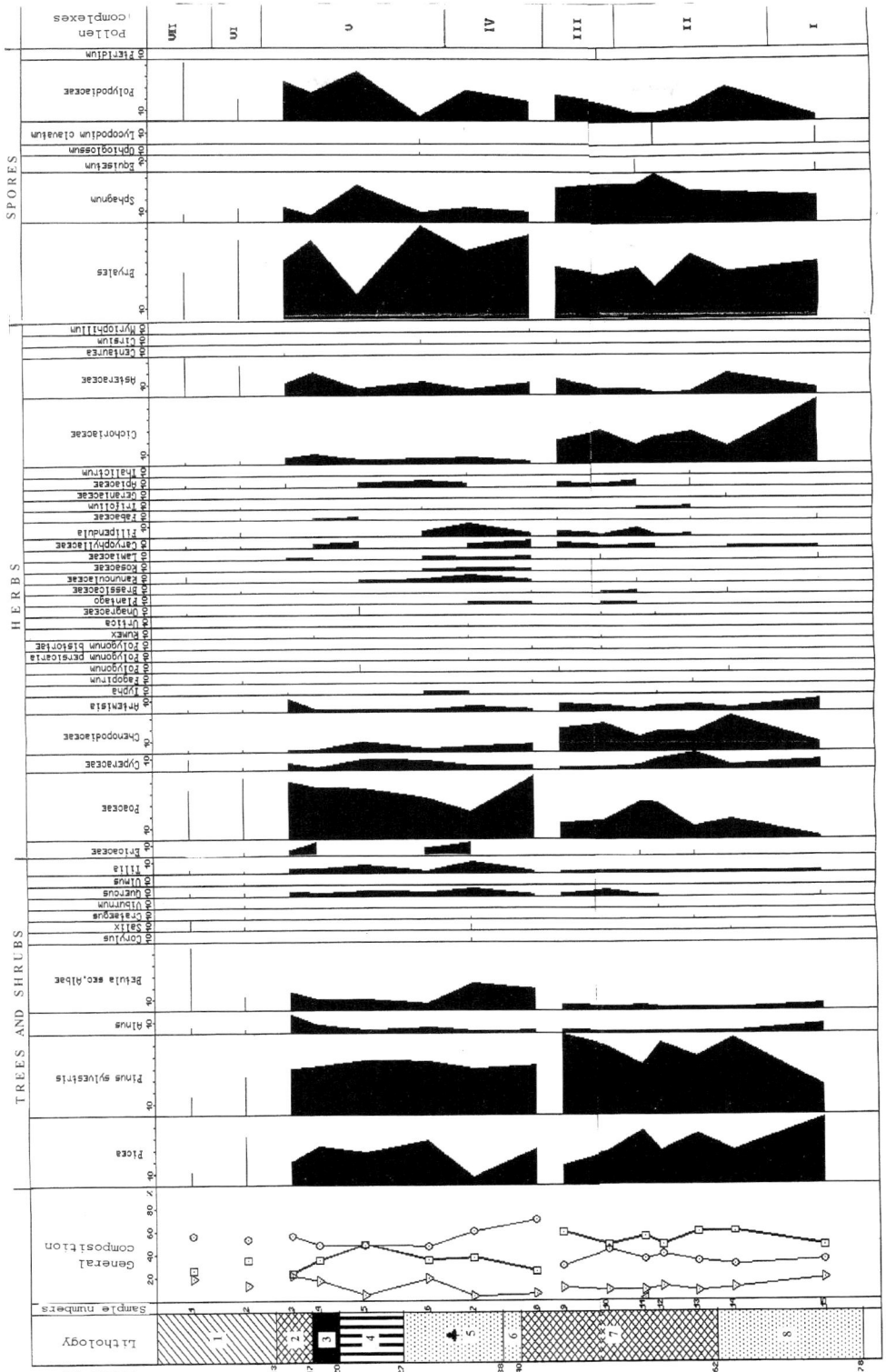

Figure 2.2 Pollen diagram of Section 2 from Ryurik Gorodishche.

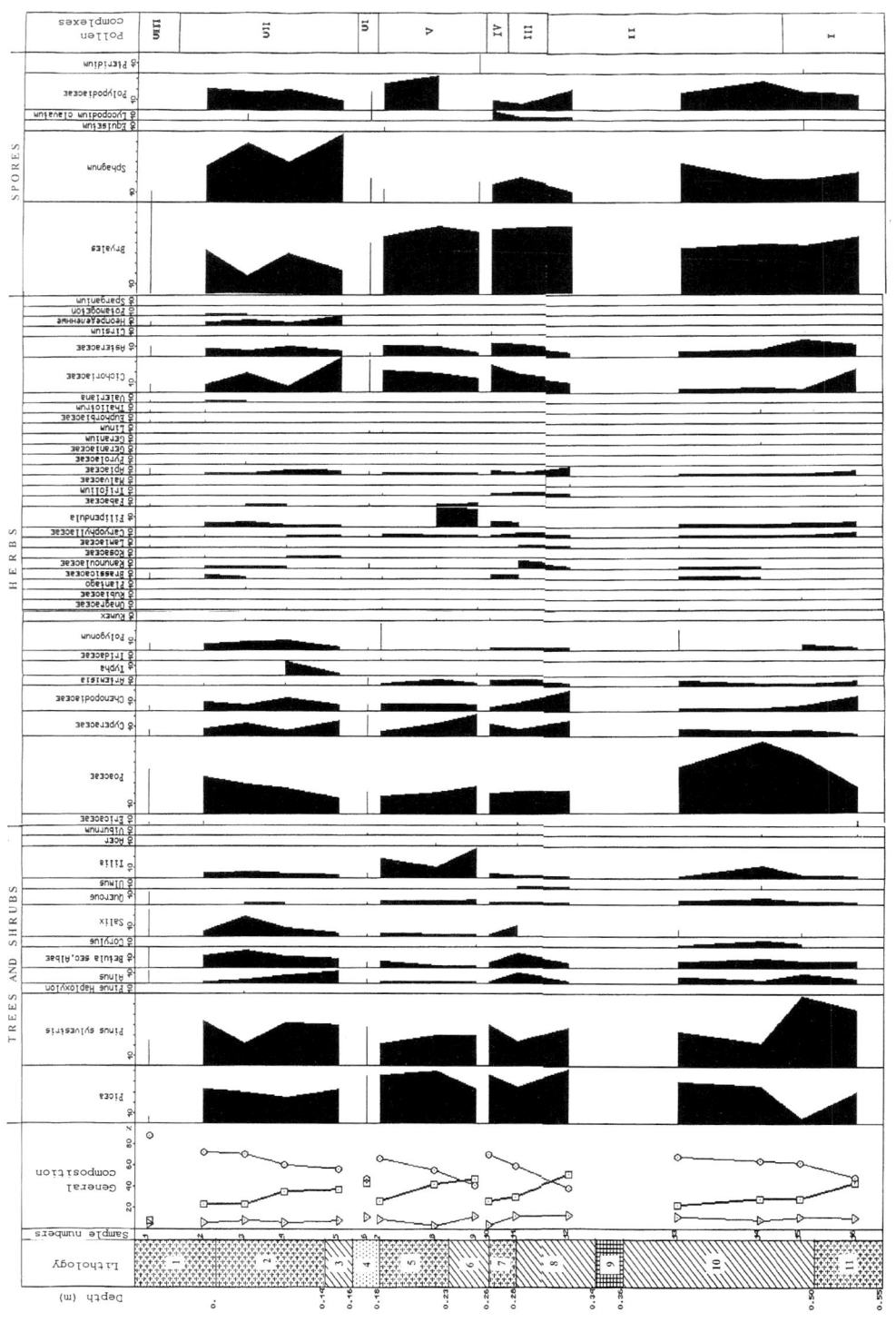

Figure 2.3 Pollen diagram of Section 1 from Ryurik Gorodishche.

In approximately the middle of the 8th century a small drop in temperature was noted, which led to more woods appearing in the territory and a decrease in the role of broad-leaved species. After this, there began a gradual rise in temperatures which lasted until the end of the 8th century. At the end of the 8th century, for all intents and purposes the point at which the settlement of Gorodishche began to take shape, there is a marked reshaping in the plant cover of the territory, which is due to human activity. The changes manifested themselves in the sharp drop in the woodland (there was a drop of as much as 28.4%), and the change from primary forest, consisting of both conifers and broad-leaved trees, to secondary forest, consisting of birch trees and very small amounts of spruce, pine and broad-leaved species. Such a rapid and large-scale decrease in the woodland could be the result of intensive felling of coniferous trees for economic purposes. At that time the role of open landscapes had become more important: these as before were filled with meadows of varying composition. Mesophilous (moderate temperature inhabiting) plant communities became widespread and may be seen as particularly important from an economic point of view. Bordering or near water, hydrophilous (water inhabiting) plants were present, as before represented by bulrush, spirea, meadow rue, sorrel, buttercups and sedges.

It is important to note the appearance of pollen from cultivated cereals of two varieties, one of which had grains that were comparatively large (45–60 μm) and the other grains that were noticeably smaller (from 25 to 35 μm) (see microphotographs on the accompanying CD). Often these grains were found in clusters, which might indirectly indicate that they had only been carried over a short distance. Determining the species of cultivated cereals is a fairly complex task as they are often severely crushed and do not present grains of a clearly defined shape, but here they are most likely to be pollen of barley, wheat and possibly rye. When comparing the pollen record here with the dated climatic data for Northern Europe (Stuiver *et al.* 1995), we can see that the beginning of the construction of Gorodishche can be related to regional data dated to the very end of the 8th century.

The beginning of the 9th century was marked by a slightly cooler period, during which the woodland of the territory increased and rose to 40%. Pine began to predominate within the woods, and it is possible that mixed sub-taiga forest was well-developed in more elevated sections of the region's terrain. The presence of cultivated cereals confirms the continued agricultural exploitation. Meadows of varying composition played an important part in the landscape as before, which indicate their significant role for animal husbandry. After a certain interval, later in the 9th century, the pollen evidence testifies to a drop in the level of Lake Ilmen and its catchment. Man's presence is demonstrated by the many wood chips and birch-bark present in this level consists of silt-like peaty deposits. Woods at that time occupied a slightly smaller area than they had at the beginning of the century, but remain the main climate indicator. This was the first of the warmest stages, when broad-leaved forest consisting of lime and, less frequently, oak and maple predominated in the vicinity of Gorodishche. The vegetation of the meadows was rich in both mesophilous species and communities of various damp-ground forbs (non-grass broad-leaved herb growing in fields, prairies, or meadows). In general these conditions could be favourable for the development of animal husbandry as well. Meanwhile, apart from the meadow forbs, the vegetation of peat levels have also been recorded; levels in which marshland shrubs from the Ericaceae family are encountered. Even sundew (*Drosera spp.*) and cattail (*Typha spp.*) appear and low shrubs such as willow are found in large numbers. During this warmer period human economic activity intensified, clearly manifesting itself both in the abundance of weeds (*Plantago*, Onagraceae, various species of *Polygonum*, Brassicaceae, *Fagopirum*, Malvaceae, Cichoriaceae) and in the interruption of the lake sediments. At the base of the section lumps of blue-grey and red clay were found, created, apparently, in order to improve the approach to the moat during the period when peaty and silt-like deposits were building up. The waterlogged lower part of the territory of Gorodishche became even more saturated with water (probably this represents the cooler stage in the middle of the 9th century).

Major changes of climate also had an impact on the composition of the primary forest. It is precisely at this time that the areas of spruce, pine and spruce/pine forest (with a very small component of broad-leaved species such as lime, oak, maple or hazel) increased. Plants associated with forest margins such as *Polygonum bistortae* also appeared and the range of the various meadow-land forbs also decreased. Due to these changes in rainfall, species composition and soil character, these forests could more appropriately be defined as southern-taiga massifs, which varied in both size and configuration.

After a time, but still in the 9th century, the environmental conditions became warmer and drier. The saturated nature of the soil in the moat was no more than slightly waterlogged. The composition of the forest plant communities also changed, although there had been a sharp reduction in their overall area: once again broad-leaved tree species assumed the dominant position and coniferous forest ceased to exist. This was a result not so much by change in climatic conditions, but by man's intensive economic activity. In addition an increase in the role of agricultural exploitation of the territory is evident in the appearance of weeds associated with ploughed fields. What we are seeing here is essentially the manifestation of a second warm period in the second half of the 9th century. Nearer the end of the century the climatic situation gradually began to change and to become colder once more. There was a marked drop in the broad-leaved species. Pine became the environment-forming plants and at the level dated to AD 889 (dendrochronological identification by N. B. Chernykh) spruce and birch had already become more important. The development of the the composition of woods served to change the structures of the adjacent herbaceous communities. At that time the balance of meadows and agricultural land was almost equal. At the very end of the 9th century the climate began to grow warmer once again. Broad-leaved species became more significant in the forests; firstly with regard to lime but also maple and hazel. The composition of plant communities in open areas was fairly varied as previously. It is likely that during this period the population of Gorodishche did not need to fell trees in large numbers to make more land available for ploughing and perhaps not at all, because the meadows of the high flood-plain were well suited for agriculture. This gave provided a major advantage over the communities of the Vologda region, which experienced a more continental climate and there had always been a higher proportion forest. Yet it is appropriate here to mention another fact as well, namely that the constant presence of small pieces of charcoal in the deposits from that interval and subsequent ones as well and also the high proportion of willow herb (Onagraceae family) in the spectra (a plant that is popularly known as "fire grass") enable us to assume that shrubs were being deliberately burnt in order to improve the quality of the ploughed land.

The rise in temperatures continued into the beginning of the 10th century. The woods formed small massifs made up for the most part of broad-leaved species and, first and foremost, of lime. The presence of birch and pine was preserved in a rather selective way. In the lower part of Gorodishche the defensive moat was filled in with deposits of silt and wood splinters, which disrupted the normal drainage of the terrain and, despite the higher summer temperatures, led to an increase in the general degree of waterlogging. It is possible that this high water content was bound up with the spring floods. Since, apart from the peat and wood-splinter deposits a layer of sand was also encountered, which could have been washed down from a higher part of the cape. The high water content in the lower part of Gorodishche manifested itself in the maximum development of the willow-beds and in the presence of cat's-tail, horsetail and spirea (see section RG4, Figure 2.1). In addition, large numbers of weeds appeared which revealed wide-ranging ecological adaptability (*Polygonum sp.*, Cichoriaceae, *Galeum sp., Artemisia*). It is possible that a heavy spring flood disrupted the ordinary existence of the local biogeocenoses. The nature of the deposits also confirms that suggestion and testifies to the fact that in the first half of the 10th century the level of water in Lake Ilmen rose and also that in the rivers flowing into it. The warmer climate continued leading to still greater development of the lime woods and, less frequently (when the balance of temperature and moisture was more favourable than usual) of oak groves. It was probably at that time that intensive felling of those few woods took place. As more of these species were being cut down, they began to be replaced by small-leaved woods, usually birch woods. Secondary birch woods began to appear and later their number continued to grow. Birch woods began to be just as dominant as the broad-leaved woods. From about the middle of the 10th century a gradual cooling of the climate was noted. In the vicinity of Gorodishche first pines appeared and then spruce as well. Changes in the balance between individual formations in the meadow vegetation were not really significant at first and agricultural exploitation of the territory continued.

The materials obtained by our research did not reflect anything worthy of comment in relation to the second half of the 10th century. We were also not able to trace in any consistent way change in the vegetation cover and specific features of the agricultural land throughout the 11th century. In the 10th century the rise in water levels had evidently been so significant that it could be clearly recorded in the uppermost layer of the 10th-century deposits. The lower layers relating to the 11th century are represented by a thin sandy layer with inclusions of gravel and charcoal. It is possible that this layer was that of the final infill used to level off the defensive moat. Consequently we have only been able to comment clearly on the character of the natural environment in the second half of the 11th century. At that time there had been a conspicuous increase in the wooded areas in comparison to the 10th century and to the degree of neglect which took place in the first half of the 11th century. Woods became the predominant feature in the landscape around Gorodishche and ploughed fields, although they still existed, occupied conspicuously less territory. This meant that near Gorodishche the forest was zonal, but did not constitute the only type of vegetation. Spruce-pine or pine-spruce woods containing small numbers of broad-leaved species were the dominant feature. On richer soils mixed spruce forests might be found and in the vegetation cover of these forests undergrowth could appear consisting of such shrubs as guelder-rose (*Viburnum*) or hawthorn (*Crataegus*). Some areas were occupied by watershed and floodplain meadows. In wetter areas there were marshes and, to judge from the spectra, sphagnum and transitional types together with wild rosemary began to play a conspicuous role with spirea along the edge of swamps. Some territories were occupied with fields of cultivated vegetation and gradually the importance of such vegetation grew.

Vegetation of this kind indicated that the climate at the time was colder than today, and that the forest formations can only be regarded as those of the southern-taiga variety. It is probable that a decline in the intensity of the economic activity of the population of Gorodishche was also to be observed. Subsequently, however, possibly after the 1070s, a new construction phase at Gorodishche began and arable land was used again, and there was a concomitant marked drop in the area covered by forest.

What gave rise to this change in the nature of the vegetation of the forest formations, meadows and ploughed land was not only the slightly warmer climate but also the economic activity that was being pursued. Because the climate was slightly drier, spruce forest played a less important role. Large areas became forested with pine woods, which were probably of a less self-contained character than before. Forest clearings began to appear. The composition of meadow vegetation became more varied than before and the areas under plough increased. It is possible that at this time animal husbandry also increased. Active work at Gorodishche led to changes in the composition of plant communites. Many weeds (goosefoot (Chenopodiaceae) and chicory (Cichoriaceae) families) began to appear around buildings and plants such as plantains (*Plantago*) and knotgrass (*Polygonum aviculare*) grew along roads. Where trees had been felled secondary birch groves began to establish. Open areas now cleared of forest were reincorporated into the general farming crop rotation. This was a period when there was a marked increase in the areas of cereal cultivation, although the meadow vegetation, as before, was characterized by a wide diversity of mesophilous forbs.

At the end of the 11th century and, essentially, at the very beginning of the 12th (dendrochronological dates of 1099 and 1105), the slightly higher temperatures continued and this led to a further reduction in the number of spruce and to an increased role of pines and birches and also of broad-leaved species. It is also important to remember the importance of cultivation in the area. Among the cultivated cereals, barley, wheat, rye and possibly oats were all noted. The agricultural economic productivity was of a fairly high level, since there are few weeds associated with ploughed fields, only spotted knotweed (*Polygonum persicaria*).

At the beginning of the 12th century the nature of the vegetation cover around Gorodishche had changed little from what it had been at the end of the 11th century. At Gorodishche itself, there are some traces of the remains of a large fire, but this was probably localised. There was some reduction in the wood-cover in the surrounding area and the nature of the woodland undergrowth had changed: the percentage of ferns increased, as had sphagnum mosses, but there were fewer other mosses than before. In the first half of the 12th century against a background of continued cooler temperatures, spruce played a more important role as forest edificatory, and there were fewer shrubs in the lowest tier of the forest. In wetter and better lit parts of the spruce forest, shrubs from the heather family (Ericaceae) grew as before with possibly blueberries or bilberries, and crowberries probably grew in the margins of pine. The composition of the meadow vegetation was less varied that it had been in previous periods. It is possible that some of the meadows might have been cultivated because of their low productivity as a meadow/graze for animal fodder, and this would have enhanced their productivity.

After an interval of no less than 15 or 20 years some major changes in the composition of the forests occurred. It would appear that the spruce and pine woods around Gorodishche had been felled and that the primary conifer forest was replaced by secondary birch woods. These changes manifested themselves particularly clearly at this time as this was the first time this had happened during the period so far studied. A major transformation had taken place in the natural vegetation within the area territory. The end of the 12th century was not, however, reflected in the sections that were being studied.

By the beginning of the 13th century primary forest consisting of pines and spruce with a few limes and oaks had re-established itself in the environs of Gorodishche. The ratio of forest to open landscape was, however, virtually the same as before. The waterlogging of this area, particularly in the lower-lying land, appears still to have been considerable. Waterlogging is indicated not only the constant presence of sphagnum mosses and horsetail, but also that of Spirea (*Filipendula*) among the herbaceous plants. The meadows and arable land continued to play a prominent role and the agricultural exploitation of the area was gradually increasing over the whole of the 13th century. Climatic changes during that century have been singled out by a number of scholars, but these changes did not lead to abrupt changes in the composition of the plant ecologies, as had been noted in earlier centuries. By this time the economic activity of the population of Gorodishche had a much greater impact on the landscape, which was exemplified by the scale of forest clearances.

The main forest massifs comprised spruce and pine with a few broad-leaved species, most frequently lime. There had been a noticeable increase in the proportion of nemoral plants when the climate had been warmer. This involved first and foremost lime and, rather less frequently, oak. In the light of dendrochronological observations, also data collected by Borisenko and Pasetskii (1983) and other historical and geological sources there would appear to have been two clearly identifiable warm periods in the 13th century: at the beginning of the century and approximately between 1265 and 1280. By the end of the century the forest around Gorodishche had been gradually destroyed and the landscape in its vicinity became essentially open. By then the only trees in the area would have been willows in the lower parts of the floodplain. Most of the meadows were tilled and cultivated by then.

The end of the 13th century was noteworthy as a period of growing economic activity, primarily of increased settlement in the area around Gorodishche, when the primary plant communities there not only ceased to dominate the landscape but even to be predominant within it.

CHANGE IN THE VEGETATION IN THE ENVIRONS OF THE MININO AND VLADYSHNEVO SETTLEMENTS AROUND LAKE KUBENSKOYE

In the Vologda Region palynological research was carried out at the sites of Minino and Vladyshnevo on the western shore of Lake Kubenskoye in order to piece together the character of the natural environment and the degree to which the territories in question had been settled and exploited. The first of these settlements is near the mouth of the River Dmitrovka and the second is slightly further away from the lake basin on a ridge which follows the whole of the lake's western shore. In the summer, the low water season, Lake Kubenskoye has a surface area of approximately 370 km². The size of the lake and the volume of water in it change to a significant degree depending upon the time of year and the water levels. The lake is 180 m above sea level (Serditov 1957). Lake Kubenskoye first came into being in the wake of glacio-dynamic processes during the so-called lobate stage in the degradation of the ice sheets of the last glaciation in the North-west of the Russian plain (*Problemy stratigrafii chetvertichnykh otlozhenii i kraevye obrazovaniya Vologodskogo regiona [Severo-Zapad Rossii]* {=*Questions of the stratigraphy of quarternary deposits and marginal formations in the Vologda region [North-West of Russia]*} 2000). One of the characteristic features of this stage is the formation of lobes at the edges of glaciers, which reflect a short-lived transgressive movement of the edge of the ice sheet.

As regards the lobe at the site of what is now Lake Kubenskoye, it had a pulsating regime, was moving at a considerable speed and during its movement exerted a significant impact on the lake bed. This enabled the formation of extruded ridges (sometimes regarded as peripheral moraines) in the space adjacent to the lateral parts of the lobe. These ridges round the basin of the Lake Kubenskoye consist mainly of lacustrine aleurites dating to between 55,000 and 15,000 BP. This undoubtedly testifies to intensive mixing while the deposits were being pushed out from under the moving ice lobe, and the creation of fundamentally new glacio-tectonic breccia formations from the original lacustrine deposits. The pulsating regime of the lobe and the considerable speed of its movement led to the breaking of the ice into separate blocks, which melted fairly fast during the degradation of the ice sheets and the relatively short warmer period. Lake Kubenskoye was formed, therefore, in the exaration (glacially dug) depression where the lobe had been, approximately 14,000 years ago.

The area round Lake Kubenskoye, being subject to major cyclonic activity and frequent influxes of Atlantic and continental air masses, is characterized by a moderately continental climate with a moderately warm summer, quite a long moderately cold winter and changeable weather patterns.

The predominant type of vegetation in the Vologda Region was forest, which covered over 68% of the territory. The primary forest in the region consisted of spruce woods. Spruce woods with *Hylocomium*, *Diocranum* and *Rhytidiadelphus* would be found in well-drained areas with podzolic loams and sandy loams. In the lower parts of the relief at poorly drained watersheds there would be spruce woods with haircap-moss, sphagnum and herbaceous-sphagnum. Along the valleys of the rivers and streams and the linear depressions spruce forest containing ferns and tall grasses was found.

Pine forest was associated with sandy podzolic soils and the most typical pine woods would be those containing cowberries or cowberries/bilberries. On flat watersheds and along the edges of oligotrophic moors, sphagnum pine forests were common. The pine woods on the 'forested terraces' of rivers and sandy plains contained lichens and were associated with poor soils. Small-leaved woods consisting of birches, aspen and speckled alder are often secondary ones, which have replaced primary spruce forest after fires or felling. Under their canopy herbaceous plants develop well. There are also many birch woods. Aspen woods are encountered less frequently and they are usually associated with more fertile soils than the birch woods.

Marshes occupy 10–12% of the territory of the Vologda Region, yet the figure for the Lake Kubenskoye area would be slightly lower. Oligotrophic moors predominate containing shrubs and sphagnum and also stunted pines: marshes containing shrubs, grasses and mosses are found less frequently and the latter often contain pines and birch-trees as well. Low-lying marshes (containing grasses or grasses and moss) often occupy the lower parts of river valleys and the shores of lakes or are to be found in places where calcareous rocks protrude at the ground surface.

Meadows along the shores of Lake Kubenskoye occupy between two and five percent of the terrain. Low-yield meadows predominate: the dry ones contain small-grained cereals and small-grained cereals in conjunction with forbs, while the low-lying meadows contain sedges, damp-loving grasses and cereals. Along the river valleys in the basin of Lake Kubenskoye some meadows with a higher yield are found in the flood-plain: meadows with large cereal plants and sedges.

The arable land, both the dry meadows and the ploughed fields, came into being in the area round Lake Kubenskoye in places where forest (mainly of spruce and pine) had been cut down.

Intensive tree-felling had been embarked upon as far back as the medieval period, as can be seen from the results of the palynological research carried out in the Minino and Vladyshnevo settlements situated on the west bank of Lake Kubenskoye. More details of the current vegetation can be found on the accompanying CD.

Pollen Results (see Figures 2.4 and 2.5 in the text and the complete set of diagrams in the accompanying CD)

In the Minino settlement palynological investigations were carried out in four sections: three of these were within the confines of the settlement itself (Sections M3, M6 and M7) and one was a natural section nearby (Section M4). In the Vladyshnevo settlement two sections were examined: one natural section (Section V2) and one from the trench excavated in 2000 in Settlement I (Section V1).

The research carried out at these sites made it possible to trace how the vegetation developed between the end of the first millennium and the 13th century and to identify stages in the primary re-emergence of the plant groupings associated with both climatic conditions and the activities of the inhabitants of the nearby settlements.

As has been noted above, the primary forest in the area under discussion consists of coniferous woods, which occupied most of the territory in the medieval period. This meant that large tracts of forest had to be felled to make it suitable for habitation, cultivation and other economic activities.

Pollen diagrams (Figures 2.4 and 2.5) show that this process was taking place as far back as the end of the 10th century. To judge from the composition and floristic features of the spectra, coniferous woods consisting of pine and spruce were replaced around the settlements with secondary plantings of birch and alder; this was probably in the wake of the felling of coniferous woods. The impact of human activity was reflected not only in the felling of primary forest but also in the appearance of weeds of anthropogenically disturbed ground, such as nettles, knotweed, hemp and chicory. This constituted a fairly short period, and at the beginning of the 11th century some of the spruce woods regenerated. An increase in spruce can be seen and, therefore, primary spruce woods clearly played a more important role in the landscape. Apart from this, the territory was becoming more waterlogged, a development evidenced by the composition of the meadow plant communities; sedge meadows were far more conspicuous than before. Subsequently less of the territory was waterlogged and this was reflected in the smaller proportion of alders in the composition of the forests.

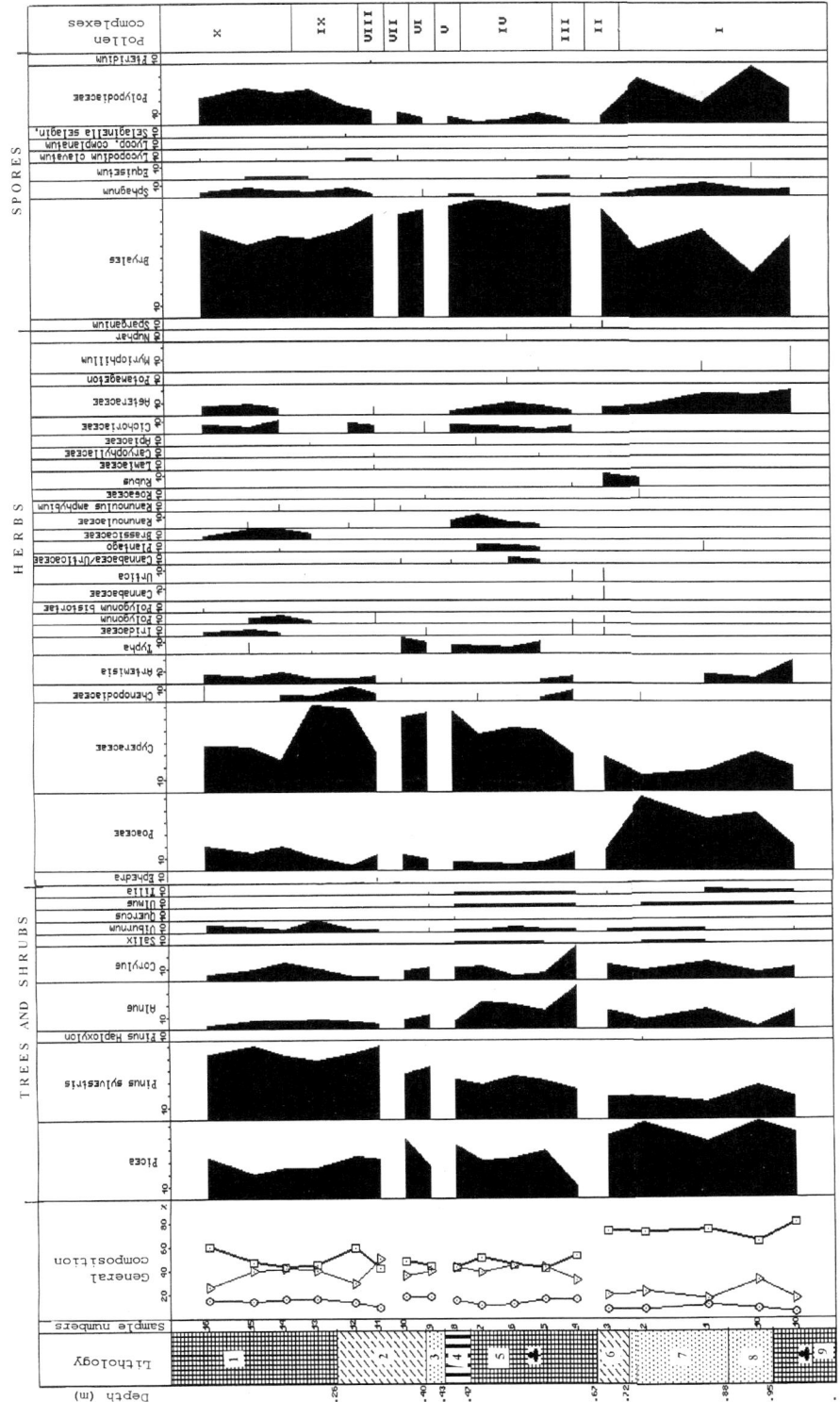

Figure 2.4 Pollen diagram of Section 4 from Minino settlement.

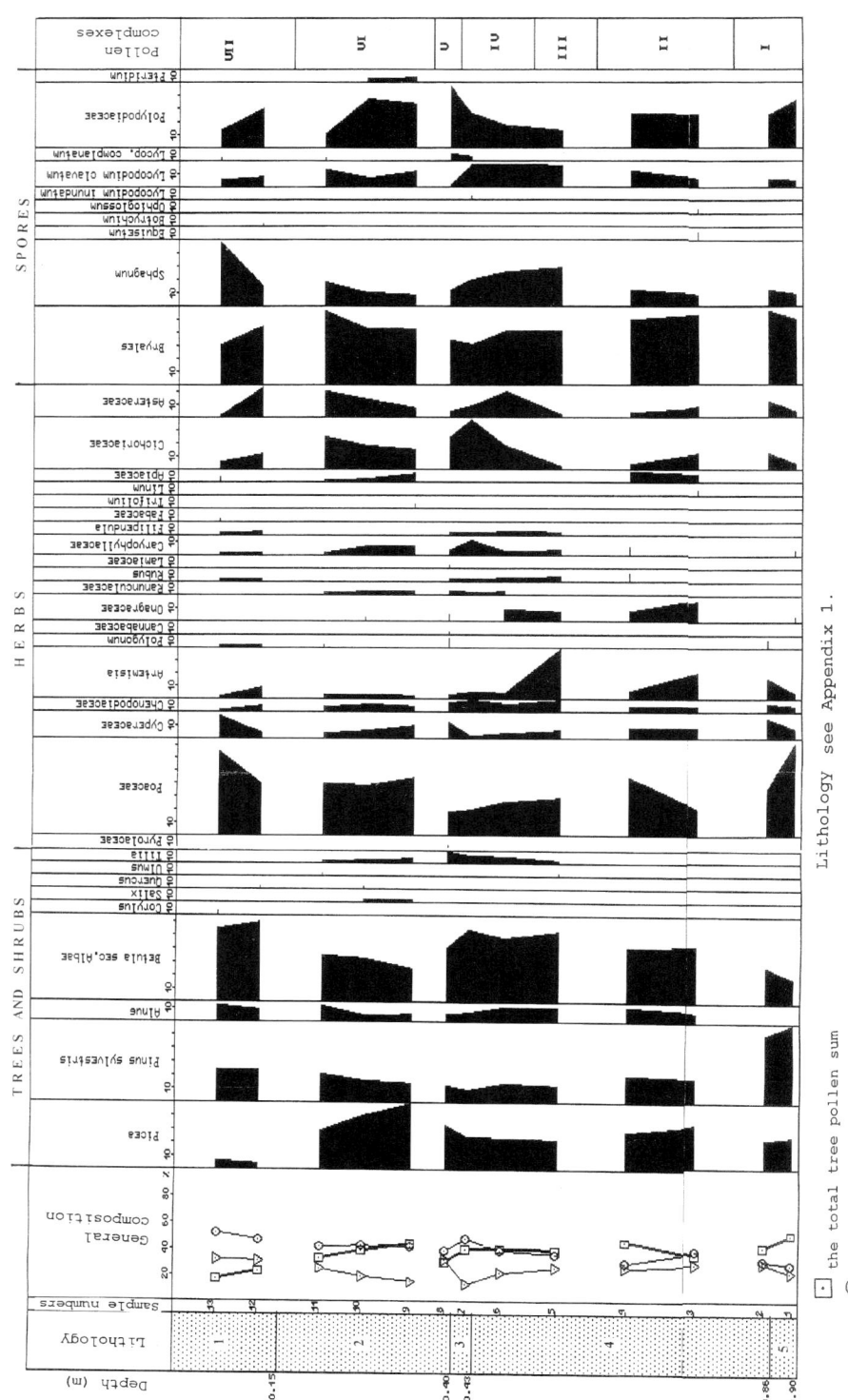

Figure 2.5 Pollen diagram of Section 3 from Minino settlement.

Human economic activity intensified during the 11th century, and substantial changes restructuring the landscape were observed. Birch woods began to play a more important role in the environs of Minino. While woods still predominated over open spaces, they were reduced in comparison with previous phases. A characteristic trait of this period was the predominance of sagebrush among herbaceous plants (39%). The majority of it was probably linked with the destruction of uncultivated lands and may indicate the creation of new clearances for growing crops. Active tree-felling started at this time and continued throughout the whole of the 11th century.

Palynological evidence which reflects the development of vegetation making it possible to state that the warmest climatic conditions were in the second half of the 11th century. Lime trees began to appear in primary coniferous forest. Near the settlement, as before, birch played a major role. The composition of meadow vegetation is diverse and includes the buttercup, pink, willow herb, aster, chicory and other families. The samples from Section M3 in the settlement of Minino include the pollen of cultivated cereals, sometimes in clusters. These are large forms with a distinct ridge round the poral aperture. These features in the morphology of pollen grains are characteristic for most cultivated species of cereals (see micro-photographs on CD). Smaller forms of cereal pollen are encountered as well, which might also have come from cultivated species, but it is impossible to draw categorical conclusions, because the pollen of some wild cereals is of a similar size.

At the end of the 11th and beginning of the 12th century a decline of up to 29% in arboreal pollen is to be observed. At the same time there was an increase of up to 32% in the sporophyte content of the samples. Herbaceous plants made up 39%. All this relates to the change in overall levels of humidity and possibly the water content of the territory under consideration, which can be deduced from the marked increase of the proportion of sporous plants in the general composition of the flora and from the major presence of spruce among the trees and of sedges among the herbaceous plants. Weeds appear in large number, which is apparently linked with the change in the ecological conditions around the settlement and possibly with the change in the way specific sections of the settled territory were being used at that time.

The composition of plant communities is close to the zonal type of that period, as regards the proportion of both specific trees and also of forbs among the herbaceous plants. Some human impact is reflected in the reduced role of woodland in the overall picture and of the predominance of birch over spruce and pine in the composition of those woods.

From this period onwards man began to have an ever greater impact on the environment of the settlement, as is made clear by the increasing reduction in woodland (the amount of tree pollen falls to 16%) and also in the increase of ploughed arable land.

At the same time the territory is becoming increasingly waterlogged. This is seen in the far greater proportion of sporophytes and, in particular, from the marked increase in the amount of sphagnum mosses, the appearance of willows and a large amount of plants from the sedge family together with the cereals.

After a certain interval, the pollen data indicates, the reappearance of spruce in the woodland composition, which testifies to the re-establishment of the primary coniferous forest. The substantial reduction in the presence of birch can be explained with reference to two factors. They could either have been gradually replaced by spruce, or they might have been selectively felled, after which the resulting clearings were tilled. The later explanation is more probable because of the gradual decline in woodlands and the concomitant rise in cultivated cereals.

Open spaces, which play an important part around the settlement, were occupied in the main by meadow forbs and weeds, among which representatives of the chicory and aster families predominated. The large amount of cereal pollen (55% of the total), suggests that large areas were being cultivated.

It is possible that at the end of the 12th century more intensive felling of primary forest began and was subsequently replaced by birch – a development which can be clearly traced in the increase (up to 60%) of birch pollen. It is at this time that intensive economic activity around the settlement becomes most obvious. In the overall picture there is a very low tree pollen content, which could be related to an increase in the settlement area. Furthermore among the herbaceous plants the proportion of cultivated cereals was considerable. It would appear that the area of ploughed land was approximately the same as that of meadow-land. At the same time the marked deviations from the natural or zonal type of vegetation led to the territory becoming more waterlogged, which, in turn, led to a sharp increase in sphagnum mosses.

In the 13th century the most widespread woods were of pine, although the role of spruce was substantial as previously. The change in the edificators of the forest components was most probably determined by the heavily waterlogged nature of the area. Pine could have replaced spruce, which does not easily withstand waterlogging.

An increase of up to 47% in the spruce pollen in the spectra from the next stage (13th and 14th centuries), points to small changes in the composition of the vegetation cover of that stage. Once again there was more spruce in the forest and a decrease in the proportion of broad-leaved trees. The nature of the meadowland and marsh vegetation remained the same.

The composition of the spectra at the end of the 14th century show that from this stage onward pine forest was the most widespread. The absence of broad-leaved species in these forests implies that these were mid-taiga pine forests including some spruce. From the climatic point of view, this was the coldest period with the highest precipitation levels in comparison with all the previous stages. The territory around the settlement became more waterlogged, as reflected in the marked increase in the amount of sedges in the meadow vegetation and in the slightly smaller proportion of spruce among the forest-forming species. The latter is probably linked with the stagnant water in the overly-moist soils to which spruce cannot adapt. The deterioration in the climatic conditions, which led to rising water levels in the River Dmitrovka and possibly also Lake Kubenskoye, was probably the reason for the decline of the settlement.

Later on the pollen spectra indicate a reduction in precipitation levels, and a slight drop in the water-table, along with a reduction in the waterlogging. In the herbaceous plants the proportion of sedge pollen was down to 25–37%. At the same time there was a renewed increase in the amount of pollen from forbs; mainly the chicory and aster families. There was also an increase in the cereal pollen of the overall sample (on average up to 18%). The general character of the composition of the forest was still close to that of the four last stages in the 13th to 14th centuries, while the increase or reduction in the proportions of spruce was determined by specifically local conditions. In comparison with the previous stages, the proportion of forb meadows increased again: the composition of this vegetation included representatives of the cabbage, buttercup, buckwheat, aster, chicory, iris and other families.

The spectra from the last stage are characterized by a predominance of spruce, spruce-and-pine and pine forests with small areas of meadowland vegetation of varying composition in between. This means that the changes in vegetation in the environs of Minino were mainly the result of the impact of man's economic activity, which began at the beginning of the 10th century.

The most substantial reshaping of the landscape in the middle of the 11th century and at the end of the 12th was linked with the felling of primary coniferous forest and its replacement with secondary birch woods. At the same time there was a gradual reduction in the areas of woodland and a gradual increase in meadowland and cultivated areas. At the end of the 12th century the proportions of ploughed and meadow-land were roughly equal, while woodland was considerably reduced. This is the time when the most significant human impact on the environment occurred.

As for natural change in the vegetation cover two facts are worth noting: first, the increase in the broad-leaved trees in the composition of the forest in the mid-11th century as a result of warmer climatic conditions and, secondly, cooler climatic conditions and increased humidity at the very end of the 11th and beginning of the 12th centuries and at the end of the 13th century. This latter fact was probably one of the reasons for the degradation of the Minino settlement.

COMPARISON OF THE SPORE AND POLLEN DIAGRAMS FROM ARCHAEOLOGICAL SITES IN THE AREA AROUND LAKE ILMEN AND LAKE KUBENSKOYE

There are certain difficulties associated with the stratigraphic correlation of the sites located near large lakes in the North-West of European Russia, such as Lake Ilmen and Lake Kubenskoye, stemming from the remote nature of the features being investigated; the differences between the two geographic locations, the nature of the geology on which habitation took shape at the two sites, and in the degree of human impact on the environments in question. The sites are, however, situated within one and the same landscape zone and have similar geo-morphological positions, giving

Research locality	Average January temperature	Average July temperature	Annual precipitation in mm	Duration of vegetative period (days)	Number of days with snow cover
Lake Ilmen area	-8 °C	18 °C	650–700	175	120–135
Lake Kubenskoye area	-11.5 °C	16–17.5 °C	500–650	170	165–170

Table 2.1 *Comparison of the main Climate Indices for the Novgorod and Vologda Regions.*

rise to many similarities in the character of their vegetation cover throughout the medieval period.

As has already been pointed out the two areas studied are located in similar landscape conditions but have slightly different climatic indices. Despite the fact that both these areas are in a zone with a moderately continental climate, the degree of impact from the Atlantic Ocean varies. In the area round Lake Ilmen, it is stronger, as can be seen from the larger amount of precipitation, the higher temperatures in both winter and summer and in the longer vegetative period and shorter duration of the snow cover (Table 2.1).

Differences were noted in the vegetation cover as well. The area around Lake Ilmen is in a zone of mixed coniferous and broad-leaved forest, while the environs of Lake Kubenskoye are in a southern taiga zone. This means that when the pollen diagrams are compared it would be difficult to expect complete parallels between these given areas. Nevertheless, comparison of the pollen data revealed certain patterns in the development of the vegetation to be found in both the area around Lake Kubenskoye and also that around Lake Ilmen.

In order to make more precise comparisons it was essential for each interval of time recorded in the pollen diagrams to distinguish between specifically local, regional and supra-regional changes in the vegetation cover of the study areas. As a rule, local characteristics manifested themselves in the diagrams in the differing compositions of meadow vegetation. Regional characteristics were noted due to changing patterns in the sub-dominants among the tree, while the supra-regional features often came to light in the different roles of specific trees species in the general composition of the flora and also in the larger role played by nemoral elements in the area around Lake Ilmen.

The concept of a pollen zone is of purely stratigraphic significance and it brings together the palynological spectra of similar composition. Yet, while working in the medieval period, it is necessary to take into account the whole composition of the spectra and to introduce correction factors when piecing together the vegetation cover of the territory under investigation, as well as to identify pollen zones. This attention to detail only serves to underline the complexity of the changes in the natural environment during the medieval period against the background of its transformation under the impact of human economic activity.

In order to chronologically compare the individual pollen sections, a table was drawn up to correlate the sections at the sites near Lake Ilmen and Lake Kubenskoye respectively (Table 2.2). This table, together with the pollen diagrams for each section, provides the most detailed picture of the character of the natural environment and how it changed over the almost five centuries of the medieval period. As a result of this study of the general conclusions drawn from comparison of the data from the various sites, it has been possible to form not only an idea of the changes in environmental conditions, but also to link these in with the question of the interaction and interdependence of nature and society.

The main palynological characteristics of the sections investigated from these two areas may now be considered. The oldest of the habitation levels studied were those exposed at Gorodishche in Section 4. Seventeen spore and pollen ranges with spectra of spores and pollen (see Table 2.2) similar in composition were identified from this section and they correspond to zones 1–17. The seven lowest palynological zones can only be discerned at Gorodishche and they relate to the development of vegetation during the 8th and 9th centuries. As has been made clear by the investigations, during this period changes took place in vegetation on a number of occasions as is reflected in the pollen diagrams. In virtually all the pollen spectra from that period pollen from herbaceous plants dominates in the general composition. Most of the spectra (zones 1, 3, 5 and 7) are characterized by pine pollen (*Pinus*) (31–49%). Birch pollen (*Betula* 7–20%) is also frequently encountered. The composition of herbaceous plants from the whole section varies little. In virtually all of the palynological zones pollen from forbs predominates: there are large amounts of pollen from moisture-loving plants such as spirea (*Filipendula*). In all of the palynological zones cereal pollen (Poaceae) (on average around 20%) is present. Only in a few samples are deviations from this composition to be found, mainly those associated with the increase in the amount of cultivated cereals.

Of particular interest are the two zones relating to the second half of the 8th century, when a high content of birch (*Betula*) pollen is present. It was precisely at this time that the settlement of what was to become Gorodishche was beginning. Changes of this kind were probably bound up with man's economic activity: with forest clearance and cultivation, which is also confirmed by the appearance in the spectra of cultivated cereal pollen and the weeds that follow in their wake. Pollen zone 6 provides a record of the warmer temperatures in the 9th century. In the relevant spectra it is the pollen of lime (*Tilia*) which predominates (39–67%). In addition oak pollen (*Quercus*) and elm (*Ulmus*) is present. Attention should also be paid to the rise in the quantity of cereal pollen (Poaceae) to 43% and this includes pollen from cultivated species. It was only towards the middle of the 9th century that a slight drop in temperatures was noted, when the role of broad-leaved species was almost non-existent.

The vegetation at the end of the 9th century can be traced from sections at both

			Lake Kubenskoye						Lake Ilmen					
Calibrated dates	Palynological Zones	Project wide Zone No.	Minino IV S. M4	Minino IV S.M3	Minino IV S.M6	Minino S.M7	Vlad. S.V2	Vlad. S.V1	Date	Palynological zones	Project wide Zone No.	Ryurik Gorod. S.RG1	Ryurik Gorod. S.RG2	Ryurik Gorod. S.RG4
			Natural section	Archaeology section	Archaeology section	Archaeology section	Natural section	Archaeology section				Archaeology section	Archaeology section	Archaeology section
			Fig 2.4 & CD 4	Fig 2.5 & CD 5	CD 6	CD 7	CD 9	CD 8				Fig 2.3 & CD 3	Fig 2.2 & CD 2	Fig 2.1 & CD 1
	Spruce, pine with some birch and alder; forbs, sedges	20					VII	VI						
	Pine with some spruce; forbs	19	X				VI	V						
	Pine with some spruce, sedges	18	IX				V							
1370± 46 AD	Pine with some spruce and a little birch and alder	17	VIII		V	IV	IV	IV						
										Pine, birch with some broad-leaved species and alder	32	VIII		
									End of 13th cent.	Pine, spruce with some birch and broad-leaved species	31	VII		
										Spruce, pine	30	VI		
										Spruce with some pine and broad-leaved species	29	V		
										Spruce, pine with some alder, birch and broad-	28	IV		

No.	Date	Vegetation	Zone a	Zone b	Zone c
27		Spruce, pine with some broad-leaved species	III		
26		Spruce, pine, broad-leaved species	II		
25		Pine with some spruce	I		
24		Birch with some pine and spruce	VII		
23		Spruce, pine with a little birch	VI	III	II
22		Pine, spruce with some birch and broad-leaved species	V		II
21		Pine with some birch and broad-leaved species	IV		
16		Spruce, pine	VII		
15		Pine with some spruce and a little alder, birch and broad-leaved species	VI		
14		Birch with some pine and a little alder	VII		
13	1170±59 AD	Spruce, birch with some pine; cereals	VI	IV	III
12		Spruce, birch with some pine and a few broad-leaved species	VI	III	II
11		Pine with some spruce and a little birch and alder	II		
10		Birch, pine with some alder	III		
9	1100±44 AD	Birch with some spruce and pine and a little alder	II		
8	1054±51 AD	Birch, spruce with some pine and broad-leaved species	V		
7		Birch with some spruce, pine, alder and a few broad-leaved species;	IV		

						Column								
		forbs												
		Birch with some spruce, pine and alder	6	III		II						III		
		Spruce, pine with a little birch	5	V						20	Pine with some spruce	III		
1011±114 AD		Spruce, pine with some alder, a little birch and some broad-leaved species	4	IV				I		19	Pine, spruce	II	I	
										18	Spruce with some pine	I		
1004±14 AD		Alder, birch, pine with a little spruce and broad-leaved species	3	III			I	I						
										17	Broad-leaved species, birch			XVII
										16	Broad-leaved species with some birch and pine			XVI
										15	Birch with some broad-leaved species and pine			XV
										14	Broad-leaved species with some birch and pine			XIV
										13	Spruce, pine with some broad-leaved species			XIII
									889	12	Pine			XII
										11	Broad-leaved species			XI
		Spruce with some	2	II						10	Pine, birch			X

Date	Section	No.	Vegetation description
	IX	9	spruce Broad-leaved species with some pine, birch and spruce
	VIII	8	Birch, broad-leaved species, birch and spruce
	VII	7	Pine with some birch
	VI	6	Broad-leaved species
	V	5	Pine with some birch and broad-leaved species
	IV	4	Broad-leaved species with some pine, birch and spruce
	III	3	Pine with some broad-leaved species and birch
	II	2	Birch, broad-leaved species and spruce
890± 54AD	I	1	pine and birch Spruce with some pine and broad-leaved genera

Table 2.2 Correlation of the Sections at archaeological sites in the Lake Kubenskoye and Lake Ilmen areas according to data obtained through palynological analysis. The dates were obtained in the laboratory of the Institute for the History of Material Culture. The calibrated dates were re-calculated using the programme CalPal (CalCurve Comparison. A comparison of INTCAL98 / CALPAL98 / CALPAL1998 / CALPAL2001 / CALPAL2003 / CalPAL2004_Jan / CalPal-Online. Updated January 2004).

sites and constitutes palynological zone 9 at Gorodishche and zone 1 at the Minino settlement. In the spectra relating to this period we find once again that a high pollen content from broad-leaved trees is typical. In the samples from Section 4 at Gorodishche, for instance, lime pollen (*Tilia* 30–48%) and oak (*Quercus* 10–40%) is often found. It is precisely at this level that the maximum figure for oak (*Quercus*) pollen is found (40%) in the composition of arboreal pollen from trees. There are also large amounts of pine (*Pinus*), birch (*Betula*) and spruce (*Picea*). At the Minino settlement a rise was also noted in pollen from broad-leaved species, which were represented by oak (*Quercus*), elm (*Ulmus*) and lime (*Tilia*). Unlike Gorodische, however, data from this site still revealed a high percentage of spruce pollen (*Picea* 55–66%) and the proportion of pine pollen (*Pinus sylvestris*) was also high (16–23%). The differences noted in the composition of the spectra can be explained with reference to the physical geography of the sites, and by changes in climate that took place at this time but which impacted differently on the plant communities in these regions.

Pollen zone 10 at Gorodishche correlates with zone 2 at the Minino settlement. In the general composition of the spectra at both sites arboreal pollen predominates: 51–60% at Gorodishche and 74% at the Minino settlement. The composition of the range of trees was changing. Pollen from broad-leaved trees was seldom encountered while there was an increase in pine pollen (*Pinus*) and spruce (*Picea*). At both sites the amount of birch pollen (*Betula*) remained high (17–33%).

In zones 11 and 12 at Gorodishche the overwhelming majority consisted of herbaceous plants (55–82%), and among these it was forbs which predominated. At the same time the two pollen zones differed from each other with regard to the proportions of the various tree species. In zone 11 broad leaved trees predominated (*Tilia* 51–69%) and in zone 12 trees were represented mainly by pine (*Pinus* 55%). For zone 12, Chernykh provided the date of AD 889 from dendrochronological data.

The period of the 10th and 11th centuries (zones 13–17) was only identified at the Gorodishche site from Section 4. The composition of the tree species of zone 13 was quite varied. Spruce (*Picea* 28%) and pine (*Pinus* 27%) were present in approximately equal measure. Birch (*Betula* 18%) and lime (*Tilia* 12%) were encountered frequently as well. Characteristic within the group of herbaceous plants was the predominance of forbs and the increase in the proportion of cereals (Poaceae 30%) and sagebrush (*Artemisia* 14%).

The next four zones (14–17) shed light on the natural conditions in the part of the 10th century during which a large amount of broad-leaved trees was noted – the dominant feature of this phase. The composition of this was mainly lime (*Tilia* 30–57%) and oak (*Quercus* 3–10%). Among the herbaceous plants forbs still predominated, while in zone 16 an important feature was the increase in cereals (Poaceae) in comparison with other zones: cereals included pollen from cultivated species. Moreover these were sometimes present in large clusters, which could indicate that the said pollen had been carried over a short distance. Essentially these conditions were favourable for the development of 'islands' of broad-leaved forest, meadows and ploughed land.

The vegetation at the end of the 10th century is illustrated by zone 3 (Sections 4 and 7) at the Minino settlement. Unlike the situation in the environs of Lake Ilmen, here it was arboreal pollen which predominated. A similar pattern was retained right up until the 11th century, when active settlement was beginning in both the areas. From that time on the amount of trees began to decrease: it reached its minimum level in the 12th century both at Gorodishche and the Minino settlement. In these alder (*Alnus* 35%) predominated. Also conspicuous was the birch (*Betula* 28%) and somewhat less so pine (*Pinus* 24%). The proportion of spruce pollen (*Picea*) fell as low as 10%. Only isolated examples of oak (*Quercus*), lime (*Tilia*), elm (*Ulmus*) and willow (*Salix*) were found. The composition of herbaceous plants was fairly varied: most frequent were forbs (38%) and sedges (Cyperaceae 30%). There were large amounts of weeds.

This evidence shows that in the period of the greatest economic activity the population of Minino destroyed large parts of the zonal forest and created as much ploughed land as possible. The large proportion of sedges and sphagnum mosses testify to the fact that the destruction of natural biocenoses led to the area becoming waterlogged.

The development of vegetation in the 11th century can be 'reconstructed' both with the help of materials from the sections at Gorodishche (zones 18–20) and also those from the Minino and Vladyshnevo settlements (zones 4–7). At Gorodishche the characteristics of this stage and subsequent ones can be gleaned from Section 2, in which only seven spore and pollen ranges were identified (zones 18–24). At the Minino settlement the various stages within this period of time can be identified within Sections 3, 4 and 6 and within Sections 1 and 2 at Vladyshnevo.

Pollen zones 4 and 5 identified in the Minino settlements (Section M4) and at Vladyshnevo (Sections V1 and V2) can duly be compared with zones 18–19 and 20 at Gorodishche (Section RG2). In the settlements of Minino and Vladyshnevo and from Gorodishche, spruce (*Picea* 30–52%) and pine (*Pinus* 27–42%) dominate the woodlands: moreover, at Gorodishche pine was encountered more frequently. As regards herbaceous plants, at Gorodishche cereals (Poaceae) predominate, mostly cultivated forms, while at the Minino and Vladyshnevo settlements there were large amounts of forbs and sedges (Cyperaceae). These spectra illustrate the gradual re-establishment of the zonal forest plant communities, although the total area of forest in the territory was still less than the zonal figure.

The next five zones (6–10) identified from the sections in the Minino settlement illustrate the natural conditions obtaining in the 11th and early-12th century. In all the zones herbaceous plants (36–44%) were predominant as previously. A characteristic feature of these zones was the large quantity of birch (*Betula*) (approximately 50%) but there is a difference to be observed between the zones when it comes to the proportions of other trees. In zones 7 and 10, for instance, in addition to birch (*Betula*), there was also spruce (*Picea*), pine (*Pinus*) and alder (*Alnus*); in zones 8 and 9 there was also a good deal of broad-leaved trees; in zone 11 birch (*Betula*), pine (*Pinus*) and alder (*Alnus*) were present. In all the zones forbs predominated and, moreover, its composition was fairly varied.

Pollen zones 6 and 7 can be compared with zone 21 at Gorodishche. In all three, the presence of birch (*Betula*) is noted, although pine (*Pinus*) predominates. In connection with the fact that in the environs of Minino large expanses of land were forested, the settlement demanded that large areas be cleared, which later became overgrown with birch trees that eventually came to constitute secondary birch woods. At the same time in the area around Lake Ilmen large open landscapes prevailed, which meant it was not necessary to fell the surrounding forests so intensively: hence the smaller percentage of birch present. In the environs of Gorodishche at that time pine forests were springing up on the sandy soils, while secondary birch woods were not as widely developed as in the vicinity of the Minino settlement.

The vegetation of the 12th century was illustrated in zone 11, identified within the section at the settlement of Vladyshnevo and in zone 22 within Section 2 at Gorodishche. Both these zones were distinguished by a high content of pine (*Pinus* 40–46%) and spruce (*Picea* 20–38%). In the group of herbaceous plants, cereals (Poaceae) predominated: these included cultivated varieties which would indicate large expanses of cultivated land. In the second half of the 12th century a large quantity of spruce (*Picea*) was present. There was also a large quantity of birch (*Betula* 32–38%). The proportion of pine (*Pinus*) was 13–17%. This is, moreover, typical both for the sites round Lake Kubenskoye (zones 12 and 13) and also for Gorodishche (zone 23). These data testify to the fact that in the second half of the 12th century temperatures had been falling somewhat in both areas under discussion and this development can also be traced in the dendrochronological data (Chernykh 1996).

The next three zones can be traced at all of the sites in this study and may be clearly compared with each other (Table 2.2). Pollen zones with a predominance of birch (*Betula* 55–60%) give way to zones in which pine (*Pinus*) is beginning to predominate (42–68%) and later spruce (*Picea* 36–47%). With regard to herbaceous plants there was a good deal of cereals (Poaceae) and weeds.

Spruce (*Picea*) and pine (*Pinus*) continued to dominate in the next four zones (27–30) as well, which can be singled out in Section 1 at Gorodishche and which illustrate the features of the vegetation in the 13th century. In addition, birch (*Betula* up to 14%) and alder (*Alnus* 11%) are encountered quite frequently. The composition of the herbaceous plants is almost the same as that found in the previous zones.

The distinctive feature of zones 31 and 32 from Gorodishche is the very different composition of the range of trees compared to what had been encountered before. Pine (*Pinus*) was most frequent (up to 44%). The amount of spruce (*Picea*) was lower than it had been in the previous zones, but it still remained fairly high (25–33%). Among the herbaceous plants forbs predominated, but higher up in the section there was an increase in the amount of cereals (Poaceae).

The last four zones have only been identified in the sections at the Minino and Vladyshnevo settlements. Arboreal pollen (45–49%) dominates the range of trees being similar to that of the preceding zone, but the composition of the herbaceous plant range is substantially different. Here sedges (Cyperaceae) are encountered most frequently and predominate this zone (68–71%). Forbs fall by about 10%. Cereals (Poaceae) constitute between 4 and 11%, sagebrush (*Artemisia*) and plants of the goosefoot family (Chenopodiaceae) account for 4%.

These spectra reflect the decline in economic activity. A gradual re-establishment of the zonal type of vegetation is to be observed taking place, although as before the low proportion of tree species in the overall composition is an echo of the disruption of natural plant families which had taken place earlier.

– 3 –

THE MININO PROJECT:
THE INVESTIGATION OF A GROUP OF
MEDIEVAL SITES IN THE BYELOOZERO
REGION OF NORTHERN RUSSIA

N. A. Makarov

INTRODUCTION

Unfortified, medieval rural settlements make up the largest category of archaeological sites in the Russian plain, but they are also the sites which have been subjected to less investigation than any other category. The total number of such settlements with habitation levels dating from the second half of the 10th to the 13th century, i.e. relating to what is deemed the classic culture of medieval Russia, comes to several thousand. On the basis of the data so far available in the central and northern parts of European Russia (that is, within the territory of the modern Pskov, Novgorod, Leningrad, Vologda, Tver, Yaroslavl, Smolensk, Moscow and Kostroma, Nizhegorod, Ivanovo and Vladimir Regions) excavations of more than 80 m² have been carried out in 62 settlements dating from the period in question (Figure 3.1). This means that only a tiny proportion of the enormous area occupied by these medieval Russian settlements have been excavated. As a result our current knowledge regarding rural settlements of the pre-Mongol period (i.e. pre-1238) has been established upon a very inadequate sample of the culture, economy and social characteristics of the settlements concerned.

This situation can to a large extent be explained by the actual nature of the medieval settlements when approached as subjects for archaeological study. Despite all the various regional and individual differences encountered, in the vast majority of cases these sites have a fairly thin cultural layer often disturbed by ploughing. Ploughing over long periods makes it difficult, if not impossible, not only to identify the stratigraphy within the cultural layer, but also to piece together the lay-out of the settlements and to make out the remains of dwellings. The results of wide-scale excavations of certain settlements undertaken in the 1950s and 1960s were to some extent a disappointment for the researchers involved, who then began to study medieval Russian villages by identifying the structure of settlements without clearing large areas, merely carrying out surveys of cultural remains, relying heavily on surface finds. The return to large-scale excavation in the 1990s required a far-reaching modernization of field-work

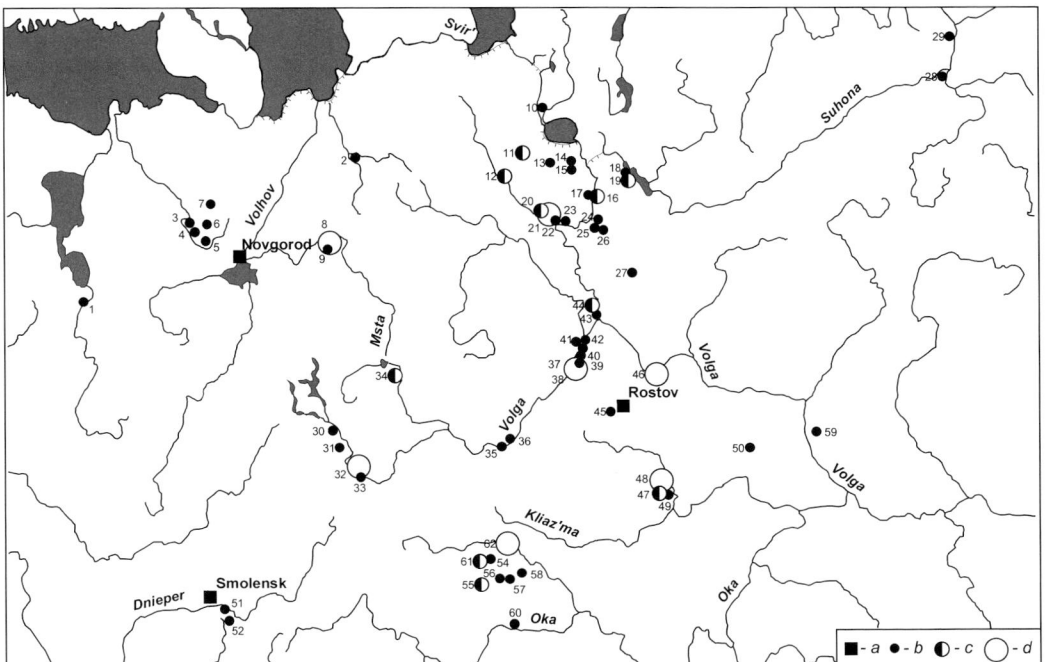

Figure 3.1 Map showing the 62 rural dwelling sites of the 10th to early 13th-century sites where excavations of at least 80 m² have been carried out and produced medieval deposits. Key: a – medieval urban centers; b – rural dwelling sites with an excavated area from 80 to 500 m²; c – rural dwelling sites with an excavated area from 500 to 1000 m²; d – rural dwelling sites with an excavated area over 1000 m². For names of sites please see the list.[1]

methods, a search for more effective ways to investigate deposits including improved collection methods of artefacts, and wider use of methods drawing on the natural sciences for the retrieval and study of palaeo-ecological remains.

THE MININO ARCHAEOLOGICAL PROJECT

One of the largest field projects devoted to the study of medieval rural settlements in the northern margins of medieval Russia to have been carried out in the last decade was the investigation of the Minino Archaeological Complex on Lake Kubenskoye 70 km from Vologda. This complex consists of three medieval rural settlements (known as Minino I, VI and VII) occupying a total area of no less than 4.5 hectares, a burial ground (Minino II), and traces of iron production. Preliminary excavations at one of the settlements in 1996 by the Onega-Sukhona Expedition of the Institute of Archaeology of the Russian Academy of Sciences marked the beginning of a cycle of field investigations that continued until 2003. Minino was approached as a model site, which might yield up materials that would shed light on general features of the medieval clan-based villages of Northern Russia, on their economy and culture, and the general environmental conditions for their existence (Makarov and Zakharov 2000; Makarov 2001; Makarov and Zakharov 2003). The selection of the Minino group of sites for wide-scale excavations lasting many years was determined by its state of preservation, the burial complexes and the landscape context (unusually good for northern settlements in this case) and by the geographical situation of this cluster of settlements on the very edge of the region in which large rural settlements dating from the late 10th to the early 13th century had been recorded by archaeologists.

The group of medieval sites near the village of Minino is on the western shore of Lake Kubenskoye at the mouth of the River Dmitrovka (also known in the past as the Karachevka) which flows into it (see Figure 3.2). All three of the settlements involved are on the main river terrace. The first of them, Minino I, occupies a ridge of land resembling a cape nearest of all to the lake: it is a terrace rising 3 m above the flood plain. The other two are situated further up river 450–500 m from the lake on pieces of land between 4 and 5.5 m above the modern water level.

Minino I

The settlement known as Minino I (Figure 3.3) and the first to be excavated differs somewhat in its overall appearance from the majority of settlements found in Northern Russia. On its surface small hillocks can be seen with large stones protruding from them, the remains of stone stoves from inside medieval buildings lying immediately beneath the turf. It is evident that the area occupied by this village had never been ploughed using modern agricultural machinery (although at certain periods horse-drawn equipment may have been used) and that the habitation levels have remained virtually undisturbed. The first major excavations of this site were undertaken in 1993 by S. Y. Vasiliev, who first discovered the site. He identified the relatively thick layer of habitation levels, the lower of which contained pottery and tools from the Stone Age and early Iron Age periods and burials of the Mesolithic and Neolithic periods. In the course of subsequent excavations it was established that the medieval settlement, which occupied a total area of 1.4 hectares, was located on a terrace above the river's floodplain, which had been settled on a number of occasions in antiquity.

In the trenches of the Onega-Sukhona Expedition a cultural layer was identified which had a thickness of between 40 and 90 cm. In the eastern section of this area the upper part of this layer was made up of medieval deposits with a thickness of 30–50 cm and lower down there were deposits from the Stone and Early Metal Ages and burials from a burial-mound of the Late Mesolithic and Early Neolithic periods. In the northern and western sections of the area the cultural layer was between 40 and 55 cm thick and dated exclusively from the medieval period. The extremely high concentration of artefacts and palaeo-ecological remains in the medieval cultural deposits and the presence of habitation levels and burials from a primitive period over a significant part of the site led those involved to contemplate the possibility of investigating the settlement within a single trench extending over a large area. Instead of that six smaller trenches were dug with a total area of 301 m² making it possible to study the cultural layer and structures and also to collect materials from different parts of the site. This approach enabled us to obtain the necessary materials for describing the lay-out and stratigraphy of the settlement and to collect a representative collection of artefacts (approximately 5,180 finds from the medieval period, without counting pottery) while preserving untouched a significant part of the site.

Minino VI and VII

Two other settlements located slightly higher up the Dmitrovka river, 250 m from Minino I, one on each side of the river, provide a striking contrast with the first site. Their cultural layer has to a significant extent been destroyed by ploughing. The small settlement known as Minino VII (with an area of 1,500 m²) occupies the edge of the main terrace on the north bank of the River Dmitrovka, which is 5–5.5 m above the water level, has only been studied using a reconnaissance trench. At the settlement known as Minino VI, on the opposite south bank of the river, an area of approximately 600 m² was cleared. This latter settlement was on a river-bank terrace 4–5.5 m high and in its western section there was a sharp slope towards the North: the central and eastern parts were flat next to the cemetery of the Dmitrovskii church, one of the parish centres on Lake Kubenskoye. In the part of the settlement free of woods or bushes, traces of the boundaries between old fields and piles of stones cleared from the fields could be seen. The reconnaissance work had revealed the presence of medieval pottery in 14 test pits within a total area of 3 hectares, but in the western part of the settlement, however, within an area of at least one hectare, the concentration of medieval pottery within the cultural layer was low. The greatest concentration of pottery and maximum thickness of the deposits were noted in the central part of the settlement approximately 80 m north-east of the Church of St. Dmitri. Excavations were carried out here in two wide trenches which crossed each other at right angles (Figure 3.4).

The cultural deposits in a major part of this excavation could be divided into two main levels, an amorphous dark-grey sandy loam containing humus (the ploughed level) 20–38 cm thick and underneath it a dark-grey (almost black) medieval habitation level consisting of sandy loam with a high humus content and large numbers of stove stones, large pottery fragments and animal and fish bones, which had not been disturbed by ploughing. In the whole excavated area a total of 72 pits containing artefacts, pottery and animal and fish bones was recorded. In all parts of the ploughed level medieval pottery predominated among the finds: among these pottery fragments round rims were found with profiles typical for the 13th and 14th centuries. In the fill of the pits cut into the natural soil most of the finds were fragments of medieval pottery, both hand-moulded and wheel-turned. The total number of finds from this excavated area was 1,730 not counting the pottery. The artefacts included objects from all periods ranging from the 11th century to recent times and among these finds household objects and jewellery from the 11th, 12th and early-13th century predominated.

Minino II

The Minino II burial-ground on the north bank of the Dmitrovka River is located on one of the sections of the main river terrace separated from the central settlement of the Minino complex by a small gulley containing a stream which runs dry in the summer. The burial-ground area, which lies 3–4 m above the river is partly overgrown by woods, while the rest is either under meadowland or built over. There are no outward indications of the burials on the surface but, to judge from finds of bones in the exposed areas, the burial-ground had stretched in a West-East direction over a distance of no less than 220 m. Only a small part of this burial-ground is now accessible for research, the part which is covered neither with woodland or buildings. The excavations of 1998–2004 were carried out in four locations in the west and east parts of the area in question. Approximately 860 m² were cleared and the remains of approximately 80 burials were examined: 63 inhumations and at least 16 cremations complete with grave-goods ranging from the second half of the 10th century to the late-12th or early-13th century (Figure 3.8) (Makarov and Zaitseva 2000, 106–121).

The remains of the cremation burials were identified from certain calcified bones found in layers of humic soil, which had been ploughed over across the whole of the excavated area in the eastern part of the burial-ground. In those layers scattered, charred medieval objects were found: misshapen glass beads, bronze jewellery and melted pieces of non-ferrous metal. Under the top humic layer and in the fill of pits, 16 more or less compact clusters of calcified human bones each weighing between 60 and 550 gm were identified as separate cremation burials.

Of the 63 excavated inhumations, 41 contained skeletons which had either not been disturbed at all or only to a minimal degree. These had been placed into flat graves and in most cases laid out on their backs in an extended position. In the rest of the burials the skeletons had been disturbed and some of the burials simply contained a collection of scattered bones in the ploughed layer. Ten of the deceased were oriented with their heads towards the West and the rest towards the East with minor deviations. In 35 of the inhumations, jewellery and parts of garments were found. In 31 there were household objects and tools. Of the undisturbed burials, 70% contained jewellery and 57% household items and tools. The abundance of artefacts has made it possible to specify fairly accurately the dates of these burials and how the use of this burial-ground developed.

The anthropological sample of the Minino II inhumations comprised 16 males including one juvenile and 19 females also including one juvenile. There were 28 individuals of undetermined sex, 26 of whom were children of various ages (Buzhilova 2009).

Historical Context

The written history of the micro-region under discussion can be traced back to the first half of the 17th century, to the land registers of the Vologda District in which 13 villages on the River Karachevka are mentioned, also the Karachevskii *stanok* (a group

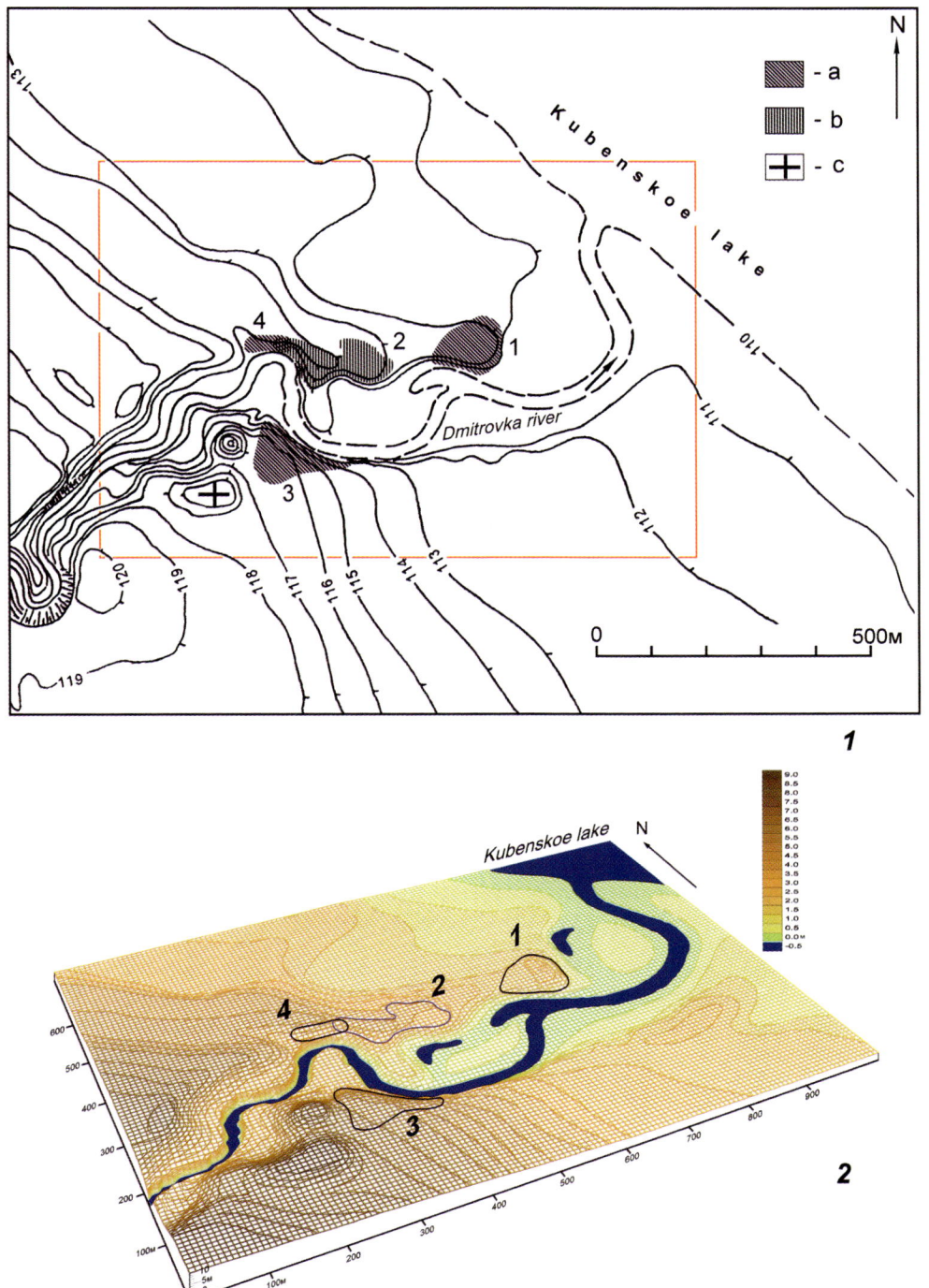

Figure 3.2 *Plan and topographical map of the Minino archaeological complex. Site 1 is Minino I; Site 2 is Minino II; Site 3 is Minino VI; and Site 4 is Minino VII. Key: a – settlement; b – cemetery; c – church (likely to be that of St Dimitri).*

Figure 3.3 *Photo of Minino I (centre left) in its landscape, looking north-east towards Lake Kubenskoye.*

of small settlements) and two parish churches with cemeteries, those of Saint Nicholas and Saint Dmitrii. The latter should be identified with the ruins of an existing church with a cemetery, while the adjacent settlement of Minino VI (Figure 3.4) should be identified with the village of Tropova known to have had a church and mentioned in the 1646 land register of the Vologda District. Karachevskii *stanok* once constituted a special administrative unit within the extensive Syamsk *volost* (smallest administrative district in pre-1917 Russia), of which the centre would evidently have been the Saint Dmitrii parish with a cemetery near Kubenskoye Lake [*Pistsovye knigi Russkogo Severa* (*Land Registers from the Russian North*) 2001, 62, 97, 120]. Although there is no direct information about a church with a cemetery at the mouth of the Karachevka river relating to any period earlier than the 17th century in the written sources, there is a mention of 'Karachevskii wasteland' in a document issued by Prince Andrei Vasilievich Menshii to Father Superior Ignatii of the Kirillo-Byelozersky monastery some 50 kms to the NW of Minino, which makes it possible to assume that the definition of Karachevskii *stanok* as a special administrative entity had taken place significantly earlier (*ASEI*, Vol. II, No. 205).

Excavation strategy

From the very beginning the excavations at Minino had been undertaken with the aim of achieving a thorough examination of the cultural deposits and recording the details of stratigraphy and lay-out. The most complete extraction of small artefacts from the cultural deposits was planned including the wide-scale use of wet sieving. Thanks to this it proved possible to collect a large sample of finds from the settlements. In addition, the sieving of deposits in the burial-ground made it possible to collect all the calcified bones and small fragments of burnt items scattered over the

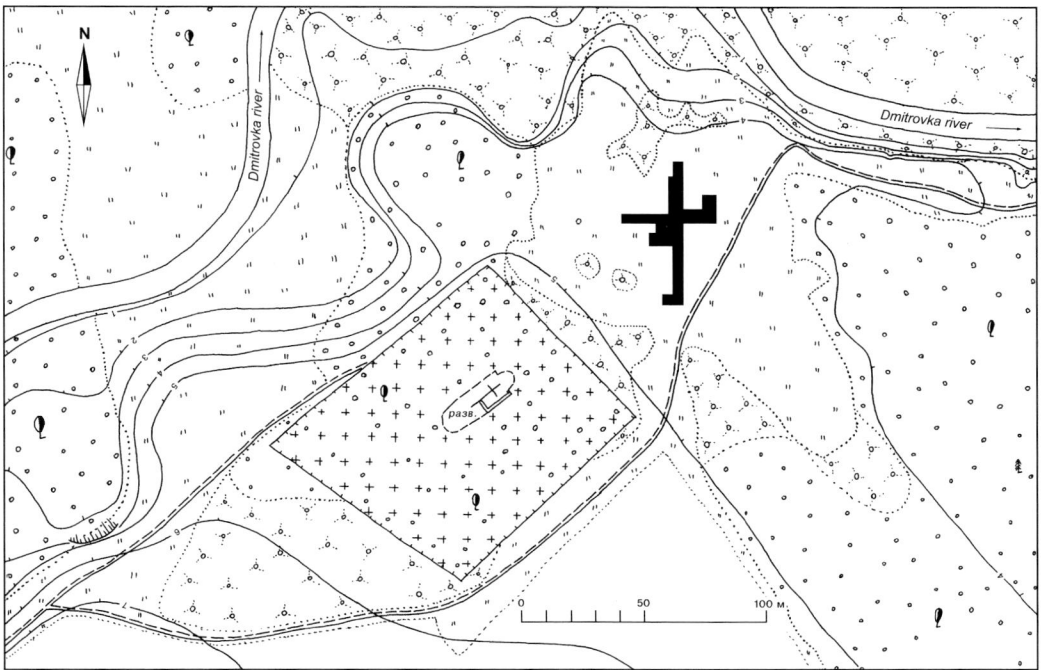

Figure 3.4 *Location of trenches for the excavation of Minino VI, lying east of the church of St Dimitri and its associated cemetery.*

burial-ground, which would not have been discernible if the earth had merely been sorted through by hand. Another key aspect of the strategy used for fieldwork at Minino was the extremely thorough collection of various kinds of palaeo-ecological materials that shed light on the natural environment of the site and on the economic activity of the inhabitants of the medieval settlements. In the excavation trenches large amounts of carpological and palaeo-zoological materials were collected and a series of samples were collected for radiocarbon dating. In addition, the deliberate collection of palynological materials from the trenches and from natural sections in the flood-plain of the Dmitrovka river near the settlements made it possible to delineate the palaeo-environment of the Minino micro-region at various periods in its history (see Chapter 2, this volume and Maltby, in press). The multi-disciplinary investigation of the settlements and the accompanying cemetery was extremely significant as it provided additional information for the study of cultural materials and the development of the exploitation of this locality by settlers.

Refined methods for investigating the cultural layer made it possible to trace the remains of seven dwellings built above ground, to identify a number of production premises linked with the processing of non-ferrous metals and to discover beneath the cultural deposits of both villages levels where ploughing had taken place during the medieval period. Yet one of the most important results of the excavations at

Figure 3.5 *Metal finds (iron and non-ferrous) from the Minino settlements.*

Figure 3.6 *Finds of metal, bone, horn and stone from the Minino settlements.*

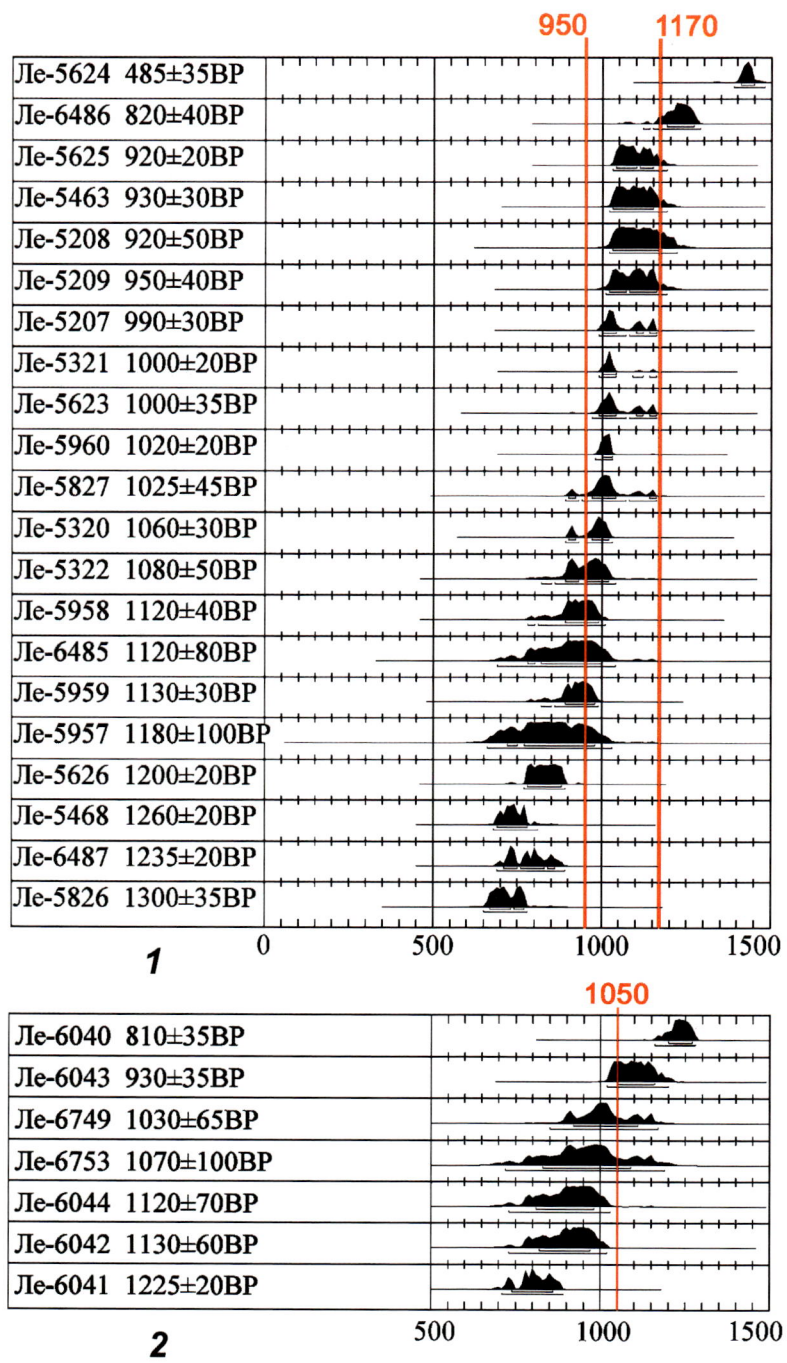

Figure 3.7 *Range of radiocarbon dates obtained from wood samples from the Minino settlements. Diagram 1: 21 samples from the settlement site of Minino I. Diagram 2: samples from the settlement site of Minino VI.*

Figure 3.8 Photograph of the excavation of the Minino cemetery.

Figure 3.9 *Finds from the Minino cemetery.*

Minino was the collection of an enormous number of artefacts, exceeding that of all other collections of artefacts from the pre-Mongol period in rural settlements of medieval Russia. For the purposes of comparison it is worth pointing out that at the medieval settlement of Vvedenskoye near Yaroslavl, where a larger area was excavated (approximately 5,000 m² and some five times greater than the excavated area at Minino), only a third of the number of artefacts was found (approximately 2,360 items). Even if we take into account the fact that finds from Minino includes sieved material, the Minino collection provides a much more complete picture of the material culture, economy and every-day life of the rural settlements in Northern Russia than do collections from other sites of a similar type.

The finds

The collection gleaned from two settlements (Minino VI and VII) consists of 1,792 objects made of glass, 1,701 objects made of non-ferrous metals (Figure 3.5.1–46; Figure 3.6.1–36), 2,758 objects made of iron (Figure 3.5.47–58; Figure 3.6.37–54), 327 objects fashioned from bone and horn (Figure 3.6.55–59), 205 from stone (Figure 3.6.60–62) and 251 objects made of clay. At Minino I approximately 4.6 glass beads, 3.8 objects made of non-ferrous metals and 6.4 made from iron were recovered from each square metre, while at the Minino VI site the concentration of artefacts was slightly lower (0.6 glass beads, 0.9 finds made from non-ferrous metals, and 1.4 iron objects). The collection includes jewellery and parts of garments, household objects, tools, weapons, trading goods and objects with cultic functions (Figures 3.5 and 3.6). The range of articles represented in the collection is most varied: from finds very familiar as regards rural settlements such as iron knives, whetstones and clay weights for fishing nets, but there are also comparatively rare objects which indicate the high level of prosperity enjoyed by the population and its wide involvement in trade: objects such as shards from Byzantine glass vessels, a lead weight bearing a depiction of a saint on one side and a three-bar, flowering cross on the other, a tiny axe used as an amulet, and ornamental appliqués for belts and belt-ends. Among the tools found the most numerous were iron knives (373 specimens) (Figure 3.6.41–44), iron needles (412 specimens) (Figure 3.6.48–52, 54), whetstones (106 specimens) (Figure 3.6.62), iron awls (97 specimens) (Figure 3.6.63), stone, clay and bone distaffs (69 specimens) (Figure 3.6.53) and fragments of axes (25 specimens). A prominent group of objects was that consisting of iron and horn arrow-heads (47 specimens), among which a group of cylindrical horn arrowheads with blunt ends stands out (eight specimens), which were used for hunting fur-bearing animals. Weapons were also represented by iron ferrules from the handle-end of spears (three specimens), rings from chain mail (six specimens) and a horn loop from a quiver. The collection also contains objects associated with fishing: 31 hooks (Figure 3.6.36), six fishing spears and 65 clay and stone weights for nets. Among the metal items of jewellery the most numerous were complete and fragmentary pendants and small bells (85 specimens) (Figure 3.6.18–25), rings (68 specimens) (Figure 3.6.10–15) and bracelets (25 specimens), parts of belt sets (56 specimens) (Figure 3.6.6–9) and wire temple rings

(49 specimens). At the two settlements 25 metal crosses to be worn round the neck were found (Figure 3.6.1, 5), which constitute the largest ever series of Christian objects fashioned from metal ever found in rural settlements of medieval Russia.

The cultural layer and the burial complexes at the Minino sites provide eloquent witness to the fact that these settlements had been part of a long-distance trade and intensive commodity-exchange network. Around half of the artefacts recovered from the settlements are imports or articles manufactured from imported materials. Among the imported items there are two fragments of glass vessels of Byzantine origin, a cross to be worn around the neck, beads and a fragment of a ring made of amber, cowrie shells, some fragments of red-burnished pottery manufactured in Volga Bulgaria and fragments of glazed pottery made in Kiev including a whole, glazed clay Easter egg and fragments of others. The cultural layer of these settlements also yielded up a small weight, part of the balance beam of a pair of scales, and a fragment of a dirham. Minino's trade links with the West have been documented first and foremost by finds of deniers minted in Friesland and Germany, specifically Jever, Utrecht, Dokkum, Emden, Regensburg, Strasbourg and Cologne between 976 and 1086. Six coins were found in burials, where they had been used as parts of necklaces and 15 coins were found in the settlements. Deniers minted after the 1040s predominated. The absence of eyelets or suspension holes in some of the coins shows that they may have been used as a means of payment rather than as ornaments.

The chronology of Minino I

Artefacts and above all glass beads make it possible to date the formation of the earliest medieval levels in Minino I to the second half or end of the 10th century. In order to confirm this early date the presence of mosaic beads in the collection of finds is important, including beads with a horizontal hole through them, large snapped beads and coiled speckled beads with loops. The uninterrupted occupation of the settlement from the 11th to the 13th century has been documented with reference to a significant number of artefacts which serve as date-indicators for that period, including glass beads and metal ornaments.

The following facts need to be taken into account when it comes to the latest date for the settlement. First, in the large collection of jewellery found in the settlement there is a whole series of different types which appeared in the last third of the 12th century, but there are hardly any items, which first appeared in the North-west or North-east of medieval Russia in the middle or the second half of the 13th century (for instance, earrings in the shape of a question-mark, ball-shaped bell-rattles containing linear slits with a single ridge in relief on them, temple rings consisting of many beads or rings with round base-plates). Secondly, among the items of wheel-turned pottery collected in the upper part of the cultural layer the types which predominate are those that were in use in the late 12th or early 13th century, but there were no pottery forms found which were being used between the middle of the 13th and the end of the 14th century. The final abandonment of the settlement should therefore be dated to the period between the very end of the 12th and the middle of the 13th century.

A total of 21 samples of organic material from the Minino settlement were selected for radiocarbon dating (Figure 3.7). Most of the radiocarbon dates obtained for charcoal and wood from the cultural layer show that the settlement was inhabited in an interval similar to the one indicated above. The main interval indicated by 15 of these specimens was 892–1260. The upper limit of the four earliest dates in this group fell within a period embracing the second half and last third of the 10th century, i.e. it coincides with the dating of the earliest beads. It is significant that 14 of these specimens were given a pre-1168 date, thus defining the period in which most activity went on as prior to the last third of the 12th century. Wood from a transect cutting through the medieval layer has been dated to the first half of the 15th century (1414–1444). Finally four of the specimens have been dated to a period between 676 and 932. This difference in the dates of the artefacts concerned could be explained either by the use of wood for construction, which was of a date very different from the date when the buildings were erected or, as is more likely, by the fact that the specimens from the very much compressed medieval layer of organic material from the lower levels had been contaminated.

The chronology of Minino VI

The appearance of the Minino VI settlement has to be dated to a period no later than the middle of the 11th century in view of the range of beads found there, including 'snapped' beads, yellow, gold and silver-coloured lemon- and berry-shaped glass beads. In the second half of the 12th century and the first half of the 13th there was a marked increase in the area of the settlement when it came to absorb territory to the South, further away from the river. Amongst the materials shedding light on probable dates in the 12th or early-13th century were crosses with small orbs at the ends of their bars, flat two-headed horse pendants, a hollow zoomorphic jangling pendant, an oval steel strike-a-light, globular, zonal and ring-shaped coiled beads in monochrome colours made from transparent and translucent yellow, green, blue, colourless and mauve glass, and also coiled opaque black and brown beads with sculpted decoration.

Although the topographic link between the medieval settlement, Minino VI, and the late medieval Church of Saint Dmitrii (or Karachevskii Church) complete with cemetery, forming the centre of the Karachevskii *stanok* does not raise any doubts, the historical picture of the transformation of an early settlement into a village complete with a church and cemetery cannot by any means be followed through regarding all its details. In the disturbed level of the settlement, pottery with profiles typical of the 13th and 14th century has been collected and a number of articles dating from the 15th and 16th centuries or even later, and in one area the remains of buildings from the 18th and 19th centuries, have been found. Important in this connection are the finds of coins from the 16th and 17th centuries (a silver *denga* of Grand Prince Ivan IV, 1533–1547, Moscow Mint; a silver kopeck of Tsar Boris Fyodorovich, 1600, Moscow Mint) and certain typical objects which were in use in the 13th and 14th centuries or as late as the 15th century: for example crosses, iron appliqués encrusted with silver used for decorating belts, an iron spoke from a spinning wheel. Our efforts, however, to identify remains of buildings or pits from the second half of the 13th, 14th or 15th century have not met with success. It has not proved possible to locate the nucleus of a settlement of that period.

Comparison of the number of objects and pottery found in the 13th–15th centuries with the materials from the preceding period testifies to a marked drop in the activities at the settlement. It is clear that in the 13th century the large rural settlement typical of the pre-Mongol period gave way to a village consisting of small properties and that the first period in the life of this village left behind it meagre and not very distinctive material remains, contrasting sharply with the materials from the pre-Mongol period. A reconstruction of the development in the life of the settlement on the basis of the archaeological data broadly coincides with the picture provided by the radiocarbon dates. Six of these fall in the interval between 721 and 1265 and, moreover, the upper limit of the two earliest dates falls within the period between the end of the 10th and the first third of the 11th century, i.e. the findings are similar to the information provided by the evidence of the archaeological materials. Important in this connection is the presence in this series of specimens of those, for which the dates fall within the period 1213–1265, i.e. dates indicating that life in the settlement continued into the first half of the 13th century. The age of one specimen (dated to 712–810) does not coincide with the date established on the basis of evidence drawn from artefacts.

The chronology of Minino II: the cemetery

In order to achieve a more precise chronology for the emergence and development of the Minino group of settlements, the distribution over time of the burial complexes in the burial-ground is important. The earliest group of burials is that with the cremations accompanied by single or several lemon-shaped beads, snapped beads and large speckled beads. A number of burial complexes can be dated as falling within a fairly wide interval of time between the second half of the 10th and the beginning of the 11th century. Yet some complexes clearly date from before the end of the 10th or very beginning of the 11th century. An example is Burial 50 where the grave-goods include striking items of jewellery of Volga-Finnish types, such as a pendant with a triangular multi-spiral base-plate, a bottle-shaped pendant and a bracelet-shaped ring of large diameter, one of the ends of which was in the shape of a socket while the other was pointed. The earliest cremations are located in the highest north-east part of the burial-ground and the relatively large number of them confirms observations to the effect that the first medieval settlement at the mouth of the River Dmitrovka must have initially been a large one. The transition from the cremation rite to inhumation in the Minino area took place at the beginning of the 11th century, although for a certain period the two rites existed side by side. The inhumations of the 11th and the first quarter of the 12th century with the heads of the deceased orientated to the East and complete with a large array of grave-goods are numerous and they were to be found throughout the burial-ground (Figure 3.8). Approximately 20 inhumations in the Minino burial-ground contained jewellery and household objects, the appearance of which, to judge from the Novgorod chronology, should be dated to the middle or the last third of the 12th century (Figure 3.9). The latest group of burials in the Minino burial-ground consists of five burials empty of grave-goods and with the deceased orientated towards the West. On the basis of the general ideas as to how the funerary rite developed in the Minino area, these should be dated to a period no earlier than the end of the 12th or beginning of the 13th century. It is highly likely that by this time the first wooden church had already been erected at the site of the St. Dmitrii, or Karachevskii church, close to which burials also took place. As we can see, the abandonment of the earliest medieval settlement at the mouth of the River Dmitrovka coincided with the period when the burial-ground, which had been used for burials for no less than 200 years, ceased to function.

CONCLUSIONS

It can thus be seen how the excavation of the settlements and burial-ground at Minino shed light on the history of the colonization of one of the rural micro-regions at the northern edge of medieval Russia, which began in the second half of the 10th century and also on the close links between that colonization and long-distance trade orientated towards the Baltic lands and the Volga region. The stable development and the economic prosperity of the Minino settlements in the 11th and 12th centuries did not continue into the period that followed. One of the settlements was abandoned and there was a significant drop in the intensity of activity in the other. As has already been noted above, cycles of this kind are typical for the development of a large proportion of the settlements of the "first wave of colonization" which were founded on the Sheksna River and Byeloozero in the 10th and 11th centuries. More detailed discussion on the economy, use of natural resources, reasons for shifts in settlement patterns and for cultural transformations should be possible after further analyses of certain categories of archaeological and palaeo-ecological materials collected at Minino.

Note

1   The names of the sites numbered on Figure 3.1 are as follows: 1 - Vybuty; 2 - Petrovskoe 3; 3 - Udraj IV; 4 - Udraj III; 5 - Udraj I; 6 - Udraj II; 7 - Zapole 2; 8 - Zarucheve IV - VII; 9 - Bor IV; 10 - Nikolskoe V on Kema; 11 - Murinovskaya pristan; 12 - Nikolskoe VI; 13 - Molebny Ostrov;14 - Dyukovo; 15 - Nefedovo;16 – Selishche-Vorkop; 17 - Andryushino-Irma; 18 - Minino I on Kubenskoe Lake; 19 - Minino VI on Kubenskoe Lake; 20 - Krivets; 21 - Octyabrsky Most; 22 - Sobornaya Gorka; 23 - Uryvkovo; 24 - Minino 4 on Yug; 25 - Minino 5 on Yug; 26 - Minino 2 on Yug; 27 - Teleshovo II; 28 -Morozovitsa I - II; 29 - Gostinskoe; 30 - Volkovo; 31 - Kholmovo; 32 - Blagoveshchenie; 33 - Struiskoe; 34 - Shitovichi 6; 35 - Pekunovskoe; 36 - Kimrskoe; 37 - Olenino; 38 - Grekhov Ruchej; 39 - Altynovo; 40 - Zolotoruche; 41 - Nesterovo; 42 - Vasilki; 43 - Ust-Sheksna 1; 44 - Ust-Sheksna 2; 45 - Shurscol II; 46 - Vvedenskoe; 47 - Ves 1; 48 - Gnezdilovo; 49 - Vasilkovo; 50 - Rybino (Strelka 1); 51 - Drosnenskoe; 52 - Yanovskoe; 53 - Savvinskaya Sloboda; 54 - Piskovo; 55 - Kutino 1 a; 56 - Zhdanovo; 57 - Pokrov 5; 58 - Novoe Syanovo; 59 - Nagovitsyno I; 60 - Priluki I; 61 - Desna; 62 - Myakinino.

– 4 –

BUILDINGS AND STRUCTURES OF THE MININO ARCHAEOLOGICAL COMPLEX

S. D. Zakharov

The building of rural houses remains to this day one of the relatively neglected subjects in the field of medieval Russian archaeology. This is not only bound up with the relatively small number of excavations undertaken so far in rural settlements. The fact of the matter is that the bulk of the settlements of medieval Russia so far investigated are sites with a cultural layer that is far from deep and which have suffered significantly from ploughing that has gone on over many years and often for many centuries. If the remains of buildings have been damaged by ploughing over long periods, this will have made it impossible to single out distinctive features of the construction work or even to establish the type and overall dimensions of the structures in question, since in the majority of cases all that will have survived are the ruins of stoves or those parts of buildings which had been sunk into the ground.

In this situation the materials obtained in the course of the excavations undertaken in the Minino archaeological complex are of major interest. The relatively good state of preservation of the cultural levels in the settlement of Minino I, the application of delicate methods of field-work, the large scale cleaning and sieving of the soil from the cultural layer and the thorough processing of the data obtained have made it possible for the first time to achieve a fairly detailed and complete picture of the special features of how rural dwellings were built in this micro-region.

BUILDINGS AND STRUCTURES

Within the settlements of Minino I the remains of no less than seven structures were recorded. These were found in three different trenches (Figures 4.1 and 4.2). Six of the buildings were dwellings (Buildings 1–6) and one had been erected for the purposes of production. The range of finds and the features of the building work enabled us to identify it as a jewellery workshop (Building 7, see Zaitseva, this volume). Careful analysis of the wealth of objects and ceramic remains and of the stratigraphic picture testify to the fact that the dwellings investigated relate to the whole range of periods during which this settlement was inhabited (Figure 4.1). The earliest structures were two houses discovered in the eastern part of the settlement (Trench 1).

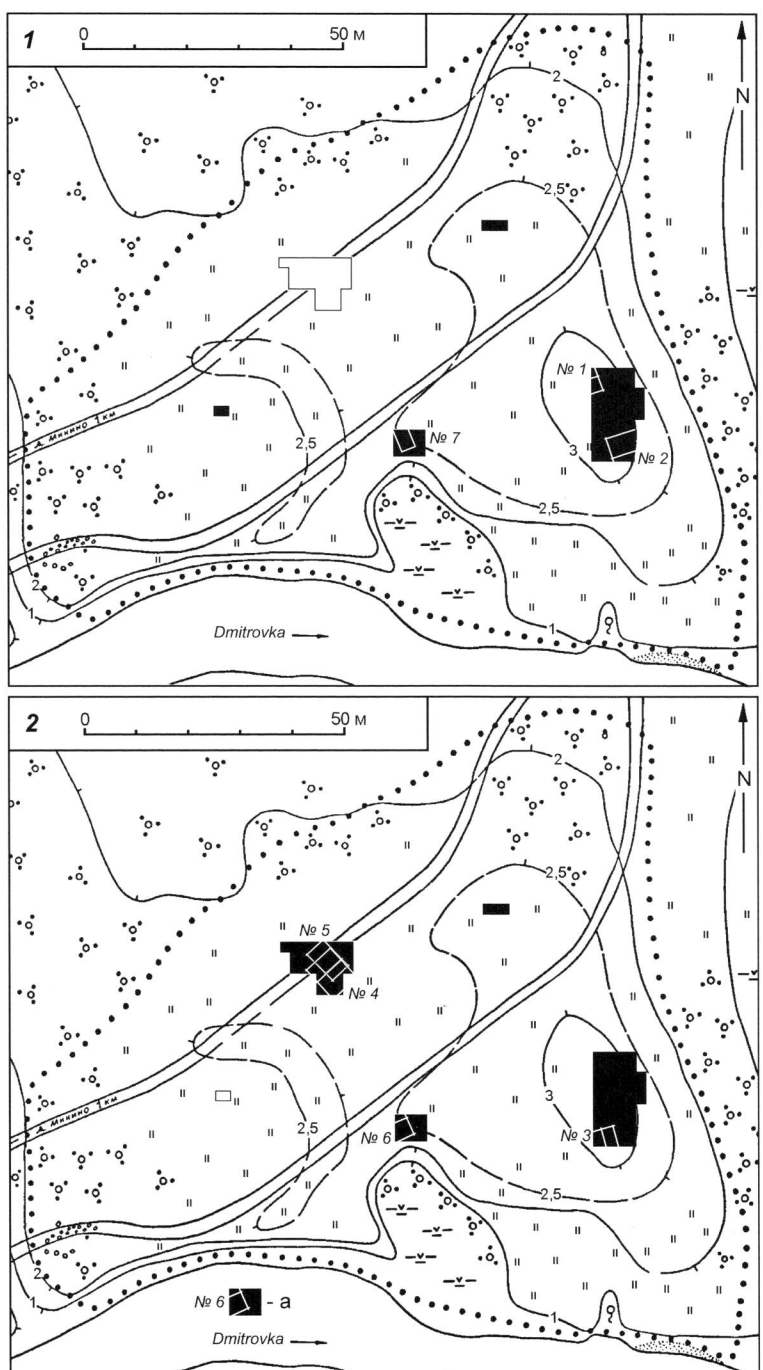

Figure 4.1 *The Minino I settlement at different stages of its existence: 1) level of the 10th–11th centuries; 2) level from the end of the 11th century to the early 13th century; (a) trenches with layers from the given period, the buildings found in them and their numbers.*

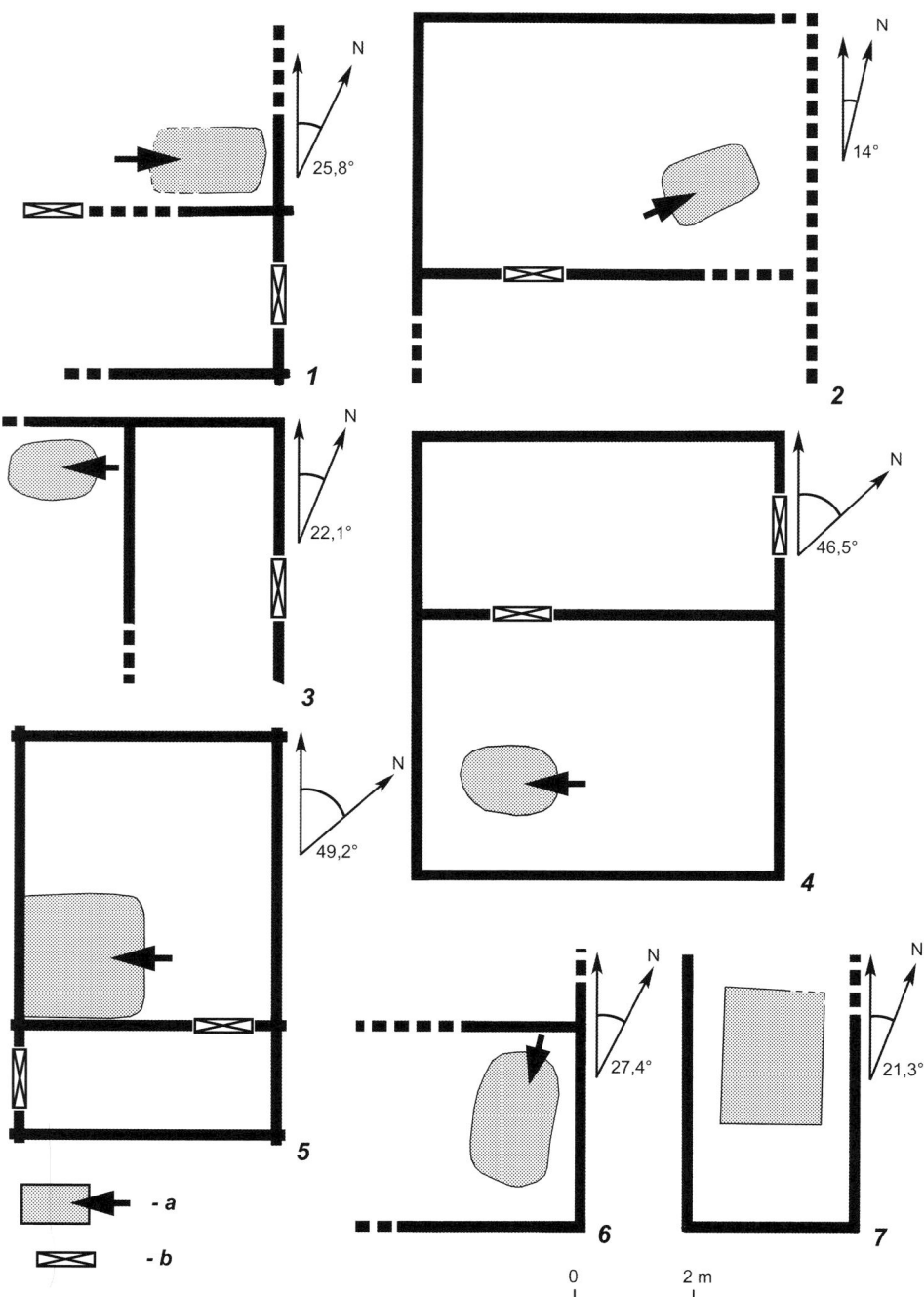

***Figure* 4.2** *Plans of buildings found in the Minino I settlement: 1) Building 1 (Trench 1);*
2) Building 2 (Trench 1); 3) Building 3 (Trench 1); 4) Building 4 (Trench 3); 5): Building 5
(Trench 3); 6) Building 6 (Trench 4); 7) Building 7 (Trench 4); (a) heating installations and the
assumed position of the opening of the firing chamber; (b) the assumed position of doorways.

No. of building	Place where sample was taken	Lab. index	Radio-carbon date (BP)	Calibrated date (AD) 1σ	Calibrated date (AD) 2σ
1	Log from the east wall	Le-5320	1060±30	976–1014	894–1026
1	Log from the wall between the rooms	Le-5321	1000±20	1016–1030	1005–1152
2	Log from the west wall	Le-5958	1120±40	892–974	822–1014
2	Isolated log from the level of the building	Le-5957	1180±100	725–975	665–1020
4	Floor fragments	Le-5624	485±35	1414–1444	1404–1466
4	Floor fragment	Le-6485	1120±80	810–1000	690–1030
4 or 5	Charcoal stain	Le-5827	1025±45	972–1150	892–1162
5	Log from stove cover	Le-6486	820±20	1185–1260	1050–1280
5	Log from the south-west wall	Le-5623	1000±35	1002–1154	982–1160
6	Log from the south wall	Le-5625	920±20	1048–1164	1039–1168

Table 4.1 The Minino I settlement: results from the radiocarbon dating of buildings.

The period when Building 2 was in use has been identified as the second half of the 10th and the 11th century and in the case of the Building 1 it was the end of the 10th and the 11th century. The end of the 11th century and the first half of the 12th century make up the period when House 5 (Trench 3) was in use. House 6 (Trench 4) was in existence in the second half of the 12th century, while the latest of the buildings investigated were numbers 3 (Trench 1) and 4 (Trench 3), which date from the second half of the 12th and the first half of the 13th century. The jeweller's workshop (Building 7, Trench 4) was in use in the 11th century and possibly at the beginning of the 12th. The dates for these buildings, which have been established on the basis of the archaeological materials found, correspond to those obtained using radiocarbon dates for five of the structures under discussion (see Table 4.1). Yet two dates relating to Building 4 lie outside that sequence. Moreover, one of them (Le-5624) was much later and the other (Le-6485) was much earlier than the time during which the building had been in use.

THE CONSTRUCTION, DIMENSIONS AND INTERNAL LAY-OUT OF THE DWELLINGS

In view of the small area of the trenches it was only possible to excavate two of the buildings in virtually their entirety: the others were only partially investigated. In addition, although Minino has survived decidedly better than other settlements in the group on account of the comparatively good state of preservation of the medieval, the large village of Minino I needs still to be numbered among sites with a so-called 'dry' cultural layer. The medieval levels at Minino are very much compressed: despite being not very thick they cover a significant chronological period. The presence of a large number of pits, which are difficult to trace in the dark cultural layer, and the unsatisfactory state of preservation of the wood, which has only been recorded in a rotten state, make it impossible in most of the trenches to divide up the cultural layer in a detailed way or to single out levels which can be given a precise date. In these conditions it has not always been possible to determine beyond doubt the contours of the identified buildings and the features of their internal lay-out, which has meant that a number of possibilities can be suggested for their reconstruction.

The most effective way for resolving this range of questions is to determine how the different categories of materials are distributed in the levels relating to the time when the buildings in question were in use. Observations concerning changes in the density of the distribution of artefacts discovered, pottery remains, animal and fish bones, fragments from the outer coating of stoves and stones used to construct them both inside and outside the best preserved buildings have made it possible to identify certain patterns in their distribution (Figure 4.3). It is important to note that the recording of many details and nuances only became possible thanks to the enormous dimensions of the collection examined, the bulk of which was obtained in the course of washing and sieving materials from the cultural layer.

It turned out that objects were lost least often in the narrow strip of terrain round the outside of the buildings, at spots where stoves had been erected and in the narrow space immediately around them (Figure 4.3.1). It should at the same time be noted that various categories of material were distributed in different way within the cultural layer (Figure 4.3.2–6). Objects were found mainly inside the houses, both in the unheated porches or *seni* and also in the heated rooms. In all cases the position of the object found in relation to the walls of the building was noted, including internal partition walls. The bulk of the animal and fish bones was usually found outside the dwellings. Clusters of ceramic material were recorded both inside the buildings and outside them, but inside the houses most such material was associated with the space immediately round the stoves.

Clusters of calcinated bones were also noticed round the stoves. In a number of cases it has been possible to draw preliminary conclusions regarding the positions of details such as doorways, which often prove elusive for archaeologists. What serves to indicate the position of these is the long-term concentration at specific spots of all categories of material.

The patterns listed above were used to investigate the other buildings which were not so well preserved. Comparison of the distribution of wood fragments from the walls of these houses and the distribution of hearth stones from the remains of stoves with the results of distributional analysis for all groups of archaeological finds has made it possible to suggest well-founded variants for the reconstruction of the dimensions of buildings, their orientation and features of their internal lay-out.

All the dwellings identified in the Minino I settlement were rectangular buildings over the ground made of rows of logs (Figure 4.2). They were made from logs with a diameter of between 20 and 25 cm. In two cases it was possible to trace the nature of

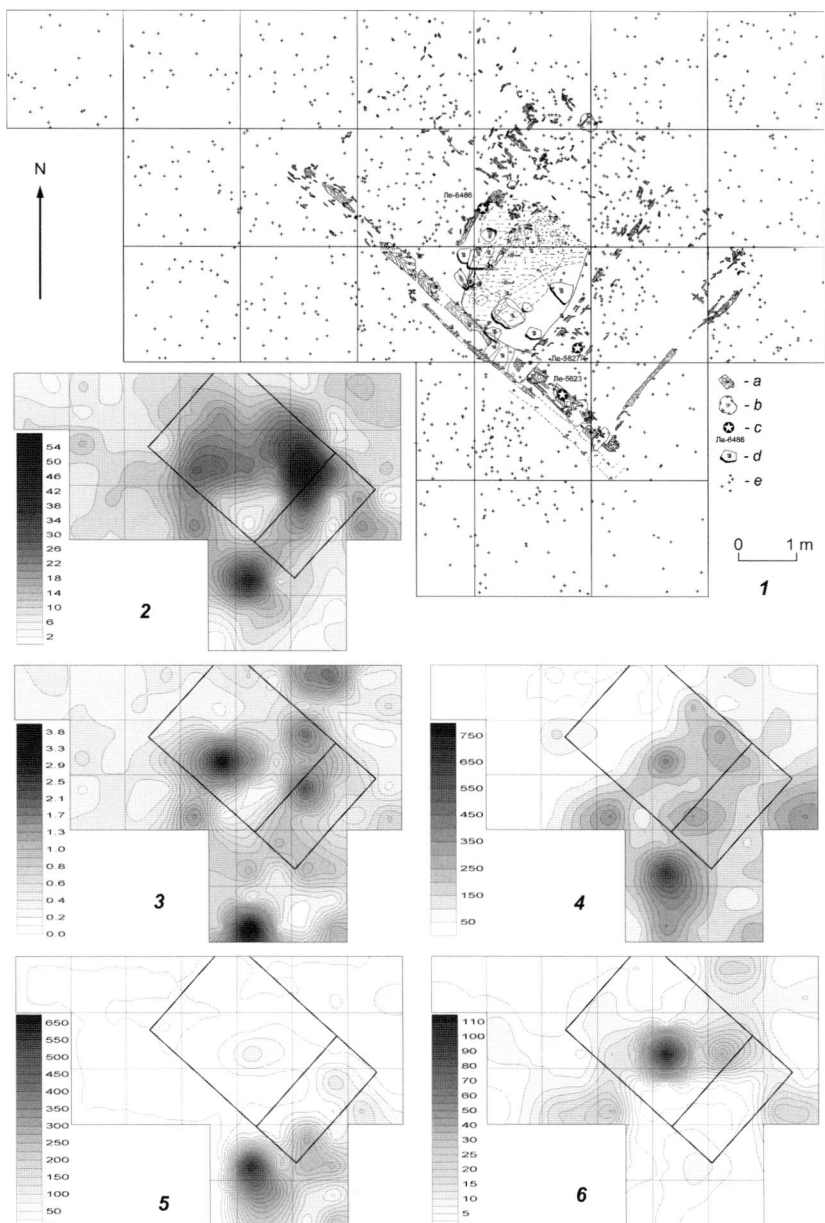

Figure 4.3 *The Minino I settlement, Building 4 (Trench 3): 1) plan with the remains of a building and the arrangement of finds in its habitation level; (a) fragments of rotted wood; (b) foundation stones; (c) places selected for radiocarbon samples and their laboratory numbers (see Table 4.1); (d) the largest stove stones; (e) artefacts found; 2–6) density of distribution of the various categories of materials in the building's habitation level; 2) artefacts (objects per m²); 3) pottery (kg per m²); 4) animal bones (gm per m²); 5) fish scales and bones (gm per m²); 6) calcified bones (gm per m²).*

the log joins. Houses 1 and 5 had joins of the *oblo* type (over-lapping, cupped joints) with logs extending 17–20 cm beyond the line of the wall. Large flat stones laid out on the ground were often used as foundation supports. This can be seen particularly clearly in Building 5, indeed the largest stone had been positioned at the point where the inner wall meets an outer wall (Figure 4.3.1). On the outside another row of thinner logs from the walls of this house and House 4 was found. These could be regarded as material from the collapsed walls of buildings, but they are more likely to be the remains of a dug-out used to keep the lower part of the house warm.

It is essential to note that all the dwellings investigated, starting from the earliest, can be reconstructed with a high level of probability as two-room buildings with an internal partition-wall ("five-walled houses"). The internal wall divided the house into two parts of unequal size. The stove was always positioned in the larger of the two rooms. Three variants for the position of the stove have been found. In the early buildings (Houses 1, 2 and 5) the stove was positioned near the internal wall and parallel to it. The opening of the stove was facing the door between the two rooms. In all cases this door was not in the middle of the internal wall, but over towards the outer wall of the building further away from the stove. In later periods of the settlement other variants for the positioning of the stove were found. In two buildings (Houses 3 and 6) stoves were found near the external walls of the dwellings parallel to them. Their openings faced the wall between the rooms. In House 4 the stove was closer to the back wall of the heated room parallel to it. The door linking the two rooms was positioned opposite the stove.

The entrance into the house in all the reliably reconstructed examples was through the unheated room (*seni*). The door was positioned in the short wall of this unheated room. Only in one case (Building 3) was it possible to suggest that there had been an outside door in the long wall of the unheated room (*seni*). It would be wrong to rule out the other possibility, namely that the entrance into this building was in the south (short) wall of the *seni*, which remained outside the confines of the trench. In those cases, when it is possible to confirm the position of both doors (the outside one and the door between the two rooms), it emerges that they were as far away as possible from each other, i.e. at opposite ends of the *seni* (Houses 1, 4 and 5).

It is likely that all the dwellings had wooden floors but remains of these have only reliably been identified in three buildings. In the *seni* and heated rooms of Houses 5 and 6 the floor was laid along the entrance axis. This is the most frequently encountered method for laying floors in dwellings in medieval Rus. In Building 4 a different method for laying out floorboards was recorded. In the *seni* the floorboards had probably been laid as above, but in the heated room they were laid across the entrance axis. Another interesting detail was noted in that particular house. In a rectangular space round the stove there was no wooden floor. This had possibly been designed to avoid the risk of fire. With the same aim in mind, the log walls had been coated with clay in the region of the stove. In the course of the excavations several clay fragments bearing imprints of large logs were found.

No. of Building	Type and Function	External Measurements (m)	Total area of interior (m²)	Internal measurements and area of Seni (m and m²)	Internal measurements and area of heated room (m and m²)	Overall dimensions of stove (m)	Dimensions of firing chamber (m)
1	Two-roomed dwelling	>4.9 × 3.3	?	2.5 × >3.1 (>7.9)	?	~ 1.9 × 1.1	~1.9 × 0.8
2	Two-roomed dwelling	>6.2 × 6.8	>39	>1.7 × 6.5 (>11.3)	4.1 × 6.5 (26.6)	1.6 × 1.1	1.4 × 0.5
3	Two-roomed dwelling	>4.8 × >4.5	?	2.3 × >4.4 (>10.1)	>2.1 × >4.4	1.5 × 1.2	1.1 × 0.6
4	Two-roomed dwelling	7.6 × 6.3	42.8	2.8 × 5.9 (16.8)	4.3 × 5.9 (25.2)	1.6 × 1.2	1.6 × 0.5
5	Two-roomed dwelling	6.9 × 4.5	27	1.7 × 4.1 (7)	4.7 × 4.1 (19.3)	2 × 2.1	2 × 0.7
6	Two-roomed dwelling	>4.8 × >3.9	?	>1.2 × >3.7	3.2 × >3.7 (>11.7)	2.3 × 1.5	1.6 × 0.7
7	One-room outhouse	>4.7 × 3	>11.8	-	-	2.3 × 1.7	?

Table 4.2 The Minino I settlement: dimensions of buildings.

The dimensions of the houses excavated varied (Table 4.2). The earliest of the houses, House 2, which had been used in the second half of the 10th and the 11th centuries, was evidently the largest. When reconstructed its width came to 6.8 m and its length to more than 6.2 m. The area of the heated room was approximately 27 m². It only proved possible to establish the complete dimensions of two buildings. The external dimensions of House 4 dated to the second half of the 12th and the first half of the 13th century came to 7.6 × 6.3 m. The internal area of the building was approximately 43 m² and the heated room accounted for more than 25 of these and the *seni* for approximately 17. The total internal area of one of the smallest houses, House 5, dating from the end of the 11th and the first half of the 12th century, came to approximately 27 m² (the heated room accounting for more than 19 m² and the *seni* for 7). It proved possible to measure the lengths of the *seni* for four houses (1, 3–5) and these ranged between 1.7 and 2.8 m. In four houses it proved possible to establish the length of the heated room and this varied between 3.2 and 4.8 m. The internal area of the heated rooms used as living space which was established in the case of three houses, varied between 19.3 and 26.6 m². Stoves occupied between 7% (in Houses 2 and 4) and 20% (in House 5) of that space.

HEATING INSTALLATIONS

Precisely the presence of stoves, over and above a specific range of household items, testifies to the fact that the excavated buildings were dwellings and not outhouses. All the heating installations discovered in dwellings from the settlement of Minino I were stoves based on similar structural principles (Figure 4.4.1–4). They had been constructed using stone and clay. The base of the structure consisted of 5–6 large stones (measuring up to 50 × 60 cm) often arranged on their narrow edge round a roughly rectangular space filled with clay. Smaller stones were placed in the gaps between the large ones and these were charred and had all the characteristics of stone chips split off by heat. In a number of cases it was noted that small stone slabs arranged so as to rest on their narrow edge were also used for this purpose.

The overall size of the stoves varied from 1.5 × 1.2 m (House 3) to 2.3 × 1.5 m (House 5) and the area they occupied varied from 1.8 to 4.2 m² (Table 4.2). The width of the internal space, in which fuel was burned, measured between 50 and 80 cm and had a total area varying between 0.7 and 1.4 m². The amounts of clay used in the construction of these stoves also varied. The total weight of the clay used for the stove in House 5 came to 532 kg (approximately 0.33 m³), while the equivalent figure for House 4 was 120 kg (approximately 0.08 m³). On the other hand the total weight of clay used for the stoves in Houses 1–3 varied between 10 and 25 kg and the clay used for the stove in House 6 did not exceed 40 kg.

In one case, for House 6 in Trench 4, the stratigraphic situation made it possible with every confidence to separate out the stones forming the collapsed material from one stove. Measurement of their volume demonstrated that for the erection of this particular stove approximately 1 cubic metre of stones had been used. Some small stones, which had been lying in a dense layer in the upper part of the firing chamber of the stove in question, had been held together with clay (Figure 4.4.4). In this same context fragments of the coating used for the stove with impressions of a coarse textile (like sacking) were also found. In the remaining stoves similar details were not recorded, but in the clay in-fill of the firing chambers of the stoves from Houses 4 and 5, particularly near the top, large fragments of coating material for the stove were found and one of the coated surfaces showed signs of having been smoothed. Sections through the in-fill of virtually all the stoves revealed thin ash-and-charcoal layers running through the clay. These can be regarded as evidence for the existence of vaults, which would mean that stoves in Houses 4 and 5 would need to be reconstructed with a clay vault, while the stove from House 6 would need to be reconstructed with a stone-and-clay vault. At the same time several observations do not tie in with such an interpretation. First of all, the only light firing of the clay which

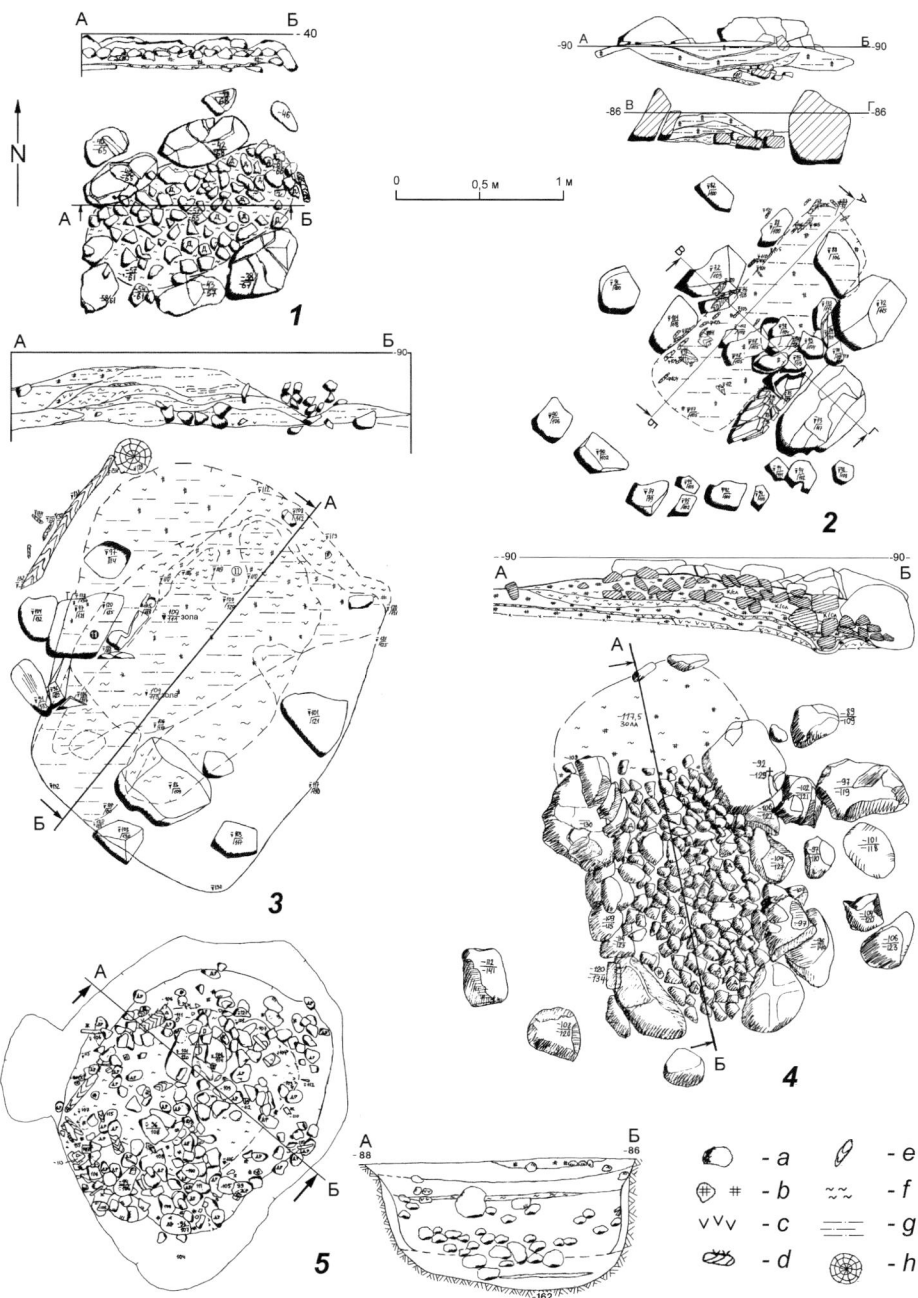

Figure 4.4 *Remains of heating installations from the dwellings in the settlements of Minino I (1–4) and Minino VI (5): 1) stove from Building 3; 2) stove from Building 4; 3) stove from Building 5; 4) stove from Building 6; 5) stove from Building 1 in the Minino VI settlement; (a) stove stones; (b) fragments of stove coating; (c) charcoal; (d) charred wood; (e) rotted wood; (f) ash; (g) loam; (h) post.*

filled the upper part of the firing chamber, then the fact that the volume of the well-fired (no longer soluble in water) clay accounted for only about 15–20% of the whole amount and in addition it has not proved possible to find a single reliable fragment of a vault. For the above reasons, the above-mentioned ash-and-charcoal layers can be regarded as traces of repair-work carried out on the stoves and this would necessitate a different reconstruction of their upper sections.

In three cases, immediately below the layer of stone and clay, fragments of rotted wood were recorded, which could be regarded as the remains of the foundation of a stove. The structure of these in the stoves from Houses 3 and 4 (Figure 4.4.1–2) remained unclear. The stove foundation from House 5 was evidently constructed using posts (Figure 4.4.3). Moreover the split logs forming two walls of this fundation could have been fixed in position by placing one end into the grooves made in the corner post and the other end into the grooves made in the logs forming the walls of the building.

No cellars or pits under stoves were traced in any of the houses in the settlement of Minino I. Yet in the settlement of Minino VI the only reliably recorded dwelling dating from the second half of the 12th to 13th century incorporated a pit under its stove of substantial dimensions (Figure 4.4.5). The dimensions of the pit, which had almost vertical walls and a round base, were 2 × 1.6 m at its upper edge and its surviving depth was 75 cm. The pit was filled with a layer containing a large number of stove stones and fragments of the stove's coating, which was interspersed with thin layers of ash and charcoal. In the upper part of its in-fill along the walls of the pit several charred wooden split logs were found lying at right angles to each other. These were probably the remains of a wooden construction (*opechek*), which had covered over the pit and on top of which the stove had been positioned. The whole stove had evidently been destroyed (probably as a result of a fire) and collapsed into the pit: for this reason it was difficult to work out how it had been constructed. Approximately 15 kg of clay and 0.45 m^3 of stone had been used to build the stove.

SPECIAL FEATURES OF THE PLANNING OF THE SETTLEMENTS

The small area of the trenches in the settlement of Minino I limits our opportunities for studying the special features of the organization of the space around the dwellings. It was possible to make the most interesting observations in this regard in Trench I. In its northern section to the East and South of House 1, several features were identified providing an idea of how the space round the house was used (Figure 4.5). Here a stain consisting of rammed earth roughly rectangular in shape was found. Within the confines of that stain the cultural layer contained a large number of animal and fish bones and various other finds. In the centre of the stained earth there was an open hearth, which had been used over a long period. To the North of it a round pit was found. To judge from the narrow strip of rotted wood on the walls of the pit there

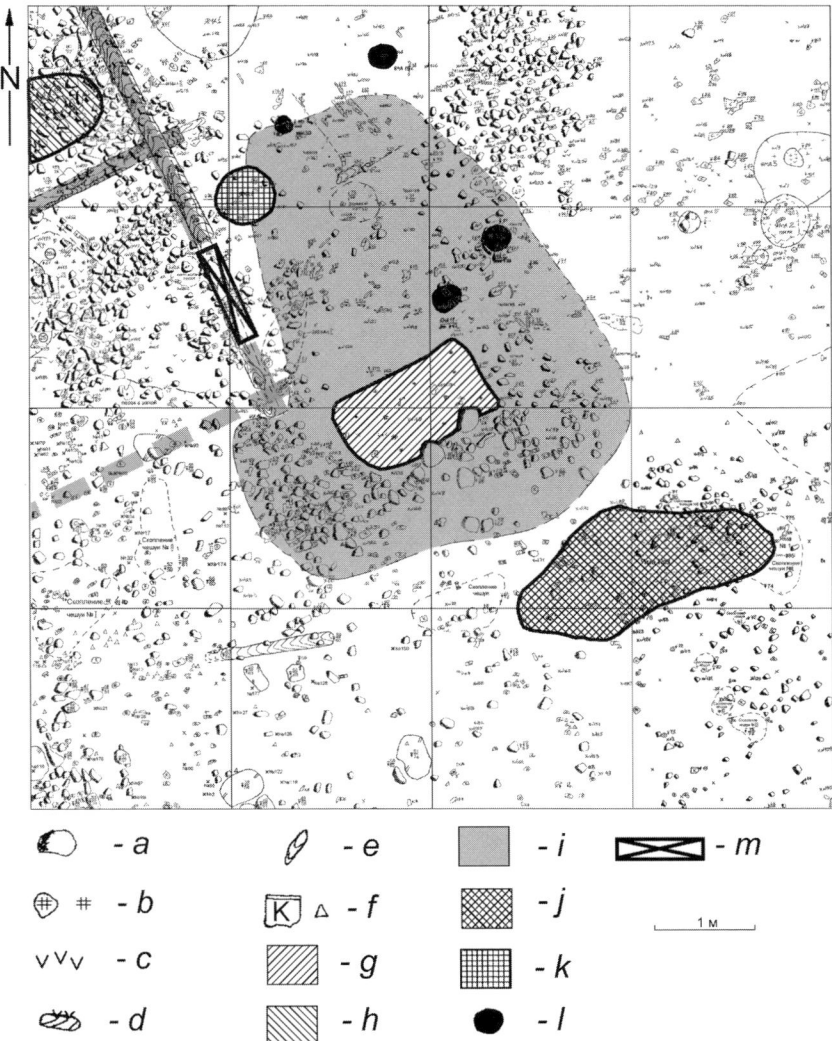

Figure 4.5 Building 1 and its vicinity in the Minino I settlement: (a) stove stones; (b) fragments of stove coating; (c) charcoal; (d) charred wood; (e) rooted wood; (f) fragments of pottery; (g) an open hearth; (h) stove; (i) stain from trodden earth; (j) rubbish pit; (k) barrel let into the ground; (l) posts from the 'canopy' roof; (m) assumed position of the doorway into the building.

had been a barrel sunk into the earth here, which had had a diameter of 60 cm. To the East of the barrel a series of post holes and split logs was found. On the south side of the hearth a large oval pit had been dug, from which we were able to extract 12 litres of fish scales and bones. In actual fact there must have been far more, since the bulk of the scales had rotted. In addition bones of animals and birds and pottery remains were found in the pit.

The complexity of the stratigraphy makes it impossible to establish which finds were without doubt of one and the same period. What would indicate that we had before us a range of structures, which had been in use at one and the same time, is the coincidence in the orientation of the various buildings, the interdependence of the boundaries and the proximity of their stratigraphic positions. If we approach the whole range of structures as belonging to one and the same complex, then the open hearth arranged next to the dwelling was most likely to have been a summer kitchen. The area around the hearth had been subjected to intensive use and it was evident that it was precisely into this area that the outside door of the building had led. In this part of the outside area near the hearth there had been some light wooden structure (possibly a lean-to roof) and a barrel sunk into the earth. On the south side of the area in question a rubbish pit bordered it, into which waste food had been thrown.

One other fact should be borne in mind. In the early levels of Trench 1 two houses were cleared (Houses 1 and 2; Figure 4.1.1) which co-existed for a period. No traces of fences or palisades separating these houses were found, which means that the question as to the existence of properties with fixed boundaries in the settlement remains an open one. At the same time it can be stated that the settlement was built up as a very tight cluster, so that the distance between the houses was approximately 8 m, i.e. it was virtually the same as the length of a house. The high density of the buildings in this settlement is also borne out by the fact that three of the six excavated dwellings had been erected on the site of buildings which had existed previously and partially or completely covered their remains.

In order to establish the general lay-out of the settlement Minino I use could be made of another source of information over and above the materials from the excavations. In the first years of the research small elevations were noted on the ground surface of the settlement. In a number of cases large stones were protruding from the tops of these. It proved possible to mark out in the plan of the site more than 40 such features (Figure 4.6). We assumed that they were debris from stoves which had been used in buildings. This assumption was clearly borne out by subsequent excavation work. Three such elevations investigated in Trenches 3 and 4 turned out to be stoves of former dwellings.

The distribution of the identified remains of stoves in the plan appears at first glance to be completely random. When attempting to find some logical system behind it all, it is important to take into account a number of important details. Firstly, by no means all the buildings containing stoves have been included on the plan: only those which are most clearly discernible on the ground surface, probably the latest of those which had stood in each part of the settlement. Some of the elevations must, without doubt, have been destroyed later on when the territory of the settlement was ploughed up. Secondly, we have no data relevant to the dating of the vast majority of the stove remains which have been marked in on the plan, since they were not excavated. They could relate to any of the periods when the settlement was in existence. These facts complicate the interpretation of the data collected so far and make the general picture

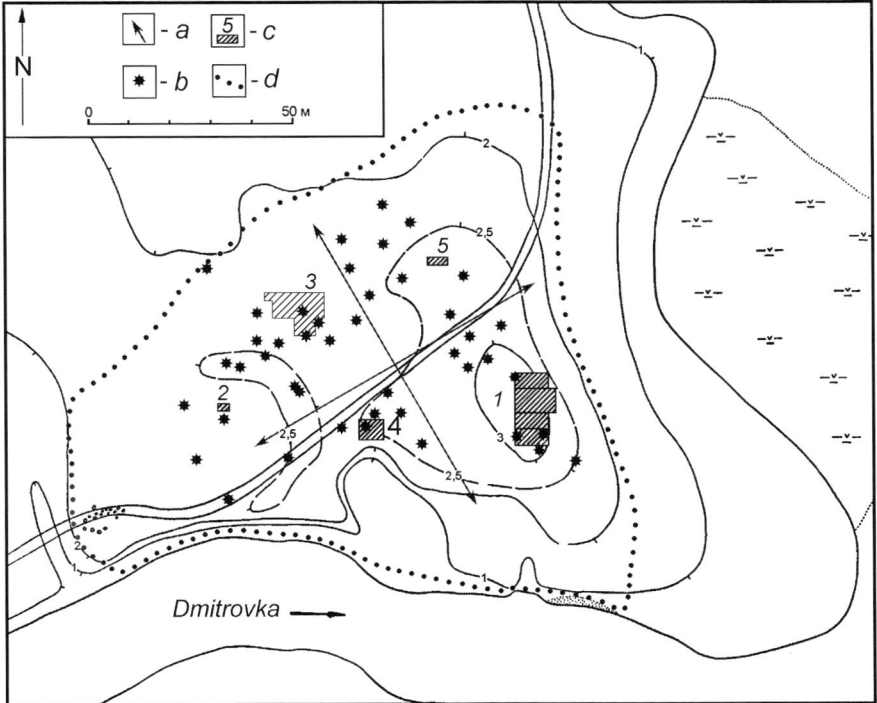

Figure 4.6 *Features of the lay-out of the Minino I settlement: (a) orientation of the buildings cleared in the trenches (average direction); (b) ruins of stoves recorded on the ground surface in the settlement; (c) trenches and their numbers; (d) boundaries of the settlement.*

significantly more confusing. An analysis of the orientation of the buildings already excavated could provide an interesting key to our understanding of this situation. Observations have shown that all the houses identified in different sectors of the site and relating to different periods of the settlement's existence share more or less one and the same orientation, namely along a NW-SE line, parallel to the shore of the lake. Furthermore, in most cases, the lengthways axis of the buildings coincides with this orientation (Figure 4.2). Linking this axis with the plan of the settlement enables us to discern a certain pattern in the arrangement of the stove remains (Figure 4.6). Several rows of buildings emerge which are perpendicular to each other. These can be clearly traced in the southern, central and northern parts of the settlement. The longest row stretching SW to NE has been recorded in the central part of the settlement.

Starting out from these observations it is possible to voice a number of assumptions regarding the lay-out of the village. After no more than a cursory examination of the shape and dimensions of the area it becomes clear that Minino I does not belong to that group of lake-side settlements in which all the houses form a single row, the most common lay-out to be found in medieval Russian villages. The lay-out of the settlement could, of course, be designated as a cluster. Yet the facts already outlined above testify to the high degree of order in the arrangement of the buildings and this, in view of the considerable density of their arrangement, enables us to classify Minino I as a settlement with a 'street' lay-out. It is interesting to note that the orientation of the longest row of houses coincides with the course of the modern road, which when it intersects the settlement, leads from the burial-ground to the shore of Lake Kubenskoye. The row of houses perpendicular to the first row leads to a section of the bank of the small Dmitrovka River, which is more convenient for human exploitation.

A different situation has been recorded in the settlement Minino VI, where the cultural layer has suffered a good deal from many years of ploughing and in general has only survived in pits extending down as far as the virgin soil. The artefacts and results of radiocarbon dating have made it possible to divide up the medieval pits as belonging to two main periods: from the middle of the 11th through the 12th century, on the one hand, and from the second half of the 12th and 13th century on the other. Analysis of the arrangement of the pits relating to the different periods within the area of the trench shows that the early materials are concentrated in the northern part of the trench close to the river bank (Figure 4.7). In the second half of the 12th century the area of the settlement grew on account of the settling of plots of land to the south far away from the river. It is to that period that the remains of the only dwelling found in the settlement situated in the southern part of the trench. The stains in the cultural layer from different periods partly overlap each other, but, bearing in mind that an area of twice the size has been excavated here as compared to the Minino I settlement, it can be stated with a good deal of confidence that dwellings in that settlement were more spaced out and at a considerable distance from each other. A major difference has also been recorded with regard to the concentration of finds in the cultural layers of the settlements. While the average concentration of finds per square metre in the excavated area of the settlement Minino I was 17, and approximately 600 gm of pottery, in the settlement Minino VI the equivalent indices were three finds and 250 gm of pottery.

Yet at the same time the identified differences in the lay-out of the settlements, the density of building and the concentration of various finds in the cultural layer should not be regarded as a reflection of significant differences in the level of life in the settlements or the subsistence systems of their inhabitants. As regards the overall range of finds and their quality, the composition of the material and osteological collections the settlements are extremely similar. A particularly important find at Minino VI was that of a small lead seal, which demonstrated that the inhabitants of that settlement possessed certain officially authenticated documents. It is possible that the main reason for the above-mentioned differences should be sought in the topographic features of the locations of the settlements. The relatively small area occupied by the large settlement of Minino I had natural boundaries and in the settlement's heyday this was probably built up almost all over. Meanwhile the opportunities for territorial expansion when it came to the village of Minino VI were virtually unlimited.

Figure 4.7 The Minino VI settlement: 1) plan of the settlement; 2) arrangement of pits from different periods in the trench; (a) pits from the middle of the 11th through the 12th century; (b) pits from the late-12th and 13th centuries; (c) medieval pits, the dates of which have not been possible to determine; (d) House 1.

It thus follows that the research into the settlement of the Minino archaeological cluster situated in the far northern margins of medieval Russia enable us to take a new look at the nature of life and the principles underlying its organization in ordinary rural settlements. The results of these investigations testify to the fact that even settlements which do not stand out on account of their size could constitute fairly complex formations similar to urban settlements regarding a whole series of parameters. Apart from the high level of the inhabitants' prosperity, as reflected in the extremely rich and vivid collection of artefacts and the recording of traces of the plying of various crafts in the villages, attention should be drawn to the existence here of two-roomed houses. Buildings of this kind, namely five-walled houses, are regarded as one of the significant elements in the house-building associated with urban culture. They have been discovered in the earliest levels at Novgorod, in the 10th and 11th-century levels at Pskov and Novogrudok and then in the 12th and 13th centuries they became extremely widespread throughout medieval Russia (Rappoport 1975, 62–67; Faradzheva 1999). Two-room dwellings of that period have been discovered in virtually all the urban centres of the forest and forest-steppe zones so far excavated, but they might be regarded as particularly typical of North-western Russia (Rappoport 1975, 95–111, 166–168). In Novgorod, five-walled houses constituted the most common type of dwelling in the course of 250 years from the time the city was founded up to the very end of the 12th or beginning of the 13th century (Kolchin and Yanin 1982, 73). In the opinion of Spegalskii (1972, 95–97) they were the main type of dwelling for the prosperous section of the population of Novgorod's *posad* or trading quarter. Thanks to the excavations at Minino it has proved possible for the first time to record reliably the fact that two-roomed dwellings were widespread in rural Russia as well. It is important to note that five-walled houses throughout the whole period of the settlement's existence and from the moment it first came into being, were the main type of built dwellings and, essentially, the only type. The sources of this tradition for the Minino micro-region are still unclear today, since we have virtually no data regarding the nature of house construction in North-eastern Rus in the early period. It is possible that the tradition of building two-roomed houses spread there from the North-west, where their wide-scale presence was recorded as early as the 10th century. What it is crucial to focus attention on, however, is the fact that five-walled dwellings, together with buildings of other types, were to be found in the early levels at Byeloozero town dating from the second half and end of the 10th century (Golubeva 1973, 69, 71–74). Interesting data have also been obtained during excavations at the settlement of Krutik which existed in the 9th and 10th centuries in the middle reaches of the Sheksna River 55 km west of Minino. Despite the poor state of preservation of the wood in the cultural layer, it proved possible to establish that the main type of building in that settlement was the log-house built above ground and scholars have succeeded in reconstructing at least one of these houses as a two-roomed dwelling (Golubeva and Kochkurkina 1991, 39).

Results obtained via analysis of the lay-out of the settlements can also be regarded as highly significant. It has been established that the way in which the Minino I settlement was built up was not spontaneous. There was a definite system underlying the overall organization of the space set aside for dwellings. This system found expression in the 'street' pattern of the lay-out – a principle which formed the basis of the territorial organization of medieval Russian towns. Given that there are no archaeologically recorded traces of settlement lands being divided up into properties, what does attract attention is the considerable density characterizing the arrangement of the buildings, which were often erected on the site of previously existing structures.

In recent years, thanks to the wide-scale excavation work, which has been undertaken in a whole series of settlements in North-east and Southern Russia it has proved possible to single out groups of structures which consist of a dwelling and various outhouses, which are usually interpreted as constituting farms or rural estates (Gonyanyj *et al*. 2003; Shpolyanskii 2003). The justification for making direct comparisons between such farms with urban properties containing groups of buildings is debatable, since the question as to the enduring nature of their boundaries in time and space remains an open one, something which is regarded as a crucial feature for the boundaries of urban properties. In the overwhelming majority of cases rural farms are made up of groups of structures and features with a variety of functions linked together by the nature of their lay-out and separated from other similar groups not by archaeologically traceable fences, but by open spaces free of buildings (Shpolyanskii 2003, 256–257). Such groups of buildings can be identified particularly clearly in those cases when farms of different date do not overlap each other. In such conditions it is difficult to speak of properties which existed for a long time within one and the same part of a settlement. Features with various functions which have been studied round the under-stove pit of House 1 in the south part of the trench in the settlement Minino VI (Figure 4.7.2) might well be the remains of a farm of this kind. Yet, given that the group of buildings has as yet only been partly excavated, the reliability of such an interpretation is still open to a certain amount of debate.

The high density of building at the Minino I site reduces the chances of being able to identify groups of buildings of one and the same date, but at the same time it might be regarded as a clear pointer to the fact that specific spatial boundaries did exist, which made it imperative to use sites that had been built on before when erecting new buildings. For this reason, when we take into account the presence of 'street' lay-outs, it could be assumed that the boundaries between various farms in that settlement were fairly stable after all, despite the fact that no traces of fences or palisades were found in the trenches. It should also be noted that the density of built structures at the Minino I site is not exclusive in any way. It matches the density of building found in certain early settlements of the Sheksna region, such as Krutik or Andryushino for instance, the status of which made them stand out from the ordinary run of rural settlements.

THE MANUFACTURE OF METAL JEWELLERY IN RURAL SETTLEMENTS ON THE NORTH-EASTERN FRINGE OF MEDIEVAL RUSSIA

I. E. Zaitseva

INTRODUCTION

Between the end of the 1970s and beginning of the 1990s a significant number of flat-grave burial-grounds dating from the 11th–13th centuries was discovered and investigated in the northern part of European Russia (Makarov 1990; Ryabinin 1997, 99–140). In the excavated burials numerous items made from non-ferrous metals were collected. The standard nature of the jewellery items of medieval-Russian and Finno-Ugrian types, the small number of local variants of jewellery items and the mixed nature of the objects with a variety of ethnic characteristics in these burials made it possible to conclude that most the items of metal jewellery which appeared in this distant region had been imported as a result of the wide ramifications of the fur trade (Makarov 1996, 174). At the same time typical 'northern' types of jewellery (horseshoe-shaped fibulae with cast heads) were identified, which bear witness to the local manufacture of objects made from non-ferrous metals (Galibin *et al.* 1986, 43 and 47; Makarov 1990, 82).

In the 1990s and since 2000 the settlements of the Minino archaeological complex have been the subject of wide-scale excavation and also a number of settlements in the middle reaches of the River Sheksna and its tributaries (Kudryashov 1996, 189–197; 2000, 44–57; 2003, 148–160). In the settlements a rich range of objects made from non-ferrous metals were collected: for example in the settlement Minino-1 occupying an area of 301 m^2 approximately 1,150 such finds were recorded. An interesting and fairly unexpected development was the discovery of areas within many of the settlements concerned of the remains of metal-working involving both ferrous and non-ferrous metals. Objects of this kind were identified in the settlements Minino-1 on Lake Kubenskoye, Krivets, Oktyabrskii Most and Minino-5 on the River Yug and Teleshovo (Figure 5.1). Isolated finds relating specifically to production were made in almost all the settlements. New finds made it possible to take a fresh look at the question of the manufacture and use of metal jewellery on the north-east margins of medieval Russia. What predominated in the apparel of the local inhabitants in various chronological periods: imported items produced in large urban centres, or items manufactured by rural craftsmen living in their environs?

It is possible to answer this question through multi-disciplinary research into the remains of production activity in the settlements, when these are unearthed in the course of excavations or into the tools discovered in these settlements and through analysis of the techniques used to manufacture jewellery items and the composition of the alloys found as raw materials or in the form of finished articles. In this article attention is focussed primarily on the materials obtained in the course of the excavations at Minino. For purposes of comparison, data are cited originating from already excavated settlements in the middle reaches of the River Sheksna and in the Byeloozero area relating to the same period and situated closest to Minino (Figure 5.1). When considering the use of alloys consisting of non-ferrous metals in this area all available data relating to sites in the north-east region have been taken into account, which are duly compared with data obtained for Novgorod and other sites from the north-western part of medieval Russia which have been subjected to similar analysis.

WORKSHOPS AND PRODUCTION COMPLEXES

Complexes from the 10th and early 11th centuries

The earliest medieval Russian assemblages linked with the manufacture of jewellery made of non-ferrous metals in the rural settlements of the north-eastern margins of medieval Russia date from the 10th and early-11th centuries. These had been investigated in the settlements of Oktyabrskii Most and Andryushino in the middle reaches of the River Sheksna (Kudryashov 2000, 46, 50–52) and that of Teleshovo in its lower reaches.

At the Oktyabrskii Most settlement two dwellings were investigated, which contained hearths in "trough-shaped" pits (term devised by Kudryashov) and the remains of wooden constructions round the perimeter, in which apart from household utensils objects were also found linked with metal-working. In one of the dwelling's hearths, both ferrous and non-ferrous metals had been processed. Iron blooms and slags were found, a chisel with a blade 5 mm wide, a driftpin for making holes, and isolated fragments of beaker-shaped crucibles, a bronze striped blank and also the whole side of a two-sided clay casting mould for manufacturing round pendants (Kudryashov 2000, 46, Figure 2.1,10). In another building bronze had been worked: a bronze blank and a fragment of a beaker-shaped crucible were found. Not far from that particular hearth the side of a limestone casting mould was found used for casting small items and a rather coarsely moulded whole ladle together with a round scoop (Kudryashov 2000, 46, Figure 2.2, 2.4). The range of tools found indicates that the

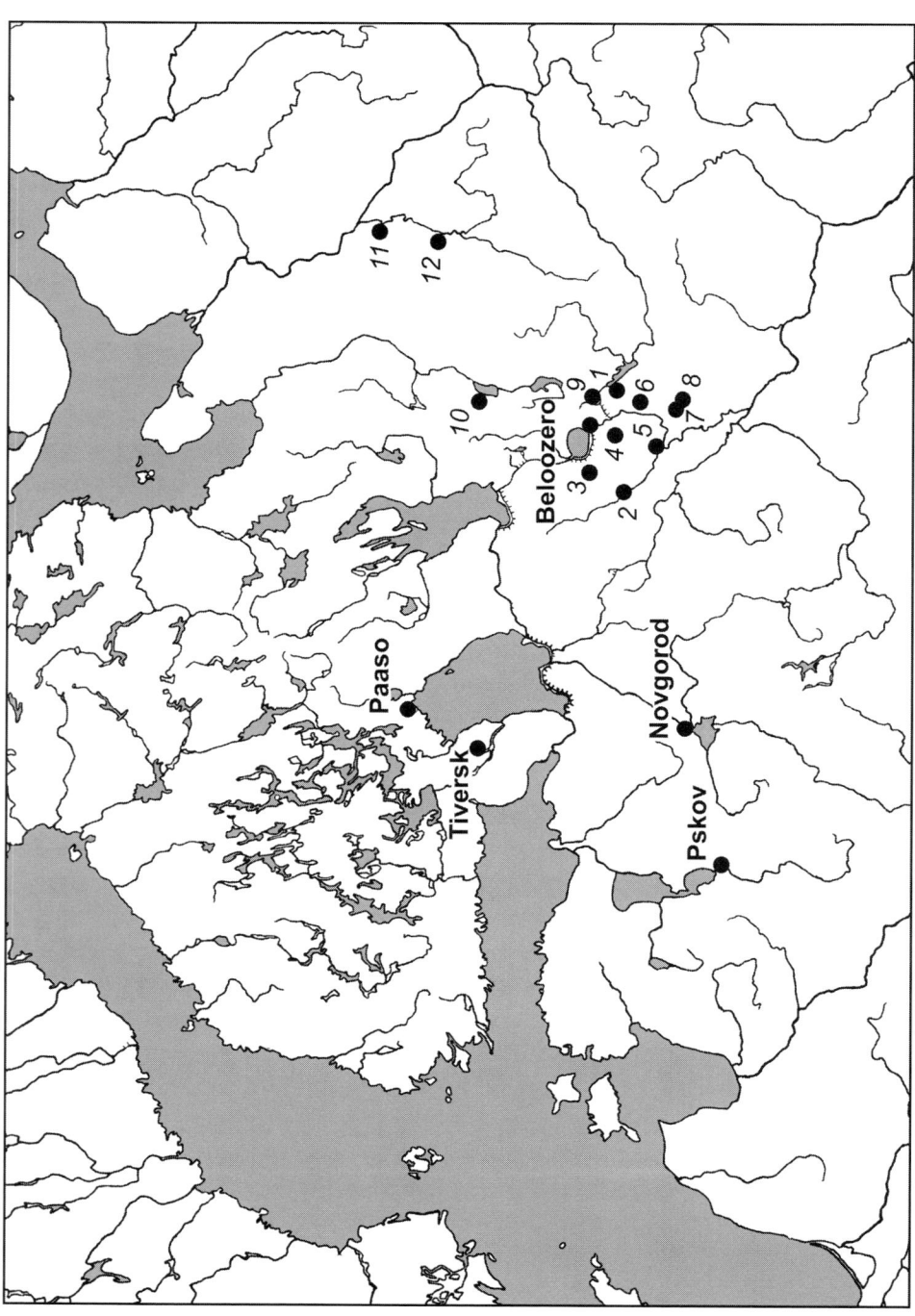

Figure 5.1 Settlements and burial-grounds in the north-eastern margins of medieval Russia between the late-10th and early-13th centuries. 1) Minino; 2) Krivrts; 3) Murinovskaya pristan; 4) Nefedovo; 5) Oktyabrskii Most; 6) Andryushino; 7) Minino 5; 8) Minino 2; 9) Nefedievo; 10) Tikhmanga; 11) Korbala; 12) Ust-Puya.

predominant technique for manufacturing jewellery had been metal-casting. It is likely that in this settlement, apart from the small articles to be sewn on to apparel various rattling pendants of various patterns used to be made using the "wax knitting" technique.

In Teleshovo (north of Moscow, about half-way to Tver) the handle of a ladle was found in the debris cleared from a hearth. There had been a considerable number of tools found in this settlement used for the cold processing of metal: three chisels, three stamps/punches with a flat working part, a burin for engraving and finishing jewellery items. 'Universal' tools were represented by a fragment of pliers and a small iron spade with a trapezoid working part. Small spades of a similar type are familiar from the Finno-Ugrian craft tradition (Golubeva and Kochkurkuina 1991, 55–58). In this settlement off-cuts from plates were found which had been used as metal raw material. There was also an interesting piece of wire, which had been forged from a strip of metal folded lengthways.

A unique find in relation to rural settlements was unearthed in Andryushino, a jeweller's small hammer 64 mm long. One of its working ends had been beaten flat, forming a roughly rectangular surface measuring 8.8 × 4.7 cm, while the other was smaller, measuring 7.3 × 2.4 mm. There were traces of cold working on the striking surfaces. At this same spot four iron tools were found with both pointed and blunt working ends. As regards raw materials, a straight piece of wire was found and fragments of metal plates.

This means that analysis of the earliest assemblages characterized by finds in households of certain objects linked with the processing of non-ferrous metals testifies to the domestic nature of this production, which had not yet reached the stage of specialization. A similar picture is also found within the extensive area of the Krutik settlement already investigated (Golubeva, Kochkurina 1991, 63).

Complexes from the 11th century

Complexes of this date, in which non-ferrous metals were worked, have been studied in the settlements of Minino-1, Minino-5 on the Bolshoi Yug River, and Krivets. It is interesting to note that at the edges of all three settlements materials have been found which were connected with iron-working. In Minino two objects date from this period. These are from a layer of grey-brown loam, containing many glass-type slags, in which are concentrated fragments of clay crucibles and ladles, drops and splashes of metal, melted plates of copper and an ingot of tin brass. Unfortunately, only the edge of this layer has been investigated in the trench in question and therefore it is not yet possible to provide a full description of it. This grey-brown layer is covered over by a building, a specialized jeweller's workshop (Building 7: Figure 5.2). It was a small log house consisting of one room with an earthen floor. The area in front of the building was covered with a layer of clay 1 cm thick. The width of the reconstructed hut was 3 m and its length was over 4.7 m, while the inside area came to more than 12 m². In the centre of the building there had stood a sizeable clay hearth or stove on

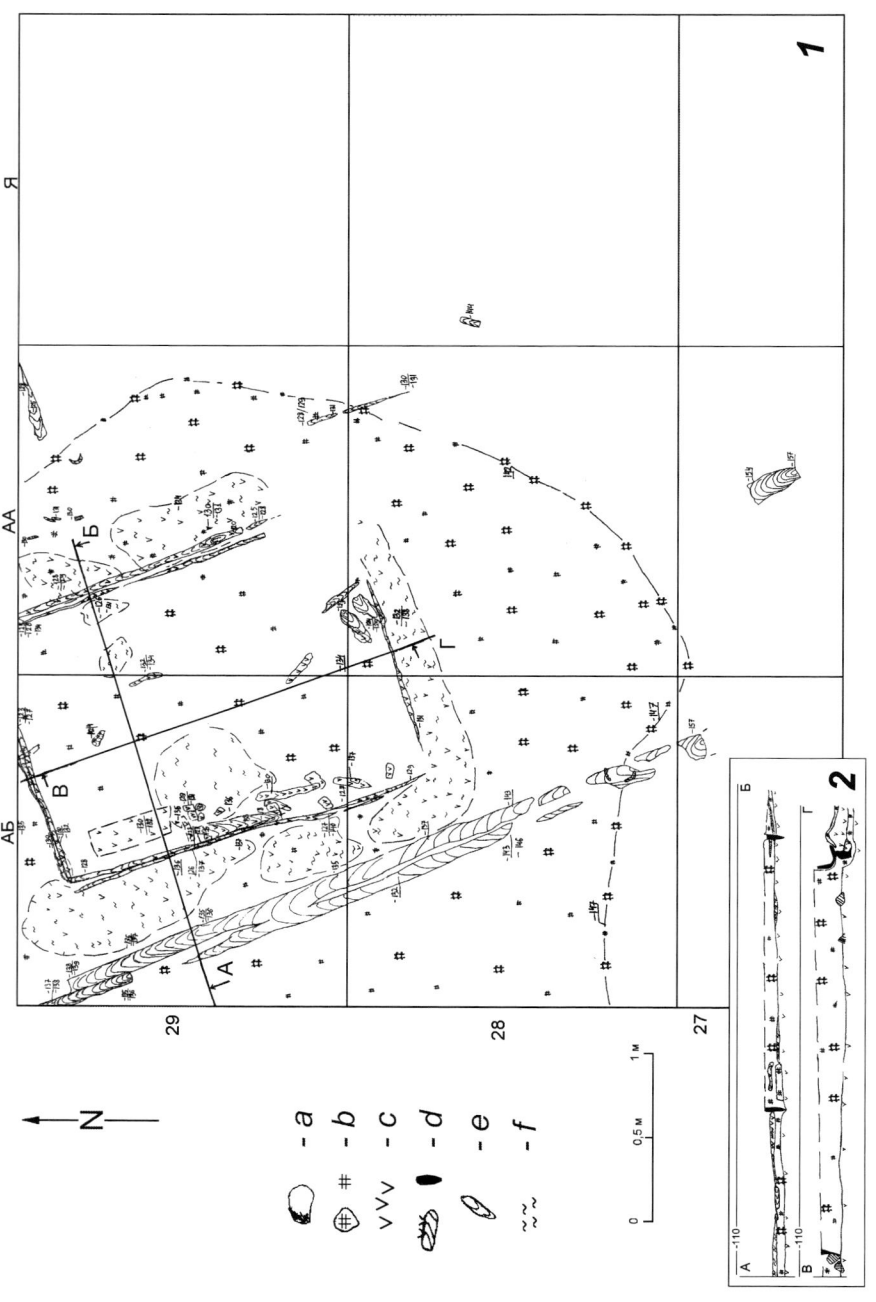

Figure 5.2 Minino I. 1. Plan of Building 7; 2. Profile A–Б and B–Г.

a clay base with a wooden outer frame consisting of thick charred split logs arranged on their narrow edge. The hearth/stove had been positioned parallel to the walls and measured 2.34 × 1.67 m and its surviving height varied between 18 and 25 cm. The distance between the base of the stove and the walls of the building was 40–50 cm. Within this space and along the south wall the base frame of the hearth/stove was on the same level as the bottom of the west wall and at a level 1–3cms further down a compacted stripe of soil could be clearly traced, which was approximately 40 cm wide and stood out on account of soot and ash inclusions which lent it a distinctive colour. This was probably the working area in which the ash and soot had been trodden underfoot. In view of the small area of Trench 4, it is impossible to identify conclusively the link between the grey-brown layer and Building 7.

Fragments of four clay crucibles and six ladles are associated with this particular assemblage. All the crucibles would appear to have been of a single type: large, tall and thick-walled 'beakers' with an oval-shaped top (or in the shape of an oval with pointed ends) and a round base and they were made of fire-proof clay mixed with sand. The thickness of the crucibles' walls was 7–8 mm. Two specimens had a surviving height of 6 and 7.5 cm respectively and on one of them could be seen traces of pliers which had been used to take hold of it (Figure 5.3.1, 2). According to observations made by Eniosova in connection with materials from Gnezdovo, crucibles of this type were 8–9.5 cm high and they had a capacity of 25–30 cm^3 (Eniosova and Mitoyan 1999, 56–57). An X-ray fluorescent analysis of the inner surfaces of the walls of the crucibles was carried out.[1] In three cases traces of silver were found in various combinations with copper and in one case copper with a small addition of lead. Another pointer to active work with silver in this workshop was provided by the find of an ingot (99% silver) in the form of a 'tablet' 14.8 mm in diameter, 5 mm thick and weighing 6.57 gm (Figures 5.3–5.8). Three ladles had survived virtually intact (Figure 5.3.3, 5, 6). From three others only the handles had survived (Figure 5.3.4, 7). Their flat-shaped scoops were oval in shape and had two spouts extending at right-angles to the handle. The sizes of the scoops varied from 5 × 1.5 cm to 8 × 4.5 cm. Analysis of residue from the walls of two ladles indicated that tin had been melted in them. Similar ladles are widely known among Finno-Ugrian antiquities. They have been found in large numbers at Krutik (Golubeva and Kochkurkina 2001, 67–68). In the immediate vicinity of the workshop another ingot of tin brass was found in the form of a bar measuring 34.5 × 4.5 × 3.5 mm (Figure 5.3.9), also drops and splashes of metal and melted copper plates used as raw material (Figure 5.3.10, 15).

At Minino-5 near the hearth of a dwelling dating from the beginning of the 11th century several pieces of melted copper were found together with copper splashes, an ingot of lead bronze in the form of a bar measuring 40 × 5.9 × 4.4 mm, a fragment of a forged blank made of tin brass and square in section and a melted incomplete belt-end. Scattered items associated with the manufacture of jewellery were found in other parts of the settlement: a handle of a red-clay ladle, a pair of forged bronze straight-jawed pincers 72 mm long and several general-purpose iron tools with linear

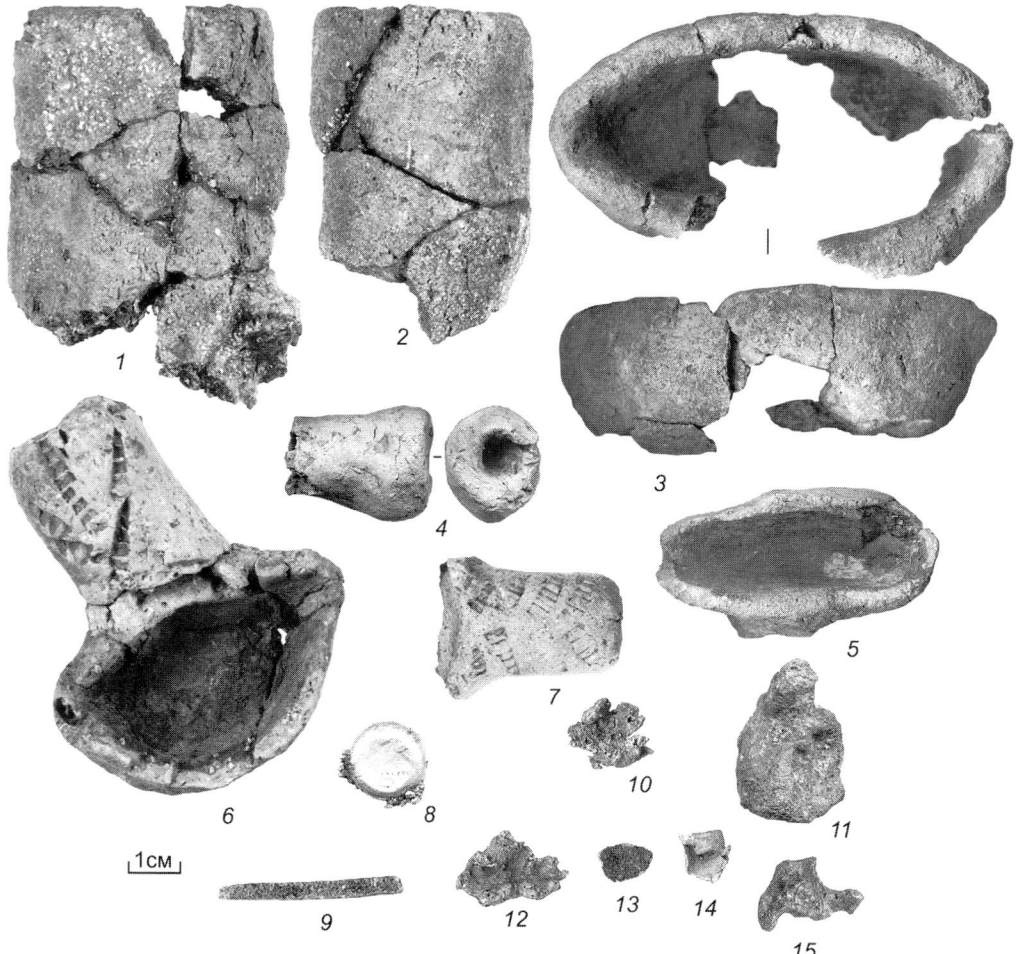

Figure 5.3 *Minino I. Finds associated with the working of non-ferrous metals from complexes of the 11th century: 1,2) crucibles; 3–7) ladles; 8,9) ingots; 10–15) splashes and production waste; 1–7 clay; 8 silver; 9–15 non-ferrous metals.*

working ends and an awl. A forged bar square in section and made of copper mixed with lead could have been used as raw material and also various off-cuts from copper plates from former vessels.

In Krivets the assemblage linked with the processing of non-ferrous metals was found inside a dwelling. Here, as well as household objects at the edge of the hearth, splashes of lead bronze were found on the ground, copper slags and melted rolled plates of varying thickness. Within the territory of the settlement numerous iron general-purpose tools were found, which could have been used for processing non-ferrous metals as well. Two of them were chisels, four were tools with pointed working ends square or round in section and a further two had straight blunt working ends. An interesting iron tool was one that was roughly rectangular in section and 16.8 mm long. Stuck on to its pointed spade-shaped end (5.8 mm wide) remains of some white metal (tin?) had survived. A tool of this kind could have been used for applying covering layers (tinning). An off-cut of twisted wire was found in this settlement, which had been clumsily covered with a thick layer of tin and also an iron tinned and lamellar bracelet.

Complexes of the 12th and early 13th centuries

Three complexes dating from this period were discovered in the settlement Minino-1. Isolated objects relating to production were found in the settlements Oktyabrskii Most and Murinovskaya Pristan.

In the Minino-1 settlement metal jewellery was manufactured during the period in question inside dwellings.[2] In Building 6, as well as household objects one fragment of a crucible was found in the shape of a flat-based round bowl 3cms high and with walls 4.5–5 mm thick with remains of copper containing a small amount of zinc on its walls, a few copper splashes and copper plates and a piece of pure tin. A whole crucible of a shape similar to that from Minino has been found in Staraya Ladoga (Davidan 1980, 64, Plates 3–7). A forged copper blank was also found here in the shape of a rectangular plate measuring 1.1 × 1.3 cm (Figure 5.4.2) and some off-cuts from copper plates and copper wire (Figure 5.4.1, 4).

The remains from production complexes linked with Building 5 (first half of the 12th century) and Building 4 (late-12th century or beginning of the 13th) are more revealing. These two structures were situated in the immediate vicinity of each other (see Figure 4.1 in Zakharov, this volume). Most of the finds connected with production were discovered outside the buildings and for the most part near their entrances. It is likely that superfluous rubbish was discarded into the street.

Building 5: With this structure the fragments of at least six crucibles and a ladle handle can be associated. Most of the crucible fragments are fairly small in size and this means that the shape of the vessels can only be guessed at. Four of the crucibles were cylindrical and had round bases (they would appear to have been high 'tumblers'). A distinction can be drawn between two kinds of cylindrical tumbler-shaped crucibles with a round base, large and small. The large tumbler crucibles (2 specimens) were made from fire-proof clay mixed with fine sand and, in some cases, organic material. They have a round base and an oval (2.5–3/3.5 cm) or round (diameter 3–4 cm) mouth. The walls of the crucible were 6–8 mm thick in their upper part and between 8.5 and 12 mm near the base (Figure 5.4.12, 13). The large tall 'beakers' were used for melting tin bronze, lead brass and low-grade silver. The metal on the walls of the crucibles from this building contains a large amount of antimony.

The small beaker-crucibles (2 specimens) were made from fire-proof clay with a small admixture of sand. An appreciable amount of organic material had also been added to the clay of these crucibles. They had a round base and a round mouth 2–2.3

Figure 5.4 *Minino I. Finds associated with the working of non-ferrous metals from complexes of the 12th and early-13th century: 1,2,9) off-cuts and blanks; 3,11) wire fragments; 4) blanks for rivets; 5) ladle; 6,12,13) crucibles; 7,8) ingots; 10) splashes; 1–4, 7–11 non-ferrous metals; 5–6, 12–13 clay.*

cm in diameter. The thickness of the crucible walls varied between 5.5 and 12 mm and they had survived to a height of 3–4 cm. Intact specimens of crucibles of this type from Gnezdovo are 5–6 cm high and have a capacity of 8–11 cm³ (Eniosova and Mitoyan 1999, 57). In these small crucibles silver was melted and also copper with small additions of lead and tin.

According to observations made by Goryunova and Eniosova tall round-based crucibles with or without a spout were fairly widespread within the territory of medieval Russia. Crucibles of this kind have been found in materials from Staraya Ladoga, Krutik, Novgorod, Ryurik Gorodishche, Gorodok on the River Lovat, Rostov the Great and elsewhere (Goryunova 1994, 63–70; Golubeva and Kochkurkina 1991, 65; Eniosova and Mitoyan 1999, 61). Crucibles of this type have been found in the fortified settlement Idnakar in medieval Udmurtia and in the cities of Volga Bulgaria (Ivanova 1998: 134–135). The chronological range for the use of these crucibles is very wide. They have been found at sites from the second half of the 1st millennium and also in materials from the pre-Mongol period.

Fragments of two crucibles are of the round-based conical type with a triangular mouth (Figure 5.4.6). They are made of fire-proof clay, to which some fine sand and organic material have been added. The thickness of the crucible walls is between 7 and 11 mm. The upper part of one of the crucibles, which has a surviving height of 4.5 cm, can be reconstructed with a fair degree of probability. Its mouth measures 5.7 × 7 cm. Although the lower part of these crucibles did not survive, it is clear that their height did not exceed their width. In one crucible of this type remains of billon and brass were found.

Round-based conical crucibles with a triangular mouth were widely used by the jewellers of Northern Russia. They made up the vast majority of crucibles found in the settlement of Krutik (Golubeva 1991, 151), predominate in Novgorod (Ryndina 1963, 213–214) and Byeloozero (Golubeva 1951, 39) and are encountered in Torzhok, Novogrudok, Polotsk and other towns. A detailed analysis of wide-mouthed conical crucibles found at sites in Northern Russia during the medieval period was undertaken by Goryunova. She believes that this type of crucible is of Finno-Ugrian origin and that its wide distribution in the towns of Northern Russia in the 12th century 'ties in well with the course of Novgorod's colonizing activity and the influx of people of Finno-Ugrian origin into Novgorod' (Goryuynova 1994, 69).

From among the raw materials in the assemblage from Building 5, copper plates were found, scraps of bronze and lead-tin wire and a rejected casting of a flat duck-pendant cut up prior to re-working (Figure 5.5.1). It is possible that zoomorphic jewellery was made in Minino. Pendants in the shape of a dog and a hollow duck found in the adjacent plot revealed major casting defects. Parts of the dog were missing as a result of not enough metal having been poured into the mould and the gaps had simply been filled with extra pieces of metal (Figure 5.5.4). Here, links in the shape of a figure-of-eight made from wire chains constituted imitations of Finno-Ugrian chains made using the technique known as wax-knitting (Figure 5.5.2, 3). In an early

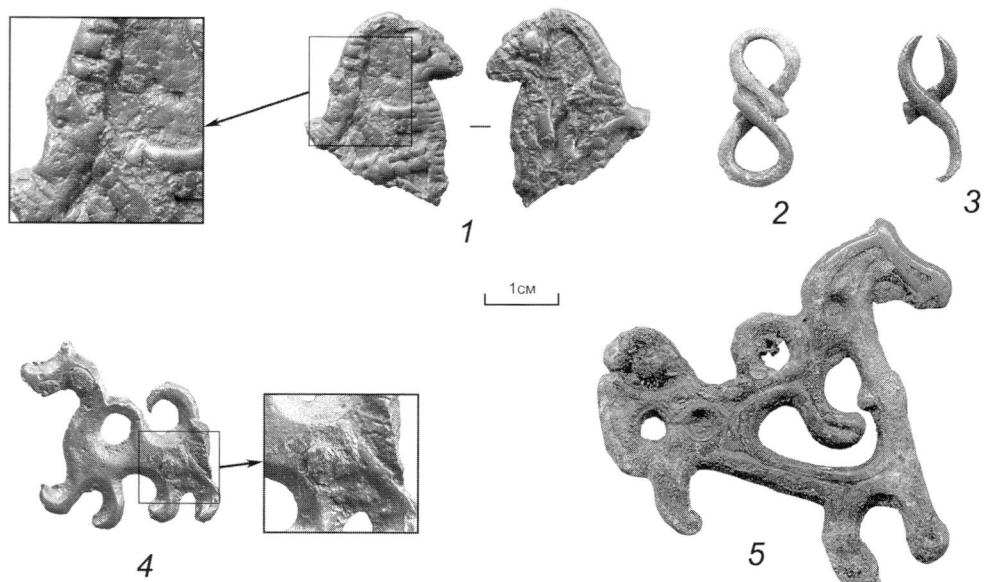

Figure 5.5 *Metal objects of local production from the Minino Complex: 1,4,5) zoomorphic jewellery; 2,3) chain links; 1–5 non-ferrous metal.*

12th-century burial in the Minino-II burial-ground there was a flat open-work horse-pendant (Figure 5.5.5). One of the hind-legs of the finished horse was undersized because its mould had obviously been used many times and the up-shot of this was that it appeared three-legged. Two similar small horses were found in burials of the Nefedievo burial-ground. It is probable that the jewellers working in Building 5 had used fusible alloys. In the building small pieces of such an alloy were found, which were of various different shapes and were waste or rejects from the casting process, and also wire off-cuts. Apart from making jewellery, the craftsmen working in this building had repaired copper vessels. In the assemblage blanks for rivets made of lead-bronze were found (Figure 5.4.4).

Building 4: Among the tools in the assemblage there are fragments of four crucibles and a ladle. The ladle was almost identical to the largest ladle from the 11th-century workshop. Its bowl measures 6 × 3.5 cm, its wall is 6.5 mm thick and the clay used contained admixtures of organic material and crushed stone (Figure 5.4.5). On the walls of the ladle remains of tin and antimony were found. Crucibles were represented by small fragments, which were not enough to make it possible to reconstruct their shape in its entirety. It is likely that they had been beaker-shaped, had had round bases and that two had been large and two small. The clay used for all the crucibles contained quite large admixtures of organic material and in two cases the clay contained sizeable

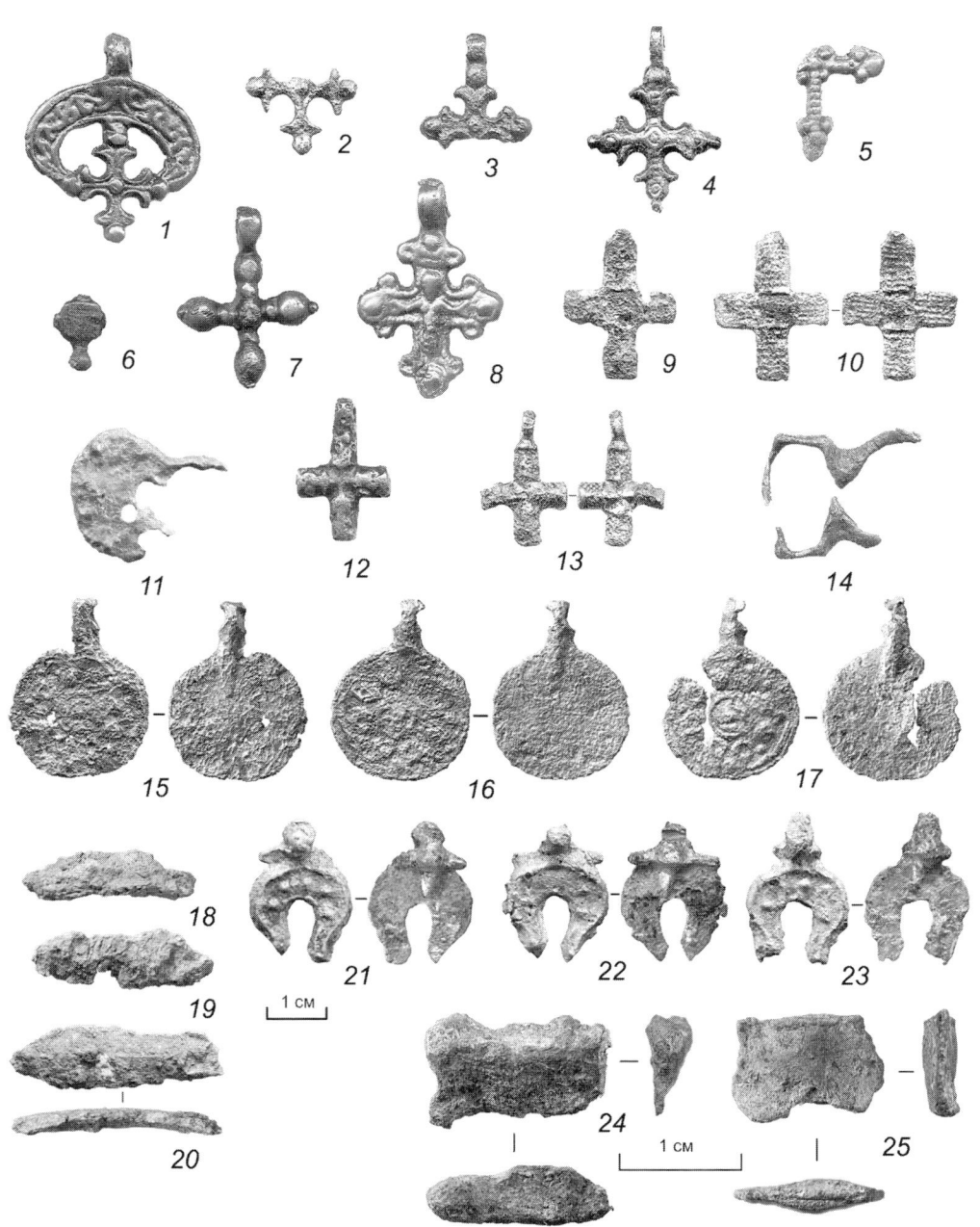

Figure 5.6 *Metal objects associated with Building 4: 1,21–23) crescents; 2–10, 12–13) crosses worn against the skin; 11,14) belt buckles; 15–17) pendants; 18–20) belt-ends; 24–25) fills from casting channels; 1, 3–8, 12, 14 copper alloy; 15–25 fusible alloys; 2, 10–11, 13, 15–25 non-ferrous metals.*

admixtures of fine sand. The thickness of the walls in most of the crucibles in the upper part is approximately 8 mm, up to 11 mm in the lower part and 5–6 mm in the case of the small crucibles. The analysis carried out on the metal from the walls of three crucibles showed that in two of them (one large and one small) tin bronze with small additions of lead had been melted and in the other copper debased with lead.

Two already partly used copper ingots and a shapeless piece of tin were among the raw materials found here. One ingot was misshapen (Figure 5.4.8), while the other had retained its original shape of a small bar measuring 23 × 5 × 2 mm (Figure 5.4.7). One end of it was semi-circular, while the other had been cut off by a tool like a chisel. Evidently, despite the fact that copper vessels were actively used as a source of copper, local craftsmen used to obtain this metal also as raw material specially prepared for jewellers. Similar small ingots of copper have been found in Staraya Ladoga (Davidan 1980, 65).

In the materials from this assemblage numerous shapeless copper splashes have been found and melted copper plates, off-cuts of wire and metal plates (Figure 5.4.9–11). As well as copper-based alloys, work with fusible alloys also played a significant role in the work undertaken in this workshop. Here two pieces of tin from the filling of channels in casting moulds (Figure 5.6.24, 25), splashes, numerous off-cuts of wire made out of an alloy of tin and lead (Figure 5.5.11).

In the workshop of Building 4, crosses worn round the neck were manufactured. Of the 18 metal crosses found in the settlement of Minino-I, eleven were associated with the workshop under discussion (Figure 5.6.2–13). Despite the fact that there are direct parallels for many of the crosses among those found in Byeloozero (Zakharov 2004, Figure 41–43), it can be assumed that some of the specimens collected up within the area containing the workshop had been made on the spot. All the crosses had been cast in two-sided moulds. Three specimens had lily-shaped ends and rhomboid centres (Figure 5.6.2–4). Two of them are of identical design. What distinguished them is the fact that one has been cast from tin-bronze, while the other has been fashioned from a fusible alloy. As regards their measurements they coincide exactly with the bronze cross to be worn round the neck enclosed in a broad crescent (Figure 5.6.1). The wax model for the crescent had been put together from two pieces obtained using an impression of the cross (on which even the loop had been retained) and one of the crescent. The place where the two parts had been fastened together is also clearly to be seen on the reverse of the article. The front of the cross complete with crucifix reveals significant casting defects, which – as in the case of the dog-pendant – had been patched up with other pieces of metal, moreover metal of a different composition. The two crosses made of bronze and a fusible alloy (Figure 5.6.12, 13) are imitations of small stone crosses of a type known as *korsunchik*, from the area of Khersones (Ukraine). They had been cast using impressions of finished articles. Two other identical crosses made of a lead-tin alloy had straight rectangular arms (Figure 5.6.9, 10). They had probably been cast in one and the same mould.

The assortment of articles from the workshop was not confined to crosses. It is

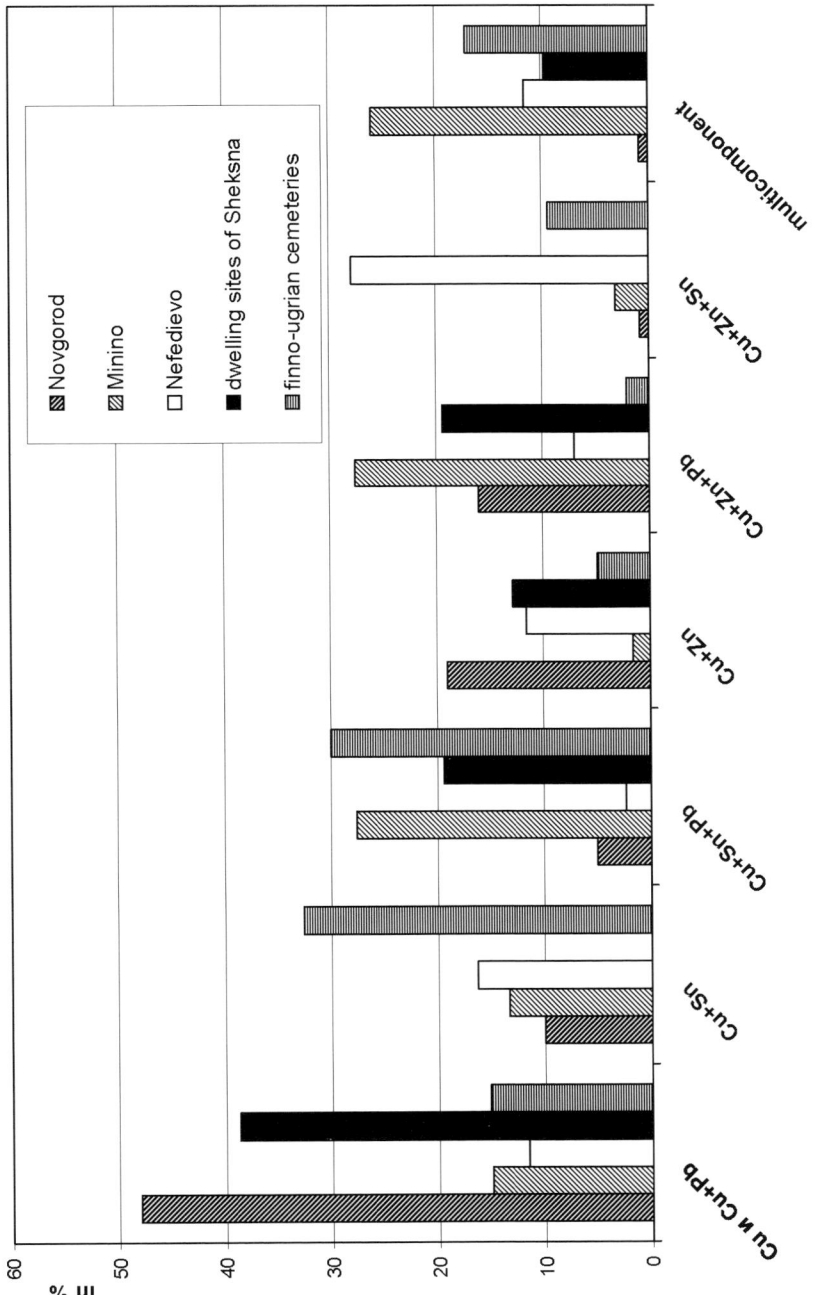

Figure 5.7 Groups of alloys found at sites in the north-eastern borderlands of medieval Russia.

possible that pendants of various types and beads made from a fusible alloy were manufactured here as well. In the area of the workshop a bead made from an alloy of tin and lead was found which had suffered from major casting defects and also three identical, disc-shaped pendants decorated with a central ring design (Figure 5.6.15–17). All the pendants had the same decorative impression which had a defect in casting at the loop. It is probable that the items had been thrown away, since the decorative motifs on them had come out very badly. It can be assumed that three identical small crescents, made from an alloy of tin and lead and found in one of the burials in the Minino-II burial-ground (Figure 5.6.21–23), had been cast in this workshop. The remains of the pouring channels had not been completely removed from the crescents even.

In the workshop metal parts for belt sets were also made. Three identical discarded belt-ends made from a fusible alloy triangular in the front and a lengthways rib down the middle were found here (Figure 5.6.18–20). They had not been properly finished. Two belt buckles had also been scrapped. One, made from a fusible alloy had not really come out right (Figure 5.6.11). The other had been made from bronze (Figure 5.6.14). The model moulded from wax had been very thin and as a result the casting had proved unsatisfactory.

At the settlement of Oktyabrskii Most fragments of two stone casting moulds were found. One of these bore a design of a round pendant and it had been made from a pinkish slate, while the other bore a depiction of a cross and was fashioned from white limestone. In one of the dwellings at the settlement known as Murinovskaya Pristan a ladle was found near the hearth. In other parts of the settlement a fragment of a thick-walled crucible with a round base was found and part of the mouth of a thin-walled crucible, and also two iron tools with linear working edges, isolated off-cuts from metal plates and parts of the latter which had been melted down.

It can thus be seen how detailed examination of what remains in production complexes has yielded finds in each excavated rural settlement in the north-east margins of medieval Russia: this would appear to demonstrate that a large amount of the metal jewellery used by the inhabitants of these ancient settlements was made on the spot. Nevertheless, this type of activity throughout the period under discussion went on mainly in individual households. The predominant technique used for manufacturing jewellery was casting using impressions from ready-made objects, i.e. replication. A considerable proportion of the jewellery was made using the technique known as wax knitting which had been widespread in the Finnish-Ugrian world.

ANALYSIS OF ALLOYS OF NON-FERROUS METALS

In the wake of over 100 years of research in Russia into the composition of alloys from non-ferrous metals used in the manufacture of medieval jewellery by specialists such as Sabaneyev, Konovalov, Naumov, Daiga, Galibin, Goryunova, Fonyakov, Koroleva and Eniosova, data from a major series of analyses of samples have been gathered from objects dating from the 10th to 13th centuries, found in both urban centres and rural settlements in Northern Russia. The availability of this comparative material provides good opportunities for analytical work in the study of the composition of metals used for jewellery and associated scrap, which have been found in settlements and in burial-grounds from the north-eastern margins of medieval Russia. The comparison of the results obtained with data from adjacent territories enables us to establish how metal jewellery evolved and the routes along which metal jewellery made its way to those outlying regions between the late-10th and early-13th century, to assess the level and nature of jewellery produced locally and the proportion that accounted for in the overall range of articles used in the North.

To this end specimens were taken for analysis from a total of 146 artefacts found in the Minino archaeological complex: the Minino-I settlement (73 specimens), the Minino-II burial-ground (55 specimens), and the Vladyshnevo-II burial-ground (18 specimens). Forty-three specimens were taken from articles found in burials in the Nefedievo burial-ground (11th and early-12th century), situated 35 km north of Minino on the Porozovitsa River, which flows into Lake Kubenskoye (Makarov 1997). Thirty-one of the specimens were taken from finds collected in settlements located in the basis of the middle reaches of the Sheksna River: Oktyabrskii Most, Krivets, Minino-5 and Minino-2 on the River Yug (10th–14th centuries). The samples were deliberately collected from articles that had been made from copper alloy. Spectral analysis using the three calibration method was undertaken in the Laboratory of Archaeological Technology in the Institute for the History of Material Culture, Saint Petersburg (for a description of the method used, see Egorkov and Shchetenko 1999, 40) and in the Vernadskii Institute of Geo-chemistry and Analytical Chemistry of the Russian Academy of Sciences.

A study was made of the composition of the metal used for the following artefacts found at Minino: bracelets (9), temple rings (8), finger rings (19), crosses (7) parts of belt sets (27), fibulae (4), crescents (2), icon pendants (2), zoomorphic pendants (6), pendants of various types (3), torques (2), jangling jewellery (17), rattle-bells (7), ɸ-shaped beads (2), spiral separator-beads (4), wire fragments (7), metal plates and lamellar loops (7), rivets (3), ingots (3), blanks and splashes (7).

Published results of spectral analysis tests on jewellery items from Finno-Ugrian flat-grave burial-mounds in northern regions of Eastern Europe were used for purposes of comparison: from Tikhmanga (46 specimens, early-12th century), Korbala (64 specimens, late-11th and early-12th century) and Ust-Puya (34 specimens from the 12th and 13th centuries) (Galibin *et al.* 1986, 52–57); conclusions drawn on the basis of research using large series of tests on materials from Novgorod (10th–15th centuries; Konovalov 1974), Pskov (10th–16th centuries; Koroleva 1996, 229–300) and also data from burial-mounds of various regions in the Novgorod lands and in the southern part of the Ladoga region (10th–12th centuries; Brandenburg 1884, 4–23) and the Izhorsk plateau (11th–14th centuries; Proceedings of the Archaeological Commission 1884,

60–87), materials from Gorodok on the River Lovat) (10th–12th centuries; Goryunova 1985) and the Karelian city-sites of Tiversk and Paaso, where Novgorod traditions were followed with regard to the use of alloys (10th–14th centuries; Vasilieva 1982, 185–188).[3]

When the artefacts were being divided up into groups, the classification used involving previously defined parameters was that general accepted with regard to metal-work (Koroleva 1997, 170–171; Eniosova *et al.* 2001, 358–371). The data gathered from each site would be broken down into groups according to the presence of the main alloying components, namely tin, bronze or zinc (Figure 5.7):

- single component – 'pure' copper (Cu);
- two components – lead bronzes (Cu + Pb), tin bronzes (Cu + Sn), double brasses (Cu + Zn);
- three components – tin-lead bronzes (Cu + Sn + Pb), tin-zinc bronzes (Cu + Sn + Zn), lead brasses (Cu + Zn + Pb), tin brasses (Cu + Zn + Sn);
- multi-component alloys (Cu + Sn + Zn + Pb).

The results of this work are presented in Figure 5.7 at the end of this article. We shall now discuss in more detail the groups classified as outlined above.

'Pure' copper

What is termed 'pure' copper is metal in which the content of each alloying element comes to less than 1%. The 11 samples originating from the Minino-I settlement turned out to have been made from 'pure' copper (15.3% of the samples from this site used for analysis). The copper was not very pure and contained admixtures. The admixture found in the largest amounts was lead. All the samples, except for one from a horse-shoe shaped fibula with plait-like decoration on its arc, were ingots (1), splashes (5), melted fragments of metal (2) or metal plates (2) and had been found in areas where manufacturing activity went on. In Trench 3 most of the finds were associated with Building 4. In Trench 4 copper articles were found both in Building 6 and also in 11th-century deposits.

A similar picture was obtained from the testing of samples taken from artefacts made of 'pure' copper collected from settlements in the middle reaches of the River Sheksna, which accounted for 12.9% of the total. The admixture of lead was larger than in the case of the Minino artefacts. What turned out to have been made from 'pure' copper were the splashes and the fragment of melted metal in Minino-5 (beginning of the 11th century), and also a metal plate and wire found in the Oktyabrskii Most settlement (11th century).[4]

There was no jewellery made of copper in the Minino-II and Vladyshnevo burial-grounds, but, on the other hand, substantial series of finds from Nefedievo (16.3%) and Korbala (23.4%). In Nefedievo there were casings made of copper, a ribbed ring, a bracelet made up of narrow plates, a twisted torque, a spiral-shaped bead and two temple rings shaped like rings worn on the finger which had originated from burials dating from the very end of the 11th, the 12th or the 13th century. In burials of the same period from Korbala the artefacts made from copper were mainly horseshoe shaped fibulae, zoomorphic pendants and metal plates.

Lead bronzes

These account for 11.1% of the total specimens from the Minino-I settlement. In the sample under discussion copper accounted for 95.3–98.4% of the alloy and lead for 1–4.2% (average lead content 2.35%). More than half the finds were associated with Building 4. All the finds from this group, except for one thick wire bracelet were plates or sheets of metal: they included a lamellar eye from a pendant, fragments of metal plates and rivets made from off-cuts which had been rolled up into a strip of metal bent to form an eye.

Most likely of all there had been no deliberate intentions of introducing lead into the melt in advance, its presence points rather to the poor refining of the copper. As regards the other admixtures, antimony was identified in samples associated with Building 5: the average antimony content was 0.48%, while the average antimony content in the 'pure' copper category had only been 0.18%. The craftsman working in that particular building had evidently been working with a batch of 'badly refined' copper with an unusually high antimony content.

Lead bronzes in the settlements in the middle reaches of the Sheksna River constitute 28% of the specimens. The average lead content came to 1.8%. If we take into consideration the fairly high lead content in the 'pure' copper group, it can be assumed that the craftsmen from the settlements in question were sent for the most part batches of copper raw material with an admixture of lead.

Most of the samples are in the form of raw material (ingots) and production waste. A belt fitting and zoomorphic horse-pendant had been cast from 'debased' copper. In the grave-goods excavated from burials there is virtually no jewellery made of lead bronze.

When studying the composition of alloys used in the manufacture of finds from Novgorod made of non-ferrous metals, Konovalov noted among them a significant percentage of objects made from 'pure' copper and copper debased by lead (Konovalov 1974, 18, 21). When recalculating the specimens using according to the selected method this came to about one third and slightly less than 15% of the samples with a copper base respectively.[5] A particularly large number of them (up to 80%) was in finds connected with manufacturing activity (also in Novgorod). Thirty percent of the objects made of 'pure' copper came from the duly analysed collection of artefacts from the Karelian city-sites of Tiversk and Paaso (Vasilieva 1982, 186–187). In Pskov 10.9% of the objects made from alloys with a copper base were made from 'pure' copper and approximately 4% of them from lead bronze (Korolyova 1996, 235–237). It is essential here to draw attention to the fact that in Novgorod almost half (48%) of the analysed specimens made of alloys with a copper base were made of copper (or contained an admixture of lead). This index was the highest for all the analysed collections in the

North of Russia. The equivalent figure for the areas to the North-east of Novgorod, namely the settlements in the middle reaches of the Sheksna River near the city was 38.7%. At the remaining sites the number of copper articles was significantly less. Analysis of the range of finds from 'pure' and 'debased' copper reveals that completed artefacts from these alloys at all the sites investigated, apart from Nefedievo and Korbala, were represented by isolated examples. Most of the selected specimens were unworked raw materials and production waste.

The quality of the copper raw material used by the local jewellers, given that medieval Russia had no copper mines of its own, depended entirely on copper obtained from elsewhere. For the north-western regions the main source of copper was from German and Swedish deposits (Konovalov 1974, 19–22; Eniosova *et al.* 2003, 240–241). Ingots from Scandinavia, Gotland and the Baltic region, which have been subjected to chemical analysis, were partly 'pure' copper and partly an admixture of up to 6–16% of lead (Eniosova *et al.* 2003, 240). For the north-eastern areas of medieval Russia copper raw materials imported from the Urals and Volga Bulgaria also played an important role: it was in the latter region that the remains of copper-smelting kilns were found dating back to the pre-Mongol and Golden-Horde periods (Polyakova 1996, 154–157): the relatively small number of analyses of the chemical composition of the artefacts concerned carried out to date, however, makes it impossible at this stage to draw any kind of conclusions. Copper pots no longer in use and cut up into pieces were often used as raw material for jewellery.

Tin bronzes

Articles made of tin bronze were found at all the sites investigated. At Minino the share of specimens made from this alloy came to 11.6%. The concentration of tin in the specimens varied between 1.7 and 16% (the average level being 8%). There was no clear norm for the introduction of tin to the alloy: in the bulk of the specimens the tin content was between 4 and 10%.

Articles made from tin bronze included belt fittings and a belt buckle, crosses worn round the neck, jangling hanging ornaments including those in the form of bells, a ring with a hexagonal plate, a round icon-pendant bearing a depiction of a warrior saint holding a spear in his right hand.

In the specimens obtained from the settlements in the middle reaches of the River Sheksna no tin bronzes were found.

As regards objects made from tin bronze, burial-grounds from three sites (Nefedievo, Ust-Puya and Tikhmanga) yielded up similar amounts between 15 and 20% of the specimens. At the same time, however, there were marked differences as regards the tin content of the alloys in question. While at Nefedievo the average tin content in the specimens was 2.2%, at Tikhmanga and Ust-Puya it was around 12%. The specimens taken from Tikhmnaga and Ust-Puya also stand out on account or their higher antimony content.

At Nefedievo there were Finno-Ugrian jangling pendants, a rattling bell, a ring-shaped bead, a temple ring and a bracelet made up of tin bronze plates. In Tikhmanga jangling pendants, lamellar finger rings, small circular and bracelet-like temple rings, a duck-shaped hanging ornament and a buckle were found all made of tin bronze.

At Korbala more than half of the analysed artefacts were made from tin bronze (51.5%). As in Nefedievo, they all contained a small percentage of tin (the average tin content in the specimens was 3.5%). Among the artefacts made of tin bronze were umbo-shaped pendants and bell-shaped hanging ornaments, horseshoe-shaped fibulae, rattling bells, belt buckles and wire rings. Examination of the chronological distribution of these finds reveals that tin bronze was used most actively in the Byeloozero area and beyond Vologda in the 11th and the early-12th century, although isolated objects made from this alloy have also been encountered in levels from all periods.

Tin-lead bronzes

Tin-lead bronzes are found everywhere apart from Korbala and they account for a large share in the samples. At Minino they account for approximately one quarter of the total. Tin content ranges between 1 and 21% and lead content between 1 and 7.5%. As regards the concentration of tin in the specimens from this sample they can be divided into two groups:

1. Bronzes with a low tin content, i.e. up to 10% (5 specimens);
2. Bronzes with a high tin content, i.e. above 10% (10 specimens).

Half the specimens contained between 1 and 2% lead, while the lead content in the others varied between 2 and 7%. It can be assumed that in most cases the relatively low lead content testifies to the fact that 'dirty' copper was used for making jewellery, rather than to the practice of using lead for making alloys.

All the objects from the group of tin-lead bronzes, apart from two wire off-cuts, were completed articles. Most of the jewellery items made from metal with a high tin content can be linked to the Finno-Ugrian 'world'. These include jangling hanging ornaments and parts of the latter, zoomorphic pendants and φ-shaped separator beads. Objects with a low tin content, temple rings made of wire, crosses worn round the neck and cruciform pendants, finger rings and belt fittings are more often medieval Russian artefacts or do not possess distinctive 'ethnic' features. Yet, the Minino tradition for manufacturing jewellery from bronze with a low tin content served to modify this picture: two horse-pendants and two duck-pendants from burials in the Minino-II burial-ground had been cast from an alloy of that kind. These articles had probably been the work of local craftsmen.

Among the finds so far analysed obtained from the settlements of the middle reaches of the River Sheksna the group of tin-lead bronzes accounted for approximately 20%. The tin content fluctuated between 7 and 16% (an average of 10.65%) and the lead content between 1.1 and 5%. In most of the specimens the lead content did not exceed 2% and coincided with the concentration of that element found in the specimens from the lead bronze group.

Half the specimens in the sample were taken from cast articles: a ring consisting of narrow plates, a bracelet made up from metal plates and the small fragment of another article, while the rest of the finds had been made from wire. Most of the finds were only given a rough date within a broad period of the 11th–13th centuries.

In the samples from the Nefedievo and Korbala burial-mounds tin-lead bronzes are only represented by isolated objects. In Tikhmanga and Ust-Puya, on the other hand, they account for 58.1% and 44.1% respectively. Most of the specimens obtained from both these sites are of bronze with a high tin content.

Tin-zinc bronze

From all the sites under discussion only one specimen was found made of tin-zinc bronze, a duck pendant from Ust-Puya.

When summing up the observations made above regarding the groups of tin and tin-lead bronzes, it is appropriate to note that using both tin and lead at the same time to make alloys was not typical of most of the sites examined. In many cases articles made using a copper base debased by lead often found their way into the group of tin-lead bronzes. By adding tin to copper, craftsmen from Tikhmanga, Oktyabrskii Most and Ust-Puya obtained alloys with a high tin content of over 10%. More common for Minino and Korbala were alloys with a more usual low tin content of below 10%.

The appearance of tin and tin-lead bronzes was first recorded in the North-east at the end of the 10th century and their use continued throughout the whole period, during which those sites were inhabited, i.e. up until the mid-13th century.

The bronzes are represented mainly by completed articles. The only specimens which might be listed as raw materials were the few fragments of wire, which originated mainly from the settlements in the middle reaches of the Sheksna River. Meanwhile the presence of these alloys in local metal-work enables us to conclude that jewellers from the Byeloozero region and from beyond Vologda deliberately made alloys from copper with tin and lead.

Tin and tin-lead bronzes predominate in the Finno-Ugrian burial-mounds of the North East accounting for 53.1% of the total in Korbala and 78.3% in Tikhmanga. In Minino their share is somewhat smaller (35.6%) and it was smallest of all in the settlements in the middle reaches of the Sheksna River (somewhat below 20%).

In Novgorod and Pskov objects made from tin bronze account for approximately 10% of all those made from alloys with a copper base. Tin-lead articles, meanwhile account for 5% of such articles in Novgorod and approximately 15% in Pskov. Typical for both groups is the low content of elements used for making alloys, but in Pskov approximately a quarter of the tin-lead articles have a tin content of over 10% (Korolyova 1996, 246). In the Karelian city-sites bronze objects account for approximately a quarter. This means that Novgorod stands apart from the other sites in the North of medieval Russia as regards the quantity of finds made from bronze alloys as well. It proved to be minimal (only 15%).

Double brass

Alloys made of copper with zinc were not in common use among the inhabitants of Minino. Only two articles made of such an alloy were found in the Minino-I settlement: a lamellar finger-ring and a fragment from a spiral made of wire round in section (11th century). Alloys of this kind are not found at all in the Tikhmanga and Ust-Puya burial-grounds.

In the settlements from the middle reaches of the Sheksna River and in the Nefedievo and Korbala burial-grounds specimens made from double brass account for 11–13% of the total. The zinc content in the finds from these settlements varied from 12.4% to 14%. Apart from completed articles there was a fragment of drawn wire and a melted piece from the edge of a vessel. The finds had been collected from 11th, 11th–12th and 13th-century levels. In Nefedievo all jewellery items from this group came from burials dating from the 11th or very early-12th century. The zinc content in the specimens collected did not exceed 8%. Spiral separator-beads and wire articles were found made of double brass. In the specimens from Korbala the concentration of zinc was fairly stable, namely 2.7–5%. The range of finds included articles of medieval Russian origin: a lyre-shaped buckle and the tongue to go with it, a horseshoe-shaped fibula, a twisted bracelet to be tied round the wrist and a horse-pendant of the Smolensk type (Galibin *et al.* 1986, 44) which would have made their way to the Northern Dvina River as a result of trade.

Lead brass

Approximately a quarter of the analysed finds from Minino had been made of an alloy consisting of copper, zinc and lead. The zinc content varied between 3.4 and 22% (average level 13.3%) and the lead content between 1 and 19% (average level 7.1%).

Approximately 40% of the articles made from lead brass had a zinc content of no more than 10%, another 40% of the articles of between 10% and 15% and the remaining 20% had a high zinc content.

On the basis of the lead content the sample could be divided into two sub-groups:

1. those with a low lead content (1–2%) accounting for 30% of the specimens;
2. those with a moderate or high lead content (more than 2%) accounting for 70% of the specimens.

It is possible that the low lead content indicates that 'dirty' copper was used.

Among the articles made of lead brass just under half consisted of articles fashioned from wire such as temple rings, bracelets, finger-rings, fibulae and fragments of the same. The remaining finds were a lamellar finger-ring, a wire torque and an imitation coil torque made from a flat band of metal, belt fittings and a belt-end, bracelets, a spiral separator-bead, a duck-pendant and also jewellery items associated with the Finno-Ugrian range of antiquities including jangling ornaments, a belt buckle and a plugged temple ring.

It can be assumed that the parts from belt sets, the duck-pendant, the bracelet made up of animal heads, the small horseshoe-shaped fibula with spiral ends and some rings had been brought to Minino ready-made. In addition to such articles, local jewellers used to obtain brass alloy in the form of wire (most of the specimens with a high zinc content were from wire or articles made of it), from which they made articles without modification of the material or which they melted down again first.

In the burial-ground the articles made from lead brass were found in burials from between the end of the 10th and beginning of the 12th century, while in the settlement they were from levels of the 11th, 12th and early-13th century.

The share of lead-brass specimens from the settlements in the middle reaches of the River Sheksna accounted for approximately 20%. The zinc content varied considerably in the range 3.6–21% (average 9.2%). The lead content was between 2.6 and 19% (average level 9.6%). All the specimens studied were probably alloys for which both zinc and lead had been used. Articles from this group found in the Minino-5 and Minino-2 settlements were of local production and included an incomplete lamellar bracelet, a forged ring made of wire round in section, an item of jangling jewellery cast using a carved wax model, a fragment from a curved wire and a forged pin. The finger-ring from Minino-2 dated from the 13th century and the other articles from a period between the end of the 10th and beginning of the 12th century.

At Nefedievo the share of articles made of lead bronze came to 7%. They included two finger-rings, one made of thick wire and the other imitation coil and a horse pendant of the Smolensk type. The finds dated either from the 11th century or from the late-12th/early-13th century. Lead-brass finds were not typical of the Finno-Ugrian burial-mounds at Tikhmanga, Korbala and Ust-Puya. Only one article from those sites, a hollow duck-pendant from Ust-Puya, had been cast from an alloy of that kind.

Tin brass

This metal is represented by four specimens from Minino. There was a finger-ring with a plate bordered by a ridge, which had a tin and zinc content of 1% each: it had perhaps been made from copper containing admixtures. In the other cases the zinc content was between 10 and 16% and the tin content between 1 and 3.2%. The other specimens were an ingot bar, measuring 33 × 3 × 3 mm with a zinc content of 16% and a tin content of 3.2%, and two rings made in Minino from one and the same batch of metal: they were made from wire round in section and with pseudo-twisting (late 11th or early-12th century).

Among the specimens from the settlements in the middle reaches of the Sheksna River there was no tin-brass. Objects of this kind were also for all intents and purposes absent from the burial-grounds at Tikhmanga and Ust-Puya.

At Korbala the jewellery items of this group accounted for approximately 10% of the total. They are distinguished by their low zinc content (on average 3.3%) and tin content (on average 2%). In addition to the jewellery items of medieval Russian types such as a horse pendant and a torque with pseudo-twisting, there was a Finnish bell-shaped pendant. It can be assumed that tin-brass was found amongst locally produced items as a result of broken pieces of imported jewellery with zinc content being melted down and then tin being added to the melt.

The site of Nefedievo stands out clearly against this general background, because jewellery items made of tin-brass there account for almost 30% of the total. The zinc content in all the specimens apart from one was low, namely 1.2–7% (an average of 3.7%), while tin content was 1–6.8% (an average of 2.3%). Two thirds of the jewellery items made from tin brass had been fashioned from wire: temple rings, both those made from beads and with an open-work sheath and others resembling finger-rings, a twisted bracelet and for the remainder ribbed and lamellar rings, a belt end and a casing.

Multi-component alloys

Multi-component alloys were found at all the sites examined, apart from Korbala. The largest quantity of these as a share of the total was found in the Minino Archaeological Complex, namely 23.5%. The share of multi-component alloys was slightly smaller at the other sites: ranging from 9.6% at settlements in the middle reaches of the Sheksna River to 17.7% at Tikhmanga.

When classifying multi-component alloys, specialists divide them into multi-component bronzes and multi-component brasses depending upon whether tin or zinc predominates in the specimen (see, for instance, Korolyova 1996, 231). Only at Nefedievo did multi-component brasses make up three quarters of all the multi-component alloys (the average zinc content in the specimens was 22.3%), while at the other sites the alloys which clearly predominated were mixed ones obtained as a result of a series of re-melts. At Ust-Puya many objects made of multi-component bronze with a high tin content (the average tin content in the specimens was 13.4%) only had a low lead and zinc content. The multi-component bronzes from Ust-Puya were obtained as a result of melting down scrap metal containing zinc and adding large amounts of tin in accordance with the local tradition for manufacturing alloys.

At Minino approximately a third of the specimens made of multi-component alloys with a high zinc content (over 10%) and a fairly low tin content (for the most part under 5%) could be classified as multi-component brasses. In most cases tin and zinc were found in more or less equal small quantities and therefore there was no point in singling out subgroups as well.

Among the examples of multi-component brasses there was the end of a forged bracelet, a lamellar ring with a wide middle section with three ridges on it and a second ring with a narrow base-plate, the hoop from a temple ring incorporating three beads, items of jangling jewellery and a trapezoid hanging ornament. Mixed alloys had been used to make jangling hanging ornaments, an ф-shaped bead and a belt fitting. The finds from Minino were dated to a period from the second half of the 10th century to the first half of the 12th. Moreover a significant number of the objects made of mixed alloys was given a more precise date: the late-10th or early-11th century.

In the group of settlements in the middle reaches of the Sheksna River multi-component alloys were represented by three specimens: two plates from Krivets and Minino-2 and a melted fragment from a jangling pendant found at the Minino-5 site. Both plates had been fashioned from multi-component brass with a high zinc content, and the jangling jewellery had been made from a mixed alloy. At this site objects were found in levels of the late-10th/early-11th century and also from the levels of the 12th and 13th centuries.

When summing up the observations made regarding the groups of alloys consisting of copper and zinc, it is essential to point out that only at Nefedievo did brass alloys predominate in the sample as regards a percentage of the whole (44.2%). In the Minino Archaeological Complex and in the settlements in the middle reaches of the Sheksna River the amounts of brasses and bronzes were more or less the same and came to about a third of the whole. In the Finno-Ugrian burial-mounds, on the other hand, bronzes clearly predominated.

Double brasses were represented in the region by a small quantity of specimens which for the most part only had a low zinc content (under 10%). The most sizeable share was that in the settlements in the middle reaches of the Sheksna River and at Korbala, where they accounted for 11–13% of the total. What had clearly led to their appearance in the region was Novgorod, since the materials found in that city accounted for 19% of the finds of double brasses among copper-based alloys. It is also worth pointing out that double brasses appeared in the settlements near the River Sheksna not only in the form of completed articles but also as raw materials. A similar picture (13.2%) is provided by Tiversk and Paaso, towns with Novgorod traditions when it comes to the use of alloys (Vasilieva 1982, 187). Finds at Korbala testify to the interest shown by Novgorod in distant lands beyond Vologda.

Lead brasses were more numerous at Minino and the settlements in the middle reaches of the River Sheksna, where they accounted for 19–23% of the finds of copper-based alloys. In Zavolochie there were only isolated examples of such objects. While in the settlements from the middle reaches of the River Sheksna alloys with a low zinc content (on average 6.8% for the period from the end of the 10th to the beginning of the 12th century) were typical, in Minino objects have been identified with both a low and a high zinc content. Apart from obviously imported jewellery made from such alloys, which had originated from the north-west, what can also be noted is the appearance of raw materials for jewellers consisting of lead brass in the form of wire, which was then fashioned into objects in local workshops.

The share of lead brasses in the range of copper-based alloys at sites in the North-west of medieval Russia and in the Baltic region is considerable: approximately 15% in Novgorod and Pskov (Korolyova 1996, 238–239), 18% in the Baltic region (Naumov 1965, 139; Daiga 1962, 62–65). According to the observations of Eniosova, typical of territories in medieval Russia were alloys with a low or moderate zinc content, obtained in the course of repeated re-melts of broken pieces of objects containing zinc, as a result of which the volatile zinc would become less concentrated (Eniosova *et al.* 2000, 104–107), while in the Baltic lands and in neighbouring regions (Pskov,

Zalakhtovie, etc.) the zinc content in most of the specimens of lead brasses was fairly high (10% or more). In the remaining part of the North-west of medieval Russia the highest concentration of zinc was found in raw materials, including wire. Wire with a high zinc content is to be found in Novgorod in 11th and 12th-century levels (Konovalov 1969, 209, 212, 214), Pskov, Gnezdovo (Eniosova 1999, 72). It also made its way as far as Minino, where not only wire jewellery was made from it, but new objects were cast from the wire after it had been melted down, including objects of Finno-Ugrian types. Lead brasses have been recorded throughout the period when the sites of Byeloozero and near Lake Kubenskoye were being used, namely from the end of the 10th century to the beginning of the 13th century.

Tin brasses, like the double ones, are not typical of the region under discussion. In Minino tin brasses appeared first as raw materials (ingots). An example of their local use is found in two finger-rings from a burial-ground, which had been made from one and the same batch of metal. This alloy was recorded in the 11th and early-12th centuries. As has already been pointed out above, a rather unusual situation was noted in Nefedievo, where more than a quarter of the specimens turned out to have been made from tin brass: moreover, jewellery items made from this alloy were found both in burials of the 11th century and also those of the late 12th century.

Tin brasses are not typical either for Novgorod or the Baltic region, where they constituted less than 1% of the total (Eniosova *et al.* 2003, 103 and Table I). The largest share (10%) which they accounted for was in Pskov (Korolyova 1996, 237–238) and Karelian city-sites (17%) (Vasilieva 1982, 186–7).

Multi-component alloys made their way as far as the north-east margins of medieval Russia in the form of completed articles (horseshoe-shaped fibulae, parts of belt sets, temple rings) and as raw materials for jewellers (plates, small bar ingots); moreover, the raw materials were represented in the main by multi-component brasses with a high zinc content. It is interesting to note that among the earliest jewellery items from Minino, relating to the late-10th or early-11th centuries and originating from burials in burial-mounds where the deceased had been cremated (Vladyshnevo-II and Minino-II), multi-component alloys and bronzes were represented by a more or less equal number of specimens, while for the later period the number of multi-component alloys declined considerably. When considering the distinctive features of bronze alloys from the North-west of medieval Russia, Eniosova and Sarachova note how widespread multi-component alloys were in "the materials from those sites, which were a long way from large urban markets for non-ferrous metals", in the burial-mounds of the Izhorsk Plateau and the Lake Ladoga region (Eniosova *et al.* 2003, 237–239). A similar situation was observed by Orlov (1988) in relation to rural sites in the Chernigov area. It is likely that the Minino settlements had not yet been drawn into the orbit of Novgorod influence, since in the materials from those sites relating to the late-10th and early-11th centuries there were virtually no objects of 'Western' appearance, although jangling pieces of jewellery and belt sets of eastern types were widely represented.

Multi-component alloys were not typical of the jewellery tradition which had come into being in Zavolochie. The quite large share of these from among the total found at Ust-Puya (over 20%) might reflect the intensive Western contacts actively nurtured by the inhabitants of the region in the late-12th and early-13th centuries and also the influx into it of large numbers of imported articles (Galibin *et al.* 1986, 46).

Observations regarding the distribution of alloys at various sites in the north-eastern margins of medieval Russia identify, despite a certain amount of similarity, specific characteristics intrinsic to each settlement and bear out completely the conclusion to the effect that a large number of small production centres had existed, each with its own special features in the manufacture of its output.

Interesting results were obtained by determining the co-efficients of the similarity between sites on the basis of the compositions of the alloys found in objects made from non-ferrous metals. To this end a co-efficient was used which had been proposed by Sher (in Kamenetskii *et al.* 1975, 74–76). Types of alloys were among the features analysed and the weight allocated to a feature was the relationship between the number of objects in each group and the overall number of specimens taken from the site in question (see Table 5.1).

The table compiled in this way for this purpose reflects a real historical situation. The sites most closely linked with Novgorod were the settlements in the middle reaches of the River Sheksna and Nefedievo. Craftsmen from the above-mentioned settlements had closer links with western sites, first and foremost with Novgorod, as sources of ready-made jewellery and also specially prepared raw materials for jewellery manufacture, i.e. small bar ingots

	Minino	Nefedievo	Tikhmanga	Settlements on the River Sheksna	Korbala	Ust-Puya	Novgorod
Minino	X						
Nefedievo	0.552	X					
Tikhmanga	0.564	0.242	X				
Settlements on the River Sheksna	0.785	0.310	0.288	X			
Korbala	0.271	0.658	0.171	0.172	X		
Ust-Puya	0.587	0.332	0.687	0.436	0.354	X	
Novgorod	0.659	0.797	0.251	0.745	0.476	0.384	X

Table 5.1 Coefficients for similarities between sites on the basis of alloy types.

and wire. Nefedievo was located at one of the most important portage routes on the way from Byeloozero to Lake Kubenskoye (Makarov 1997, 57). Minino occupied an intermediate position as it were. On the one hand it provided evidence of strong ties with Novgorod and the settlements in the middle reaches of the Sheksna River, reflecting the western thrust of its commercial links, while on the other there were indications of quite close links with the Finno-Ugrian burial-mounds of Tikhmanga and Ust-Puya, reflecting contacts in an easterly direction. The jewellery traditions of Korbala based on the creation of tin bronzes and working with 'pure' copper proved to be a law unto themselves.

Chronological patterns are also of interest here. In the initial period of Minino's existence in the late 10th and early 11th centuries, bronzes and multi-component alloys predominated in jewellery manufacture, which were associated with the Finno-Ugrian production tradition. Double and triple brasses, indicative of commercial contacts with a western orientation, do not appear before the beginning of the 11th century. It is significant that not only ready-made articles were imported into this distant north-eastern region, but also raw materials direct. Craftsmen did not go out of their way to change the composition of the raw material they received which contained zinc, but simply went ahead and manufactured their own articles from it.

In the 12th century in a situation where brasses still retained their importance, the number of bronzes began to grow rapidly in local metal-working involving non-ferrous metals. This can be noted in particular in materials from Minino where approximately a third of the analysed objects turned out to be made of bronze, in particular crosses worn round the neck and also zoomorphic and jangling hanging ornaments, the production of which was probably well established in the settlements. Similar patterns in the use of alloys have been noted in relation to the workshops of Novgorod (Eniosova *et al.* 2003, 232).

The craftsmen of Minino were far more skilful in their work with bronze alloys, than when fashioning brass. This comes most strikingly to the fore in their attachment to bronzes with a low tin content, which were so popular in the North-west of medieval Russia. When working with raw materials which had a high tin content, including scrap from broken jewellery, they were able to lower the concentration of tin. Nevertheless, working with raw material without changing its composition was a more widespread practice among metal-smiths making jewellery to meet mass demand. Work of this kind came to predominate in the manufacture of jewellery even in such major centres as Pskov (Korolyova 1996, 256).

CONCLUSION

Analysis of production complexes, in which non-ferrous metals were worked combined with research into the composition of the metal used in ready-made articles and that of production waste found in settlements from the middle reaches of the Sheksna River and the area around Byeloozero and Kubenskoye Lake have shown that metal-working with non-ferrous metals was going on in virtually all the settlements so far examined. Jewellery was made during the whole of the period under examination, that is, from the second half of the 10th century to the first half of the 13th. Despite the fact that the manufacture of jewellery was carried on mainly as a craft within individual households, it can be assumed that the production of local workshops supplied the needs of the local population to a considerable extent, although the importing of objects from further afield also had a significant role to play. Local production was not aimed at putting out large series of articles of one and the same type: on the contrary, rural craftsmen used to make small numbers of jewellery items copying imported models, which had caught their customers' eyes (items which had been cast with impressed designs). Virtually all categories of jewellery items were manufactured, even crosses worn round the neck, which were an essential possession at that time and later came to represent 'markers' for the process of Christianization of the inhabitants of outlying territories. Series of standardized items might well make their way to outlying areas from major urban centres.

The geographical location of Minino half-way between Novgorod and remote Zavolochie is also reflected in the range of jewellery items used there, which combined types typical of both the north-western regions of medieval Russia and also the eastern Finno-Ugrian regions. The overall chronological patterns in the use of types of alloys worked in Minino and Novgorod, determined the role of the latter as one of the major purveyors of raw materials and models of ready-made articles to the borderlands.

By way of conclusion it is appropriate to point out that significant differences in the manufacture and use of metal jewellery are to be found in the north-western margins of the Novgorod Lands, in the Vodskaya Piatina[6] and along the north-eastern borders of the medieval Russian state. While in the Vodskaya Piatina an unusual self-contained "local variant of Novgorod culture" had taken shape (Ryabinin 1997, 60) with its own traditions for the manufacture and wearing of jewellery made from broken pieces of old jewellery items, which were melted down many times over as local jewellers did not have access to pure raw materials (Eniosova *et al.* 2003, 236–237), the situation in the North-east was exactly the opposite: craftsmen were able to work with jeweller's raw materials direct, but they did not create new types of jewellery replicating instead articles from central workshops which came their way.

A list of samples studied as part of this survey and the results of their analyses are included in a table in the accompanying CD to this volume.

ACKNOWLEDGEMENTS

The author would like to thank the director of the Archaeological Museum, part of the Cherepovets group of museums, A. V. Kudryashov for the opportunity to use unpublished materials from his excavations, and N. V. Eniosova for her help in carrying out X-ray-fluorescent analysis of the crucibles.

Notes

1   The test was carried out in the Geological Faculty of Moscow State University.
2   It is possible that special buildings nearby were used for manufacturing jewellery. However, the small area excavated so far has not yet made it possible to draw any definite conclusions.
3   When these calculations were being made for all these sites only alloys with a copper base were used, the total number of which was taken as 100%.
4   The dating for these samples taken from excavations led by A. V. Kudryashov was carried out by the archaeologist in charge.
5   The recalculation of the specimens for the whole range of samples taken in Novgorod was carried out by N. V. Eniosova and T. G. Sarachova (Eniosova *et al*. 2000, 103).
6   The Vodskaya Piatina was one of the five historic districts of Novgorod Land dating to the late 15th century, if not earlier. Each district is believed to have been linked originally to one of the five Ends of the town in that its administration was conducted from there. The Vodskaya Piatina covered the area from the Volkhov to the Luga Rivers (Editor).

– 6 –

MEDIEVAL POTTERY FROM THE MININO ARCHAEOLOGICAL COMPLEX

M. L. Mokrushin

The collection of pottery from Minino contains over 45,000 fragments,[1] of which 65% are hand-made and 34% are wheel-turned, while a little over 1% of the vessels may be called slow-turned (or wheel-finished) pottery. The bulk of the collection consists of pottery from the main site in this group, Minino I, with over 31,000 fragments (69% from hand-made, 31% from wheel-turned and 1% from slow-turned vessels). Hand-made pottery also predominates in the materials from the Minino Il burial-ground (92% of the 3,225 fragments concerned) and the sites known as Vladyshnevo I and II (100% of the 1,430 fragments). A different situation is to be found at Minino VI, where 58% of the 9,717 fragments are wheel-turned, 42% hand-made and slightly over 2% slow-turned.

While the collection was being sorted, it proved possible to reconstruct and draw, as if complete, 66 of the vessels and the upper part of a further 91. Of the vessels concerned 106 were hand-made (45 of the 'complete' vessels and 61 of the upper parts), 20 slow-turned (13 and 7) and 31 wheel-turned (8 and 23). Virtually all the vessels were cookpots. The absence of the other categories of household pottery can be explained by the fact that they had probably been made from other materials such as wood, birch-bark or metal.

THE HAND-MADE POTTERY

Hand-made pottery consists of clay with an admixture of medium-grained (0.5–1 mm) and large-grained (over 1 mm) crushed granite. In a number of cases the presence of grog and organic admixtures in the form of husks from cereal grains was noted in the clay. One fragment was found in the fracture of which traces of burnt fish scales were to be discerned. On the basis of the nature of the breaks in the vessels only one method of production was recorded: they were made from horizontal bands of clay using a coiling technique. Traces of ash, coarse-grained sand and crushed

Figure 6.1 Decorative elements (1) and types of decorative compositions (2) on hand-made pottery from the Minino group of sites at Lake Kubenskoye (numbers of the elements correspond to those in Table 6.2).

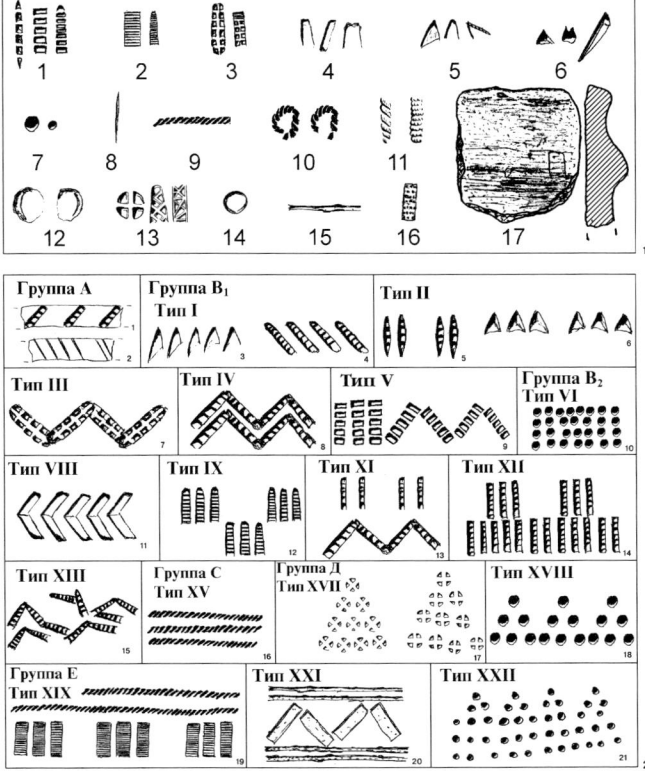

granite having been scattered on the bases of some of them were duly noted. From the way the surface of the vessels had been worked, the pottery can be seen to have been carefully smoothed: in most cases the clay had been thoroughly prepared and the firing was of good quality, so that is why these vessels could be described as either 'smoothly moulded' or 'roughly moulded'. Characteristic of vessels in the latter category are their uneven surface, grains of the filler protruding conspicuously from that surface and clear traces of the careless smoothing and moulding of the vessel by hand (imprints of fingers). The firing of such vessels would be uneven and the clay in the fracture would prevent a three-layered 'sandwich'. The colour of the fragments would vary from pale-brown to dark-grey.

All the hand-made vessels in the collection could be divided into three groups on the basis of their diameter at their widest point: (1) large vessels with a diameter of 33–36 cm; (2) medium-sized vessels with a diameter of 13–29 cm and (3) miniature vessels with a diameter of 8–10 cm. The variation regarding the size of the pots is linked most probably with their function. It can be assumed that the large vessels were used mainly for storing liquid and dry products, while medium-sized pots (these accounted for the majority, namely approximately two thirds of the reconstructed

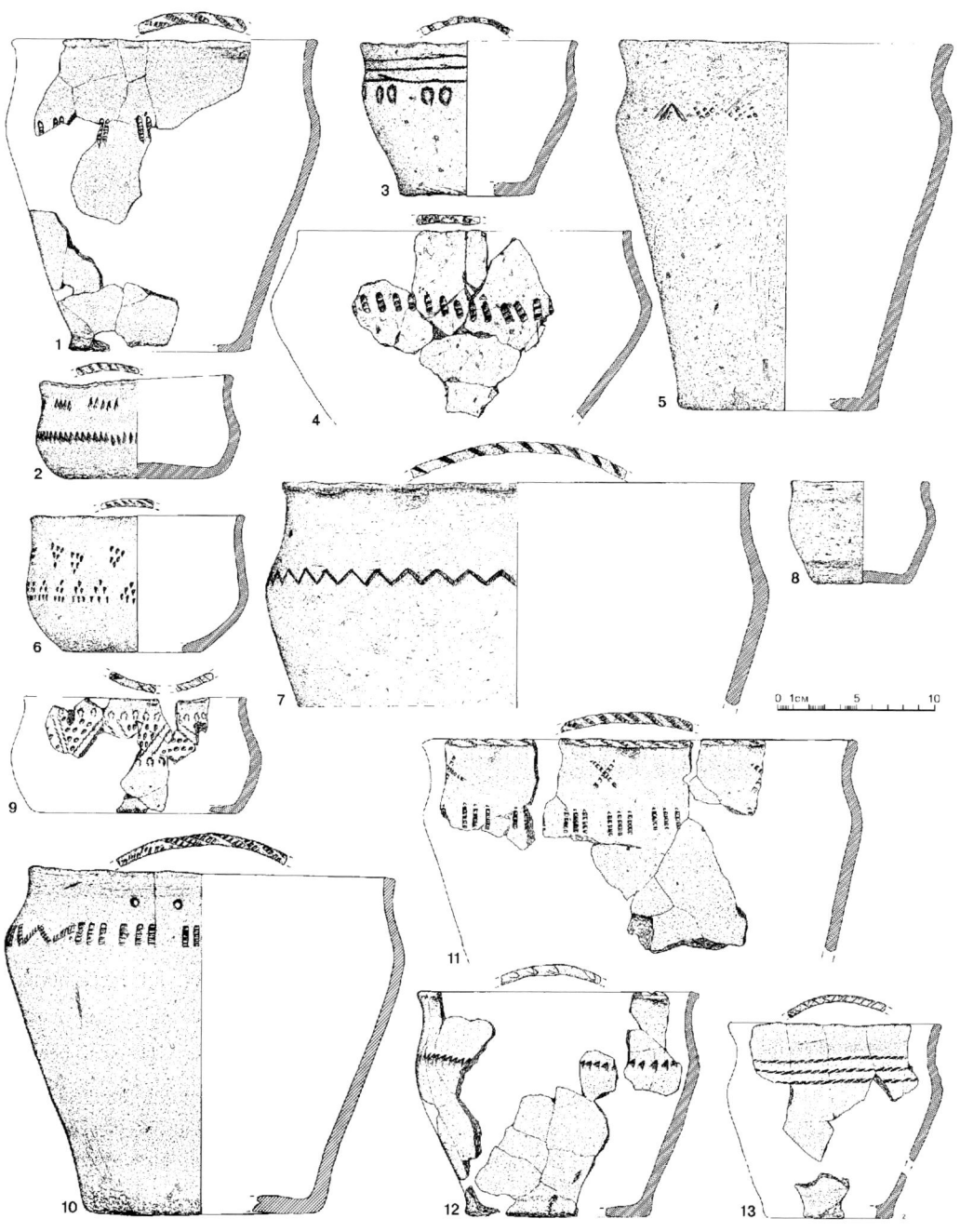

Figure 6.2 Minino. Medieval hand-made pottery vessels from the end of the 10th century to the early 11th century.

vessels) were, to all appearances, used most frequently for cooking food, indeed many of them had traces of soot. Some of them had probably been used for table-ware as well. In some cases, vessels, which had cracked during use, had been repaired: on five of the reconstructed vessels and on a number of separate rim fragments traces of repair were recorded, i.e. pairs of holes right through the vessel walls (see, for example, Figure 6.2.10; Figure 6.3.8).

For the typological analysis, 106 restored and graphically reconstructed vessels and their upper parts were selected (62 specimens from Minino I, 28 specimens from Minino II, 10 from Minino VI and six from Vladyshnevo I). The classification of the vessels was carried out on the basis of the general typological scheme elaborated for the assemblages of hand-made pottery within the whole of the area east of Lake Onega (Makarov 1989). Criteria for identifying a type were differences in vessel shapes and the nature of the profiling in their upper parts, taken as the basis for the variants. In addition, the main proportions of the vessels were also taken into account, namely the correlation between their maximum width, overall height and the diameter of their base.

Of the seven types regarded as the main ones in the range of pottery found in the area east of Lake Onega, six are encountered in the collections from Minino under discussion here, which together account for 89.6% of the total number of vessels examined. A detailed description of the main types has already been published on a number of occasions (Makarov 1989, 84–88; Makarov 1991, 130–135) and so it would seem admissible here merely to present the table demonstrating the distribution of the main types in a comparison of the assemblages from the central part of the Byeloozero region and the whole collection of hand-made pottery from the area east of Lake Onega (see Table 6.1). As can be seen from the table, the predominant type of this kind of pottery in Minino was the Type I pot (Figure 6.2.1, 3, 4, 7, 10–13). Parallels for vessels of this kind are widespread among Volga-Finnish antiquities and these date from a period no later than the 10–11th century, while certain of the vessel shapes (Figure 6.2.1, 10, 11) were common within a wider territory of the forest zone of Eastern Europe, including the north-western regions round Lake Ilmen and along the River Volkhov (Plokhov 2002, 141–154). The significant share consisting of vessels of this type in the Minino collection is explained by the fact that the bulk of the hand-made pottery from the sites Minino I and Minino II consists of materials dating from the very end of the 10th and the 11th century. It was precisely in that period that vessels of Type I predominated in the settlements east of Lake Onega (Makarov 1989, 88).

The second largest group in the collection is that of jar-shaped vessels (Type IV) (Figure 6.3.2). This stems from the fact that in the 11th and 12th centuries they came to constitute the predominant type of hand-made pottery for the whole region (Makarov 1989, 89). Numerous parallels for jar-shaped vessels can be pointed to in the range of Baltic-Finnish antiquities and they were also widely represented in the sites of North-western Russia of the medieval period, where they are considered as associated with the local Finno-Ugric population (Makarov 1989, 90). The significant proportion of

Site	I	II	III	IV	V	VI	VII	Rare specimens	Total number of vessels
Total collection from the region to the east of Lake Onega (end of 9th–12th centuries)	37.3	10.7	6.8	26.6	3.4	4.4	2.3	8.5	1,246
Total collection from Minino (end of 10th to early-13th centuries)	33	1.9	9.4	20.8	-	17.9	6.6	10.4	106
Byeloozero (late-10th to 12th centuries)	12.4	4.3	2.1	59.7	2.6	7.7	8.1	3	233
Krutik (end of 9th and 10th century)	55.1	12.2	7.6	7.3	4.3	2.5	-	11	682
Vladyshnevo I,II (late 10th and beginning of 11th century)									
Minino I,II (end of 10th and beginning of 11th century)	34.4	2.2	8.9	20	-	16.7	7.8	10	90
Minino VI (mid-11th to 13th centuries)	20	-	10	20	-	40	-	10	10

Table 6.1 Percentage compositions of the assemblage of hand-made vessels. Data relating to the Krutik settlement are cited from Makarov 1991, 129–165 and data from Byeloozero from Makarov 1989, 88. The area to the east of Lake Onega includes the following sites: Byeloozero, Krutik, Vasyutino, Nikolskoye I and V, Kemskiye kurgany, the Kisnema and Popovo burial-grounds and the Popadino and Malyi settlements (Makarov 1989, 84, 88).

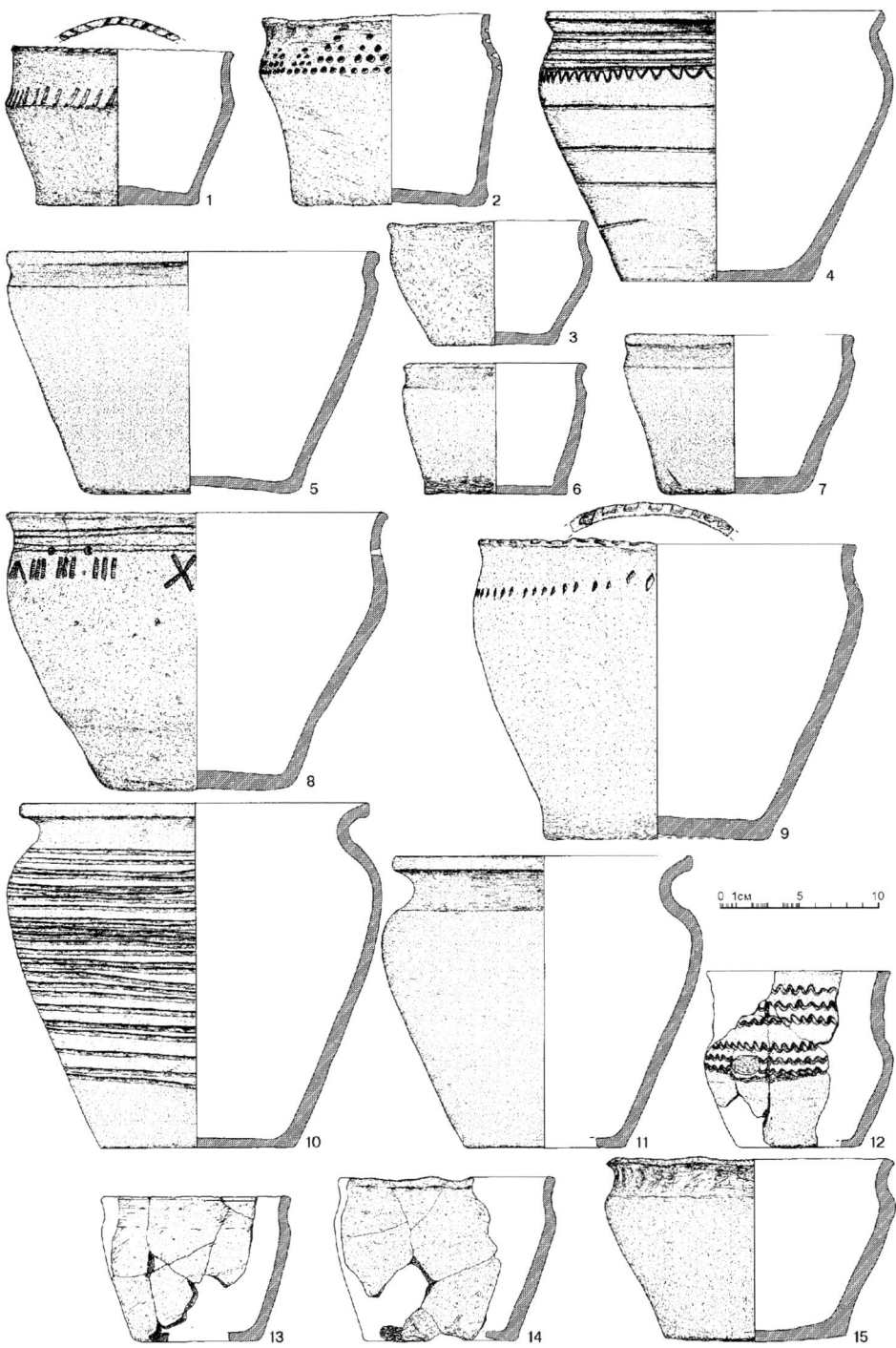

Figure 6.3 *Minino. Medieval pottery vessels from the middle of the 11th century to the first half of the 12th century.*

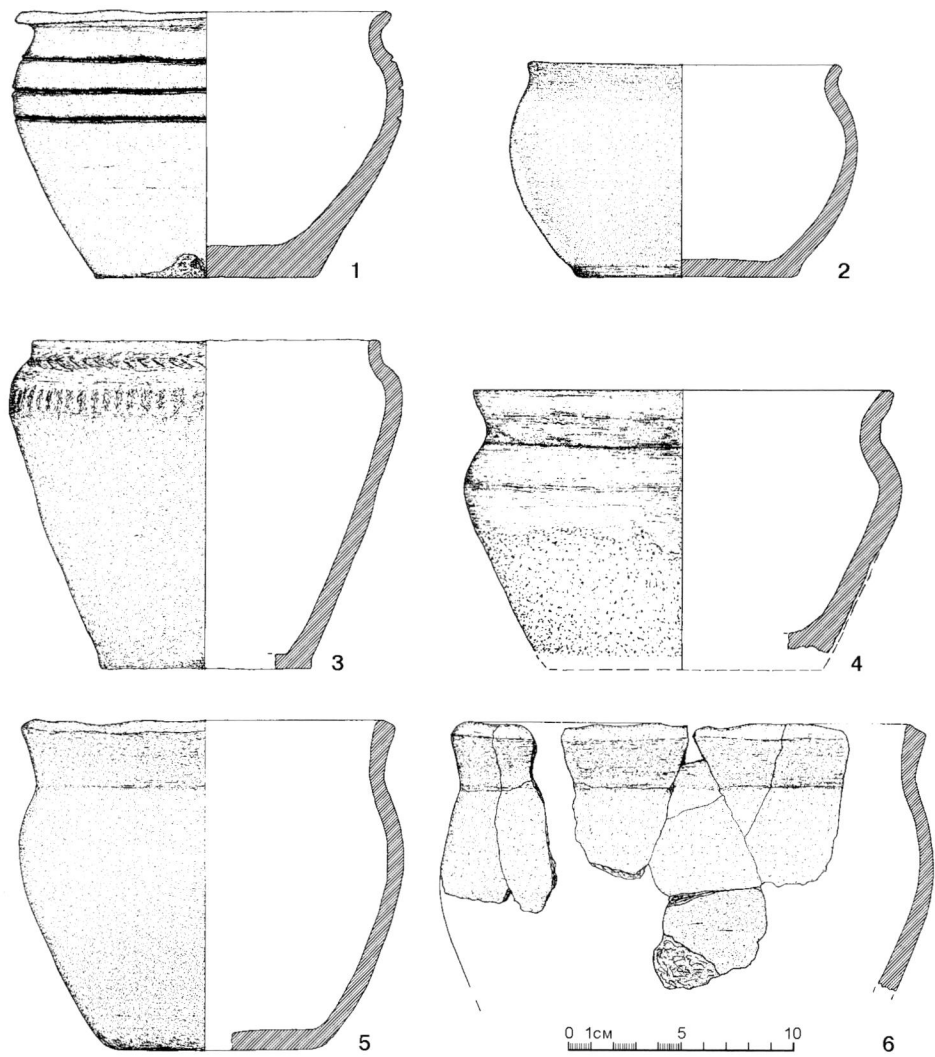

Figure 6.4 Minino. *Medieval pottery vessels from the mid-12th century to the 13th century.*

the Type VI vessels can be explained by the fact that this type, which had no definite ethnic associations, became widespread in those regions, where hand-made pottery continued to be used in the 11th and 12th centuries, after it was no longer being manufactured in most of the territory of medieval Russia (Makarov 1989, 90) (Figure 6.2.8; Figure 6.3.3, 9). Type 3 vessels are similar to Slav pottery from the Lake Ilmen region and along the Volkhov valley (Makarov 1989, 89–90) (Figure 6.2.5).

A comparatively small number of Type II vessels and the complete absence of Type V vessels in the collection can be explained by the archaic nature of these types of hand-made vessels encountered mainly at sites dating from the middle or end of the first millennium AD (Makarov 1989, 90). All parallels for Type VII vessels originate from burial-mounds in the south-western part of the Byeloozero region and the Lake Ladoga region, which date from the end of the 10th, the 11th or early-12th century (Makarov 1989, 90–91).

Apart from the seven main types referred to above, unusual shapes of hand-made vessels were also found in the collections from the sites being investigated, accounting altogether for slightly over 10% in total. Most of these shapes are represented by single specimens, the share of which comes to less than one percent of the collection (see, for example, Figure 6.4.3). Of particular interest is a small group of four bowl-shaped vessels (3.2%), which were found within the Minino burial-grounds. Three vessels, which it proved possible to piece together, were found in the Minino II burial-ground (Figure 6.2.2, 6, 9) and also scattered fragments of a fourth in the Vladyshnevo II burial-ground. They were bowls with almost straight sides, a high neck and a smooth transition from the body to the thick flat base and with its maximum width in the lower part of the vessel. The rim is straight or turned slightly outwards, while the upper edge is rounded or sloping slightly outwards. The diameters of the rims of the reconstructed vessels vary between 12 and 14 cm. All the vessels are decorated. Numerous parallels for the bowl-shaped vessels are to be found in the collections of the Kamsk-Vychegodskii Krai, an area in which this vessel-shape is the predominant one and sometimes the only one that has been recorded (Makarov 1983, 23–24). Similar vessels are also to be found in the pottery assemblages from Byeloozero, the Yaroslavl part of the Volga region and the area south of Lake Ladoga (Makarov 1983, 20–23). The vessels in question can be compared to Type II.

A strikingly distinctive feature of the hand-made vessels from medieval sites near Byeloozero is the varied decoration and the substantial number of decorated vessels. The decoration on the hand-made vessels from the vicinity of Lake Kubenskoye has features which are very similar to those from the Byeloozero area. Among the reconstructed vessels from Minino decorated vessels account for some 63% (67 out of 106). This enables us to assume that over half of all the hand-made vessels from the sites being investigated were decorated. The decoration was applied exclusively to the upper part of the vessels: the top edge of the rim, the neck, the shoulder. In 64% of cases the decoration covered the edge of the rim and the shoulder of the vessel, only the shoulder in 27% of cases and only the rim in 9% of cases.

Among the decorative patterns there are very simple ones and also quite complicated compositions in the form of multi-tiered bands made up of elements repeated several times over (as a rule of one and the same type) or combinations of the latter. Decorative elements consisted of impressions made with comb-like stamps or stamps with figures on them, indentations of various shapes, impressions of cord or simply fingers, notches and incised lines (Figure 6.1.1). When calculating the number of examples of decorative elements, each decorated fragment was considered as a unit, but if it proved possible to establish that several fragments belonged to one and the same vessel; then the vessel rather than each of the fragments was taken as the unit. As a result 1,218 specimens were singled out from the overall number of decorated fragments in the collection: it was presumed that these 1,218 specimens belonged to different vessels.

A complete and detailed description of the decorative elements found on the pottery from Byeloozero has already been undertaken (Golubeva 1973, 151–154; Makarov 1985, 81–84) and so it would seem appropriate here merely to point out the general percentage compositions of decorative elements in comparison with the main sites in the Byeloozero area (see Table 6.2). As can be seen from the table, among the decorative elements from all the sites, imprints of comb-like stamps predominate. The total share of various indentations, which are described by scholars as decorative elements peculiar to Byeloozero, is also quite significant (Makarov 1985, 149). In the Minino collection all the decorative elements typical for hand-made pottery from Byeloozero are present to a greater or lesser degree with the exception of imprints from cord wound round a stick.

In order to carry out an analysis of the decorative compositions, 121 specimens were selected from among the larger fragments originating from the upper parts of vessels and also among the vessels reconstructed either in part or in their entirety. Five main groups have been identified (broken down later into 23 types) in the existing typology relating to hand-made pottery from the Byeloozero area (Makarov 1985, 85–92).

Group A embraces the patterns used to decorate merely the rim of a vessel and its outer edge, patterns consisting of a simple series of elements (Figure 6.1; 6.2.1–2), Group B pottery has patterns consisting of one or more bands formed from a simple series of elements. This group has been sub-divided into two sub-groups: B1 vessels on which one-tier bands are found (Types I–V) (Figure 6.1; 6.2.3–9) and B2 vessels with two-tier or three-tier bands (Types VI–XIII) (Figure 6.1; 6.2.10–15). Group C vessels have decorative patterns consisting of straight, horizontal or wavy lines, in which each line forms a separate tier, that at the same time constitutes the basic element in the pattern (Types XIV–XVI) (Figure 6.1; 6.2.16). Group D vessels bear patterns, which do not have a clearly defined structure consisting of tiers: the constituent elements form figures in which the symmetry is based on a vertical axis and which are separated from each other by intervals or arranged close together (Types XVII–XVIII) (Figure 6.1; 6.2.17–18). Group E vessels bear patterns made up of decorative elements from Groups B, C and D (Types XIX–XXIII) (Figure 6.1; 6.2.19–21).

In addition, on two bowl-shaped vessels two variants of decorative compositions were found, which can be considered rare. The first is a two-tiered pattern stylistically similar to Type IX but consisting of figures from Group D executed using deep indentations (Figure 6.2.6). The second is a more complex variant of Type XXII: bands of pattern as from Sub-group B1 in the form of cord imprints at the top and bordered at the bottom by figures from Group D, which in their turn are separated from each other by double imprints made using cord, which form a zigzag line (Figure 6.2.9).

No.	Decorative element	Krutik (3,598)	Byelozero (1,246)	Minino I,II (1,010)	Minino VI (165)	Vladyshnevo I,II (43)
1	Combed	40.9	49.5	42.9	27.3	53.4
2	Small-toothed	0.3	3.2	1.8	–	2.3
3	Framed	1.1	10	0.9	–	2.3
4	Flat-bottomed indentations	6.6	6.5	9.4	14.5	7
5	Flat triangular indentations	7.7	6	10	15.2	7
6	Deep indentations	9.1	3.2	9.6	6.1	–
7	Dimpled	1.1	1.3	2.9	1.2	–
8	Notched	16.1	7.6	15.2	32.7	14
9	Cord lines	3.2	1.5	3	0.6	2.3
10	Cord loops	0.7	0.3	1.2	–	2.3
11	Pattern from cord wrapped round a stick	9.6	2.6	–	–	–
12	Finger indentations	0.1	1.3	0.5	1.8	4.7
13	Figured	1.2	0.3	1.1	0.6	–
14	Ring-shaped	0.7	3.9	0.8	–	–
15	Incised	0.1	0.6	0.4	–	4.7
16	Hatched	0.4	0.1	0.1	–	–
17	Ridge in relief	1.2	2	0.2	–	–

Table 6.2 *Percentage compositions of decorative elements (in brackets are the number of fragment specimens).*

The spread of types within the sample of decorative compositions is illustrated in Table 6.3. From this table we can see that 82% of the total number of the decorative compositions to be found in the Byeloozero area is represented at Minino. Although in general there are a considerable variety of decorative compositions, the predominance of the simple patterns of the first three types is a feature which the Minino collection under discussion here has in common with the key reference collections from Krutik and Byeloozero.

The fact that the Minino collection contains almost all the decorative elements and compositions in the table makes it possible to include the sites round Lake Kubenskoye in the distribution area of the decorative range specific to the Byeloozero area. This range has certain features in common with the pottery assemblages of the Kamsk-Vychegodskii Krai, which includes parallels for almost all the decorative elements and most of the compositions (73% of the types identified) (Makarov 1985, 97).

THE SLOW-TURNED POTTERY

This group of pottery items occupies a position halfway between hand-made and wheel-turned pottery as far as the technique used for its manufacture is concerned. Slow-turned (or wheel-finished) pottery accounts for approximately one percent of the total number of identified fragments. This stems from the fact that it is difficult to single out examples from this group in the general range of Russian medieval pottery because it exhibits features associated with techniques used for making both hand-made and wheel-turned pottery. This means that certain fragments of vessels from the group under discussion might be classified as belonging to either of the other two groups. Traces of 'correction' can be clearly observed – above all on fragments from the upper parts of vessels – and the total number of such fragments is usually small. In the whole collection from the Minino group of sites there are 31 whole vessel shapes and seven upper parts of slow-turned vessels: these constitute 13% of the total number of vessels analysed. In the collection from Minino I there are six vessels with a complete profile and four upper parts. On the basis of the features of these shapes and the proportions of the vessels in this group, five types were singled out, which were then divided into two main groups as far as their technological features were concerned.

The first group consists of vessels bearing traces of 'correction' involving a hand-driven potter's wheel. For vessels of this type we can refer to the first and second stage in the development of the functions of the potter's wheel (RFK-1 and RFK-2 according to Bobrinskii's classification), when the wheel was used as a tool for partial or complete smoothing over of a hand-made vessel (Bobrinskii 1978, 33–34). Vessels of this type are distinguished by their well-smoothed surface in their upper part, the even edge of their rim and, as a rule, by an absence of decoration.

Type 1 (two complete shapes): pots with a body in the shape of a truncated cone, with maximum width in their upper third, with a clearly defined or slightly sloping

Groups	Types of composition	Krutik (496)	Byeloozero (404)	Minino I.II (98)	Minino VI (15)	Vladyshnevo I,II (8)
A		8.7	2.2	8.2	6.7	–
B1	I	38.3	33.9	37.8	53.3	62.5
	II	15.1	6.5	12.3	6.7	–
	III	13.1	27.1	9.3	13.2	–
	IV	2.2	3.1	–	–	12.5
	V	2.6	2.5	1	–	–
B2	VI	1.6	2.8	2	6.7	–
	VII	0.6	0.9	–	–	–
	VIII	1.6	0.9	2	–	–
	IX	0.8	0.6	2	–	–
	X	0.6	2.2	–	–	–
	XI	1.2	2.8	1	–	–
	XII	2.2	5.9	6.1	–	12.5
	XIII	1.6	0.6	2	6.7	–
C	XIV	–	0.3	–	–	–
	XV	0.6	1.5	1	–	–
	XVI	0.2	0.3	–	–	–
D	XVII	3	1.2	1	6.7	–
	XVIII	0.2	1.5	1	–	–
E	XIX	3.4	0.6	7.2	–	12.5
	XX	1	–	–	–	–
	XXI	1	2.2	1	–	–
	XXII	0.2	0.6	3.1	–	–
	XXIII	–	–	–	–	–
rare	rare	–	–	2	–	–

Table 6.3 *Percentages of types of decorative compositions (in brackets are the number of fragment specimens).*

shoulder and a short out-turned rim, the edge of which is sliced diagonally (Figure 6.3.15). The diameter of the mouth is 16–18 cm. The shape and proportion of these vessels are similar to those of Type VI of the hand-made ones.

Type 2 (seven complete shapes and one upper part): pots with only a faintly pronounced profile and a body in the shape of a truncated cone. Their maximum diameter is in the top quarter. Their rims were short, straight and slightly thickened (Figure 6.3.5–7, 13, 14). The diameter of the mouth is 12–24 cm. In their shape and proportions these vessels are similar to Type 4 of the hand-made ones.

Type 3 (one complete shape and one upper part): pots with an oval-shaped body, the maximum width of which is slightly above the middle of its height. The rim has a diagonally cut edge and is thickened and turned slightly outwards (Figure 6.4.5, 6). The diameter of the mouth is 16–20 cm.

The second group is represented by vessels, which from the technological point of view relate to the third stage in the development of the functions of the potter's wheel

(RFK-3), when the turning of the wheel serves not merely to smooth surfaces but is also used for profiling, in part, the rim (Bobrinskii 1978, 34). As regards the vessels' shape, the vessels in this group are already closer to wheel-turned vessels and to all appearances they constitute imitations of advanced wheel-turned shapes.

Type 4 (two complete shapes and five upper parts) is represented by pots of squat proportions: their maximum width is in the third quarter of their height, they have a curved shoulder and their walls narrow towards the base. The neck is hardly discernible and the rim with a rounded edge turns sharply outwards (Figure 6.4.1, 2). The diameter of the mouth is 13–19 cm. Three of the vessels are decorated: one with deeply incised lines, one with a single wavy line and the third with impressions from a wide comb-like stamp.

Type 5 (one complete shape) is a vessel with a body in the shape of a truncated cone: its maximum width is slightly below the upper third of the height, it has a clearly defined shoulder, a low and vertical neck and a rim with an edge sliced horizontally and turned outwards (Figure 6.4.4). The diameter of the mouth is 18 cm.

Slow-turned pottery was found mainly in the assemblages from Minino I and Minino VI dating from between the early-12th and the 13th century, in which it accounted for between a third and half of all the medieval fragments. In the Minino II burial-ground, a Type 1 vessel was found in a burial dating from the first half of the 12th century and two vessels of Type 4 in burials dating from between the middle of the 12th century and the beginning of the 13th century.

THE WHEEL-THOWN POTTERY

When this was being manufactured the main filler used was crushed granite: for the most part of the fine (not above 5 mm) and medium-grained variety. In addition some crushed minerals containing mica and sand were added to the clay, which had not been the case with the hand-made and slow-turned vessels. In a few exceptional cases, very coarse-grained crushed limestone and grog were recorded in the pottery fragments. All the vessels had been made on a manually-driven wheel which was used for profiling the main part of the vessel and also for part of the construction of the vessel's hollow body by drawing up clay from a specially prepared hand-made lump. This process corresponds to the fourth and fifth stages in the development of the functions of the potter's wheel (RFK-4 and RFK-5) according to Bobrinskii. Most of the surviving fragments of the bases bear traces of having been sprinkled with sand and fine granite and in a number of cases these are present on the rim. No examples of smooth bases having been sliced off the wheel with a knife or thread were encountered in the collection. The firing as before was in most cases uneven and resulting in the three-layered 'sandwich' fabric. The colour of the fragments varied from beige to dark-brown. Some of the wheel-turned vessels which stood out from the rest on account of high-quality finish and firing can be classified as imports.

In the settlements of the Minino group only 16 fragments of bases with impressions of stamps were found and two fragments of bases with technical traces of the shaft and head of the wheel. Nine of these are from Minino VI. Unfortunately the only remains of depictions which have survived are some unintelligible fragments and only in five cases is it possible to assume that circles had been depicted on them.

Eight reconstructed vessels with a completely restored profile, 23 upper parts of vessels (making it possible to judge what the vessel shape has been) and 175 rim fragments were selected for typological analysis. A typological table was used for this classification, similar to that used for the study of wheel-turned pottery from the centre of the Rostov-Suzdal Lands (Kadieva 1996). On the basis of the differences in neck shapes, four main groups of vessels were singled out: Group I – pots with a low neck turned outwards; Group II – wide-mouthed vessels with a low vertical neck turned outwards; Group III – vessels with a high straight (funnel-shaped) neck turned outwards; Group IV – pots with a high straight vertical neck or one which slopes slightly inwards, often with some ridges on the outside. Vessels from one and the same group, but differing in body shape are classified as separate types: conical (A), bi-conical (B) and oval (C). Ten main rim variants were singled out on the basis of features pertaining to the finish of the rim edge.

All the wheel-turned vessels encountered in the collection are of medium size: their diameter at its widest point does not exceed 27 cm even for the largest. The vast majority of the vessels are from Group I – 70% of the total (Type IA – 12 vessels, Type IC – 5 vessels) (Figure 6.3.4, 10, 11). Vessels of Types IIA, IIIA and IVA all account for 10% of the collection (Figure 6.3.12). Among the rims modifications, Variant 7 (32%) predominates; Variants 9 (23%) and I (15%) are encountered quite frequently. Variants 4, 8 and 10 are represented to an equal extent, accounting for approximately 10% each. Variant 5 is only represented by isolated examples (2%). All the vessel types and rim variants mentioned above were quite widespread in medieval Russia and could be found in all the main pottery assemblages of the 11th–13th centuries (Kadieva 2003, 317).

In the majority of cases, wheel-turned pottery was decorated (the share of decorated vessels among those which were reconstructed came to 77%). Incised decoration predominates consisting of straight and wavy lines. In addition, indentations were found in some cases and also impressions made with comb stamps or a small toothed wheel (or drum). The decorated zone of these vessels was usually at the level of their maximum diameter, but often the decoration covered the whole body and sometimes the neck as well.

THE EVOLUTION OF THE RANGE OF POTTERY FROM THE MININO SITES

Observations regarding the statistical spread of ceramic materials in the various sectors of the Minino I site and the identification of certain dated objects and assemblages both there and at the Minino II and VI sites of similar date make it possible to draw the following general conclusions about the main stages in the development of the pottery assemblage under discussion.

In the initial stage of its formation (end of 10th to the beginning of 11th century), it was made up entirely of hand-made pottery. This is demonstrated by materials both from Vladyshnevo I and II and also from a number of early pits at the Minino I and Minino II sites. Most of the pottery assemblage consisted of Type I vessels and more than half of these were decorated. The specific character of the pottery assemblage from the sites east of Lake Onega dating from the late 10th or 11th century consists first and foremost in the enduring co-existence of eastern and western types of hand-made pottery (Makarov 1989, 91). A similar picture is also to be observed with regard to materials from the Minino collection, which are of later date than the above. In addition, as early as the second half of the 10th century at Byeloozero, decoration already constituted a clearly defined and consistent range of elements and compositions for which the Minino collection provides a complete parallel. Furthermore, from the Krutik materials it is clear that for more than a century in the life of that settlement this range remained fairly stable (Makarov 1985, 155). Thus both the sets of circumstances cited above make it possible to assert that, even at the beginning of the settlement's existence, its pottery assemblage constituted a well-established enduring range of hand-made pottery shapes and decorative techniques for it.

The appearance of wheel-turned pottery can be dated to the first half or middle of the 11th century. In the assemblages dated to the 11th century the total share of wheel-turned pottery does not come to more than 10–15%. In the bottom level of Trench 4 it accounts for even less than 5%. Use of the potter's wheel in the settlement itself is confirmed by the appearance of slow-turned pottery of Group I in assemblages dating from the period between the middle of the 11th century and the beginning of the 12th century.

In the course of the 12th century the share of wheel-turned pottery increases on average to 60 or 70% of the total number of fragments and, according to data obtained in Trench 3, it was already in excess of 80% in the second half of the 11th or at the beginning of the 12th century. In this period there was a marked decrease in the number of decorated hand-made vessels and only the simplest decorative compositions were being used. Types IV and VI are by this time the predominant forms of hand-made pottery. It is worth noting that in burials dated to the 12th century, slow-turned pottery is replacing the hand-made variety.

The range of wheel-turned pottery from Minino (first and foremost from the Minino I settlement) characterizes the features of the material culture of the Lake Kubenskoye region, which grew up on the basis of a variety of cultural elements of Slav, West-Finnish and East-Finnish origin. The pottery collection from Minino is similar to the pottery assemblages from the Byeloozero region and this similarity is to be found not only in the range of the main shapes for hand-made pottery, but, in particular, in the nature and degree of its decoration. A significant feature of the pottery assemblage examined in this article is the long use of hand-made pottery, which was being made right up until the end of the 12th or beginning of the 13th century, when the tradition of making hand-made pottery had long been a thing of the past in the central regions of Northern Russia, including the region around Lake Ilmen. This means that, despite the considerable importance of the colonization for the outermost margins of northern medieval Russia, economic links with the West and the cultural influence of the Baltic lands, the culture of this region in the 10th–12th centuries was advancing and generating its own individual features which manifested themselves vividly in its pottery assemblage.

Note

1   In all calculations only identifiable fragments have been taken into account.

7

GLASS BEADS FROM THE MININO ARCHAEOLOGICAL COMPLEX

S. D. Zakharov

INTRODUCTION

In the course of excavations at sites of the Minino archaeological complex an enormous collection of artefacts was amassed including approximately 9,770 objects (Table 7.1). Of these 3,717 were made of glass and there were also 26 stone and amber beads (Table 7.2). Glass articles and stone beads were present in the collections from all the sites investigated. Among the glass articles the most numerous were beads, which accounted for more than 98% of all the glass finds (3,652 items). Apart from beads, seven finger-rings were found, five inlays, nine buttons, three fragments of glass vessels and 41 unidentified objects. The most varied collection was that of finds from the Minino I settlement, where examples of all the recorded categories of glass items from the Minino complex were discovered. In the Minino VI settlement, over and above beads, finger-rings were found and buttons in the Minino II burial-ground.

Glass beads constitute the largest category of finds and not only when it comes to glass items. These items account for more than 37% of all artefacts collected from the sites of the Minino complex (Table 7.1). The average share for this type of find in the assemblages from the Minino settlements was 25.3% and it was significantly higher with regard to the burial-ground, namely 66.2%.

The excavations at Minino involved wide-scale washing and sieving of the earth using a variety of sieves (Zakharov 2001; Makarov 2001, 15). It was thanks to the application of these methods and their on-going improvement that over a third of all the glass items were obtained.

	Minino I Settlement	Minino VI Settlement	Total	Burial-ground Minino II	**Total**
Excavated area in m²	301	588	889	860	
Burials	-	-	-	~81	**~81**
Medieval Finds	~5180	~1670	~6850	~2920	**~9770**
Glass beads	1394	337	1731	1921	**3652**
Share of glass beads (%)	26.9	20.2	25.3	66.2	**37.4**

Table 7.1 Share of glass beads in the materials from the excavations at the sites of the Minino Archaeological Complex.

BEAD CLASSIFICATION AND CHRONOLOGY

The table devised by Z. A. Lvova, based on the nature of the techniques for manufacture, was used as the basis for the classification of these glass beads (Lvova 1968, 64–94) (Table 7.3). In the Minino collection four main groups of beads have been recorded,

Material	Find Category	Minino I settlement	Minino VI settlement	Burial-ground Minino II	Total	%
Glass	beads	1,394	337	1,921	**3,652**	**98.3**
	rings	5	2	-	**7**	**0.2**
	inlays	5	-	-	**5**	**0.1**
	buttons	7	-	2	**9**	**0.2**
	vessels	3	-	-	**3**	**0.1**
	objects	38	1	2	**41**	**1.1**
	Total	**1452**	**340**	**1925**	**3,717**	**100**
	%	**39.1**	**9.1**	**51.8**	**100**	
	Total	**1,792 (for Minino I and VI)**	**1,792 (for Minino I and VI)**	**1925**		
	%	**48.2**		**51.8**		
Stone	Beads	16	3	7	26	100
	%	**61.6**	**11.5**	**26.9**	**100**	
	Total	**19 (for Minino I and VI)**	**19 (for Minino I and VI)**	**7**		
	%	**73.1 (for Minino I and VI)**	**73.1 (for Minino I and VI)**	**26.9**		

***Table 7.2** Glass items and stone beads from Minino. General composition of the collection by site. Rings = finger-rings; objects = unidentified fragments.*

Position	Feature	Number of recorded variants of feature
1. Group	Technique of manufacture	6
2. Sub-group	Presence of decoration	2
3. Class	Shape of bead in cross-section	7
4. Variety	Main dimensions	2
5. Section	Technique for applying decoration	9
6. Sub-section	Kind of decoration	36
7. Type	Shape of bead in lengthways section	19
8. Sub-type	Number of parts	5
9. Sort	Colour	15
10. Sub-sort	Transparency of glass	3

***Table 7.3** Classification of the Minino glass beads.*

Group: Technique of manufacture	Sub-group: Presence of decoration	Number	%	Total	%
Coiling	Undecorated	2,542	69.60	3076	84.22
	Decorated	534	14.62		
Pulled tube	Undecorated	457	12.51	555	15.20
	Decorated	98	2.68		
Mosaic	Decorated	7	0.19	7	0.19
From layered glass	Decorated	5	0.14	5	0.14
Single wrap-round of glass sheet	Undecorated	1	0.03	1	0.03
Undefined	Decorated	7	0.19	8	0.22
	Undecorated	1	0.03		
Total		3,652	100	3652	100

Table 7.4 Distribution of the Minino glass beads according to techniques of manufacture and presence of decoration.

which are told apart on the basis of the following features: coiled beads, beads made from a pulled tube, mosaic beads and beads made of layered glass. In addition one bead was found which had been made from a sheet of glass which had been wrapped round a hard rod, but it did not prove possible to ascertain the technique used for manufacturing some of the beads.

Beads are divided into sub-groups on the basis of whether or not they have been decorated. The shape of the horizontal section (over the groove or thread) provides the basis for dividing the beads into seven classes. Later in the diagram an additional feature was incorporated: two separate types of bead were singled out on the basis of dimensions (height and maximum diameter), i.e. a distinction was drawn between larger and smaller beads. A distinction of this kind can be used, when examining beads with the naked eye, and later confirmed with reference to statistics. The dividing line between the two groups was 5 mm for the maximum diameter and the diameter for the bulk of the smaller beads was 3.5–4 mm (Zakharov 2004, Figure 28). In addition certain distinctions were observed in other features of beads from the two groups: the smaller beads were all undecorated, round in horizontal section and they were made using extended tubes or a coiling technique.

The larger beads were divided up into nine sections on the basis of the nature of their decoration and how it was applied and sub-sections were classified based on different kinds of decoration. Types were identified on the basis of the shape of the lengthways section of the larger beads (along the groove for the thread), sub-types on the basis of the number of parts, sorts on the basis of colour and sub-sorts on the basis of the transparency of the glass (Table 7.3).

The quantities of the beads from the various groups and sub-groups are presented in Table 7.4. The most numerous beads in the collection are coiled beads (3,076 specimens), of which four fifths are undecorated, i.e. they are made from glass of a single colour. In second place are beads made from an extended tube (555 specimens) and the correlations between the number of decorated and monochrome beads are the same in this group too. The remaining groups of beads are represented by isolated finds.

The considerable typological diversity, the relatively well-devised time-scale and the existence of groups with a narrow date range enable us to consider glass beads as one of the most important chronological indicators. The role beads play for dating purposes is enhanced in the case of sites like Minino, where they are represented by statistically significant series. On the other hand, the materials from Minino, where more than half the finds came from funerary complexes, can also be used for narrowing down the chronological range for certain types of beads. The most interesting results we have been able to achieve so far have been for three types: small coiled beads, bi-trapezoidal bright blue beads with 1:1 proportions and beads which we have referred to as "tablet-shaped" (Figure 7.1).

The coiled beads have not yet been the focus of detailed attention from scholars. According to calculations by Y. M. Lesman made in relation to the habitation levels at Novgorod, such beads did not appear before the second decade of the 12th century (Lesman 1984, Table 1). In Minino this variety of glass bead was the most numerous (1,227 specimens: Figure 7.1A). The earliest find of a yellow opaque small bead was noted at the Minino I site in a pit dating from the second half of the 10th or from the beginning of the 11th century, but its isolated nature means that it could have made its way into the complex by chance. The earliest finds of coiled small beads in this burial-ground were recorded in a burial, which had been deposited in the second quarter of the 11th century. Indeed four kinds of small bead were found in this complex straightaway (Figure 7.1A, 20, 34, 37). The coexistence of several varieties of small beads was also noted in other burials, where they were represented in statistically significant series. The comparison of the findings after assessing the distribution of small beads in various funerary complexes in the burial-ground and in the settlements made it possible to assume that the earliest varieties of small coiled beads in Minino were a green transparent (or translucent) bead (Figure 7.1A, 15–21), a black bead (olive-coloured in thin sections) (Figure 7.1A, 34–36) and another black bead (brown in thin sections) (Figure 7.1A, 37). Their appearance can be associated with a time no later than the beginning of the 11th century. A yellow opaque small bead (Figure 7.1A, 4–14) is probably of a slightly later date, but definitely within the first half of the 11th century. The upper limit for the use of small coiled beads as interpreted on the basis of the Minino material is impossible to establish, since they are also found in the uppermost levels of the Minino I settlement dating from the first half of the 13th century. It is possible that the small black beads (brown in thin sections), which stands out on account of the good state of preservation of the glass, disappeared before the others (Figure 7.1A, 37).

Coiled bi-trapezoidal beads with proportions in the ratio 1:1 made of blue transparent and semi-transparent glass (Figure 7.1B) were dated by M. V. Fekhner

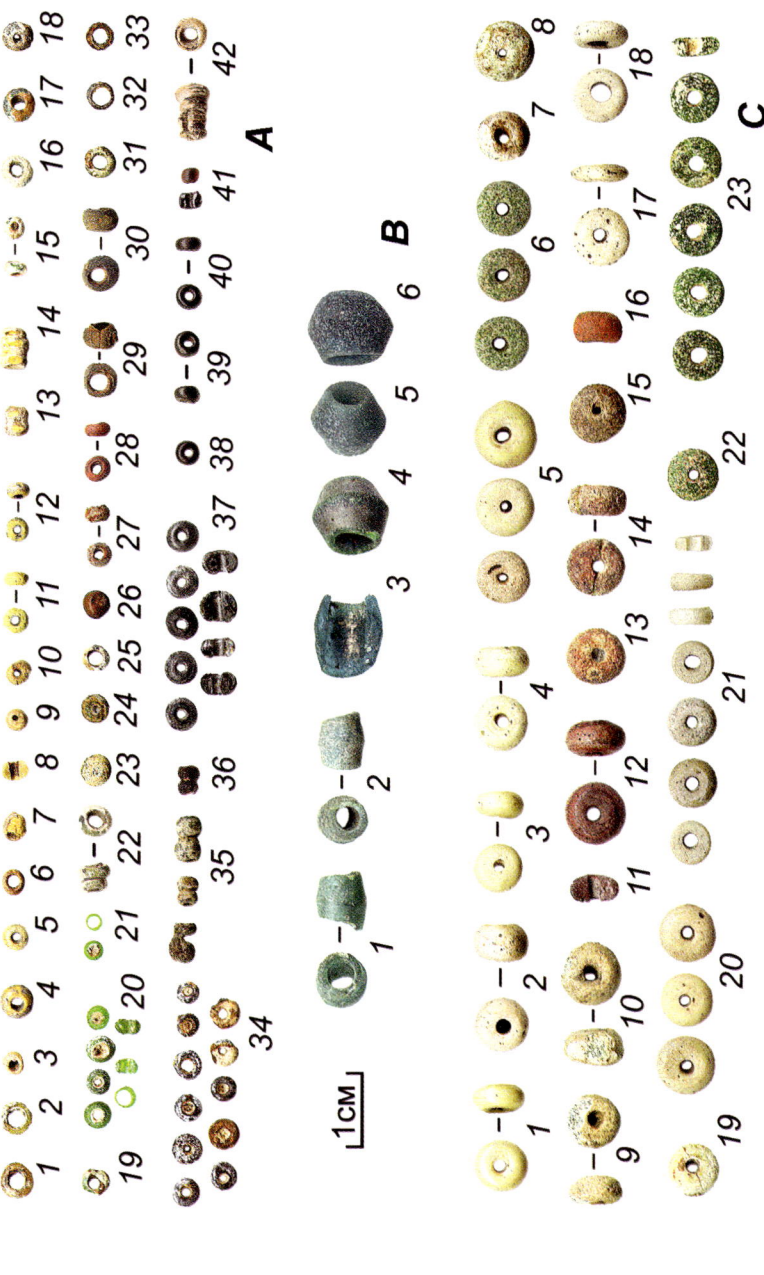

Figure 7.1 *Some types of coiled glass beads from the excavations of the Minino Archaeological Complex: A) small beads; B) Bi-trapezoidal blue beads with the proportions 1:1; C) 'tablet'-shaped beads.*

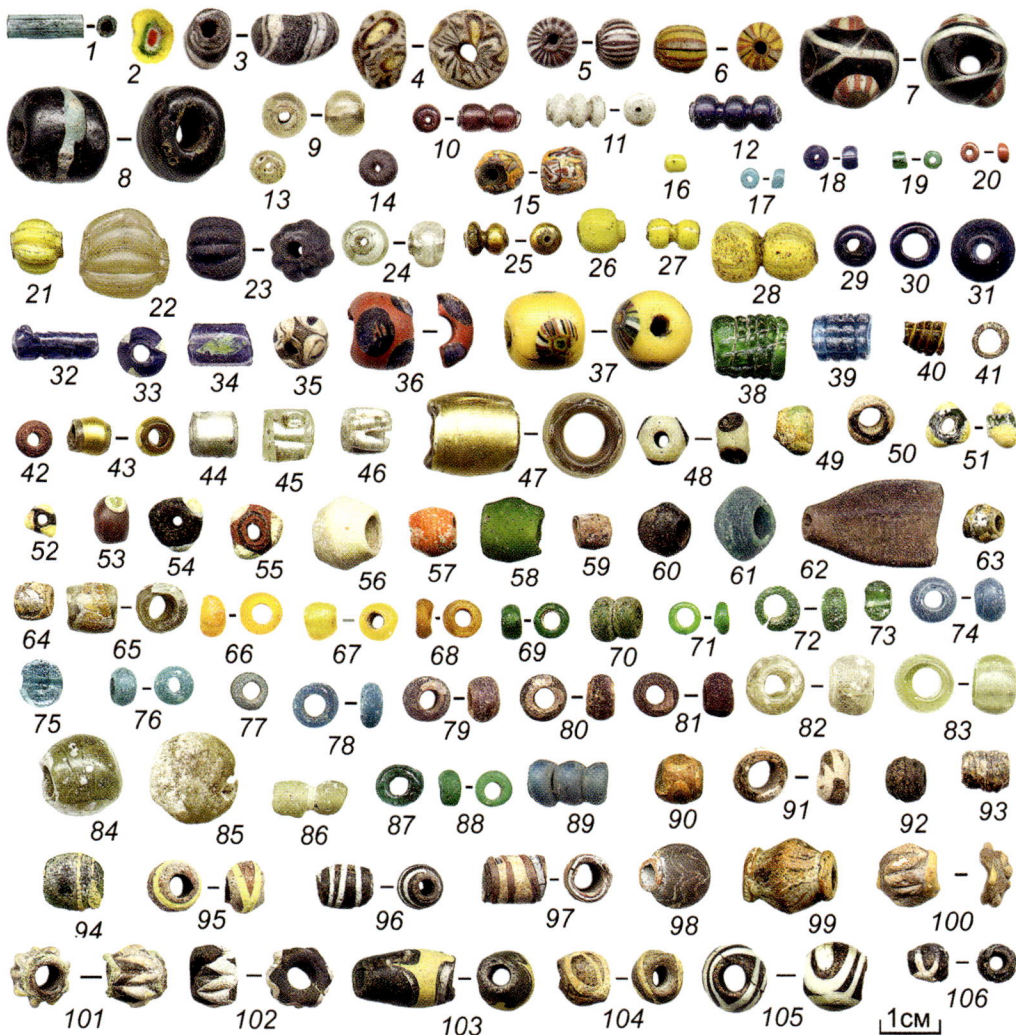

Figure 7.2 *Main chronological groups of glass beads from the excavations of the Minino Archaeological Complex: 1–8) beads of the 10th and early-11th centuries; 9–15) beads of the 10th to the mid-11th century; 16–37) beads of the 10th and 11th centuries; 38–42) beads of the 11th and early-12th centuries; 43–55) beads of the 11th to the mid-12th century, (this group includes the beads in Figure 7.1C); 56–60) beads of the 11th and 12th centuries; 61–62) beads of the 11th–13th centuries,(this group includes the beads in Figure 7.1A,B; 63–106) beads of the 12th and 13th centuries. Beads 1, 2, 11–13, 15–22, 25–27, 30, 34, 36–37, 41, 43–45, 47, 48, 58, 65, 72–77, 82–84, 89, 94–98, 101, 103–106 are from Minino settlement I; Beads 3–10, 14, 23–24, 28–29, 31–33, 35, 38–39, 42, 46, 52–55, 56–57, 61–64, 66–71, 78–81, 87–88, 102 are from the Minino II Burial-ground; Beads 40, 49, 50, 51, 59–60, 85–86, 90–93, 99–100 are from Minino settlement VI.*

to the 11th–12th centuries (Fekhner 1959, Appendix VI). According to information provided by Y. L. Shchapova, these beads were found in Novgorod in 12th-century levels and, with reference to more precise data provided by Y. M. Lesman, in spits dated to 1116–1281 (Shchapova 1956, 170; Lesman 1984, Table 1). At the same time reliable data exist demonstrating that blue bi-trapezoidal beads existed in the first half and middle of the 11th century (Makarov 1997, 121, 125; Safarova 1998, 71, 87, Table 7) and the Minino materials, including 52 finds of such beads, confirm that date. The earliest burial containing such beads was one dating from the third quarter of the 11th century (Figure 7.1B, 5–6). At the Minino VI settlement the beads in question were encountered in funerary complexes dating from a period from the middle of the 11th century to the beginning of the 12th. At the Minino I settlement one bead was found in a pit dating from the 11th century, but they were found in the largest numbers in the levels from the late-11th and 12th century. It therefore follows that, as regards the Minino materials, the dating for blue trapezoidal beads (with proportions in the ration 1:1) can be determined as falling between the mid-11th and mid-13th century: when data from other sites are taken into account this period can be extended somewhat, from the second quarter of the 11th century to the third quarter of the 13th century.

During the classification of monochrome zonal and ring-shaped coiled beads, a group was identified which was regularly distinguished from the others on the basis of the narrow groove for its thread (diameter of groove is equal to 10–25% of the maximum diameter of the bead) and often stood out on account of the existence of large areas round the groove (Figure 7.1C). All beads of this kind (361 specimens) were made of yellowish-white, green or reddish-brown opaque glass. Study of the Minino materials has shown that beads of this kind, referred to for the sake of convenience as "tablet-shaped", stand out not merely because of their common type, but also on account of their shared date. In the Minino II materials the earliest finds of "tablet-shaped" beads were recorded in a burial from the second quarter of the 11th century and this applied to all three sorts mentioned above. More often than not, however, they are found in burials from the third quarter of the 11th or the first half of the 12th century. At Minino I beads of this kind were most numerous in levels from the late-11th and early-12th century, while at the Minino VI settlement they were recorded in funerary complexes dating from the mid-11th century to the early 12th century. If these data are taken into account then the 'tablet-shaped' beads can be dated from the 11th to the first half of the 12th century.

In order accurately to specify the chronology of various objects, levels and trenches and in order to achieve an understanding of the general dynamics underlying the development of the Minino archaeological complex, all the glass beads were gathered together in chronological groups. The composition of the groups and their dating were determined on the basis of chronological diagrams, which exist today in medieval Russian archaeology and the combinations of different kinds of beads in the Minino complexes were also taken into account. Eight such groups were singled out and, in addition, approximately 8% of the beads remained outside the confines of the identified groups (Table 7.5, Figure 7.2).

No.	Chronological Groups	Number	Chronological Periods	Total for Period	%
1	X–early-11th c.	71	I		
2	X–mid-11th c.	117	I		
3	X–XI c.	514	I	702	19.2
4	XI–early-12th c.	60	II		
5	11th–mid-12th c.	624	II		
6	11th–12th c.	22	II		
7	11th–13th c.	1,285	II		
8	12th–13th c.	683	II	2,674	73.2
9	Undated	276	-	276	7.6
	Total	**3,652**			**100**

Table 7.5 Chronology of the glass beads from Minino.

As can be seen from Table 7.5 the bulk of the Minino beads stem from the period which can be defined as the 11th–13th centuries (more than 73%). If it is taken into account that glass beads constitute the largest category of finds at Minino, then it is likely, at least during the above-mentioned period, that beads played a very important part in the material culture of the inhabitants of Minino. Similar results were also obtained during investigation within the town of Byeloozero, the central settlement in the region. Beads accounted for approximately 29% of all the artefacts (Zakharov 2004, Table 3.34). In order to assess the scale and understand the reasons behind this concentration of glass beads in the cultural layer of Byeloozero and Minino, it is essential to compare the data obtained with the findings from excavations undertaken at other medieval sites. Given that the number of beads in funerary complexes could reflect not merely their actual role in the life of the local population, but also other patterns (cultural traditions, special features of the funerary rite and so on), only the materials from settlements were taken into considerations.

COMPARISONS WITH OTHER SETTLEMENT SITES

Assessing the concentration of one or other type of find in the cultural layer of a settlement can be done in a variety of ways: calculating the number of articles per unit of area or volume or their share in the overall assemblage of finds. Preliminary analysis of the data collected so far has shown that when the first or second methods were used, the duration and intensity of activity at a site (within its investigated section) could have an enormous influence on findings. This also applies to the state of preservation of the wood involved, since this considerably increases the thickness of habitation levels. This state of affairs complicates assessment and interpretation of the data obtained to a significant degree. A more objective assessment of the degree of concentration of finds in the cultural layer can be expressed in terms of their share in the overall assemblage of finds. Yet this last method is not without its shortcomings.

The main one of these stems from the inconsistencies in the lists of objects included by different scholars in lists of artefact collections. In order to obtain comparable results we endeavoured not to use information about sites where any categories of finds (such as unidentified iron objects) were not included in the composition of the artefact collection. In addition, articles made of wood, leather, textiles and birch-bark were excluded from the total number of finds, since the amount of the above-mentioned artefacts depends first and foremost on the properties of the cultural layer, which may either help to preserve these artefacts or the opposite.

When collecting information for this study, data were collected regarding the chronology of the sites, the total number of finds and the quantity of glass beads. The collection of sites for comparison was determined not only by the criteria mentioned above, but also by the range of the available evidence about the excavations that had been carried out. Preference was given to sites, for which detailed publication of the relevant excavations already exist, or field reports on the excavations which are complete with detailed inventories of the find collections. Unfortunately, it did not prove possible in all cases to select sites which met even this limited range of criteria. For this reason the materials used for a number of sites (such as Ladoga, Pskov and Novgorod) do not always cover the whole period of their existence.

It is essential to note one other detail as well, which it is important to take into account in relation to further analysis. At the early sites the number of beads is usually higher than at those with later levels. This specific feature regarding the distribution of glass beads was noted several decades ago by Shchapova in relation to materials from Novgorod (Shchapova 1956, 178–179) and has since been confirmed by other scholars (Lvova 1968, 64–65; Leontiev 1998, 147). For this reason, when we were relying on dates provided by other scholars we tried, wherever possible, to single out two chronological periods: an early one and a later one, taking as the hypothetical dividing line between them the beginning to middle of the 11th century. This served to narrow down still further the range of the sites used for comparison of materials.

The results of the work duly carried out are presented in the tables accompanying this chapter.[1] These tables encompass information gathered from 36 settlements; 25 urban sites and 11 rural settlements. The following urban sites have been included in the table: Staraya Ladoga (Ryabinin 1985;1973–5, 1977, 1981–82, 1984–85), the city-site on the river Syas (Boguslavskii A-1996–97; Machinskaya A-1989),[2] Krutik (Golubeva, Kochkurkina 1991), Byeloozero on the basis of results obtained from the collection of surface finds in 1990–1997 (Zakharov 2004, Table 3) and from excavations led by L. A. Golubeva (Golubeva 1973; 1952, 1957–60), Rostov (Leontiev 1998; 1989–96), Gnezdovo,[3] Mangazeya,[4] Asote (Shnore 1961), Novogrudok (Gurevich 1981), Idnakar (Ivanova 1998), Titchikha (Moskalenko 1965), Vladimir (Zharnov 1997), Pskov (Labutina A-1980), Staraya Ryazan (Mongait A-1966–68, 1970; Darkevich A-1969), Serensk (excavations of T.V.Nikolskaya 1966, 1971), Bolshoye Gornalskoye (Kuza A-1972–73; Uzyanov A-1973), Moscow (excavations in the Zaryadie district) (Dubynin A-1954–55, 1957), Rostislav,[5] Novgorod, the Nutny excavation (Gaidukov 1992),

Smolensk (Avdusin, A-1957; Urieva 1991), Voin (Dovzhenok *et al.* 1966), Yaropolch (Sedova 1960), Voishchina (Ibid). Apart from these, the following rural settlements have also been included : Blagoveshchenie (Oleinikov A-1985–86); settlements in the Minino archaeological complex – Nikolskoye VI (Bashenkin A-1983), Ust-Sheksna 2 (Rykunov, Rykunova 1994; Ibid., 1997; Rykunov A-1992–94, 1996; Rykunova A-1995), Gnezdovo; Ves 1 (excavations by Moshenina 1986–1990), Timerevo (Dubov A-1974), Gnezdilovo 2 (Lapshin 1989), Shitovichi 6 (Oleinikov A-1989–90), Vvedenskoye (Prazdnikov 1996, 1997, 1999) and Oznobishino 5 (Shpolyanskii 2003).

The data on the Minino settlements have been combined together in the table. As regards the large settlement Minino I, only those trenches and parts of the cultural layer have been taken into account, which it proved possible to identify clearly as belonging to one or other of the two chronological periods. For Minino VI, where there was a significant amount of finds from different periods in the ploughed level that was difficult to date, only those materials were included which without any doubt can be assigned to the medieval part of the complex, namely the pits immediately above the virgin soil.

The overall quantity of finds at the sites in the sample presented in Table 7.6 varies within a very wide range from 150 to several thousand artefacts. For this reason when comparing the proportion of beads in the collection from various settlements it is essential to take into account not merely the absolute size of that index, but also the confidence intervals, within which that index might vary. Given that the calculated share of beads in the assemblage from each site is none other than the frequency with which beads were found expressed as a percentage, the following formula was used, which made it possible to establish the confidence intervals for the frequencies (Fyodorov-Davydov 1987, 74–75):

$$p', p'' = \frac{wn + \frac{1}{2}t^2 \pm t\sqrt{w(1-w)n + \frac{1}{4}t^2}}{n + t^2}$$

in which p′ and p″ are the upper and lower limits for the confidence intervals; w is the share of beads in the assemblage from each site; n is the total number of finds at the site; t is the Student co-efficient used for the confidence level 0.95, the size of which depends on the unit n. The use of confidence intervals makes it possible to assess the share of beads in the materials from the site in question as directly dependent on the size of the sample. Furthermore, if 'the confidence intervals for different objects do not overlap each other, it can be said that the shares of those objects in the general totality differ from each other considerably' (Fyodorov-Davydov 1987, 75). It is possible to present these data in a more visible way in a graph (Figure 7.3), in which the confidence intervals are represented as vertical lines and the actual calculated shares of glass beads as short horizontal lines intersecting them.

No.	Site	Chron. Period	Total No. of finds	Glass beads	Share of beads (%)	Confidence intervals
1	Staraya Ladoga	I	2,773	1,875	67.6	65.9–69.3
2	City-site on the River Syas	I	261	153	58.6	52.6–64.4
3	Krutik	I	822	431	52.4	49.0–55.8
4	Byeloozero	I	266	130	48.9	42.9–54.9
		I–II	1,633	294	18	16.2–19.9
		II	12, 335	3,568	28.9	28.1–29.7
5	Rostov	I	658	271	41.2	37.5–45
		II	1,178	43	3.7	2.7–4.9
6	Gnezdovo	I–II	3,327	662	19.9	18.6–21.3
7	Mangazeya	–	1,711	338	19.8	17.9–21.7
8	Asote	I	849	112	13.2	11.1–15.6
		II	3,194	394	12.3	11.2–13.5
9	Novogrudok	I	499	55	11	8.6–14.1
		II	7,182	86	1.2	1.0–1.5
10	Idnakar	I	2,177	247	11.3	10.1–12.7
		II	3,111	173	5.6	4.8–6.4
11	Titchikha	I	701	71	10.1	8.1–12.6
12	Vladimir	II	1,200	54	4.5	3.5–5.8
13	Pskov	II	616	27	4.4	3.0–6.3
14	Staraya Ryazan	II	1,658	70	4.2	3.4–5.3
15	Serensk	II	1,905	75	3.9	3.2–4.9
16	Bolshoye Gornalskoye	I	571	21	3.7	2.4–5.6
17	Moscow	II	171	6	3.5	1.6–7.4
18	Rostislav	II	700	20	2.9	1.9–4.4
19	Novgorod	II	1,888	46	2.4	1.8–3.2
20	Smolensk	II	2,842	69	2.4	1.9–3.1
21	Voin	I–II	1,973	33	1.7	1.2–2.3
22	Yaropolch	I–II	3,366	55	1.6	1.3–2.1
23	Izborsk	I–II	3,377	23	0.7	0.5–1
24	Borodinskoye	II	1,197	8	0.7	0.3–1.3
25	Voishchina	II	1,302	2	0.2	0–0.6
26	Blagoveshchenie	I–II	620	240	38.7	35.0–42.6
27	Minino settlements	I	918	293	31.9	29.0–35.0
		II	4,059	1,151	28.4	27.0–29.8
28	Nikolskoye VI	I	294	78	26.5	21.8–31.9
29	Ust-Sheksna 2	II	~400	82	20.5	16.8–24.7
30	Gnezdovo	I	1,919	373	19.4	17.7–21.3
31	Ves 1	I–II	1,654	107	6.5	5.4–7.8
32	Timirevo	I	272	15	5.5	3.4–8.9
33	Gnezdilovo 2	I–II	389	20	5.1	3.4–7.8
34	Shitovichi 6	II	620	27	4.4	3.0–6.3
35	Vvedenskoye	II	2,365	75	5.2	2.5–4
36	Oznobishino 5	II	151	3	2	0.7–5.7
Total			79,071	11,876	15.1	14.9–15.4

Table 7.6 Share of beads in the artefact collections of analysed sites (Nos. 1–25 are towns and Nos. 26–36 are rural settlements).

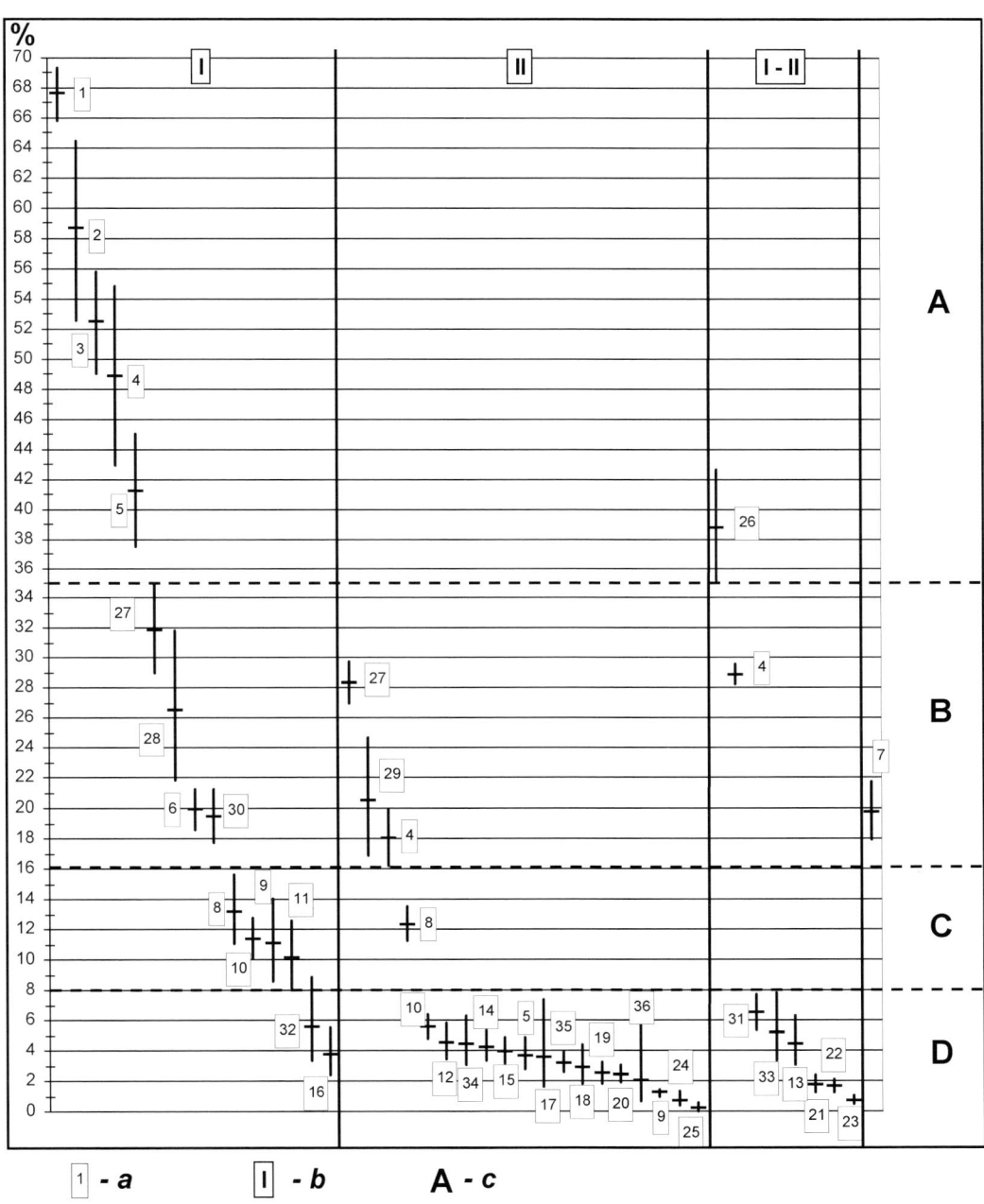

Figure 7.3 Graph to show the distribution of settlements according to the share of glass beads in their artefact collections: a) the site number (this corresponds to the site numbers as listed in Table 7.6); b) groups according to chronological period; c) groups according to share of beads in artefact collections.

When analysing the graph it can be noted that in those cases when the overall size of the artefact collections do not exceed 400–500 finds, the confidence intervals fluctuate to a large extent making it far more difficult to single out compact groups. The four main groups of lines which do not intersect and within which the confidence intervals overlap, may be singled out quite clearly (Figure 7.3A–D). The limits of the identified groups are only exceeded once – in the case of Timerevo settlement (number 32). It is possible that this is linked with the small overall number for the finds from that site, but it would be wrong to rule out the possibility that it belongs to another group or that it occupies an intermediate position. Nevertheless, given that the one exception to the integrity of the established groups is negligible, it can be said that the difference between the groups with regard to the share of glass beads in the artefact collections is significant.

We shall attempt to assess the distribution of the compared sites in groups. In the first place, there is the change in the quantity of beads over time noted previously which can be clearly discerned. Only settlements which had been in existence in the early period or levels relating to that period at sites which existed for a long time, were placed in Group A, where beads accounted for a share of between 35 and 69% of all finds taking into account confidence intervals. The only exception is the large settlement Blagoveshchenie (No. 26), the materials from which proved impossible to divide up according to the two above-mentioned chronological periods. It would appear that the bulk of the recorded finds from this large settlement relate to the early period, since, in all cases, when the chronological periods are identified, the share of beads in the early levels is higher than in the late levels, regardless of the type of settlement or its location.

The share of beads at sites of the first chronological period varies considerably, but only at two of the 15 early settlements does it come to less than 8% (Group D). The picture changes radically in the second chronological period (II). The bulk of the sites relating to the second period (II) – 15 out of the total 19 – belong to Group D with a share of beads amounting to less than 8% of the finds. Against this background sites, at which there were far more beads, between 16 and 30%, Group B sites stand out very clearly. It is precisely into this group that Minino and Byeloozero fall. If we take into account the general trend towards a decrease in the share of beads, the fact that there did exist in the second period sites, where beads continued to occupy an important place in artefact collections, is definitely worthy of note. Yet, for the Minino group of settlements, this index remains stable throughout both periods (the confidence intervals intersect). The index for the share of beads is fairly high as well in the materials from Byeloozero, which relate to the second period (II). This is particularly so if we bear in mind the collection of artefacts obtained in 1990–1997. This collection consisting of many thousands of objects is made up of surface finds, which makes sorting it chronologically into the two periods outlined above very difficult. Yet, the detailed chronological analysis already undertaken demonstrates that the bulk of the collection relates to the second period (Zakharov 2004, 40–61 and 69–85).

BEADS AND THE FUR TRADE

The results of the mapping work presented in Table 7.6 bring to attention certain geographical patterns. Sites with artefact collections containing a larger share of beads in the first, and in particular in the second period, clearly tend to be in the northern areas of the territory under discussion (Figure 7.4). Lvova, after carrying out a detailed study of the composition and special features of the distribution of glass beads within the territory of Northern Europe, devoted several articles to working out the reasons for the significant concentration of beads in these areas during the early period (Lvova 1968, 91–94; 1977; 2003). Thorough analysis of this enormous quantity of material enabled this scholar to conclude that the fur trade was the underlying factor for this phenomenon. In her opinion beads were one of the important commodities in the chain of non-equivalent exchange that can be summarized as follows: beads – furs – silver. Indeed beads were acquired in large quantities, by weight, in Ladoga. Here they were sorted, divided up into smaller amounts and then via a network of settlements, such as the city-site on the River Syas, they were conveyed to areas where fur-bearing animals were hunted, so that they might be exchanged for furs (Lvova 1977, 107; 2003, 152–153).

In this connection it is important to note that Rostov and Byeloozero, very early towns which were trading centres for medieval North-Eastern Russia (Leontiev 1997, 216–217; Zakharov 2004, 127–139), fall into the same category as Ladoga and the city-site on the River Syas . Still more significant, however, is the fact that Krutik is also in that group, a settlement which had been in existence in the 9th and 10th centuries in the middle reaches of the River Sheksna. Materials from the excavations undertaken at that settlement – thanks to the good state of preservation of the faunal remains – made it possible for the first time to record archaeologically the fact that there had existed an enormous amount of fur-bearing animals in the northern margins of medieval Russia, which were hunted for the fur-trade. In the impressively large osteological collection from Krutik the bones of wild mammals predominate: they account for more than 66% of all the identifiable individuals. The predominant species is beaver, which accounts for 78% of the total number of wild animals and more than 50% of all the mammals identified (Andreyeva 1991, 182–183). There is no doubt that Krutik was one of those settlements, whose inhabitants were directly engaged in obtaining various types of produce from the local forests, and first and foremost furs (Zakharov 2004, 108–111, 119). One of the commodities which the inhabitants of Krutik would have obtained in exchange for furs would have been glass beads, the share of which in the collection of artefacts from the site in question amounts to more than half the total number of finds.

The patterns identified by Lvova and since confirmed by new data were based on an analysis of materials from early sites. It is, however, hardly likely that it would be inappropriate to apply them to the sites where the share of beads remained considerable in the second chronological period as well. This is particularly so if we take into consideration the overall trend for a decrease in the number of beads

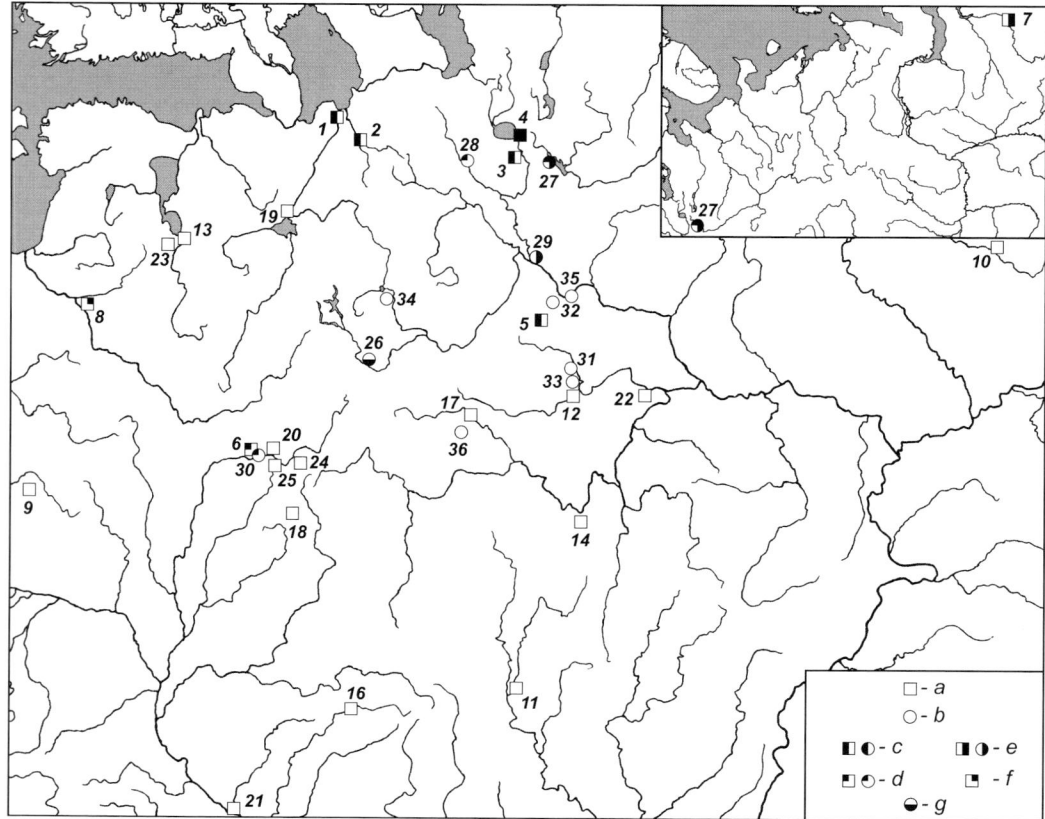

Figure 7.4 *Share of beads in the artefact collections of the settlements: a) urban sites; b) rural settlements; c) settlements relating to Group A in the First Chronological Period; d) settlements relating to Group B in the First Chronological Period; e) settlements relating to Group B in the Second Chronological Period and Mangazeya; f) settlements relating to Group C in the Second Chronological Period; g) settlements relating to Group A, the materials from which it proved impossible to divide up according to chronological period. The site numbers on the map correspond to their numbers in Table 7.6.*

at that time. A reliable argument in favour of that suggestion can be provided by the osteological materials obtained during the excavation of the Minino settlements. Despite the fact that the first settlement at Minino appeared at the time, when life at Krutik was already on the decline, the correlation between various types of mammals in the faunal remains collections from these settlements turns out to be extremely similar. Wild mammals predominate at Minino (over 64%) and among these the species most widely represented is the beaver (more than 54% of all wild mammals) (see Savinetskii in Maltby forthcoming). The only substantial difference is the larger share of squirrel bones in the Minino levels. Attempts to assess patterns of change in the correlation of the main mammal species at various stages in the existence of these settlements reveal not only that the observed processes are all moving in the same direction, i.e. the increase over time of the share of domestic animals and the reduction in the share of wild animals, first and foremost beaver, but also the very similar numerical values (compare the data cited by Savinetskii and by Zakharov 2004, 110).

At the same time it is impossible to overlook the fact that the share of beads in the early materials from Ladoga and the materials from Krutik is twice as high as in the collections from Minino and Byeloozero relating to the second chronological period. When seeking to interpret this fact, it is essential to use data from the post medieval period collected by Lvova. In her work aimed at reconstructing the nature of the trade in beads in Ladoga and the surrounding area, this scholar made use of a large number of written sources, which provide a detailed picture of how the fur trade was organized in the 17th–19th centuries in Siberia. One of the main types of commodity in those operations was the glass bead. In the seventeenth century glass beads were imported from Holland to Arkhangelsk, where they were sold in gross by weight by the 'pood' (1 'pood' = 16.38 kg: Trans) or even the ton. These beads were then taken to Siberia and sold there, no longer by weight, but by the thread or individually, to the local population in exchange for furs in the form of the so-called "sovereign's wages" (Lvova 1977, 108; 2003, 152–153). These transactions which amounted to no more than non-equivalent barter, often involved a number of stages. Moreover the price of the furs while they were being bought up and sold on by various middle-men increased many times over, according to Lvova's observations as much as 60 times (Lvova 1977, 109, Note 24).

One of the important centres for this trade was the town of Mangazeya, which came into being in 1601 on the River Taz in Western Siberia. The fact that the basis for its existence was the active trade in furs and mammoth tusks is evident, not only from the numerous written sources, but also from the town's rapidly growing prosperity and its no less rapid decline later on. This town which had had as many as 2,000 inhabitants at the beginning of the 1620s ceased to exist soon after the Royal Decree of 1627, which prohibited the use of the sea-route leading to Mangazeya, the main route linking it with the rest of the country (Belov *et al.* 1980, 1981; Chernosvitov 1994), so as to deny access for foreigners to the fur stocks of Siberia. For the subject under discussion here, it is important to turn to the materials yielded up by the excavations of that town. Analysis of these has shown that the considerable part played by glass beads in relation to the fur trade that is clearly recorded in the written sources has left revealing traces in the collection of artefacts from Mangazeya. Here glass beads account for approximately 20% of all objects found, i.e. this site falls in the same group (Group B) as that to which Byeloozero and Minino belong in the second chronological period.

This means that the significant share of beads in the artefact collections from Minino and Byeloozero in the first and second chronological periods, just as their significant share in the collections of artefacts from the early levels at Ladoga and Krutik, can be regarded as a clear indicator of the active involvement of their inhabitants in the fur trade. There is little doubt that glass beads were not the only valuable commodity and definitely not the most valuable one acquired in exchange for furs. It is no mere coincidence that the collections of artefacts from virtually all the large settlements, in which there is an above-average share of glass beads, stand out as rich and diverse. As at Minino, these collections contain numerous imports and silver coins, while the range of goods bought and sold there and that of various prestige items reflect the prosperity of the inhabitants. Glass beads, however, first and foremost because of the large numbers involved, can probably be regarded as some of the clearest indicators of locations where furs were traded in the northern part of Eastern Europe.

It is also interesting to trace how the geographical distribution of sites with significant numbers of glass beads in their artefact collections changes over time. During the first chronological period all the settlements, including Ladoga, played a stable role in relation to the most important trade routes (Figure 7.3). For Ladoga and the area south-east of that trading centre, which have yielded the highest indices for concentrations of glass beads, it is precisely this period, i.e. the 9th to the beginning or middle of the 11th century, that can be regarded as its heyday (Lvova 2003, 152; Boguslavskii 1993, 142–146, Figure 1). During the following chronological period a clear shift has been recorded regarding the areas with an above-average concentration of beads to the East and North-East, i.e. towards the River Sheksna and Byeloozero. It seems likely that in the 11th–13th centuries it is precisely these territories that became the main areas for the hunting of fur-bearing animals and the fur-trade. It is thus hardly a coincidence that precisely this time, the 12th and early-13th century, was the period of greatest prosperity for the town of Byeloozero itself and the rural settlements in its vicinity (Makarov *et al.* 2001, 87–92; Zakharov 2004, 94).

Notes

1   The numbers of the sites in the tables correspond to those on the map (Figure 7.4) and the graph (Figure 7.3).

2   All references in this paper cited as A followed by a year refer to unpublished archives. A full list of all these unpublished sources may be found in the CD that accompanies this volume in the section related to this chapter.

3   The calculations for Gnezdovo were carried out using inventory entries for individual finds for the years 1974–1998, stored in the Archaeology Department of Moscow State University. The author is sincerely grateful to T. A. Pushkina and N. V. Eniosova for the opportunity granted him to make use of unpublished materials.

4   The calculations were carried out using the collection from the excavations of M. I. Belov during the period 1968–1973 stored in the State Historical Museum (Moscow).

5   Excavations carried out in 1992–1997. The author is sincerely grateful to V. Y. Koval to the opportunity granted him to use unpublished materials.

8

THE NATURAL ENVIRONMENT AND SETTLEMENT PATTERNS OF THE LAKE ILMEN REGION IN THE LAST THIRD OF THE FIRST MILLENNIUM AD

I. I. Yeremeyev

INTRODUCTION

An essential prerequisite for a comprehensive 'reconstruction' of the process of settlement of the Ilmen region by Slavs in the first millennium AD is a study of the natural environment of the Ilmen basin. After encountering questions relating to the historical geography of the Novgorod Lands and the early history of Novgorod, both historians and geographers usually stress first and foremost the advantageously strategic position of both the city and its environs within the system of East European waterways (Shver *et al*. 1985, 4; Nosov 1999, 162). The unique nature of the ecosystem, within which the city took shape, tended to be relegated to the background, although it had been noted on more than one occasion by scholars (e.g. Nosov 1991, 6). At the present time the need for a more detailed analysis of the geography of the region has become more and more obvious both to historians and geographers (see, for instance, *Ekosistema ozera* [Ecosystem of Lake Ilmen] 1997, 4).

Analysis of the medieval geographical environment and the way it evolves needs to be especially thorough in relation to questions concerning Slav migration into the area around Lake Ilmen. There is little doubt that in the early stages of Slav colonization when the geopolitical factors which shaped the rise and flowering of Novgorod in the medieval period were not yet of decisive importance for determining settlement patterns, natural conditions played a key role in the selection by the Slavs of places where they would live.

THE CENTRAL PART OF THE LAKE ILMEN REGION: THE GEOGRAPHICAL DEFINITION OF THE REGION TO BE STUDIED

The idea of the 'central part of the Lake Ilmen region' is not a geographical term in the strict sense of the word. The need to single out this concept stems mainly from the tasks involved for those engaged in historical and archaeological research. According to the written sources, one of the Slavonic tribes which played a central role in Russian medieval history known as the Slovenes, settled near Lake Ilmen in early medieval times. Whichever way this formulation from the chronicles is interpreted, it remains clear that the model for 'Slovene' material culture can be found and studied most reliably of all in the Lake Ilmen basin.

The territory, which will be discussed below, incorporates first the Lake Ilmen basin and then parts of the Ilmen region immediately adjacent to that basin. This paper attempts to describe the territory moving anti-clockwise round a 'clock-face' with Lake Ilmen at its centre and starting out from the city of Novgorod.

The area where we commence this description embraces the upper reaches of the River Volkhov right down as far as the mouth of the Malyi Volkhovets. Further on, moving in an anti-clockwise direction, we come to a space bordered on the West by the River Veronda and in the north by an extensive stretch of woods and swamps, where the Rivers Veronda and Veryazha rise. South-west of the Lake Ilmen basin the area of interest to us includes the so-called Ilmen Glint on the south bank of the River Shelon in its lower reaches. To the south of the Lake, the area includes the basins of several small rivers flowing into it such as the Rivers Krupka, Makov and Tuleblya and also the lower reaches of two larger rivers, the Psizha and Perekhoda. In the south-east we include in the central part of the Lake Ilmen region the River Lovat from the mouth of the River Shubinskaya Robya, the lower reaches of the Pola as far as the mouth of the River Larinka and the deltas of the Pola and Lovat. East of Lake Ilmen it is as well to include the lower reaches of the River Msta (until the point where the River Kholova flows into it), the basins of small eastern tributaries of Lake Ilmen, namely the Kolpinka, Volozha, Sytinka, Zamlenka, Vitna and Nisha rivers. They all rise in the large, thinly settled marshes, which at the beginning of the medieval period would probably have been completely uninhabited, between the River Kholova and the *plavni* (low parts of downstream valleys of Russian rivers covered with reeds and trees) on the eastern shores of Lake Ilmen. Then we come to the delta of the River Msta, the marshes of the interfluve between the lower reaches of the Rivers Msta and Vishera and the waterlogged stretches of woodland in the interfluve of the Vishera and Volkhov.

LAKE ILMEN AND THE LAKES AND RIVERS OF THE REGION

One of the first scholars to embark upon a professional study of the Ilmen region was Domrachov, who described the subject of his research as a shallow lake 'with an extremely faintly marked depression and with very gently sloping banks, some of which are being eroded while others are being built up' (Domrachov 1926, 357). Its average depth is approximately 3 m. Its surface area with average water levels is approximately 45 × 35 km.

The catchment area of the lake's basin is 67,216 km². The lake is fed mainly by the

	Absolute water level in metres	Maximum depth in metres
Lowest level	16.5	3
Average level	18	4.5
High level	21.3	6.5
Highest level	23.4	10

Table 8.1 *Fluctuations in the level of Lake Ilmen prior to the construction of the Volkhov electric-power station (based on data obtained by Sokolov 1926).*

rivers flowing into it (*Razvitie* [Development] 1975, 101), moreover 57.2% of that comes into the lake in the spring (*Ekosistema ozera Ilmen* 1997, 22). This means that during the lake's flooded state in the spring its surface area and depth increase threefold, a unique phenomenon for lakes in north-western Russia. The range of seasonal fluctuations in the water level is a massive 6 m.

Sokolov assembled data on the fluctuations in the water levels of the lake between 1881 and 1924, when the Volkhov electric-power station was built, raising the level of water in the lake.

The Poozerie region and also the southern shore in the area of the Ilmen Glint are hardly flooded by the spring melt waters, but the flooded sections of the banks of the Malyi Volkhovets are quite considerable. The most extensive flooded areas are those on the sloping eastern shores of the lake in the deltas of the Lovat and Msta rivers.[1] This situation gave rise to the view that the lake was the result of the constant flooding of the rivers flowing over a flat plain (Domrachev 1925, 56; 1926, 353; Prasolov 1925, 5). The existence of an actual lake basin was only demonstrated conclusively in the 1920s (Sokolov 1926, 167).

The rivers which flow into Lake Ilmen do not have clearly defined valleys and they overflow their banks covering a wide area at high water. Even today it is not completely clear at what speed alluvial deposits are building up in the deltas of the larger rivers which flow into it. Nevertheless, these factors enable scholars to number Lake Ilmen among the country's "dying" natural reservoirs (*Razvitie* 1975, 100).

VEGETATION

At the present time the central part of the Lake Ilmen region can in the main be classified as belonging to the zone of mixed coniferous and broad-leaved forest at its northern extremity (sub-taiga). To the north of Novgorod the southern taiga begins, but does not have clearly defined edges (*Razvitie* 1975, 152–153).

At the time immediately prior to the appearance of Slavs in the north-west, the forest consisted mainly of spruce and broad-leaved trees, with some oak, lime, maple and elm throughout the area. Today, when we hear the word Ilmen, this conjures up a picture of an enormous open plain, flood-plain meadows intersected by rivers, ploughed fields on sloping hills and dotted about along the lake shore bushes and occasional clumps of small trees. Yet the Lake Ilmen region only began to look like this a few hundred years ago. In the mid-17th century the banks of the lake were still covered with forests which could be used for building timber. That was precisely how the eastern shore of the lake appeared in the well-known set of drawings by Augustin von Meierberg (1662) for example.

As late as the early-19th century there were still remains of oak groves to be found on the southern shore of the lake near the delta, as noted by Ozeretskovskii (1812, 489, 490). At that time there were also islands of pine forest of a type suitable for building timber near the western shore of the lake between Novgorod and the mouth of the Shelon River (Ozeretskovskii 1812, 525). There were extensive forests on the eastern shore of the lake as witnessed by Ozeretskovskii, who in 1805 had to make his way along a forest path to go from the village of Gosttsy to the mouth of the River Nisha (Ozeretskovskii 1812, 513). Information regarding the forest cover of parts of the eastern shore near the delta of the River Msta as late as the beginning of the 20th century is provided by accounts of elderly inhabitants from the Ilmen region (Navoloki Historical and Ethnographic Museum 1990, 5). Small oak groves, noted by scholars within the area of the Msta delta near the Mshashka River in the 1920s (Anufriev 1925, 29), have survived to the present day. In the 1920s there were still patches of oak forest to be found in certain parts of the Lovat delta. Finally, in that same period, the last remains of valuable conifer woods (spruce and pine) were noted along with some oak to the west of the lake in the River Veronda area and north of the mouth of the Shelon River (Gelfer 1927, 20).

Zhekulin, using toponymic data and historical documents, drew attention to a concentration of place names associated with broad-leaved species to the south and south-west of Lake Ilmen (*Razvitie* 1975a, 20–22). It has been established that the above-mentioned areas near the lake are today the most open as a result of intensive agriculture.

The modern-day vegetation found in the areas near the lake has been almost entirely transformed as a result of human activity. The indigenous woods have been replaced by small-leaved species (birch, aspen) and bushes. Viburnum and alder are also to be found and in the flood-meadows willow beds are widespread. For the most part expanses of open countryside predominate consisting of flood meadows and ploughed fields.

CLIMATE

The climate of the central part of the Lake Ilmen region is classified as moderate continental, similar to a maritime climate. The summers are comparatively warm and the winters mild with frequent thaw periods. The average temperature in July is 17.5–18° C. The frost-free period lasts longer here than anywhere else in the Ilmen basin and, according to a variety of estimates it is between 130 and 150 days. The annual

1923			1924										
VIII	IX	X	XI	XII	I	II	III	IV	V	VI	VII	VIII	IX
+1.2	+0.4	+0.7	+0.3	-0.6	+0.1	+0.2	-0.5	-0.6	-1.0	+0.5	+0.4	+1.1	+1.2

Table 8.2 The difference between average monthly temperatures in the upper reaches of the Volkhov Rover and the central part of the Lake Ilmen region based upon readings taken at Khutyn and Troitsa during 1923/1924 (as published by Domrachev 1926).

precipitation is relatively light amounting to 650–700 mm and between 425–450 mm of this rain falls during the warm period of the year (*Ekosistema ozera Ilmen* 1997, 24).

Lake Ilmen exerts an extremely significant influence on the climate in the territory adjacent to it. This has a positive impact on agriculture in the confines of its basin. This shallow expanse of cloudy water, at the bottom of which there is a thick (up to 10 m) layer of silt deposits, heats up well in the summer–autumn period and gives off the heat accumulated during the spring and early summer (*Ekosistema ozera Ilmen* 1997, 24), creating a relatively favourable micro-climate during the vegetation growing period, which is longer on the shores of Lake Ilmen than in areas further away from the lake. A hundred and fifty years ago Eikhvald noted that "the climate on the western and southern shores of the lake is not as severe as it is far away from the lake: this is why apples, pears, plums and cherries ripen much better in Korostyn, than in Staraya Russa" (Eikhvald 1856, 27). It is also worth noting that there were large apple orchards in the delta of the River Msta known from late medieval written sources.

An indication of the above phenomena is provided by recordings made in the 1920s of the difference between average monthly temperatures during the summer–autumn period along the shore of the lake (at Troitsa, north of the lake) and in the Khutyn area, according to the Khutyn meteorological station. During the June–November period the difference in temperatures could be as much as 1.2° C (see Table 8.2).

The area considered the warmest in summer is the eastern shore of the lake (*Razvitie* 1975, 63) but the influence of Lake Ilmen on the climate of Poozerie is considerable as well. The cloud cover and the level of precipitation here in the summer are less than in parts of the Ilmen region further away from the lake. In general, the central part of the Lake Ilmen region is that best suited for agricultural activity in the whole of the territory of the Lake Ilmen basin.

AREAS MAKING UP THE CENTRAL REGION ROUND LAKE ILMEN DIFFERENTIATED ON THE BASIS OF THEIR PHYSICAL GEOGRAPHY

Predominant in this area is the overall flat lacustrine relief of the Ilmen Depression, where erosion is limited. This area, which extends beyond the study zone, is the so-called Ilmen Glint. Here the average absolute height above sea level is 20–30 m. The territory is extremely water-logged: its surface consists mainly of alluvial lake sands, sandy loams and clays. The soils are derno-podzolic. In the river deltas alluvial meadow soils are often found. Characteristic of the marshy areas are gley and podzolic soils. Although the external appearance of the relief is uniform within the confines of the indicated area discussed in the previous section of this chapter, it is possible to single out a number of geographical areas which differ as regards their predominant landscape. These nine areas are described in detail in the section for this chapter on the accompanying CD.

EARLY MEDIEVAL SETTLEMENT ON THE SHORES OF LAKE ILMEN

If the antiquities of the Ilmen low lands are regarded as parts of a whole and taken together with their landscape context, it is possible to single out a number

of natural/archaeological micro-districts. When describing these we shall keep to the same sequence used above, when the geographical conditions of the Ilmen Basin were being discussed, i.e. we shall move round Lake Ilmen in an anti-clockwise direction (see Figure 8.1).

Micro-district 1: Settlements in the flood-plain landscapes found in the upper reaches of the Volkhov River

These settlements are located as a rule on low elevations in the flood-plain, separated from each other by the wide, water-logged flood-plain. At the present time within an area that extends for approximately 20 km there are up to 15 settlements containing hand-made pottery dating from the 8th to 10th centuries. A separate count is required for settlements that came into existence from the 10th century. In the region containing the sources of the Volkhov River, there are two fortified settlements which appeared in the 9th century, namely Kholopii Gorodok and Ryurik Gorodishche.

Micro-district 2: Settlements in the alluvial landscapes of Poozerie

These settlements are located on hills between narrow gullies, once channels of ancient deltas. Between Peryn and the mouth of the Veryazha, 16 settlements with early medieval hand-made pottery have been recorded over a distance of some 20 km. Two settlements, Georgii and Sergovo, had fortifications.

Micro-district 3: On the south bank of the Shelon River in its lower reaches

A concentration of settlements is to be found in the western part of the so-called Ilmen Glint, an area on the south bank of the River Shelon, where Devonian clays and limestones protrude at the modern ground surface. The settlements here (to judge

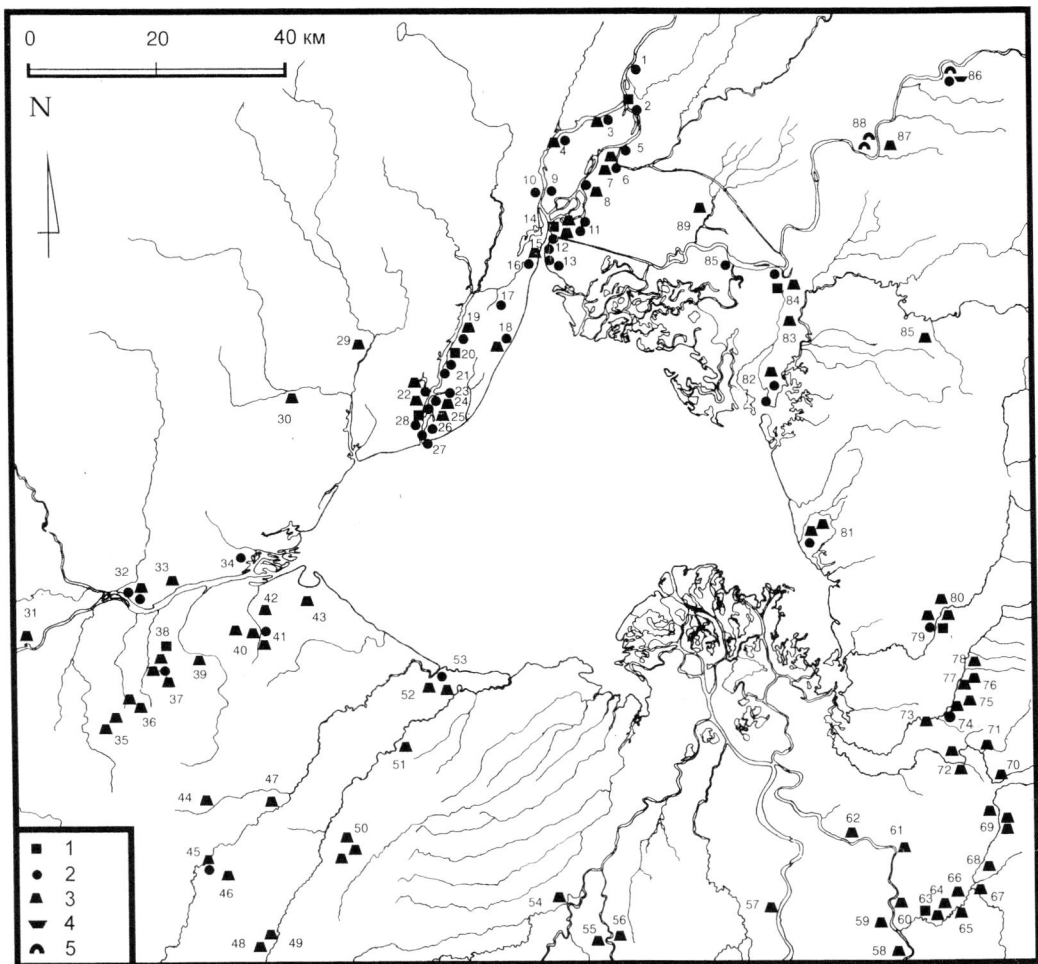

Figure 8.1 *Archaeological sites dating from the second half of the first millennium AD in the environs of Lake Ilmen.*

Legend: 1 – fortified settlement; 2 – settlement; 3 – sopki (large burial mounds); 4 – flat-grave burial-grounds; 5 – other burial-mounds.

Sites: 1 – Slutka; 2 – Kholopii Gorodok; 3 – Khutyn; 4 – Derevyanitsy; 5 – Myza Speranskogo; 6 – Rodionovo; 7 – Ushersko; 8 – Volotovo; 9,10 – Velikii Novgorod; 11 – Sitka; 12 – Spas-Nereditsa; 13 – Shilka; 14 – Ryurikovo Gorodishche; 15 – Peryn; 16 – Prost; 17 – Rakomo; 18 – Beregovye Moriny; 19 – Moiseyevichi; 20 – Georgii; 21 – Vasilievskoye; 22 – Zaval; 23 – Khotyazh; 24 – Lyuboezha; 25 – Goroshkovo; 26 – Zabolotie; 27 – Erunovo; 28 – Sergovo; 29 – Okatovo; 30 – Bazlovka; 31 – Velebitsy; 32 – Bor; 33 – Shimsk; 34 – Golino; 35 – Lyubyni; 36 – Dubrovo; 37 – Solonitsko; 38 – Gorodtsy; 39 – Luki; 40 – Kolomo; 41 – Gortsy; 42 – Malaya Viton; 43 – Bolshaya Viton; 44 – Yazvino; 45 – Gorodtsy; 46 – Rakitno; 47 – Parnik; 48 – Mikhalkovo; 49 – Gorki; 50 – Gopstezh; 52 – Podteremie; 52 – Solobsko; 53 – Ustreka; 54 – Perevoloka; 55 – Kotovo; 56 – Chirikovo; 57 – Rogashevo; 58 – Borki; 59 – Dubki; 60 – Pola; 61 – Shchechkovo; 62 – Manuilovo; 63 – Seltso I; 64 – Vypolzovo; 65 – Krutets; 66 – Malyi Toloknyanets; 67 – Yablonovo; 68 – Dvorets; 69 – Lorinka; 70 – Lutovnya; 71 – Sopki; 72 – Dubrovo; 73 – Rostani; 74 – Ryabutki; 75 – Olisovo; 76 – Grigorovo; 77 – Seltso II; 78 – Bolshie Buchki; 79 – Gorodok; 80 – Terebusha; 81 – Veisko; 82 – Navolok; 83 – Yamno; 84 – Bronnitsa; 85 – Kholynya; 86 – Kobylya Golova; 87 – Glebovo; 88 – Ryshevo; 89 – Mshashka.

from the arrangement of the burial-grounds) stretched in a line along the high south edge of the valley of the River Shelon formed by an escarpment consisting of pre-Quaternary rocks. Set further back in the plateau to the south of the river and running along the valley there is a band of sandy-loam and light-loam soils, which were built up on fluvio-glacial deposits. It can be assumed that it was precisely these soils that had attracted the Slav agricultural population who settled here. On the other hand, the rendzinas, which formed on the Devonian limestones covered by thin layers of boulder loams, could also have attracted the population, although tilling them would have involved much more work.

It is not easy to calculate the precise number of settlements in this area, because it has not been studied in any detail. The overall number of burial-sites relating to the 8th–10th centuries that have been recorded enables us to state that there would have been at least 13 early medieval settlements over a distance of 26 km from the village of Lyubyni to that of Korostyn. In this micro-district one fortified settlement has been recorded near the village of Podgoshchi (which is now destroyed). The date of the fortified settlement has not been clearly established. Its location within the cluster of settlements dating from the last quarter of the first millennium AD makes it possible to assume that it was in use during that period. One other fortified settlement was possibly in existence then, near Korostyn on the shore of Lake Ilmen. At the beginning of the 19th century the toponym "gorodok" was used in relation to a steep section of the shore east of that village (Ozeretskovskii 1812, 534).

The natural and demographic potential of this micro-district was, without doubt, considerable, and it could have played an important role in the central part of the region round Lake Ilmen. Unfortunately we know very little about the settlements in the lower reaches of the River Shelon.

Micro-district 4: On the southern shore of Lake Ilmen

The section near the mouth of the River Psizha has been treated as a separate area for the purposes of this study. As regards the features of its physical geography, it is similar to the previous micro-district, although it is some distance removed from it. According to the available data, a large medieval settlement was located near the mouth of the River Psizha. It was probably not the only one in the area. Unfortunately, the micro-district has not yet been studied in adequate detail. It is likely that eventually the settlements at the mouth of the River Psizha may come to be regarded as forming the eastern edge of Micro-district 3.

In the academic literature the opinion is put forward to the effect that this micro-district should be regarded as an important place "on the journey from the Varangians to the Greeks" (Ershevskii and Konetskii 1985). But it should be noted that, due to the prevailing winds, it would seem unlikely that coastal sailing took place round Lake Ilmen. The mouth of the Lovat is at almost the same distance from the mouth of the Psizha River as it is from the source of the Volkhov River. It goes without saying that any settlement is drawn into a network of communications to a greater or lesser degree, but we are of the opinion that the micro-district at the mouth of the River Psizha should be considered first and foremost in the context of the settlement of the south-western part of the Ilmen region for agricultural purposes.

Micro-district 5: The Interfluve of the Rivers Pola and Mayata

There is a group of settlements established near rivers flowing into Lake Ilmen from the south-east. The settlements are located at the point where the fluvio-glacial landscapes of the Ilmen Basin meet those of the moraine plain, which extends in the direction of the Valdai Upland. From the geographical point of view this micro-district resembles not so much the specific landscapes characteristic of the Ilmen Basin but rather has features typical of the outer margins of the Valdai Upland. It is likely that this state of affairs was to a considerable degree what led to the influx into the district in the 8th and 9th centuries of people who were adherents of the culture involving *sopki* and preferred the landscapes of the margins of moraine ridges to other natural conditions in the north-west of Russia.

In this micro-district over a distance of 36 km from the station at Pola as far as the middle reaches of the River Mayata there is a total of no less than 27 settlements. Here also, near the village of Ryabutki, there is one of the two largest burial-grounds made up of *sopki* in the central part of the Ilmen Region (the other was near the village of Volotovo near Novgorod). Bearing in mind that, to judge from the data obtained through studies undertaken in the area where the River Volkhov rises and in Poozerie, a considerable number of the early medieval settlements in the central region around Lake Ilmen did not have any cemeteries consisting of burial-mounds in their vicinity, it is possible to anticipate that many more settlements will be discovered here eventually. This will mean that the already considerable demographic potential of this micro-district will stand out still more clearly against the backdrop of the other zones of early medieval settlement in the central part of the Lake Ilmen region.

This micro-district is known to have contained two similar, early medieval fortified settlements. They were near the modern villages of Seltso and Gorodok. Both of these fortified settlements were in existence in the 9th century.

Micro-district 6: Eastern area adjacent to Lake Ilmen

A small group of settlements evidently existed on the ridge near the villages Zamlenie and Veisko. The historical name of this part of the terrain near Lake Ilmen, Sytinskii Ugol (Sytinka Corner), reflected the fact that it was in the margins, isolated from the rest of the world. Two burial-grounds containing *sopki* have been recorded here and one settlement containing hand-made pottery. Being surrounded by flood plains and swamps, Sytinka Corner has been investigated less than any other micro-district in the central region around Lake Ilmen, as far as its archaeology is concerned. Geographical descriptions of this micro-district enable us to predict that several new early medieval settlements will be discovered here in due course. Yet it is important to remember that no fortified settlements have been recorded here and open settlements are unlikely to have been numerous because of the comparatively weak grounds, as regards the nature of the soils and local resources, for settling this particular micro-district. It is therefore highly unlikely that it played a significant and independent role in the early history of the region inhabited by Novgorod Slovenes.

Micro-district 7: Bronnitskaya Ridge

A group of medieval settlements was founded near the Bronnitskaya Ridge in the interfluve of the Msta and Nisha rivers. Four settlements have been identified, which can be assumed to date from the 8th–10th centuries. One of them near a place called Yamno has only been recorded in connection with the *sopka* located there. There is little doubt that properly focused investigation of this micro-district with its favourable conditions for land cultivation and fishing would enable scholars to achieve a significant increase in the number of recorded settlements. In this micro-district in the early medieval period there had only been one fortified settlement near the village of Bronnitsa, known as one of the strongest fortresses in the region around Lake Ilmen. The rich natural resources in the lower reaches of the Msta, the unusually important strategic position/situation of the micro-district, given its strong fortifications and the geographical isolation of the neighbouring micro-districts, makes it possible to regard the Bronnitskaya Ridge as having been an independent territorial and political unit in the era of the Early Slav settlement of the Ilmen Basin. At the same time this small territory restricted the prospects for growth in the region and its location on the route for the peat trade, which passed down the River Msta, destabilized the political situation, a fact that would have robbed this micro-district of any political independence it might have enjoyed.

SETTLEMENT PATTERNS IN THE EARLY MEDIEVAL PERIOD IN THE ILMEN BASIN

The above-listed natural/archaeological micro-districts vary considerably in the size and character of their natural resources. It would appear that at the time when the Slavs reached Lake Ilmen they had, to a greater or lesser degree, been settled by the indigenous pre-Slav population. In order to understand which micro-districts were settled by the Slavs and how they were settled by Slavs, further study is essential.

The natural/archaeological micro-districts identified above coincide in the main with the sub-divisions of the Ilmen Basin based on their physical geography, which have been outlined above. At the same time we cannot fail to note that three areas within the central region round Lake Ilmen settled in the early medieval period for purposes of agricultural exploitation stand out – the interfluve of the Rivers Veryazha and Shelon (apart from the narrow strip of land along the north bank of the River Shelon); the delta of the Lovat River and the delta of the River Msta. All three of these areas are not high above sea-level and are characterized by unusually high humidity and an unstable hydrological regime. This means that the creation of a stable network of settlements there would have been unlikely even in the relatively dry climate of the 8th and 9th century.[2]

Despite the undeniable link between large clusters of early medieval settlements and relatively dry parts of the Ilmen Basin, among the large natural/archaeological micro-districts certain settlements stand out as not really belonging to any of these micro-districts. Some isolated *sopki* recorded on swampy soils in the lower reaches of the Rivers Msta (also known as the Mshashka), Veronda (Vazlovka), Nisha (Balozha) enable us to assume that over time our views of the settlement patterns in the Ilmen Basin will undergo some amendment. We might assume, for instance, that in the future early medieval settlements will be discovered on the Vzvadsk Ridge, which is similar in its natural characteristics to the Bronnitskaya Ridge. Other factors pointing in this direction are results of analysis of the geographical context and also the famous hoard of 10th-century coins found in the village of Podborovka, not far from Vzvad. It is, however, unlikely that the system of sub-divisions of the Ilmen Basin will undergo radical change, since it is based on existing physical-geographical boundaries.

It is at this stage difficult to say which Early Slavonic social and political structures underpinned the micro-districts we singled out and what the hierarchy of the latter was. Without claiming to have achieved a final resolution of these questions, it is possible to assume that in the territory that was being colonized in the 8th and 9th centuries and which consisted of quite clearly defined different geographical areas, small territorially based tribal groupings would have taken shape, little "Slavinias" referred to in the earliest of the chronicles as "clans" with their own settlements, where the leaders of the tribe or clan would live and sometimes popular assemblies would exist.

Taking into account the ancient demography and natural potential of the largest of the micro-districts and also the presence of fortified settlements within them as possible military-cum-administrative centres that served as a consolidating factor, it can be assumed that the total number of settlements in the Ilmen Basin at the time of its Slavonic colonization was originally divided into five groups. Possible territorially independent micro-districts which might well have emerged are the following natural/archaeological micro-districts: the area where the River Volkhov rises (Micro-district 1); Poozerie (Micro-district 2); the lower reaches of the Shelon river (Micro-district 3); the area between the Rivers Pola and Mayata (Micro-district 5) and the Bronnitskaya Ridge (Micro-district 7).

It is necessary to stress that the approach outlined in this article with regard to the identification of historical-geographical areas is only justified if we view the settlements of the central region round Lake Ilmen as parts of a single entity, which had taken shape round one of the largest lakes in Europe. This approach is not the only one possible. In particular, some of the natural/archaeological micro-districts could be viewed as marginal parts of agglomerations along rivers (the Lovat, Msta, Shelon and so on). Yet, as we see it, the aptness of our method is shaped by the chronicles themselves, which single out precisely Lake Ilmen as the geographical nucleus of the region of the Slovenes.

The Early Slav population all over the north-western part of medieval Russia is known to have shown a preference for lacustrine and flood-plain landscapes. Yet only the shores of Lake Ilmen provided opportunities for a considerable concentration of agricultural population in the last third of the first millennium AD. The gently sloping relief of Poozerie, the fertile and light alluvial soils, the favourable lake-side micro-climate – all this together provided a unique ecological niche in the natural environment of north-west Russia. Moreover, this niche was large enough to absorb a significant number of settlers.

After Slavs had settled the region round Lake Ilmen for all the above-listed reasons and which determined the historical development of this region, the first conditions began to emerge which would play a key role in the development of a North-Russian state with its centre first in the lower reaches of the Volkhov river (Staraya Ladoga) and later at the spot where the Volkhov rises (Gorodishche/Novgorod). What came to play the key role in this process was not the wealth of the natural sources in some or other tribal territories. In this respect the upper reaches of the Volkhov were not nearly as important as Poozerie, the lower reaches of the River Shelon and even parts of the Pola and Mayata interfluve. What began to emerge as the key factors were geo-political and strategic ones ensuring optimal control of trade routes and convenient conditions for administering the surrounding territories. The military power of the North-Russian state was based not so much on its local resources, which were determined by the natural characteristics of the micro-districts discussed above, but military strength from Varangian contingents and an economic base stemming from outside the local economic base, such as Kufic silver. In the final analysis these were the factors which shaped the political and economic prominence of Ryurik Gorodishche and later that of Novgorod at the source of the River Volkhov.

Notes

1 Changes in the life of the lake resulted from the construction of the Volkhov electric-power station, which caused (from 1926 onwards) an appreciable rise in its water levels. This rise turned out to be not very significant, just as the scientists had predicted who had been carrying out research before the construction work began (Stepanov 1927, 136; Prasolov 1927, 347). At the present time the average level of the water in Lake Ilmen is accepted as 18 m above sea level, just as before the construction of the Volkhov dam (see Table 8.1). Nevertheless, comparison of the low eastern shore on maps of the general land survey in the last quarter of the 18th century (Topographical diagram of Medieval Novgorod 1828) and modern maps (Novgorod Region, 1997) brings to light some differences in the configuration of the shore-line. In the Msta delta the eastern shore of Lake Ilmen turned out to have been flooded by the Lake to a distance of up to 2 km from the average water line in the 18th century. A stretch of beach in the coastal part of the delta disappeared under water. Some of the lakes in the Msta delta turned into inlets of Lake Ilmen (for example, the largest of them, Lake Arkadskoye).

2 A case on its own in the south-western part of the region around Lake Ilmen is the above-mentioned chain of hillocks on the north bank of the Shelon river shortly before its mouth. Here

on a line joining Shimsk and Golino there is a small area convenient for cultivation containing an early medieval settlement near the village of Golino and another settlement within the territory of modern Shimsk (in this case only its *sopka* has so far been recorded). In the future we can possibly expect the discovery of new settlements in this area.

9

BRONZE WORKING AT RYURIK GORODISHCHE AND OTHER SETTLEMENTS IN THE REGION NORTH OF LAKE ILMEN IN THE 9TH AND 10TH CENTURIES

N. V. Khvoshchinskaya

INTRODUCTION

The area near the source of the River Volkhov and the neighbouring territory of Poozerie north-west of Lake Ilmen were settled at the end of the first millennium by one of the groups of Eastern Slavs. This is reflected in the dozens of settlements along the banks of the River Veryazha, in the upper reaches of the River Volkhov and its tributary, the Volkhovets (Nosov 1990, 173–183). In early medieval times this whole area had been the most populous and economically developed of the territories making up the Novgorod Lands. This is due to a large extent to the light fertile soils, which were easy to cultivate and also to the extremely advantageous geographical location at the crossroads of medieval water routes vitally important for trading in Eastern Europe. In this zone of settlement, Ryurik Gorodishche (hereafter Gorodishche) emerged as the most important centre of population in the second half of the 9th century. It became the first pre-urban settlement of a non-agrarian type in the area round Lake Ilmen (Nosov 2001). It is no coincidence that precisely at Gorodishche elements of the cultures of various peoples of Eastern Europe and Scandinavia were interwoven: here they were re-worked to a certain extent and then spread to the immediate surroundings of the site and later into other parts of medieval Russia as well. The output from craft production at Gorodishche made its way into rural settlements, where local artisans mastered and adopted new techniques. Gorodishche came without doubt to influence the development of craft production in the area round Lake Ilmen and, in particular, the development of the jeweller's craft of copper alloy metalworking (see Figure 9.1).

Excavation of a number of rural settlements undertaken round Lake Ilmen has revealed that a certain share of the objects fashioned from non-ferrous metals were manufactured on the spot in many of these settlements. Yet it should be emphasized

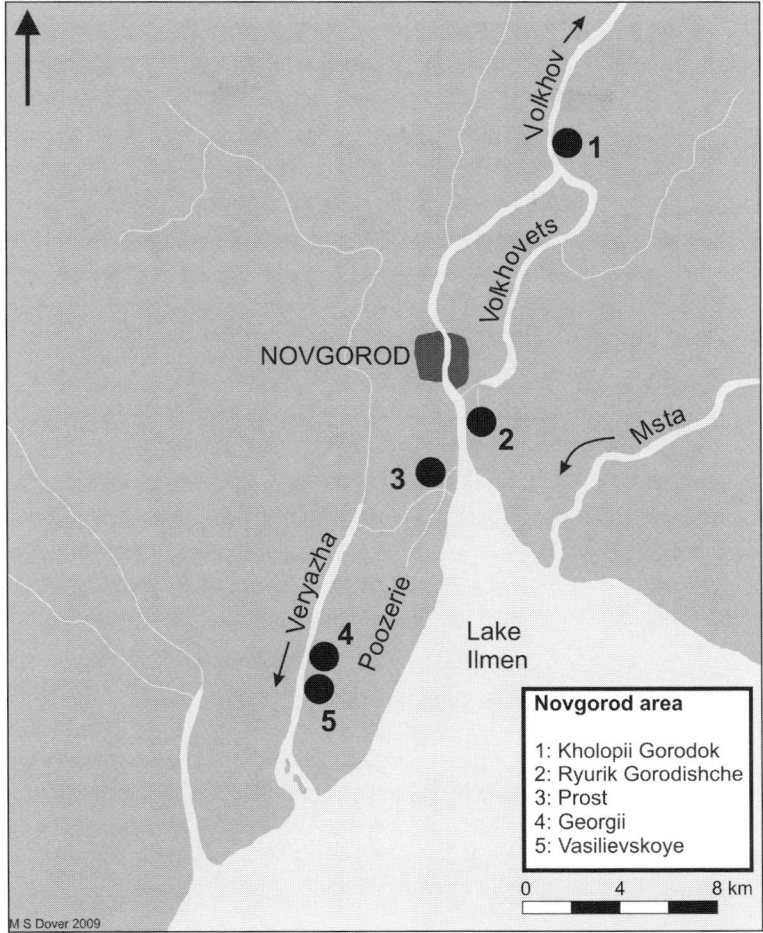

Figure 9.1 Map of the study area showing the location of Ryurik Gorodishche and other contemporary, pre-Novgorod sites.

that despite the extensive areas already excavated here, materials testifying to bronze casting in the 9th and 10th centuries in the settlements of the northern area around Lake Ilmen (known as Poozerie) are so sparse that they cannot in any way be compared with the materials obtained during the study of Gorodishche itself. Nevertheless, we shall dwell in some detail on these to begin with.

THE EVIDENCE OF COPPER ALLOY OBJECTS FROM SITES IN THE VICINITY OF RYURIK GORODISHCHE

An interesting complex was excavated in the settlement near the present-day village of Vasilievskoye on the River Veryazha in Poozerie. A total area of 500 m² has been investigated in the settlement. Chronologically speaking its main cultural deposits relate to the second half of the 10th century (Nosov and Plokhov 2002, 164–165). During excavation work, part of an area not taken up by dwellings was found in the central part of the settlement. In a structure sunk into the natural soil remains of a furnace were found, which could be interpreted as an iron smith's, if we bear in mind the context of the finds. It is, however, possible that it was also used for smelting non-ferrous metals, since a fragment of a stone mould had been found next to the furnace. The impression on the mould is so unclear, that it is difficult to say what would have been cast in it (Nosov and Plokhov 2002, 161–163, Figure 2.7). Some groups of buildings containing hearths might also have been used for work with non-ferrous metals. An indirect indication of this is provided by a fragment of the upper part of a crucible which was found on one of the hearths. Several small fragments of tumbler-crucibles were found in the settlement. A fragment of a clay nozzle and a bronze ingot from among the finds could also be regarded as the remains of bronze-casting. The ingot was trapezoidal in section, which is characteristic of articles of that kind and it measured[1] 4.2 × 1 × 0.7 cm (Nosov and Plokhov 2002, 161, Figure 2.5). Ingots used as a method for storing raw materials will be discussed in more detail below. All that might be pointed out at this stage is that raw material for bronze-casting in the Poozerie area would appear to have come from Gorodishche, or at least moulds for casting it have been recorded there.

Apart from the Vasilievskoye settlement, two more sites in Poozerie provided materials that testify to the existence of the production of articles from non-ferrous metals. These were the fortified settlement of Georgii on the River Veryazha and the settlement of Prost at the spot where the small river Prost flows into the Volkhov. The Georgii settlement dates from the second half of the 9th or the early 10th century and the Prost settlement from the 8th to the 10th century, although finds have been recorded at Prost going back to the era of the Early Metal Age (Nosov and Plokhov 2002: 169, 174–176). In the fortified settlement of Georgii an area of more than 600 m^2 has been excavated and the equivalent figure for the settlement of Prost is close to 1000 m^2. Although the areas which have been the subject of archaeological investigation are fairly large, no production complexes have been discovered at either site. All that indicates that the inhabitants of these settlements were engaged in bronze-casting is the small number of finds of fragments of ladles (three at the Georgii settlement and one in the Prost settlement) and a few crucible fragments.

Gorodishche in the middle of the 9th century was a settlement of a kind quite different from the settlements in its immediate vicinity when it comes to craft production and, in particular, to bronze casting. It should be noted that the Prost settlement, one of the largest in the area north of Lake Ilmen, was located opposite Gorodishche on the west bank of the River Volkhov and, as mentioned above, traces of intensive craft production were not found there.

The available materials, which testify to the processing of non-ferrous metals in the early period of Gorodishche's history, i.e. at the time when the settlements Prost, Vasilievskoye and Georgii were in existence, overshadow the far less informative evidence obtained during excavations in the Poozerie area or indeed in the upper reaches of the River Volkhov. In this connection it should be noted that at the settlement and fortified area of Kholopii Gorodok, where excavations were undertaken over a total area of 386 m², no finds were made which were linked with the processing of non-ferrous metals. There must, without doubt, have been close economic ties between Gorodishche and the population of its environs. Poozerie had always been Novgorod's 'granary'. These relations began to take shape when Gorodishche came into being as a centre for craft production and trade. The rural population would have brought food products there and in exchange they would have received the output of the craftsmen working in Gorodishche. That is the only way to explain why so little material relating to bronze casting has been found in the rural settlements of the Poozerie region and in the upper reaches of the River Volkhov, despite the extensive areas there which have already been excavated. At the same time it is precisely from Poozerie that rare articles are found, which would appear to have made their way to this rural locality via Gorodishche in its role as commercial intermediary (for instance a twisted iron torque, an equal-armed fibula of the Valsta type, beads from the Northern Caucasus, etc.) and also articles which had come directly from the workshops in Gorodishche itself. We would number among finds in the latter range the bronze ingot already mentioned from the settlement of Vasilievskoye cast by a professional artisan, since there is no blow hole to be seen. There are also three open-work round pendants in the Borre style that are discussed in more detail below in connection with the mould in which they were cast, which has been found at Gorodishche.

THE EVIDENCE FROM RYURIK GORODISHCHE

From a stratigraphic point of view, the habitation levels at Gorodishche and the material in them singled out for mention here can be clearly divided into two chronological periods: the late-9th to the 10th century and the 11th to 12th centuries. It is the manufacture of jewellery relating to the earlier period that is the subject of this paper. When at the end of the 10th or beginning of the 11th century Gorodishche was losing its predominant position in the region, it was Novgorod itself which assumed that role and also became the centre for craft production, which dictated the fashion for bronze jewellery and supplied mass-produced articles not merely to the city's immediate environs but also further afield. From the 11th century onwards, Gorodishche materials (many crucibles of various shapes and sizes, slags, casting moulds and rejected cast bronze items) need to be examined in the same context as the Novgorod finds, thus complementing them. This is an aspect of research into the Novgorod material. On the other hand, only the materials from Gorodishche and Staraya Ladoga, in their capacity as the first urban centres in the Volkhov region (Nosov 2001), provide a unique opportunity for tracing the emergence of craft production in the centre of the area being settled by the Slavs and the trends that are to be observed in that process.

In this context, it is important to remember that Gorodishche is, in places, a badly damaged site, a significant portion of which was removed by the Siversov Canal in the early 19th century. Unfortunately, it is precisely this area of the promontory which may have had significant numbers of production complexes, although we will never know for certain.

The artefactual evidence

Investigations have been carried out at this particular settlement for many years and over this time have emerged a specific group of finds that testify to the presence of well-developed jewellery production among the population of this settlement even in the early period of its existence. It is above all the small casting moulds, the jewellery tools, crucibles and ladles which make up this category of finds.

Five small moulds (three stone ones and two clay moulds) date from the 9th to 10th centuries. All the stone moulds were made from soapstone or steatite, which was fairly rare within the territory of medieval Russia. In the opinion of Stalsberg (2003, 118), articles manufactured from soapstone came to medieval Russia from Norway or the extreme south-west of Sweden. According to her data, nine finds made of soapstone have been recorded within the territory of medieval Russia (six in Staraya Ladoga and one each from Kiev, Gnezdovo and Gorodishche).[2] Yet deposits of soapstone are to be found, to use a geological term, all along the Baltic Shield, that is, across the extensive territory incorporating Karelia, Finland, Sweden and Norway. In addition, the stone used for making the casting moulds found at Gorodishche differed in both colour and texture from the type of soapstone found in the area suggested by Stalsberg. Two of the moulds on visual examination appear to have the same structure and to be dark-grey, almost black, in colour. They would seem to have come from one and the same place and to have served the same purpose and not by chance: they both appear to have been used for casting ingots of non-ferrous metal. The third mould was designed for making parts of pendants and was reddish brown in colour. The stone from which it had been made clearly came from a different deposit.

One of the small moulds earmarked for casting ingots of non-ferrous metal consisted of a small slab of a somewhat irregular shape (6 × 3.7 × 2.1 cm), in the wide surfaces of which recesses for the reproduction of four rectangular-shaped ingots of varying sizes (5 × 1 × 0.8 cm; 3.1 × 0.5 × 0.5 cm; 3.1 × 0.7 × 0.9 cm and 4.4 × 0.8 × 1 cm) and also for one ingot semi-spherical in shape (diameter of 1.2 cm; depth 0.75 cm). In addition recesses for two other ingots semi-spherical in shape (diameter of 1.4 cm; depth 0.7 cm) had been cut out of the two long side surfaces of the slab. Among the rectangular recesses only the largest had been made with especial care. It was trapezoidal in section with a flat base and virtually vertical walls. The remaining recesses had been carved out with less care and one of the round side recesses had an extremely small rectangular recess cutting across it, which meant that only three rectangular and two curved recesses could have been used for properly made ingots. It should also be noted that the rectangular impressions carved out of the opposite flat sides of the slab, were so

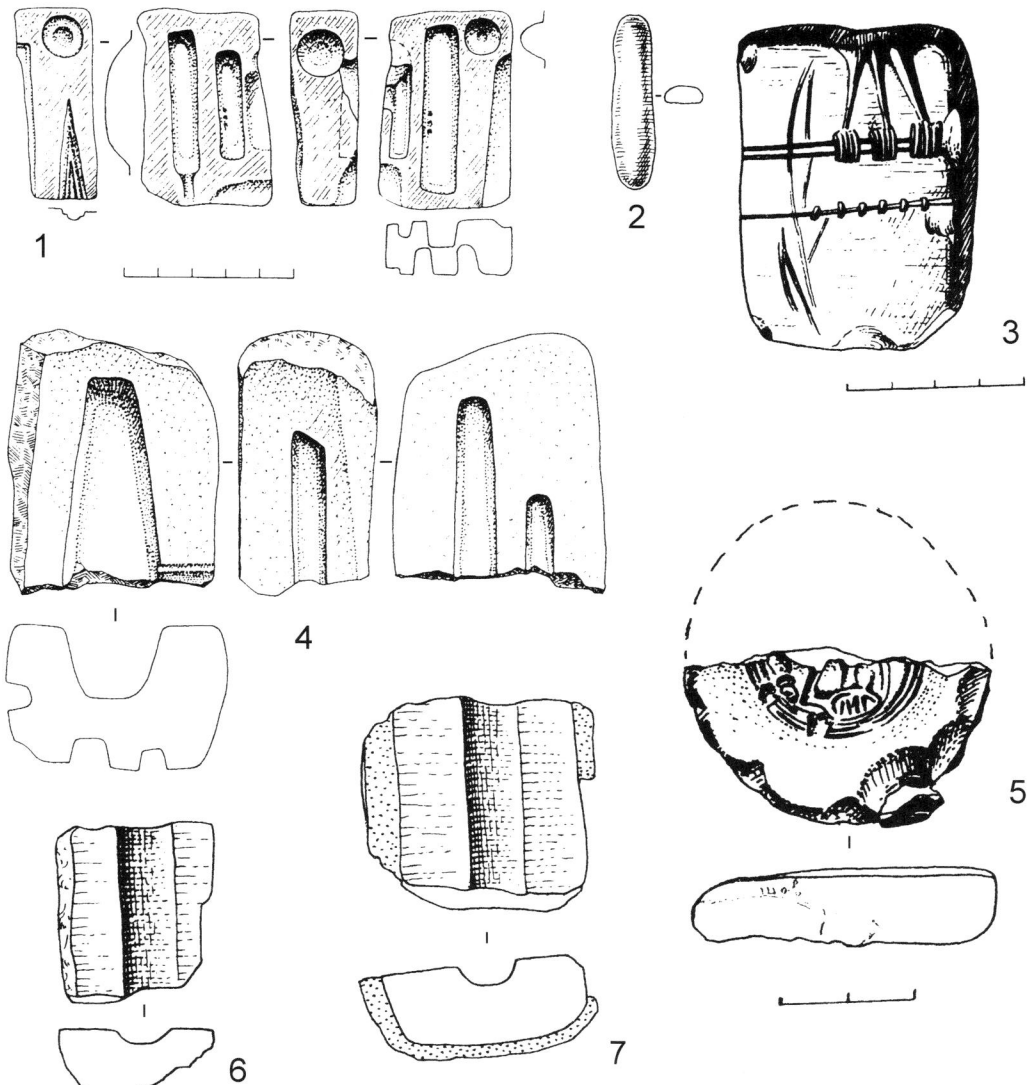

Figure 9.2 *Finds from Ryurik Gorodishche associated with non-ferrous casting: 1, 4, 6, 7) stone moulds for casting ingots; 2) a bronze ingot; 3) a soapstone mould for multiple use; 5) a clay disc-shaped mould for pendant making.*

close to each other in one case that a crack had formed between them. On the small stone slab, apart from clearly defined impressions, there were various recesses with no really clear function (for example, a wedge-shaped recess on one of the side edges and a rectangular one at the edge of a flat side) and also dents.

The second small mould for casting ingots was of far larger dimensions (Figure 9.2.4). Only part of it has survived, which is of irregular shape (7.5 × 6.1 × 2.67 cm). At the present time it is difficult to determine what the size of the missing part would have been. The mould had been designed for the casting of four ingots, the impressions of which had been cut out from the two flat sides of a stone and one of its side surfaces. As we do not know the actual length of the ingots, we shall only cite their width and depth (i.e. their thickness): the largest ingot on the flat side in its widest part measured 2.7 × 2.1 cm; the ingot cast on the side of the stone measured 0.9 × 0.75 cm in width and the two ingots cast using the second flat surface of the stone measured 0.8 × 0.68 cm and 1.3 × 0.75 cm. All the ingots were trapezoidal in section.

The slabs made of soapstone used for casting ingots of non-ferrous metals were used on quite a wide scale in Northern Europe during the Viking era. Materials relating to this subject have been examined in detail in an article by Kirpichnikov and Eniosova (2004, 290–296). It is worth pointing out that Scandinavian researchers when discussing sites, at which small moulds have been found on a mass scale (for instance, at Hedeby with 234 specimens of which 67 were intact), single out from among them small moulds, which were carved from pieces of objects that had been used previously for other purposes in so-called 'secondary moulds' (Resi 1979, 64–67). It is possible that the first small mould from Gorodishche had been just such a 'secondary' artefact. Even if we consider round recesses as moulds for casting 'counters' of a regular hemi-spherical shape, which could perfectly well have been used as blanks for jewellers' raw material, it is nevertheless still not clear what the wedge-shaped cut-out was designed for or the pared edge: they could have been traces of the preliminary working of the stone.

To this range of finds there also belong two fragments of a mould for casting ingots which were discovered at Gorodishche in 2005 (Figure 9.2.6, 7). The fragments do not fit together, but they were recorded near each other (Quadrant 61, Level 3) and without doubt were from one and same two-part mould. In both cases the width of the recess (and therefore also the ingot) was 7 mm. One fragment of the mould measured 2.75 × 3.45 cm and the recess was 4 mm deep, while the second measured 2.5 × 2.3 cm and the recess was 2.5 mm. In order to join the two parts of the recess together the usual method was probably used, namely the upper parts of the mould were coated with clay. This upper layer of clay was of a different colour and was more homogeneous.

The actual idea of storing and distributing non-ferrous metals in ingots is linked by most researchers with the North-European metal-working tradition (Kirpichnikov and Eniosova 2004, 295). It is worth mentioning that ingots of non-ferrous metals are encountered at sites in Eastern Europe far more frequently than the small moulds used for their manufacture. Whole ingots and fragments of the latter have been found at Staraya Ladoga (Davidan 1980, 62, 65, Plate 2: 1–4, 6, 7, 10), at the settlement site of Sarskoye (Leontiev 1996, 128, Figure 50: 1, 3, 4, 7–11), at Gnezdovo and Timerevo (Kirpichnikov and Eniosova 2004, 295), and at the settlement of Krutik (Golubeva and Kochkurkina 1991, 69, Figure 34.2). Mention might also be made of the hoard found at the settlement of Vyzhegsha, which was made up for the most part of 16 tin-lead ingots (14 intact ones, one fragment and a misshapen one) (Leontiev 1996, 205–207). Ingots of bronze have also been recorded at Gorodishche as well and three of these have been studied. They had all been cast in open moulds. One of the bars had been found while sorting through the in-fill at the base of a building, in which among other things a hoard of Arabic coins had been discovered, dating from the end of the 860s (Nosov 1990, 92). Two others were surface finds, which means that they might have been of a later date. The ingot found in an excavation trench measured 5.2 × 1.2 × 0.5 cm, it was segment-shaped in section and had curved edges (Figure 9.2.2). The two others differed from each other as regards type. One was a wedge-shaped ingot that had been made using a small mould (5.6 × 1.8 × 0.4 cm). On its wide side a trace of how the metal had been cut could be discerned. The second ingot (measuring 23.8 × 0.7–1 × 1 cm) was melted at one end while at the other it was still clearly trapezoidal in section, echoing the contours of the casting mould.

A close examination of the material shows that the ingots appear to have been made in both open and closed moulds. Normally, when metal was poured into an open mould, shrinkage took place and a cavity would appear in the upper surface of the ingot (see Davidan 1980, 62, Table 2: 1–4, 6, 10; Leontiev 1996, 128, Figure 50: 1, 7–11, etc.). However, in the ingots from Gorodishche, no shrinkage cavities can be seen, indicating that the quality of the casting of this material demonstrates that they had been made by professional artisans. Ingots of this quality after casting in open moulds 'are achieved on condition that the caster reduces the period of crystallization to a minimum, does not overheat the melt and heats the mould enough for the nuclei of crystals to begin to form on all sides simultaneously' (Minasyan 1994, 169). Yet the find of a small clay mould would indicate that ingots of non-ferrous metal were being cast in closed moulds, but in that case the ingots would have been round in section.

As we have already pointed out, apart from the two moulds made for casting ingots, another had also been produced which constituted one of the sides of a two-part mould designed for multiple use (Figure 9.2.3). It was made of soapstone and can also be numbered among the early artefacts. As has been pointed out convincingly by Shcheglova (2002, 134, 135), moulds of this kind were designed for 'the manufacture of small, mainly flat layered or open-work jewellery using simple geometric shapes made of tin-lead alloys involving low temperatures'. In one part of the mould impressions of the articles themselves would be cut out with the decoration on the obverse, while on the other small dents would be made for the eyelets of such items. In order to make the hole in such 'eyelets' a groove would be cut through the centre of the dent into which wire made of refractory material would be inserted, when the piece of jewellery was being cast. As far as we can tell, what was found at Gorodishche was precisely the 'reverse side' of such a casting mould. On one side the impressions for simple eyelets have been cut out, through which a groove passes, but there are no pouring channels to go with them, which means that it would have been impossible to use these moulds: on the other hand at the same time three impressions for the manufacture of fluted eyelets had been cut. Through these passed two grooves for wires and there were pouring channels. Fluted eyelets of this kind were widely used for various round zoomorphic pendants and crescent plates (Uspenskaya 1967, 107, Figure 18.1, 3; Sedova 1981, 25, Figure 6.3, 11).

An important find for shedding light on the jeweller's art as practised among the inhabitants of Gorodishche during the early period of the settlement's existence was that of half a clay mould (Figure 9.2.5). What we have is part of a side from a two-part mould, hand-moulded from clay and in the shape of a disc (diameter 4.4 cm; thickness 0.9 cm) which has been well fired: in its centre the design for a round open-work pendant has been impressed. Disk-shaped clay moulds for the manufacture of round pendants have also been recorded among the materials from the excavations at Ladoga (Davidan 1980, 61–62, Plate 2: 14, 15) and Byeloozero (Zakharov 2004, 227, 228, Figure 252.2, 3). Before the casting, in order that the two sides might close tightly, the groove between them was coated with clay, which explains why on the side edge of the disk a seam has survived at the spot where the sides of the mould were separated and a piece of clay from the coating has stuck. Although the imprint of less than half of the pendant has survived on the clay, the nature of the decoration makes it clear what the rest of the silhouette of the pendants would have been like, namely pendants of the Gnezdovo type that were decorated with Scandinavian zoomorphic motifs in the Borre style. To judge from the surviving part of the decoration, specifically from the even edge of the fluted triple ribbon, which is grasped by animal paws, the pendant is of the Riddarholmen type (Group B) according to the classification devised by Callmer (1989, 24, 27, Figure 3.25). In his opinion this type of pendant was particularly widespread in the 9th and 10th centuries within the territory of Eastern Scandinavia and Eastern Europe. When analysing mass-produced pendants from the Gnezdovo hoard, Minasyan (2002, 119–120) drew the conclusion that some of the pendants had not been made in keeping with an original model, but in keeping with a reproducible defective specimen, which had undergone slight repairs. In its turn the model from this group, after a certain amount of modification, came to provide the basis for a further series. Mass production of this kind in relation to open-work pendants indirectly demonstrated that they had been produced locally in Eastern Europe. The small casting mould found at Gorodishche demonstrates this beyond question.

In this connection three similar open-work pendants found by collectors of antiquities in the Poozerie area near Lake Ilmen and recently acquired by the Novgorod Museum are of interest. They are far from high-quality castings. Two of them were quite obviously made using impressions from replicas of an original model. Certain details of the decorative composition had not been well executed and instead of holes as part of the design, which lent pendants the lightness of open-work patterns and accentuated the interwoven zoomorphic designs, all there was to see were small misshapen round holes. The centre where they were manufactured was most probably Gorodishche.

Two-sided clay moulds were used to produce a series of objects. In order to achieve a high-quality impression in clay, it was imperative for a craftsman to have at his

 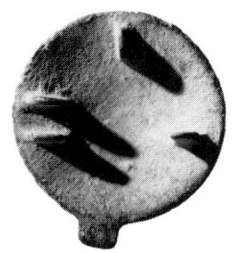

Figure 9.3 A small, round bronze brooch (Jellinge style) found as a stray find from a field within the area of Ryurik Gorodishche in 1997.

disposal either the original item or a special model (Minasyan 2002, 118,119). In view of this, an object found in 1997 by a collector of antiquities, A. N. Smetanin, in a ploughed field at the top of the hill where Gorodishche is located, becomes the focus of special interest. It was a small round bronze fibula from Scandinavia (diameter 2.7 cm), convex in profile (Figure 9.3). The basis for the decorative composition on the obverse of the fibula consisted of the bodies of two four-legged animals, stylized so that they looked like long ribbons: the bodies were elongated and interwoven to form figures of eight, so that each animal was holding the tail of the other in its open jaws. The faces of the animals were depicted in profile, their noses in the form of a loop, their eyes were ring-shaped and their ears sloped backwards. One face was slightly simpler than the other. The legs of the animals formed another interwoven pattern. The shoulders, positioned where the ribbons twisted, were picked out with a spiral pattern. The ribbons worked in relief depicted the bodies of the animals which had a decorative in-fill consisting of diagonal notches. In the centre of the decorative composition was a raised rhombus. The edge of the fibula was bordered by a thin double ribbon also decorated with notches. In general, the depiction on the obverse of the article was relatively flat. Only the legs of the animals were singled out with some degree of relief.

As regards the character of its decoration the fibula had been executed in the Jellinge style and was reminiscent of clasps from Birka of Type I AI, according to the classification devised by Jansson (1984, 60–61, Figure 8.2). What makes this fibula remarkable, however, is not the rare style of the finish, but the fact that it was never used for the original purpose for which it was designed, namely as a clasp. Two factors point to this. First, the tongue of the pouring channel had not been sawn off. Second, two plates had been cast to hold the pin in place and there was another longer one for the clasp and there was a ledge for the loop (from which the chains and pendants would have been suspended). Yet neither the ledge for the loop nor the plates for fastening the pin in place had been drilled and the plate designed for the clasp had not been bent, i.e. a virtually finished article had not been completed.

The fibula looked as if it had been taken out of the casting mould and bore no traces of subsequent working. At the same time it should be stressed that the casting of the article had been successfully carried out, particularly as regards the working of the decoration on the obverse, so this article should not be dismissed as production waste. It is also difficult to imagine that such a high-quality object had been lost immediately after its manufacture in a Gorodishche workshop.

The most acceptable explanation for the situation outlined above can be provided if this particular fibula is regarded as a model or template for casting a series of similar articles. The production of fibulae using wax models required the carrying out of a relatively difficult procedure in order to obtain a two-sided clay mould for casting (see for example Catalogue 1992, 198–199) and in the end the mould was broken. Any clay mould could only be used once. If a craftsman was using a model, then the situation became significantly simpler. With the help of the available original image, the obverse of the article complete with decoration would be impressed on one side of the clay mould and the reverse on the other. The fact that the plate of the clasp was not curved and that no attempt had been made to insert a small peg into the pin-holder demonstrate clearly that what we have here is a model for mass production. It was essential for a craftsman to mould the layered parts of a device for the pin in a clay mould, which he had indeed been trying to do, when making an impression of the reverse of the article under discussion. This made his work for moulding the second side significantly easier. If that were the case, there was justification for leaving the pouring channel without sawing it off, so as to make it clear where the pouring channel was positioned on the sides of the new mould. The model itself could have been made either on the spot in Gorodishche or it might have been brought in from Scandinavia as a special order for a local craftsman.

A special group of finds directly linked with bronze casting is made up of the failed castings for bronze jewellery, i.e. of production waste. In 1965 Korzukhina (1965, 45–46) published the fragment of a fibula found by S. N. Orlov on the Gorodishche river bank which is subject to erosion. Despite the unclear nature of the depiction on the fragment, the outlines of two heads can be traced, in the upper part that of a man with a moustache and in the lower part that of a beast facing in the opposite direction (Figure 9.4.2). By all appearances this is a failed casting of an article that the craftsman concerned did not finish working on.

Korzukhina pointed out (1965, 45–46) that there was a parallel for this particular unfinished fibula in the materials from the Gnezdovo burial-ground (Figure 9.4.1) and that the fibula itself had probably been made somewhere in Eastern Europe, since despite the typically Scandinavian motif used in the decoration, fibulae of this shape have not been recorded within the territory of Northern Europe. It is possible that the fibula from Gnezdovo had come from the workshop of Gorodishche.

Another rejected casting, most probably of a fibula of a type difficult to define, was recorded as a surface find in 1970 (Figure 9.5.1). The edges of the object were uneven and its surface was covered by dents and lumps. On the upper half, decoration could

Figure 9.4 Fibulae: 1) bronze fibula from the Gnezdovo burial-ground; 2) stray find from the riverbank at Ryurik Gorodishche of a casting of a bronze fibula.

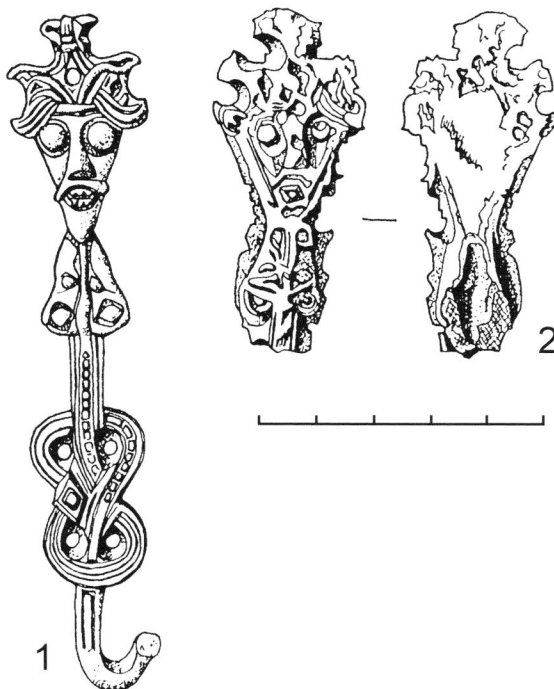

be traced consisting of interwoven ribbons worked in relief (a motif characteristic of Scandinavian jewellery) and there were two holes right through it at the sides. In the centre the outlines of an animal's face can be made out. Towards the bottom the object narrowed and in that part of it on the reverse two ledges could be discerned, which would evidently have been from the pin-holder (Nosov 1990, 157, Figure 62.6). It is unlikely that this was part of a rejected casting for an equal-armed fibula, as suggested by Nosov. The object is rather reminiscent of the fibula examined and published by Korzukhina, but its full identification remains unresolved for the present.

Among the rejected castings is a ring-shaped fibula (Figure 9.5.2) with decoration in the Borre style (Nosov 1990, Figure 44.1). It is badly blurred which suggests that the article was not made using the original, but probably a secondary replica. The fibula was found during excavations led by M. V. Shorin on the south bank of the Siversov Canal in a brown layer containing organic material, part of which was covered by wooden planking. The date given on the basis of dendrochronology for the log, on which the planking had been laid, was AD 900 (Nosov 1990, 47).

The range of objects which for some reason or other were not completed included three hooks (two of which are illustrated in Figure 9.5.3, 4) for fastening men's foot-cloths known as *onuchi* (for wearing inside boots or bast shoes: Trans). This means that they would never have been used for the originally intended function. In Birka a pair of hooks of this kind was found near the feet of a male burial (Burial No. 906) with their eyelets pointing downwards. It was assumed by those excavating the site

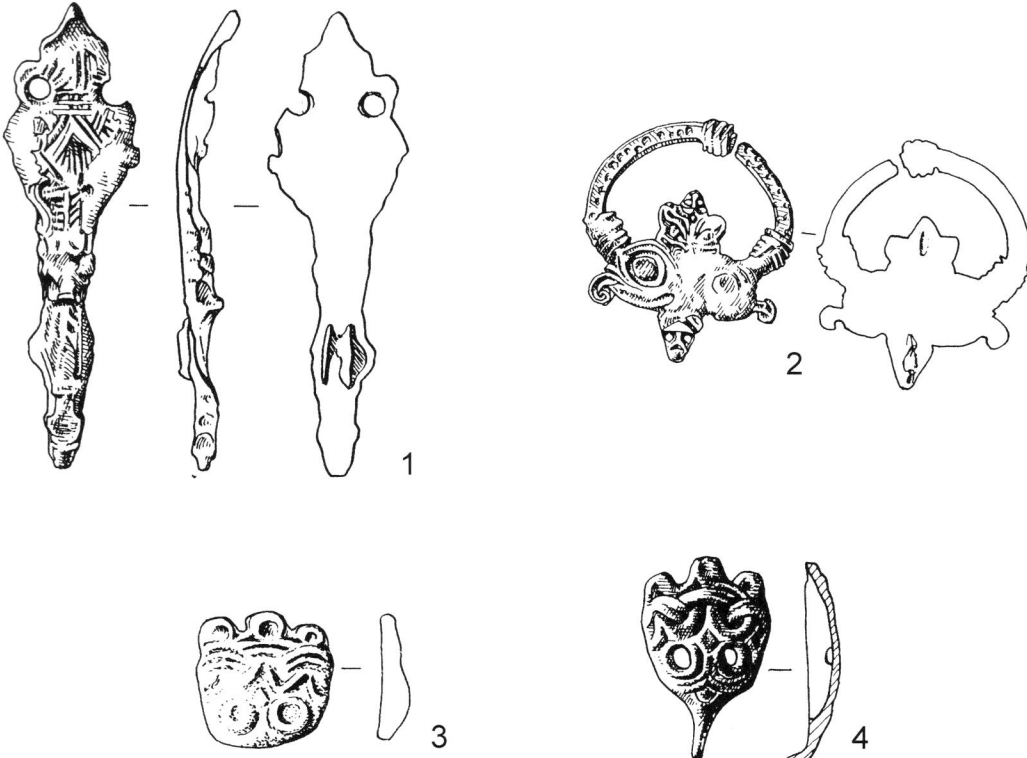

Figure 9.5 *Possible rejected copper alloy castings found at Ryurik Gorodishche: 1, 2) fibulae; 3, 4) hooks.*

that the hooks had been sewn on to the strips of the woollen foot-cloths through the eyelets and the foot-cloths in their turn would have been fastened in place using the actual hook to attach them to cloth trousers (Arbman 1943, 353, Figure 304.6). One of the hooks found at Gorodishche was discovered during excavations carried out in 1985, while the other two were surface finds.

The hook found by excavators was distinguished by the elegance of the depiction of an animal mask on it. It had evidently been repaired, since on the nose of the mask a secondary hole had been drilled and traces of soldering could be seen on the reverse. The second hook of slightly larger dimensions had been found in 1989 on the ground surface in the cape area of Gorodishche. Nosov assumed that both items had been production waste, since the first hook was without the crucial part, namely the hook itself, while the actual hook part of the second item was so thin and fragile that there would have been no point in completing work on the item (Figure 9.5.4). In the opinion of the excavator these finds 'bore witness to the manufacture of such elements of apparel on the spot in Gorodishche' (Nosov 1990, 162). However, Jansson called into doubt the local production of objects of this kind, drawing attention to the rarity

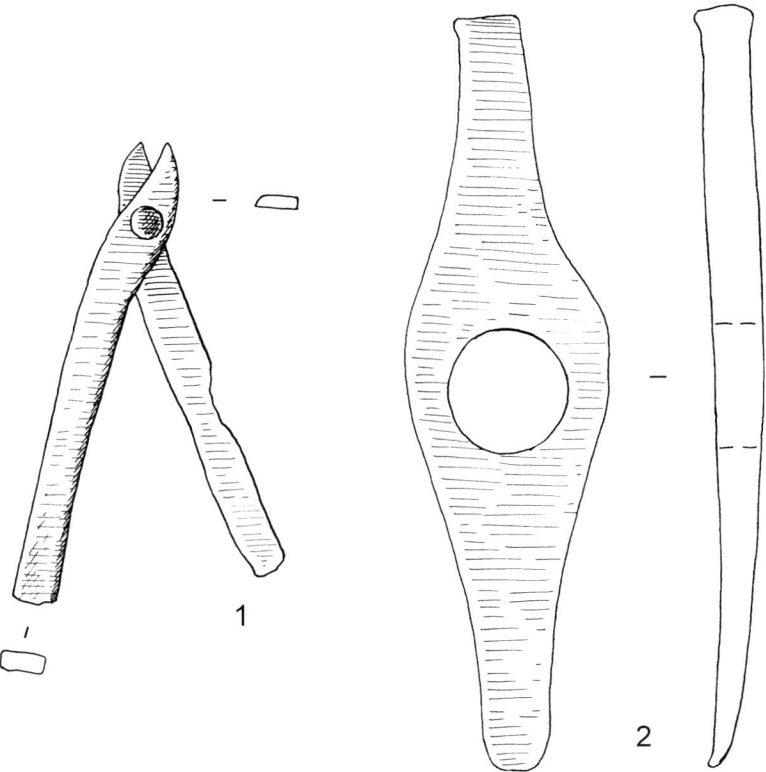

Figure 9.6 *Possible jeweller's tools found at Ryurik Gorodishche: 1) scissors and 2) hammer. The length of the scissors is 7.7 cm and the head of the hammer is 13 cm long.*

of such jewellery items, both in the territory of Scandinavia itself and also in Eastern Europe (Jansson 1999, 29). Yet an additional find made in recent years at Gorodishche rules out any doubt regarding the fact that the hooks for men's foot-cloths had been manufactured by craftsmen in Gorodishche. What we have encountered is definitely production waste. In the case of the last hook described, there had not been enough metal with which to cast it and for that reason the whole of the lower part complete with the actual hook did not materialize (Figure 9.5.3). The depiction in relief on the obverse of the mask had been executed extremely carelessly and was blurred. There is no doubt that the impression in the mould had been made using a replica of the original item and this further demonstrates that it had been produced locally.

A small iron hammer (Figure 9.6.2) and a pair of scissors (Figure 9.6.1) found in the early levels at Gorodishche have been classified as jeweller's tools. The scissors for cutting metal were found in the level immediately above the natural soil at a depth of 90–110 cm. They consisted of two halves held together by a rivet. Their extremely small size (length 7.7 cm; width of the blades 8 mm) demonstrate without doubt that the tool in question could only have been used for cutting thin sheets of non-

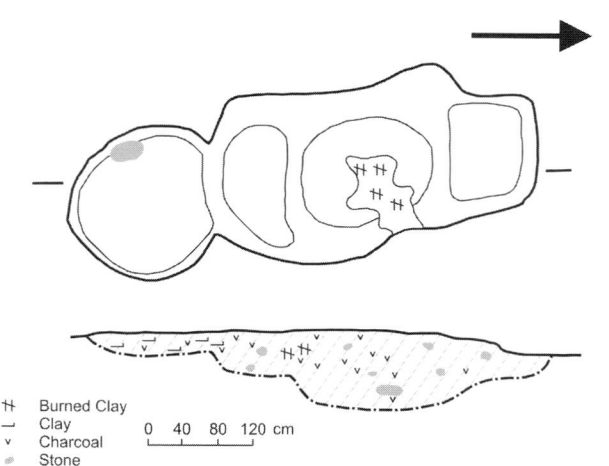

Figure 9.7 Production complex for a possible jeweller's workshop, Ryurik Gorodishche.

++ Burned Clay
—   Clay
v   Charcoal
⌀   Stone

0   40   80   120 cm

M S Dover 2010

ferrous metal. The actual shape of the scissors was extremely simple. Iron scissors of this kind, usually large in size, are encountered quite frequently, both as individual finds and also in hoards together with other metal-working tools in the territory of both Northern and Eastern Europe (Leontiev 1996, Figure 49:6; Ryabinin 1985, 59, Figure 21:2; Müller-Wille 1977, 153; Arbman 1962, 202; Catalogue 1992, Nos. 94–95). As regards measurements, scissors from the Estonian settlement of Kivivare are the closest parallels (Aun 1975, 82, Plate VIII–1).

In a level dating from the second half of the 10th century, a small iron hammer was found (length 13 cm; thickness 1 cm) with a central hole for a wooden handle (diameter 2 cm). The head of the hammer was round in shape (diameter 1.8 cm) and the top of the pin had a sharp edge rather like a chisel (width 1.7 cm). Similar small hammers were used to forge jewellery items. They are found in the collection of jewellery tools from both Novgorod and Staraya Ladoga (Ryndina 1963, 222, 223, Figure 15:4,5; Repnikov 1948, Plate 1: 22). Small hammers of similar shape were widespread in medieval Western Europe (Arbman 1962, Table 1, 2; Catalogue 1992, 250–251, Nos. 94–95; Graham Campbell 1980, No. 415).

Recent structural evidence for a jeweller's workshop

In 2006, when the central part of Gorodishche was being investigated, a group of features were found which, for the first time, could definitely be interpreted as the remains of a jeweller's workshop (Figure 9.7). Part of these features consisted of a trough-like pit 3 m long, between 1.4 and 1.6 m wide and comprising three parts. At its centre was a depression 64 cm deep and 1.6 m long. To either side of this depression, at the pit's northern and southern ends, were two smaller depressions each of approximately 70 cm in length. The north depression was 40 cm deep and the southern one 30 cm deep. On the north-eastern slope of the central depression part of a furnace was found with pieces of densely packed, fired clay surviving in places (measuring from 12–14 cm and 4–5 cm in thickness). All this appears to have been contained within a wooden structure with the furnace at the edge of the building. When the building disintegrated, the furnace appears to have slipped along the wall. To judge from the total amount of stone and clay remaining, the furnace was not large (see Figure 9.7). Furnaces of this kind were usually heated with charcoal and animal bones were sometimes added as a flux. In this regard it may be no coincidence that so many bones were found in the infill of this building. The furnace would have served for melting bronze in crucibles, unlike larger iron-smithing forges made of stones.

The main production feature therefore consisted of a pit in front of a furnace, where the smith stood, ledges up against the pit which served as work surfaces, and the furnace at the edge. The in-fill of the complex consisted of black humic material containing charcoal with inclusions of animal bones, stones and clay. On the basis of the proportions of hand-moulded and wheel-turned pottery, the assemblage may be dated to the mid-10th century, but in the opinion of the pottery specialist, V. M. Goryunova, analysis of the typology of the early wheel-turned pottery suggests a date in the last quarter of the 10th century. As regards the nature of the construction of the workshop itself that incorporated these features, little can be said, as organic remains do not survive on the hilltop of Gorodishche. Yet there is no doubt that the part of this structure that once existed above ground was longer and wider than the area occupied by the below ground features described above. The measurement of the part above ground would have been no less than 2 to 2.5 m by 4 to 4.5 m, most likely a small, log-constructed house.

Up against the south side of this structure was a small pit 1.4 m in diameter and 20 cm deep. However, it is not clear whether or not it was associated with the complex described above. A fragment of an iron, leaf-shaped arrowhead, rhomboid in section, and a round, crystal bead were found in the fill of the pit.

The production complex discussed here was reminiscent of the Type 2 installations for craft production identified by Goryunova in the manufacturing area of Gorodok on the River Lovat. In her opinion that group of buildings contained a sizeable pit, oval in plan, in front of the furnace at one of the edges of which or on a ledge a small furnace-cum-hearth had been set up. Characteristic features of constructions of this type were light roofs made of poles (Goryunova 1988, 51). In our case, the furnace was at the edge of the pit and the small steps at the side, which Goryunova describes as 'ledges in the wall', were used to work on. Similar bases for production installations oval in plan have also been identified during excavations at the settlement of Gnezdovo.

Further evidence at Gorodishche that this complex was used for non-ferrous metalworking is provided by the find of a *lyachka*, a spoon used for pouring non-ferrous metal into moulds. The handle of the spoon would have been wooden and does not survive, but the bowl was 6.6 cm long, 3.8 cm wide and 3.7 cm high. It had been very crudely made and upon closer examination was found not to have been modelled as was the common practice, but had been cut out from a piece of clay.

In addition, fragments of crucibles were found in the western part of a large, early medieval building constructed up against the north-east side of the workshop. These fragments had clearly been associated with the earlier craft complex but were found in later, mixed deposits together with material dating to the end of the first millennium AD. The dating of the complex to the 10th century on the basis of the pottery is supported by other finds, such as a half-dirham, a bronze pin from a ringed-pin (the end of which was in the shape of an animal's face in the Borre style), a fragment of a bronze oval brooch, and a bronze pin from a penannular brooch.

This production complex was located virtually on the edge of the settlement's ditched enclosure, and lying immediately outside the confines of the defences of the early fortified settlement. As work in 2007 has revealed, this area was the location of various production processes. Other material from cultural deposits of 10th century date had slipped into the ditch producing patches of stones and clay from collapsed furnaces along with numerous crucibles, slag and iron bloom.

DISCUSSION

As can be seen from the material collected from the early period of the history of Gorodishche, craftsmen were manufacturing quite complex items of Scandinavian appearance. Only clay moulds could have been used for producing them. In this connection we come up against a paradoxical situation. So far, during many years of excavation at the settlement, all that has been found is a fragment of a single clay mould for casting a round open-work pendant of a Scandinavian type. Yet during excavations at Ribe in Jutland, for instance, over 3,000 fragments of small moulds have been found (Brich Madsen 1984, 31; Jensen 1991, 34) and at Birka, during the 1991 and 1992 excavation seasons alone, more than 4,300 fragments were found (Ambrosiani et al. 1994, 115).[3] The fact is that small clay moulds were made individually and were only used for casting a single article, after which they were broken (Brich Madsen 1984, 36; Minasyan 2002, 118). It is precisely for this reason that there have been so many mould fragments in centres of production and that a range of models was essential for each craftsman, since its availability made possible serial production in the manufacture of complex items from non-ferrous metals.

What also attracts attention in this connection is that, unlike the situation in Scandinavia, clay moulds are not to be found in large numbers not only at Gorodishche, but also at other settlements in Eastern Europe (such as Staraya Ladoga, Gnezdovo, Timerevo, and Gorodok on the River Lovat). Moreover, to judge from the finds of casting rejects, crucibles and ladles, in all of those trading and craft-production centres, bronze-casting was well-developed, items of Scandinavian appearance were being manufactured, and small moulds, which constituted the most mass-scale material connected with this type of production, ought to have been present in large numbers.

Despite the hundreds of finds of crucibles and ladles and their fragments at a number of settlements in northern medieval Russia (Davidan 1980, 59–61; Kirpichnikov and Sarabyanov 2003, 65; Goryunova 1994, 61; Eniosova and Mitoyan 1999, 55), clay moulds for casting were isolated phenomena. On the basis of the data known to us, it can be pointed out that in Ladoga approximately ten moulds have been found (Davidan 1980, 59–61; Plokhov 2003, 292–304), one at Gorodishche, two at the settlement of Gorodok on the River Lovat (Goryunova 1974, 79, Figure 25.15; Goryunova 1978, 144, Figure 2.18), seven in Gnezdovo (Eniosova 1998, 74–77) and the list could be extended further. Attention has already been drawn in the academic literature to the disproportion in the correlation of fragments from clay moulds to other finds, which serve to characterize medieval jewellery production in Eastern Europe. Eniosova, for instance, noted that although stone and clay moulds for casting were being used everywhere, in the territory of the Baltic region, medieval Russia, Poland, Volga Bulgaria and the lands of the Golden Horde stone moulds predominated, while in Northern and Western Europe, on the other hand, the clay mould was more common (Eniosova 1998, 67–68). Yet, we can only agree with this interpretation of the situation in part. It is indeed the case that the Slav peoples who began settling extensive territories in Eastern Europe in the second half of the first millennium AD, unlike the Finns, the Balts and the Scandinavians, manufactured simple bronze jewellery on a small scale. Widespread among the Slavs up until the 11th century were various small and flat items of jewellery or simple convex items, which were cast in stone moulds from fusible metal. In this respect the material collected by Shcheglova (2002, 134–150) is quite revealing. As we have already pointed out, among the numerous settlements dating from the end of the first and beginning of the second millennium in Eastern Europe, those which stand out as having evidence for the production of items of Finno-Scandinavian and Baltic appearance (namely Ladoga, Gorodishche, Gorodok on the River Lovat, and Gnezdovo) are all large trade and craft centres, mainly situated on major waterways (see map, Figure 9.8).

The manufacture of certain types of three-dimensional jewellery worked in relief, which was widely used by Germanic and Finnish peoples, could not have been made in stone moulds, because it is virtually impossible to cut out interwoven zoomorphic patterns of complex design with raised parts and protruding heads even in soft stone. This means that in centres where jewellery of this kind was produced it would have been natural to expect large amounts of clay moulds: both two-piece moulds and also those consisting of one piece using the lost-wax method. There is, however, no available evidence for this.

There are a number of factors which might help to explain this situation. First, the fragments of clay moulds constitute a specific kind of archaeological material, which often consists of little more than amorphous small pieces of poorly fired clay, which easily crumble when touched and do not attract the appropriate amount of attention from researchers during excavations.[4] Moreover, they are difficult to pick out from the cultural layer, if the material from it is neither washed nor sieved. In this connection a

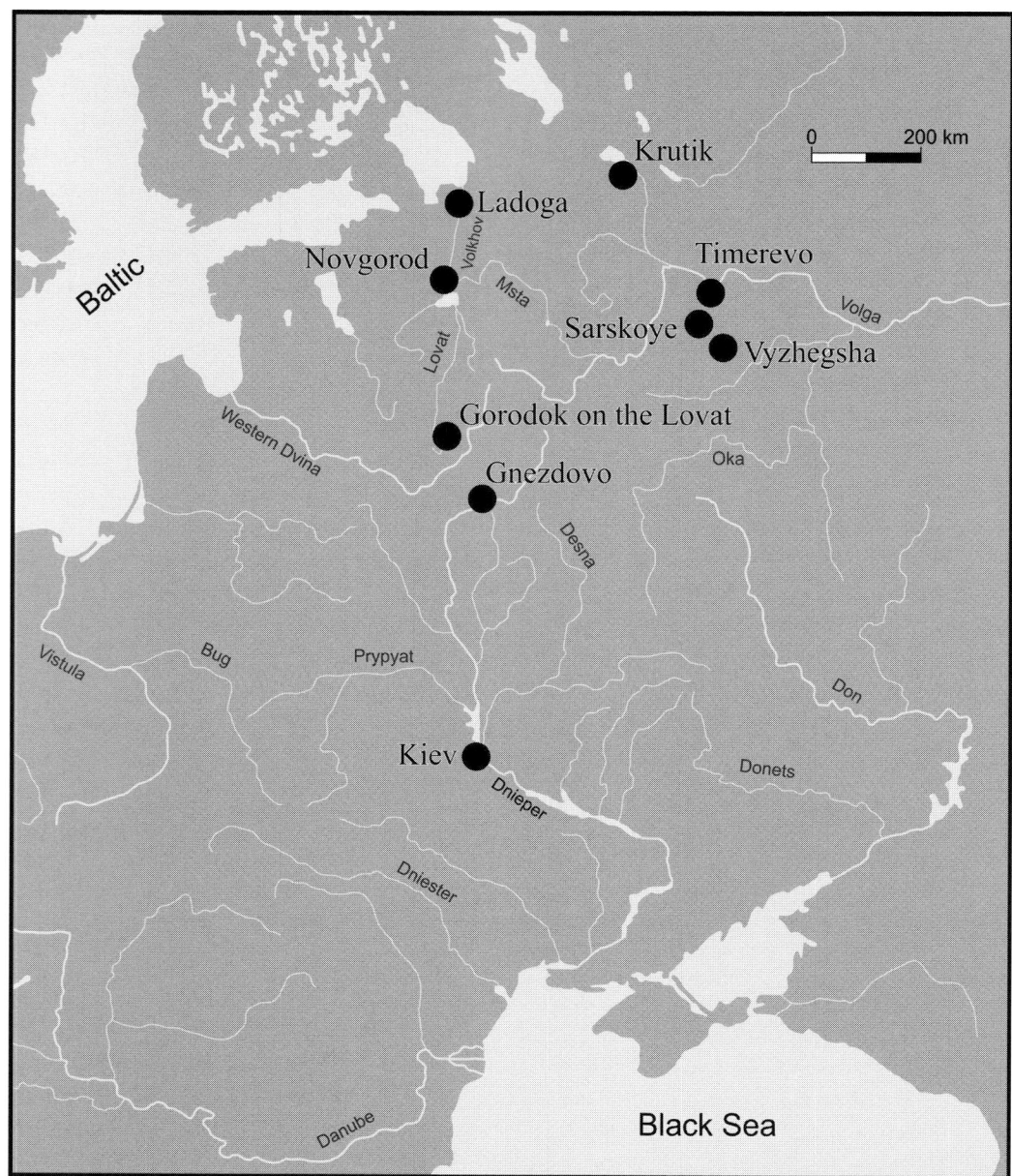

Figure 9.8 *Location map for settlements discussed in the text as having evidence for the production of items of Finno-Scandinavian and Baltic appearance.*

revealing example is provided by the case of the excavations undertaken by H. Stolpe at Birka in the 1870s, when only ten fragments of clay moulds were found. When the task of washing the in-fill from his trenches was undertaken in 1991, Ambrosiani immediately obtained more than 1,300 such fragments (Ambrosiani *et al.* 1994, 115).

It is quite clear that material from the habitation levels of many medieval settlements during investigations by Russian archaeologists is still not being washed or sieved, although in Western archaeology this practice has long been universal. Second, in settlements with a thick cultural layer (Ladoga, Gorodishche, Novgorod, etc.) small pieces of lightly fired clay become wet, which reduces them to unidentifiable fragments. Third, bronze-casting was not concentrated in all parts of a settlement and by no means at all sites. Many years of washing and sieving material from the habitation levels in the southern part of Gorodishche, at the fortified settlement of Georgii, and the settlement of Prost in the Poozerie have not yielded up materials comparable to those from Birka or Ribe. It should also be noted that in Gnezdovo four of the seven moulds were found during one and the same field-season, i.e. they would appear to have been concentrated within a particular area of the site.

This means that in the 9th and 10th centuries Gorodishche was the centre of an extensive area north of Lake Ilmen (Poozerie and the upper reaches of the Volkhov River) in which the production of articles made from non-ferrous metals was concentrated, which served to determine fashions for a significant section of the local population. It is possible that the output of the craft workers from Gorodishche spread not merely within the immediate vicinity of their production base, but also travelled far along various trade routes. At any rate the level of production skills in the settlement was quite high and corresponded both technically and technologically to those found in the early urban settlements of Eastern and Northern Europe. This fact, along with the material evidence, indicates the high social status of the population of Gorodishche. Finally, the transfer of the centre of craft production at the very end of the 10th or beginning of the 11th century from Gorodishche to Novgorod ushers in a new era in the relations between the emerging centre of Northern Russia, namely Novgorod, and its adjacent territories.

Notes

1 In all cases measurements are given in the following order: length × width × thickness.
2 The number of objects cited in the articles by Stalsberg is open to criticism: for example, she lists among the soapstone articles a small casting mould from Staraya Ladoga designed for casting ingots. In an article devoted to this mould, Kirpichnikov and Eniosova (2004, 290) point out that this particular artefact had been carved from micaceous slate. On the other hand she does not take into consideration two small moulds found at Ryurik Gorodishche.
3 Eniosova (1998, 79), in her article devoted to the cast moulds found at Gnezdovo, cites an even larger number of fragments and intact clay moulds recorded in settlements of Scandinavia.
4 A revealing example of this is the recent case when Plokhov found among pottery fragments excavated in Staraya Ladoga in 1940 a fragment of a clay mould for casting a Scandinavian 'Valkyrie' pendant, which had not been noticed during the original excavations (Plokhov 2003, 292–304).

10

FERROUS METALLURGY IN THE TERRITORY AROUND LAKE ILMEN AT THE END OF THE FIRST AND THE BEGINNING OF THE SECOND MILLENNIUM AD

S. E. Toropov

The study of questions regarding the production and processing of iron and iron-based alloys during the medieval period has long been recognized as important for the archaeology of Russia and for archaeology world-wide. Metallurgy and metal-working constituted one of the key sectors of the economy in the medieval period. The state of this sector is an indication of the general level of economic development in the medieval community at any particular period of its existence. Iron and iron-carbon alloys, steel and cast iron were and remain the most widely used metals. Apart from the physical and mechanical properties of iron, which make it a material suited to the manufacturing of tools, the popularity of iron in the medieval period stemmed from the fact that the raw material was widely available everywhere (ores from bogs, meadows and lakes) and also from the relative ease, from the technological point of view, with which it could be obtained and then processed. The last of the above-mentioned factors makes it possible to study the craft of iron-working within a narrower regional context. Narrowing down the geographical context for the purpose of our research enables us to focus closer attention on the local peculiarities of the processes involved in the emergence and development of the craft, the technology of iron production, the distribution of the finished product and so on.

Over several decades successful research has been being carried out into various aspects of iron-working in several Russian craft centres of the medieval period, first and foremost urban centres. In this work the main method used has been that of archaeological metallography (e.g. Zavyalov *et al.* 2001). A monograph by a team of authors has been devoted to the fruits of many years' research by Russian scholars: it presents the overall picture and interpretations of all the data so far amassed on the techniques and technology used for processing ferrous metals in Eastern Europe since the earliest beginnings of this craft and up until the medieval period (Terekhova *et al.* 1997).

When it comes to the study of ferrous metallurgy in medieval Russia, the situation appears slightly different. The monograph by Kolchin (1953) is to this day the only general and thorough study of this question. In the decades that followed other pieces of research were to appear summarizing the materials available in this field for specific regions of medieval Russia, mainly in the wooded steppe zone. Medieval iron-working in that region of Russia is deeply rooted in the traditions of cultures pre-dating the Russian one (Voznesenska *et al*. 1996).

The region around Lake Ilmen played a key role in the history of Novgorod and the Novgorod Lands, particularly in its early stages. Yet, at the same time, we need to recall that questions relating to the emergence and development of metallurgy and metalworking in this region during the medieval period have hardly been studied at all. Without, however, resolving those questions and identifying regional features it is impossible reliably to assess the importance of Novgorod as the most important economic centre of Northern Russia.

One of the main factors contributing to this situation is, in our opinion, the extremely meagre range of available sources. Yet traces of iron extraction and iron-working in the form of slag, pieces of charred clay coatings, ore from bogs and sometimes even fragments of metallurgical nozzles are encountered as surface finds in the habitation levels of most settlements and urban sites dating from the end of the first and beginning of the second millennium AD pertaining to the Culture of the Pskov-Novgorod Long Mounds, the *sopki* culture, or to the Medieval Russian period. Extension of the available range of sources is directly dependent upon the number of settlements and the extent of the excavations carried out. Another contributory factor is the poor state of preservation of the remains of structures for iron production, which sometimes make it impossible to interpret them correctly.

At this point in time the only available publication touching upon this subject remains a short article by Orlov (1984) devoted to archaeological research carried out within the territory of the St. Antony Monastery in Novgorod in which reference is made to some medieval rural settlements with traces of iron production.

THE SITE EVIDENCE

The purpose of this article is to introduce in a systematic way information regarding the archaeological sites dating from the end of the first and beginning of the second millennium AD, at which clear traces of metallurgical production and associated structures have been discovered in the course of archaeological investigations in the territory round Lake Ilmen. Below there follow short descriptions of these sites and the objects found at them.

The **Shilovo-X** settlement (Figure 10.1.1) situated 1.7 km south-west of the village of Shilovo in the Khvoininskii District of the Novgorod Region on the south-eastern shore of Lake Bolshoye Kuzino. It was discovered by local historian G. I. Ivanovskii in 1970 and the same year it was surveyed by S. N. Orlov (1970). In a test-pit measuring 2 × 2 m Orlov discovered Neolithic pottery, fragments of hand-moulded undecorated vessels, a significant quantity of 'impurities from bloom iron' and fragments of

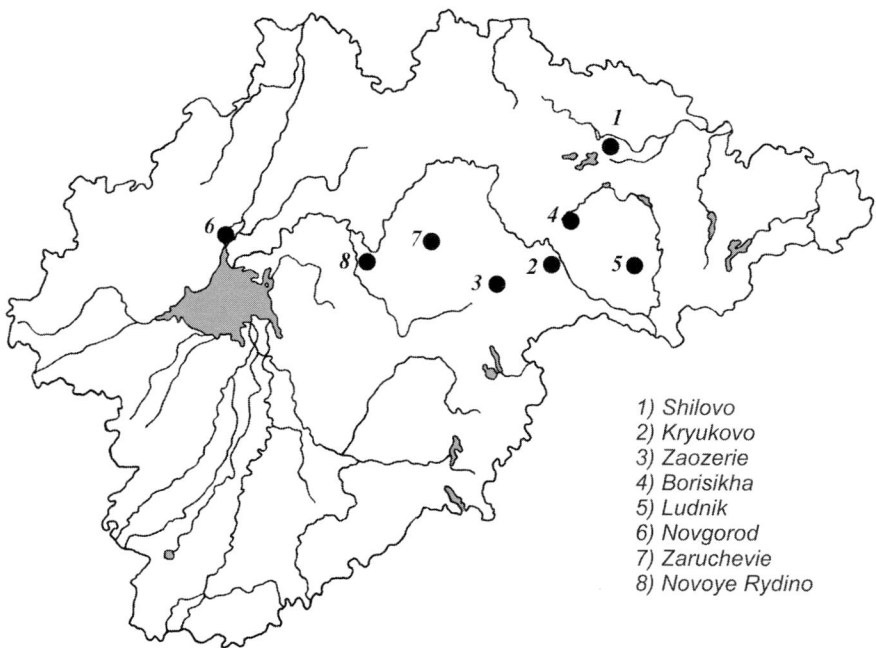

1) Shilovo
2) Kryukovo
3) Zaozerie
4) Borisikha
5) Ludnik
6) Novgorod
7) Zaruchevie
8) Novoye Rydino

Figure 10.1 *Archaeological sites of the late first and early second millennium AD with recorded remains of iron-smelting production in the area around Lake Ilmen: 1) Shilovo; 2) Kryukovo; 3) Zaozerie; 4) Borisikha; 5) Ludnik; 6) Novgorod; 7) Zaruchevie; 8) Novoye Rydino.*

medieval wheel-turned pottery. The thickness of cultural deposits did not exceed 30 cm. The territory of the settlement was ploughed thoroughly several decades ago. It is difficult to provide precise dates for the remains of metal production on the basis of data currently available. Next to the settlement there is a fortified settlement and a medieval burial ground. The overall chronological framework for the life of the site is from the Neolithic to the Late Medieval period.

A settlement by the small **Lake Kryukino** (Figure 10.1.2) situated 2–3 km east of the town of Borovichi in the Novgorod Region. It was discovered in 1958 by M. M. Alexeyev from the staff of the Novgorod Museum. The site forms part of one of the largest complexes in the territory round Lake Ilmen pertaining to the Culture of Long Mounds and contains up to 100 burial mounds. This settlement was surveyed by Orlov (1959, 1971–72) and Milkov (1988; 1989). Orlov noted the large quantity of slag in the cultural layer of the settlement, although in the most closely investigated areas, no structures linked with iron production were identified. In general the site has been assigned a date in the first millennium AD (Toropov 1997).

The group of sites near the village of **Zaozerie** (Figure 10.1.3) in the Okulovka District of the Novgorod Region, 8 km south-west of the town of Okulovka. It consists of a settlement and an area in which traces of iron-smelting and remains of a burial-ground pertaining to the Culture of Long Mounds were recorded. The sites were discovered in 1982–1985 by a Novgorod expedition under the direction of V. Y. Konetskii. In 1985–88 the same expedition carried out excavations which covered all the sites in the group to varying degrees (Konetskii 1985–1988). Work was mainly concentrated on the settlement, which extended SW–NE along the shore of the lake. Traces of large-scale metal production were recorded in the form of a solid layer of slag up to 30–40 cm thick in the north-eastern part of the settlement. Some 40 m further towards the north-east outcrops of lacustrine iron ore were discovered consisting of a monolithic layer exposed in the channel of a stream, which flowed into the lake. Given that the excavations were first and foremost of a rescue type and that the main research was concentrated in the settlement part of the site, after the upper level of the site had been excavated, the trench was conserved so as to preserve the features revealed. Along with other objects a collection of fragments from metal-working nozzles was transferred to the stores of the Novgorod Museum. The materials obtained from the excavations of the settlement, first and foremost the pottery, made it possible to limit the chronological range of the life of the settlement to the first millennium AD and to identify a number of cultural-chronological stages associated with the antiquities of the Early Iron Age, with the Culture of Long Mounds and the period of the Slavic colonization of the region. At this stage it is impossible to say with which stage in the life of the settlement the appearance and functioning of iron-smelting are associated until further field research is carried out.

The settlement at **Borisikha** (Figure 10.1.4), near the villages of Duboviki and Priozerie in the Borovichi District of the Novgorod Region, is situated on the northern shore of Lake Poleno. There are two *sopki* nearby. In 1960 the site was discovered and surveyed by Ivanovskii and Orlov. In the cultural layer of the settlement a large quantity of fragments of hand-moulded and wheel-turned pottery was discovered and also pieces of metal slag and 'smelted vitreous' clay coating (Orlov 1960). The site dates from the end of the first or early second millennium AD.

A group of late first or early second millennium sites is situated at **Ludnik** (Figure 10.1.5), located two km south of the village of Podchinnaya Sopka in the Borovichi District of the Novgorod Region, on the bank of the River Limandrovka not far from where it flows into Lake Limandrovo. The group of sites includes a settlement with traces of large-scale iron-smelting and a burial-ground consisting of one *sopka* and eight other burial-mounds. The sites were discovered in the 1960s by Ivanovskii and Orlov. In 1976 these scholars undertook small-scale rescue excavations of the settlement, in the course of which the remains of a blast furnace for the production of iron were discovered. Unfortunately, it is virtually impossible to form an opinion of its construction, as no report was compiled on these investigations. In the written sources of the Novgorod Museum only diary entries and an inventory of the finds survived. Among the latter were listed fragments of metallurgical nozzles from bellows, fragments of tiles from the base of a furnace, and hand-made pottery.[1] The finds have not survived and the sites themselves were destroyed in the course of land-improvement work in the 1980s.

St. Antony's Monastery, Novgorod (Figure 10.1.6). In the course of rescue excavations in 1973–1974 and archaeological surveys carried out in the area where new blocks of the Novgorod Pedagogical Institute within the territory of the monastery were being built, Orlov recorded the remains of mass production of iron as follows: 'Within the area studied during the excavations and in part of the trench we collected no less than 50 tons of just large pieces of iron slags and discarded blooms. Dozens of squeezed puddle balls or fragments of the latter, models for semi-finished iron ploughshares and skillets, shingling tongs and stone anvils were found. Stocks of charcoal were also discovered and a number of bases for furnaces together with pits in front of the furnaces. Piles of collapsed bricks and pieces of clay coating with melted surfaces were observed. Fragments of small blast pipes were found as well' (Orlov no date, 152). The researcher also noted that 'the production of iron here, within the territory of the monastery grounds, began no later than the 12th century, before the territory became part of the property of the St. Antony Monastery' (Orlov no date, 154). Apart from in the grounds of the above-mentioned monastery, Orlov also recorded a number of areas within the territory of the modern town of Novgorod, where the production of ferrous metallurgy might well have developed in the medieval period. These were in the flood-plain of a stream which flows into the river Vitka (in the Thirtieth Anniversary of Great October Park), near the *Byelaya Bashnya* (White Tower) in the Lyudin End and at the mouth of the River Pitba (Orlov no date, 155). Clarification of these assumptions requires additional archaeological investigations.

The above review touches upon the archaeological sites around Lake Ilmen, where clear traces of iron production had been recorded. For various reasons, however, not a single production complex was recorded. In the meantime, a further two iron-smelting centres dating from the 10th/11th century were discovered in the 1990s in the basin of the River Msta, when rescue archaeology was being carried out. We shall now describe these in more detail.

The Zaruchevie-IV settlement

The Zaruchevie-IV settlement (Figure 10.1.7) situated 2.7 to 3 km south of the village of Zaruchevie in the Okulovka district of the Novgorod Region, was the core of the largest group of archaeological sites dating from the end of the first or beginning of the second millennium AD in the basin of the River Volma, a southern tributary of the River Msta. The group of sites also includes a second settlement, a burial-ground consisting of *sopki,* isolated *sopki*, a group of burial-mounds pertaining to the Culture of the Long Mounds and a medieval Russian cemetery dating from the 11th–12th centuries. In 1979–1982, 1986 and 1989–92 rescue archaeological work was carried out by expeditions of the Novgorod Museum (led by Konetskii) and of the Institute of Philosophy of the USSR Academy of Sciences (led by Milkov) at various sites within the group before a road was built nearby (various authors, see endnote).[2]

The excavations of 1990 cleared a production zone in the outskirts of the *Zaruchevie-*

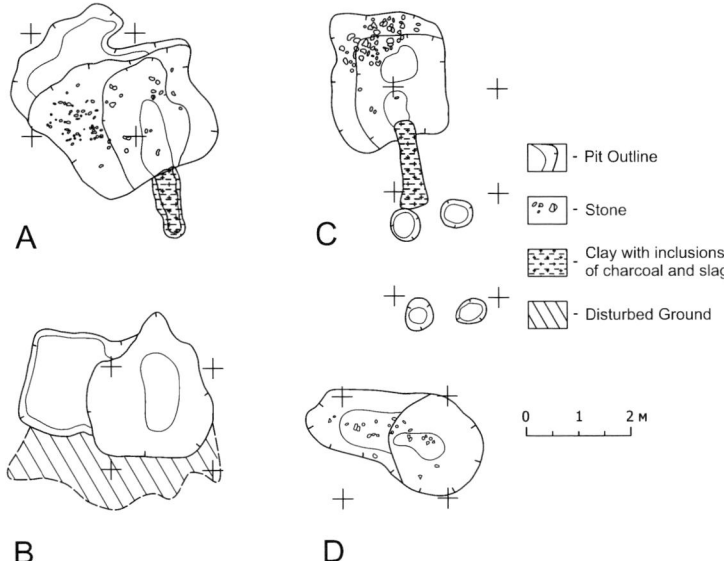

Figure 10.2 *Remains of metal-working furnaces A to D in the settlement of Zaruchevie-IV.*

IV settlement. The central, residential part of the settlement had been almost completely destroyed the year before the excavations by quarrying. In the area where excavations were carried out, the cultural layer had survived only in a fragmentary state and for this reason research was focussed on the remains of installations sunk into the natural soil. The overall area cleared in four separate trenches came to 2,012 m². A further 550 m² were cleared beyond the confines of the area containing habitation levels on the edge of a quarry that had been dug out. Within the whole cleared area 71 pits in the natural soil were recorded and 25 of these could, in our opinion, definitely be classified as belonging to installations of an industrial character (Milkov 1990).[3] There is no doubt that not all of them lend themselves to interpretation, but some clearly constitute the remains of blast furnaces for smelting iron. We shall now attempt to describe some of them on the basis of drawings and the text of the field report.

Complex 1 (Pit No. 1, Trench I) (Figure 10.2A). Of this installation all that has survived is a pit sunk into the natural soil to a depth of between 90 and 120 cm, which was roughly square in shape, measuring 2.1–2.4 × 2.6–3.2 m. The walls were in the form of uneven 'steps' and arranged so that the shorter sides of the pit had a NW–SE orientation. Up against the pit on the NW side there was a shallow step irregular in plan and measuring 2.7 × 0.9 m. Up against the pit on the SE side there was a layer of clay 40–50 cm thick, rectangular in section and elongated in shape. It measured 1.2 × 0.4–0.5 m. The upper part of the layer was charred and contained a grooved recess 15–20 cm long which was filled with small pieces of charcoal and pieces of slag.

The in-fill of the pit consisted of dense very dark sand containing a large amount of charcoal, soot, pieces of clay, slag and charred stones. Towards the bottom of the pit another layer of clay (14 cm thick) was recorded. When the in-fill was examined, 350 fragments of early wheel-turned vessels were found, a certain amount of pieces of hand-moulded pots and also a fragment of a stone globular distaff, a bi-conical distaff made of pink slate, a plate made of non-ferrous metal, an iron pin and a rhomboid iron plaque with a hole in the middle. Judging from this group of finds as a whole the installation could be given a date in the 10th or 11th century.

Complex 2 (Pits Nos. 12, 16–19, Trench II) (Figure 10.2B). It is most probable that this complex consists of the remains of an installation, which as regards its construction and functions was similar to the one described above. From this one as well a pit measuring 2 × 2.2–2.6 m had survived, which was roughly rectangular in shape, but which had straight rather than 'stepped' sides. It is possible that this function had been filled by the floor of the pit in its northern section, which was raised in comparison to the southern section. The south wall of the pit was cut through (just as in the previous case) by a layer of clay rectangular in section (35 × 50 cm) and measuring 1.7 m × 40–60 cm. Its upper part was in the shape of a groove filled with pieces of charcoal and small pieces of slag.

The in-fill of the complex consisted of dense sand containing humus and was full of charcoal, ash, burnt stones, pieces of clay coating, slag and 'bloom waste'. Near the bottom of the pit a layer of clay was also recorded. In the in-fill a rhomboid-shaped arrowhead with shaft was found and also small fragments of hand-moulded and also early wheel-turned vessels. The date assigned to the complex was similar to that used for the previous pit.

To the south of the clay groove two pairs of post-holes were cleared (Nos. 16–19), which could well have been part of an above-ground construction for this same installation.

Complex 3 (Pit No. 4, Trench II) (Figure 10.2C). Just as in the case of the two previous installations this one also consisted of a ditch roughly rectangular in shape and measuring 3.7 × 2–2.8 m, which had been let into the natural soil down to a depth of between 90 cm and 1 m. The western half in the form of a 'step' was almost rectangular in shape, measuring 1.7–1.9 × 1.6 m: it had a flat base and was 30 cm deep. It did not prove possible to establish whether a layer of clay with a groove had been located up against this pit, because the eastern edge of the pit, where it might have been, was beyond the wall of the trench.

The in-fill of the complex was complicated in structure. In the upper part it consisted of dense dark sand containing humus with inclusions of charcoal, burnt stones from a furnace, pieces of coating and slag. This layer covered over another thin layer found in both parts of the pit, a thin layer of clay mixed with charcoal, soot and small pieces of slag. The thickness of the layer was between 8 and 15 cm. In the western half of the pit this layer lay immediately above the natural soil, while in the eastern half it covered a layer of grey sand between 20 and 30 cm thick, in which a large amount of slag and bloom waste was recorded. At the very bottom of the pit a thin layer of pale sand was cleared between 17 and 30 cm thick, which was separated from the layers above it by a thin charcoal layer containing a large amount of small pieces of slag. The surface of the natural site at the bottom of the ditch had been exposed to heat.

In the in-fill of the complex 12 fragments of hand-moulded vessels were found, small undiagnostic pieces of early wheel-turned pottery, an iron plaque measuring 1 × 1.2 cm and a knife with a broken tang. On some pieces of the coating taken out of the in-fill impressions of rods 6–10 cm in diameter had survived.

Complex 4 (Pit No. 1, Trench III) (Figure 10.2D). In this instance the surviving part of the installation also consisted of a ditch let into the earth complete with a 'step', but it was of a different shape and dimensions. It was a pit elongated in plan and measuring 3.5 × 1.3–2 m extending in a W–E line. The eastern part of the ditch had been sunk into the natural soil to a depth of 90 cm. The western half, which performed the function of a 'step', was between 50 and 60 cm deep.

The lower part of the pit's in-fill consisted of dense dark sand containing humus and filled with pieces of charcoal, charred stones and slag. Further up this level was covered over by a porous layer of grey humus without any inclusions of charcoal or slag. When the in-fill was being examined, a fragment of a plate made of non-ferrous metal was found and also fragments of hand-moulded pottery.

As for the function of the installations described above, in our opinion the researcher carrying out these excavations was perfectly justified in interpreting them as 'constructions of one and the same type let into the natural soil used as iron-smelting furnaces' (Milkov 1990, sheet 38). The functions of Complexes 1 and 2 are self-evident. It is most likely that each of them was 'a dug-out pit for an iron-smelting furnace, the section of which above ground had been destroyed through ploughing…' (Milkov 1990, sheet 8). In other words these were pits in which slags were collected in front of permanent furnaces. The clay grooves served to drain away the melted slag into the slag-collector. Functionally similar slag drains have been recorded at the fortified settlement of Raikovetskoye (Molchanovskii 1934, Kolchin 1953, 29).[4] Structural features of the furnaces themselves are virtually impossible to reconstruct. All that can be said is that they were made of stones, clay, and possibly elements of a wooden frame, as can be inferred from the impressions of poles on surviving pieces of the clay coating. In Complex No. 2, next to the slag drain, four pits were recorded which contained traces of posts that could have served to strengthen the furnace walls or to support some other kind of structure.

Interpretation of Complexes 3 and 4 are bound, in our opinion, to be more ambiguous. On the one hand, they do not differ fundamentally from Complexes 1 and 2 and it would appear that they performed the same functions as the slag-drains in front of stationary furnaces located above ground. At the same time they do not incorporate any such important structural elements as channels for draining off slag. Other features worth noting are traces of the natural soil having been exposed to heat in the pit of Complex 3, which had not been recorded in any other cases and the elongated shape of the pit for the slag collector in Complex 4. The range of finds from the in-fill of Complexes 3 and 4 is also different. While in Complexes 1 and 2 early wheel-turned pottery predominated, in the in-fill of the pits from Complexes 3 and 4 there were far more fragments of hand-moulded vessels, which might indirectly testify to their earlier date.

It is therefore highly probable that the complexes described above constitute different variants in the evolution of one and the same type of permanent metallurgical furnace built above ground commonly found in the given region in the 10th and 11th centuries.

Another structure linked with the technological process of metal production was discovered at the very edge of the settlement in Area VI (Milkov 1990, sheet 37–38). It was a pit of rectangular outline measuring 2.8 × 2.1 m and 40 cm deep with a SW-NE orientation. The upper part of its in-fill consisted of dense black sand and along the flat floor of the pit and up its walls over the whole area there was 'a burnt level containing small burnt pieces of metal. The level containing charcoal was between 50 cm and 1 m thick. Below that it was visible everywhere that the natural soil had been exposed to heat. No artefacts or pottery were discovered here' (Milkov 1990, sheet 38). It is highly likely that the installation in question was a pit for burning charcoal.

We have described only part of the production complexes which have been discovered at the *Zaruchevie IV* settlement. The interpretation of the other installations would require that specialized research be undertaken and that is not the task we have set ourselves here.

Sites near the village of Novoye Rydino

A furnace of a different structure but relating to the same epoch was investigated in 1999 by an expedition led by the author of this article working at a settlement near the village of Novoye Rydino in the Krestetskii District of the Novgorod Region (Figures 10.1.8, 10.3).The group of archaeological sites near the village of Novoye Rydino is situated in the lower reaches of another tributary of the River Msta, known as the River Kholova. It consists of a multi-level settlement, a burial-ground containing six large burial-mounds and also a group of two *sopka*-like mounds and a small burial-mound. The settlement located at the eastern edge of the modern centre of population on the steep left bank of the River Kholova was an important local centre at the end of the first millennium AD and the beginning of the second millennium. Its high status is borne out by data in the written sources and also by the find of a seal from the Prince's administration dating from the late 12th or early-13th century.[5] The thickness of the habitation levels in the settlement were as much as 80–90 cm, of which 20–40 cm were untouched levels dating from the 10th–13th centuries.

Research carried out in 1999 was confined to rescue-archaeology work. A small trench with a total area of 70 m² was let into the part of the settlement next to the river bank, which had been badly damaged by floods. The cultural layer in this particular area was full of inclusions of charcoal, burnt clay, pieces of slag and clay coating. Remains of the furnace above ground were recorded in the cultural layer within a radius of 4–6 m from the centre of the installation in the form of layers and 'lenses'

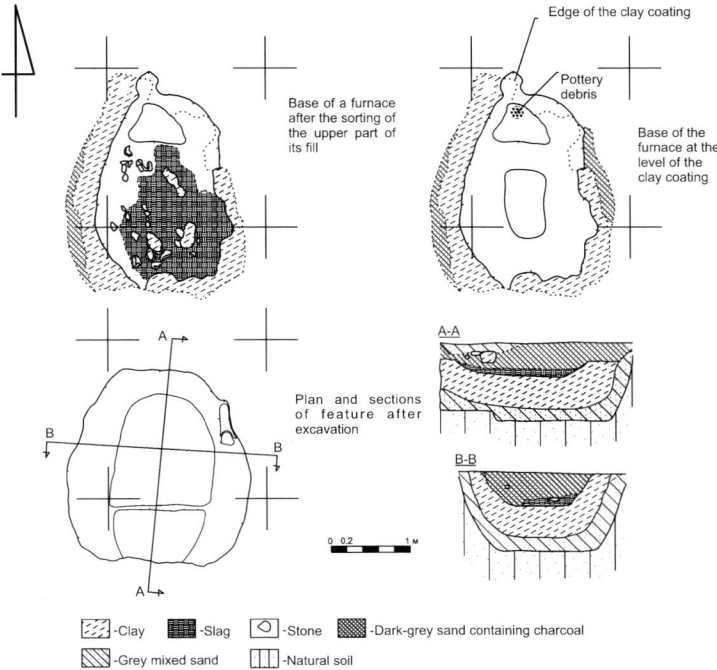

Figure 10.3 *Plans and sections of a blast furnace in the settlement of Novoye Rydino.*

of burnt clay containing a large amount of stones, also isolated clusters of charred stones. The base of the furnace at a level immediately above the natural soil could be made out as a system of stains, among which the base of the walls for the dome of the furnace was identified in the form of a 'horseshoe' measuring 2 × 2.8 m.

The base of the installation had been laid out in a pit 80–90 cm deep. The shape of the pit in plan was approximately oval. The long axis was orientated along an N–S line. The external measurements were 1.2–2.3 × 2.4 m. The base was flat with a small 'step' in its southern part. The measurements of the base were 2.1 × 0.9–1.3 m and the height of the step was 10–12 cm. The southern edge of the ditch had been destroyed when the river bank collapsed: the north-east corner had been cut across slightly by a large pit of evidently later origin.

The main in-fill of the pit in its upper part was a dense dark-grey sand containing humus and filled with inclusions of charcoal, pieces of metallurgical slag and slag-covered clay coating. In the upper part of the in-fill in the southern half of the trench a layer of grey-yellow mixed sand was noted, which was 13–15 cm thick. For an analysis of slag and clay fragments from this site, see Martinón-Torres and Rehren, this volume.

When the dark-grey in-fill containing charcoal was examined, in the south and central parts of the pit some scattered stones measuring 4–15 cm and 'islands' of charred clay were recorded. Under the dark-grey in-fill in the south-east and central

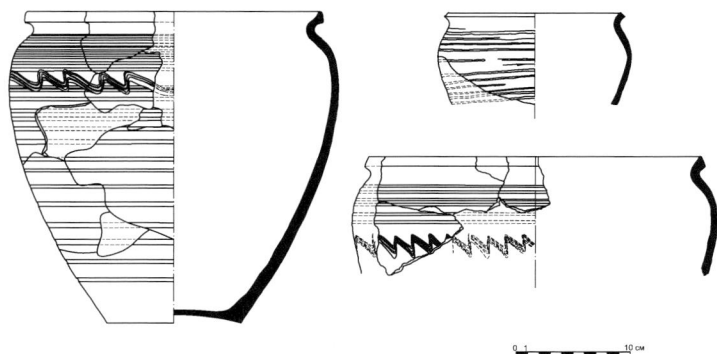

Figure 10.4 Pottery from the clay level in the settlement near the village of Novoye Rydino.

parts of the furnace a melted mass of metallurgical slag was recorded in the form of a lens measuring 1.4 × 1.6 m and 20 cm thick. The base and the walls of the pit were covered with a solid layer of clay 18–40 cm thick on the walls and 36–56 cm thick at the base. In the north part of the pit the layer of clay formed a ledge measuring 50 × 70 cm and 20–30 cm high. The nature of the surface of the clay level bears witness to the fact that it had been exposed to high temperatures.

Between the level of the clay and the walls of the pit a thin layer of grey-yellow mixed sand was recorded the thickness of which was between 6–8 and 25 cm. It had probably taken shape during the construction of the installation. Individual finds from within the in-fill of the trench were two indeterminate objects made of ferrous metal, a whetstone and two fragments of clay air-blast nozzles. The pottery finds consisted of 59 fragments of hand-moulded and 628 fragments of wheel-turned vessels. In the layer of the clay coating in the north part of the pit pieces from a further three early wheel-turned vessels were found (Figure 10.4), which had perhaps been deliberately broken during the construction of the furnace. On the basis of the nature of the pottery material and the stratigraphy in this part of the site the installation was dated to the 11th century.

It is probable that this had been a stationary blast furnace of large capacity.[6] Given that its lower section had been let well into the natural soil, we can assume that there had been a large pit with a slag collector in front of the furnace essential for letting out the slag and making it easier for the furnace to function. The pit in front of the furnace could have been on the south side of the installation, but then destroyed by erosion of the river bank. The placing of the working area of the furnace below the level of the ground surface was a deliberate step on the part of its builders, since it probably enabled them to increase the draught, reduce the height of the installation above ground, further to consolidate the walls of the furnace and facilitate access to the vent at the top of the furnace.

The construction in the 11th century of a technologically fairly complex installation, evidently designed for long-term exploitation bears out the status of this particular site as a local centre in the early medieval period and confirms the fairly high level of development of iron-working at this time.

When drawing this review to a conclusion, it is essential to point out that further study of the history of ferrous metallurgy and iron-working in rural settlements around Lake Ilmen at the end of the first and beginning of the second millennium AD will significantly extend our picture of the nature and level of craft production in the region as a whole. At the current stage of research, efforts should concentrate on extending the data base of these types of sites.

Notes

1   'Inventory of archaeological finds from the rescue excavations in the Borovichi District, Novgorod Region near the village of Pochinnaya Sopka at Ludnik in 1976', *OPI NGOMZ* (Dept of Written Sources in the Novgorod State Regional Museum and Historical Reserve), File 10, Inventory 1, Storage Unit 72, K.P. 38136 (142–143).

2   V. Y. Konetskii, (1) 1979: 'Report on work carried out within the Novgorod Region', *Arkhiv IA RAN* (Archive of the Institute of Archaeology of the Russian Academy of Sciences), P. 1, No. 7895; (2) 1980: 'Report on research carried out by the Novgorod Museum', *Arkhiv IA RAN* (Archive of the USSR Academy of Sciences), P.1, No. 8573; (3) 1981: 'Report on research carried out by the Novgorod Museum', *Arkhiv IA RAN* (Archive of the Institute of Archaeology of the Russian Academy of Sciences), P.1, No. 8514; (4) 1982: 'Report on research carried out by the Novgorod Museum in 1982', *Arkhiv IA Ran* (Archive of the Institute of Archaeology of the Russian Academy of Sciences), P.1, No. 9067.

   V. V. Milkov (1) 1980: 'Report on the conduct of Archaeological Work in the Novgorod Region by a team from the Novgorod Museum', *Arkhiv IA RAN* (Archive of the Institute of Archaeology of the Russian Academy of Sciences), P.1, No. 7741; (2) 1986: 'Report on the conduct of Archaeological Work in the Novgorod Region by a team from the Novgorod Museum', *Arkhiv IA RAN* (Archive of the Institute of Archaeology of the Russian Academy of Sciences), P.1, No. 11561; (3) 'Report on the conduct of the Excavation of the Archaeological Complex near the village of Pleso-Poterpelitsa in the Borovichi District'; (4) 1990: 'Report on the conduct of Excavations of the destroyed burial-mounds and settlement not yet fully investigated near the village of Zaruchevie in the Okulovka District and of the destroyed burial-mounds near the village of Dregli in the Lyubytinskii District and on the reconnaissance work carried out in the Khvoininskii and Borovichi Districts of the Novgorod Region', *Arkhiv IA RAN* (Archive of the Institute of Archaeology of the Russian Academy of Sciences), P.1, No. 15069; (5) 1991: 'Report on the conduct of Archaeological work in 1991 (excavation of the burial-ground near the village of Zaruchevie in the Okulovka District , *sopki* near the villages of Brod-Luchki in the Valdai District, the burial-ground near the village of Dregli in the Lyubytinskii District and reconnaissance work in the Khvoininskii, Borovichi and Kholmskii Districts)', *Arkhiv IA RAN* (Archive of the Institute of Archaeology of the Russian Academy of Sciences), P.1, No. 16655; (6) 1992: 'Report on the conduct of Excavations of the Burial-ground near the village of Zaruchevie in the Okulovka District and on reconnaissance work in the Borovichi, Khvoininskii and Valdai Distri cts in 1992', *Arkhiv IA RAN* (Archive of the Institute of Archaeology of the Russian Academy of Sciences), P. 1, No. 17667.

   A. A. Frolov, S. V. Mesnyankin, S. E. Toropov 1995: 'Some Findings from archaeological research in the vicinity of the villages of Zaruchevie and Bor (Okulovka District)', *Novgorod i Novgorodskaya zemlya* (Novgorod and the Novgorod Lands. History and Archaeology Series), Issue 9, Novgorod, pp. 71–82.

3   For Trench 1 these were Pits Nos. 1–2; for Trench II, Pits Nos. 2–4, 10–12, 15–19; for Trench III, Pits Nos. 1–2, 18–24, 25; for Area VI, Pit No. 1. See: V. V. Milkov, 'Report for 1990', Sheets 5–39.

4   F. N. Molchanovskii, 1934 'Metal-working in the Ukraine in the 12th and 13th centuries based on materials from the fortified settlement of Raikovetskoye', *PIDO* (Questions on the History of Pre-Capitalist Societies), No. 4, p. 86.

5   For more detail on the group of sites near the village of Novoye Rydino, see: V. Y. Konetskii, 1995: 'Questions and Prospects for Micro-regional Historical-Archaeological Research (taking as an example the lower reaches of the River Kholova)', *Proshloye Novgoroda i Novgorodskoi zemli* (The Past of Novgorod and the Novgorod Lands), 1995, 7–9.

   E. V. Toropova, 1998 'Report on rescue-archaeology excavations near the village of Novoye Rydino in the Krestsy District of the Novgorod Region in 1998', *Arkhiv IA RAN* (Archive of the Institute of Archaeology of the Russian Academy of Sciences); S. E. Toropov, 1999 'Report on the rescue-archaeology excavations near the village of Novoye Rydino in the Krestsy District of the Novgorod Region in 1999', *Arkhiv IA RAN* (Archive of the Institute of Archaeology of the Russian Academy of Sciences); I. Y. Ankudinov, 1999 'A Historical-geographical commentary on Novgorod Birch-bark Document No. 390', *Ocherki feodalnoi Rossii* (Essays on Feudal Russia), Issue 4, Moscow; S. E. Toropov and E. V. Toropova 2000 'Excavation of a Medieval Russian Settlement near the village of Novoye Rydino in 1999', *Novgorod i Novgorodskaya zemlya* (Novgorod and the Novgorod Lands), Novgorod, 54–56.

6   But for an alternative view on whether or not this site presents evidence for a blast furnace, see the article by Martinón-Torres and Rehren, this volume [editors].

11

ANALYTICAL STUDY OF IRON SLAG FROM THE NOVGOROD HINTERLAND

M. Martinón-Torres and Th. Rehren

INTRODUCTION

The hinterland of Novgorod is known to have provided much iron in the past, most likely smelted with the traditional bloomery process. In an attempt to learn more about the technical detail of the smelting process we analysed several slag samples collected near an excavated furnace site in the Novgorod Region. This report presents the analytical results of optical microscopy, scanning electron microscopy with energy-dispersive spectrometry, and X-ray fluorescence spectrometry. The interpretation concludes that the slag originates from a typical bloomery process, smelting a very clean iron ore. This result matches the metallographic investigation of iron objects from medieval Novgorod (Jeffery and Rehren, this volume), and fits well into the general understanding of early iron production in northern Europe.

Approximately two kg of slag were collected for sampling and analysis through field walking from the fields immediately surrounding the excavation site of the medieval furnace near Novoye Rydino village, Krestetskii District, in the Novgorod Region (see Toropov, this volume). It is uncertain whether they all belong to the same production period or represent different phases of activity on the site, but they are all likely to be from local metal production. A few fragments had burnt clay attached to them, probably fragments of the furnace structure; several sherds of domestic pottery were collected as well, but not included in the analysis here.

The slag fragments mostly consisted of dark brown to black fragments of a maximum weight of 60 g, some of them with a brown shade but none severely rusty. They are rather dense but contain some rounded or elongated vesicles. They often show charcoal impressions or, occasionally, small fragments of charcoal or burnt clay adhering to them. Their surface generally shows no clear flow structure. Only a few smaller slag samples showed a shinier look and a flow-like texture. The size and scarcity of the latter suggest that they are drips solidifying inside the furnace rather than deliberate tap slag. Overall, their morphology suggests that the slags formed and solidified inside a furnace; indications of slag tapping are absent (Figure 11.1).

Five slag fragments and one sample of vitrified clay were selected as representative and subjected to instrumental analyses. For bulk quantitative chemical compositions,

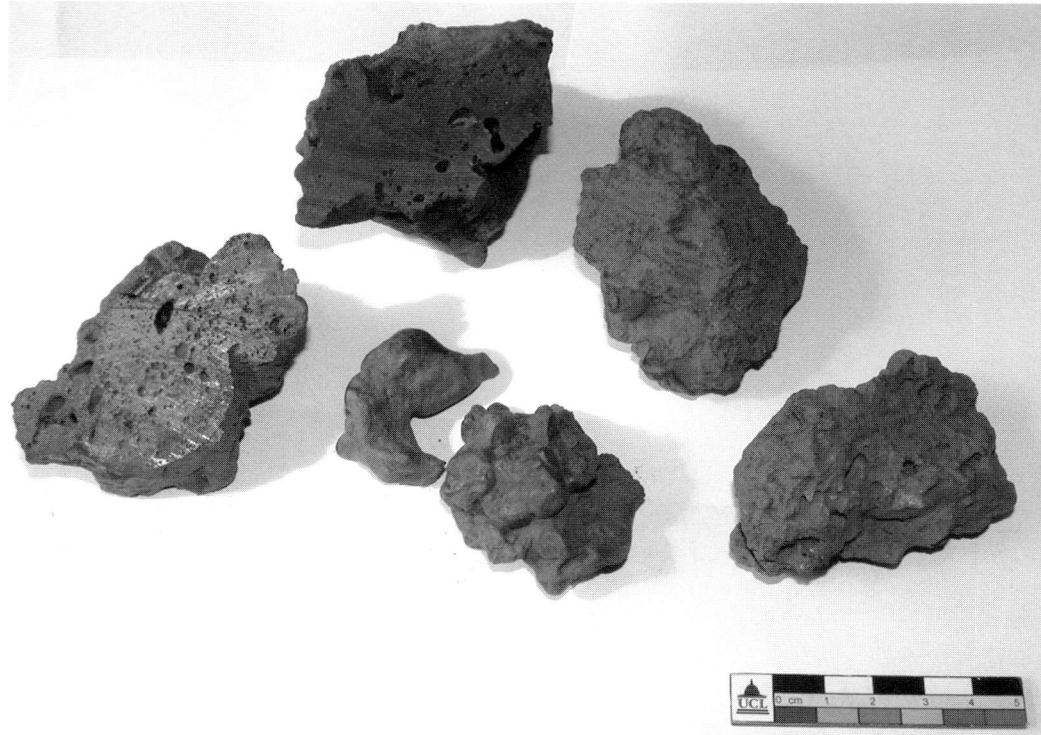

Figure 11.1 Some of the slag fragments. The samples sectioned from the left are No. 3 and No. 4. Note the shinier, flow-like samples in the centre.

the slag samples were prepared as pressed powder pellets mixed with wax, and analysed by polarising energy dispersive X-ray fluorescence (ED-XRF), using a Spectro Lab XPro 2000 instrument, and an evaluation method optimised for iron-rich materials (cf. Veldhuijzen 2003). Three of the slag samples, and one of the vitrified ceramics, were also mounted in epoxy resin and polished for optical and electron microscopy. A Philips XL30 scanning electron microscope with an attached Oxford Instruments energy-dispersive X-ray microanalyser (SEM-EDS) was employed for imaging and phase analysis. The XRF and SEM-EDS data is reported as element oxides with oxygen determined by stoichiometry. The XRF data then is reported as measured, while the SEM-EDS data is normalised to 100 wt% to account for variation in beam intensity and sample porosity.

RESULTS

All the slag samples analysed showed high FeO levels, around 75 wt%, and between 15 and 20 wt% SiO_2 (see Table 11.1). This means that the slag would have had a low

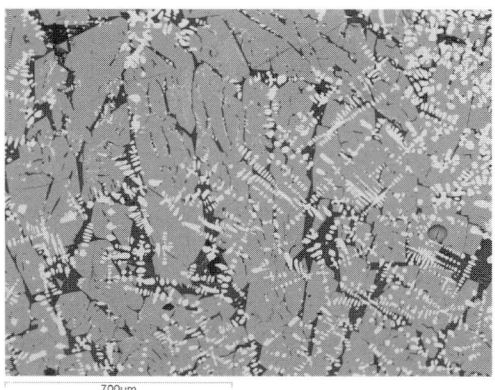

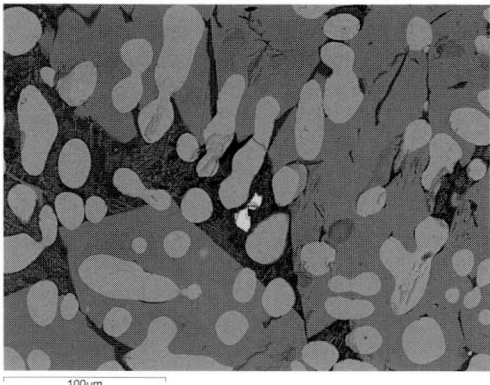

Figure 11.2 *Microstructure of slag sample of the first group, showing elongated fayalite with some skeletal features (light grey) cut across by dendritic wüstite (white). (No. 3, BSE, 80×).*

Figure 11.3 *Detail of the microstructure of slag sample No. 2, showing slightly elongated, blocky fayalite (mid grey) and rounded wüstite (light grey). Note the barite inclusion (white) in the glassy matrix (No. 2, BSE, 400×).*

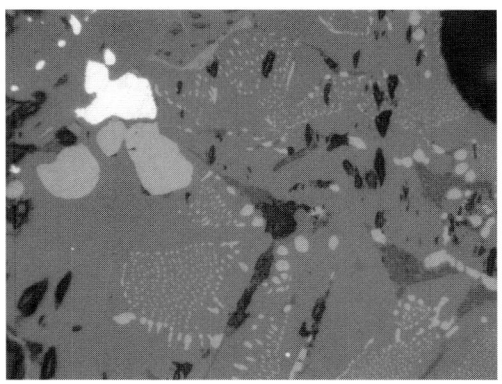

Figure 11.4 *Detail of metallic iron (bright white) and eutectoid intergrowth between wüstite (light grey) and fayalite (mid grey). Dark grey is glassy matrix and black areas are voids. The bluish grey streak near the iron is probably iron hydroxide resulting from corrosion. (No. 2, PPL, 200× enlarged, width of image is ~300 μm).*

viscosity and hence easily separate from the metal, although at the expense of keeping a considerable amount of iron oxide from the ore in the slag. In addition, they show moderate to low amounts of alumina (<2.5 wt%), lime (2 wt%) and potash (<1 wt%), reflecting a relatively limited contribution of furnace lining and fuel ash to the slag formation. Soda and magnesia are below half a percent each. On the basis of their manganese, phosphorous and barium content, however, the slag samples analysed can be separated in two groups, which appeared macroscopically undistinguishable.

The first group is comprised of samples Nos. 2, 3 and 5, which fall in a very narrow compositional range, where the concentration of the diagnostic oxides is very low (see Table 11.1). Phosphate is below 2 wt%, manganese oxide is below half a percent and the barium content is in the ppm range for all three samples.

Their microstructure, as observed in specimens Nos. 2 and 3, is rather similar to

	Na₂O	MgO	Al₂O₃	SiO₂	P₂O₅	SO₃	K₂O	CaO	TiO₂	V₂O₅	Cr₂O₃	MnO
	%	%	%	%	%	%	%	%	%	%	%	%
NOVG #2	0.37	0.49	2.23	20.65	1.28	0.06	0.76	1.73	0.1	-	0.01	0.28
NOVG #3	0.42	0.29	2.42	21.53	0.86	0.1	0.77	1.04	0.08	-	0.01	0.23
NOVG #5	0.34	0.28	2.05	19.96	1.8	0.09	0.41	0.96	0.07	-	0.01	0.25
NOVG #1	0.48	0.31	2.07	17.87	4.72	0.11	0.85	1.54	0.1	0.02	0.02	1.05
NOVG #4	0.12	0.25	1.61	13.83	3.1	0.17	0.68	1.82	0	0.04	0.03	18.26
BCS-CRM 301-1 (reference)	0.07	1.73	4.26	7.4	0.8	1	0.32	22.6	0.16	-	-	1.25
BCS-CRM 301-1 (XRF)	-	1.37	4.11	7.4	0.68	0.55	0.33	20.68	0.12	0.09	0.02	1.12
ECRM 681-1 (reference)	0.09	1.48	10.62	17.81	2.02	0.26	0.59	3.92	0.49	0.14	0.06	0.28
ECRM 681-1 (XRF)	0.34	1.17	11.92	17.26	1.96	0.34	0.54	3.65	0.39	0.13	0.07	0.27

	FeO	NiO	CuO	ZnO	SrO	Y₂O₃	ZrO₂	BaO	CeO₂	Nd₂O₃	TOTAL
	%	ppm	ppm	ppm	ppm	ppm	ppm	ppm	ppm	ppm	
NOVG #2	76.73	-	43	23	35	13	128	425	25	-	104.75
NOVG #3	74.97	-	28	18	31	10	87	217	11	-	102.74
NOVG #5	79.08	-	42	25	4	17	102	263	16	-	105.31
NOVG #1	74.58	-	15	18	23	60	185	2076	44	38	103.91
NOVG #4	71.53	32	0	107	58	77	138	33659	55	1121	114.46
BCS-CRM 301-1 (reference)	30.63	-	-	-	-	-	-	-	-	-	70.22
BCS-CRM 301-1 (XRF)	31.61	73	14	157	287	70	122	48	163	-	68.09
ECRM 681-1 (reference)	42.74	204	-	-	-	-	-	-	-	-	80.50
ECRM 681-1 (XRF)	42.11	40	6	388	1161	131	343	142	445	115	80.17

Table 11.1 (*opposite*) *Chemical composition of the slag samples from Novgorod as obtained by ED-XRF. The bottom rows present a comparison of the certified values and the analytical results for standard reference materials, shown here to illustrate the instrument's accuracy. All results given are averages of three measurements made on pressed powder pellets of the relevant samples (continued on the facing page).*

each other and typical of iron smelting slags (Bachmann 1992, 30–33). They consist of mostly fayalite, with small wüstite dendrites, sometimes containing minor amounts of silica, alumina and/or titania, and occupying up to 40 vol% of the specimens observed. In addition, there are some regions of eutectoid intergrowth of fayalite and wüstite, and small particles of metallic iron. In some areas, the dendritic structure of the wüstite is preserved, but the iron was reduced to metal (and, in some cases, subsequently corroded to iron hydroxide by post-depositional processes). This observation supports the original interpretation of these as furnace slag from solid-state iron smelting, the bloomery process (see Pleiner 2000; Nørbach 2003; Joosten 2004) (Figures 11.2–4).

Fayalite grains show a relatively elongated shape and partly skeletal structure, especially in No. 2. This feature, together with the small size of the dendrite arms of the wüstite, indicates a relatively fast cooling, despite the fact that some of these samples preserved clay fragments still adhering to them, presumably from the furnace wall. This may be taken as an indication that the furnace was dismantled in order to retrieve the iron bloom, hence allowing cool air to enter and a much quicker solidification of the slag inside the furnace. Fayalite crystals contain minor concentrations of magnesia and lime, but elements such as alumina, phosphate, lime and potash are mostly concentrated in the glassy matrix, where iron oxide and silica levels are around 30 wt% each, and alumina and lime appear in concentrations around or above 10 wt% each (Figures 11.2–4, Tables 11.2–3).

The second group is formed by specimens Nos. 1 and 4. Compositionally, they stand out in their higher manganese oxide concentrations, which appear directly proportional to the higher barium levels. Phosphate is also higher than in the previous group (≥3 wt%), and so are impurities at the trace level such as vanadium, yttrium and neodymium. This is compensated by a lower bulk silica concentration, well below 20 wt% (see Table 11.1).

The microstructure of specimen No. 1 shows what seem to be two different layers of deposition within the furnace, which can also be noticed macroscopically in cross section. One contains feathery to skeletal grains of fayalite and dendritic wüstite, indicative of a relatively fast cooling, and may correspond to the last steps of smelting

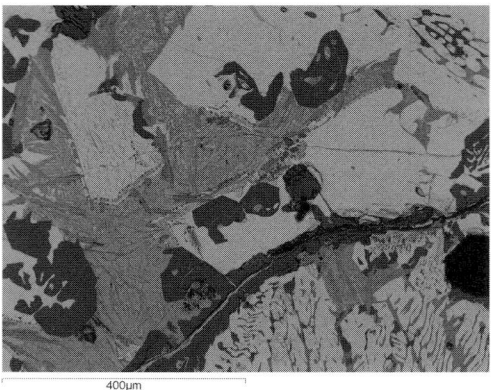

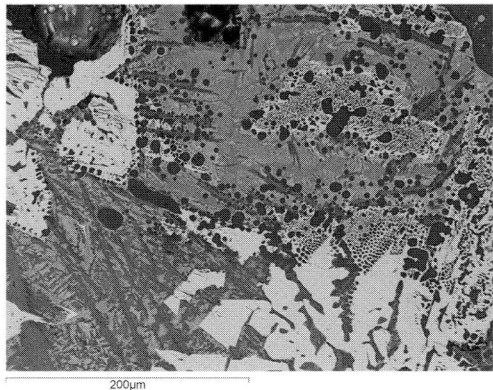

Figure 11.5 *Detail of slag from the second group showing interface between two layers. The bottom layer (probably deposited later) shows skeletal grains of fayalite (light grey). The top layer shows more developed crystals of fayalite with subhedral leucite (dark grey) on the grain boundaries. Note the presence of acicular iron-rich calcium phosphates (mid grey) within the glassy matrix (No. 1, BSE, 150×).*

Figure 11.6 *Detail of the microstructure of No. 1, showing a liquid-liquid separation, with un-mixing of a leucitic melt (see darkest phases), following the crystallisation of fayalite (light grey) (No. 1, BSE, 300×).*

Figure 11.7 *Section through a furnace wall fragment, showing increasing vitrification and bloating by high temperatures towards the inner surface (right), as seen in the large bloating pores (Sample No. 6, maximum width 2.5 cm).*

	Na₂O	MgO	Al₂O₃	SiO₂	P₂O₅	K₂O	CaO	FeO
Wüstite			0.5	0.2				99
Fayalite		1.0		30			0.3	69
Fayalite		0.8		30			0.5	68
Glassy matrix	2.3		16	38	4.4	7.3	8.7	23
Glassy matrix	0.8		17	40	2.9	11.3	6.4	22

Table 11.2 SEM-EDS analytical results for some phases shown in Figure 11.2.

	Na₂O	MgO	Al₂O₃	SiO₂	P₂O₅	SO₃	K₂O	CaO	FeO	SrO	BaO
Barite						34			3	5.3	58
Wüstite			0.6	0.6					98		
Fayalite		1.0	31	31				0.5	68		
Fayalite		1.0	31	31				0.5	67		
Glassy matrix	0.9	12.8	7.2	35	7.2		5.8	10.4	28		

Table 11.3 SEM-EDS analytical results for some of the phases illustrated in Figure 11.3.

	Na₂O	MgO	Al₂O₃	SiO₂	P₂O₅	SO₃	K₂O	CaO	TiO₂	MnO	FeO
Dark leucite			20.6	57	0.9		15.5				5.8
Dark leucite		0.5	20.4	57			15.9				6.4
Acicular calcium phosphate		0.7	3.3	16	36		1.5	32.6			9.4
Acicular calcium phosphate					48			43.3			9.1
Fayalite top layer		0.8		33				0.6		1.0	65
Fayalite top layer		0.8		32	1.3					1.2	65
Fayalite bottom layer		1.4	0.8	33	1.2		0.6	0.7		1.4	61
Glassy matrix			7.9	33	11.1	1.0	1.5	9.4	3.5		33

Table 11.4 SEM-EDS analytical results for some of the phases illustrated in Figure 11.5.

	Na2O	MgO	Al2O3	SiO2	P2O5	K2O	CaO	MnO	FeO
Darkest globules	0.7		11.9	66		7.7	3.1		10.2
Darkest globules			13.0	66		9.0	2.8		9.7
Acicular calcium phosphate		0.9	2.3	12	39	1.5	37		6.8
Fayalite		1.9		32			0.8	1.6	63
Fayalite		4.2		34				2.2	60

Table 11.5 SEM-EDS analytical results for some of the phases illustrated in Figure 11.6.

	Na2O	MgO	Al2O3	SiO2	P2O5	K2O	CaO	TiO2	FeO
Ceramic composition	0.5	0.8	11.7	77	0.6	3.5	1.1	1.1	4.0

Table 11.6 Chemical composition of the furnace wall fragment as obtained by SEM-EDS. Figures given are the average of three measurements of areas of ~1 mm².

immediately prior to dismantling the furnace. The other layer, probably deposited before, shows a more developed crystalline structure, with subhedral fayalite crystals (containing manganese oxide), subhedral leucite forming at the grain boundaries, and areas of a liquid-liquid exsolution, with un-mixing of a leucitic melt following the crystallisation of fayalite and the resulting enrichment of alumina, potash, phosphate and lime in the residual melt. In addition, acicular crystals of iron-rich calcium phosphate appear forming in the glassy matrix. The absence of an oxidation skin of magnetite between the two flow layers indicates that this sequence was deposited within the furnace, under reducing conditions, and therefore does not represent evidence for tapping slag (Figures 11.5–6, Tables 11.4–5).

The formation of potassium- and aluminium-rich phases such as leucite is sometimes related to a more substantial contribution of the furnace wall, melting during the high temperature process and being absorbed in the slag, and/or to a large contribution from the fuel ash. However, it is worth noting that the bulk compositions as obtained by ED-XRF show similar low concentrations of these elements for all the slag samples, thus the presence of these phases in specimen No. 1 may be simply a reflection of longer cooling times and clearer separation of the two phases.

The higher concentrations of manganese oxide, phosphate and barium, together with the different impurities pattern between the two

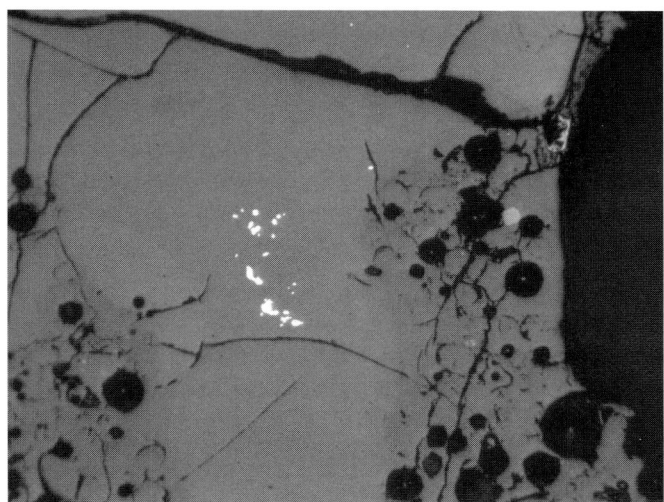

Figure 11.8 Detail of metallic iron within silicate inclusion of the ceramic indicating strongly reducing conditions throughout the ceramic (No. 6, PPL, 50×, width of image is 1.3 cm).

slag groups, remain to be investigated in detail, as they may be related to the use of a different type of ore. Given that clay-related oxides such as alumina, potash and lime are at comparable levels in both slag groups, the differences in slag compositions cannot be explained as resulting from a simple dilution effect through variable contributions of melting clay. To illustrate this relationship between ore and slag composition, we use data from Ganzelewski (2000). In this extensive study, analyses of bog ores from the German/Danish border typically have several weight percent of phosphate and up to one percent of manganese oxide; the related slags have typically three to five percent phosphate and around one to two percent manganese oxide. The geological and climatic setting of that region is relatively similar to the situation around Novgorod, resulting in comparable bog ore formations. However, some differences in composition between the German/Danish ore and the ore from around Novgorod are to be expected, and obvious in the data for minor and trace elements such as barium and the rare earth elements.

Finally, investigation of the ceramic sample shows obvious vitrification and bloating through high temperature, and a chemical composition akin to that of other ordinary clays, hence it does not seem to have been selected on the basis of a special refractoriness. However, as noted above, none of the slag analysed shows an important contribution of clay components, thus it seems that only a limited amount of furnace wall would have melted during the smelting process. It may be of significance to note that some of the free iron within mineral inclusions in the ceramic appears to have been reduced to the metallic state, indicating the strongly reducing conditions throughout the ceramic (Figures 11.7–8, Table 11.6).

CONCLUSION

The analytical study confirms that this assemblage originates from the smelting of iron from bog ore, using the traditional direct or bloomery process, which entailed a significant loss of iron into the slag but was nevertheless effective. The slag is of good quality, containing very little metallic iron and normal amounts of free iron oxide as wüstite. Its external shape and crystal morphology indicate that the slag formed inside a non-tapping furnace; the absence of large slag blocks rules out the use of pit furnaces as used frequently in earlier Polish and Scandinavian contexts (Bielenin 1976; Ganzelewski 2000; Pleiner 2000).

The slag composition particularly of the samples with increased manganese, phosphate and barium concentrations matches the composition of slag inclusions recently identified in late medieval knives from Novgorod (Jeffery and Rehren, this volume). It thus appears that these production remains from the hinterland might be related to consumers in the Novgorod settlement. In any case, it seems reasonable that both products (i.e. the slag reported here, and the knives analysed by Jeffery and Rehren in this volume) may originate from a very similar, if not the same, bog ore.

Another interesting aspect is the presence of two slag groups with clearly different geochemical signatures, which points to some variability of the ore source, and/ or the use of different ores. However, due to the lack of more analyses and better contextualised and dated samples, it is not possible to state whether this represents synchronic or diachronic variation.

Within the samples received and studied, we found no evidence of tap slag, which is typically formed when molten slag is drawn off through an opening near the bottom of a shaft furnace, so that it flows away and solidifies preserving a characteristic texture. More importantly, the confirmation of these as remains of bloomery smelting is of significance, in view of the recent excavation of a seemingly very large furnace base in the vicinity of these finds. The diameter of this furnace base, of above one meter, might have suggested the utilisation of a more advanced technique, i.e. blast furnace-based iron smelting, introduced in Northern Europe and Scandinavia in the Late Middle Ages and resulting in a more economic exploitation of ores. It is known, however, that blast furnace slag would appear mostly glassy, much poorer in iron oxide, and richer in lime, than seen in the slag samples analysed. Hence, the introduction of blast furnace technology in Novgorod remains to be documented, and is unlikely to be represented from this site.

12

INVESTIGATING SOCIAL CHANGE IN 12TH–13TH CENTURY NOVGOROD USING SLAG INCLUSIONS

D. Jeffery and Th. Rehren

INTRODUCTION

In 1959 Boris A. Kolchin published an in-depth study of iron artefacts recovered in the excavation of Novgorod. His analytical work has stood for the last 50 years as a landmark in archaeometallurgical research and, as with any insightful work, points the way to further research. One question centres on Kolchin's analyses of knives; Kolchin identified a rapid shift in the preference for particular construction methods within the final years of the 12th and the beginning of the 13th century. Kolchin posited an economic shift in demand for iron knives, which resulted in larger scale production, which in turn caused the preference for an apparently simpler form of knife.

Such a rapid and essentially complete abandonment of previous techniques is strikingly abrupt and accordingly L. S. Rosanova and V. I. Zavyalov (1990) proceeded to replicate Kolchin's analyses on a larger body of knives excavated more recently since his study with results that generally confirm Kolchin's findings. Rosanova and Zavyalov propose instead a correlation between the preferred construction method and cultural association of the smith. This is based on data gathered from the northern and southern regions of Russia, which indicates preference for particular construction methods that may correlate closely with cultural affiliation. It seems worth noting that the Chronicle of Novgorod does not record a major shift in the cultural makeup of the population. However, it is reasonable that a significant flux and shift within a trade such as blacksmithing could occur without a comment in the Chronicle. In the hope of uncovering further corollary evidence for one of these proposals, the present work was undertaken to consider whether a parallel to the shift in construction techniques could be detected in the chemical composition of the slag inclusions.

With this narrower area of focus, the hypotheses that this study aimed to test were: 1) that there exists a statistically significant difference in composition of slag inclusions between the 12th and the 13th century and 2) that there exists a statistically significant difference in the compositions of slag inclusions due to the raw materials selected for different methods of construction (that is, smiths preferring to use different methods of construction also selected to use different raw materials). To test these hypotheses, metallographic samples were first photographed using a reflected light microscope to create maps of the polished surface. This was followed by analysis of slag inclusions in the metal with the scanning electron microscope using energy dispersive spectroscopy to gather chemical compositions. The data were then analysed statistically.

The study of iron at Novgorod

The metalwork recovered at Novgorod is extremely remarkable both for its quantity and its excellent preservation. This is largely due to anaerobic waterlogged conditions and the high phosphorous content of the soil. Additionally, the dendrochronology available from the abundant preserved timber at Novgorod provides an excellent and very precise framework of dates within which to study a shift in artefact construction techniques.

Kolchin's 1959 text is remarkable both in the number of artefacts studied and the quality of the analysis. Kolchin was able to analyze a substantial fraction of the iron material excavated at the site including the careful analysis of 304 knives recovered from the Nerevsky site (Kolchin 1959, 48). In 1959, 1444 knives had been recovered from this site, and of those knives 109 were complete with handles intact and 1130 were complete with tangs. Only 205 were considered to be seriously damaged. Of the undamaged knives 304 were analyzed and of these 195 were subjected to microstructural analysis. Of those, 109 were treated with an acid etchant. It is these 195 knives that Kolchin used to discuss the development and change of the blacksmith's craft in Novgorod. Unfortunately, Kolchin provided no details as to how or why these 195 knives were selected and in what way they can be considered to represent the larger body of knives excavated at Novgorod. Kolchin indicated the age of the layer from which each sample was excavated and, as a credit to his thoroughness, subdivided the overall number of knives according to their century for comparison.

Figure 12.1 summarizes the analysis done on these knives by Kolchin and shows clearly the transition that he observed from one type of construction to another. Figure 12.1 also illustrates the skew in Kolchin's data which is an issue of sample choice and presentation that can be seen to be more fundamentally problematic when one considers Kolchin's interpretation of the data. The information as presented in this figure would signify that the numbers of knives excavated that related to the 12th and 14th centuries was almost twice what archaeologists actually uncovered. Kolchin interpreted this rapid transition from one technique of knife construction to an apparently simpler technique and the accompanying increase in number of knives recovered as indicative of the lowering of quality standards to meet greater production demands (1959, 52). While there are a number of issues with this interpretation, at the heart is the question of why the transition from one form to another is so extremely rapid. The data Kolchin presented in Figure 12.1 could strongly support the idea of increasing production, but much of this support may be bias from sample selection and interpretation. In the years since Kolchin's work, further metallographic analyses

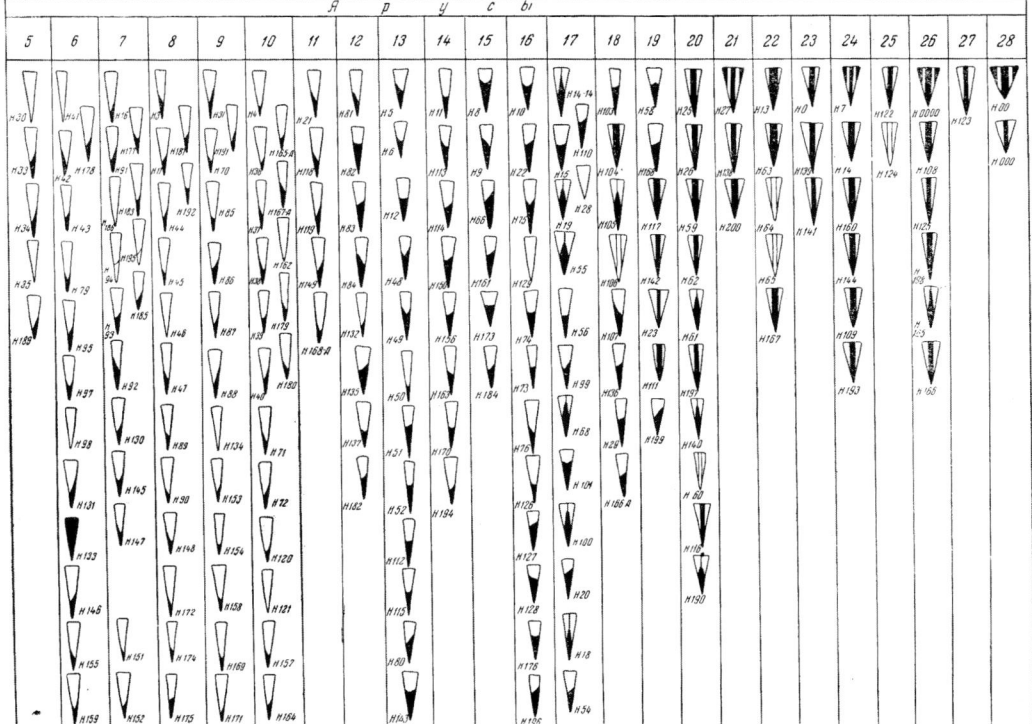

Figure 12.1 Kolchin's table of knife construction methods. White represents low-carbon iron and black represents steel. Layered welding, initially used exclusively, is completely abandoned by column 17 (Kolchin 1959, 50, Fig. 36).

of archaeological materials began to challenge the percentages of each construction type in relation to the others as identified at Novgorod. In order to evaluate Kolchin's interpretation it was necessary for further research to be conducted.

Because of the comprehensiveness of Kolchin's study and the respect held for Kolchin himself, it was a number of years before another major analysis of iron metalworking at Novgorod was performed. It was not until 1989 that Rozanova and Zavyalov conducted a programme of analyses studying knives from the Troitsky sites VI, VII and VIII, all located in the Lyudin End of medieval Novgorod. The Nerevsky trenches, which Kolchin studied, were located to the north of Troitsky in the Nerevsky End, so it was recognized at the outset that there may be some variation from Kolchin's findings simply because the area of the city was different.

Unlike Kolchin's work, Rozanova and Zavyalov's study focused solely on knives as they sought to evaluate Kolchin's conclusions. Their study encompassed 350 knives, 332 of which underwent micro-structural analysis. They do not report any information regarding what portion of the total number of knives from the excavations this represents or how the numbers of knives studied from each century relate to the

Technology	Century					
	X (2nd half)	XI	XII	XIII	XIV - BegXV	Total
3-layer packet	13	7	12	7	3	42
5-layer packet	2	1	0	1	0	4
In-welded	5	2	14	8	1	30
Butt-welded	1	1	13	40	42	97
Scarf-welded	1	0	5	29	31	66
Entirely of iron	0	0	0	11	10	21
Entirely of steel	0	3	4	12	15	34
Cementation	0	0	1	1	5	7
Packetized	0	0	1	4	12	17
Total	22	14	50	113	119	318

Table 12.1 Rozanova and Zavyalov's selection of samples organized by century and construction method. This is their table translated into English (Rozanova and Zavylov 1990, 179).

total number recovered from that time period. They acknowledge at the outset that the selection of samples was conducted sporadically from 1981 to 1987 and was based more on the artefact's possessing good preservation and a clear find location than on an organized sampling strategy. Thus, similar to Kolchin's work, the analyses appear to be unequally distributed across the 10th to early 15th centuries. The results reported by Rozanova and Zavyalov (see Table 12.1) generally support Kolchin's data, but they do smooth the curve from one form to another by making it a shift in proportions rather than a complete abandonment of an older technology.

In the time since Kolchin's work was done, a great many sites across Russia and Eastern Europe containing iron artefacts have been excavated. Rozanova and Zavyalov thus benefit from a wide database of comparative information that was unavailable to Kolchin. In other papers, both Rozanova and Zavyalov have identified separate smithing traditions in the Northern and Southern regions of the former USSR (Zavyalov 1989, Rozanova 1990). The Southern regions tend to favour the welded-on (butt-welded and scarf-welded) and all-iron or all-steel forms of blade construction, while in-welded and 3 and 5-layer packet knives are more common on Northern sites (see Figure 12.2). This becomes very interesting in the study of Novgorod as there seems to have been a relatively abrupt shift from Northern styles of knife construction to Southern Russian methods that may be tied to some major cultural change within the ironworking industry and, by extension, the city as a whole. Another aspect which has been developed since Kolchin's work, and upon which Rozanova and Zavyalov briefly touched, is the relationship of blade form to construction method. This was not considered in this study, but could provide further evidence for or against a shift from Northern to Southern smithing traditions.

Rozanova and Zavyalov's general confirmation of Kolchin's results encourages the present author that further analysis of these knives could realistically lead to clearer understanding of larger cultural changes within Novgorod at this time. The present work thus focuses on discovering whether the change in preferred construction method could be correlated to a shift in materials selection. If this is found to be the case, then additional research into iron raw materials and a survey of change within other crafts, such as wood- and glassworking, should be undertaken in order to better characterize the extent and nature of the changes taking place in the cultural makeup of Novgorod's population.

For this work, a selection of Rozanova and Zavyalov's polished samples were primarily analysed using a scanning electron microscope (SEM). A Jeol 35 SEM fitted with an Oxford Link energy dispersive spectrometer (SEM-EDS) was used to study the slag inclusions in each section and characterize them according to their major and minor elements.

5-Layer Packet

3-Layer Packet

In-Welded

METHODOLOGY

This study followed the research of Rozanova and Zavyalov in focusing on knives as a prolific, universal tool in which important aspects of the blacksmith's craft can be studied. The research of Rozanova and Zavyalov dealt with a very large number of knives dating from the founding of Novgorod through to the early 15th century, but in order to test the specific hypotheses of this project the present study focused on a much smaller selection of these knives covering only the 12th to 14th centuries. In this study, 29 individual blades were analyzed, but each of the blades was further subdivided according to the number of discrete pieces of iron metal used in its construction based on the illustrations of Rozanova and Zavyalov. Each of these sections was treated as a separate sample for both information gathering and later processing of the data. Thus, from the 29 knives studied there are 66 discrete pieces of iron represented.

Butt-Welded

Scarf-Welded

Figure 12.2 Several major construction methods used at Novgorod (after Kolchin 1959).

The analytical work of Kolchin, Rozanova and Zavyalov under consideration focused on optical microscopy of the polished cross-sections of these knives, using etchants in order to bring out the microstructure and chemical composition of the samples being studied. A great deal of information regarding the conditions under which the iron was produced and possibly the forging conditions is available in the bits of slag trapped within the iron matrix. The present study used the reflected light microscope only in the limited capacity of taking digital optical micrographs at 20X to construct image maps. These maps were then used both to provide a map for finding slag inclusions of appropriate size and to indicate the location of a slag inclusion which was excited for X-ray analysis. Given more time it would have been useful to conduct image processing to quantify the average size of slag inclusions, their aspect ratio (elongation) and the ratio of slag to metal within each segment of iron as an additional descriptor to be used with the chemical compositions in characterizing each piece.

The figures published by Rozanova and Zavyalov clearly show the construction method of each sample and these illustrations were used in order to determine the appropriate areas in which to study the slag inclusions. In selecting inclusions to excite, preference was given to inclusions toward the centre of a specific section of the knife in order to avoid any changes that may have been introduced due to welding flux or corrosion. This proved very difficult with the steel sections, since inclusions large enough for sampling were often either not present or only present at the borders. Not surprisingly the statistical treatment of steel samples was therefore unhelpful and the steel samples were not used in any of the significant data sets. Analyses were taken at 20kV and, in an attempt to minimize the effects of the subsurface reaction volume, all inclusions analyzed were at least 2µm in the smallest dimension and generally they were on the order of 3–4µm in the smallest dimension. Slag inclusions were generally single-phase in appearance and the sample point was set as near the centre of the inclusion as possible to keep the reaction volume within the inclusion. Five or more analyses were taken in most of the iron sections studied, but in a very few instances only one or two analyses were taken in specific sections.

As the X-ray spectra were being gathered, a slag inclusion generating a spectrum with a high percentage Fe content (generally more than 75%) was skipped over immediately as it was unlikely to contain as much minor element information. All X-ray analyses were performed by selecting an inclusion at 40X and then zooming to 4,000X magnification and manually setting the scan on the Jeol 35 to a point in the centre of the slag inclusion. The only advantage of such a high magnification was to be certain that the dot was centred on the slag inclusion; the volume of the material which would be excited to produce X-rays remained unchanged.

Once all of the X-ray spectra had been gathered they were carefully considered to select appropriate elements for quantification. For standardization purposes all spectra were processed using the same set of elements, although not all elements are present in all samples. The elements selected were: Na, Mg, Al, Si, P, S, K, Ca, Ti, Mn, Fe and Ba. All results were combined using stoichiometry with oxygen and normalized to 100% since all the slag inclusions were determined likely to be in an oxidised state. The iron was assumed to be FeO although it was more likely to be a mixture of Fe_2O_3 and FeO, but the Isis software package used for quantification does not allow for such a calibration. Isis was set to use these parameters and process all the spectra at once as a batch, outputting a .tsv file which was then imported into Microsoft Excel for processing.

Having collected the spectra and quantified them, it was necessary to organize the data into a manageable order for analysis. To categorize these samples according to method of construction, the groupings proposed by Rosanova and Zavyalov (1990, 179) were used here with some modifications. Some very similar groups have been combined for ease of comparison when discussing this smaller portion of Rosanova and Zavyalov's complete set of samples. Groups missing from this sample set have been removed from the modified categorization. The types are listed here in Table 12.2 according to the most predominant types.

Once the data had been organized within Microsoft Excel and properly labelled

Table 12.2 *The construction method typology as implemented in this study. Modified from Rozanova and Zavyalov (1990, 179).*	Type I	3-layer and 5-layer packets
	Type II	In-welded
	Type III	On-welded (Scarf & butt welds)
	Type IV	Entirely of iron
	Type V	Cementation

according to century and type, conditional formatting was applied to give ranges of numbers. This served to both highlight outliers and draw attention to potential patterns in the data. This immediately identified two spectra that were too radically disproportionate to be utilized in the full data set. These are 5494s3 and 5484e1, which were subsequently excluded from all calculations. Looking at this same data set, it rapidly became apparent, as mentioned above, that there was a dramatic difference between the numbers of points collected for each area. In order to avoid skewing the statistical analyses toward those samples with more data points, it was deemed necessary to average the weight percent of each oxide for each iron section and do all analyses based on the averaged numbers. The choice to average masked the variation existent within the individual sections, but still seemed the most appropriate method of making the sections comparable.

Finally, in order to perform the statistical processing of the data, the averages of the sections were copied into Minitab 14 as specific groups of data. For example, when testing whether a correlation according to century could be identified, only the knives from two centuries could be compared at any given time therefore a data set containing only knives from the 12th and 13th centuries would be copied to Minitab for analysis. Each of these data sets was subjected to several different statistical methods, but only discriminant analysis results were found to be useful and these will be used for interpretation below.

Statistical techniques

Statistical methods were employed in order to deal with the large amount of data gathered. In this particular study discriminant analysis was expected to be the most useful method from the outset, although several other common statistical techniques were tried first.

Discriminant analysis is a technique intended to test the fit of samples within a predetermined grouping and was found to be very useful in testing the sets of data for all three hypotheses. When using discriminant analysis the provided predictors are considered (in this case, weight-percentages of specific oxides) and used to create the parameters for each grouping, such as type or century. The method then states how well each of the points in a group fits within its predetermined group or if it would better fit into another group. It is possible to then cross check the group assignments by taking each entry out, one at a time, and testing it to see which group it would best fit now that they have been populated. Cross-checking was used for all of the analyses discussed below.

Using discriminant analysis against the ratios of minor element oxides to major element oxides as recommended by Buchwald and Wivel (1998, 74) (SiO_2/FeO, SiO_2/Al_2O_3, Al_2O_3/CaO and K_2O/MgO) there was no discernible pattern and when they were combined with the element oxides as predictors they tended to decrease the accuracy of the predictions. In the end all of the useful groups of predictors were formed using some or all of the following oxide weight percents: %Na_2O, %MgO, %Al_2O_3, %P_2O_5, %SO_3, %K_2O, %CaO, %TiO_2, %MnO and %BaO.

THE RESULTS OF ANALYSIS

The full results of the quantification are not provided here and, since the results of the statistical analysis show a need for a very large number of elements, the summary table below (Table 12.3) is rather substantial. Artefacts are arranged first according to the century of their deposition and then time within the century (that is, early, middle, or late) and then by lab number. The Type column refers to the method of construction and Iron identifies whether Rozanova and Zavyalov identified a section as uncarburized iron or steel. The lower detection limit for most of these elements is approximately 0.1%, so values below 0.1% should not be trusted.

The oxides SiO_2 and FeO were omitted from the calculation (although included in the table) as they were observed to have little useful impact on correctly predicting group membership. 5504e and 5504Fe were omitted from the testing of the date hypotheses because of the lack of information regarding their deposition timeframe, but they were used in testing the construction type hypotheses. For most of the analytical work the columns to the right were used as labels within Minitab in order to divide the samples according to construction method, time of deposition, and the type of metal in the surrounding matrix.

Interpreting the data

The analysis was focused on characterizing slag inclusions within the different iron constituent layers in order to test the hypotheses stated in the introduction which are: 1) that there exists a consistent difference between the chemical composition of slag inclusions in artefacts produced in the 12th versus the 13th centuries and 2) that knives of different construction type will have a corresponding difference in slag inclusion chemistry.

Date of manufacture

Differentiation according to date of deposition has been a very simple matter in the archaeology of Novgorod because of the excellent stratigraphy and dendrochronology. As in most archaeological excavations, it has generally been assumed at Novgorod that the knives were manufactured within a very brief timeframe before their date of deposition and while there are possible flaws in this assumption it is not within the scope of this work to challenge it. Using the data already gathered within the present study, it is possible to apply the clear chronology of artefacts to discover if there is a broad change in the chemical composition of slag inclusions over time. The data was accordingly organized into groups based on date information received from Zavyalov (pers. comm.), which is slightly revised from the 1990 published data as the dendrochronology for the Troitsky sites was completed after that time.

The full data set was subdivided into three subsets in order to test this hypothesis. The data from the 14th century had to be left out because there were too few samples representing that century. Thus, the first data set consisted of all the samples from the 12th and 13th centuries; the second data set comprised all iron samples from the first data set and the third set consisted of all steel samples from the first data set. Only the results from analysing the second data set (the iron sections) are discussed here since the first and third data sets, when subjected to the same tests, did not return any useful results. This seems a reasonable step as most of the steel inclusions were extremely small and frequently positioned so close to the weld as to cast doubt on their origin as smelting slags.

To test the first hypothesis, the oxides which gave reasonably good agreement with the true groups when used as predictors were found to be $\%Na_2O$, $\%MgO$, $\%Al_2O_3$, $\%P_2O_5$, $\%SO_3$, $\%K_2O$, $\%CaO$, $\%TiO_2$ and $\%MnO$ with the initial match being 100% and the cross-validation being 86%. An additional six groups of oxide predictors returned results of 100% to 92% for the initial grouping and between 83% and 72% for the cross-validation (see Table 12.4). These numbers seem consistent enough to justify stating that there is clearly a distinction between the chemical composition of the slag inclusions in knives of the 12th century as compared to that of knives from the 13th century. This observation is further remarkable when it is considered that data set 2 held only 14 sections from the 12th century and 22 from the 13th century and the results were nevertheless sufficiently distinct to provide a high level of accuracy. These observations clearly support the idea of a major shift in ironworking at the transition of these centuries.

It is worth noting that in every case the cross-validation overall percentage correct was pulled down severely by sections attributed to the 12th century. This may be because there were fewer of these sections to create a solid grouping, but from Kolchin's data (Figure 12.1) the transition in construction methods began in the mid-12th century. If a correlation exists between the shift in slag inclusion composition and the preferred material of smiths choosing alternate construction methods, then it could be expected that many of the 12th century sections would group with the 13th century sections. In order to explore this the author generated a number of bivariate scatterplots, which showed that with several oxides (Na_2O, CaO, MgO, TiO_2) there was a tight cluster among 12th century samples and 13th century samples tended to overlap and spread out significantly, which overlap is apparently resolved by multivariate plotting of the data. As further research, it would be very worthwhile to expand this body of data to include the other samples studied by Rozanova and Zavyalov and make use of

Metallic Group	Na$_2$O	MgO	Al$_2$O$_3$	SiO$_2$	P$_2$O$_5$	SO$_3$	K$_2$O	CaO	TiO$_2$	MnO	FeO	BaO	Cent	Type	Iron
5481a	0.74	0.65	4.18	23.96	2.25	0.08	0.60	0.89	0.12	6.45	59.83	0.24	XII	I	Fe
5481b	0.63	0.50	6.86	26.06	2.24	2.68	4.78	0.85	0.10	8.20	46.48	0.62	XII	I	Fe
5481c	0.75	0.91	9.96	46.10	0.53	0.11	3.23	9.22	0.56	3.60	24.59	0.47	XII	I	St
5483e&s.e	0.69	2.19	7.57	60.00	0.15	0.19	2.41	11.26	0.39	5.76	8.33	1.07	XII	I	St
5528e	0.54	1.81	3.14	31.39	7.44	0.42	1.20	8.55	0.03	9.30	34.21	1.98	XII	III	St
5528s	0.78	1.69	1.76	30.07	8.68	0.69	1.25	8.58	0.04	6.32	38.05	2.11	XII	III	Fe
5529e	0.85	0.61	5.16	70.10	0.39	0.19	3.55	2.44	0.29	1.11	14.64	0.68	XII	III	St
5529s	0.85	0.81	2.71	23.27	9.80	0.34	1.10	4.24	0.03	3.14	52.98	0.73	XII	III	Fe
5493e	1.26	0.82	4.07	31.45	3.27	0.17	1.33	3.64	0.25	1.00	52.61	0.17	XII	I	St
5482c	0.83	1.87	4.96	60.08	0.32	0.20	4.66	7.48	0.23	0.74	17.88	0.76	XII	I	St
5482l	0.62	0.33	1.35	19.13	7.36	0.13	0.43	1.64	0.04	15.79	51.27	1.92	XII	I	Fe
5482r	0.75	0.63	2.85	27.94	7.64	0.45	1.79	2.99	0.11	18.43	32.28	4.15	XII	I	Fe
5497e	0.72	0.79	1.70	23.82	3.89	0.21	1.33	4.45	0.03	14.69	42.62	5.75	XII	I	St
5497s	0.66	0.84	1.19	28.46	2.92	0.29	1.03	4.39	0.03	15.74	39.30	5.17	XII	II	Fe
5503Fe	0.81	1.70	1.35	29.21	10.29	0.81	1.22	4.93	0.05	11.83	34.53	3.37	XII	II	Fe
5503St	0.78	0.73	3.96	66.24	0.11	0.15	2.76	3.46	0.20	3.98	15.60	2.07	XII	II	St
5498e	1.04	1.58	12.48	59.18	0.19	0.17	5.75	5.84	0.42	0.82	11.31	1.22	XII	II	St
5498l	0.87	0.79	5.82	35.14	7.77	0.33	2.04	4.06	0.10	9.48	31.92	1.71	XII	II	Fe
5498r	0.94	0.79	5.74	33.35	7.11	0.28	1.62	3.92	0.11	9.41	35.13	1.62	XII	II	Fe
5498b	0.91	0.64	5.78	33.01	7.70	0.25	1.58	3.56	0.10	8.22	36.76	1.49	XII	II	Fe
5502c.1-8	0.70	1.50	4.77	57.28	0.17	0.19	5.62	6.45	0.32	3.04	18.27	1.68	XII	II	St
5502l.9-14	0.63	0.57	2.33	22.60	13.62	1.71	0.90	4.89	0.05	9.24	37.62	5.84	XII	II	Fe
5502r.15-20	0.69	0.58	2.41	20.57	11.07	1.36	0.96	5.41	0.04	8.80	42.16	5.97	XII	II	Fe
5502b	0.68	0.62	3.20	32.33	6.16	0.66	1.59	4.31	0.11	7.51	38.05	4.81	XII	II	Fe
5480c	0.96	1.83	4.75	45.67	0.67	0.17	3.40	8.47	0.23	0.64	32.83	0.40	XIII	II	Fe
5480r	1.15	0.65	3.25	26.70	6.48	0.19	1.01	3.31	0.14	5.66	50.78	0.68	XIII	II	St
5480l	1.19	0.80	3.79	31.61	5.41	0.29	1.38	3.65	0.11	6.20	44.69	0.89	XIII	II	Fe
5494e	0.56	2.32	4.22	57.85	0.33	0.24	3.23	12.91	0.17	0.43	17.34	0.43	XIII	I	St
5494s	0.93	0.66	3.34	15.08	6.29	0.28	1.03	1.65	0.26	3.60	50.96	0.55	XIII	I	Fe
5495e	0.76	0.62	4.41	81.38	0.05	0.31	3.05	3.48	0.25	0.88	2.95	1.86	XIII	I	St
5499e	0.56	1.37	2.97	48.99	2.37	0.15	2.85	5.03	0.14	10.97	22.33	2.28	XIII	III	St
5499s	0.84	1.09	0.79	23.43	8.67	0.46	0.64	2.31	0.01	8.69	50.97	2.15	XIII	III	Fe
5500Fe	1.10	0.60	5.37	20.73	2.43	0.27	0.67	1.91	0.09	7.23	58.65	1.00	XIII	II	Fe
5500Fe13.e	2.49	0.17	0.05	0.65	0.16	5.56	0.37	2.33	0.01	0.00	88.66	0.00	XIII	II	St

Metallic Group	Na₂O	MgO	Al₂O₃	SiO₂	P₂O₅	SO₃	K₂O	CaO	TiO₂	MnO	FeO	BaO	Cent	Type	Iron
5501e1	0.75	1.96	5.72	44.71	0.82	0.14	3.76	8.64	0.36	1.55	31.33	0.25	XIII	I	St
5501e.r	0.80	1.66	4.05	29.30	3.52	0.26	2.88	6.94	0.18	1.73	48.61	0.18	XIII	I	Fe
5530c	0.83	1.19	4.59	60.68	0.18	0.16	4.91	5.81	0.25	5.70	10.64	5.08	XIII	II	St
5530I	0.66	1.10	0.52	21.25	15.03	0.43	1.23	6.37	0.01	7.03	42.96	3.45	XIII	II	Fe
5530r	0.75	0.93	0.34	15.01	17.87	0.36	0.90	3.63	0.03	4.98	53.24	2.01	XIII	II	Fe
5527a	0.81	0.45	2.31	16.21	5.61	0.16	0.78	1.59	0.03	6.24	65.06	0.77	XIII	V	Fe
5527b	0.80	0.42	4.33	16.09	9.25	0.25	1.15	2.16	0.06	7.06	57.48	0.98	XIII	V	Fe
5484e&s	1.06	1.13	3.45	27.43	4.10	0.34	0.85	2.23	0.12	7.56	44.43	3.08	XIII	IV	Fe
5496ae	0.76	0.73	3.48	51.20	0.22	0.19	2.47	3.19	0.14	3.59	32.07	1.95	XIII	III	St
5496as	0.74	0.74	2.46	25.87	10.91	0.72	2.04	5.79	0.07	5.39	43.08	2.18	XIII	III	Fe
5496b	0.87	0.80	2.26	23.63	10.20	0.67	1.74	5.98	0.05	5.97	45.60	2.26	XIII	III	Fe
5505Ae	1.01	0.72	6.49	70.70	0.12	0.08	3.32	2.78	0.29	0.22	13.87	0.43	XIII	III	St
5505As	0.62	1.23	0.97	18.01	16.10	1.11	1.16	7.99	0.03	10.06	39.65	3.13	XIII	III	Fe
5505B	0.66	1.68	0.82	19.94	11.87	0.54	0.85	4.98	0.02	10.46	46.12	2.07	XIII	III	Fe
5144e&st	0.83	0.99	6.50	72.17	0.16	0.20	4.40	3.70	0.24	1.65	7.97	1.22	XIII	II	St
5144Fe&s	0.87	1.29	2.44	34.42	5.78	0.94	1.77	6.08	0.08	3.98	40.45	1.91	XIII	II	Fe
5148ae.1-8,10-14	0.70	1.84	9.72	66.22	0.10	0.17	4.25	8.80	0.49	0.64	6.66	0.46	XIII	I	St
5148al.15-19	0.84	1.63	5.97	36.93	9.02	0.37	3.63	11.26	0.24	3.22	25.88	1.03	XIII	I	Fe
5148ar.9,20-23	0.85	0.62	5.91	20.56	13.25	0.41	4.66	10.74	0.24	1.70	39.64	1.42	XIII	I	Fe
5148b	0.76	1.04	5.06	29.30	9.18	0.42	2.82	7.43	0.21	2.80	40.26	0.73	XIII	I	Fe
5149ae	0.77	1.18	7.42	69.28	0.16	0.16	4.62	5.03	0.28	0.53	10.14	0.43	XIII	I	St
5149as	0.96	1.40	12.80	30.59	4.21	0.24	2.18	7.93	0.12	7.19	29.29	3.08	XIII	I	Fe
5149b	0.88	1.40	12.08	27.26	6.85	0.38	1.70	6.96	0.16	7.74	31.89	2.71	XIII	I	Fe
5147e	0.89	2.13	2.26	29.69	1.43	0.34	1.36	1.65	0.17	1.40	58.61	0.16	XIII	III	St
5147s	1.07	0.48	3.80	28.84	3.35	0.17	1.42	2.32	0.09	6.90	50.89	0.68	XIII	III	Fe
5150aFe	0.76	1.73	5.55	53.14	0.44	0.21	3.27	6.06	0.21	1.01	27.07	0.55	XIII	III	Fe
5146e	0.87	0.46	4.37	66.75	0.35	0.13	2.16	1.85	0.24	0.13	22.57	0.23	XIV	III	St
5146s	0.87	0.25	1.38	12.64	17.74	0.26	0.70	1.64	0.06	0.63	63.61	0.26	XIV	III	Fe
5145e	0.90	0.45	3.44	37.20	4.68	0.24	3.29	4.57	0.20	0.71	43.85	0.46	XIV	III	St
5145s	0.89	0.50	2.34	21.83	16.66	0.44	0.96	2.44	0.06	2.29	51.05	0.54	XIV	III	Fe
5151a	0.75	1.05	2.84	46.00	4.62	0.18	2.17	5.37	0.15	1.33	34.81	0.73	XIV	IV	Fe
5151b	0.91	1.71	5.39	56.17	0.11	0.66	2.93	6.25	0.29	0.59	24.52	0.48	XIV	IV	Fe
5504e	0.56	0.66	1.88	44.94	1.98	0.46	0.95	2.18	0.07	7.38	37.56	1.40		III	St
5504Fe	0.68	0.91	1.46	27.42	8.95	0.41	1.30	6.11	0.03	12.74	35.25	4.75		III	Fe

Table 12.3 Averages of chemical compositions of minor elements in the slag inclusions studied.

the very precise dating available to test for differences between the first and second halves of the 12th and 13th centuries.

METHOD OF MANUFACTURE

Kolchin, and later Rozanova and Zavyalov, identified construction types by which the data can easily be categorized and compared. The research of Zavyalov (1989), Rozanova (1990) and others clearly demonstrates preferences for particular construction methods used in knife-making that are typical of regions and cultural groups. The hypotheses for this study state that a significant difference in the chemical composition of slag inclusions exists which can be correlated with the construction method used. Of particular interest would be a significant difference between artefact types I and II versus types III and IV, since the percentages of these particular artefacts present at a site could now be attributed to the cultural group that occupied the site. Such a difference could further strengthen the argument for a major shift in the cultural makeup of the ironworking community of 12th to 13th century Novgorod

Table 12.4 Summarized results of discriminant analysis. Note that generally XII (12th century) shows lower percentages.

Predictors
$\%Na_2O$, $\%MgO$, $\%Al_2O_3$, $\%P_2O_5$, $\%SO_3$, $\%K_2O$, $\%CaO$, $\%TiO_2$, $\%MnO$

Initial Classification	XII	XIII	Overall
Percentage Correct	100%	100%	100%
Cross-Validation	**XII**	**XIII**	**Overall**
Percentage Correct	64%	100%	86%

Predictors
$\%Na_2O$, $\%MgO$, $\%Al_2O_3$, $\%P_2O_5$, $\%SO_3$, $\%K_2O$, $\%CaO$, $\%TiO_2$, $\%MnO$, $\%BaO$

Initial Classification	XII	XIII	Overall
Percentage Correct	100%	100%	100%
Cross-Validation	**XII**	**XIII**	**Overall**
Percentage Correct	64%	91%	81%

Predictors
$\%Na_2O$, $\%MgO$, $\%P_2O_5$, $\%SO_3$, $\%K_2O$, $\%CaO$, $\%TiO_2$, $\%MnO$

Initial Classification	XII	XIII	Overall
Percentage Correct	100%	96%	97%
Cross-Validation	**XII**	**XIII**	**Overall**
Percentage Correct	71%	91%	83%

Predictors
$\%Na_2O$, $\%MgO$, $\%Al_2O3$, $\%P_2O_5$, $\%SO_3$, $\%CaO$, $\%TiO_2$, $\%MnO$, $\%BaO$

Initial Classification	XII	XIII	Overall
Percentage Correct	93%	100%	97%
Cross-Validation	**XII**	**XIII**	**Overall**
Percentage Correct	64%	91%	72%

Predictors
$\%Na_2O$, $\%MgO$, $\%Al_2O_3$, $\%SO_3$, $\%K_2O$, $\%CaO$, $\%TiO_2$, $\%MnO$, $\%BaO$

Initial Classification	XII	XIII	Overall
Percentage Correct	100%	100%	100%
Cross-Validation	**XII**	**XIII**	**Overall**
Percentage Correct	64%	77%	72%

Predictors
$\%Na_2O$, $\%MgO$, $\%SO_3$, $\%CaO$, $\%TiO_2$, $\%MnO$

Initial Classification	XII	XIII	Overall
Percentage Correct	93%	91%	92%
Cross-Validation	**XII**	**XIII**	**Overall**
Percentage Correct	57%	82%	72%

by indicating that different iron was preferred by blacksmiths using particular construction methods.

Data sets were formed based on the type of construction method used and drawing from the full pool of 66 iron sections. Because there were so few samples of types IV and V it was necessary to exclude them from the analyses. Thus, the first data set for this hypothesis consisted of 61 sections of types I, II, and III (Table 12.5). This first data set was then subdivided according to composition of iron or steel into the second and third data sets respectively. A fourth and fifth data set were formed by subdividing the second data set (iron) into 12th and 13th centuries, but they proved to be too small for analysis.

In processing the data using the statistical regime outlined above, none of the statistical methods were able to determine any meaningful correlation within the data. When using discriminant analysis, each of the data sets outlined above was used in conjunction with a variety of different oxides, but regardless of which groups were used and which oxides were selected as predictors, it was impossible to obtain an accuracy above the mid-70 percent range for the initial test and the second was usually near 50 percent. From this data, it is impossible to support the hypothesis that the slag inclusions are different within different types of knives. However, it seems a larger data set is actually necessary in order to conclusively test this hypothesis as the full data set was divided into five types, two of which were then discarded. The remaining three data sets consisted of approximately 20 samples each. The further subdividing into iron/steel and century seemed to exacerbate the problem so that even if a difference existed, the numbers of samples were so small as to be statistically indistinguishable because of the error associated with such small sample sets. This hypothesis still deserves further testing with a larger data set, but it cannot be supported with the present data set.

Table 12.5 *Group assignments of sections shown in Table 12.3 above.*

Metallic Group	Cent	Type	Iron	Data Sets
5481a	XII	I	Fe	1,2,4
5481b	XII	I	Fe	1,2,4
5481c	XII	I	St	1,3
5483e&s.e	XII	I	St	1,3
5528e	XII	III	St	1,3
5528s	XII	III	Fe	1,2,4
5529e	XII	III	St	1,3
5529s	XII	III	Fe	1,2,4
5493e	XII	I	St	1,3
5482c	XII	I	St	1,3
5482l	XII	I	Fe	1,2,4
5482r	XII	I	Fe	1,2,4
5497e	XII	II	St	1,3
5497s	XII	II	Fe	1,2,4
5503Fe	XII	II	Fe	1,2,4
5503St	XII	II	St	1,3
5498e	XII	II	St	1,3
5498l	XII	II	Fe	1,2,4
5498r	XII	II	Fe	1,2,4
5498b	XII	II	Fe	1,2,4
5502c.1-8	XII	II	St	1,3
5502l.9-14	XII	II	Fe	1,2,4
5502r.15-20	XII	II	Fe	1,2,4
5502b	XII	II	Fe	1,2,4
5480c	XIII	II	St	1,3
5480r	XIII	II	Fe	1,2,5
5480l	XIII	II	Fe	1,2,5
5494e	XIII	I	St	1,3
5494s	XIII	I	Fe	1,2,5
5495e	XIII	I	St	1,3
5499e	XIII	III	St	1,3
5499s	XIII	III	Fe	1,2,5
5500Fe	XIII	II	Fe	1,2,5
5500Fe13.e	XIII	II	St	1,3
5501e1	XIII	I	St	1,3
5501e.r	XIII	I	Fe	1,2,5
5530c	XIII	II	St	1,3
5530l	XIII	II	Fe	1,2,5
5530r	XIII	II	Fe	1,2,5
5496ae	XIII	III	St	1,3
5496as	XIII	III	Fe	1,2,5
5496b	XIII	III	Fe	1,2,5
5505Ae	XIII	III	St	1,3
5505As	XIII	III	Fe	1,2,5
5505B	XIII	III	Fe	1,2,5
5144e&st	XIII	II	St	1,3
5144Fe&s	XIII	II	Fe	1,2,5
5148ae.1-8,10-14	XIII	I	St	1,3
5148al.15-19	XIII	I	Fe	1,2,5
5148ar.9,20-23	XIII	I	Fe	1,2,5
5148b	XIII	I	Fe	1,2,5
5149ae	XIII	I	St	1,3
5149as	XIII	I	Fe	1,2,5
5149b	XIII	I	Fe	1,2,5
5147e	XIII	III	St	1,3
5147s	XIII	III	Fe	1,2,5
5150aFe	XIII	III	Fe	1,2,5
5146e	XIV	III	St	1,3
5146s	XIV	III	Fe	1,2
5145e	XIV	III	St	1,3
5145s	XIV	III	Fe	1,2
5504e		III	St	1,3
5504Fe		III	Fe	1,2

Figure 12.3 Example bivariate plot showing the overlap of samples from the 12th and 13th centuries.

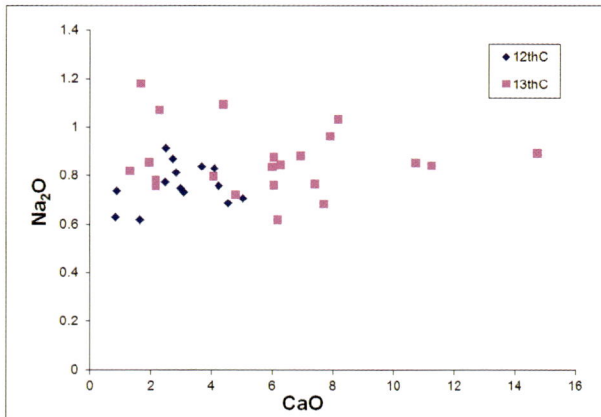

CONCLUSIONS AND FURTHER RESEARCH

Medieval Novgorod played a significant role in the regional political struggles of the first half of the second millennium AD and through its unique environmental conditions is now playing a significant role in telling the stories of the common people who built her streets and churches. In attempting to understand the development of this great city the study of technological choices within the ironworker's craft may be providing insight into patterns of migration and technology transfer in the 12th and 13th centuries. To this end, this project was conducted to test the following hypotheses: 1) that there exists a statistically significant difference in composition of slag inclusions between the 12th and the 13th century and 2) that there exists a statistically significant difference in the compositions of slag inclusions due to the raw materials selected for different methods of construction. Based on SEM-EDS and statistical analysis, there appears to be a significant change in the compositional makeup of the slag inclusions in the uncarburized sections of knives dating from the 12th to the 13th century from medieval Novgorod. Thus, the first hypothesis is solidly supported by the statistical analysis, which indicates a major shift in the raw materials being used to produce these knives. Further research should now focus on whether this is due to a shift in the ore source used to produce the iron or a change in the process used to extract the iron.

The second hypothesis asserts that the slag inclusions in knives produced using different construction methods would exhibit different chemical compositions. If a difference in the composition of inclusions could be found to correlate with construction method it would then be reasonable to posit that the smiths who preferred to use a particular method also preferred a particular iron. However, this hypothesis was not confirmed by analysis of the data. It is thus possible to say that it is unlikely the observed difference in the chemical composition of slag inclusions between the 12th and 13th centuries is the result of a shift in the quantities of knives produced by using specific iron sources for specific construction methods.

From this work it seems clear that a major shift in the nature of the iron used at Novgorod for the production of knives took place between the 12th and 13th centuries.

This change likely reflects either a change in the source of ore being selected by the iron smelters or an alteration in the extractive process being used. If the hypothesis of Rosanova and Zavyalov is true, that there is a shift in the cultural makeup of the ironworking community, it is entirely reasonable to expect a change in either or both of these parameters as a different cultural tradition of ironworking is pursued.

Another interesting possibility, which deserves further research, is the potential importation of fined iron being produced in blast furnaces to the west. Novgorod's position as a major trading centre would have made it possible for smiths to access this new imported iron and the slag inclusions in fined iron could be expected to have compositions quite different from those in bloomery iron.

Further research on iron at Novgorod should make even better use of the tight chronology available and, using a larger set of data, attempt to determine if there is a specific half century (e.g. 1250–1300, 1275–1325) during which the shift in iron composition primarily occurred. It would also be worthwhile to expand the study to other neighbouring sites which favour the Northern or the Southern traditions and determine whether the slag inclusions from Novgorod would group with those of other sites. Lastly, the implications of the technological shift from one construction method to another, originally identified by Kolchin, should have deeper roots in the socioeconomic environment of 12th and 13th century Novgorod. This is a very important aspect of the meaning of this analytical data and a dialogue should develop with archaeologists studying other aspects of Novgorod's history, particularly other crafts such as woodworking and pottery, in order to bring this socioeconomic change into clearer focus.

Acknowledgements

The authors are deeply grateful to V. I. Zavyalov for his generosity in allowing his samples to be taken from Moscow to London for study. Additional thanks are owed to N. V. Eniossova and the archaeology faculty at MGU for graciously hosting the first author's stay in Moscow and to IAMS (the Institute for Archaeo-Metallurgical Studies) for providing funding for the trip. Thanks are also due to Simon Groom and Kevin Reeves for their patience and interested support in this project. The first author is also tremendously indebted to Thilo Rehren and Clive Orton for their careful tutelage in developing the skills needed for this work and their patience with the unexpected events that have complicated the completion of this paper. Most importantly, the first author must give his deepest thanks to Aurie Jeffery for her patience and support in this work and her hours of careful editing. The research reported here was completed in 2004, before several more recent significant publications on slag inclusions in iron artefacts were published. Unfortunately, these could therefore not be considered in this study.

13

METAL MELTING CRUCIBLES
FROM MEDIEVAL NOVGOROD

N. Eniosova and Th. Rehren

INTRODUCTION

Systematic archaeological excavation of medieval Novgorod has brought to light a wide range of evidence for metalworking from the middle of the 10th to the late 15th centuries. More than 30 jewellers' workshops have been excavated in the five Quarters (or Ends) of the medieval town (Kolchin 1985, 261). The most frequent finds of manufacturing evidence are crucibles: they appear in great numbers of individual fragments and at least 40 complete vessels. Well-preserved structural remains of streets and properties allow a very precise dating of workshop complexes and artefacts by dendrochronological methods.

There are no indications of primary metal processing in medieval Novgorod: non-ferrous and precious metals reached the town by various routes from Western and Eastern Europe, Byzantium and the Middle East. A detailed analytical investigation of 900 copper-based objects and metalworking debris from Novgorod made by Konovalov (2008) revealed the chemical characterization of the alloys used.[1] The material discussed below complements this by providing evidence of metal melting, refining and casting. The relationship between finished artefacts, metalworking debris and metallic residues from the crucibles offers a unique research opportunity, based on decades of archaeological work.

METHODOLOGY

The 120 samples from Novgorod were examined at the Department of Archaeology, Moscow State University, by optical microscopy with reference to details of their construction, fabric and the preserved traces of metal. The major part of examined samples contains metalliferous deposits instead of original metal. The identification of the metal nature was based on non-destructive ED-XRF qualitative analyses, using an instrument and software ArtTAX (Röntgenanalysen-Technik) fitted with a Mo target and semiconductor detector (Figure 13.1). Typical analytical conditions were a tube voltage of 50 kV and a current of 700 µA. Each spectrum was recorded for 180 seconds. The measuring head contains a video camera recording a sample surface

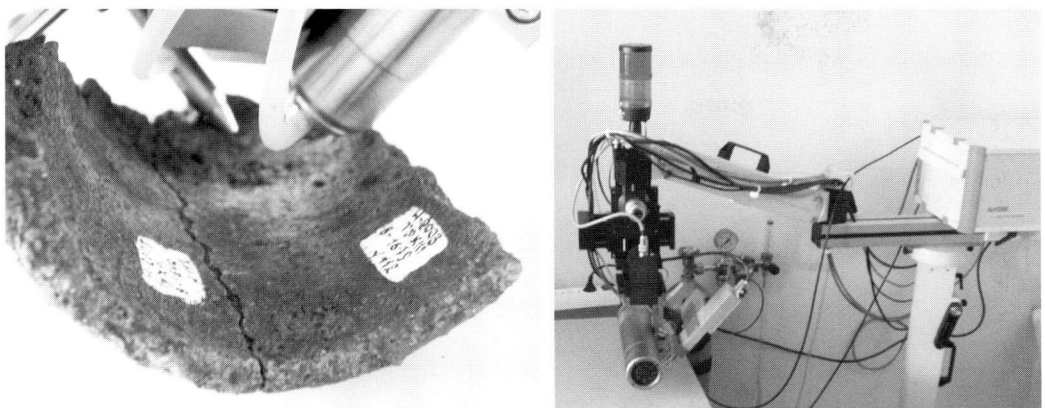

Figure 13.1 ED-XRF ArtTAX system with a sample positioning laser spot delimiting the position of the incident X-ray beam on the sample surface.

area of approximately 6 × 4 mm. A sample positioning laser spot is used to delimit the position of the incident X-ray beam on the sample surface (Figure 13.2). Small metal prills have been analyzed with a 0.2 mm collimator. The scan/mapping device has been set up to analyze large areas of the inner and outer surface of crucible sherds.

In practice, the chemical composition of metallic elements detected in crucible residues differs in many ways from its true composition due to the complicated structure of the crucible slag and its heterogeneity, as well as the influence of metal corrosion and metal surface enrichment (Bayley 1992, 817–818; Dungworth 2000, 83–86). However, with caution qualitative results can be interpreted to estimate what metal or alloy was melted in the crucible.

In addition, two polished cross-sections of crucible bodies were analysed by optical and scanning electron microscopy (SEM) at the laboratories of the Institute of Archaeology, UCL, for the compositions of ceramic fabrics and slags.

CHRONOLOGICAL VARIATIONS

About 80% of finds derive from the Nerevsky and Troitsky sites, situated on the St. Sophia (the West) side of the river Volkhov, and the Duboshin site situated on the Trade (the East) side of the city (Figure 13.3). On the basis of morphological features crucibles are classified into 12 main types.

From the early deposits of Troitsky and Nerevsky sites (mid 10th to late 11th centuries) there are predominately open cylindrical crucibles, conical vessels with a wide triangular mouth, open flat-bottom spoons with long tubular handles, open and lidded boat-shaped vessels, and shallow dishes (Figure 13.4). They vary in height, diameter and clay fabric. The volume of the early crucibles is estimated to be from 4 up to 50 cm^3, equivalent to a metal weight of between 30 and 400 grams.

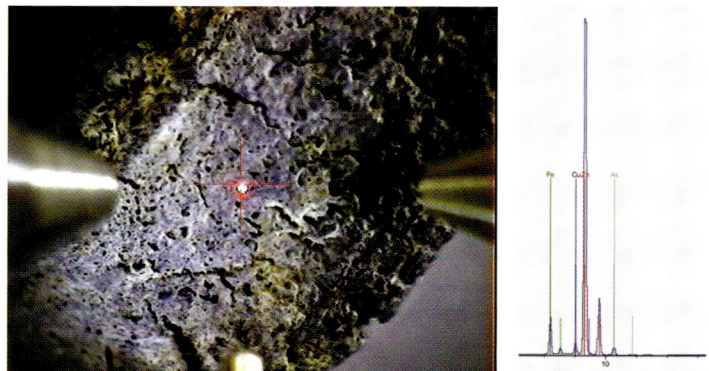

Figure 13.2 *A sample surface area of approx. 6 × 4 mm with positioning spot and the X-ray spectrum of the crucible lid (Troitsky XII, Property E, late 11th century).*

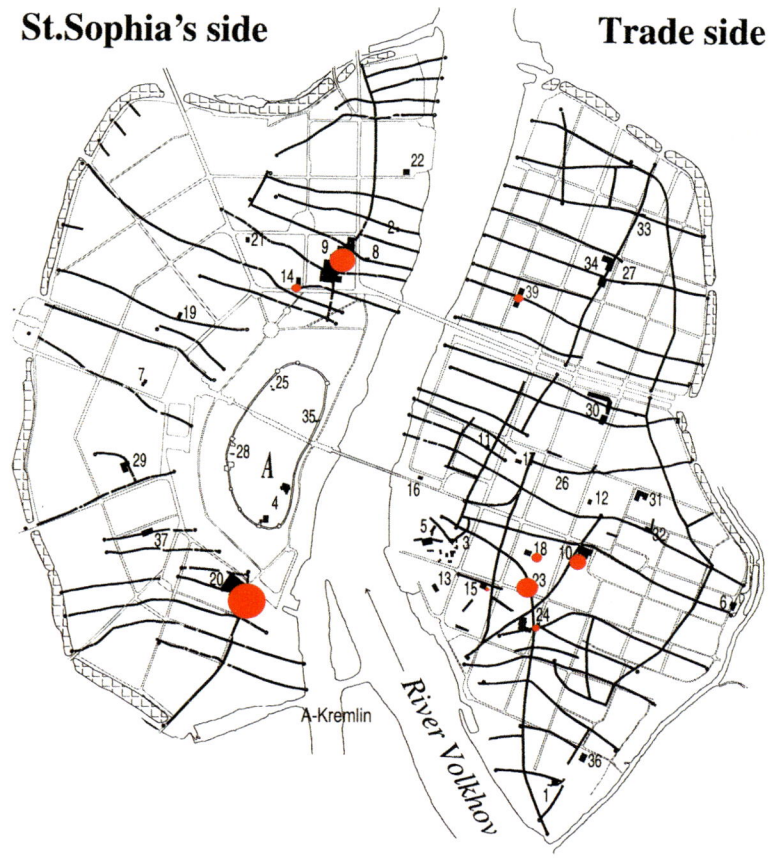

Figure 13.3 *Plan of medieval Novgorod showing the location of excavations as well as distribution and relative concentrations of crucibles. Sites: 9 – Nerevsky, 10 – Ilynsky, 14 – Tikhvinsky, 15 – Mikhilovsky, 18 – Kirovsky, 20 – Troitsky, 23 – Duboshin, 24 – Nutny, 39 – Nikitinsky.*

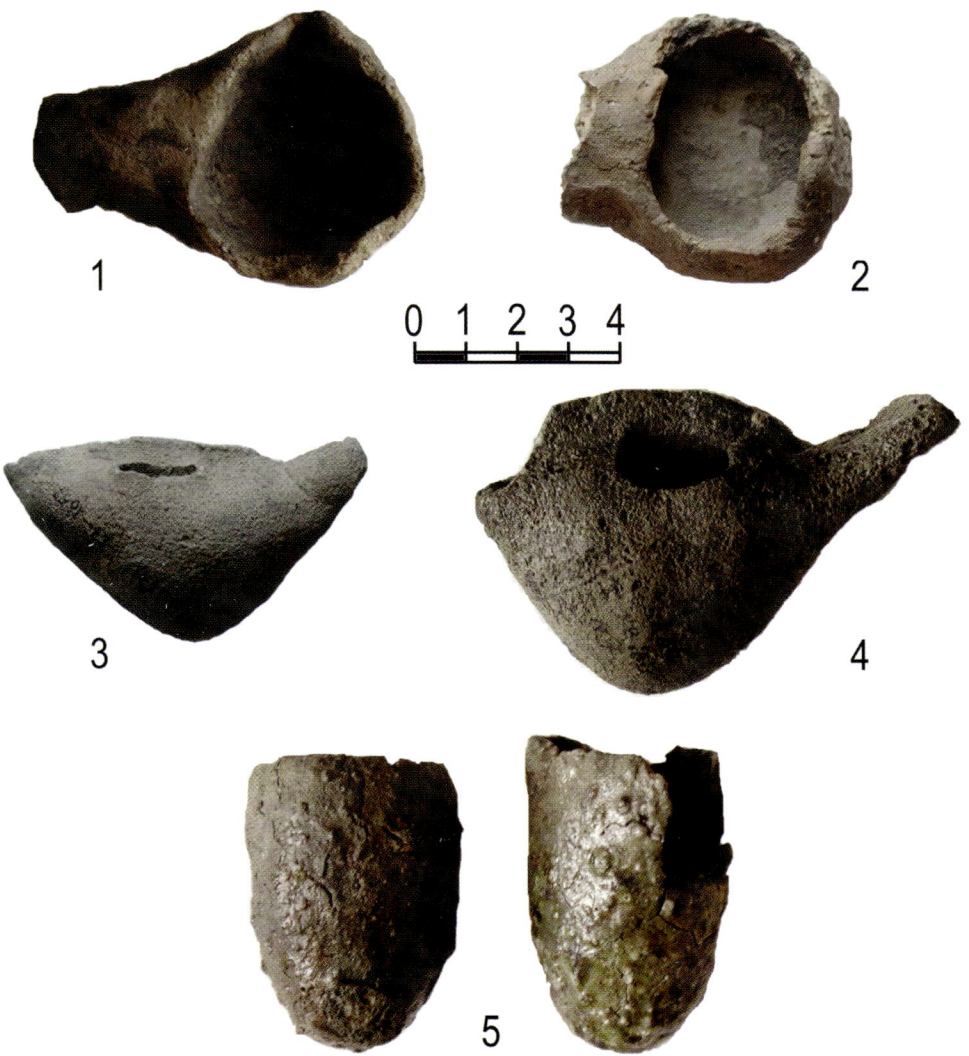

Figure 13.4 *Selection of crucibles from the Nerevsky site, Novgorod (10th–11th centuries): 1–2) open flat-bottom spoons with tubular handles; 3) 'sealed' boat-shaped vessel; 4) boat-shaped vessel with a solid handle; 5) cylindrical crucibles.*

Analysed examples of crucible charge show brass (Cu-Zn), ternary brass (Cu-Zn-Pb), impure copper, silver and pewter. The range of artefact composition is very similar, except for silver samples that have not been identified among the jewellery and metalworking debris, and bronze samples have not been found among the crucible residues (Figure 13.5). There is no particular type of metal or alloy processing in the open cylindrical crucibles and conical vessels with a wide triangular mouth. On the other hand, a group of open flat-bottomed spoons with tubular handles is a

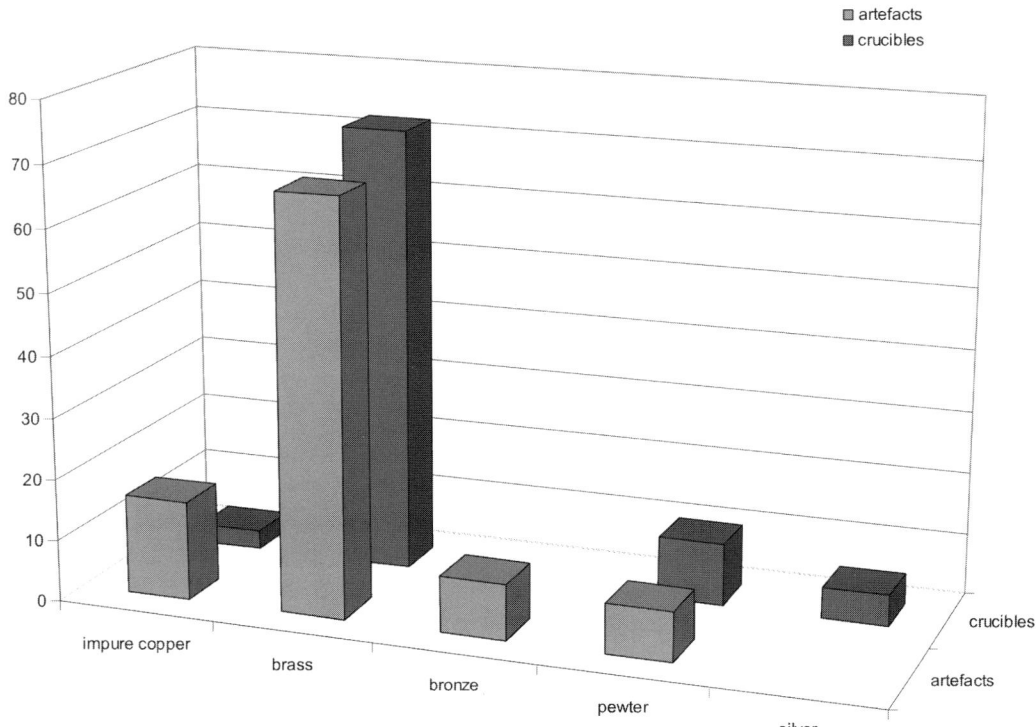

Figure 13.5 *Composition of artefacts and crucible residues (10th–11th centuries).*

good example of special purpose melting vessels (Figure 13.4.1, 2). They have been made of non-refractory red or grey clay and have no traces of vitrification or even high temperature effects. No slag or visible metal remains have been detected on the inner surface of the spoons microscopically. However, XRF analyses show that these crucibles contain lead, tin or pewter.

Shallow dishes with diameters of 55–65 mm and height of 20–25 mm were intended for small-scale silver testing or refining (Bayley 1992, 748–749). They have been made of low refractory grey clay with low alumina and high potash, soda and lime concentrations, tempered with quartz grains and charcoal. Their vitrified upper surfaces appear olive-green and dark red indicating that these dishes were heated directly from above (Figure 13.6). Silver, lead and copper were detectable on the upper surface of the shallow dishes (Table 13.1).

Source	Na_2O	MgO	Al_2O_3	SiO_2	K_2O	CaO	TiO_2	Fe_2O_3	CuO	Ag_2O	PbO
Ceramic fabric	1.34	0.53	3.60	49.58	2.48	0.64	0.25	1.83	21.00	4.94	13.80
Metal slag	1.28	0.50	1.93	29.68	0.98	0.72	0.27	1.93	36.85	8.38	17.48

Table 13.1 *Average composition of ceramic fabric and metal slag of the shallow dish (SEM/EDX analyses normalized to 100wt% for all elements).*

"Sealed" boat-shaped vessels provided with a handle placed horizontally to their back edge and with a narrow slit on the top were intended for silver refining and melting (Figure 13.4.3, 4). In contrast to the dark grey ceramic fabric of most melting vessels tempered with medium-coarse quartz grains (Figure 13.7.1), the latter group of crucibles is made of fine white or grey-light clay (Figure 13.7.2). They were used as a jeweller's container for safe keeping of silver scrap; silver remains were identified inside the crucibles. The spout of the filled vessel was struck off only before the melting of the metal, probably once the vessel was full or a small amount of silver needed.

The dynamics of the metal craft development seem to start changing during the 12th to 13th centuries when one can see an increase of the availability of metal in Novgorod (Rybina 2001, 231). The amount of non-ferrous and precious metal objects suggest that they were produced on a large scale. This increase in availability is also testified by the increase of crucible volumes up to 100 cm^3 and a wide range of alloys found in the metal melting vessels of different shapes, volumes and functions (Figure 13.8). Besides brass, copper and tin-lead alloys there are now tin-bronze (Cu-Sn), leaded copper (Cu-Pb), gunmetal, sterling and debased silver and gold. The range of artefact composition, however, does not change much over the earlier period (Figure 13.9).

The largest dateable assemblage of crucibles comes from the Troitsky site. Over 120 sherds and 4 complete cylindrical round-bottomed crucibles come from property E, dated to the late 11th–early 12th century (Figure 13.10). They show a remarkable standardization with the same height (94–95 mm), diameter (45 mm), wall and bottom thickness (5 and 10 mm), volume (60 cm^3) as well as a dark grey, charcoal-tempered fabric of fine clay with a small amount of quartz. The slags inside of these crucibles are very rich in zinc oxide and contain copper and lead. Undoubtedly, all these vessels were used for brass melting. Some of them had round lids preventing zinc evaporation (Figure 13.10.2). The dark violet ceramic fabric of the lids is tempered with abundant quartz grains, amounting to around 70% by volume. The main metallurgical contamination is zinc oxide, reaching up to 57% by weight together with copper and lead oxides in lower concentrations (Table 13.2).

Source	MgO	Al_2O_3	SiO_2	K_2O	CaO	TiO_2	Fe_2O_3	CuO	ZnO	PbO
Ceramic fabric	0.77	20.56	68.74	2.27	2.09	1.25	3.79	0.35	0.69	-
Metal slag	0.94	1.4	30.80	0.19	0.40	0.09	4.29	0.14	57.13	1.76

Table 13.2 *Average composition of ceramic fabric and metal slag of the cylindrical round-bottomed crucibles (SEM/EDX analyses normalized to 100wt% for all elements).*

The late 12th to early 13th centuries were a period of flourishing metalworking activity on Property A of the Troitsky site, which belonged to the priests and artists of St. Sophia's Cathedral. About 20 small crucibles were found among goldsmiths'

Figure 13.6 *Shallow dish fragment from the Nerevsky site, Novgorod (Property B, early 11th century).*

and painters' tools, ecclesiastical and ordinary items (Kolchin *et al.* 1981, 129–135). The boat-shaped vessels were made of fine, white clay and partly closed (Figure 13.8.4). The chemical analyses of the metal prills inside these crucibles allowed us to identify debased gold and silver as well as drops of mercury. The combination of gold and silver with mercury indicates amalgam preparation. This was possibly applied to the richly decorated icon frames made of copper and found at the same workshop.

Over the course of the 14th to 15th centuries the wide variety of crucible forms and their significant quantities provide the evidence for thriving metalworking activity in the town. Open round-bottomed cylindrical or conical vessels of different size and open boat-shaped crucibles predominate in these late deposits (Figure 13.11).

Large stoneware crucibles were introduced to the casting technique in the late 14th to early 15th centuries (Figure 13.12). A remarkable concentration of stoneware melting vessels was found on the Duboshin site in the upper layers dated to the period *c* 1392–1415 (Gaidukov 1997, 63). They were also found at the workshops of properties

Figure 13.7 Crucibles: 1) open boat-shaped crucible showing the ceramic fabric with abundant quartz grains ((Troitsky XII, Property E, mid-11th century); 2) 'sealed' boat-shaped crucible made of fine white clay.

Figure 13.8 *Selection of crucibles from the Troitsky site, Novgorod (12–13th centuries): 1–2) shallow dishes for silver cupellation; 3) open boat-shaped vessel; 4) small crucibles from the priest's workshop (Property A).*

B and E on the Nerevsky site, dated to 1382–1429 and from the Troitsky Property E dated to the mid 15th century (Zasurtzev 1963, 71–72; Yanin *et al.* 1996, 7). All crucibles were large enough to hold several kg of bronze, indicating an industrial scale of casting activity during the last centuries of the Novgorod republic. Remarkable concentrations of metalworking debris including copper alloy ingots, wire and scrap derive from the late deposits. Written sources testify that non-ferrous metals came

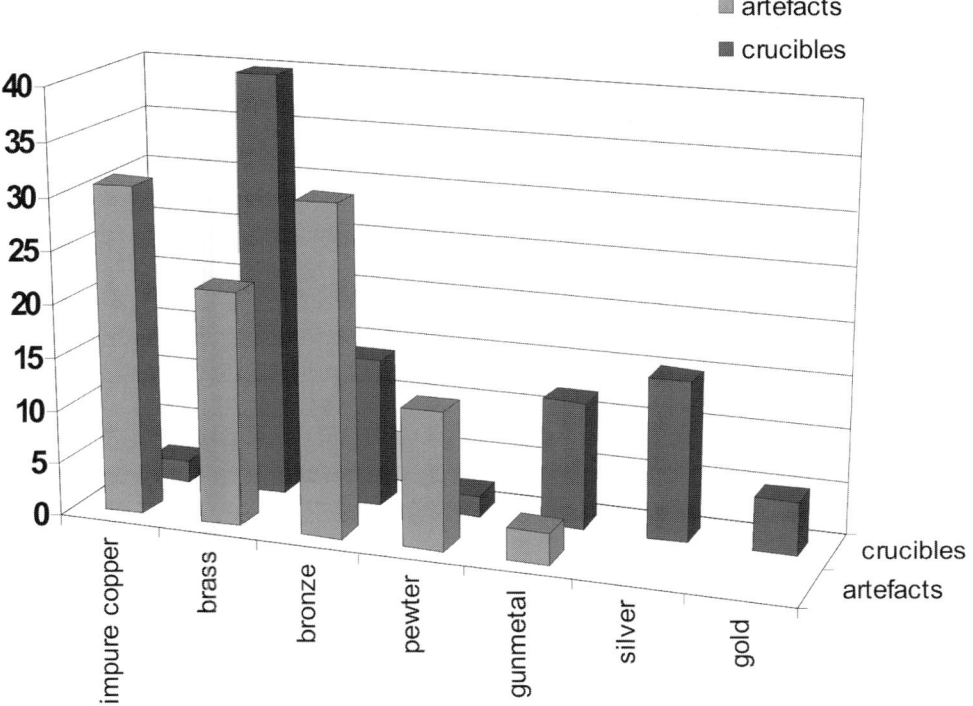

Figure 13.9 *Composition of artefacts and crucible residues (12th–13th centuries).*

to Novgorod market as irregular lumps and regular ingots, wire hanks, fragments of vessels and cauldrons and reused scrap packed in big stave-built vessels (Choroshkevich 1963, 314–315). A large-size lead ingot with the stamp of the Polish king Kazimierz the Great weighing at least 151 kg discovered during excavations on the Ilynsky site allows us to estimate the scale of metal import into Novgorod in the 14th century (Yanin 1966, 324).

Lidded crucible forms continued to be in use up to the 14th century but never occurred in the 15th century. In contrast to

Figure 13.10 *Crucibles from the Troitsky site, Novgorod (Property E, late 11th to early 12th century). Standard cylindrical round-bottom vessels with lids for brass melting.*

219

Figure 13.11 Selection of crucibles from the Nerevsky site, Novgorod (14th–15th centuries). Cylindrical and conical vessels of different size.

the previous periods there are no open flat-bottomed spoons with tubular handles for lead/tin melting and shallow dishes for silver testing and cupellation. Analysed examples of the crucible slags and metal remains revealed that jewellers used small vessels for the melting of gold and silver, while large crucibles were used mainly for bronze, leaded bronze and gunmetal. The compositional range of analysed objects, ingots, scrap and waste metal shows a different distribution; they include impure copper, brass, bronze and pewter (Figure 13.13).

SUMMARY

The intensive archaeological study of medieval Novgorod over the past 75 years has produced over 3000 single crucible fragments and 40 complete vessels providing evidence of metal melting, refining and casting in the workshops situated in the five Quarters (or Ends) of the town. This study focuses on the investigation of the chronological distribution of the crucibles, their fabric, and the chemical characterization of the metal and alloys melted in vessels of different shapes and sizes. A total of 120 samples from the Nerevsky, Troitsky and Duboshin sites were examined by optical microscopy with reference to details of their construction, fabric and the preserved traces of metal slag and metal prills. The identification of the metal was provided by non-destructive ED-XRF qualitative analyses. The range of metallic residues from the crucibles, in contrast to the range of almost 900 copper-based objects'

Figure 13.12 *Large stoneware crucibles from the Duboshin site, Novgorod (late 14th–early 15th centuries).*

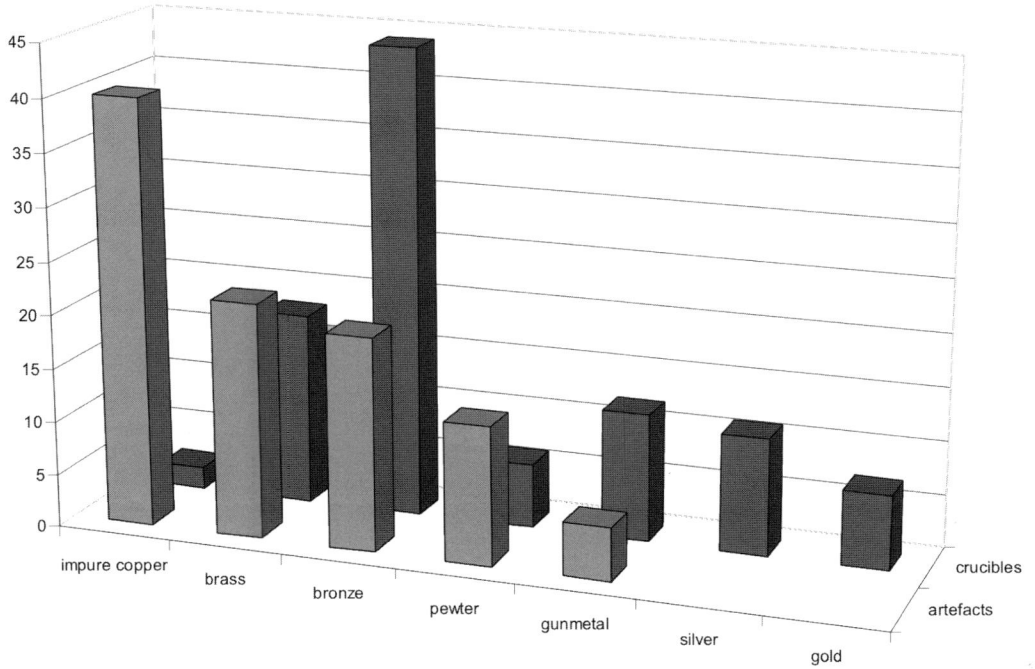

Figure 13.13 *Composition of artefacts and crucible residues (14th–15th centuries).*

composition, provides an interesting research opportunity for an estimation of the raw materials that came to jewellers' workshops from different sources.

On the basis of morphological features, the crucibles may be classified into 12 main types. From the mid-tenth to late eleventh centuries there were open cylindrical crucibles, conical vessels with a wide triangular mouth, open flat-bottomed spoons with long tubular handles, open and lidded boat-shaped vessels and shallow dishes. Analysed examples of crucible charge show brass (Cu-Zn), ternary brass (Cu-Zn-Pb), impure copper, silver and pewter. The range of artefact composition is very similar, except for silver and bronze samples.

The dynamics of the development of the metal craft seem to start changing during the 12th to 13th centuries when one can see an increase in the availability of metal in Novgorod. The amount of non-ferrous and precious metal objects suggests that they were produced on a large scale. This increase in availability is also testified by the increase of crucible volumes up to 100 cm³ and a wide range of alloys found in the metal-melting vessels of different shapes, volumes and functions. Besides brass, copper and tin-lead alloys there are now tin-bronze (Cu-Sn), leaded copper (Cu-Pb), gunmetal, sterling and debased silver and gold. The range of artefact composition, however, does not change much compared with the earlier period.

Over the course of the 14th to 15th centuries the wide variety of crucible forms and their significant quantities provide the evidence for thriving metalworking activity in the town. Open round-bottomed cylindrical or conical vessels of varying size and open boat-shaped crucibles predominate in these late deposits. The increase in crucible volume testifies to an increase in the importation and availability of raw materials for non-ferrous metalworking from the 12th to the 15th centuries.

CONCLUSIONS

The analyses of crucibles from Novgorod have shown a great variety of crucible forms, sizes and fabrics. There is some clear correlation between forms and alloy types; the shallow dishes and small boat-shaped vessels made of fine white clay were solely intended for precious metal working, and the early lidded tubular crucibles with a porous fabric are mostly used for brass melting. Open flat-bottomed spoons with long tubular handles were well fitted for lead, tin and pewter melting at low temperatures, not requiring particularly refractory ceramics. The relatively late, large stoneware crucibles were predominantly linked to bronze. On the other hand, gold, silver and pewter were all identified in both big and small cylindrical and conical vessels made of fine, medium coarse and coarse fabrics, indicating an opportunistic crucible manufacture, probably for small-scale, ad-hoc castings. There seems to be a general trend towards larger size cylindrical and conical crucibles from the 12th to the 15th centuries.

The increase of crucible volume testifies to an increase in the importation and availability of raw materials for non-ferrous metalworking. During the 11th and 12th centuries a growing metal market in Novgorod was supplied by Gotlanders. Within a century Novgorod became a part of the Hanseatic system and the main gate in the Russian-European metal trade.

Acknowledgements

The authors wish to thank the Novgorod State Museum and the Novgorod Archaeological Research Centre for providing the samples to be analysed, Dr Robert Mitoyan from Moscow State University (Dept. of Geochemistry) who kindly assisted in ED-XRF analyses, and Dr Natalia Ryndina from Moscow State University (Dept. of Archaeology) who provided us with archaeological information on the Nerevsky site crucibles from her personal archive. This research forms part of the INTAS project 00-154 "Craft production, environment and landscape: an archaeological study of the centre/periphery relationships based on the evidence of the exploration and processing of natural resources in medieval Novgorod and its region" and their support is gratefully acknowledged.

Note

1   Konovalov (2008) obtained his data for ten major (Cu, Sn, Pb, Zn) and minor (Ag, As, Sb, Bi, Ni, Au) elements by optical emission spectroscopy.

14

THE PRODUCTION OF TEXTILES IN NOVGOROD FROM THE 10TH TO THE 14TH CENTURIES

E. K. Kublo

INTRODUCTION

Textile items do not constitute the largest group among the archaeological finds obtained from the habitation levels of medieval Novgorod. Nevertheless the material accumulated so far has made it possible to carry out a systematic analysis of this category of finds and to draw certain conclusions regarding the technical features of the manufacture of textile items in chronological order and also to determine the ratio of local to imported textiles.

Techniques used for manufacturing textiles in the medieval period have long been a subject of interest to researchers. One of the early Russian articles on this subject worthy of mention here is the article by Tikhonov (1931). The year after an article came out by Voskresenskii and Tikhonov (1932). These articles dealt with finds from excavations in burial-grounds consisting of burial-mounds, in which certain details of clothing had survived thanks to the proximity of oxidized bronze. Prior to the 1950s virtually all articles on such subjects had been based on materials from burials and it was only after the beginning of wide-scale archaeological excavations in Novgorod that it became possible to form a picture of the enormous diversity of medieval textiles from a chronological point of view. While the range of textiles from burial-grounds was determined by the traditions of the funerary rite, the cultural deposits relating to the 10th–15th centuries preserved fragments of everyday clothes and other textile items which would not have made their way into burials.

An article by Chernyikh (1958) was devoted to the collection of textiles from the Nerevsky excavation (1951–1962), in which the author investigated textile finds from 1951–1956. A few years later Nakhlik (1963) produced a fundamental study which contained a classification of textiles and a detailed examination of techniques used for their manufacture. Considerable space in this article was devoted to the identification of imported specimens, to which end the author referred to works on the history of medieval cloth production elsewhere in Europe.

It should be pointed out straightaway that virtually no vegetable fibres have survived in Novgorod's archaeological deposits and yet it was linen that provided the basis for clothes and many other everyday items. We also know that hemp, willow, lime and even spruce were used for the production of fibres. In the Novgorod Kremlin excavations of 2004 parts of footwear were found, in the soles of which thick threads had survived used for sewing soles on to vamps and counters. Anatomical investigations of these threads revealed that they consisted of willow and spruce fibres.[1] Admittedly these finds relate to the 16th and 17th centuries and it would be inappropriate to link that technique to an earlier period. We can only assume that these late finds point back to an earlier tradition.

Most of the textile fragments which have survived were made from sheep's wool and only a few were of vegetable origin or made from silk fibres.

Later in this article we shall provide a description of the textile finds from the Troitsky excavation, where work began in 1973 and continues to the present day (2008). During the last 30 years this has been the largest excavation within the territory of Novgorod: approximately 10,000 m² has been excavated. Several medieval properties have been cleared in their entirety and the earliest levels date from the first half of the 10th century. Finds from other excavations in Novgorod will be referred to where relevant.

This study requires a wide review of the excavated textile collection, as well as its composition. We shall also consider the various methods used for manufacturing the different kinds of textiles and their technical features.

For this study 390 specimens have been examined: of these three were made from vegetable fibres, nine of silk, while the others were fragments of woollen cloth, knitted or looped items, and also individual fibres and felt. Most of the specimens were fragments from woven wool items, a total of 330 in all; belts, cords and separate threads accounted for 28 of the items; items looped with a needle for 14; felt insoles and pieces of felt for six. The classification was based on the above-mentioned article by Nakhlik (1963) in which he divided textiles into four varieties (or sorts) depending upon the density of the weave. Similar criteria had been used for identifying textiles by Geijer (1938) for textiles from Birka.

The four sorts are described as follows from coarsest to finest:

Sort IV included textiles with a thickness between 0.6 mm and 2 mm from coarse thick yarn with a large amount of coarse fibres and with threads that were between 0.5 and 2 mm thick: the density of the weave was up to 10 threads per cm for the warp and up to 8 threads per cm for the weft, i.e. there were no more than 18 threads per cm² although in isolated instances there were eight threads per cm in the warp and four threads in the weft. The yarn for this group of textiles was made up of short fibres (between 1.5 and 3.5 cm long) and the shortest of these were the finest not exceeding 14 microns of soft, downy fibres. Of the longer fibres, the coarse ones had a thickness of up to 50 microns. This kind of yarn was used not only for making cloth but also for knitted and knotted items such as socks, stockings, mittens, headwear and belts.

Sort III consisted of textiles with a thickness between 0.6 and 1.2 mm of a more even yarn: the threads in the warp were between 0.16 and 0.3 mm (an average thickness of 0.24 mm), while the thickness of the weft threads ranged from 0.3 to 0.8 mm (average thickness 0.35 mm). This meant that the overall density of the weave taking the warp and the weft together was up to 27 threads per cm²: up to 15 warp threads and up to 12 weft ones. Frequently, however, different ratios of the numbers of threads in the warp and weft were encountered, when there might be 13–14 threads in the warp and 5–6 threads in the weft per cm². The threads of the warp in textiles of this sort were more even and more often than not they consisted of medium fibres. In one pitch of the twist there might be 16–18, while the threads of the weft could include soft/downy, medium and coarse fibres and the total number of fibres in one pitch of the twist could come to between 70 and 150. The textiles in question were of a 3/1 twill weave.

Sort II consisted of textiles with up to 37 threads per cm²: up to 22 threads in the warp and up to 15 threads in the weft per cm. The thickness of these threads varied between 0.45 mm to 1 mm. This category also included a group of textiles of exactly the same type as we saw in the case of Sort III: the warp threads were thin (0.16 to 0.30 mm) while the threads of the weft were fairly thick (between 0.16 and 0.80 mm). Some fragments of textiles of this type bore traces of having been turned under along their edges. This category also included textiles with a 3/1 or 4/1 twill weave in which the threads of the warp and weft were of approximately the same thickness (0.12 to 0.26 mm in the case of the warp and 0.15 to 0.35 mm in the weft). The quality of the yarn did not differ in any way from the yarn of the preceding group. Evidently these textiles were made of local raw materials, but more carefully processed fibres were used for the warp. In this group there were several fragments of textiles classifiable as belonging to Sort II as regards the density of the weave, while the quality of the wool used would indicate that they belonged to Sort I.

Textiles classified as belonging to **Sort I** were of high quality and their average thickness was 0.5 cm: they were made of fine fibres and evenly spun threads between 0.06 and 0.14 mm thick in the warp and between 0.08 and 0.2 mm thick in the weft, so that the overall density of the weave was over 37 threads per cm². Table 14.1 demonstrates the spread of the various Sorts according to date.

As can be seen from the table the largest number of finds was obtained from the 12th-century levels, followed by those of the 13th century, while the smallest number of textile fragments was that found in 14th-century levels. Here it should be pointed out that the 14th-century levels in the Troitsky Excavation do not provide a complete picture of the formation of those particular levels, since the organic materials from the upper layers in that part of Novgorod have not survived well. It is possible that this

	Sort I	Sort II	Sort III	Sort IV	Total amount
14th cent.	6	5	12	11	34
13th cent.	9	15	22	16	62
12th cent.	27	15	40	33	115
11th cent.	13	8	8	15	44
10th cent.	7	9	23	16	55
Total no. of finds	62	52	105	91	

Table 14.1 Spread of textile finds according to date.

is linked with the level of the water table. The levels of the 10th and 13th centuries, meanwhile, in particular the 10th-century ones, constitute quite thick layers filled with organic remains. The largest amount of textile finds is that from the 12th century and, among those, textiles of Sort III predominate when it comes to density of weave, i.e. they are most common textiles.

It should be noted that the word 'sort' implies only a level of quality and nothing more and that density of weave and quality do not always correspond. Quite often specimens are encountered in which the threads of the weft are 2 to 3 times thicker than the threads of the warp and incorporate fibres of varying composition. In such cases there might be 10 threads of the warp and 4 to 5 of the weft and such textiles are known as textiles of uneven density and, moreover, this feature can be found in all four Sorts. In respect of textiles of Sort I, textiles of uneven density account for 43% of the total, for Sort II textiles the equivalent figure is 55%, for Sort III textiles 48% and 46% for Sort IV textiles. This can be explained by the fact that the use of thick weft threads significantly accelerates the weaving process. Yet, as a rule, the weft threads are twisted loosely and those of the warp tightly: this is no coincidence in so far as the threads of the warp need to be stretched tightly and evenly on the loom. The loosely twisted threads of the weft render the cloth soft and even in those cases when the thickness of the warp threads and that of the weft threads are identical or almost identical, the weft threads are loosely twisted, with rare exceptions.

LOOM WEAVING

The most widespread types of weave are plain and twill, the latter type used mainly for manufacturing linen cloth, of which we have virtually no remains. In this regard, however, we can to some extent rely on ethnographic data as a source of reference. From Table 14.2 it can be seen that the largest group of finds is that of woollen textiles

	Полотняное 1/1				Простая саржа 2/2, 1/2				Мелкоузорчатая саржа			
	I	II	III	IV	I	II	III	IV	I	II	III	IV
X	4	3	1		5	13	10	15		1	3	
XI		2	3	3	8	4	10	22	2	1		1
XII		3	2	4	25	20	32	26	3	1	2	3
XIII			3	2	14	12	26	10			1	
XIV		2	3	1	1	3	8	9	1			2

Table 14.2 Occurrence of the main types of weave for Sorts I–IV in chronological order (10th to 14th centuries). The left hand column shows Plain Weave 1/1; the middle column is Simple Twill Weave 2/2 and 1/2, and the right hand column shows Finely Patterned Twill.

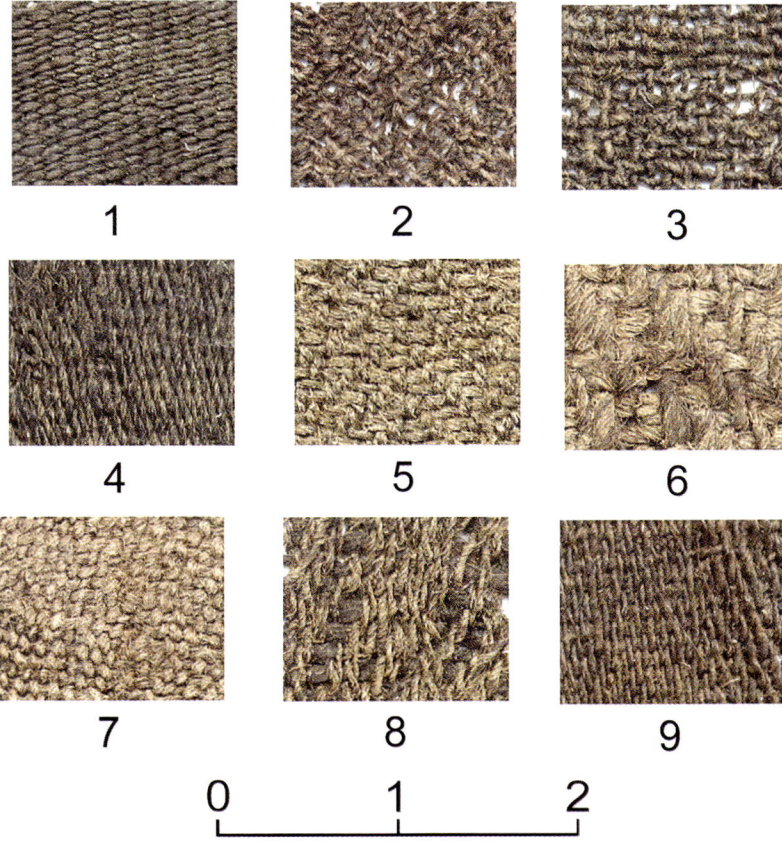

Figure 14.1 Weave techniques: plain (2,3); twill (1,4–6); complex (7–9).
1) N-90, Troitsky X, Spit 3, Quadrant 1144, late-11th or early-12th century; 2) N-86,
Troitsky VIII, Spit 14, Quadrant 770, 11th century; 3) N-87, Troitsky VIII, 10th century; 4)
N-90, Troitsky X, Spit 6, Quadrant 1042, mid-13th century; 5) N-87, Troitsky VIII, Spit 21,
Quadrant 666, 10th century; 6) N-93, Troitsky IX, Spit 13, Quadrant 904, 12th century; 7)
checked weave, N-96, Troitsky XI, Spit 10, Quadrant 1268, late-11th century; 8) diamond
weave, N-96, Troitsky XI, Spit 7, Quadrant 1253, 12th century; 9) checked weave, N-86,
Troitsky VIII, Spit 12, Quadrant 672. 12th century. The scale is in cms.

of a simple twill weave: the number of finds of a plain weave is far smaller and smaller
still is the number of textile fragments with a finely patterned weave, i.e. a complex
twill.

The simplest weaving technique is that for a plain weave in which single warp and
weft threads alternate and the front and reverse sides of the cloth appear identical
(Figure 14.1.2, 3). This method produces the firmest and most durable of textiles. In
the collection of textiles we examined, a plain weave was found in only 36 of the 330
specimens, including open-weave textiles, to which reference will be made below. If

the warp threads are significantly thinner than the weft threads, then a horizontal rib will appear lending the cloth an appearance reminiscent of a rep weave. A fragment of cloth of this type dark-brown in colour was found in the 10th-century levels in the Troitsky excavation (H-87, Spit 23, Quadrant 705).

In the overwhelming majority of textile items we find a twill weave, which does have a characteristic diagonal ridge moving from bottom to top and left to right. In some cases, however, it might go in the opposite direction and then the weave is known as reverse twill (Figure 14.1.1, 4). The angle of the slope of the rib depends upon the thickness of the threads and the density of the weave. If the density of the warp and weft threads is the same, the angle of the sloping ridge will be 45°. The repeat of a twill weave is indicated with a fraction, in which the numerator indicates the number of warp threads and the denominator the number of weft threads. If warp threads predominate on the front surface of the textile, the twill is known as warp twill and indicated by the number 2/1, while if weft threads predominate, the twill is referred to as weft twill and indicated by the number 1/2. If the numbers of warp and weft threads are the same with a difference of only one thread, then the resulting twill is 2/2. Twill weaves can have many variants depending upon the change in the direction of the binding points along the warp, which make it possible to decorate the front side of the textile. There were a total of 21 specimens with a finely patterned design. Eight fragments had a 'herringbone' design (Figure 14.1.5, 6) and in five instances this was found on textiles of Sort IV, while the three other specimens were of Sort II and III textiles. The date range was 11th–14th centuries. All the features of these textiles made it clear that they were of local production. Textiles with a finely patterned weave were probably not used for everyday outer garments, at least in so far as the simple townsfolk were concerned. This can be seen from the complete absence of such patterns worked in coarse wool. A design with a rhomboid pattern was found in six textile fragments: two of these were of Sort I, one of Sort II and three of Sort III, while Sort IV was not represented at all. They fell within the same chronological framework as the textiles with a 'herringbone' design. The two fragments of Sort I had been woven from yarn of high quality, which was thin and even both in the warp and weft. The thickness of the thread in these specimens was between 0.13 and 0.2 mm and the thickness of the fibres was between 15 and 20 microns.[2] One fragment has been dated to the 14th century and another to the 12th and they were both from the Troitsky excavation. The quality of these two specimens makes it possible to classify them as having been produced abroad, but the finely patterned technique in itself is not the defining factor.

SPINNING THREAD

Since we know that spindles and distaffs were found in levels as early as the 10th century, there is every reason to assume that the yarn for woven articles was spun using both spindles and distaffs and that threads were obtained twisted in different

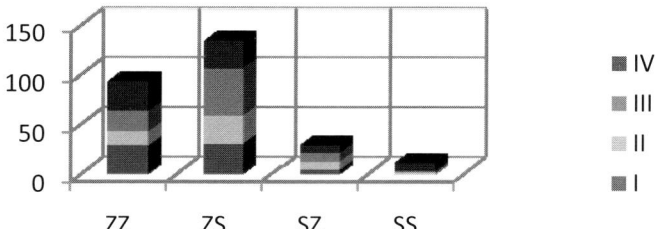

Figure **14.2** *Correlation between different sorts of textile and spinning methods. The Roman numerals on the right designate the textile Sort; the figures in the vertical row to the left indicate the number of specimens; ZZ indicates warp and weft threads twisted to the right; ZS indicates warp threads twisted to the right and weft threads twisted to the left; SZ indicates warp threads twisted to the left and weft threads twisted to the right; SS indicates warp and weft threads twisted to the left.*

directions depending upon the purpose for which the future cloth was being manufactured. More often than not textiles are found in which the warp has been twisted to the right and the weft twisted to the left. In Figure 14.2, a diagram is provided showing the relative amounts of the Sorts of textiles and the main methods used for twisting warp and weft threads.

From the diagram it emerges that the twisting of threads in different directions was used for all sorts of textiles including coarse woollen textiles of Sort IV. This shows that the use of the technique of spinning could not be used as an indication of imported textiles, since all spinners knew how to twist spindles in different directions. Three fragments in which a more complicated method was used for twisting both the warp and the weft were not included in the diagram. One of these from the 10th-century levels in the Troitsky VIII excavation (Spit 21, Quadrant 666) has a warp thread twisted to the right and the two-ply weft thread twisted to the left, each of which has been twisted to the right. As regards the density of the weave, this is a textile of Sort III. The second fragment, also identified as Sort III, was found in 1975 in Troitsky III (Spit 15, Quadrant 131). In the warp of this textile single threads twisted to the right alternate with double threads, each of which is twisted to the right before the two are then twisted together to the left. Here the weft is twisted to the left. In the third fragment the threads of both the warp and the weft are double and twisted together to the right after each of the two individual threads has first been twisted to the left. This was a textile of Sort IV found in Troitsky VII (Spit 2, Quadrant 575) in 10th-century levels. As regards the quality of the yarn all these woollen textiles could be identified as coarse woollen, ordinary woollen or open-weave, namely as cloth of particularly high quality and felted.

Figure 14.3 *Fragment of textile with a looped edge: N-87, Troitsky VIII, Spit 20, Quadrant 754, No. 47. 10th century.*

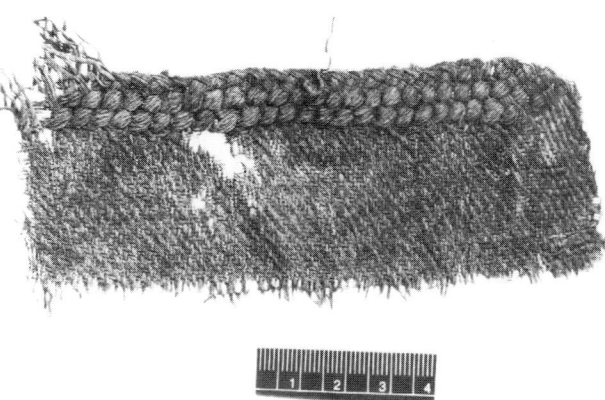

WOOLLEN TEXTILES

Coarse woollens

Items of Sort IV and some of Sort III belong to this category. As regards quantity this is the largest group, it accounts for more than half of all the textile finds. As a rule, these are textiles with a 3/1 or 4/1 twill weave. It can be stated with confidence that these were textiles of local manufacture in so far as they had been made of the same raw material which was used for manufacturing felt and simple looped items. From these textiles outer garments were made as is indicated by the nine fragments with traces of shaping or hemming. Many of these textiles have been dyed shades of brown of varying intensity: the tones range from golden brown to dark brown. Only a few fragments were found of textiles which had not been dyed.

Ordinary woollen textiles

These have a weave with a density ranging from 27 to 37 threads per cm^2 and, as far as the quantity of all these textiles is concerned, they occupy second place. As regards the density of the weave and the quality of the raw material they can be classified as textiles of Sorts II and III. Nine fragments were of a plain weave and in one of them the threads of the weft were twisted from two separate threads to the right, while each of those two threads had been twisted to the left. Many of the textiles of this group had a twill weave of any number of variants – from the simple to the complex: combinations or sequences of simple weaves were used to form a pattern consisting of stripes, squares or small geometric figures (Figure 14.1.7–9). This group included the largest number of fragments with traces of shaping. In the 12th-century levels of the Troitsky excavation two fragments were found with a 'diagonal' fold, which had perhaps been the bottom edge of a skirt or a flared shirt, although the latter alternative is less likely. Also of interest is a fragment of an item from Troitsky relating to the mid-11th century, the edge of which ended in a plait (Figure 14.3) worked by hand

Figure 14.4 *Open-work textile with traces of shaping: N-79, Nutny, Spit 11, Quadrant 25, No. 27. 12th century.*

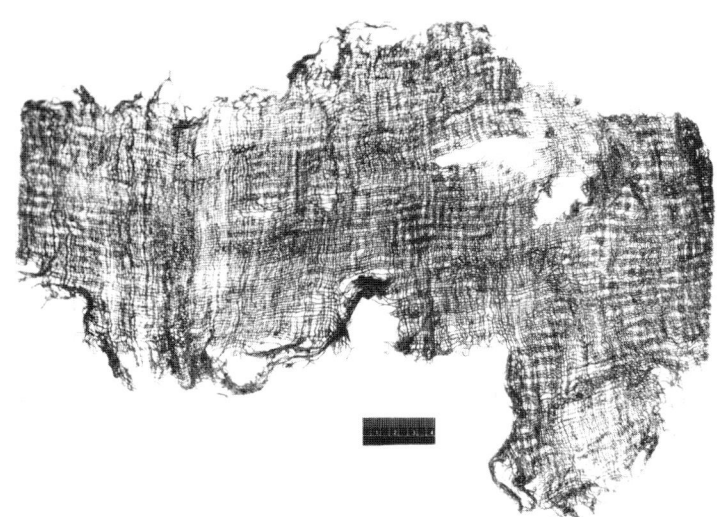

using the ends of warp threads. The technique for this weave involved a reverse 3/1 twill weave. It is likely that this fragment was part of a garment for which the plaited edge was meant to be visible. It could have been from a headscarf or a shawl worn over the shoulders. Shawls of that kind, also known as *villaine*, were found during excavations of Livonian burials dating from the 10th–13th centuries in the West of Latvia (Zarina 1988).

'Open-work' textiles

These constitute a separate group of textile items. They are known as 'open-work' textiles because the structure of the weave of the threads is not packed together, as in the case of all the other textiles, but incorporates spaces formed by the omission of several threads both in the warp and in the weft (Figure 14.4). Most scholars working in this field suggest that these spaces formed as a result of the disappearance of threads of vegetable origin, which did not survive in the cultural layer. Unfortunately, no remains of such vegetable threads have survived in these textiles, although indirect confirmation of their existence has been found. The actual fact of a combination of woollen and vegetable threads does not raise any doubts. This is borne out by a textile fragment, possibly of a belt, of the 12th century found in the Troitsky VIII excavation in 1985, in which threads from a woollen weft had survived, while there were only traces remaining from the warp (Figure 14.5). Combinations of woollen and vegetable threads are also known to us from ethnographic data.

In all the fragments so far found the combinations of gaps have been rather varied. Sometimes there are rows of them along the warp, but more often the gaps form small or large squares, for the formation of which two shuttles were used: wound on to one shuttle was a woollen thread and on to the other a linen thread. The woollen and vegetable threads of the warp were also combined in a definite sequence.

Figure 14.5 (above) Fragment of a textile item with traces of warp threads having fallen out: N-85, Troitsky VIII, Spit 6, Quadrant 716, No. 182. 12th century.

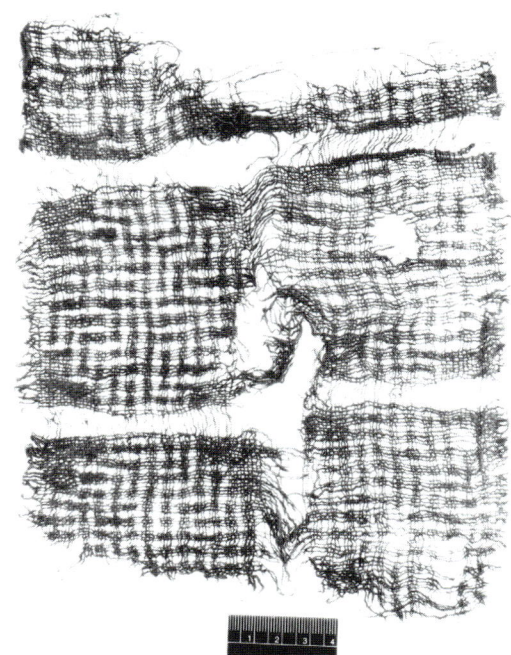

Figure 14.6 (right) Open-work textile: N-83, Troitsky VII, Spit 5, Quadrant 550, No. 29. 14th century.

From among the ordinary open-work textiles two fragments from Troitsky attracted special attention. One of these was found in 1983 (Figure 14.6) in 14th-century levels. The textile consists of large and small squares formed by alternating gaps and woven sections. The large squares measure 10 × 10 cm and they are separated off from each other by wide vertical and horizontal bands, in which only the woollen threads of the warp have survived, while the vegetable threads of both the warp and the weft have not survived. Each large square, in its turn, has been divided up into small squares consisting of four warp threads and four weft threads. Here attention needs to be turned to the weaving technique. In all the corners of the large squares plain weave can be clearly discerned, without any omissions or loss of threads, while the small gaps in each square have been formed by moving the threads of the weft apart and introducing additional threads which have not survived. This is reminiscent of the technique of patterned weaving familiar to us from ethnographic data, when some of the threads from the warp fixed to a separate rod and an additional weft thread would then be inserted into the resulting space. A specific kind of pattern was produced in the textile with the help of these additional threads. This technique in weaving had a purpose in those cases when the additional threads were coloured. In this way a thin and festive textile with large squares was achieved complete with a coloured pattern. The second specimen of a textile of this kind from Troitsky found in 1989 in 13th-century levels was identified as a small but intact part of apparel (Figure 14.7.2). This was a square piece of grey-green textile folded under on three sides, while the fourth side formed the edge of the textile complete with small loops, which had been made

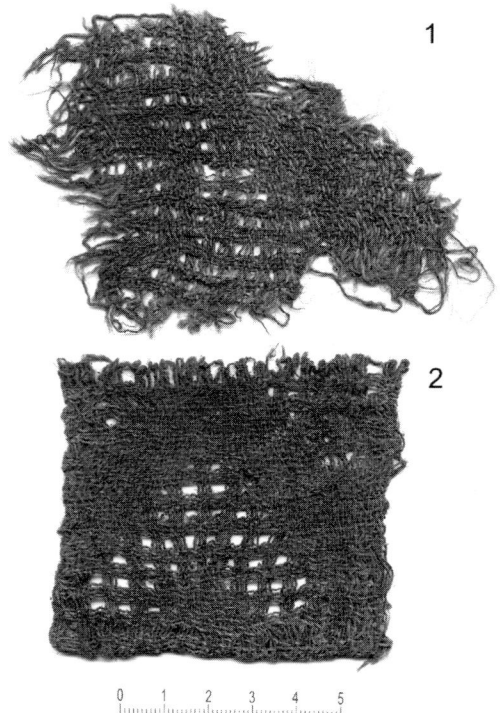

Figure 14.7 *(left) Open-work textiles: 1) N-79, Nutny, Spit 11, Quadrant 25, 14th century; 2) N-89, Troitsky IX, Spit 2, Quadrant 837. Mid-13th century.*

using a weft thread when the shuttle was turned. The threads of the warp along the edge were probably of vegetable origin and when they disappeared only the weft threads remained. As in the case of the previous specimen the gaps in the weave were formed by the introduction of an additional heddle.

Thirteen examples of open-work textiles were found in the Troitsky and Nutny excavations at Novgorod: of these three were dated to the 11th century, two to the 12th, four to the 13th, one to the very end of the 13th or beginning of the 14th and two to the 14th century, while one fragment was found in a drainage ditch outside the established stratigraphy. The thickness of the threads for the warp and the weft in these textiles was almost identical, between 0.15 and 0.23mms, but the density of the weave did not come to more than ten threads in the warp and eight in the weft. It is possible that the function for which these textiles were made did not require a particularly close weave. The threads were twisted in one and the same direction, either ZZ or SS. The weave of the threads as a rule was plain but some fragments were found with a combined weave (a combination of plain and twill weave), which created an additional woven pattern. As regards the quality of fibre, the 'open-work' textiles using the combined technique differed from the simple ones. In the former fine fibres predominated: soft/downy fibres with a thickness of between 4 and 14 microns and with a length of up to 7 cm. A fragment of this kind of textile was found in the Nutny excavation in 1979 in 12th-century levels (Spit 11, Quadrant 25) (Figure 14.7.1). Squares with small gaps in them are interspersed here with vertical wavy stripes. Nakhlik (1963) singles out this particular group of textiles: "Textiles of this type, which are found everywhere in the excavations, and pertain to the Early Medieval period in Russia, are found together with textiles executed using the patterned technique: they constitute specimens representing the highest technical and artistic achievement in Russian weaving of that period".

All these textiles were dyed and were of shades ranging from greenish grey to dark brown and even black. What indicated the function for which they had been made were surviving fragments with traces of their having been shaped and hemmed together. Some of them had traces of having been turned up along the edges, along the weft or warp threads or along a 'diagonal' and could have been used as armholes, sleeves or neck openings. The least that could be said was that the fragments were textiles of different colours worn for special occasions: perhaps they had been used for both garments and headscarves or shawls. The latter possibility was favoured by the specialist in medieval Russian textiles, V. P. Levashova (1966, 115) who stated: "In the burial-mounds of the central plain the remains of woollen open-work textiles, also incorporating linen threads, were common finds. Often the remains of these textiles were found round the skull".

We have inadequate data as yet on the first appearance and subsequent development of the technique used for 'open-work' weaving, which is commonly held to have advanced from the simple to the more complex. From Table 14.3 it emerges that the most complex combined technique for 'open-work' textiles existed as early as the 11th century, while simple 'open work' with a plain weave appeared later, but it is difficult to accept this hypothesis.

Weave techniques

	Plain	Patterned	Combined
11th century	2		1
12th century	2		
13th century	3	1	
End of 13th or beginning of 14th century	1		
14th century	1	1	

Table 14.3 *Occurrence of open-work textiles in chronological order.*

High-quality textiles

These were characterized not only by density of the weave (totaling more than 37 threads per cm^2) but also by the quality of the yarn itself. More often than not these were textiles of Sort I, but there are small amounts of Sort II and Sort III textiles in which the weave is not so close, but the yarn is still of high quality. This group of textiles should be examined taking due account of the location of its production. Unfortunately, it is not possible for us to compare the fleeces of English merino with the wool from Novgorod sheep, but it is precisely the fibre which is the crucial indicator of imported textiles, in so far as the technique for spinning and weaving cannot be used as an indicator.

For the purpose of comparative analysis fibres from high-quality and ordinary textiles were used, including those from open-work textiles, a fragment of 10th-century sheep-skin from the Troitsky VIII excavation and fibres from coarse woollen items, in relation to which it is difficult to imagine that they could have been imports. The fibres were examined to establish their length and thickness, although these indicators should only be used with caution, since the state of preservation of the textiles being examined significantly distorted their original parameters. Investigations using a microscope demonstrated that the coarse and medium fibres could split lengthways and therefore provide incorrect indices regarding thickness. Nor was it easy to determine the original length of twisted fibres because of their heightened fragility, particularly at places where they were interwoven. As a result of all this it was virtually impossible to identify one or other fibre as being from a thin English fleece or a Spanish merino one. The task facing us was to compare what was without doubt local material with material which could easily have been imported in view of its high quality, since there would have been no point in importing commodities which could have been produced locally.

The composition of the fragment of 10th-century dark-brown sheepskin found in Troitsky VIII (Spit 23, Quadrant 722) turned out to contain soft/downy, medium and coarse fibres. The thickness of the finest soft fibres ranged between 14 and 21 microns, while that of the coarsest warp ones ranged from 45 to 50 microns. The length of the fibres turned out to be a useful indicator: the longest of them did not exceed 3 cm. It would be wrong, of course, to base judgements regarding the whole of the Novgorod flock on a single fragment of sheepskin, but we have not yet encountered any further fragments. Approximately similar findings were made regarding the specimens of coarse woollen and knitted items, apart from the fact that the latter contained some fibres up to 3.5 cm in length. What did emerge, however, was that it was quite wrong to maintain that it is not possible to manufacture thin even threads from such short fibres. Most of the textiles of Sorts II and III were made of precisely such fibres, but, unlike the textiles made of coarse wool, they contain only a few warp fibres: some of them consist exclusively of soft/downy and medium fibres. These are textiles of good quality perfectly suitable for garments, headscarves, shawls and other items of everyday use.

Imports

We shall take it as read that imported textiles are of high quality, but we shall at the same time bear in mind that not all high-quality textiles were imported. The main distinctive characteristic could be the length of the fibres, in so far as we did not succeed in finding any fibres over 3.5 cm in length in the coarse woollen or knitted items or the fragment of sheepskin. On the other hand in some of the high-quality textiles the fibre length was between 4 and 7 cm and the thickness of the fibres was between 5 and 14 microns. The wool in these items was frequently not homogenous, that is, it incorporated both soft/downy and medium fibres, although in some cases there were only soft/downy ones.

Textiles that can be classified as imports make up approximately 16% of the total and their chronological spread is illustrated in the diagram below (Figure 14.8). This group also includes textiles for which it was difficult to determine the length of the fibres, but as regards their quality they were similar to those described above. The diagram also includes silk textiles, which will be discussed later in this chapter.

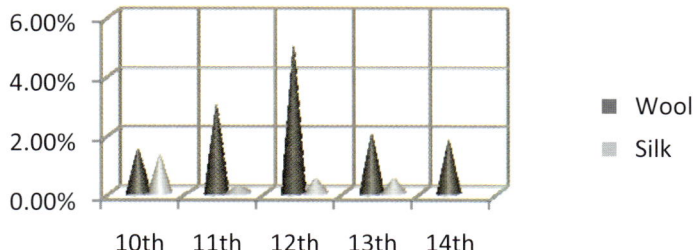

Figure 14.8 Chronology of imported textiles (10th to 14th centuries) as a percentage of textiles found; blue is wool, purple is silk.

The largest amount of imported textiles was in the 12th century, but in this connection we should recall that these statistics do not always reflect a true picture of the use of organic objects, insofar as the formation of deposits in various parts of the town depended on a whole range of circumstances, such as the intensity of economic activity within the given area, the number of fires, the level of the water table, and so on. Given that the 14th-century levels were not entirely accessible for investigation purposes, some finds made in the Nutny excavation in 1989 were also used in this study, in particular, fragments of dyed felted cloth.

The written sources make mention on a number of occasions of various textiles produced abroad. In birch-bark document No. 125 dating from the 14th century (Artsikhovskii and Bokovskii 1955, 59), for example, a mother asks her son to buy her some "good *zendyants*" – a word used to denote a cotton textile produced near Bukhara in the settlement of Zendan, which explains the name. In the collection of textiles which has been the object of our study no textiles made of cotton have been found, but that is without doubt a result of the special features of the habitation levels at Novgorod which has not preserved fibres of vegetable origin. Often textiles were referred to by their colour: '*rudavshchina*' was a reddish-brown textile; '*chermen*' was a red textile; '*zelen*' was a green textile. In birch-bark document No. 713 dating from the end of the 12th century, we read: "how much red cloth (*chermen*) do you have, how much reddish-brown (*rudavshchina*) do you have and good blue cloth" (Yanin and Zaliznyak 2000, 13). When using these terms the people of that period had in mind quite specific textiles, but we, on the basis of colour alone, cannot link them either with a place of production or with those fragments which we discover during excavations. In birch-bark document No. 722 (dating from the end of the 12th or beginning of the 13th century) nets, cloth and canvases are mentioned, but the text is not linked with trade or with production (Yanin and Zaliznyak 2000, 21). In a birch-bark document from the middle of the 13th century (No. 765) a certain Danila asks his brother Ignat to find him some clothes. "I'm walking around naked. I have no cloak or anything else!", he writes (Yanin and Zaliznyak 2000, 61). He therefore asks his brother to send him a "reddish-brown" (*rudavyi*) cloak and promises to give him the money for it after a sum has been deducted for some cloth or other. This is a rare instance of clothes actually being mentioned.

More concrete information on the subject of textiles being imported into Novgorod is provided by official documents, including contracts between Novgorod and other cities of the Hanseatic League, charters and other documents concerning commercial organizations, religious documents and contracts belonging to Russian princes, and also customs registers, commercial records and lists of commodities. From these documents it emerges that trade, not only in textiles but in other commodities as well, depended to a large degree on both Novgorod's relations with commercial centres in Western Europe and also on competition between West-European producers.

Dyed textiles should be numbered among the important categories of commodities imported into Novgorod. At the end of the 13th and in the 14th century Flanders was the main centre for cloth production in Europe and from there through Champagne cloth was sent all over Europe: cloth made its way to Novgorod through the Livonian towns of Riga, Reval (now Tallinn) and Pernau (now Pärnu, Estonia). The heyday for cloth production in Flanders was in the 14th century and continued into the 15th, until new textile centres appeared both in Flanders itself and also in England, which began manufacturing cheaper cloth products than before. These circumstances led to a rise in the price of wool and the ousting from the markets of traditional textiles from Flanders (Khoroshkevich 1963, 174–5). The rapid rise in cloth production in Europe was bound up with the growing demand in the market, and to a considerable degree this was the growing demand from the Russian market. It was no coincidence that most of the finds of imported textiles were from levels of the 14th century, the heyday of the Novgorod republic. Most popular of all in Novgorod and Central Russia was one of the most expensive varieties of cloth, namely cloth manufactured in the town of Ypres, the oldest centre for cloth production in Flanders. Together with another expensive variety of cloth, *Scharlaken* (in German: *skorlat* in Russian), it attracted the attention of the most prosperous sections of Novgorod society. *Scharlaken* (modern Scharlach) was produced in Northern Europe and the main centres for its production were the towns of Ghent and Brugge. Yet these expensive textiles accounted for a smaller share of Russian imports than the cheaper varieties of cloth, which were nevertheless of good quality. Of these, the cloth purchased most regularly was *popering* cloth, which was also produced in Flanders, not far from Ypres. Coarser cloth known as *votola* made its way to the Novgorod market from Germany, where it was known as *watmel* or *watmal*. It is likely that these textiles were more affordable for the townspeople (Khoroshkevich 1963, 194). Some specimens of imported textiles are listed in Figure 14.9. A typical feature of the imported textiles is the combination of different coloured threads both in the warp and in the weft (Figures 14.9.1–3, 14.10).

Felted Textiles

It is appropriate to consider separately felted textiles, nine specimens of which were found in the collection we examined. In general there were far more such specimens but many of them had acquired a felted surface as a result of long use and if a researcher lights upon a small fragment, it is easy to identify it incorrectly. As regards the quality of the raw material and their external characteristics, these textiles can be divided into three groups. The first group comprises thin dyed textiles with an even felted surface on both sides. The thickness of such textiles would be between 0.8 and 1 mm, while that of the fibres would be between 8 and 25 microns and it is the fine fibres which predominate. There are three specimens from this group and one of them, green in colour, dates from the 13th century, while the other two, which are red, date from the 14th century.

Group II of these dyed textiles differs from the first in that its pile is longer and it is somewhat thicker, that is up to 2 mm: the fibres, however, are virtually identical to those of Group I. There are three examples, one of them is green and dates from the 12th century, while the other two are both red and date from the 14th century (Figure 14.9.7,8).

Group III comprises textiles which have a felted surface on only one side. There are three specimens from this group as well. One of them is black in colour and was found in 12th-century levels, while the other two are both green and date from the 14th century. What sets them apart is the somewhat loose structure of the weave and the wool which is not all of the same kind: as well as thin soft fibres, fine, downy ones are also found (Figure 14.9.9).

While Groups I and II can be regarded as consisting of imported textiles, there are doubts regarding Group III. All that can be said with any confidence is that the fibres in those textiles are of higher quality than the fibres found in locally produced items made of coarse wool. Given that we know that not only fine cloth was imported, but coarse cloth as well, it may be assumed that textiles from Group III were also imported textiles.

From the written sources we know that ready-made textiles were imported into Novgorod (woollen cloth, silk, cotton) but we have never come across any mention of raw material or semi-manufactured articles being imported. This question arises in connection with a particular find made in the Troitsky V excavation in 1979 in 13th-century levels (Spit 7, Quadrant 313). It consisted of a skein of spun threads black in colour and folded together: they had never been used either for weaving or for needlework, which accounted for their state of preservation and made it possible to study the fibres. It turned out that the threads consisted of soft/downy and medium fibres with a predominance of the first variety. The thickness of the threads ranged from 0.24 to 0.28 mm, the thickness of the fibres from 4 to 6 microns and their length from 4 to 13 cm. In so far as such threads had not been found in local textiles, they can definitely be regarded as imported and from that it would follow that not only textiles were being imported but yarn as well. It which case it may be suggested that the open-work textile with a combined weave referred to earlier (Figure 14.7.1) had been manufactured in Novgorod or some other production centre in medieval Russia from imported threads.

Figure 14.9 *Imported textiles: 1) N-91, Troitsky X, Spit 6, Quadrant 1199. 13th century; 2) N-80, Nutny, Spit 23, Quadrant 74. 12th century; 3) N-83, Troitsky VI, Spit 26, Quadrant 448. 10th century; 4) N-86, Troitsky VIII, Spit 11, Quadrant 701, end of 11th/beginning of 12th century; 5) N-83, Troitsky VI, Spit 26, Quadrant 480. 10th century; 6) N-93, Troitsky IX, Spit 13, Quadrant 903. 12th century; 7) N-79, Nutny, Spit 13, Quadrant 71. 14th century; 8) N-79, Nutny, Spit 13, Quadrant 18. 14th century; 9) N-79, Nutny, Spit 13, Quadrant 39. 14th century. The scale is in cms.*

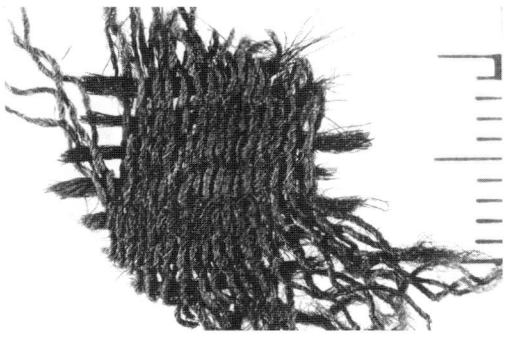
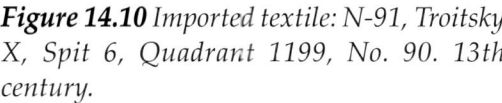
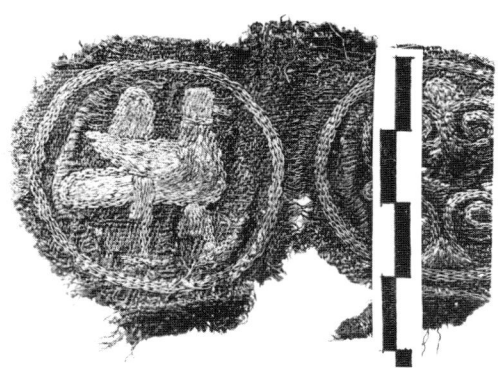

Figure 14.10 *Imported textile: N-91, Troitsky X, Spit 6, Quadrant 1199, No. 90. 13th century.*

Figure 14.11 *Fragment of a collar with the depiction of a bird from the burial-ground at Derevyanitsy. Silk embroidery on taffeta. 12th century.*

SILK

While the import of woollen textiles was associated with the countries of Western Europe, silk textiles made their way to Novgorod from the countries of the Mediterranean, Byzantium and the Middle East. There was wide demand for these textiles in the Russian market not only in the towns but also among the rural population. This can be deduced from finds in medieval burial-grounds in Central and North-western Russia. More often than not silk textiles were used for trimming clothes: for collars, cuffs and for headwear. Apart from monochrome textiles with no pattern (taffeta), parts of garments made from thick silk with multi-coloured patterns in the weave were encountered as well and also garments embroidered with silk and gold or silver thread. Byzantine trimmings made of silk or gold-inwoven ribbon were also used to finish garments.

As early as the 11th century special workshops had existed in many Russian monasteries where patterns or whole scenes were embroidered on silk. For the most part these workshops carried out commissions from monasteries and made church vestments for priests and items required for performing religious rituals. In the 11th and 12th centuries the technique most widely used for this embroidery was 'underside couching', when silk or metallic threads after a long stitch on the right side were pulled through on to the left side with a needle and then a short stitch was made. On the right side of the article the threads would be arranged packed closely one up against the other, forming a 'solid' cushion. Another technique for such embroidery appeared at the end of the 12th century known as 'couching', when the threads forming a pattern, would be arranged in sequence on the front surface of the item and fixed in place with silk threads. Both spun and drawn gold threads are encountered.

Figure 14.12 *Woven silk ribbon and a fragment of a collar with a depiction of angels. Embroidery in gold threads on taffeta. 12th century.*

For ordinary townspeople textiles with silk and gold-thread embroidery were something extremely rare, but the fact that such items were used among the ordinary, albeit relatively prosperous, population is confirmed by finds from excavations of burial-grounds. An example of this is provided by 12th-century finds from the flat-grave burial-ground near Novgorod (Konetskii 1984). These were fragments of two collars and a woven silk ribbon. On one of the collars alternating depictions of birds and the Tree of Life had been embroidered with untwisted silk using the 'underside couching' technique (Figure 14.11). On the other fragment, figures of angels and semi-circular arcs separated off from each other by small pillars have been embroidered in spun gold threads and untwisted silk, again using the 'underside couching' technique (Figure 14.12). Along the right-hand and some of the upper edge, part of a plaited pattern has survived. The embroidery of both collars was on brown silk cloth with a canvas lining (Ignashina 2003).

The silk textiles most frequently found in urban levels are taffeta and damask. In the *Dictionary of the Living Russian Language* by V. I. Dal, taffeta is defined as a smooth fine silk textile from Persia and damask as a shot silk textile from China, i.e. with a pattern woven into it. In the collection we have studied there are nine specimens of silk textiles. Four of them date from the 10th century and the rest from the 12th century. Three examples of taffeta were found: they were of plain weave and from twisted threads: only in one instance did twisted and non-twisted threads alternate in the warp and the weft. They were all brown in colour, but as has been established through special analyses the original colour had been yellow or orange (Figure 14.13.2). Two

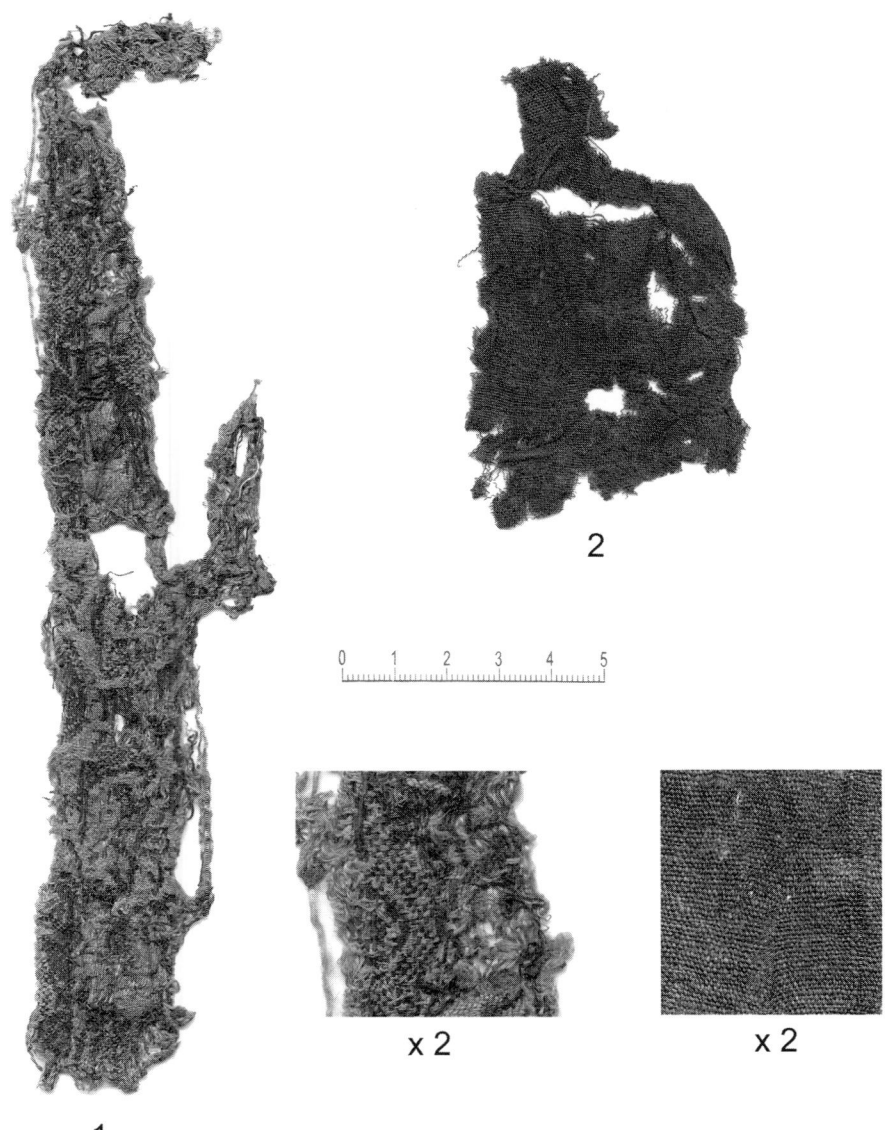

Figure 14.13 Silk textiles: 1) N-87, Troitsky IX, Spit +4, Quadrant 835. 14th century; 2) N-80, Nutny, Spit 15, Quadrant 76. 14th century.

of them had probably been used for collars: one fragment from the Troitsky VIII excavation measured 7.5 × 4.5 cm and bore traces of having been hemmed on both sides of its length, while the second fragment from Troitsky IX consisted of two pieces measuring 17.5 × 3.7 cm and 17.5 × 1.5 cm joined by a side seam (i.e. it had been sewn together from two halves).

Figure 14.14 *Cuff of a sleeve with a silk lining: N-9, Troitsky XI, Spit 11, Quadrant 1257, No. 64. Early 12th century.*

In four cases damask was found with untwisted silk in the warp and twisted silk in the weft. One of the fragments was green, one orange, one red and a fourth was woven from three different coloured threads, which were yellow, yellowish-pink and pale brown. The sizes of the fragments do not enable us to draw any conclusions about what they were used for. An exception to this is presented by the remains of the orange damask, which had been sewn on to the cuff of a woollen sleeve (Figure 14.14). This find dating from the beginning of the 12th century was made in Troitsky XI (Spit 11, Quadrant 1257). Another find from the Troitsky excavation in the 14th-century levels can be identified as a collar (Figure 14.13.1). Finds of silk textiles in an urban habitation level testify to their having been used by the citizens of Novgorod, while their use mainly for finishing garments indicates that they were likely to have been very expensive. There is no doubt that the upper echelons of society and religious leaders were able to wear silk garments and garments embroidered with gold and silver threads.

CLOTHING

It is worth making special mention of what the people of Novgorod wore. If we attempt to imagine the appearance of a male or female inhabitant of the city in the medieval period, what we would see first and foremost is a man well shod in leather boots, with a wooden spoon kept in a leather case inserted into the top of his boot, with mittens knitted or made of embossed leather, with a knife in a leather case stuck into his belt and a round cap made of felt on his head. His female counterpart would be wearing leather shoes decorated with embroidery worked in threads of different colours. She would be wearing metal or glass bracelets, beads and pendants for the finishing touches to her apparel, items which could be both seen and felt. As for her actual garments we can merely refer to written sources and depictions from the period, which provide only the most general picture of the costume of that time. In birch-bark document No. 765 already mentioned we find the expression '*myatele rudavo*' which Zaliznyak has translated as "brown-red cloak". It would seem that it will never be possible to link written statements of this kind either with graphic sources or with archaeological materials. What archaeologists have, as a rule, at their disposal are small fragments of woven garments, sometimes retaining traces of shaping and hemming. On the basis of some of these fragments it is possible to put forward suggestions as to the shape of individual parts of garments.

The collection that has been the object of our study includes 47 pieces of textile with traces of shaping. Apart from fragments which have been impossible to assign to one or other specific garment, there are some pieces which can be reliably identified, such as pockets, cuffs, collars and other small parts of garments. Fragments are also encountered from which a curved piece has been cut out, typical for the armhole into which a sleeve would be inserted. Parts of sleeves are also encountered. In 12th-century levels at Troitsky IX, a fragment of a sleeve was found measuring 21 × 6.5 cm, which broadened out towards the top, although its upper part had not survived. To judge from the side seams, it had been part of a sleeve sewn together from two pieces. The lower part of the sleeve was formed by the edge of the textile and had not been hemmed. The textile was of an ordinary variety of 3/1 twill weave. The collection includes a total of five finds complete with traces of shaping, which can be considered as sleeve fragments. One of them, to which reference has been made earlier, was an open-work textile but the part which has survived is not enough to indicate whether it was a sleeve or the armhole for a sleeve, since the upper and lower parts of the item have not survived (Figure 14.4). The edge of the armhole has a hem 0.7 cm wide. This

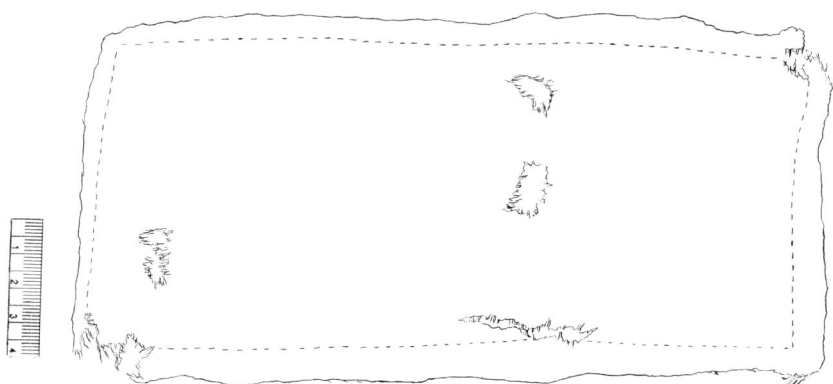

Figure 14.15 *Hemmed garment part: N-92, Troitsky IX, Spit 8, Quadrant 956, 12th century.*

find enables us to assume that open-work textiles were used not only for headscarves and shawls, but also for women's garments.

The smaller trimmings for garments have survived better and these include collars, pockets and cuffs. Two appliqué pockets dating from the 12th and 13th centuries have survived in their entirety: both were found in the Troitsky excavation. One of them is brown and measures 15 × 15 cm. On three sides it has a hem 1 cm wide and on the fourth a hem 2.5 cm wide. The second is red and measures 13.5 × 10 cm and all its edges have a hem 1 cm wide. Some of the garment parts, despite the fact that they have survived in their entirety, cannot be reliably identified. One such is a rectangular piece of brown textile measuring 17 × 9 cm and hemmed on all sides, which was found at Troitsky IX in 12th-century levels (Spit 9, Quadrant 975), which is unlikely to be a pocket, since there is too great a difference between width and length, but it could easily have been a flap covering a pocket from above. It is possible that a lining had been sewn on to it from the left, since this side of the fragment has a felted, not a worn surface and has a hem on three sides only 0.5 cm wide, which would not have been practical for sewing a pocket on to a garment. One further textile item which has survived intact consists of a rectangular strip of dark-brown cloth of twill weave measuring 20 × 10 cm and with a hem on all sides 0.6–1.2 cm wide (Figure 14.15). It is possible that it was part of a reinforced band to which buttons were attached. The textile was dark brown of twill weave and as regards the density of that weave it was classified as belonging to Sort II. Apart from appliqué pockets, internal pockets also existed, while on the front of garments slits provided access to them. A fragment of a garment with just such a slit was found at Troitsky IX in 12th-century levels (Figure 14.16). This was an outer garment made from a non-dyed coarse woollen textile with a 2/2 twill weave. A similar find also from Troitsky was dated to the 10th century (N-87, Troitsky VIII, Spit 23, Quadrant 685, No. 70). In this case the textile of twill weave was thinner (2/1) and probably of local production. The length of the slit was 11 cm and its edge had been turned under with a hem 1 cm wide.

Figure 14.16 *Slit for a pocket: N.93, Troitsky IX, Spit 11, Quadrant 923, No. 54. 12th century.*

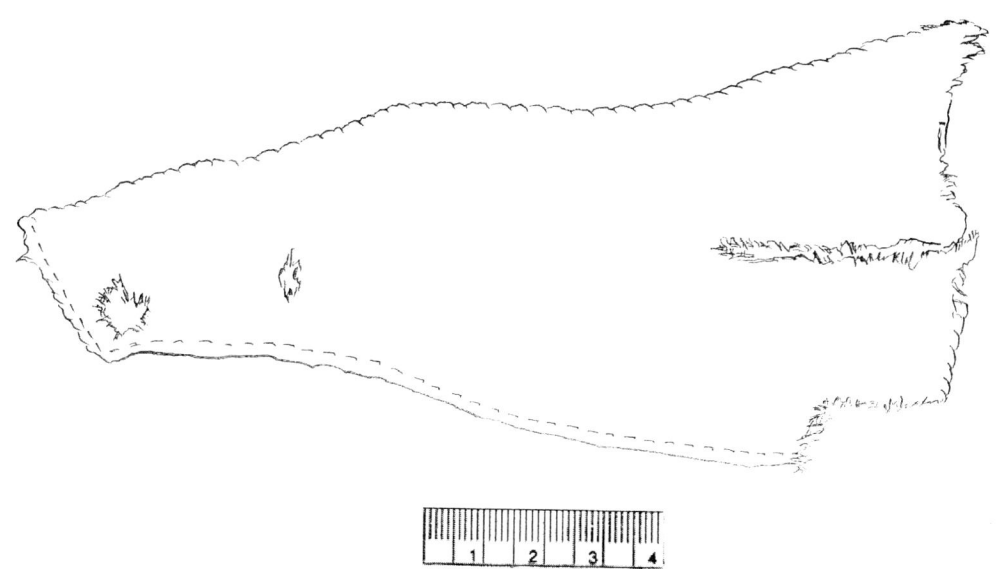

Figure 14.17 *Fragment of a collar: N-92, Troitsky X, Spit 9, Quadrant 1119, 12th century.*

We do not have at our disposal complete woollen collars, but some of the garment fragments might be identified as belonging to this category. One of them was found in 12th-century levels at Troitsky X and consisted of a strip of dark brown textile tapering towards the end (Figure 14.17). To judge from the surviving seams, it was half of a collar, to which a similar second half would have been joined and then both of them would have been sewn on either to the back of the neck or to a facing using a

Figure 14.18 *Cuff of a sleeve: N-92, Troitsky IX, Spit 8, Quadrant 816, No. 13. 12th century.*

'herringbone' seam. A further find dating from the 12th century and discovered in the Nutny excavation in 1980 (Spit 22, Quadrant 12) might also be classified as a collar. It was a strip of plain-weave textile measuring 28 × 7.5 cm, on three sides of which traces of turn-under hems had survived, while the fourth side was torn. The reversible seams indicate that the collars had been double, like modern ones.

With regard to costume details, mention should also be made of sleeve cuffs: two early/13th-century finds from Troitsky can be identified as such. One of them is the complete half of a cuff but with its central part missing (Figure 14.18). Traces of seams with a very small turning have survived, which points to there having been a very fine lining, possibly one made of silk. The major missing part makes it impossible for us to work out the original shape in its entirety, but it is clear that the cuff had not consisted of a straight strip but was more likely to have been triangular in shape. It is possible that the top of the cuff had been curved and the corners trimmed as well. This red textile showed traces of felting in some places on the reverse side. The second such find was half of a high cuff with a partially preserved silk lining (Figure 14.14). The woollen textile was red in colour and the silk lining orange. There were some traces of felting resulting from long use.

When it comes to larger components of costume it is worth referring to gussets and strips with the remains of side seams or with a hem along the edge. A strip of this kind was found at Nutny in 12th-century levels (Spit 22, Quadrant 44). It was 79 cm long and 8–10 cm wide. The lower edge had been cut diagonally and turned under. One of the short sides of this strip still retained traces of a 'straight' seam, while the

Figure 14.19 *Fragment of a gusset: N-84, Troitsky VII, Spit 1, Quadrant 669, 14th century.*

other was torn. It is possible that this fragment had been from a flared skirt. There are several gussets which might also be classified as belonging to skirts. One of them consisting of two fragments had survived with a length of 21 cm. It was dark-brown and of 3/1 twill weave with traces of seams at the side edges (Figure 14.19). A further two gussets found in 11th- and 12th-century levels at Troitsky had retained traces of hemming along the bottom edge (N-86, Troitsky VIII, Spit 14, Quadrant 750 and N-92, Troitsky IX, Spit 8, Quadrant 857). The width of the hem was 1.5–1.8 cm. Both gussets had been cut out of thick textile of Sort IV with a 2/2 twill weave in a herringbone pattern.

A find from the Nutny excavation in 1979 provides some idea of the complexity of costume in Novgorod (Figure 14.20 a and b). This consists of several parts from a single garment: of these a collar (1), facing for a collar (2) and pieces of hemmed textile for a lining underneath a loop (3) and a button (4) can clearly be identified. The function of the remaining parts is not totally clear. One of them could have been a yoke or a back (6), but it is not evident what it had been made for and a small armhole had been hemmed along its right edge, although there is unlikely to have been a patch involved. It is possible that the presence of small rectangular and wedge-shaped pieces reflect not so much whims of fashion but efforts to economize on woollen cloth. What is definite is that garments were worn for a long time until they began to fade and become matted: this is borne out by the above mentioned pieces of textile.

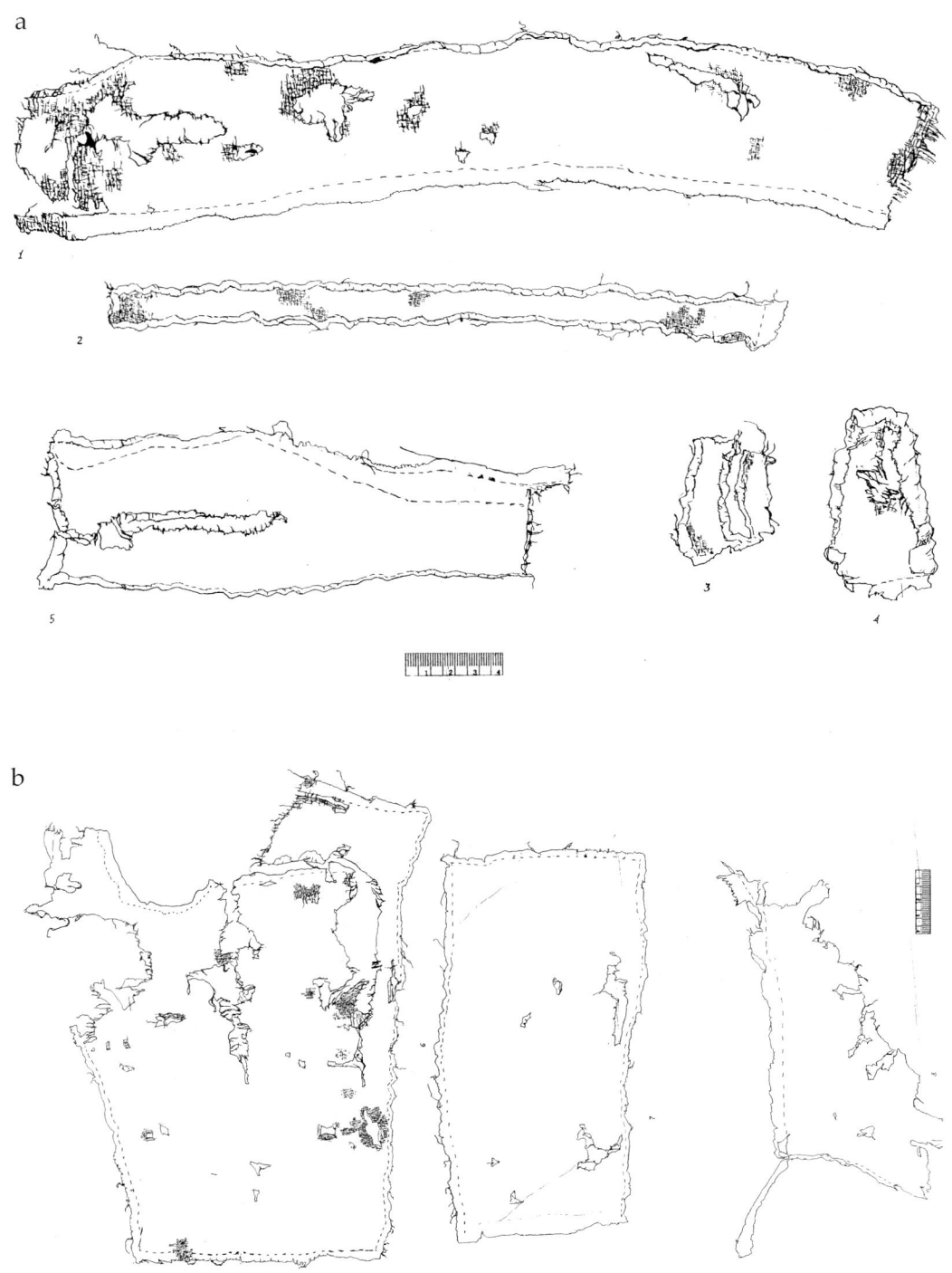

Figure 14.20 a and b: *Garment parts: N-79, Nutny, Spit 14, Quadrant 8, 13th century.*

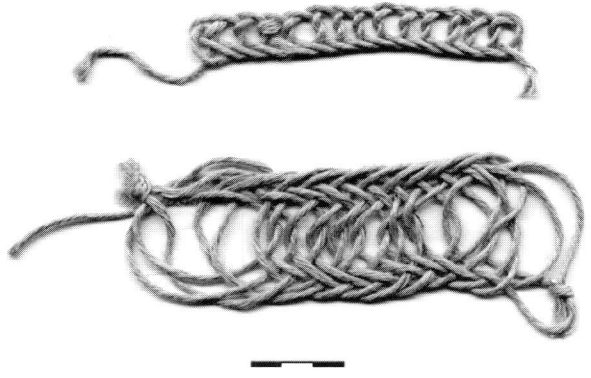

Figure 14.21 Reconstructions made by using two different methods of looping: the upper one is looped very simply and the lower specimen is more complicated, incorporating a raised rib in the final product.

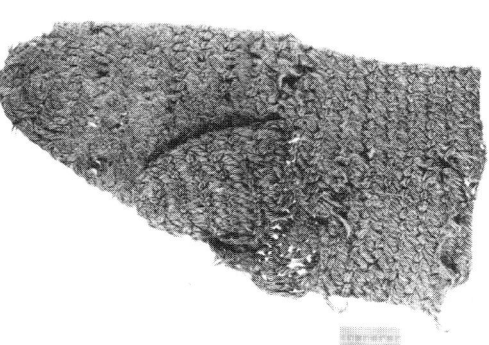

Figure 14.22 Mitten: N-73, Troitsky, trial trench. No date.

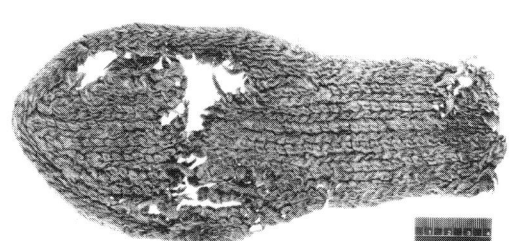

Figure 14.23 Insole: N-84, Troitsky VIII, Spit +1, Quadrant 800, No. 8. 14th century.

With regard to the rest of the garment pieces, what cannot fail to attract attention are items made of cut pieces of thread looped together using a needle. The technique used for looping of this kind still lives on in the Poozerie area near Novgorod: the only difference to be noted is that in medieval Novgorod two methods for this looping had been current, while only one of these has come down to us, the simpler of the two. In Figure 14.21 a reconstruction of the two methods is provided: the upper one is looped very simply and the lower specimen is more complicated, incorporating a raised rib in the final product. The most frequent finds from the category of looped items were mittens and socks (Figure 14.22).

Unlike the ethnographic ones, 'archaeological' mittens and socks were knitted in the round, apart from a single item, in which the looping using a needle went forwards and backwards. This was an insole found at Troitsky in 14th-century levels (Figure 14.23). Among the looped items, an article of particular interest is a cap or helmet with an open top, a peak and a round collar incorporated in its entirety into the cap, which has been plaited in the round (Figure 14.24). To put on this cap it would have been necessary first of all to pass your head through the circular collar.

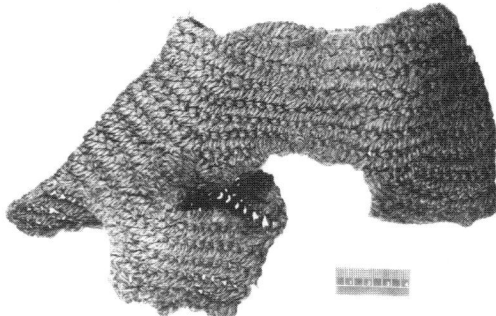

Figure 14.24 (above) Cap or helmet: N-73, Troitsky Excavation, Spit 10, Quadrant 15, No. 43. 12th century.

Figure 14.25 (right) Braided belts: 1) N-79, Nutny Excavation, Spit 13, Quadrant 41. 14th century; 2) N-89, Troitsky IX, Spit +1, Quadrant 846. 14th century; 3) N-80, Nutny, Spit 22, Quadrant 34. 12th century.

The small dimensions of this item raise some doubts, indicating perhaps that it must have belonged to a child. The open top could either have been a consequence of the hair-style of the wearer or there could have been a top made of some other material which did not survive.

Other important items in the apparel of both men and women are belts, the creation of which involved a variety of different techniques: looping by hand, looping using rods, on a tablet or weaving with a loom. The collection of belts is quite wide-ranging. Their outer appearance depended not only on the technique used for manufacture, but also on the quality and colour of the yarn used. Apart from belts of simple brown shades, some belts were made from coloured threads: yellow, green and red, although the dyes tended to fade after being exposed to acids in the soil. All methods used to make belts are well-known from ethnographic data (Figure 14.25).

DYES

Most of the woollen textiles were dyed various shades of brown, ranging from greenish brown to dark brown. There is no doubt that exposure to mineral dyes influenced

Figure 14.26 Textile dyed with madder: N-79, Nutny, Spit 13, Quadrant 18, No. 2. 14th century.

Figure 14.27 Textile dyed with blue indigo and yellow flavonoids: N-79, Nutny, Spit 13, Quadrant 39, No. 74. 14th century.

the colour of textiles: non-dyed textiles became darker and dyed ones changed their colour or lost their original colour altogether. It is possible that some dyes dissolved completely in the moist habitation levels. In order to determine the dyes used 22 specimens of woollen textiles and 4 silk ones were selected for analysis.[3]

The research methods used were: microscopic, micro-chemical and thin-section chromatography. MIKMED-1 and MBS-2 microscopes were used.

Threads of the warp and the weft were examined separately. Results showed that all the textiles represented in the sample had been dyed with red, blue, yellow or green dyes. The original colour of the five red samples, two of those green in colour and one black one were duly confirmed. All the remaining textiles, which appeared to be various shades of brown to the naked eye, turned out to have been dyed originally and the colours were able to be established. Red dyes turned out to be the fastest and four of these were of vegetable origin, while one was of animal origin. The vegetable dyes belonged to the class of anthraquinones, for which the roots of tinctorial madder (*Rubia tinctoria*) provide one of the sources. The dye of animal origin contained kermesic acid, which was obtained from insects (*Kermes vermilio*). Potassium alums were used as mordants. Two of the red textiles had a felted surface (Figure 14.26) while the others were ordinary textiles most likely of local production.

The composition of green dyes involved yellow flavonoids and blue indigo and the mordant for them was provided by potassium alums. The vegetable source of indigo was woad (*Isatis tinctoria*), tinctorial knotweed (*Polygonum tinctoria*) and plants with an indigo content such as Indigofera. As regards yellow dyes of the flavonoid class, quercetin and luteolin were discovered, which are found in many plants, and datiscin, which is present in so-called bastard hemp (*Datisca cannabina*). One of the green textile fragments was a piece of well-felted cloth (Figure 14.27) and two others were in the category of fine high-quality textiles.

The original colour in three fragments of brown textiles of high quality was revealed with the help of a yellow dye. One of them had been found at Nutny (Spit 12, Quadrant 293) in 14th-century levels. It was a textile of complex weave with a 'diamond' pattern. The second fragment from Troitsky VIII dated from the end of the 11th or beginning of the 12th century (Figure 14.28): it was from a textile of 3/1 twill weave. The third fragment was from Troitsky XI (Spit 10, Quadrant 1268) and was found in levels of the late-11th century: the textile was of complex weave with a pattern of 'squares'. All three fragments were from textiles manufactured abroad.

Brown and black dyes come from the category of tanning substances, but also contain flavonoids with an iron mordant. The sources of tanning substances were gall (gallnuts), oak bark (from *Quercus robur*), chestnut (*Castanea sativa*), birch bark (*Betula alba*), and tanner's sumac (*Rhus coriaria*). One of the specimens (Figure 14.29) pale-brown in colour had been dyed using quercetin with an iron mordant. Examination of a further textile fragment black in colour revealed the presence of phenyl carbonic acids and tanning substances, including gallic acid (Figure 14.30). In some textiles a number of different coloured threads were used: for instance, in a textile specimen from Troitsky XI found in 10th-century levels, in the warp one yellow thread and one dark-brown thread alternated, while the weft was pale-brown (Figure 14.30).

Orange dyes contain yellow flavonoids and red anthraquinones. This colour was discovered in two silk textiles, one of which was the lining of the above-mentioned cuff (Figure 14.14).

The methods for dying appear to have been as follows:

- one source of dye used with different mordants;
- to achieve a range of shades, dying was repeated several times, one after the other in one and the same vat;
- cloth was dipped into several sources of dye for different colours used one after the other.

CONCLUSION

From the whole collection of archaeological textiles found in the excavation trenches of Novgorod to date, only one third has been discussed in this chapter.

Nevertheless, this third adequately reflects the range of types of medieval textiles in Novgorod and ratios of the different types. In Novgorod, as everywhere else, textiles of vegetable origin are a great rarity: in other words we have to bear in mind that most of such textile material has not come down to us. In this chapter we have looked at woollen textiles and a small quantity of the silk ones which we had at our disposal.

For the basis of our classification we referred to the work carried out by Nakhlik (1963) in which textiles were sub-divided into four sorts depending upon the density of the weave and the quality of the raw material used. The classification is somewhat arbitrary given that high quality of raw material does not always coincide with density of weave.

The techniques for weaving were sub-divided into three main types: plain, twill and fine-patterned (or complex). Moreover all types were found throughout the period from the 10th to the 14th century and in textiles of Sorts I to IV. It was not established that certain techniques were characteristic of imported textiles. The same can be said with regard to the way threads were spun.

As regards the quality of yarn, all woollen textiles can be differentiated as follows: coarse woollen, ordinary woollen, open-work, high-quality and felted cloth. Identification of imported specimens from among the overall collection is bound up with the issue of quality and here it is important to determine the criteria used when approaching this problem. In so far as the technology of spinning and weaving does not give rise to any decisive indicators, the most reliable approach to this question would seem to be analysis of the raw materials used, first and foremost fibre length. Analysis of the wool in low-quality items revealed that no fibres were found longer than 4 cm. It is logical to suggest that fibres with lengths ranging from 5 to 13 cm came from sheep which were not bred in Novgorod.

Figure 14.28 *Yellow textile: N-86, Troitsky VIII, Spit 11, Quadrant 701, No. 76. Late-11th or early-12th century.*

Figure 14.29 *Pale-brown textile: N-91, Troitsky IX, Spit 7, Quadrant 930. No. 39. 12th century.*

Figure 14.30 Black textile: N-79, Nutny, Spit 14, Quadrant 8, No. 7. 13th century.

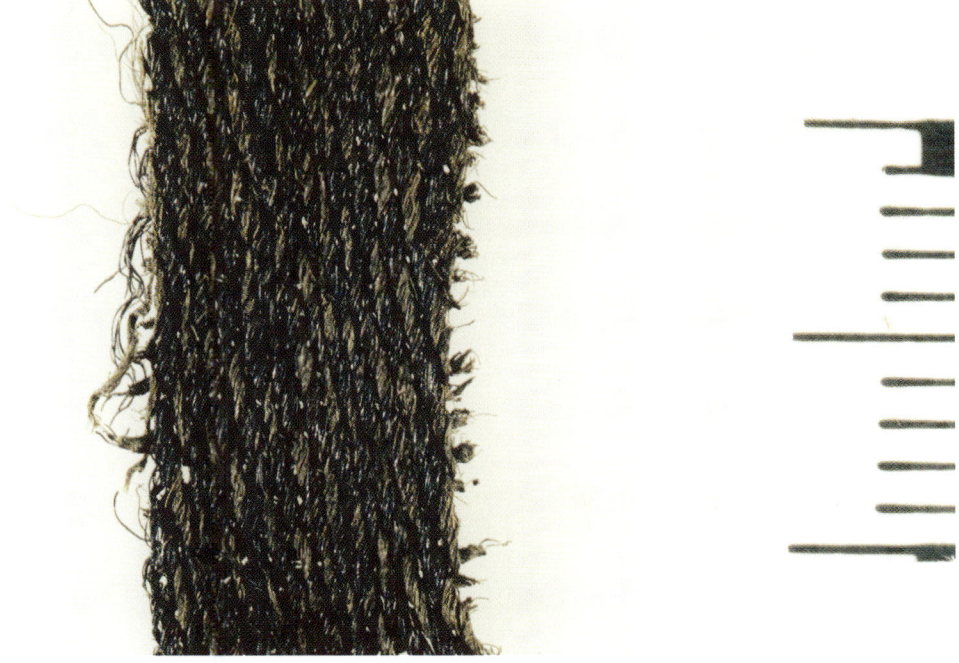

Figure 14.31 Textile with different coloured threads: yellow and dark brown in the warp and pale-brown in the weft: N-83, Troitsky XI, Spit 26, Quadrant 448. 10th century.

Apart from woollen textiles, silk and cotton textiles also came into the imported category. While no items made of cotton fibres were found in the collection under examination, there was a small amount of fragments of silk textiles and in certain cases they could be associated with specific parts of clothing, such as collars or cuffs.

Some information about certain parts of clothing can be gleaned from woollen textiles as well, but they do not enable us to trace the development of costume over time. While there are direct parallels found in ethnographic material for technical methods used in weaving and looping, when it comes to the design and cut of clothes, not only practical considerations need to be taken into account, but most probably fashion as well.

The analysis of the presence of dyes revealed that nearly all the textiles had been dyed and had originally been various shades of yellow, blue, red, green, orange and black.

Notes

1   This research was carried out by M. I. Kolosova, Candidate of Biological Sciences and a member of staff in the State Hermitage Museum, St Petersburg.
2   The thickness of the thread was measured in millimetres and that of the fibre in microns.
3   This study was undertaken by the senior chemist heading the laboratory for physico-chemical research into materials in the Department of Scientific Expertise of the State Hermitage Museum, Saint Petersburg, L. S. Gavrilenko, to whom I should like to express my profound gratitude.

15

VARIETIES OF TIMBER USED TO MAKE WOODEN ARTEFACTS IN NOVGOROD: A SHORT CASE STUDY[1]

L. N. Solovyova

The Novgorod Lands have, since time immemorial, been rich in forests. According to the general survey of 1836, the forests in the Novgorod province occupied 60% of the whole territory: the north-eastern and eastern districts were the ones most richly endowed with forests (Kolchin 1968, 11). It should also be noted that coniferous species, mainly spruce and pine, clearly outnumbered the deciduous species. Species which grew in the Novgorod Lands were elm (*Ulmus* and *Ulmus scabra*), oak, maple, birch, aspen, willow, alder, ash, lime, hazel, rowan, apple, pear, bird-cherry (*Padus*), spindle-tree (*Euonymus*) as well as spruce (*Picea*), pine and juniper. Imported species were also used such as yew, boxwood, walnut, beech, chestnut, larch, fir (*Abies*) and cedar. The trees had a cambium, built up over many years, which occasionally forms a layer of secondary timber. It is characterized by a structure that is not homogenous and for that reason it is usually investigated using three sections – one horizontal and two lengthways ones. Distinctions are drawn between the core, the sapwood year rings, vessels and their size (in deciduous species), medullar rays, resin ducts (in the case of some conifers) and also a number of anatomical features, which are relatively constant. The physical properties of the timber, such as sheen, colour, weight, texture, hardness and others, are secondary features stemming from the main anatomical ones. They are not constant and can only be used as supplementary features of the species.

The excavations which have been going on for more than 70 years in Novgorod have provided archaeologists with unique material – a large range of finds made of organic material, which were part of the every day life of the early inhabitants of Novgorod. Wood was the key material for making household and other objects in the medieval period and right up until very recently. Virtually everything was made of wood: from streets and dwellings to furniture, various essential small articles and domestic utensils used on a daily basis. Vessels for eating out of were no exception in this respect.

In the medieval period many kinds of timber were used and selection of wood for various purposes was by no means arbitrary. For construction work pine and spruce were used in the main and for making table-ware wood from deciduous trees was preferred. A total of 429 wooden finds from the Fyodorovsky and Duboshin excavations held in the Novgorod Regional Museum and from the Slavensky excavation held in the State Historical Museum were selected and analysed and of these 355 proved to have been made from the wood of coniferous species. Firstly, it should be noted that spruce and pine in the medieval period made up most of the woods in Novgorod and its environs and, therefore, timber from those trees was the most accessible and relatively cheap to use. Secondly, wood from spruce and pine trees is ideally suited for both building work and the manufacture of objects, as regards its physical-cum-mechanical properties. Pine wood is easy to work, it is moderately desiccative and soft and not over brittle. It is a heartwood species and its core is seldom destroyed by fungi. Spruce trees produce light, soft and relatively desiccative timber. In addition it is of an attractive white shade, sometimes with a yellow tinge. Juniper trees provide all-purpose timber for wood-working: it is of moderate weight and moderately desiccative, it is durable and hard. Juniper wood does not dry out too quickly and is easy to polish: its sheen and attractive brownish colour give it aesthetic appeal.

Timber from deciduous trees also filled a niche in the wood-working of medieval Novgorod. It disintegrates quickly when exposed to the air and succumbs more easily than conifers to attack from fungi: for this reason it was used mainly for making household objects. The selection of maple as a raw material for making carved vessels was also no coincidence. Timber from maple trees was of a shiny white, sometimes with a yellowish tinge. The year-rings are clearly visible in all sections divided off by a narrow, dense and dark stripe, which can be made out quite easily in all the sections. The dense, shiny and homogenous structure of maple timber stands out on account of its decorative quality and it is easy to work. It is heavy, fairly desiccative, dense, hard and fairly resilient. Ash was used for making lathe-turned vessels as a rule: it was resilient, hard and relatively desiccative. Despite the rich supply of timber in the local forests, wood was not wasted and it was used rationally. For the manufacture of small articles any remnant pieces might be used, as can be seen from the wide range of wood species used. Staves, for instance, might be made of yew (Nerevsky-78, Duboshin 34–39 No. 6), while a spade might be made of beech (Nerevsky-78, Duboshin 33–8, No. 10). Wood-working tools used were also of high quality: "socketed adzes" with an articulated handle; lathe cutters with hook-shaped blades for inner grooves in the objects being worked and with a straight blade for the working of external surfaces; manual cutting tools for making spoons; carving tools with blades of more complex shapes (Kolchin 1968, 15). Wooden utensils would be classified according to the way their surfaces had been worked: carved, chiselled, lathe-turned and woven if made from birch-bark or willow.

CARVED WOODEN UTENSILS: SPOONS, SCOOPS, LADLES AND TURNED VESSELS

Spoons were articles of a distinctly individual character and came in a great variety of shapes and sizes. Nevertheless, they can be divided up into a number of different varieties. Kolchin singled out two groups of spoons: simple 'soup' spoons and spoons of more intricate shapes.

As a rule, spoon handles were decorated with carved designs. Sometimes, however, the carved or painted decoration might extend into the bowl. Usually spoons were carved from soft flexible deciduous species of wood. According to the data collected by Kolchin with the help of his analysis of the materials found in the Nerevsky excavation, spoons made of maple accounted for 65% of the total, those made of other deciduous species for 28% and only 7% of the spoons were made from wood of coniferous species. However, when examining the material from the Fyodorovsky excavation the picture obtained is the opposite: the percentage of conifer species used is significantly more than that of deciduous varieties (74% of the articles have been manufactured from wood of coniferous species). Only 3 of the 10 spoons had been carved from deciduous timber, two of which were made from maple. For the Duboshin excavation we do not have a sufficient range of samples at our disposal, but the percentage of deciduous wood used is 49%, while coniferous is 61%. Only the materials from the Slavensky and Nerevsky excavations reveal a clear predominance of deciduous species and this is the case in relation to the manufacture of spoons as well, which are made from maple, among other deciduous species (see Table 15.1).

Scoops are utensils for serving water and other drinks at table. They can be divided up into a number of groups on the basis of the handle shape: the earliest scoops from the 10th, 11th and 12th-century levels have curved zoomorphic handles (with the depiction of a dragon's head or less frequently that of a ram). In the 12th century these were replaced by scoops with straight handles round in section: small scoops with short flat handles and a carefully worked bowl to hold half a litre also belong to this group. The flat top of the handles is sometimes decorated with carving. In the 13th and 14th centuries the overall size of the scoops increased slightly. A special group of scoops are made of rootstock that can hold up to half a litre.

Like spoons, scoops were also made from wood of soft deciduous species. According to data collected by Kolchin based on materials from the Nerevsky excavation, 15 of the 46 specimens had been carved from maple wood, nine from birch, four from ash, four from spruce, three from pine, three from oak, two each from alder, willow and elm, and one each from lime and hazel.

Ladles. A ladle is like a deep spoon in shape: as a rule it has been carefully finished and has a long handle (120–130 cm). Kolchin divided ladles into two groups on the basis of their handle shape: ladles with a straight handle and with a handle with a special hook making it possible to suspend it from the edge of a bowl.

Carved vessels. In the 10th–11th centuries the people of Novgorod used carved bowls on a regular basis. Their diameter did not exceed 20 cm or their depth 5 cm. In some cases the bowls had a flat handle 3–4 cm in length. The material used for making these was as a rule from deciduous trees: maple, alder, birch and lime. Bowls made of spruce and pine were also sometimes encountered.

Turned vessels were used throughout Novgorod – cups and bowls of various shapes,

Spoons (153 in total)

	Fyodorovsky Excavation	Duboshin Excavation	Slavensky Excavation	Nerevsky Excavation
Number of samples	10	1	14	129
Pine	1		1	7
Spruce (*Picea*)				
Juniper	5	1		9
Ash	1			4
Maple	2		8	84
Alder			2	1
Aspen			1	
Birch			1	9
Willow			1	2
Fir (*Abies*)				1
Cedar				1
Mountain-ash				3
Apple-wood				3
Pear-wood				2
Bird-cherry				1
Spindle-tree (*Euonymous*)				1
Walnut				1

Carved vessels (51 in total)

	Fyodorovsky Excavation	Duboshin Excavation	Slavensky Excavation	Nerevsky Excavation
Number of samples	2			49
Pine	1			4
Ash	1			1
Spruce (*Picea*)				7
Boxwood				1
Maple				12
Birch				8
Lime				4
Alder				3
Willow				2
Aspen				1
Elm (*Ulmus*)				2
Hazel				3
Mountain-ash				1

Turned vessels (148 in total)

	Fyodorovsky Excavation	Duboshin Excavation	Slavensky Excavation	Nerevsky Excavation
Number of samples	2	3	4	139
Pine		1		5
Juniper				2
Lime				2
Aspen				3
Hazel				3
Mountain-ash				1
Apple-wood				1
Maple				45
Birch				8
Ash	2	1	1	44
Alder		1	3	25

Ladles (1 specimen)

	Fyodorovsky Excavation	Duboshin Excavation	Slavensky Excavation	Nerevsky Excavation
Maple	1			

Wickerwork boxes (1 specimen)

	Fyodorovsky Excavation	Duboshin Excavation	Slavensky Excavation	Nerevsky Excavation
Pine		1		

Table 15.1. Summary tables for the comparison of species of trees providing timber for articles found in the Fyodorovsky, Duboshin, Slavensky and Nerevsky excavations within Novgorod.

vessels for serving and drinking, containers and boxes. Turned utensils were relatively simple to manufacture and they had played a part in Novgorod households as early as the 10th/11th centuries. The preferred wood for turned vessels was ash, which was particularly hard and resilient. In addition, it had an attractively smooth and white texture. Maple, alder or wood from trees of coniferous species was used less frequently for such work.

Both carved and turned vessels were seldom decorated, but carved bowls are found with traces of red or yellow paint on them. Carved bowls small in size made of burrs or rootstock also stand out on account of their particularly attractive or original appearance.

In 13th and 14th-century levels fragments of wickerwork vessels were found: these were made of pine twigs twisted in a spiral and then with pine withes woven between them. So far no complete examples of wicker vessels have been found.

On the whole, the choice of timber for the manufacture of each kind of article is seen to follow particular patterns. Yet timber from trees that were not typical for a specific kind of output might also be used, merely because they had happened to be accessible at the time. Isolated examples of spoons made from the wood of bird-cherry or walnut have been found as has a turned vessel made not of the traditional ash, but from light and very soft lime-wood.

Note

1   Editors' Note: For a full account of the use of wood in medieval Novgorod see Brisbane and Hather (2007).

16

FAIR AND FOUL: ANALYSIS OF SUB-FOSSIL INSECT REMAINS FROM TROITSKY XI–XIII, NOVGOROD (1996–2002)

E. Reilly

INTRODUCTION

The analysis of insect remains from archaeological deposits (archaeoentomology) is a well-developed discipline in Britain (e.g. Osborne 1971; Hall and Kenward 1990; Smith *et al.* 1997). To a lesser extent it has been used in Ireland, The Netherlands, Denmark, Sweden, Iceland/Greenland and North America on prehistoric, medieval and post-medieval archaeological material (e.g. Bain 2001; Barrett *et al.* 2007; Buckland *et al.* 1994; Hellqvist and Lemdahl 1999; Kenward 2005; Reilly 1994, 2003, 2005; Schelvis 2000). However, in general, it is an under-utilised tool in environmental archaeology outside of Britain, despite the very valuable information that archaeoentomological studies have shed on wider archaeological, ecological and biogeographical issues (e.g. Whitehouse 2006).

As part of the most recent INTAS project of archaeological research at Novgorod (INTAS-00-154), insect remains analysis was added to the range of bio-archaeological proxies being utilised. The main research aim of the project was centred on a detailed analysis of 'Centre/Periphery relationships' based on evidence of the exploitation and processing of natural resources in medieval Novgorod and its region (Brisbane 2001). Many well-preserved insect remains were noted during macro- and micro-scale analysis of samples from earlier excavations at Novgorod (Monk and Johnston 2002). Remains of insects are preserved in large numbers in some types of archaeological deposits, usually where there is anoxic water-logging. It was intended that the study of insects, in conjunction with other biological evidence, could further elucidate important information about local environmental conditions within the town of Novgorod including importation of raw materials and processing of animal and plant remains on site.

This paper will look at a range of samples from Troitsky XI, excavated from 1996 to 1998 and a small number of samples from the most recent excavations of Troitsky XIII (2001 to present). Only one sample was available from Troitsky XII (1998–9) and while basic statistics are included in Tables 16.2 and 16.3, the number of insects recovered was too small for detailed analysis. Table 16.3 includes the complete species list and is included on the accompanying CD.

METHODOLOGY

Seventeen samples from deposits in different context complexes from Troitsky XI, XII and Troitsky XIII were analysed (Table 16.1). These were either taken on site by the author or from stored bulk samples that were previously analysed for plant remains (see Monk and Johnston 2002). Bulk soil samples generally measured between four and six litres in volume. Samples are listed in Table 16.1 in approximate stratigraphic order and are grouped according to the context complex they come from.

All but one of the seventeen samples analysed for insect remains were subject to the paraffin flotation method (Kenward 1980; Kenward *et al.* 1986). For most of the Troitsky XI samples, this involved the recombining of stored flots produced during flotation for plant remains and then subjecting this to paraffin flotation. All of the Troitsky XIII samples were sub-sampled and processed for insect remains in the normal way.

Insects were extracted onto damp filter paper and identified using a range of keys and the Gorham and Girling comparative collections at the University of Birmingham. Most of the beetles recovered could be identified to at least genus level and many to species level, despite the perceived difficulty of geographical variation in genera or species. Identified species along with their primary ecological information adapted from the BUGSCEP ecological database (Buckland and Buckland 2006) are listed in Table 16.3 on the accompanying CD (nomenclature follows Lucht 1987). The habitat information from individual taxa is then grouped into ecologically-related groups. These groups are based on an archaeological interpretation of their ecological information and these are illustrated in Figures 16.1 and 16.2. The index of diversity (Fisher's alpha; Fisher *et al.* 1943) is calculated for all samples with total number of individuals greater than 20, and detailed along with other basic statistics in Table 16.2.

Interpretations of insect remains are based on groups of species considered to represent past communities (*cf.* Kenward 1978; Robinson 1991). Direct comparisons with modern insect communities is difficult as some species that are now rare or not found in nature were formerly abundant on intensively-occupied sites and also because some species not expected to exist in urban environments once flourished in medieval towns (e.g. waterside beetles, see Kenward and Hall 1995).

In order to understand the archaeological implications of ancient insect assemblages it is important to define, as far as practicable, the communities that existed in the past. Assuming that all caveats in relation to pitfalls for interpretation based on modern ecological information are taken into consideration (see Kenward 1975), this method has proved to be very beneficial for archaeological contexts and analysis here is based primarily on the approach outlined in Kenward and Hall (1995) and Carrott and Kenward (2001), without necessarily replicating the nomenclature used in these studies.

Troitsky XI		
Context/Context Complex	**Sample No**	**Description**
Context 33	1a	Woody build-up under Building 1. 1998 UCL excavation. Grid 1279/spit 28. Excavated using single context recording. *ca.* 930 AD
Context 34	2a	Woody build-up under Building 1. 1998 UCL excavation. Grid 1280/spit 28. Excavated using single context recording. *ca.* 930 AD
Context 79	3	From a woody 'sealing layer' above floor of Building 1. 1998 UCL excavation. Grid 1265/spit 21. Excavated using single context recording, *ca.* 930 AD
Byre deposit in Structure 155 (Property R)	91	Byre within building. Grid 1254/spit 20 (construction level 27). *ca.* 970–990AD
South wall of Structure 88 (property I)	64	1996 excavations. Grid 1257/spit 8. *Not paraffin floted. ca.* 1205–1225 AD
Structure 88 (inside)	49	1996 excavations. Grid 1240 /spit 8. *ca.* 1205–1225 AD
Roadside edge	54	1996 excavations. Northwest side of road 13. Grid 1295/spit 8. *ca.* 1245–1270 AD
Property boundary, east of Structure 83/85	48	1996 excavations. Grid 1258/spit 8. *ca.* 1290–1330 AD
Troitsky XII		
Context 13	3a	Build-up below wall of Building 3/4. 1998 UCL excavations. Excavated using single context recording. *ca.* mid-12th century AD
Troitsky XIII		
Inside building	9	Grid 1778, spit 4/5. Sample comes from layer stratigraphically earlier than 6/7. *ca.* early 13th century
Within building	6	Grid 1778/spit 4. Construction level 5/6. Appearance of building debris, brick, plaster, wood. *ca.* mid-13th century
Within building	7	Grid 1778/spit 4. Organic deposit same as 6. Against E–W post. Mixed deposit. *ca.* mid-13th century
Fill between two buildings	2b	Grid 1778/spit 4. Construction level 5/6. Disturbed material. *ca.* mid-13th century
Fill between two buildings	3b	Grid 1778/spit 4. Construction level 5/6. *ca.* mid-13th century
Fill between two buildings	4	Grid 1779/spit 4. Construction level 5/6. Disturbed material. *ca.* mid-13th century
Workshop floor? within building	5	Grid 1683/spit 4. Lots of leather fragments. *ca.* mid-13th century
Leather working area or midden	8	Grid 1649/spit 4. Area of dumped leather off-cuts covering a number of grids. *ca.* mid-13th century

Table 16.1 Samples analysed for insect remains.

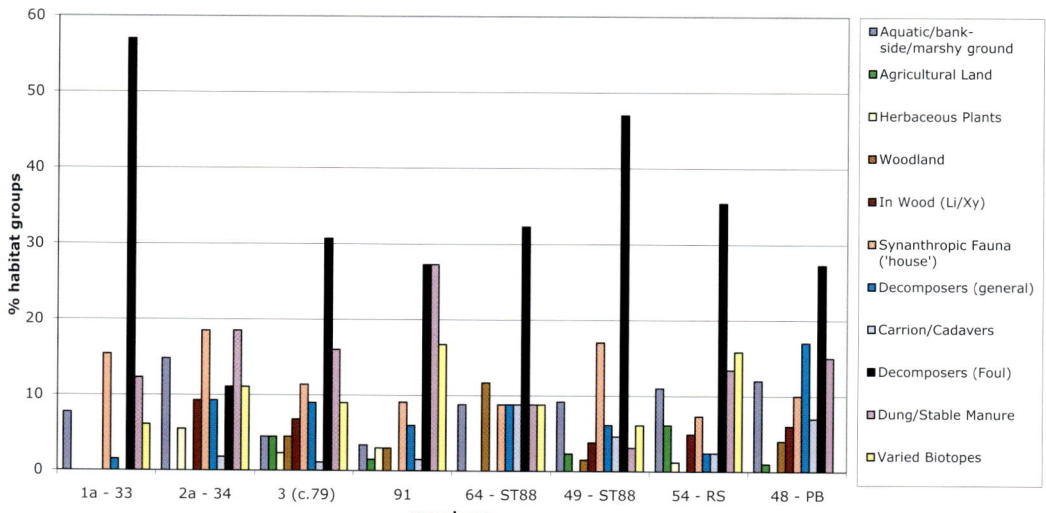

Figure 16.1 *Habitat groups represented in insect death assemblages, Troitsky XI, Novgorod.*

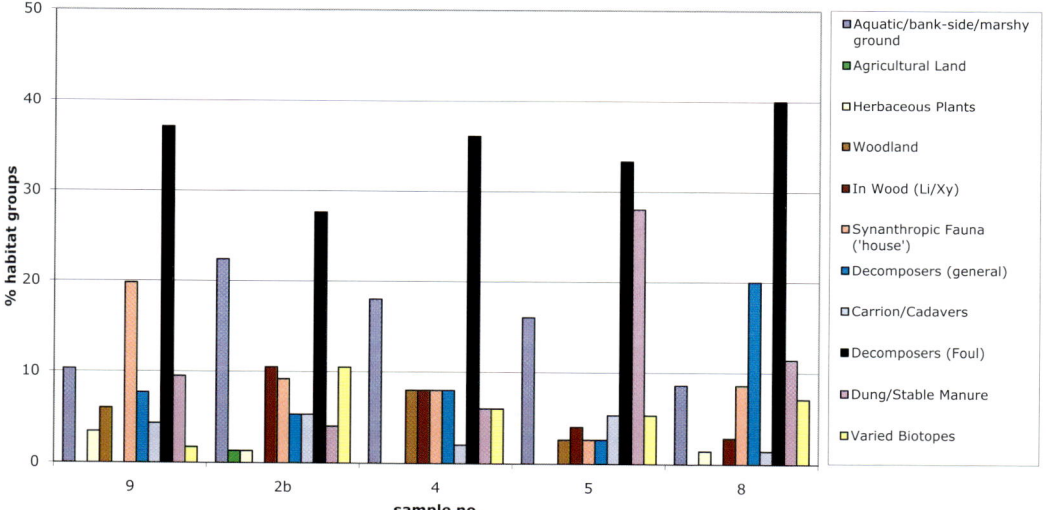

Figure 16.2 *Habitats groups represented in insect death assemblages, selected samples only, Troitsky XIII, Novgorod.*

ANALYSIS

A total of 1049 individuals representing 120 taxa were identified in seventeen samples from the three Troitsky sites. Four samples produced less than twenty individuals each and are excluded from detailed analysis. The total assemblage was dominated by 'foul decomposer' species (35%) with 'dung/stable manure' species the next largest group (13%); 'house fauna' and 'aquatic/bank-side/marshy ground' species were next with 11% of the total fauna each. All other habitat niches form between 1.3–8.5% of the total assemblage.

Troitsky XI (Figure 16.1)

The earliest levels analysed in this paper came from Troitsky XI and the section of the site excavated by a team from University College London (Reynolds and Sudds 2001).

10th century

Samples 1a, 2a and 3 were taken from woody layers under Building 1. Samples 1a and 2a (contexts 33 and 34) were from woody layers deliberately spread before the frame of the building was laid out and continued to build up beside the frame. Sample 3 (context 79) was from a layer of woody material deliberately spread between the walls, before the floorboards were laid. It was made up of a great deal of woodworking waste, plant remains and animal bones. This material was probably partly deliberately laid down to level the ground and protect the floorboards from rot by removing them from direct contact with the ground (Reynolds and Sudds 2001). It may also have been carried out for insulation or to create warmth. The insects identified from these samples were probably derived from two main sources: those incorporated into the material deliberately laid down before the floorboards and frame were laid and the gradually accumulating rubbish falling through the floorboards from the household activities carried out above. A number of artefacts were excavated from within context 79 including the head of a wooden club decorated with carved concentric circles along with more functional items, including a split willow stem used to bind a barrel and a wooden whisk (Reynolds and Sudds 2001).

Two of the assemblages, 1a and 3, were quite similar in make-up and both had low to moderately low index of diversity values (Table 16.2). The insect remains consisted primarily of decaying vegetation indicators, with a higher percentage of species associated with foul conditions (Figure 16.1). Sample 2a had a higher index of diversity, simply indicating a more mixed origin for the assemblage. It had lower numbers of foul decomposers and higher percentage values of house fauna indicators.

Many of the species recovered in Sample 1a and 3 are commonly found in cess-pits in Viking or medieval contexts in other urban centres (Kenward and Hall 1995; Reilly 1994, 2003), however, a number are found in decaying material with a higher moisture content, indicating wet conditions under foot. These species include *Anotylus rugosus*, *A. complanatus* and *Oxytelus sculptus*. Some 18% of the assemblage in Sample 2a was made up of species indicating what is commonly known as the 'house fauna' (e.g. Kenward and Hall 1995) or species that have become associated with human habitation including *Cryptophagus* spp., *Lathridius* spp. and *Ptinus fur* (Hellqvist and Lemdahl 1996). Percentages for this group were also quite high in 1a and 3. The 'house fauna' also includes species that inhabit fouler conditions too and are associated with human cess-pits, dried skins and leather such as *Dermestes* sp., the larder beetle.

Sample number/context	1a - 33	2a - 34	3 (c.79)	91	64 - ST88	49 - ST88	54 - RS	48 - PB	3a	9	6	7	2b	3b	4	5	8
Excavation No	TRXI	TRXI	TRXI	TRXI	TRXI	TRXI	TRXI	TRXI	TRXII	TRXIII	TRXIII	TRXIII	TRXIII	TRXIII	TRXIII	TRXIII	TRXIII
Total No. Individuals	65	54	88	66	34	130	82	99	18	116	3	7	76	16	50	75	70
Total No. of Taxa	22	33	35	28	17	43	39	44	13	40	3	6	39	14	28	36	33
Index of Diversity (α)	12	38	22	19	14	23	30	31	n/a	22	n/a	n/a	34	n/a	28	28	26
Aq/bank-side/marshy ground	5	8	4	3	3	12	9	12	2	12	0	1	17	3	9	12	6
Agricultural Land	0	0	4	1	0	3	5	1	0	0	0	0	1	0	0	0	0
Herbaceous Plants	0	3	2	2	0	0	1	0	0	4	0	0	1	0	0	0	1
Woodland	0	0	4	2	4	2	0	4	0	7	0	0	0	0	4	2	0
In Wood (Li/Xy)	0	5	6	0	0	5	4	6	1	0	0	0	8	0	4	3	2
Synanthropic Fauna ('house')	10	10	10	6	3	22	6	10	2	23	1	0	7	1	4	2	6
Decomposers (general)	1	5	8	4	3	8	2	17	2	9	0	1	4	4	4	2	14
Carrion/Cadavers	0	1	1	1	3	6	2	7	1	5	0	1	4	2	1	4	1
Decomposers (Foul)	37	6	27	18	11	61	29	27	4	43	2	2	21	8	18	25	28
Dung/Stable Manure	8	10	14	18	3	4	11	15	3	11	0	0	3	2	3	21	8
Varied Biotopes	4	6	8	11	3	8	13	0	3	2	0	2	8	3	3	4	5
% Presence of habitats																	
Aq/bank-side/marshy ground	7.7	14.8	4.5	3.4	8.8	9.2	11	12	-	10.3	-	-	22.4	-	18	16	8.6
Agricultural Land	0	0	4.5	1.5	0	2.3	6.1	1	-	0	-	-	1.3	-	0	0	0
Herbaceous Plants	0	5.5	2.3	3	0	0	1.2	0	-	3.4	-	-	1.3	-	0	0	1.4
Woodland	0	0	4.5	3	11.7	1.5	0	4	-	6	-	-	0	-	8	2.6	0
In Wood (Li/Xy)	0	9.3	6.8	0	0	3.8	4.9	6	-	0	-	-	10.5	-	8	4	2.8
Synanthropic Fauna ('house')	15.4	18.5	11.4	9.1	8.8	17	7.3	10	-	19.8	-	-	9.2	-	8	2.6	8.6
Decomposers (general)	1.5	9.3	9	6	8.8	6.1	2.4	17	-	7.7	-	-	5.3	-	8	2.6	20
Carrion/Cadavers	0	1.8	1.1	1.5	8.8	4.6	2.4	7	-	4.3	-	-	5.3	-	2	5.3	1.4
Decomposers (Foul)	57	11.1	30.7	27.3	32.3	47	35.4	27.3	-	37	-	-	27.6	-	36	33.3	40
Dung/Stable Manure	12.3	18.5	16	27.3	8.8	3.1	13.4	15	-	9.5	-	-	4	-	6	28	11.4
Varied Biotopes	6.1	11.1	9	16.7	8.8	6.1	15.8	0	-	1.7	-	-	10.5	-	6	5.3	7.1

Table 16.2 Basic statistics on habitats represented in insect death assemblages, all samples, Troitsky XI, XII, XIII, Novgorod (samples listed in approx. stratigraphic order from earliest to latest and grouped according to context complexes).

While the overall impression from the assemblages in 1a and 3, in particular, is of foul decaying material the number of true 'dung' feeders is actually quite small and although some human cess indicators are present only two true 'outdoor' or farmyard dung beetles, *Aphodius ater* and *A. granularis,* are present in any of the assemblages. Overall, this is in keeping with assemblages from an indoor location and made up of material derived from household rubbish.

A small but significant group of woodland, timber and wood debris insects are found in these three contexts. *Hylastes* spp. (Sample 3) is a wood-borer and is exclusively found on pine, spruce and other coniferous species (Lekander *et al.* 1977). *Hadrobregmus pertinax* (Sample 2a) is a typical wood-borer of old wooden houses in Scandinavia and Northern Russia, where the wood has been attacked by rot fungi (Vittanen and Pulkkinen 1989), particularly re-worked coniferous wood. *Lyctus brunneus* (Sample 2a) is a destructive wood-borer with a palaearctic distribution (Koch 1989). *Pityogenes chalcographus* (Plate 1 on CD) is a small bark beetle common in both spruce and pine (Lekander *et al.* 1977). *Pityophagus ferrugineus* (Sample 2a) is found under bark of dead pine (Alexander 2002). *Glischrochilus hortensis* is found generally in woodland debris, particularly under bark and among rotting wood and leaves (Alexander 2002). It is also found among compost material with some wood content and this pre-flooring material would appear to have been an ideal habitat. *Cerylon histeroides* is also found under bark or in dead stumps of both coniferous and deciduous trees (Bullock 1993). There are a number of species present that occupy woodland mosses and might have been brought on site with firewood or pre-worked timber.

Apart from woodland indicators, the number of 'outdoor' species is relatively low although nearly 15% of the assemblage of Sample 2a was made of species from aquatic and/or marshy ground habitats. Approximately 7% of Sample 3 was made up of species that feed on various herbaceous plants, urban and agricultural weeds. These are probably primarily accidental inclusions brought in with foodstuffs and water-side plants used for flooring or bedding. This low level of 'outdoor' indicators is a common feature of insect assemblages derived from 'indoor' contexts.

Sample 91 came from a byre within structure 155, Property R, and was dated to approximate AD 970–990. This interesting insect assemblage would appear initially to reflect the use of this space for housing animals. High numbers of fly puparia were noted during processing although these were not identified. Foul decomposers and species indicating stable manure such as *Cercyon unipunctatus* (Plate 2 on CD) and *Platystethus aerinarius* dominate the assemblage (*sensu* Hall and Kenward 1997). Comparing the graph from this assemblage to those from Building 1, above, it is clear that the assemblage is derived from somewhat different sources (Figure 16.1). Most notably, the presence of wood-borers, 'house fauna' indicators and drier decomposers are generally lower in Structure 155 than in any of the three assemblages from Building 1. The only anomalous finding is the lack of true dung beetles (only one example of *Aphodius* sp.). However, the large number of *C. unipunctatus*, *C. quisquillus* and *Platystethus arenarius* are all indicative of animal dung.

Early to mid-13th century
Samples 49 and 64 are dated to the early and mid-13th century. Sample 49 was taken from inside Structure 88, dated to AD 1205–1225. Plant remains included a range of weeds and ruderals and plants of grassy places such as *Dianthus* sp. (Monk and Johnston, this volume).

It was the richest sample in terms of insect remains of any sample examined (130 individuals). However, the index of diversity was slightly lower than previous samples as the assemblage was dominated by two species, *Carpelimus bilineatus* (Plate 3 on CD, foul decomposer, damp conditions) and *Atomaria nigripennis* ('house fauna'). Overall, the foul decomposer group made up 47% of the assemblage, followed by the 'house fauna' at 17% and aquatic/marshy ground species at 9%, reflecting a mixed origin for the assemblage. *C. bilineatus* is tolerant of a wide range of ground conditions but is usually indicative of long-lived damp organic layers in urban archaeological contexts (Kenward and Hall 1995). *A. nigripennis* is a mould feeder in drier conditions and is almost certainly from an indoor source. A number of water beetles are present, including *Ochthebius* sp. and *Cymbiodyta marginella*, possibly reflecting pools of muddy water on the ground surface or imported water for household use (Kenward 2005; Barrett *et al.* 2007). A small but similarly significant group of wood dependent beetles were recovered from this context, including *Hadrobregmus pertinax*, *Dendroctonus* sp., *Hylastes* sp. and *Lyctus brunneus*, again reflecting both structural wood and recently arrived 'natural' wood sources.

Sample 64 was taken from material built up against the south wall of Structure 88. It had a small insect assemblage with a low index of diversity indicating a more restricted range of origins. The identified plant remains included apple and cherry, bilberry, flax and a few damp ground plants (Monk and Johnston, this volume). Millet and husk fragments were also found. Hop and cannabis, were identified and the flax and cannabis may indicate processing for textiles.

The insect assemblage was dominated by foul, wet decaying vegetation indicators, which is not unexpected for a deposit forming 'outdoors' (Figure 16.1). A smaller number of 'house fauna' and generalist decomposer species were also present, as well as a small number of mossy, wood detritus-indicating species. The assemblage may indicate changing conditions under foot at this location and perhaps the addition of drier material to cope with a particularly wet area. The house fauna species present would occupy various niches in human structures from roofing to bedding material. The more foul decaying vegetation group is made up primarily of one species, *Platystethus arenarius*. This species is found in all kinds of dung, both animal and human, but also in carrion, and liquefied or putrified vegetable material (Hall and Kenward 1990). Significantly, it is also found in mud along riverbanks and in general is highly tolerant of wet conditions (Kenward and Hall 1995). This would appear to indicate that either much of the material at this location was highly putrified or there was a high degree of dung or human cess incorporated. There are few other dung indicators, however, so the evidence points towards the former explanation. Indeed the outdoor element of the overall assemblage was quite low, with no plant feeders and few aquatics.

Late 13th/early 14th century
Samples 54 and 48 came from late 13th/early 14th century levels in Troitsky XI. Sample 54 came from a roadside edge (Level 13), dated to AD 1245–1270. A very high frequency of wood and other woody fibre was noted during processing. Plant macrofossils recorded included disturbed ground plants from the dock, goosefoot and nettle families, and lots of damp ground plants including water plantain, reed, pondweed and sedges (Monk and Johnston, this volume.).

This rich insect assemblage had a moderately high index of diversity, which indicated very mixed origins for the material found in this roadside location. This is to be expected given the potential for inclusions from a number of outdoor contexts as well as general household rubbish that may be ejected from buildings onto the roadside. Again, the highest percentage presence was the decaying/foul indicator group including species such as *Platestethus aerinarius*, *Anotylus complanatus* and *Carpelimus fuliginosus*. Indeed the high percentage presence of this group throughout all the samples from Trotsky XI has wider archaeological implications, which shall be addressed again later (see Discussion). Here, however, there are also many outdoor indicators giving a better impression of overall wetness including aquatic species like *Hydroporus* sp., *Cymbiodyta marginella* and *Helophorus* sp. Many species tolerant of damp, marshy conditions such as *Cercyon laminatus*, *Pterostichus strenuus* and *Carpelimus bilineatus* are also present. The evidence from the plant remains would appear to correlate with these findings (Monk and Johnston 2001 and this volume).

There are also dung feeders such as *Aphodius conspurcatus* and *A. fimetarius*, which would be found on domestic animal dung, as well as many species indicative of human waste. A significant percentage of the overall assemblage is also made up of species belonging to the house fauna group, although a number of them are common in human cess-pits. Clearly, however, the material at the roadside is derived from many sources and appears to be primarily muddy and wet.

A small but significant woodland debris/timber element was found in this assemblage including *Priobium carpini* (Plate 4 on CD), a central European Anobid ('woodworm') beetle found in dry timber of conifers and broad-leaved trees (Barclay 2005). *Ips typographus*, was also recovered. This species is found exclusively on pine, spruce and larch and geographically is most common across Northern Europe and Russia (Lekander *et al.* 1977). It attacks thicker barked, debilitated trees (particularly storm or frost damaged trees) or un-barked timber. It may have been found in structural timber at this time but it is not considered synanthropic. It is more likely to have come from the felled timber that was brought on site to be used in construction. A third interesting wood-dependent beetle identified in this assemblage was *Carphoborus* sp. (Plate 5 on CD), a small bark beetle of which there are nine species across Europe. Three species are known from the general Leningrad (St Petersburg) region and surrounding regions but all are extremely rare today (Mandelshtam and Popovichev 2000). *C. cholodkovskyi* is found in pine and there have been no recent records from the region; *C. minimus* is also found in pine and is thought to be regionally extinct, while *C. rossicus* is found in spruce and is regionally rare (Mandelshtam and Popovichev 2000). It was not possible to identify this beetle to species but the habitat preferences of all three fit with the dominant construction wood of choice in medieval Novgorod.

Sample 48 was taken from beside a property boundary dated to AD 1290–1330, another 'outdoor' context. The plant remains recovered included lots of fruit, blackberry, raspberry strawberry, apple, cherry and bilberry, as well as millet, wheat and oat; all evidently food-waste. Also, plants of disturbed ground and damp ground, similar to Sample 54 above, were recovered.

The insect assemblage from this sample was quite rich and also had a high index of diversity, again, a feature of 'outdoor' contexts (Figure 16.1). The biggest representation within the assemblage came from the foul decaying vegetation group, however, there was also a high percentage of species that could not be identified beyond genus. This is often the case with outdoor material that has been reworked and trampled, for example. Aquatic species and species of herbaceous plants or weeds were recorded as well as species indicating hummic soil or fully decomposed plant material. The foul group was once again represented by a large number of *Platestethus aerinarius* and along with other cess, dung and carrion indicators, such as *Trox scaber* (Plate 6 on CD), would appear to point to the presence of both human and animal waste material in the soil matrix of this context. The presence of human waste, in particular, would seem somewhat unusual given its location beside a property boundary but it is possible that very foul conditions from a combination of decaying plant matter, animal dung and pools of water could combine to provide suitable habitats for most of the foul-preferring species noted in the assemblage. Equally, however the combination of fruit seeds observed in the plant remains may represent the 'fruit salad' often observed from cess-pit fills in both Britain and Ireland (e.g. Geraghty 1996).

A similar suite of wood-boring species to other samples discussed was present including the most common synanthropic wood-borer, *Anobium punctatum*. A number of *Hylastes* spp were recovered from this context. As discussed above, it is a pine-dependant though probably not synanthropic. It may have been a casualty of wood working on site.

Troitsky XII

A single sample from Troitsky XII was analysed as part of this study. Sample 3a was taken from below the wall of buildings 3/4 during 1998 (Reynolds and Sudds 2001). This sample produced a very small insect assemblage with a number of dung beetles, foul decomposers and wood-dependent species (Table 16.2). While the findings reflected those of other contexts examined in Troitsky XI and XIII, discussed below, the assemblage is too small to assess further.

Troitsky XIII (Figure 16.2)

Early/mid-13th century

Eight samples in total were analysed from this site. Due to the timing of the sampling visits, all of the samples come from early to mid-13th century levels. However, at least three context complexes were sampled dating to this period with some stratigraphic differences noted within them. There are also useful comparisons that can be drawn between these samples and those from the same period in Troitsky XI.

Samples 9, 6 and 7 came from within the southernmost corner of two buildings in the southeastern corner of the site (Grid 1778/1779). Sample 9, dated to the early 13th century, was from a layer stratigraphically earlier than 6 and 7, dated to the mid-13th century.

Only one of these three samples, Sample 9, produced sufficient insect remains to warrant detailed analysis (Table 16.2; Figure 16.2). It had a moderate index of diversity showing admixture of insects from a number of different sources but was dominated by insects from the fouler end of the decomposer spectrum. While the 'house fauna' element was quite high at 20%, the majority of the assemblage represented damp, foul conditions with elements of dung or stable manure and some evidence for the presence of carrion or cadavers, possibly discarded bones. The genus *Philonthus* spp. was present in large numbers and many members of this genus are indicators of foul conditions. Also present were carrion/cadaver species such as *Hister impressus*, *Dermestes* sp., *Trox scaber* and *Omosita colon* (Plate 7 on CD) and abundant fly puparia. The overall impression of damp ground conditions are implied by the presence of various riparian ground beetles such as *Bledius subterraneus* and *Pterostichus strenuus* and wetland plants (possibly being used as bedding or fodder) are indicated by the presence of *Prasocuris juncii*. Indeed, all samples from Troitsky XIII are characterised by high percentage presence of damp/marshy ground indicators.

As a deposit derived from an indoor location it is generally fouler than might be expected or when compared to Sample 2a, from 10th century levels in Troitsky XI. However, it is similar in profile to Sample 49, an 'indoor' deposit from 13th century levels in Troitsky XI and it is possible that the deposit from which Samples 9 and 49 were derived related to abandonment of the structures or their use not for human habitation but for animals. Neither Sample 6 nor 7, which are stratigraphically later than 9, can shed any light on this perplexing issue due to the tiny assemblages recovered.

Samples 2b, 3b and 4 came from between two buildings in the southeastern corner of the site (Grid 1778/1779), both dating from the early to mid-13th century. The interior of one of these buildings was sampled (see Samples 9, 6 and 7 above).

Two of these samples, 2b and 4, produced good assemblages and their habitat information is illustrated in Figure 16.2. The deposits from which these samples came can be seen as 'outdoor' midden material or general organic build up between the structures. Both produced similar moderate to high index of diversity values, reflecting the mixed origins of the insect assemblages. Both are dominated by foul decomposers, a now familiar picture from this period in Troitsky XI and XIII but with high percentage presence of marshy ground indicators such as the ground beetles *Dyschirius globosus* and bare, riverine clay-indicators such as *Bledius subterraneus*.

Sample 2b, in particular, has a small but interesting assemblage of wood dependent beetles, most notably the Bostrychid beetle, *Stephanopachys substriatus* (Plate 8 on CD), which was also recovered from Sample 4. This is a borer in various species of pine, often attracted to burnt wood (Hyvarinen *et al.* 2006). It was also recovered from woody layers beneath Building 1 in 10th century levels of Troitsky XI (Sample 2a). Overall, the prevailing damp, foul ground conditions represented by Sample 9 from inside a building are reflected in the assemblages from these 'outdoor' deposits. Again, this would hint that either prevailing living conditions inside and out were uncomfortable, damp and smelly or that the 'indoor' Sample 9 is in fact from an 'outdoor' setting, whether byre or abandonment phase.

Samples 5 and 8, while originating in slightly different parts of the site both relate to a possible leather workshop, tentatively identified in the middle of the site (Figure 16.2). Sample 5 is from a floor layer within this workshop (Grid 1683), while Sample 8 came from a large spread of leather off-cut and waste material, further to the north (Grid 1649). This whole area may have been part of a larger industrial complex, with the area where Sample 8 was taken from a midden of general waste material.

Both samples had good assemblages with moderate diversity indices (Table 16.2). Both were dominated by foul decomposer species. However, Sample 5 had a very high percentage dung/stable manure signature and a small but significant carrion/cadaver signature (*sensu* Hall and Kenward 1997). In particular, the dung beetles were primarily those that would be found in animal manure rather than human faeces such as *Cercyon quisquillis* and *Aphodius fimentarius*. The carrion/cadaver indicators included *Acritus nigricornis*, a small beetle frequently found in tannery pits elsewhere (e.g. Buckland *et al*. 1976), *Necrodes littoralis*, *Dermestes* sp., *Sipha* sp. and *Omosita colon*, variously found in carrion, on old bones and on dried animal skins. Combined with a reasonably high animal dung signature, this could be evidence for butchery, storage of skins for later leather working or furs for trade. As discussed by Hall and Kenward (1990) in relation to the Colonia, York and Kenward (2005) in relation to Viking-age Viborg, Denmark, tanning is not likely to have taken place within the habitation areas of the town. Therefore, these 'carrion/old bones/skins' indicators occurring together are more indicative of piles of old bones (perhaps discarded butchery waste) or leather working.

Sample 8 has a similar range of species present but with a less coherent butchery signature. This may be due to the fact that the sample was taken from a midden of waste material, which contained waste from other sources, therby diluting the carrion/cadaver species group. A higher percentage presence of 'house fauna' was noted from this sample than Sample 5, as well as a higher presence of generalist decomposers species such as *Carpelimus fuliginosus* and *Xantholinus linearis/longiventris*. This probably reflects the more mixed origin of this deposit.

The woodland/dead wood signature for both samples was small but two interesting species are present that were not present in other samples. *Dorytomus longimanus*, a weevil found on poplar, birch and willow (Bullock 1993) was present in Sample 5 while *Xyloterus lineatus*, a bark beetle found in various conifer species was found in Sample 8 (Alexander 2002). A fragment of *Dorytomus* elytra was also noted in Sample 4 from within a building (see above). The presence of *X. lineatus* is not surprising given the dominant use of pine and spruce in house construction (Tarabardina 2001, 2007). Stenotopic wood-dependents of other tree species, including birch and poplar, were not common from any level examined. Tarabardina (2007) noted that deciduous tree species made up only 1% of building timber excavated in Troitsky XI and 2% of building timber excavated in Troitsky XII. This pattern was probably also true for Troitsky XIII.

DISCUSSION: MORE FOUL THAN FAIR?

The ecological information from the insect assemblages proved to be very informative and had immediately discernible signatures. The similarity with suites of insects commonly seem on urban sites of this time elsewhere in Europe is striking while particular patterns unique to Novgorod have emerged that require further analysis. In particular, the dominance of species that inhabit the fouler end of the decomposing spectrum in all deposits, both indoor and outdoor, is a feature not seen in contemporary Viking-medieval dated sites such as Dublin (Reilly 2003), York (e.g. Hall and Kenward 1995), Viborg, Denmark (Kenward 2005) or Kaupang, Norway (Barrett *et al.* 2007) but was noted during previous analysis of insect remains from an exposed excavation baulk at Troitsky X, Novgorod (Hellqvist and Lemdahl 1999). The explanation offered by Hellqvist and Lemdahl was the proximity of the site to the river and the possibility of frequent flooding episodes that kept the ground surface wet and provided an impetus for building up the town rapidly (Hellqvist and Lemdahl 1999).

However, despite the proximity of the settlements of both York and Dublin to rivers and a similar rapid build-up of the urban layers this dominance of foul decomposers, other than in cess-pit contexts, is not often seen. The only parallels are in those contexts where there is a possibility of the presence of stable manure or animal waste products, such as the early 10th century levels at Essex Street West and a house/byre structure in Back Lane, Dublin (Reilly 2003).

Analysis of plant remains from Troitsky XI and XIII shows high numbers of aquatic plant taxa including *Ranunculus scleratus* and *Alisma plantago-aquatica* in certain contexts through all periods, particularly in the earliest-dated levels and again in the late 12th/early 13th century (Monk and Johnston, this volume). A combination of the known underlying dampness of the area and the presence of stable manure or animal waste products on site might explain the dominance of foul-preferring species.

Therefore, a close relationships between humans and animals, animal waste and by-products, during the history of the Troitsky area, are suggested by the insect assemblage. The singular importance of wood and wood-working was also clearly demonstrated in the insect assemblages, in particular the central role of pine and spruce in house-building.

Animal husbandry and 'foul' indicators
Dung beetles were a common element of the insects assemblages from Troitsky XI and XIII. In the earliest levels from Troitsky XI, Sample 91 came from a building, which was described archaeologically as a 'byre'. This had a high number of animal dung indiators, as well as other beetles indicative of stabling of animals (Hall and Kenward 1997). These include indicators of 'meadow' or pasture, such as *Chaetocnema cf. concinna*. From later deposits in Troitsky XIII, Sample 5 had a similarly high range of dung beetles, again possibly indicating stabling of animals. In general, this ties with the indications given by the plant remains, which showed a signficant presence of damp meadow and hay plant species in many 'byre' contexts (Monk and Johnston 2001 and this volume). The presence of such plants on site could be due to human transport of the raw material but possibly they were incorporated into dung through the grazing of animals in wet meadows close to the town.

This niche group is separate from, but related to, the dominant foul decomposer group found in all samples, which in general indicated wet, muddy and relatively foul ground conditions underfoot. Opportunistic plants of disturbed and waste ground were the dominant element of the plant macrofossil assemblages (Monk and Johnston 2001 and this volume). Animal bone evidence indicated there were huge numbers of discarded bones on site and a significant amount of gnawed bones, indicating the presence of dogs (Maltby and Hamilton-Dyer 2001). The presence of certain beetles associated with old bones and carrion were a small but significant element of the insect fauna (see further discussion below).

The presence of bare ground and riparian ground beetles in some of the samples would suggest that intermittent flooding took place or, at least, the watertable was very high at particular times in the past. Aquatic, bank-side and marshy ground species form a signficant percentage of the assemblages from Sample 2a (Troitsky XI, 10th century) and 2b and 5 (Troitsky XIII, 13th century).

Taken together, this range of material would have provided many suitable niches for scavanging and opportunistic decomposing beetles and flies tolerant of damp conditions, explaining their dominance of all assemblages recorded here.

Butchery and leather working indicators
A small number of species present in three or four of the samples indicate the presence of cadavers, probably skins or hides of animals (Samples 48, 49, 9 and 5), including *Catops* spp., *Dermestes* sp., *Hister impressus*, *H. cf. striola*, *Necrodes littoralis*, *Silpha* sp., *Trox scaber* and *Omosita colon*. Unfortunately, both *Catops* spp. and *Dermestes* sp. were very fragmented and not identifiable beyond genus in some of the 'outdoor' samples (48, in particular). This probably indicates that they were re-deposited here as part of

ejected household waste. Hall and Kenward (2003) have suggested that some of these species found in association with bark remains are possible evidence for tanning. However, a combination of these species found in certain contexts in Viking-age Kaupang and Viborg are thought more likely to be indicative of stored skins or furs (Kenward 2005; Barrett *et al.* 2007)

The presence of a diverse range of such taxa in one sample, Sample 5, from within a building along with a significant animal dung/foul insect assemblage, seems to indicate the presence of both primary butchery waste and hides of animals. A similar combination of species was recorded in samples from Saxon-dated pits, thought to be butchery pits, in Southampton, England (Buckland *et al.* 1976) and from 19th century wharf-front deposits in Quebec, Canada (Bain 2001). Sample 5 came from a deposit where huge numbers of leather fragments were excavated. A midden of rubbish outside this property produced more leather off-cuts but a sample from this material (Sample 8) had fewer animal hide beetles, although the number of foul decomposers was very high. Both samples had plenty of dung beetles specifically indicating animal dung or stable manure. It may be that the building had a duel purpose i.e. stabling of horses, for example, and a hide- or leather-working workshop also. Alternatively, the stable may have been used as a dumping area for leather off-cuts during its final use phase.

The number of cadaver indicators was higher than in the assemblages recorded from Troitsky X or Ryurik Gorodishche by Hellqvist and Lemdahl (1999). However, in those instances, samples were taken from sections and not directly from excavated contexts and so could easily have missed certain kinds of features/structures.

Woodworking and house building
Another interesting element of the fauna was the number of wood-dependent species present. The assemblage was a mixture of synanthropic (i.e. human dependent) species such as *Anobium punctatum, Hadrobregmus pertinax, Priobium carpini* and 'natural' woodland species such as *Stephanopachys substriatus, Hylastes* spp., *Trypodendron lineatum, Pityophagus ferrugineus, Pityogenes chalcographus, Carphoborus* sp. and *Ips typographus.* Soil studies from the base of cultural layers in Troitsky XI clearly indicated the presence of mixed woodland prior to the construction of the town (Alexsandrovskaya *et al.* 2001). Charcoal fragments of oak, lime and birch were present, probably representing the local dominant tree taxa. However, the overwhelming signature from the insect assemblages was of pine and spruce, the main species of wood used in the buildings of Troitsky and elsewhere in Novgorod (Tarabardina 2001, 2007) and well-represented in the woodlands of its hinterland. Interestingly, woodland-indicators were more frequently encountered here than in either Kaupang or Viborg (Kenward 2005; Barrett *et al.* 2007).

Urban sites of this period present a particularly problem to the archaeo-entomologist when examining wood-dependent species (Reilly 2003). Are *all* of these species living in the artificially-created 'woodland' niches of houses, property boundaries and roads or are some simply casualties of wood-working processes? Species such as *A. punctatum* have a long, continuing and acrimonious relationship with humans and their homes and still occupy structural wood to this day. *Priobium carpini* is particularly widespread in Fennoscandia and Russia associated with structural timber (Barclay 2005). *Lyctus brunneus* has also been closely associated with human structures, probably for centuries (Hickin 1968). However, other wood-dependent beetles have never become truly synanthropic and are generally only found in natural environments today (e.g. Reilly 2005; Whitehouse 2006). These species should be able to inform the archaeologist of construction practices, in particular, if de-barking or storage was occurring on site or off-site.

Other writers have suggested that wood was felled for construction and left to season off-site (Khoroshev and Sorokin 1992), possibly stripped of branches and roots ('topped and tailed') and then transported to site for use in construction (Reynolds and Sudds 2001). Interestingly, no leaf-defoliating beetles were recovered from any of the deposits, which one might expect if branches and leaf litter were present on site. This would appear to corroborate the theory of off-site preparation of logs.

Most of the non-synanthropic wood-dependent beetles recorded at Troitsky are bark beetles. These beetles generally live under the bark or within the sapwood of various tree species shortly after felling (Dajoz 2000). The level of moisture they tolerate varies and therefore some are restricted to more seasoned wood, others to freshly cut wood and *S. substriatus* is found in burnt wood, usually up to two years after burning (Hyvarinen *et al.* 2006). The cutting of trees and leaving them to season *in situ* would probably explain the presence of many of these beetles on site as this delay would have afforded them time to invade the felled wood. The evidence of copious wood-working debris on site from the excavations at Troitsky XI would explain how they became incorporated into floor and midden layers (Reynolds and Sudds 2001). The insect evidence would suggest this was also the case for Troitsky XIII, at least in the later period for which samples were examined.

Khoroshev and Sorokin (1992) noted the presence of nineteen different tree species among the construction and worked wood at the Lyudin end of Novgorod, although pine and spruce were the dominant trees. Pine and spruce-dependent beetles dominated the wood-dependent taxa recorded here (six out of a total of eleven taxa) from Troitsky XI and XIII. Pine and spruce beetles also dominated the wood-dependent taxa from Troitsky X and Ryurik Gorodishche (Hellqvist and Lemdahl 1999).

Synanthropy

The construction methodology of housing in Novgorod might also explain one other curious phenomenon encountered in the insect evidence, namely the low overall percentage presence of house fauna (11.6%). Kenward (Barrett *et al.* 2007) discusses the proportionally low level of 'synanthropic' insects at Kaupang, Viborg and Buiston crannog compared to contemporary or near-contemporary sites elsewhere e.g. Deer Park Farms, Northern Ireland (Kenward and Allison 1994) and Coppergate, York (Kenward and Hall 1995) as being possibly indicative of short-term or intermittent occupation. However, the percentage of synanthropes from Novgorod is lower than all of these sites and yet the archaeological evidence clearly shows that the Troitsky area was intensively occupied for many centuries. The low level of synanthropes at Novgorod, therefore, is possible evidence that the raised wooden floors negated the need for a build-up of deep litter layers, such as those seen at Coppergate or Deer Park Farms. Without this continuous build up of 'dry' organic matter many of the familiar 'synanthropic' insects from such sites, especially *Aglenus brunneus*, did not become established.

A final thought: preservation and taphonomy
Preservation of insect remains in general was excellent and it was possible to identify most of the insects present to at least genus level. Interesting archaeological questions arise from very fragmented, unidentifiable material, in particular, possible evidence for re-working and secondary deposition or longevity and trampling of the deposit *in situ*. Very often, so-called 'outdoor' samples produce a lot of fragmented material and this was the case with a number of samples such as 64 and 48. As much of the material in these deposits were formed from both outdoor elements and possible house fauna it is clear that mixing had taken place over time. However, the nature of the excavation methodology from which most of these samples came, i.e. spits of fixed 20 cm depth, may mean that some of the species diversity and mixing noted in the samples is a product of taphonomy, in particular mixing of contexts during sampling. This is something that has to be taken into consideration when looking at any of the samples, except 1a, 2a, 3 and 3a which were excavated using the single context system.

The issue of taphonomy is one that has exercised the minds of all the environmental archaeologists working at Novgorod. It is often tempting to extrapolate too much from the presence of particular species but when taphonomic factors are not taken into consideration it can potentially lead to erroneous conclusions.

The sampling methodology devised tried to take account of the potential taphonomic problems of the spit system of excavation, however, one can never be sure that admixture of deposits has not occurred. Therefore, it is heartening to note that the profile of the assemblages from the context-based excavation by the UCL-led team is not dissimilar to that from the assemblages taken from the spit samples (Figures 16.1 and 16.2). The main environmental indicators are similar including the dominance of foul/decaying species across context types while the outdoor samples show the right balance of both potential indoor and outdoor origins, as noted in urban 'outdoor' samples from other sites across Europe (*senus* Kenward and Hall 1995). The indoor samples, meanwhile, display a higher percentage presence of house fauna with fewer outdoor species. In this respect, while some mixing of contexts is inevitable due to the spit system of excavation, the eye of the specialist taking the samples has ensured for the most part that the samples reflect a particular event horizon.

SUMMARY

Seventeen samples were examined for sub-fossil insect remains (Coleoptera - beetles) from 10th and 13th century deposits, Troitsky XI and 13th century deposits, Troitsky XIII as part of INTAS-00-154. Preservation was excellent for the most part and a picture of underlying damp and muddy ground conditions, copious decaying plant and animal matter, dung/stable manure and wood-working waste was identified from the insect assemblages. Tentative evidence for butchery and leatherworking were indicated from a suite of insects recovered from a building and associated midden deposit in Troitsky XIII. The dominance of pine and spruce as the construction wood of choice for Medieval Novgorod's residents was reflected in the wood-dependent beetles recovered.

Acknowledgements

I would like to acknowledge the assistance and encouragement of the following: Mark Brisbane, Margaret Gowen, Jon Hather, Penny Johnston, Katharine Judelson, Harry Kenward, Mark Maltby, Michael Monk, Linzi Simpson, David Smith, Russian colleagues particularly Peter Gaidukov, Alexander Sorokin and the supervisors and staff of Troitsky XI–XIII. I would like to express particular gratitude to Professor Paul Buckland for help in identifying a number of the beetles from Novgorod.

Finally, but most importantly, I would like to thank my husband Rónán for his support and patience.

– 17 –

PERSPECTIVES ON NON-WOOD PLANTS IN THE SAMPLED ASSEMBLAGE FROM THE TROITSKY EXCAVATIONS OF MEDIEVAL NOVGOROD

M. Monk and P. Johnston

BACKGROUND TO THE STUDY

Since the late 1950s, when Kiryanov undertook a study to identify the main cultivated plants from the Novgorod excavations, there has been an awareness of the important insights that could be gained about medieval agriculture and diet from the organic debris that make up the deep archaeological deposits of this incredible site (Kiryanov 1959 and 1967; Kiryanov in Thompson 1967, 87–92; also general studies for northern Russia Kiryanova 1979). While this project was large in scale (identifying numerous carbonized grain and cultural plant remains), its focus was not the mass of plant debris, including wood waste, which made up the major part of the anoxic deposits that formed the archaeology of this unique site. A study of this organic debris could offer considerable potential not only to provide detail of on site activities but also the environment in which these took place.

An exploratory statement of the potential of the Novgorod deposits for environmental study, along with other contexts in the region, was initiated by the Christian-Albrecht University of Kiel in Germany with the Universities of Uppsala and Stockholm in Sweden and published in 1993 (Alsleben *et al.* 1993). Alsleben has subsequently undertaken systematic sampling of a number of other sites of mostly earlier date in the region with the intention of exploring changes in crop husbandry through time, especially those associated with the Slavic people (see this volume and Alsleben 2001). A more specific programme of environmental work, targeting the Novgorod excavations at Troitsky was initiated in 1994. Funded by INTAS, the aim was the investigation of the relationship between Novgorod and its hinterland. The systematic plant remains study of Troitsky XI, which forms the basis of the present paper, was part of this study. Preliminary results of the work were published by us in 1996, 1998 and in a collective work in 2001 (Monk 1996; Johnston and Monk 1998; Monk and Johnston 2001). The taxa lists and other supporting data are to be found in a CD-ROM within this volume.

Sampling and Extraction

Bulk samples of between four and six litres of dug deposit were taken from different context complexes, as identified by ourselves but by reference to the excavators. Sampling was therefore strictly on the basis of judgement. Three to four litres of each sample were passed through a series of geological sieves with the aid of water. The purpose was to fractionate (but not mechanically break down) their content into manageable sizes for quantitative assessment and description. In addition one litre sub-samples were taken from the primary samples and micro-processed, also using wash-over but using three brass laboratory sieves of decreasing mesh sizes: 1 mm, 500 and 250 microns. A further sub-sample of between 50 and 250 ml (depending on scanned incidence of remains) was taken from the organic material retained on each sieve. This was then sorted using a stereoscopic microscope with a magnification range between ×7 and ×12.5. A micro-scale description was made of the deposit content to complement the macro-scale description and identifiable remains were extracted.

As noted, the samples were taken on site from various context complexes and these included: (i) building interiors – above and below floors; (ii) within cavity walls of buildings; (iii) yard areas; (iv) areas exterior to buildings and between them; (v) boundary fences; and (vi) edges and surfaces of roads. The density of remains extracted per sample varied from between 600 to 3,000 items per litre of sampled deposit, although the actual number of extracted remains was much less, given that most micro-sorted samples were for the most part less than a litre in volume.

Nature of the Deposits

The deposits consisted of varying amounts of, mostly, fibrous plant material, the majority of which were plant stems and wood fragments (including many chips from constructional carpentry). These showed varying degrees of abrasion, encrustation and decay. The macro-description that accompanied the sampling and primary processing of the samples also noted a broad size range, but generally small amounts of charcoal, except in areas of burning as around the ovens. Overall there was very little inorganic material, with occasionally some fine silt and sand. At the micro-scale, noted during the sorting the fine fraction of the processed samples, there was a moderate to high incidence of finely fragmented plant material, including both fibrous (wood and stems of herb plants) and vegetative remains, in amongst which there was a largely moderate to high incidence of anaerobically preserved, distinctively shaped, seeds and fruit remains.The discussion of the analyses of these remains forms the focus of this study.

In addition the samples taken produced occasional charred grains. In a couple of cases where the deposits were mostly burnt, more charred grain was found (for example samples 19 and 81 on Troitsky XI and samples 1–3 on Troitsky XII). The incidence of faunal remains, while often present, also varied from one sample to another and included small mammal bone, small bones of large mammals and fish bones. At the micro-scale the faunal evidence was in the form of insects, including especially fragments of beetles and fly pupa (see Reilly this volume and Endnote 1).

The Identifiable Remains

The identified seed and fruiting body remains are listed for each sample and are to be found on the accompanying CD-ROM.

The samples came from spatially distinct context groupings and from stratigraphically definable horizons. Overall the remains from all horizons and different contexts can be grouped on the basis of whether their presence can be interpreted in a primarily cultural way or on the basis of the plant habitat information that can be deduced. From such a division the following groups have been distinguished:

(i)   remains of cultivated plants
(ii)   remains of those plants that may have been intentionally gathered
(iii) remains of plants from disturbed or waste ground
(iv) remains of plants of damp ground and standing water

PLANTS: THEIR HABITAT, ITS INTERPRETATION AND SITE ACTIVITIES

The majority of the identified seeds, fruits and grains were from plants that either grew on or within the immediate hinterland of the site. They represent several different habitats. The gathered seeds and fruits were mostly from under-story plants that grew around the edges of woodland and may also have formed field margins. A further significant group of remains represent plants that would grow close to slow flowing water and in damp meadows.

The Spatial/context Complex Representation of Diaspores of Plants of Disturbed and Nitrogen Rich Ground

A significant number of seeds present were from plants that are what are now termed 'ruderals' to be found in disturbed ground around human habitations and in fields as crop weeds. While many plants can become weeds of cultivated ground, depending on specific local conditions, the majority of those identified as being present (specifically in the Troitsky XI samples) were what might be called 'classic weeds' including several members of the Polygonaceae family (*Polygonium aviculare, P. persicaria, P. lapathifolium/ lapathifolia, P. persicaria/maculosa* and *Fallopia convolvulus*), the ubiquitous *Chenopodium album* as well as *Chenopodium glaucum-rubrum, Silene nutans, Stellaria media, Circium* sp, *Urtica dioica, Urtica urens, Galeopsis tetrahit, Lapsana communis, Spergula arvensis, Anthemis cotula* and *Papaver rhoeas* (habitat data based on entries in Clapham *et al.* 1981, 39, 80, 83, 94, 101, 206–8, 212, 291, 331, 340–42, 345; Tutin *et al.* 1964, 68, 78–9, 81, 93, 94, 134, 146, 154, 164, 248). All the above, except *Papaver* sp, *Spergula arvensis and*

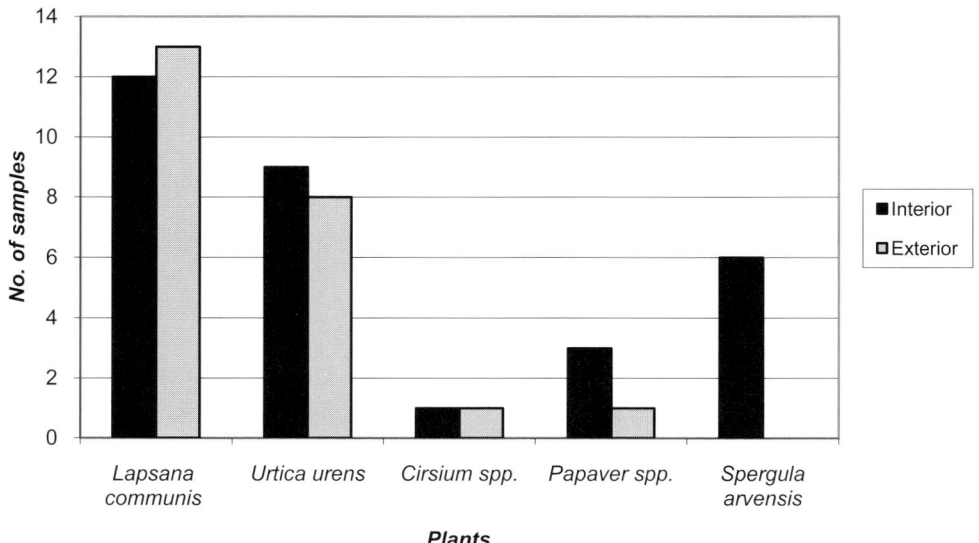

Plants

Figure 17.1 *Distribution of infrequent weeds.*

Cirsium sp., were found throughout the samples irrespective of time, context, feature type, etc.

It is perhaps no surprise that *Chenopodium album* was found in 57 of the Troitsky XI samples and four of the nine samples from Troitsky XIII. It is quite an adaptable plant and may well have thrived in the conditions on site (see below for discussion). This could also have been the case for *Polygonum/ P. lapathifolium/lapathifolia, P. aviculare* and *Urtica dioica* (noted in Clapham *et al.* 1981, 212, 250–1,257; Stace 1995, 144, 226, 230).

Of those weed plants listed that do not have the same frequency, specifically *Papaver* sp., *Spergula arvensis* and *Cirsium* sp., the majority occurred within buildings (six out of six contexts for *Spergula arvensis* and three of four for *Papaver* sp.;) as indicated in Figure 17.1. However, on Site XIII both *Spergula arvensis* and *Papaver* sp. came from samples taken between two closely set building walls (*Spergula arvensis* in sample 6 and *Papaver* in samples 1 and 4). In the case of *Cirsium* sp. one sample was from within a building while the other was between the walls of the building that produced *Spergula* and *Papaver* sp.

For two further weeds, *Lapsana communis* and *Urtica urens*, which have a moderate incidence of remains in the samples, seem to be found almost evenly in exterior and interior contexts on Site XI. On Site XII only one sample produced both species and this was taken from within a building (ELS[1] sample 16 from below the south wall of structure (3)/(4). On Site XIII *Urtica urens* came from two of the nine samples (samples 2 and 5 – one between buildings and the second within a building). *Lapsana communis* was found at a reasonable incidence within five samples, only one of which was within a building (sample 5). (See below for a discussion of possible habitat adaptation of *Lapsana communis* and *Urtica urens*).

Taking all the weed species together it does seem that there was a preference for crop processing waste to accumulate within buildings or, alternatively, it is possible that straw containing these seeds as contaminants was being used for bedding inside the buildings. For the most part, as far as the rest of the species in this habitat grouping are concerned, there seems to be little significance in their distribution. This may mean, as implied earlier, that these plants, although deriving from rural waste and cultivated areas, had become naturalized in the town and were contributing their seeds to the steadily accumulating debris that also included byre and household waste (see below for discussion of this possibility).

Of all the samples taken from Site XI, only nine did not produce any evidence of cereals or millet (samples 4, 50A and B, 59, 62, 85, 99, 100 and 103). However, several of these produced seeds of plants that could occur as crop weeds, in particular sample 103 that produced *Spergula arvensis, Lapsana communis, Polygonum aviculare, P. lapathifolium, Silene nutans, Galium palustre, Chenopodium album* (although see below for discussion of the latter species and its more likely habitat choice in this context). On Site XIII three of the samples (6, 7 and 9 – all from between the walls of two buildings) did not produce remains of cereals or millet, though they all produced weed species. Sample 2 on Site XIII was also devoid of cereals and millet apart from fragments of straw.

Cereals and millet were absent from Sample 103 on Site XI but it did produce a high incidence of wetland species particularly *Alisma plantago-aquatica. Spergula arvensis* was found in three other samples on Site XI that not only produced evidence of cereals (straw or glumes or grains) but also produced seeds of other plants that, within their range, could be described as weeds. These were samples 5, 57 and 86. Sample 5 produced evidence of *Raphanus raphanistrum, Stellaria* sp., *Galeopsis* sp., *Anthemis tinctoria* and *Senecio* sp. Sample 57 contained *Fallopia convolvulus, Silene nutans, Lapsana communis, Chenopodium album,* but also millet husks and cereal straw. Sample 86 in common with 57 also had *F. convolvulus, C. album, Silene nutans* and *Lapana communis* and *Galeopsis* sp. as well as cereal straw and millet husks. This sample also produced evidence of emmer wheat (*Triticum dicoccum*) glumes and barley (*Hordeum* sp.) rachis. There were, in addition, 17 samples from Site XI that, although they did not produce evidence of other cereals did contain millet including its husks. Several also had a range of weed seeds. These samples included 5, 48A and B, 49, 60, 64, 73, 75, 83A and B, 93, 94, 95, 97, 98, 104, 106 and ELS 13 Site XII. It may be of some significance that all these samples (other than sample 5) came from the older deposits on the site. Other than this, there seems to have been no pattern in terms of the contextual location of weeds and chaff remains.

Alsleben has expressed some degree of surprise to the authors of this study that no finds of *Agrostemma githago* have been made, especially given its association with the increased adoption of rye cultivation on sites in western Europe from the 10/11th century and the adoption of a three field rotation system (see discussion of later medieval samples from Site XII below and Endnote 2). Perhaps the explanation for this lies in the cropping regime practiced. Early germinating weeds such as *Agrostemma githago* were associated with winter-sown crops such as rye (*Secale cereale*). Possibly the absence of *Agrostemma githago* in the Novgorod samples indicates that rye was not sown until spring, perhaps because of the harsh winters in this region (see Endnote 3).

However, Almuth Aleleben (pers comm) has pointed out that other areas of northern Europe, with similar climatic regimes to this area of Northern Russia, plant rye in the winter and would have *Agrostemma githago* as a contaminant. Kiryanov in earlier reports viewed rye as being winter sown and while there is no mention of *Agrostemma githago* the point is made that 75% of the weed seeds in the rye crops are from plants that are said to indicate winter sowing, including Nipplewort (*Lapsana communis*) and wild oat (*A.fatua*) (see Endnote 4).

In the latter case there seems to be confusion with *Bromus secalinus* which is a key contaminant of rye crops and a usual indicator of winter sowing (Kiryanov in Thompson 1967, 90). Alsleben has noted in our discussions that an earlier study, by Linkola of recent plant communties north of Lake Ladoga in Finland, did not mention *Agrostemma githago* as a weed contaminant of rye (Linkola 1916). It is therefore possible that a completely different suite of weeds, as implied by Kiryanov, are associated with winter sown crops in this area. Alsleben is also of the opinion that the length of the fallow period could be a factor in the almost total absence of *Agrostemma githago*. The samples from one context on Site XII (see below and Alseleben this volume) did however have a high incidence of grasses especially *Apera spica venti*, but also the presence of *Rhinanthus* (yellow rattle), a plant common in meadows and pastures, which might imply that the rye was sown in fields that had sufficiently long fallow period for grasses to be come established from nearby meadows. Kiryanov notes that rye was sown in fallow fields and perhaps in Novgorod's case these areas to the south were also former meadows (Kiryanov 1967, 90).

The Spatial Context of Diaspores of those Plants associated with Damp/Wet Ground

The majority of the identifiable plant remains in the samples can be compared with plants that can be found in damp areas and natural meadows in the present: habitats that still exist to the south west of Novgorod today (known as the Poozerie). Many of these plants, as represented by their seeds, could also have become naturalized on the site during the time of occupation. These included *Ranunculus sp., (R. repens; R. acris; R. scleratus), Thalictrum flavum, Oenanthe aquatica, Apium* sp. (*inundatum* and *graveolens*), *Mentha arvensis* and *M. aquatica, Bidens tripartita, Alisma plantago-aquatica, Potamogeton* sp., *Juncus* sp., *Typha* sp., *Eleocharis palustris, Carex* sp, *Filipendula* sp. Of these the most frequently identified species and taxa, irrespective of context, were *Ranunculus scleratus, Mentha* sp., *Alisma plantago-aquatica, Juncus* sp., *Eleocharis palustris* and *Carex* sp. Most of these had a particularly high frequency, although the actual numbers per sample varied considerably. The species with the highest frequency throughout were *Ranunculus scleratus* and to a slightly lesser extent *Alisma plantago-aquatica*; the former producing a particularly high incidence in three byre samples and two road samples on Troitsky XI (sample numbers 89, 90, 91, 93 and 106). *Ranunculus scleratus* also had a significant presence in three of the nine samples from Troitsky XIII (samples 2 and 3 from between two buildings and notably sample 5 from within a structure with leather off-cuts). Samples 73 (an exterior sample from between a building and a property boundary) and 102 and 103 (both building interiors at a low level in Site XI's stratigraphy) produced the highest incidence of *Alisma plantago-aquatica*. Only in one sample on Site XIII (sample 9) was *Alisma plantago-aquatica* significantly present. Both species occur in quite damp situations on mud or, in the case of *Alisma plantago-aquatica*, in shallow water, both highlighting the quite damp conditions underfoot on or near the site (see Endnote 5).

Ranunculus scleratus is also known to be a common nitrophilous plant occurring in moist to wet nutrient rich open ground on the edge of areas of muddy standing water, in other words areas that could be inundated with water from time to time, possibly colonizing areas as the water receded (Hall *et al.* 1983, 214; Tüxen 1950, 108; Poli and Tüxen 1960; and see below for further discussion).

In addition *Eleocharis palustris* occurs in similar locations but particularly in marshy ground and ditches. *Eleocharis palustris* had a consistent presence in most samples from all sites with particular significance in samples 17, 58 and especially 62, 63, 80 and 84 for Site XI and sample 9 for Site XIII).

Of the lesser represented genera, *Potamogeton* sp., the pond weeds, as their name implies, are also to be found in shallow water in ponds and puddles, further reinforcing the interpretation of the local habitat and the surrounding area. The incidence of this plant across the site was relatively low, except in sample 63 and ELS sample 79 from woodworking waste in a wall cavity on Site XI, where it was very frequent. The distribution of *Eleocharis palustris* on Site XI indicated a significant preference for interior locations. The same is true for the distribution of two other species *Ranunculus acris* and *Thalictrum flavum*, but far less so. Both are common species of meadows and both were found at a low incidence in a number of contexts (see Figure 17.2). Amongst them, both species, were found in byre samples 89 and 91, highlighting the likelihood that at least this deposit included 'saved' hay and, unlike the others from which these species and the others (discussed above) were found, was not a mixed infill but was an *in situ* deposit. The study of the insect remains from one of these samples (91) produced a high incidence of species that would occur in the foul conditions associated with stable manure although there was a lack of true dung beetles (see Reilly this volume). The likelihood that these samples included plants from a damp field edge is suggested by the high incidence of *Bidens tripartita* (particularly in sample 89), a plant found locally in ditches, ponds or streams (Clapham *et al.* 1981, 383; Stace 1995, 890).

There was relatively little overlap in terms of high frequency of the different

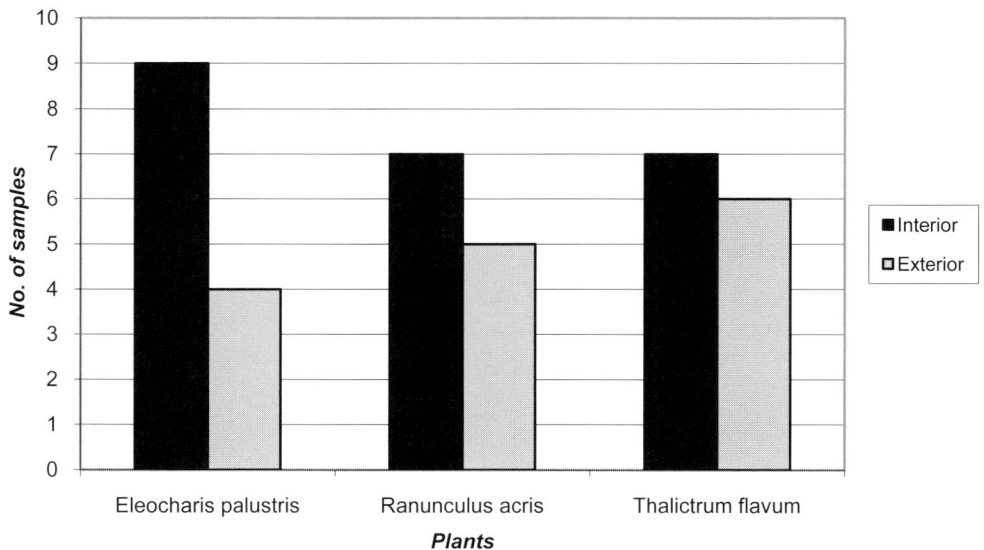

Figure 17.2 *Distribution of damp-land plants.*

wetland species across the site. However, there was some overlap, for example in sample 62, which produced a significant incidence of *Eleocharis palustris*, *Juncus* sp., and *Alisma plantago-aquatica*. Sample 63 also produced an overlap for *Potemegeton* sp, *Juncus* and *Ranunculus scleratus* and *Bidens tripartita*. There was also a significant overlap in wetland species in the byre samples (89–93, especially 89).

Chronological Changes in Proportions of Seeds from Damp Land

An interim statement on the nature of the plant remains in deposits from Troitsky XI by Monk and Johnston (2001, 116), suggested that there was a "relatively higher incidence of seeds from plants of damp ground in the lower deposits on site, as might be expected given the lower topographical position of these deposits." The statement was instinctual rather than statistical and required further investigation. To this end, a graph of the variation in the percentage of damp land plants against time was plotted (see Figure 17.3).

The results imply that although the earliest samples contained relatively high proportions of seeds from damp land plants, these were gradually declining as time progressed. There are, however, anomalous results from early 13th century samples where suddenly the number of damp land plants increased again.

Stratigraphic information suggests that the site flooded periodically and its low-lying situation explains the higher frequency of damp land plants in the earliest samples. The results plotted here generally support the idea that the retrieval of seeds from damp land plants decreased with time; as cultural material accumulated at the site, the level of the site rose and the frequencies of damp land plants in the samples

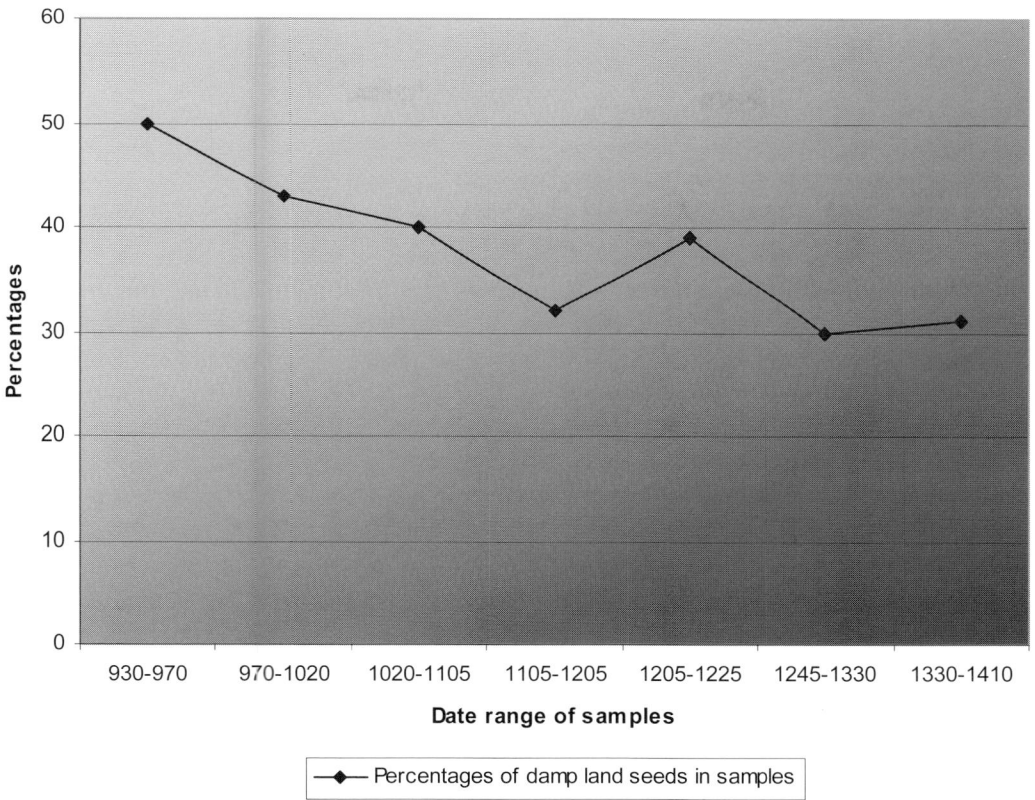

Figure 17.3 Percentage of damp-land seeds in samples (omitting sample 62).

decreased. This suggests that a significant quantity of the damp land seeds retrieved were from plants that were growing in the immediate area. However, the picture is probably complicated by the importation of material from nearby damp meadows, for example material used for roofs and floors in the buildings, for animal bedding and for fodder. This brief examination of the percentages of damp land plants illustrates that a purely chronological method can produce a significant incongruity, a danger inherent in any approach that ignores a contextual understanding of the samples. This point has also been made in the examination of the insect remains from the site, (e.g. Reilly and Johnston 2002 and Reilly this volume). Consideration of the context of the macro remains is vital to the interpretation of the results (see Figure 17.2).

Other Species Represented by a Low Incidence of Seeds

On the basis of the presence of their seeds a number of other species were found in the Troitsky samples, but for the most part these were at a low incidence. Their habitats covered the same range as those plants more numerously represented and included (a) waste and cultivated ground; (b) damp areas and areas of shallow water; (c) grass and heath land; and (d) woodland margins. Amongst these plants the 'ruderal' and waste ground group are well represented by *Rumex crispus* (sample 52), *Atriplex* sp., particularly *A. patula* (samples 49, 50A and B, 52, 54A and B, 57, 60, 61, 62, 63, 74, 75, 106, 107, 108 and ELS samples 34 and 77), *Raphanus raphanistrum* (sample 5) and *Potentilla* sp., (samples 1, 2, 3, 4, 5, 17,19, 29, 48A and B, 50A, 52, 61, 54A and B, 57, 58, 59, 62, 63, 74, 83A and B, 84, 88, 91, 95, 97, 99, 100, 101, 107, 108 and ELS samples 13 and 34; Site XIII – samples 1, 2, 3, 5 with *Potentilla anserina* from samples 2, 4 and 9). Several species do come into various habitat groups but would be common in grassy places and these included *Rumex acetosella* (sample 58 on Site XI and 1, 2 and 6 from Site XIII), *Stellaria gramineae* (samples 4, 5, 19, 48A, 52, 106 and 108; sample 6 from Site XIII), *Dianthus* sp., (sample 48A from a boundary fence, 49, 62, 86, 91 and 103) and various members of the Gramineae family (e.g. cf *Bromus* sp, cf *Lolium* sp.) from samples 3, 17, 48A, 50A, 57, 61, 62, 72, 73, 81, 84, 86, 87, 90, 92, 97, 98, 103 and 104. Of the grasses the most frequently identified group were members of the *Setaria* genus including *Setaria viridus* (samples 86 and 87 from Site XI), *Setaria glauca* (72, 83A and B, 97 and 98 from Site XI) and *Setaria* sp. (samples 85, 90, 98, 103, 104, 107 and ELS 22, the last a fill of a stove). The other species were only represented in individual samples from Site XI and Site XIII. A couple of species, each found at a low incidence, would fit with respectively, a damp ground community and a community that might be expected on wood margins or in open woods. These include in the former environment *Rumex hydrolapathum* (sample 103) and *Sonchus* sp., (samples 48A, 54A and 108 from Site XI) and in the latter one *Rumex conglomerates* (sample 104 from Site XI and sample 1 from Site XIII) and *Stellaria holostea* (samples 3 and 50A).

Seeds and Fruits from Woodland Plants

Apart from those plants whose fruits were gathered, as discussed below (principally members of the Roscaceae family but also *Vaccinium* sp. and *Corylus avellana*) few woodland margin or open wood and heath plants are represented in the collections, despite the very high incidence of constructional timber on the site. Two examples that did occur and may have originally been woodland margin species were *Urtica urens* and possibly *Lapsana communis* (but for the latter see habitat range outlined by Küster 1991, 21).

However, Wieswerowa, in her study of medieval deposits from Cracow, makes the point that *Urtica urens*, while a woodland/forest plant by nature has adapted to synanthropic situations (Wieswerowa 1979, 185). In addition Geraghty (1996) has noted, referring to a study by Wyse Jackson and Sheehy Skeffington in Ireland, that *Lapsana communis*, was an increasingly common weed in medieval samples especially from those located on boundaries. It may have originally been a woodland margin and hedgerow plant that found favourable conditions in waste and cultivated ground (Wyse Jackson and Sheehy Skeffington 1984, 130). It is possible that this 'migration' happened during medieval times as former woodland areas became increasingly taken into cultivation (see Endnote 6).

A Phytosociological Interpretation of the Remains (see Endnote 7)

It was noted that *Ranunculus scleratus,* while being a damp land plant, has also been observed on the continent to be a nitrophile and has been found in association with *Chenopodium rubrum, Polygonum hydropiper and Bidens* sp., in such nutrient rich, though polluted, margins of water bodies, especially in areas with standing water like ponds. These plants are especially characteristic of the phytosociological class Bidentetea tripartite (Lohmayer *et al.* 1962; Shimwell 1971). Although the Novgorod samples did not produce seeds that were clearly *P.hydropiper* (tentatively identified examples in samples 52 and 54B on Site XI). Apart from in three samples (89, 91 and 93, two byre samples and one from a road edge), *Bidens tripartia* only occurred infrequently. *Chenopodium glaucum/rubrum* occurs in recently exposed nutrient-rich muddy areas, especially in and around dirty farmyards, and was a frequent find, as it was at Fishamble Street, Dublin (Geraghty 1996, 37). Its presence, along with *Ranunculus scleratus,* in a number of samples (17 samples from Site XI especially 93, 94, 97, 99, 100, 101, 102) could then be taken to clearly imply the existence of such conditions in and around the site, especially during the earlier period. In his discussion of the finds of this plant on the Lloyds Bank, Pavement site in York and its place in communities defined by the phytosociological approach, Hall has pointed out that it was seen as a characteristic plant of the Rumicetum maritimi association of the Bidens tripartite class of plants. He quotes Tüxen in describing the habitat where this association of plants is most likely to be found as nitrogen and nutrient (nitrophilous) rich open areas on periodically flooded muddy perimeters of various types of polluted water bodies and ponds, including cattle ponds and drained fish ponds found in areas adjacent to human settlements. All the plants in this group are also to be found in bogs and sewage soakaways, drying ponds, ditches, marshes and muddy areas in pastures (Hall *et al.* 1983, 214–215; Tüxen 1950, 110). The situations in which the colonisation of these plants was most likely to develop are in the late summer/early autumn (Wieserowa 1979, 182). *Ranunculus scleratus* is so commonly found in such associations that Tüxen even feels that the name of the group should be changed to Rununculetum scelerati (Hall *et al.* 1983, 214–215; Tüxen 1950, 110).

The plants in this group would find a very suitable natural habitat in the backwaters of a river flood plain. The identification of such a habitat, from the presence of this and other similar plants discussed above, is not surprising given the location of the Troitsky site so close to the river Volkhov, with areas of standing water close to it that are still definable in less built-up locations in this locality today. Wieserowa has noted the occurrence of members of this community in medieval samples from the Market Square excavations in Cracow (Wieserowa 1979, 182–3), as have Lynch and Paap in their study of several samples from medieval deposits in Lübeck (Lynch and Paap 1982, 345 and 354: in this group they also included Alisma plantago-aquatica, Eleocharis palustris, Mentha aquatica, Stachys palustris and Lycopus europaeus). Barrett et al. have similarly identified in particular Ranunculus scleratus, and what they describe as other swamp taxa, in samples from the early medieval site at Kaupang (2004, 8 and 2007, 291).

Beněs *et al.* (2002, 116–117) in their discussion of a plant remains study of the town defences of medieval Prague noted that the wetland/swamp plants (including *Lycopus europaeus, Bidens tripartitus, Eleocharis palustris, Carex* sp., and *Chenopodium polyspermum*) were frequent in the waste and dung layers. In the case of *Eleocharis palustris*, while they concede that it could have grown locally, they felt it was most likely brought to the site in this material.

As noted above another species that has a significant presence in Novgorod and several other similar dated sites in northern Europe is *Alisma plantago aquatica*, water plantain, which, while not a true aquatic species, occurs in swamp areas on the edge of stagnant or slow flowing water. It was also noted in the Staraya Ladoga samples and from Market Square, Cracow (Aalto and Heinäjoki-Majander 1997, 26; Wieserowa 1979, 177). In the Cracow study it was included in the phytosociological group Phragmitetea along with *Typha* sp. (Wieserowa 1979, 177). Its presence in Novgorod would fit more closely the habitat suggested by the presence of *Ranunculus scleratus* (see Endnote 8).

In terms of the phytosociology groups identified by Wieserowa in the Cracow plant remains assemblage, there are some other parallels that can be drawn with the Novgorod remains. As was the case in the Cracow collection there would appear to have been some members of at least one further present day ruderal group and two communities that would be defined as field weed groups (see Endnote 7).

The Potentilla polygonetalia grouping is characterised by members of the *Potentilla* genus and Polygonum family but especially *Polygonum aviculare, Rumex crispus, Plantago major, Sagina procumbens* and *Rorrippa* cf *silvestris*. It is *P. aviculare* and the *Potentillas generally* (probably including *P. anglica, P. tormentilla and P.erecta*) that were found present together (though in smaller numbers) in the Novgorod samples (identified in samples 29, 54 A and B, 84, 91, 96, 98 and ELS 34). The type of habitat that this plant group characterises includes yards, roadways and trampled areas, all present in medieval Novgorod, as the archaeology of the site has demonstrated. The two other phytosociological weed orders identified in the Cracow study, some of whose members were common in the Novgorod samples, were the Secali violetaia arvensis and Rudero-Secalietea associations. Included in the former and found in the Novgorod samples were *Lapsana communis, Polygnum convolvulus, Silene* sp., *Sinapis arvensis, Spergula arvensis*, and *Galeopsis tetrahit*. The species that occurred in the latter order, Rudero-Secalietea, included *Chenopodium album, Galeopsis tetrahit Polygonum lapathifolium, P. persicaria and Stellaria media* (Wieserowa 1979, 184–187). Hall has argued that since the natural habitat of these weed plants was disturbed ground, it is likely that they would have found suitable niches on most early urban sites and, by implication, we should not be surprised by their presence (Hall *et al.* 1983, 216). This could include plants that would not be considered urban colonizers today, for example *Anthemis cotula, A. tinctoria*. In addition, pioneering plants of bare-waste places were present in the Novgorod samples. Hall has noted the presence of *Anthemis cotula* in yard areas around buildings in villages within various parts of Europe. Similar habitats would have been typical of early urban centres in the past

(Hall *et al.* 1983, 216). Hall *et al.* further points to the work of Steiner and Kinzel (1980) who have noted that *Chenopodium album*, often taken to have been a nitrophile, is also a pioneer species of abandoned areas (Hall *et al.* 1983, 216). As it was likely that the deposits in such areas were also nitrogen rich, as would have been the case on the early urban sites, there is little wonder that it occurs in such significant numbers on sites like Novogord. Indeed presently this plant is rampant on previously excavated areas of Troitsky!

Presence and Distribution of Remains of Cultural/Cultivated Plants: The Grains

Overall the incidence of cultural plants was low, but their presence was consistent throughout. These plants included the following grain crops: barley (*Hordeum* sp.), wheat (*Triticum* sp.), oats (*Avena* sp.), rye (*Secale cereale*) and millet (*Panicum millaceum*). A few samples did, however, produce a higher incidence of charred cereals including samples 19 and 81 on Site XI and sample 1 for Site XII. Millet was mostly represented by the presence of husk fragments, occurring in samples 1, 2, 52, 58, 64, 90, 95 on Site XI and ELS 13 on Site XII. Overall, apart from millet, the cereals were usually only represented by a few individual charred grains. In waterlogged deposits non-charred grain is seldom preserved because its relatively thin testas are fragile and will decay unless anoxic conditions develop very quickly after deposition (see elsewhere for discussion of differential preservation at Novgorod and Körber-Grohne 1964 for reference to this phenomenon of anoxic deposits). For the most part, where it was possible to identify the wheat present, it was a hulled species. On the basis of the presence of its characteristic glume bases, it would appear to have been emmer (*Triticum dicoccum*) as in samples 61, 86 and 108. While barley was mostly indeterminate to species it was occasionally possible to identify the hulled form, as in sample 96 on Site XI and sample 5 on Site XIII. The absence of flower parts made it impossible to suggest which species of oats were present. Rye was also represented in a number of samples (for example samples, 2, 3, 19, 52, 64, 108 on Site XI and samples 1 to 3 from Site XII).

The spatial and temporal distribution of these plants within the sampled deposits and contexts varied. Temporally the earliest deposits (Site XI samples 67–96) contained almost entirely wheat and barley. However, one incidence of rye rachis was found in sample 108 at the base of the stratigraphy on Site XI and the latest deposits contained all four cereals (wheat, barley, oats and rye). A reasonable incidence of oats was noted in the samples from the middle of the stratigraphic sequence on Site XI (samples 33–65). Rye also made an appearance at a low incidence in these samples (as a rachis fragment in sample 52 and a possible grain in sample 64). This perhaps ties in with the fact that rye does not appear to be mentioned in the birch bark documents until after AD 1200. After that date it is more frequently mentioned (Rybina 2001, 127 and see below). While rye grains are evident in later dated samples (for example samples 2, 3 and 19), their actual incidence on Site XI remains low.

Millet is ubiquitous throughout the Site XI sequence and in samples from Sites XII

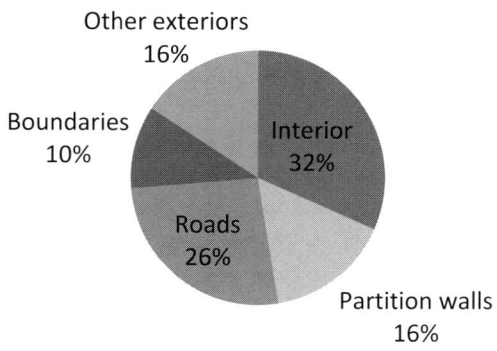

Figure 17.4 *Distribution of millet.*

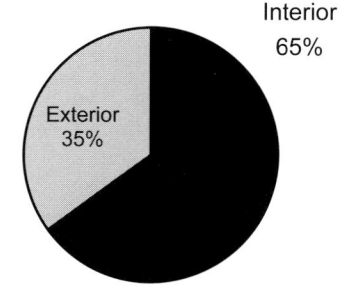

Figure 17.5 *Distribution of cereals.*

and XIII. In terms of spatial distribution, millet was present throughout the range of contexts. On its own, without any association with cereals on Site XI, it occurs within buildings (6 instances, 31%), within partition walls (3 instances, 16%), on roads (5 instances, 26%), in or along property boundaries (2 instances, 11%) and other areas exterior to buildings (3 instances, 16%). There were marginally more exterior contexts associations than interior ones overall. However, the largest % of all the context groupings was building interiors (see Figure 17.4).

Millet also occurred with cereals in a similar range of contexts including six instances within buildings. In addition, while cereals were present (in the form of preserved glume bases/spikelet forks and a rachis fragment), millet had a relatively high incidence in three samples from a byre deposit (samples 89, 90 and 91). Overall in this context, as well as in others, it is the husks of millet that were mostly represented. In this instance the remains could have been animal fodder, bedding residue or manure (but see discussion by Hall and Kenward 1998, 123–6 and Kenward and Hall 1997, 663–673). Davidson (1999, 506) suggests millet was used for livestock in the recent past. There seems to be a reasonably broad distribution of the cereals wheat, barley, rye and oats found in different context groupings, e.g. property boundaries, within houses, and house exteriors. However, there was a marked absence of association of cereal remains with roads (e.g. sample 58). While there was an even spread of these remains between interior and exteriors there does seem to have been some increased incidence of barley in house/building interiors (samples 19, 74, 86, 96 on Site XI and sample 5 on Site XIII).

Taking all the remains of grain crops together, there also seems to have been an association of them within buildings rather than exterior areas on Site XI, although this result is, admittedly, based on a small sample (Figure 17.5). This simply reinforces the expected presence of charred grain close to, if not within, buildings. Because the amounts of grain in the samples were mostly relatively small, it is not easy to make an interpretation of their presence beyond casual loss and charring during domestic processing. Sample 19 from Site XI however, produced a higher than average amount of charred grain. It mostly consisted of barley but the incidence of wheat was almost as high (17 as against 20 identifiable grains), with a few grains of rye. While there was a mixed grain content it had few seeds of other plants (just 2 sedge seeds of the Cyperaceae family) suggesting that whatever its purpose and derivation it had been processed and any chaff and weed seeds removed. By contrast the mass of charred grain from samples 1 and 2 from Site XII (associated with floor boards of a building), examined by the present authors and particularly by Almuth Alsleben, produced not only a very high incidence of mostly charred and partially charred rye grain (and rachis) but a relatively low incidence of other species including barley (the six row hulled type) and bread wheat but by contrast also a broad range of weed seeds (Alsleben 2001, 111 and this volume). Particularly significant was the presence of seeds of the grasses family including *Apera spica-venti, Poa annua, Bromus secalinus* and *Lolium* sp. Of these the most frequent was *Apera spica venti* which, according to Šikula (1979, 112), is a widespread weed of cereals. Growing on light soils it is found at all altitudes. This grass produces a large number of seeds that are dispersed before the infested crop is harvested. Its seeds also germinate early, in the autumn, but they can be destroyed if the ground is ploughed before spring sowing. Its presence in such numbers in this instance may therefore indicate that this was not done or that the rye crop was sown in the autumn and this plant emerged with it (see Notes 3 and 4 for discussion of the rye sowing regime).

The other weeds of cultivation and field edges included *Chenopodium album, Chenopodium glaucum/rubrum, Polygonum convolvulus, Lapsana* sp., *Rumex acetosella, Spergula arvensis, Stellaria mediea, Urtica urens. Urtica dioica* and *Carex* sp. (Alsleben pers comm and this volume). The incidence of these and those other species also present are listed on the CD ROM. The high incidence of weed seeds in this sample, mostly rye crop, would suggest that the grain it contained had not been primarily processed prior to the charring fire or, that the weed contamination was so high that it was destined for animal feed rather than human consumption.

The issue of the extent to which the grain that arrived on the site was already processed is one that cannot be addressed by only one such large sample. The detailed accounts of food produce that appear in the birch-bark documents would suggest that considerable organization was involved in the distribution of grain, which would therefore indicate systematic primary and secondary processing, probably involving the use of mills. However, un-ground grain did arrive on the site, as indicated by the presence of the charred grain. Ethnographic sources indicate that grain was processed to assist in chaff removal and for domestic purposes using large wooden pestles and mortars (Baranov *et al.* 1999, 324–5).

As noted earlier, in several samples from Site XI, the presence of cereals is indicated by finds of chaff elements and straw. As shown in Table 17.1, the most frequent finds were straw node fragments.

In addition to that shown within Tables 17.1 and 17.2, the presence of a high incidence of millet chaff at a high incidence could be linked to the fact that it was the

	No. of instances
Straw fragments, nodes & rachis internodes	32
Rye rachis fragments	2
Barley rachis fragments	2
Wheat glume bases, spikelet forks & rachis fragments	3
Rachis indet.	3

Table 17.1 Presence of cereals as indicated by chaff elements and straw. Number of instances of the different elements identified.

Straw fragments, nodes & rachis internodes	Samples 17,57, 61, 72, 74,83A, 86, 87, 89, 90 , 91, 107
Rye rachis fragments	Samples 29, 108
Barley rachis fragments	Samples 52, 74
Wheat glume bases, spikelet forks & rachis fragments	Samples 86, 91, 108
Rachis indet.	Samples 101, 102

Table 17.2 Presence of cereals as indicated by chaff elements and straw by sample.

only grain/seed crop processed in the household, as mentioned in the Prague report on medieval samples (Beneš *et al.* 2002, 113).

The content of samples 89 to 91, and certain aspects of this context, clearly indicated that it was a byre deposit and it is likely also that several of the other samples listed were in part derived from such deposits and may represent animal food waste and animal bedding (see below for further discussion in relation to the wild plant species present and cautionary remarks from Kenward and Hall 1997; Hall and Kenward 1998; and Reilly this volume).

Hops, Hemp and Flax

A further two plants whose presence on site, noted from finds of parts of their fruiting bodies, is likely to have been a result of their cultural status are hops and hemp, respectively *Humulus lupulus* and *Cannabis sativa*.

Hemp was found in 17 samples from various contexts on Site XI including interiors and exteriors of buildings, partition walls, yard areas, a byre deposit, a boundary fence and property boundaries. There is a higher incidence of finds in exterior locations and particularly along property boundaries. By contrast hops are often found within buildings including on their floors, within partition walls and also within the byre deposit. They were also found in a limited range of external contexts such as along a boundary fence, between two buildings and in road samples (see Figure 17.6). This contrast in distribution between hemp and hops may have some significance, although it is unlikely that the plant remains from all samples were from *in situ* deposits (see Endnote 9).

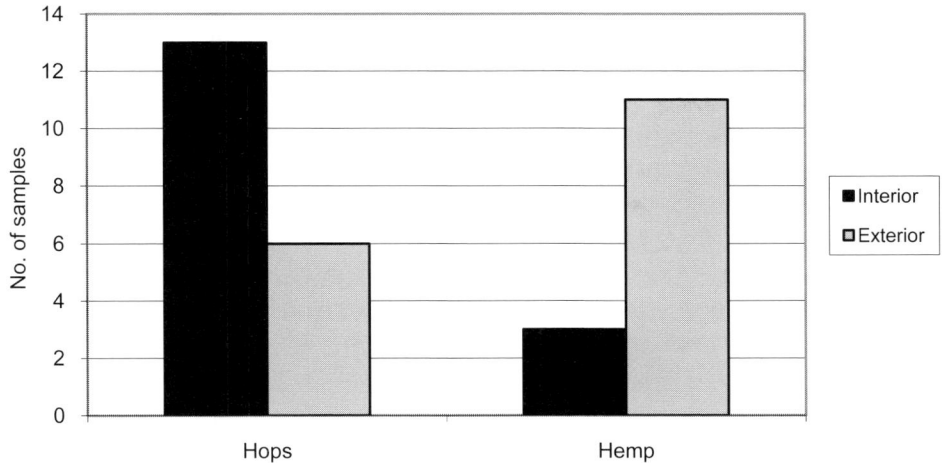

Figure 17.6 *Distribution of hops and hemp.*

Overall these two species were only found in small amounts. Exceptions include hemp in sample 1 on Site XIII and hops in ELS 2A and 2B and 6, where fragment counts for hop remains were in double figures.

Flax was a rare find in Novgorod, only being present in two samples: sample 64 from beneath a wall and sample 108 associated with an unusual, small building at almost the lowest stratigraphic position on Site XI.

Fruits, Nuts and Gathered Plants (Figures 17.7 to 17.13)

It is the case that many of the plants, whose presence is suggested by the finds of their diaspores, could have been gathered for various uses not least to supplement the diet. In particular amongst them were hazel *Corylus avellana* (represented by the presence of their nut shells), wild strawberry (*Fragaria vesca*), wild raspberry (*Rubus idaeus*), apple pips (*Malus* sp.), the sour cherry (*Prunus cerasus*) and the bilberry (*Vaccinium myrtillus*).

Wild strawberry was found in a number of samples across a range of contexts. The samples include property boundaries (four samples), building interiors (12 interiors including 2 byre samples) and one road. It could be said that wild strawberry was pretty ubiquitous throughout the site. Hazel nuts were found to be present on Site XI in a number of samples, as follows:

Hazel Nut fragments on Site XI
Structures and Partition Walls	6 (Samples 4, 62, 64, 65, ES 6 and 34)
Building interiors	5 (Samples 52, 60, 81, 94, and ES 33)
Boundary fences	3 (Samples 48b, 83a and b, and 97)
Roads	4 (Samples 54a and b, 58, 93, and 100)

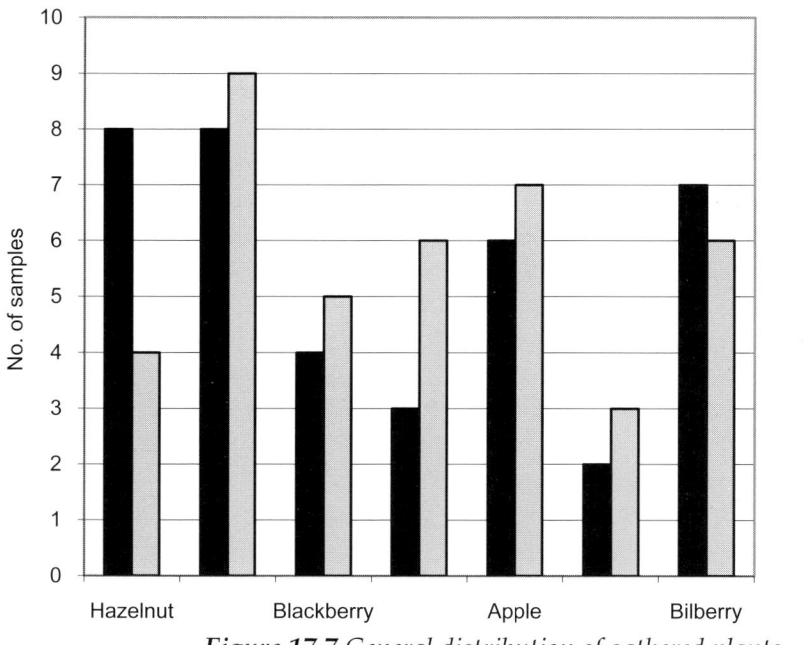

Figure 17.7 General distribution of gathered plants.

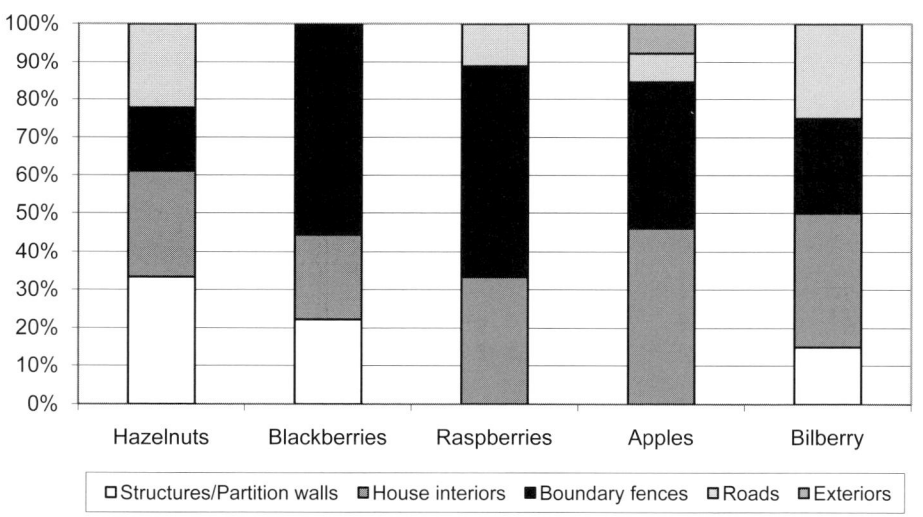

Figure 17.8 Distribution of hazel nut fragments and fruits.

Therefore eleven of the samples were from within buildings, including as part of the structures, six were known to be from exterior locations (three from property boundaries and four from road surfaces).

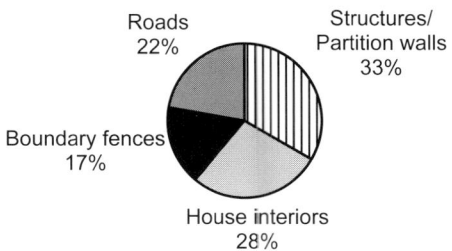
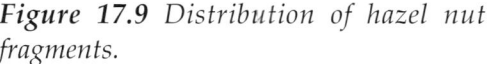

Figure 17.9 Distribution of hazel nut fragments.

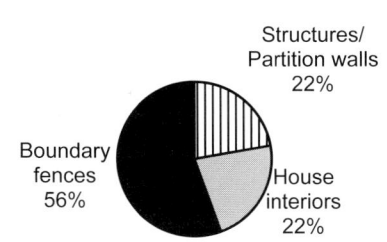

Figure 17.10 Distribution of blackberry drubes.

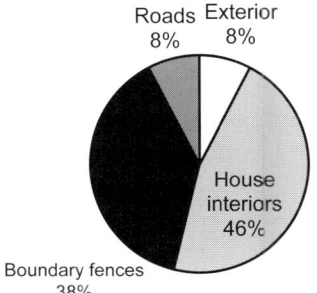

Figure 17.11 Distribution of apple pips.

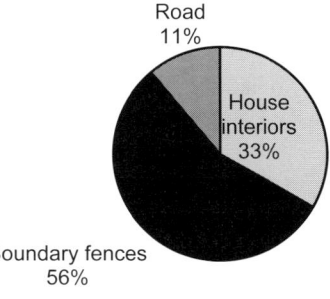

Figure 17.12 Distribution of raspberry drubes.

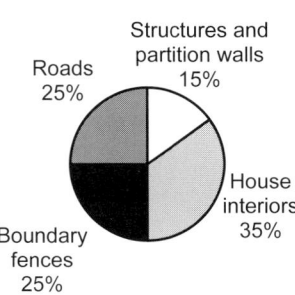

Figure 17.13 Distribution of bilberry seeds.

Blackberry (*Rubus fruticosus*) was also found across a wide range of contexts on Site XI and one sample from Site XIII.

Structures and Partition walls 2 (Samples 62 and ELS 34)
Building Interiors 2 (Samples 19 and 74)
Boundary fences 5 (Samples 1, 48B, 73, 83A and B, and 92)

Apple pips were also found in a range of samples including:
Building interiors 6 (Samples 64, 74, 85, 89, 91, ELS 34A and B)
Building exteriors 1 (Sample 95)
Boundary fences 5 (Samples 1, 2, 48A and B, 83A and B, and 97)
Roads 1 (Sample 93)

Raspberry (*Rubus ideaus*) was found in a similar range of samples on Site XI and Site XIII as follows:
Building interiors 3 (Samples 17, 29, and 5 Site XIII)
Boundary fences 5 (Samples 1, 2, 3, 48A, 83A and B)
Roads 1 (Sample 54A)

In all the above cases, but especially raspberry and apple, there is a bias towards property boundaries.

This would mean that the finds of apple were found almost equally from boundary samples (5 examples) and from within building (6 examples) and one each from a road and a building exterior. If the latter two are added to those samples from exterior contexts then this would mean a slight majority of remains were from exteriors.

The finds of the sour cherry, were similarly located though the number of samples with remains were fewer: they included samples 1 and 4 (property boundaries), 17 (within a house), 48A and B (boundary fence) and 64 (beneath wall of a building). Again it seems that the balance of remains was along boundary fences.

The bilberry (*Vaccinium* sp.), whose presence is represented by its seeds, is also very likely to have been gathered and consumed on site. It was found to be present in a number of samples on Site XI.

Structures and Partition walls	3 (Samples 64, 75, ELS 13)
Structure interiors	7 (Samples 60, 74, 89, 90, 103, 104, 108)
Structure exteriors	3 (Samples 52, 61, 95)
Boundary fences	5 (Samples 48A and B, 73, 83A and B, 97, 98),
Roads	5 (Samples 58, 93, 100, 101, 106)

Again the balance of the remains came from exterior contexts (13 instances with five from property boundaries or near them, the others were from a yard area, exterior to a building and roads). By contrast there were seven samples with bilberry that were from within buildings.

In summary the distribution of remains would suggest an almost even spread of remains from the interior and exteriors of buildings. However, there was some variation with hazel nuts being more frequent within buildings and associated with their structures. The other fruit species (including strawberries, raspberries and sour cherry), by contrast, indicated a bias to building exteriors. This was particularly the case for raspberries and blackberries with a significant balance of the exterior finds occurring close to property and other boundaries. Bilberries occurred marginally more in exterior locations, though their highest contextual distribution was within buildings.

Overall there would seem to have been some minor level of patterning in the disposal of food waste during medieval times in Novgorod (that is, if the deposits are considered to be even partially 'in situ' (see Endnote 8). Why this would be is not clear accept perhaps that some of the gathered plants were being used in culinary dishes and therefore their waste was more likely to occur within buildings in areas of primary processing whereas others were consumed directly in exterior areas and the residues dumped/discarded close to the property boundaries. It is possible that the distribution of these remains reflects either defecation practices or the deposition of such excrement. Reilly's study of the insects from one of the property boundary samples (48) would seem to indicate the presence of species that could inhabit human as well as animal dung. Although she feels the presence of human fecal material is unlikely in such a location and instead has argued that the foul conditions were as likely the result of a combination of decaying plant debris in a situation that also included dung and standing water (Reilly this volume). It is also possible that the concentration of blackberry and raspberry pips along property boundaries results from 'droppings' of birds sitting on the fences of these boundaries, where indeed these plants may have been growing anyway. However it does seem that all the gathered plants, identified via the presence of their seeds, would be found in woodland edges or field margins and it is more likely they were brought onto the site rather than have become naturalized there (see discussion of comparanda below).

Wild Plants having known Medicinal and Other Uses Represented by their Seeds

A number of identified remains in the samples came from plants known to have medicinal properties which, according to documentary sources, where utilised in the past. Their contexts on the site however, were not indicative of such usage and in the absence of such evidence it is difficult to make the case based on this study that they served such a purpose in medieval times at the Troitsky site, especially as several of them are also common weeds of disturbed or waste ground in urban environments. A particular case in point is henbane *Hyoscymus niger*. In discussing its presence in the samples from Fishamble Street, Dublin, Geraghty (1996, 41) cites Roesdahl (1982, 162), who mentions that the plant was used by the Vikings for its medicinal value and was thought to have magical properties. Its seeds were, for example, found in high incidence in association with a Viking age burial at Fyrkat in Denmark (Jensen 1991, 338; from Roesdahl and Nordqvist 1971). Robinson refers to its value as a painkiller in the context of being found on Viking age sites in Denmark (Robinson 1994, 547) and stresses that its growth may have been encouraged (Robinson 1987, 206–207). Hjelmqvist also recovered a few seeds of this plant from 11th to 12th and 13th century deposits in Lund, noting that it might have been cultivated in medieval times for external medical use (Hjelmqvist 1991, 246). However, finds of *Hyoscymus niger* were only made in small numbers in samples 1 from Site XI and samples 2 and possibly 4 from Site XIII.

Another plant whose seeds has been found in the samples, and could have been utilised for its medicinal properties, is self-heal, *Prunella vulgaris*. *Prunella* sp., was found in samples 5, 17, 19, 50A, 54A, 61, 64, 74, 86, 89, 91, 98, 100, 107 from Site XI and samples 7 and 9 from Site XIII. Hall and Kenward have urged caution in making such interpretations both because of the lack of independent contextual information and because it was only certain parts of the plants that were used medicinally (Hall and Kenward 2003, 126).

Other wild plants that could have been utilised, not least for food, included wild celery *Apium graveolens,* which was found in small numbers in samples 88 and 102 from Site XI and also a higher frequency in sample ELS 79 from the same site (see Endnote 10).

Geraghty notes that it could have been used to flavour food but like the other plants mentioned that had potential uses it would have found suitable habitats for growth in and around the town (Geraghty 1996, 39). Evidence of other plants used for flavouring has also been found including especially caraway (*Carum carvi*) and possibly rough chervil (cf *Chaerophyllum bulbosum*). Both *Apium* sp. and *Carum carvi* were found in several samples, particularly the former. All their contexts were from interiors of buildings.

The Evidence from the Birch-Bark Documents and Other Sources

A unique feature of the archaeological remains from Novgorod is the finds of birch-bark documents. Almost a thousand of them have been recovered from the excavations to date. They are written in an early form of Cyrillic script and have been translated by Zaliznyak (1995). While they cover a range of subjects most of them deal with tribute, taxation, debt and communications about trade or exchange. In a good number of cases various plants, mostly cultivated, are mentioned. Rybina and Konetskii have discussed this information (Rybina 2001; Konetskii 2003). The most frequently mentioned plants are cereals, although these are not mentioned in the earliest, 11th-century documents (Rybina 2001, 127).

Rye has the most numerous mentions (65 times in 34 texts: Rybina 2001, 127; Konetskii 2003), followed by oats (20 instances in 13 texts: Konetskii (2003) and then barley (18 references in 13 texts: Konetskii 2003). Rye seems to increase in importance through time, based on the frequency of references in the documents from the 12th/13th centuries onwards, whereas barley diminishes through time, though remaining significant.

According to Kiryanov, oats became increasingly more important from the 15th century (Kiryanov 1967, 90). Konetskii suggests oats had usurped barley as the crop of the forest zone by the 11th century (Konetskii 2003). Barley is also mentioned in later documents in the context of malt for brewing (Rybina 2001, 127). Oats seem to be regarded as peasant food but were also used as fodder for horses (Rybina 2001, 127). Wheat is occasionally mentioned (14 instances in 12 texts: Konetskii 2003). The first reference to wheat was in the later 12th century and the last in the 15th century (Rybina 2001, 127). Millet remains were the most commonly identified cultural plants found in the samples, yet they do not appear to be unequivocally mentioned in the birch-bark documents. However, Konetskii has discussed the use of the words *pshenka,* which derives from *pes* and *pesh* – 'to grind' – (the word gives rise to pestle), and notes that while the word is often used to describe wheat, in one document its context might suggest another form of grain being ground. This could have been millet (Konetskii 2003). Perhaps it is because millet is so ubiquitous that, in complete contrast to rye (which began cultivation as a novelty), it had little or no value as tribute or in taxation transactions. The 19th-century Russian composer Rimsky Korsakov, in his study of Russian folk tales, noted the frequent reference to millet as a food stable. This inspired him to incorporate the 'millet chorus' in his opera *The Snow Maiden* in which the men sang 'and we sowed and we sowed the millet' to which the woman replied '…and we pound it and we pound it' (Redwood 1989, 126).

The only other cultivated plant that is referenced in the birch bark documents and found (though not frequently) in the samples is flax (Rybina 2001, 128). In terms of fruits and nuts there is only one reference and that is to sour cherries: also found in a number of the samples. The birch bark documents, while they contain extremely important information about economic behavior in medieval Novgorod, are quite partial when it comes to information about utilized plants by comparison with the evidence from the archaeobotanical record.

COMPARISON WITH OTHER EARLY AND LATER MEDIEVAL URBAN SITES IN NORTHERN EUROPE AND SCANDINAVIA

There are few contemporary or even near-contemporary medieval urban sites in Russia comparable to Novgorod that have been extensively sampled for plant remains. Therefore comparable sites within Russia are limited and primarily confined to the earliest levels in Staraya Ladoga. Outside Russia, the plant remains from other early urban centres that have been studied include Cracow and Gniezno in Poland, Birka and Lund in Sweden, Ribe and Aarhus in Denmark, Hedeby and Lübeck in Northern Germany (also the later Hansa towns of Northern Europe), Prague in the Czech Republic, Amsterdam in the Netherlands, Perth in Scotland, York, Winchester, London, Norwich and Southampton in England and Dublin, Cork and Waterford in Ireland.

Obviously, sites within the same geographic region would provide the best comparisons, in particular those within the former Slavic areas such as Staraya Ladoga and the Polish sites. However, archaeobotanical assemblages from medieval sites across Europe are relevant because plant remains studies from all medieval towns hinge on the relationship between the urban centre and the rural hinterland. A hinterland approach has mostly been a key focus of animal bone studies by comparison with research on plant remains from early urban settlements (Prummel 1983; Crabtree 1996; Wigh 2001; O' Connor 2004). There are however some notable exceptions which include, to an extent, Geraghty's study of the plant remains from Viking Age Dublin (Geraghty 1996); more so van Haastor's (1994) overview of Lübeck; Griffin (1988) and Schia 1994 for Oslo; Hall's work (with Kenward and O'Connor) in York, for example Hall *et al.* (1983); and Barrett *et al.* (2004) and (2007) for Kaupang. Tierney and Hannon (1997) for Waterford also aspired to such an approach.

Cultivated Plants: Hops (Humulus lupulus), Hemp (Cannabis sativa) and Flax (Linum usitatissimum)

At Staraya Ladoga the preliminary study by Aalto and Heinäjoki-Majander (1997, 21) of the 10th/11th century levels produced a range of remains, the most frequent economic plant of which were hops. The authors argue that, even at this early stage, hops were being used to flavour beer and the practice could have developed in this area of Eastern Europe following influences from further east (Alato and Heinäjoki-Majander 1997, 21, 26–7; Hansson and Dickson 1997, 209; Behre 1983, 51–53 and 187). However, there are many early discoveries of hops in the north and west. For example, finds of hops have been made in early deposits from Birka, Hedeby (Behre 1984, 115–122), and 8th century deposits at Ribe (Jensen 1985; Robinson *et al.* 1993, 1–16; Robinson 1994, 546). There are also early discoveries of hops from Kaupang in 8th/9th century pits (Barrett *et al.* 2007, 291 and 304), the 10th century Graveney boat in Kent (Wilson and Conolly 1978,147), Whitefriars Street, Norwich in late Saxon 10th/11th century deposits (Ayers and Murphy 1983, 41); Wolin (9th to 12th century, Alsleben 1995, 192, 206 and 215); Lund (11th century and 12th to 14/15th century deposits, Hjelmqvist 1991, 246), 13th century levels from Grosse Petersgrube in Lübeck (Lynch and Paap 1982, 344) and 14th century deposits from Prague (Beněs *et al.* 2002, 116), as well as in the later levels at Coppergate, York (Kenward and Hall 1995). Later still in the Medieval Period it was only the female parts of the hop plant that were used to flavour beer, therefore preventing the development of the fruiting bodies, and in consequence less likelihood of finding them in archaeological deposits. Ninth century documentary sources indicate that rent and renders from French monasteries included hops for flavouring beer and numerous hop gardens are mentioned in the annals of an abbey at Freising in West Germany from later that century (Levillain 1900; Bitterauf 1967: I, 666–715; Wilson and Conolly 1978, 147). In addition, a recipe from an Anglo-Saxon leech book (a medicinal hand-book) comments on the use of hops (Cockayne 1864, 172; Wilson and Conolly 1978, 147). There are therefore clear archaeobotanical and documentary indications that hops were used to flavour beer across northern and western Europe from an early period. During later medieval times trade in hopped beer was a key feature of the exchanges networks set up by the Hanseatic League (Alsleben 2007, 22).

Beer is mentioned in Russian texts from the 11th century onwards with various terms used to denote a hopped ale (Smith and Christian 1984, 75). From the 13th century in Novgorod, hops were a regular item of trade and prices fluctuated considerably, indicating that demand sometimes outstripped supply. A similar scenario was seen at Pskov (Smith and Christian 1984, 78). However, according to the record of foreign observers, by the late 15th century in Russia the brewing of beer, making of mead and using hops were all restricted. This was an attempt to control social order (Smith and Christian 1984, 84). Despite this, domestic brewing continued into the 16th century and hops were mentioned on a par with grain in custom charters (Smith and Christian 1984, 101).

Another plant used to flavour beer in more coastal areas of northern Europe was bog myrtle (*Myrica gale*), which rivaled hops in those areas as a flavouring until later medieval times. There are examples from Scandinavia, for instance the find of its pollen with malted (sprouted) barley in probable 13th century brewery deposits from Bergen (Krzywinski *et al.* 1983, 153). Alsleben has also noted that it was used to flavour beer in the Rhineland and the northern coast of Germany in medieval times (Alsleben 2007, 22). Being a plant that occurs in more maritime districts of Europe it is hardly surprising that it was not found in the assemblage from Troitsky.

There was a small amount of evidence at Troitsky to indicate the use of oil and fibre plants such as hemp and flax. Finds of the remains of these plants have been from a number of later early medieval and medieval urban sites across Europe. For the most part the more eastern sites have both species present, with a greater frequency of hemp. This was the case at Novgorod where there was considerably more hemp than flax (see Endnote 11). Similar results were obtained from Staraya Ladoga, where there were 'many charred and non-charred seed fragments of ...hemp and some fragments of flax capsules' in the early deposits (9th/10th century) that have been studied so far (Aalto and Heinajoki-Majander 1997, 13).

While flax was used for making linen, hemp was particularly good for rope making and for the production of durable textiles. For example, there were finds of hemp rope in early excavations at Staraya Ladoga (Aalto and Heinäjoki-Majander 1997, 21; Ravdonikas 1950). It is also likely that both flax and hemp plants were being used for oil as well as fibre. The seeds of flax were ground for linseed oil, one of the important vegetable oils used during fasts in medieval and post-medieval Russia (Smith and Christian 1989, 5). Hanseatic traders exported linseed oil from Russia during the later medieval period (Péhaut 2000, 457). The edible seeds of hemp are not narcotic and from them good quality oil can be pressed. Frying the seeds for food is practiced to this day in areas of Poland and the Volga region of Russia and these regions are also places where the oil from the seeds is used for cooking (Davidson 1999, 377–8). Before an 18th century gastronomic revolution, it is thought that most Russian dishes were cooked in hempseed oil, 'which made all the dishes taste much the same' (Figes 2002, 164). Even until recently, the former USSR was the main world producer of hemp seed. Vaughan, in a study of oil producing seeds, has noted that the states of the former Soviet Union produced an average of 250,000 tons of hemp seed annually up to 1970 (Vaughan 1970, 23).

Polcyn in his 1994 general survey of early and later medieval Polish sites states that un-charred flax seeds and capsules were common finds in waterlogged deposits. He states that flax was the main early medieval fibre crop and that hemp has been found in similar contexts, suggesting that it was used to produce thick, cloth fragments examples of which were found at Gniezno (Polcyn 1994, 535). Polcyn also sumises that the seeds of flax were being used for the production of oil.

Both hemp and flax were present in the medieval deposits in Oslo and Trondheim (Jensen 1991, 341; Griffin 1988 and Griffin and Sandvik 1991). At Trondheim, there was sufficient evidence to suggest that flax was processed on site. At Kaupang, flax and hemp were both present in the plant assemblages although the impression is that there was greater representation of hemp in the collection. The achenes were also broken suggesting that they had been processed for their oil, in the same way as may have been the case at Novgorod (Barrett *et al.* 2004, 9). In addition Lynch and Paap reported that although present in small numbers, flax and hemp are both represented in an early 13th century deposit. They comment that their presence along with gold of pleasure (*Camelina sativa*) could have been either for their oil or fibre (Lynch and Paap 1982, 348, 357). However, *Camelina sativa* is a characteristic weed of flax crops (Fitter *et al.* 1993, 84; Hall and Kenward 2003, 119).

Both hemp and flax were occasionally found at York (Hall *et al.* 1983, 205) and also at Norwich (Ayers and Murphy 1983, 40), although in general the medieval sites in the West seldom produced evidence of hemp. On the other hand they often have a high incidence of flax. For example Fishamble Street, Dublin where it is likely that the flax was 'ribbled' on site, i.e. the seed capsules were removed (Geraghty 1996, 45–47). Flax was also a regular and relatively frequent find in samples from other Irish medieval towns, for example Waterford and Drogheda, but only an occasional find in samples from Cork (Tierney and Hannon 1997, 857, 861, 869, 873, 889 and 892; Mitchell and Dickson 1985; McClatchie 2003, 404, 405). Flax was also found at Kirk Close in Perth where Robinson is of the view that it was used to produce oil, even though a single flax fibre was found in a sample from elsewhere in Perth at South Metheven Street (Robinson 1987, 206). In his 1994 assessment of plant remains from Viking age sites in Denmark, Robinson noted that flax was only an occasional find. There was no mention of hemp in his assessment (Robinson 1994, 544–5). It seems from Behre's study that while flax seeds and capsules were present at Hedeby, hemp achenes were not (Behre 1983, 24–5, 186).

Other oil plants include members of the *Brassica* family (namely *Brassica napus* and *campestris*). Opium poppy, *Papaver sominferum,* can also produce oil (Wieserowa 1979, 188–9). While there were no finds of the latter in the Novgorod samples there were a few seeds identified as *Brassica,* although it was not possible to identify them to species with any confidence.

Cultivated Plants: Cereals

In the case of cultivated plants, all sites produced varying incidences of cereals. These were preserved both by waterlogging and carbonization. In some urban deposits these included bran fragments, as was the case in samples from Waterford and Perth.

However, the relative numbers of cereal remains in waterlogged samples from early urban sites were low. The cereals present included oats, barley, bread wheat and rye, as, for example, Dublin where the main cereals were six-row hulled barley and oats (Geraghty 1996, 48–9).

Rye rose in significance during early medieval times, though it may have been grown on poor soils since the Roman period, having come into Europe as a weed of other cereals prior to this (Behre 1992, 142–150). By the 10th/11th to 12th centuries its occurance in archaeobotanical samples is particularly pre-eminent for southern Scandinavia and the Slavic areas, including the sites of Gorodishche, Novgorod, Cracow and Gniezno. Sites where it has been noted include Aarhus (Fredskild 1971 and Jensen 1991, 338), Viborg (Jensen 1991, 338), Hedeby (Behre 1983, 19–20), 12th/13th century deposits at Cracow (Wieserowa 1979, 187); Gniezno (Polcyn 1994, 534); and Gorodishche (Alsleben 2001, 108–9). In addition, studies on some early urban sites outside this region have recorded less significant quantities, for example Waterford (Tierney and Hannon 1997, 890) and Perth (Robinson 1987, 205) where it is believed it was not widely grown. The significance of rye in Novgorod is indicated by the numerous references to it in the birch-bark documents (see above and Rybina 2001, 127). One of the two significant deposits of charred grain found during the course of the project on TroitskyXII was dated to late medieval times and was dominated by rye (see above and Alsleben 2001, 111 and this volume).

Many of the sites produced few incidences of wheat and these were mostly indeterminate to species (Robinson 1987, 202). At Cracow there were some grains of bread wheat *Triticum aestivum* in the early medieval deposits (Wiesrowa 1979, 187). Elsewhere in Poland, as at Gniezno, barley was a more frequent find and, where identifiable, it was the six-row type, but wheats were also noted. Two types were distinguished, *Triticum vulgare* and *Triticum compactum* (Polcyn 1994, 534). While rye and barley were most frequently found on the Danish sites, there were very occasional finds of bread wheat, *Triticum aestivum*. The medieval deposits from Trondheim, Oslo and Bergen mostly produced evidence of barley and oats, with a small amount of rye in the case of Bergen (Jensen 1991, 341 and Krzywinski *et al.* 1983, 153). Earlier dated Viking age carbonized bread loaves from Närke and from graves in Birka in Sweden seem to have been made from hulled barley, but some included bread wheat (*T. aestivum*). There were also a few examples of emmer and even einkorn (*Triticum dicoccum* and *Triticum monococcum*). One loaf was made entirely from rye and another from a mix of rye and wheat. A further one was made from pure oats and other loaves were made from a mix of cereals (Jensen 1991 reporting the work of Hjelmqvist 1983 and 1984).

The evidence for cereals in Novgorod and the earlier sites in its hinterland seems to indicate variations on this theme. While barley, oats and rye were significantly present (particularly rye after the 10th century and later oats) there is clear evidence of the hulled wheats, emmer and spelt. The presence of these species was especially noted at Prost and Georgii in the 8th to 10th century (Alsleben 2001, 108–9). In addition the presence of emmer wheat, along with *Triticum vulgare*, had been previously reported by Kiryanov for the 7th/8th century deposits excavated at Staraya Ladoga (Kiryanov in Thompson 1965, 89). In Novgorod the incidence of wheat was less in the samples, but the presence of probable emmer was noted from occasional finds of its un-charred characteristic spikelet forks and glume bases (samples 86 and 91 on Troitsky XI, see Monk and Johnston 2001, 114). Of the western European sites surveyed, only in the

Waterford samples were there a possibility that the cultivation of hulled wheats (possibly spelt) continued into medieval times (Tierney and Hannon 1997, 861, 873, 889–90). Overall the cultivation of the hulled wheats diminished in Western Europe during the earlier part of the first millennium AD, but it seemed to continue longer in areas further east. Alsleben has noted that the glumed wheats, emmer and spelt as well as millet continued to be grown along with other cereals on the glacially derived soils of the Southern Baltic into medieval times but in Germany, by the time of the Hanseatic League towns, emmer cultivation had ceased and spelt cultivation had become confined to southwest Germany (Alsleben 2007, 19 and 22). In addition, Wasylikowa *et al.* have argued that hulled wheat cultivation became less common in Poland after the 10th century AD. This change is less clear for other areas of eastern and central Europe (Wasylikowa *et al.* 1991, 225, 228 and 230).

Millet was a cultivated species that, while not present on western medieval sites, occurred in variable quantities on northern European/southern Scandinavian and on eastern European sites. These sites include Cracow (Wieserowa 1979, 187), Hedeby (Behre 1983, 23–4, 186), various Viking age sites in Denmark (Robinson 1994, 544–5) and various Polish sites (Polcyn 1994, 534). As in the Novgorod samples, millet was the most ubiquitous find from Staraya Ladoga (Aalto and Heinäjoki-Majander 1997, 21) especially during the first half of the 10th century. Polcyn says that by the end of the 11th century it became the most popular grain for bread making and was called the 'Slavonic grain' (Polcyn 1994, 534).

Plants Indicative of the Local Environment

Taking an overview of the representation of the groupings of the plant remains from Novgorod by comparison with those from other early to late medieval urban sites, there are some similarities but also contrasts that may reflect temporal variations but are more likely to reflect differences in preservation, context and biogeographical location.

However, as would be expected, one common feature is the presence of plants that colonize ruderal, nitrogen rich and disturbed ground. A number of these would have been weeds of cultivation but, as put forward by Kenward and Hall (1983, 216), they could have become naturalized in these early towns. Geraghty drew on a point made by Robinson in 1979, in her discussion of the Viking age plant material from Dublin, suggesting that the net input of organic material created a large fermenting dung heap and consequently a warm nitrogen rich environment for colonization by many different weed plants. This in turn would have provided a reservoir of former weed type plants in the locality (Geraghty 1997, 70–1; Robinson 1979, 113–4). While these ruderal weeds do differ from site to site the grouping of such plants represents one of the common themes in the samples from the deposits on these early and later medieval sites (Dublin, York, Perth, Cork, Waterford, Hedeby, Kaupang, Lübeck, Birka, and Bergen). Included amongst them are members of the Polygonaceae (persicaria and dock), the Chenopodiaceae (goosefoot/ orache) and Caryophylaceae (the Pinks) families (Geraghty 1996, 72–109; Hall *et al.* 1983, 215–6; Robinson 1987, 207; McClatchie 2003, 403–411; Tierney and Hannon 1997, 856–878; Behre 1983, 59, 62–3, 65, 97; Barrett *et al.* 2004, 41–2; Lynch and Paap 1983, 344; Hansson and Dickson 1997, 210–211; Krzywinski *et al.* 1983).

Gathered Plants and Cultivated Fruits

Another common feature of the plant remains from all these early urban sites, from Viking age times onwards, is the presence of gathered hedgerow plants such as blackberry, wild raspberry, wild strawberry, members of the *Prunus* genus including cherry, damson, and sloe (but less so for Novgorod because of its location), wild apple, hops, bilberry, bog myrtle, hazel nuts, acorns, rose hips, bird cherry, wild strawberry and in the case of Hedeby, because of its location, beech mast (Behre 1983, 51, 187). As well as Hedeby other sites with such evidence include Ribe (Robinson 1994, 546), Kaupang (Barrett *et al.* 2004, 8 and 2007, 291), Lübeck (Lynch and Paap 1983, 347), London (Jones *et al.* 1991, 348 and 381), Norwich (Ayers and Murphy 1983, 40), Dublin (Geraghty 1996, 38, 67); Perth (Robinson 1987, 206), Waterford (Tierney and Hannon 1997, 889 and taxa lists 857–878), Cork (McClatchie 2003, 400–1, 403–13), and Trondheim (Jensen 1991, 342). This would seem to highlight the fact that these plants (or rather their fruiting bodies) were not only making an important contribution to human nutrition but were also indicative of woodland within the near hinterlands of these incipient urban centres.

   In addition it is also important to stress that it is during this period, and particularly after the 12th century, that various fruits were being grown systematically in orchards. While the beginnings of orchard husbandry in post-Roman northern Europe was linked to ecclesiastical institutions, its full development paralled the development of urbanism in medieval times. Many of the urban sites listed above that produced remains of gathered plants have also produced remains of cultivated orchard crops. In the case of Novgorod, while it is possible that the pips of apples that were found in the samples were domestic species, the only certain orchard plant would have been the sour cherry (*Prunus cerasus*).

Exotics

A significant feature of the plant remains assemblage from the Troitsky sites is the absence of imported fruits or nuts. This is especially curious because such finds, particularly of walnut and possibly almond, have been made on earlier excavations in the city. These earlier finds, archived in the Novgorod State Museum, were reported on by Kiryanov and Kolchin in Thompson 1967, 7–8).

Kiryanov traced the changes in the frequency of walnut fragments from the 10th to the mid-13th century, indicating a steady increase in their incidence in time until the beginning of the 12th century after which there was a dramatic fall off (Kolchin as outlined in Thompson 1967, 7–8). Alsleben has also reported shells of walnut from the Gorodishche excavations, which she noted would be an indicator of the status of its occupants relative to those people living at near contemporary sites where no such finds were made (Alsleben 2001, 111).

Overall, while imported fruits and nuts are found in some medieval urban deposits that date before the 15th/16th centuries, their occurrence is minimal. Finds of walnut along with silver fir were the only imports noted in the samples studied by Behre from Hedeby, for example. Although the deposits also produced peach stones and grape pips these were not considered by him to have been significant imports (Behre 1983, 187, 43–4). Jensen, reporting on the work of Griffin and Sandvik, noted finds of walnut as an important feature of the Trondheim collection (Jensen 1991, 342). Ayers and Murphy also report finds of walnut and grape from the late Saxon/early Norman excavations at Whitefriars Street, Norwich (Ayers and Murphy 1983, 40) and Jones *et al.* report on figs and grape pips from a pit dated to the 12th century at Milk Street in London (Jones *et al.* 1991, 348). In addition Polcyn refers to the occurrence of walnuts from several sites in Poland. He also noted the incidence of peach stones and grape pips at Gniezno, raising the possibility of the local cultivation of vines (Polcyn 1994, 535–6). Wieserowa identified a small number of walnut shells, grape pip and fig seeds from the late medieval deposits on the Market Square site in Cracow. She speculated that the figs were grown locally but does not raise the question about the importation of the walnuts or grapes (Wieserowa 1979, 190).

Excavations in Oslo have produced remains of imported plants including fragments of walnuts shells, grape pips and fig seeds (Jensen 1991, 341). The upper fill of a 13th century latrine in Bergen produced a high incidence of fig seeds (Krzywinski *et al.* 1983, 161–2). Samples of medieval date in Lübeck produced grape pips. Fig was particularly evident in post-medieval deposits (Lynch and Paap 1982, 349). Figs and grapes can of course grow in sheltered places in northern Europe (see Endnote 12).

In addition walnut was identified from Viking age samples in York and from medieval Perth (Hall *et al.* 1983, 179; Robinson 1987, 206), though its status as an imported species at this time is unclear. The likelihood is that it was probably introduced into Britain by the Romans, although its pollen is known from an earlier date (Godwin 1975, 248). In Ireland, later early medievel and later medieval deposits from Cork, Dublin and Waterford have all yielded imported plant evidence, principally again walnut but also, from the Cork and Waterford samples, grapes and possibly figs (McClatchie 2003, 401, 404, 407, 408 and 411; Geraghty 1996, 50, 52 and 70; Tierney and Hannon 1997, 859, 863, 874 and 892). In addition the 13th century deposits in Dublin produced a Stone Pine cone (*Pinus pinea*) (Geraghty 1996, 53). The maritime location and an active trade with South-west France and Spain probably would explain these imports. By comparison with these contemporary and near contemporary urban sites, the samples from Troitsky, if the evidence is representative, suggest a more limited taste for such imported plants (from more convivial climates) on the part of those people living in this part of Novgorod in medieval times than elsewhere in the city.

SUMMARY AND CONCLUSIONS

This project was intended to reawaken an interest in the study of the archaeobotany of medieval Novgorod. The genesis of this focus on the non-wood macro remains from the site can be traced back to the work of Kiryanov and Kolchin from the late 1950s to the late 1970s. The current study has raised a number of issues and identified a number of themes, some of which have been partly developed in this phase of archaeobotanical work. This study has successfully prospected the considerable potential for a follow-up of dedicated systematic archaeobotanical research that needs to centre on a greater contextual understanding than was possible for this limited project of the formation history of the deposits that make up the Novgorod sequence (see Endnote 13). Without this contextual understanding the significance of the distributional and chronological patterns in the macro-plant remains record will not be fully realized.

A key part of the sampled plant remains assemblage can be directly interpreted in cultural terms and this has a direct bearing on the theme of this volume. However, the presence of the majority of remains cannot be explained in this way in the first instance as they were first and foremost part of the local vegetational environment that has arisen from the influence of local and regional biogeographical factors and the activities of people. For the latter reason a significant complement of the remains from across the Troitsky excavations, and through time, was made up of seeds and fruits of plants that can best be described as ruderals, i.e. weeds of waste, disturbed and nitrogen rich ground (the kinds of habitats that develop around all human habitations). Some of these plants may have become naturalized at Troitsky. This could have begun before the earliest stage in the urbanization of the area when the land use was both tillage and meadow farmland (see above and Aleksandrovskaya *et al.* 2001). Subsequently there could have been the deposition and colonization by plants that were brought into the developing urban environment as animal feed, bedding or as weeds of processed crops.

These plants could well have included various members of the Polygonaceae, Chenopodiaceae and Caryophylaceae families. However, one member of the last of these, *Agrostemma githago,* known as a common weed of rye, was significantly absent. Despite Kiryanov's 1967 suggestion that rye (for which there is plenty of evidence from Novgorod) was winter sown, the absence of *Agrostemma githago* might suggest either a different sowing regime or a longer fallow period. Spring sowing is a possibility, especially since such a practice is preceded by intensive tillage that could destroy winter germinating weeds like *Agrostemma githago*. However, Alseben has pointed out to the authors that an ecological study further north, in Finland around Lake Ladoga, noted that *Agrostemma githago* was a weed of oats, presumably sown in the spring (Alsleben pers. comm., and Linkola 1916). It may simply be that this region is beyond its natural range and, as suggested by Kiryanov, other weeds were indicating a winter sowing regime (Kiryanov 1967, 90). Equally, as postulated by Alsleben, its absence could be as much to do with a longer fallow regime as occurs elsewhere in northern Europe, where it regularly occurs as a crop weed as discussed above.

In the case of one large charred grain assemblage from a late dated context on Troitsky XIII, while it did produce a few instances of *Agrostemma githago*, they were insignificantly present by comparison to the high incidence of species such as the grass *Apera spica venti*. This is a plant that is also susceptible to being severely restricted in its growth potential by intensive tillage but, like *Agrostemma githago*, it tends to germinate in the autumn.

Despite the significant presence of seeds of ruderal and weed plants, those seeds with the highest frequency were from plants characteristic of swamp ground conditions including water meadows and locations beside very slow flowing or stagnant water (particularly *Ranunculus sceleratus*). Such habitats would include areas periodically inundated with water. These conditions would be expected in the locality with the seasonal range of the Volkhov and its tributaries leading to regular over-bank flooding during the early spring melt, creating the natural water meadows that are still characteristic of the district to the south and east of Novgorod today. As with the weeds of disturbed ground the plants producing these seeds could have adapted to suitable habitats in the developing urban environment.

A study of the buried soils at the base of the stratigraphic sequence produced evidence for damp meadow conditions in that part of the excavated area at Troitsky that had not been cultivated, including most of the area of Troitsky XI (Aleksandrovskaya *et al.* 2001, 17–20). Equally, given the contexts of some of the samples (for example, byre deposits for samples 89 to 91) these swamp plants with their seeds, as with the ruderals, could have been brought in with animal fodder or for bedding (Reilly this volume). A chronological study of the incidence of them in the Troitsky XI samples indicated a decrease in frequency of damp land plants through time, which may suggest that the plants were naturalized in this relatively low-lying situation. However, as deposits accumulated, the on-site habitat of these plants almost certainly diminished.

Although the overall instance of cultural plants, particularly cereals, was low they were a consistent feature. In a few instances burnt destruction deposits produced a high incidence of cereals, and in one case associated weed seeds. An exception to this low incidence pattern was millet, particularly the presence of their husks. The high frequency of these millet husks stands in contrast to the references to this crop in the birch-bark documents. All the other grains are mentioned and most especially rye, but there seems to be no unequivocal reference to millet. The explanation for this may be related to millet's ubiquity, perhaps reflecting the fact that it had little value as food rent or tribute, a central concern of many of the birch-bark documents. Millet has been a common component in the diet of the Slavic peoples, including the Russians ever since, being mentioned in many Russian folk tales. Following the interpretation made of a similarly high incidence of millet from medieval Cracow, it may have been the only food grain completely processed in the domestic household. In this context however, the highest incidence of millet remains (though mostly husks) on the Troitsky sites was from exterior rather than interior locations. This pattern is most likely related to the disposal of waste but may also hint to the use of millet chaff to feed animals in the yard areas. Davidson in a general study of food plants makes reference to millet being used to feed livestock (Davidson 1999, 506).

Most of the cereal remains occurred as charred grains and indicated the presence of all the main genera, wheat, barley, oats and rye. Apart from one late destruction deposit on Troitsky XII, mentioned earlier, there was a relative absence of chaff elements. The only other exception to this was a few instances of preserved (by water-logging) glume bases of emmer wheat, cultivated to a quite late date in this region by comparison with Western Europe. These remains are most likely to represent waste from a final stage in crop processing, although their use for fodder or bedding cannot be ruled out (see Endnote 14).

The likelihood however, is that primary cereal processing for human food was taking place away from the site. The high incidence of charred remains from sample 19 (from within a building) produced mainly grains of wheat and barley (perhaps suggesting mixed cropping) with few seeds of other plants. However, the large destruction deposit from Troitsky XII, containing a very high frequency of remains, produced not only a very large number of rye grains but also produced a high incidence of a wide size range of weed seeds, suggesting minimal cleaning before being brought to the site (Alsleben 2001, 111 and Alsleben pers comm). This deposit could be 'the exception that proves the rule' but it is perhaps too difficult to draw a sound conclusion from such a few high incidence samples. Pre-culinary processing may have been taking place close to cooking areas (see Endnote 15). While the distribution of cereal remains occurred within buildings, there was no particular association with internal ovens.

In addition to the bread-making grains two other cultural plants, hemp and hops, were significant by their presence, though again not in large numbers (except sample 2 from Troitsky XIII). The contrasting distribution of these remains on Troitsky XI, with hops mainly coming from interior contexts and hemp from exterior locations, raises the question of whether the deposits from which they came were *in situ*, as well as questions about what uses the plants were put to. Hops are most usually associated with flavouring beer, a practice that seems to have been known from at least the 9th century, but they can also be used to produce a dye and the young shoots can be eaten. Hemp has medicinal and drug properties, but had a common usage in medieval times for fibre and for rope making. The fragmented achene/nut-lets might suggest another practice, namely oil extraction. Despite the predominant exterior location of the nut-lets it is very possible that, as is known for more recent culinary sources, hemp oil was used for cooking (Smith and Christian 1984 and see above). Evidence for another oil-bearing plant, flax, was minimal. Apart from one very significant sample taken towards the base of the stratigraphy on Troitsky XI, which produced a high incidence of seed capsules as well as seeds, there were very few finds of flax in the collection.

An important element in many samples was the remains of gathered plants including shells of hazel nuts, drubes of wild strawberry and raspberry, apple pips and bilberry seeds. The distributional study of these remains across and within

Troitsky XI probably had little significance, although it does seem that raspberries, bilberries and apple remains were frequently located along boundary fences and may represent a variation in discard practices.

There are many similarities and some contrasts between the archaeobotanical finds from Novgorod and other developing late early medieval and later medieval urban settlements in NW Europe. One area that is particularly similar is the presence of such gathered fruits from woodland margin plants suggesting an important and continual link with such locations in the immediate hinterland of these sites (see Endnote 16). The presence of sour cherry in a number of samples distributed throughout the sequence is an important indicator, as elsewhere in northern Europe, of the development of orchard husbandry, which seems to have paralled increasing urbanization throughout the region (Alsleben 2007, 25).

Comparisons have also been drawn between the range of ruderal and weed plants and indeed the presence of damp-land species. The presence of plants from such habitats reflects both the low-lying location of these early urban sites and the land use prior to their development which in the case of Novgorod was most likely both damp meadowland and tillage fields.

The incidence of remains would also be influenced by the nature of deposits. Hall *et al.* (1983), Kenward and Hall (1995; 1997) and Hall and Kenward (1998) have discussed such deposits in the context of their work in York and in particular discussed the possibility that they represented stable/byre debris, mainly given the presence of so-called 'dung and slum' species in the insect collection. It has, however, been difficult to make this interpretation in Novgorod, though it is believed that deposits represented in samples 89–91 were definitely *in situ* byre debris. The incidence of insects characteristic of foul conditions in stable manure would seem to confirm this interpretation (see discussion of the insects from sample 91 in Reilly this volume). Overall the insect study carried out by Reilly of a range of samples across both Troitsky XI and XIII has cast important light on the nature of the deposits and the living conditions at the time the site was occupied. The study would also seem to confirm the interpretation of an overall damp to wet marshy environment with pools of standing water on and close by, as is also indicated by the presence of *Alisma plantago aquatica, Ranunculus scleratus* and *Eleocharis palustris*. In addition, the insect evidence has confirmed the presence of animals living on the site (at least for a time before they were butchered). This evidence lends support to the suggestion, made earlier, that some of the damp land floral remains could have derived from animal feed (from hay) in their dung or in the bedding material used in on-site byres (Reilly this volume).

The low incidence of grain crop remains (partly influenced by the preservation conditions, except where there were destruction deposits), is also a characteristic of other early urban sites. In addition, in a number of examples from NW Europe, hops and hemp are similarly consistently found. One difference between many of these sites and the remains from Troitsky is the lack of imported exotics in the latter case, though such remains (mainly of walnut and almond) have been found in deposits from the earlier excavations in other parts of Novgorod. Is this simply the result of sample bias or does it reflect a real situation on Troitsky, perhaps influenced by cultural choice or by social status? It seems that the dietary preference of the inhabitants of this part of Novgorod was for local produce, although this interpretation serves to beg this question for future studies on this site and elsewhere in Novgorod.

Explicit hinterland research has not been a common theme in archaeobotancial studies in the past. However, there are exceptions (see above for references to such work). In the case of Novgorod, the study of the environmental, as well as the artefact assemblages, has been very much influenced by a defined hinterland approach: the city's relationship with the so-called Novgorod Lands, both near and far. The results of the current study would suggest that the predominant proportion of the organic deposits that go to form the site and the identifiable non-wood plant remains content were sourced locally. The remains of the cultural plants, in particular the cereals, but also the millet, were probably grown from the area to the south west of Novgorod. This area is known as the Poozerie, where earlier dated sites (such as Prost and Georgii) have produced cereal remains (Alsleben 2001, 108–9 and this volume). The area to the south also supported deciduous woodland (the most northerly area for such trees in this region) from which many of the gathered plants found in the deposits were likely to also have been obtained including hazel nuts, wild strawberries, raspberries, apples and wild hops (but see Endnote 1). The common incidence of bilberries on the site would indicate the heath areas in woodland clearings to the north of the city were also being exploited.

The selected discussion of comparable, similarly dated, early urban sites across Europe indicate a not unexpected common theme namely that local sources for gathered plants were consistently exploited, highlighting the fact that it is from the 'rural hinterlands' that these early towns emerged and were continually sustained. It is perhaps true to say that the continuity of occupation of such early urban sites across the whole of Europe was far more dependent on their immediate hinterland than their far flung contacts and the exotic material that demonstrated such links. It is a lesson to us that we should not create an unbalanced interpretation by over-emphasizing this imported evidence to the detriment of the overwhelming influence of the immediate hinterland.

Acknowledgements

Our special thanks go to a number of people who have helped in this project at different stages or throughout. In particular we would like to single out Mark Brisbane (for eternal optimism, his second to none people skills, and patience in so many ways not least as series editor of these volumes). In addition we wish to acknowledge the tremendous help and support from our environmental archaeological colleagues on the project Mark Maltby and Ellen Hambleton (for their good humour and companionable support as well as thoughts on the animals), Sheila Hamliton-Dyer (for her breadth and depth of knowledge in all things environmental and for being a great 'team player'), Eileen Reilly (for her knowledge and enthusiasm for all things insect wise), Almuth Alsleben (for practical help and advice on identification and for helpful discussions on several issues not least the *Agrostemma githago* problem, cropping regimes and plant remains from Hanseatic league towns). We must also single out several other people without whom the project would not have worked. These include Kathy Judelson and Lyuba Smirnova whose translation and language skills were so fundamental to the project as a whole. In addition we wish to acknowledge the contribution of Eamon Cotter (for being there in the early days of the project and for his fine singing voice), to several years of Bournemouth students (for their continued help with the processing), Judith Monk (for allowing MM to disappear to Russia for several weeks each summer and for editorial advice), to John (for feeding us on several occasions in the final stages of completing this report and for allowing PJ to disappear to Russia for the period of the project).

We would also like to extend our thanks and acknowledge the support of our Russian colleagues particularly Peter Gaidukov (for being consistently helpful and engaged in what we were doing and to allow us to disrupt the work on his site to take samples), Evgeni Nosov (whose belief in what we could bring to the Novgorod project made it all possible), the late Alexander Khoroshov (for agreeing to allow us to work on the material from the incredible sites at Troitsky that he directed, but also his good humour and support of the project throughout), Elena Rybina (for opening up the world of birch bark documents to us), and to Valantine Yanin (for his in-depth knowledge of Novgorod).

Several seasons of site supervisors and Russian students on Troitsky XI, XII and XIII allowed us to dig holes in their areas and provided contextual data whenever we asked for it, in particular Lyuba Smirnova, Gena Dubrovin and Misha Petrov (whose command of American English allowed us to develop a rapport and understanding with the excavation teams on Troitsky XII and XIII) and Alexander Sorokin for discussing Troitsky XII and XIII and for sharing his insights with us. To our colleagues from the Institute of Archaeology, in particular Andrew Reynolds, Jon Hather and Martin Comey for being there at a critical stage in the project.

We would particularly wish to thank Andrew Bleasdale for permission to refer to his unpublished thesis on the ecology of rye cultivation on the Aran Isles and the advice from Gordon Hillman on the possibility of a spring sowing regime for rye in the Novgorod region. Thanks also to INTAS, the Society of Antiquaries of London and Bournemouth University for providing funding and to the Department of Archaeology, UCC for its support.

Endnotes

1. The woodland insect fauna found to be present in Reilly's study were species associated with coniferous forest, with almost no species associated with broad-leaved deciduous trees, even though these trees were present in the area to the south of Novgorod in the past according to recent pollen studies and are still extant in some areas today (Spiridonova and Aleshinskaya this volume). The suggestion here is that the unidentifiable fragmented vegetative material in the non-wood macro-plant assemblage did not come from the leaves of broad leaved trees but came from either plants associated with coniferous forest or, more particularly, those plant species brought to the site for insulation, bedding or animal feed (see Reilly this volume).

2. Kiryanova has argued that initially rye and oats came into this region of North West Russia as weeds of spring-sown crops before being taken on as crops in their own right. When this happened, rye was sown in the winter (Kiryanova 1979, 85).

3. An ecological study (Bleasdale undated) of traditional non-herbicidal spring-sown rye cultivation and its associated weed flora on the Aran Isles, Ireland, also indicated an absence of *Agrostemma githago*. A comparison between those weeds present in the late dated charred sample from Troitsky XII (identifications by Alsleben), indicated some similarity with the species in the rye fields on Aran for the most frequently identified taxa (over 17 individuals). These included *Avena* sp. (*A. fatua* and *A. strigosa* in the Aran fields), *Brassica rapa, Chenopodium album, Lolium temulentum, Lolium perrene, Poa annua, Fallopia convolvulus, Spergula arvensis* (eight of 13 commonest taxa in the Troitsky XII sample).

4. Kiryanov has made reference to an entry in the Novgorod Chronicle for 1127 that notes that rye was winter sown. The question is whether such an entry is made because it represents the norm or the exception (Kiryanova 1967, 90).

5. In an ecological survey by Haslam in Britain, *Alisma plantago-aquatica* was noted as being a characteristic plant of slow flowing channels, including in the vicinity of man-made dykes (Haslam 1978, 249–251).

6. In this context Ankudinov discusses the meaning of the word '*suki*' as it appears in the birch-bark documents. It would appear to refer to 'a cleared patch of land'. He argues that it could have arisen to describe increasing clearance of areas around Novgorod for the cultivation of cereals, particularly rye as it became increasingly favoured after the 12th century (Ankudinov 2003). Both *Urtica urens* and *Lapsana communis* have been found in samples 48A, 60, 96 and 100. Though there is little significance in this association and little association with other plants that might be found in woodland or woodland margin.

7. This exercise is undertaken here, but in doing so we bear in mind the cautionary comments in taking such an approach in archaeobotany of in particular Küster. However, in order to help illuminate details of the habitat choices of certain plants, identified as present from their seeds (particularly those from damp-land locations and human created habitats), and to draw on parallels with studies that have used this approach, we believe this discussion has some value. We fully recognise that it is not possible to suggest that the phytosociological groups made reference to here can be said to be present in and around Novgorod in medieval times, because the evidence is based on such a narrow range of plant remains from the archaeological collections, many of which can occur in more than one phytosociological group (Hansjörg Küster 1991, 17–26 especially 18–19). However, this approach may have more validity for anthropologically created habitats that, as has been pointed out by Alsleben (2007, 17) following Hellwig (1990), share many similarities across Europe (according to phytosociological classification these human-influenced assemblages are called thanatocoenose). But as Alsleben has rightly pointed out, the full value of this data can only come about if the archaeobotanical evidence is well supported by good archaeological contextual information (Alsleben 2007, 17).

8. The insect study undertaken by Reilly has noted the varied but consistent presence of species associated with swamp and aquatic locations (samples 48 and 54 on Troitsky XI and samples 1 to 9 on Troitsky XIII).

9. One of the site directors at the Troitsky excavations, Alexander Sorokin, has argued, from his interpretation of the archaeological evidence, that there was a regular and rapid build up of refuse on either side of the buildings and when each went out of use the roof was taken off and the walls taken down to the level that the organic refuse had built up on the outside of them. The interior of the building was then used as a dump for the adjoining properties. If this interpretation is correct it would suggest initial buildups within buildings were *in situ* but then re-deposition from elsewhere would have taken place including residue from activities outside that property altogether (Sorokin pers comm). A varying range of insect fauna that are either characteristic of interior or exterior locations were found in most samples, though the mix was less in those contexts from within buildings (Reilly this volume). Such evidence further highlights the difficulties in defining the extent to which the Novgorod deposits accumulated *in situ*.

10. *Apium* sp.was found in samples 62, 98, 103 (with significant presence), ELS 13 and sample 2 from Site XIII.

11. A factor that might have had some influence in this bias is soil conditions. Flax prefers dry soils, although it does grow well in oceanic climates, as in Ireland. By comparison, hops do better on damp, though well-aerated, soils (Alsleben 2007, 24).

12. In her discussion of the plant remains evidence from the North German Hanseatic towns, Alsleben noted that the regular occurance of figs and grapes in deposits from these towns would seem that they could have been afforded even by people from the lower orders of society (Alsleben 2007, 26 and 30).

13. The potential for this approach was explored by the UCL excavation team's involvement in the Troitsky excavations in 1998 (Reynolds and Sudds 2001, 31–46).

14. Davidson has noted that hulled wheat, like emmer and spelt, is presently used to feed animals (Davidson 1999, 845).

15. Baranov *et al.* (1999, 265) noted, in near recent times in peasant households in Russia, the final cleaning of the crop (and even after milling) involved the use of sieves (*nochva*).

16. Groenman-van Waateringe (1994, 156) has similarly made this point in her general study of medieval dietary evidence from not only urban sites, but also castle and monastic sites in Holland.

Note

1   ELS = Environmental London Sample, being samples collected by the excavation team led by Dr Andrew Reynolds from the Institute of Archaeology, UCL.

– 18 –

THE PLANT ECONOMY OF NORTHERN MEDIEVAL RUSSIA

A. Alsleben

INTRODUCTION

The investigation of plant macrofossils, i.e. seeds and fruits of cultivated and wild plants, helps to provide an understanding of the nutritional economy of former peoples and communities. When charred or water-logged organic remains were incorporated in human deposits, such as cultural layers, postholes, pits or other archaeological features, we can obtain information about the occurrence, usage, preference and consumption of certain grains, pulses, oil and fibre plants, fruits, nuts and herbs. In particular, closed complexes of plant remains are valuable to us, because, according to their degree of weed contamination, they may reflect all the different steps of crop-processing from harvest to grain storage. This type of data from more than 50 urban centres in North-western Russia has been studied by A. V. Kiryanov (1959) and N. A. Kiryanova (1992) and more recently by E. Y. Lebedeva (2005) and by V. V. and A. V. Tuganaev (2001). To gain a complete picture of food processing and consumption requires information concerning both the archaeology and the environmental factors. In a regional context, comparative archaeobotanical studies of urban centres and rural hinterlands are of special interest because they help to put light on the limited documentary evidence we have for this period of such things as exchange processes, trade and taxation. For instance, some of the famous birch-bark documents from Novgorod touch upon the question of which crops were liable for taxation (Rybina 2001). Interestingly, all cereals were mentioned except millet, but which nevertheless occurs in the archaeological record, sometimes in large amounts.

In the second half of the first millennium AD Slavonic farmers arrived in the vast territories of the North-western Russian plain with a scattered Finno-Ugrian population. Their economy was based on pasturing and arable farming. By the time fortified settlements were established in the region of Lake Ilmen, slash-and-burn cultivation was replaced by cultivation of an enlarged variety of crops on permanent fields. The introduction of rye was one important new development which occurred later than it did in North-western Europe (Behre 1992). In a further step the territory south of Lake Onega was colonized when the demand for natural resources such as wood, fur, wax and honey increased. The observed developments in agriculture are not solely the result of the Slavonic colonization, but are also defined by slightly different

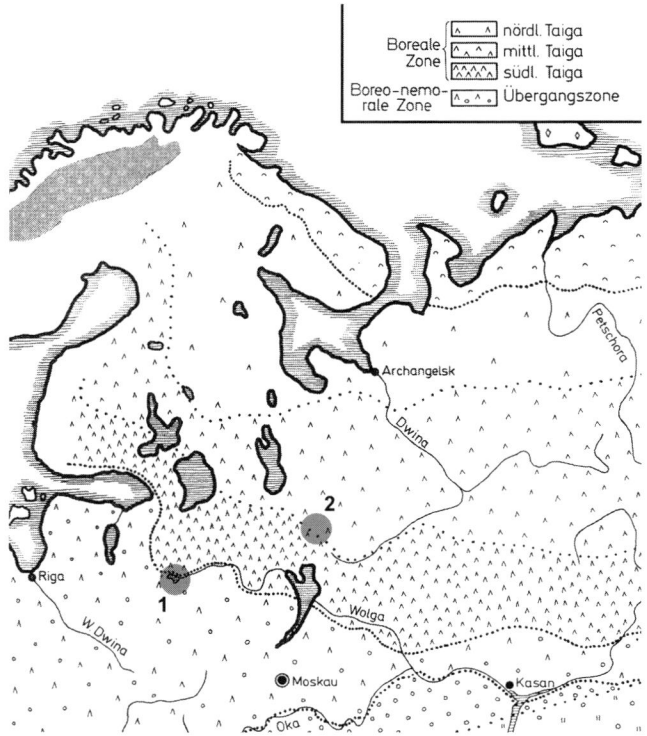

Figure 18.1 *Forest vegetation zones of Northwest Russia. Location of the study areas: 1 = region of Lake Ilmen at the border of broad-leafed forest and southern coniferous forest (southern Taiga); 2 = region of Lake Byeloe and Lake Kubenskoe at the northeastern border of southern coniferous forest (Walter 1974, 9, modified).*

environmental, mainly climatic, factors in the two investigated regions. Botanically, both areas belong to the boreal forest zone dominated by coniferous trees but differ in their composition of broad-leaved trees, due to the decreasing oceanic influence in climate towards the northeast (Figure 18.1). Even small differences in temperature were decisive in the way that people in the Lake Ilmen region enjoyed a varied range of basic crops, whereas in the area of Lake Byeloe and Lake Kubenskoye they had to be content with a frugal diet, based on two staple crops, barley and rye.

ARCHAEOBOTANICAL INVESTIGATIONS IN THE REGION OF LAKE ILMEN

Lake Ilmen is situated in a flat plain with a high ground-water level. On the southern and the eastern shores extensive estuaries of the rivers Lovat and Msta create marshy land unsuitable for habitation, apart from some island-like small hills within the plain. Adjacent to the western bank a small strip of land, known as Poozerie, rises high enough to be suitable for arable farming (Figure 18.2). In this area around Lake Ilmen and the river Veryazha, seasonal flooding provides nutrient-rich meadows when the water recedes. The first Slavonic farmers were attracted by these favourable conditions for arable farming and cattle-breeding on Poozerie. Here two settlements

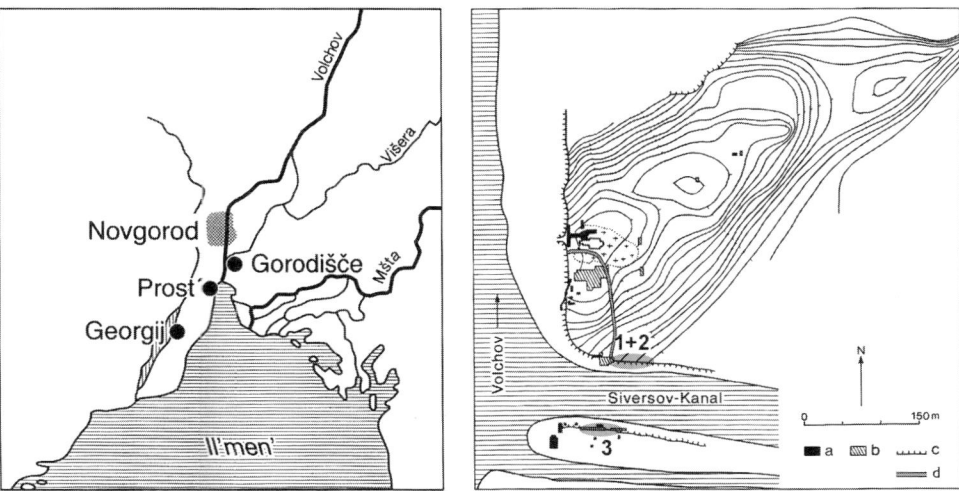

Figure 18.2 *Novgorod hinterland: The location of samples taken for analysis of macro plant fossils. Topographic situation of Ryurik Gorodishche (right). Excavations 1995–2002: Trench (1) and profile of the northern terrace scarp (2); south of Siversovov Canal (3). Key: a = excavations 1901–1970; b = excavations 1975–1985; c = modern terrace scarp; d = ditch. (Alsleben 2001, 107; Nosov 2001, 36).*

have been studied archaeobotanically: Prost in the east and Georgii in the west of this area. In Prost the excavated archaeological structures are dated mainly into the second half of the first millennium AD, with some back to the sixth century AD. Georgii is round about 100 years later. The plant macrofossil data of these two sites has been published previously, in parts (Alsleben 1997, 2001a, b).

PROST

Prost is one of the oldest Slavonic settlements on Poozerie, but it is singular because of its close proximity to a pagan cult site, Peryn. Numerous pits, some of them with burnt stones indicating the presence of dwellings, contained charred (fossil) fruits and seeds of cultivated and wild plants. Archaeological information on soil samples are summarized in Table 18.1. The archaeological dates of the cultural layers cover a time span of some 300 years. That means the results of the studied crop assemblages may be seen as reflecting the use of cultivated plants, i.e. cereals, from the 6th to 9th/10th century AD. Table 18.I (on CD) provides the complete results of the investigation of plant macrofossils. The main crops in Prost were emmer wheat *Triticum dicoccum* followed by barley *Hordeum vulgare* and spelt wheat *Tr. spelta*. The portion of oats *Avena* sp. is comparatively high with a value of nearly 6%. Oats are a high-quality fodder for horses, so in this connection it should be discussed if people in Prost kept horses for the

No.	Lab. No.	Square	Date	Description of structures	Culture plant (charred)
P1	98/1	85, 86, 87, 88, 99	8th	foundation of dwelling "A"	Tr.dic., Tr.sp.; chaff 78%
P2	99/14	230, 231	6th–9th	pit XIII, upper part	Tr.dic., Hord.; chaff 43%
	99/15	230, 231	6th–9th	pit XIII, lower part	
P3	99/10	160, 161	6th–9th	pit VIII	Sec., Tr.dic.; chaff 79%
P4	99/11	167, 168, 174, 175	6th–9th	pit IX	Hord., Pan.; grains 99%
P5	98/2	182, 183	6th–8th	foundation of dwelling "B"	Hord., Tr.dic.; Av.; grains 87%
P6	98/5	117, 118	8th?	pit I	Hord., Tr.dic., Pan.; small sample
	98/6	116	6th–8th	pit II	"
	99/1	119, 126	9th ff.	black layer over pit III	"
	99/2	96, 119, 125, 126	7th–8th	pit III, upper part	"
	99/3	96, 119, 125, 126	7th–8th	pit III, lower part	"
	99/4	126	7th–8th	pit III	"
	99/5	126, 127, 133, 134	8th/9th	pit IV	"
	99/6	127, 134	8th/9th	pit IV	"
	99/7	124, 125	6th–9th	pit V	"
	99/8	129, 130, 136, 137	9th/10th	pit VI	"
	99/9	143.144	6th–9th	pit VII	"
	98/3	181	6th–8th	pit X	"
	98/4	190	6th–8th	pit XI	"
	99/12	216, 240	6th–8th	pit XII, upper part	"
	99/13	216, 240	6th–8th	pit XII, lower part	"
	99/16	229, 230	6th–9th	pit XIV, upper part	"
	99/17	229, 230	6th–9th	pit XIV, lower part	"

Table 18.1 Prost. Information on samples. Plant macrofossils. Av. = Avena; Hord. = Hordeum; Pan. = Panicum; Sec. = Secale; Tr.aest. = Triticum aestivum; Tr.dic. = Triticum dicoccum; Tr.sp. = Triticum spelta.

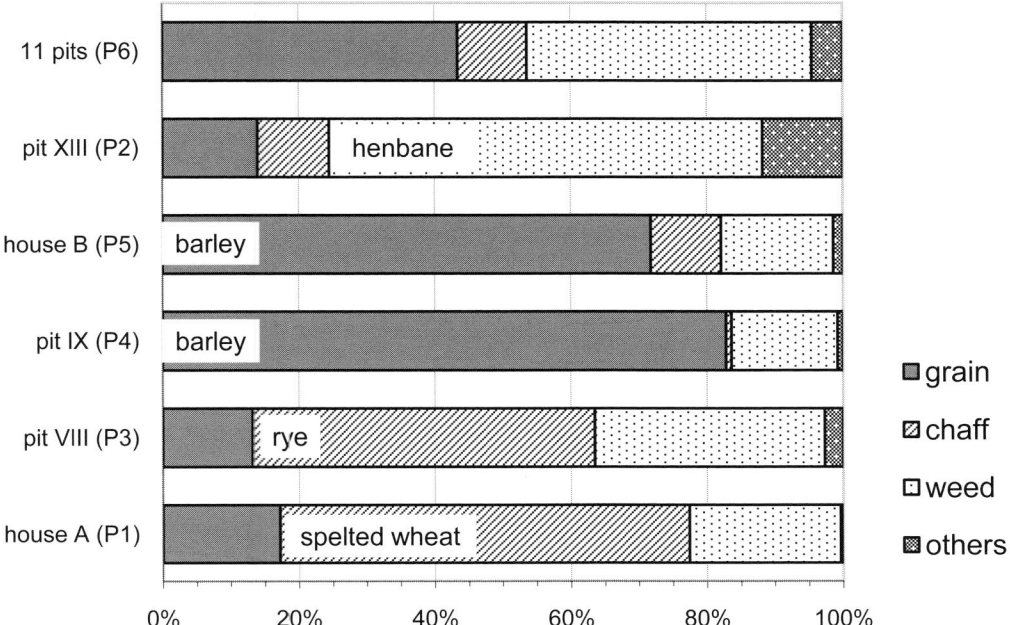

Figure 18.3 Prost: Plant macrofossils. Relative abundances of grains, chaff and weeds in the samples.

nearby place of Peryn. Stallions or geldings are said to adopt the function of an oracle within this pagan cult (Keiling 1994). The other cereals, bread wheat *Tr. aestivum,* rye *Secale cereale,* and common millet *Panicum miliaceum* appear frequently but in small numbers in the material. The dominance of barley, the occurrence of emmer, and the lack of rye are typical of traditional iron-age agriculture in the North, which lived on in the oldest Slavonic arable farming (see below; Table 18.6). Crops were probably sown in late spring, because indicators of winter-cultivation are missing within the group of wild species.

Concerning temporal development, no significant differences are visible within the fossil plant material. But some samples (P1 – P5) differ in their composition of grains, chaff and weeds (Figure 18.3). Two samples are rich in chaff: House A (P1) contained mainly the glume bases of the spelted (or glume) wheats, i.e. emmer and spelt. In Pit VIII (P3) fragments of the ears of rye reached a portion of nearly one third of the whole plant remains. House B (P5) and Pit IX (P4) are rich in grains which comprise in both cases mainly barley. Weeds are the main component of Pit XIII (P2) and here henbane makes up a large part at 30%. Spikelet forks, glume bases and fragments of the rachis, end products of crop-processing (threshing and winnowing), should not be expected to occur in cultural layers of dwellings. In this way the frequent record of them in House A is conspicuous. On the other hand, the chaff from dwelling A consists of the glume bases of spelted wheats and to get the pure grain a second step of milling

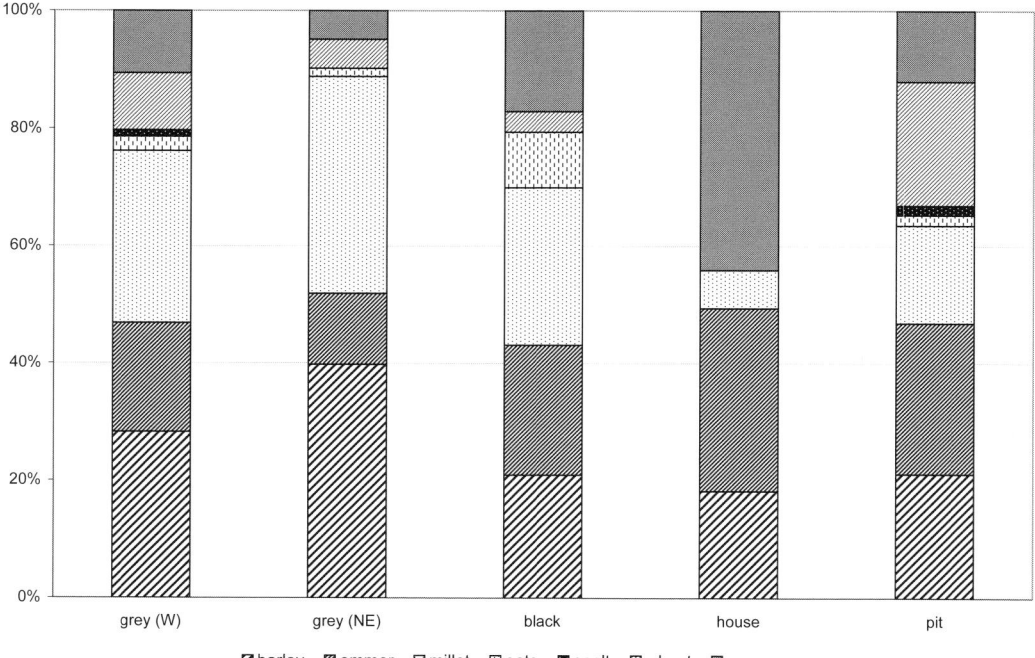

Figure 18.4 *Georgii: Plant macrofossils. Proportion of crops in the different features and layers.*

is necessary. This had most likely been done in or near the houses. Emmer and spelt as well as barley from House B are residues of preparing food. The high portion of ear fragments of rye together with many seeds and fruits of wild species in Pit VIII (P3) must be explained differently. Rye belongs to the naked cereals, which means parts of the ears are removed by the crop-processing techniques. The composition of plant remains in Pit VIII is typical for such processes. Additionally, because rye is recorded only by chaff and not by grain, it is very likely that rye is still a weed probably tolerated in the fields of Prost.

GEORGII

The fortified settlement of Georgii is situated at the western side of Poozerie. It belonged to a chain of settlements of the second half of the first millennium AD, strung along the bank of the river Veryazha, a water-route which was used by former traders to avoid shipping across Lake Ilmen (Nosov 1992). The settlement developed over already cleared and ploughed land, as shown by plough-marks of a one-shoed ard conserved below layers deposited during the medieval period. They show a criss-crossed system of dark lines in the clear subsoil. The covering anthropogenous deposits can be divided into an older grey and a younger black layer, but the analysed plant material does not differ significantly between the two (Table 18.II on CD and Alsleben 1997). The main plant remains were barley, emmer and millet as the results show from several samples taken from the grey layers in the northeastern part of the site and under the rampart in the west (Figure 18.4).[1] With some caution a tendency can be extracted from the archaeobotanical results: rye *Secale cereale* slowly displaced barley in the upper black layer in the house, and in a northern pit. Compared to Prost, common millet was more important at Georgii and seems to be a new element in the agriculture of the region of Lake Ilmen, probably introduced by Slavonic farmers.

In total, people in Georgii cultivated a rich and balanced spectrum of seven cereal species, as well as peas *Pisum sativum*, beans *Vicia faba* and lentils *Lens culinaris*. Different demands of the cereals on climatic and edaphic conditions enabled farmers to choose the most suitable crops, as the weather determined. For instance, spelt wheat is less sensitive to climate than bread wheat. Millet *Panicum milliaceum* needs a dry and hot, but only short, summer season. In comparison with it the vegetation period of rye is quite long but because of its tolerance against cold temperatures it could have been a suitable crop for winter-cultivation. Indeed, here, as in Prost, no wild species typical for the fields of winter crops were found in the samples, which also suggests that a crop-rotation system was not in use by the time of the 10th century. Rye had not found its place as a crop in its own right by this time. No burnt staples had been excavated in Georgii or Prost, but the natural capacities of the region are rich and offer many opportunities for the cultivation of crops. There can be little doubt that arable production on Poozerie had the potential to serve the local population as well as the needs of a local market.

RYURIK GORODISHCHE

In contrast to the medieval settlements on Poozerie, the hillfort of Ryurik Gorodishche was built on a small cape immediately to the north of Lake Ilmen between the marshy plains of the estuary of the river Msta to its south and the outflow of the rivers Volkhov and Volkhovets ('the little Volkhov'). The hill covered around 10 ha of land which was not flooded in late spring. The centre of the hillfort was situated on the prominent east bank of the Volkhov, from here overlooking the northern part of Lake Ilmen. Gorodishche was naturally guarded by its topographical situation, but in the east a 10 to 12 m wide ditch separated the central higher part from an inhabited lower area. Unfortunately, the archaeological deposits are heavily disturbed by erosion on the western edge of the cape, by medieval and later buildings and by World War II activity, which partly destroyed the centre, and by the construction of the Siversovov Canal, which disturbed and mixed deposits from most of the southern area of Gorodishche. Therefore undisturbed cultural deposits of the 10th century and older could only be excavated in limited parts to the north and south of the Siversovov Canal (Figure 18.2; and see Nosov 1992).

Figure 18.5 *Ryurik Gorodishche, profile of the northern terrace scarp east of the trench. Stratigraphy of Square 10 with dwelling "B" (above) and Square 8 with dwelling "A" (below). a = stratum of ploughmarks; b = brown culture layer; c = mixed brown/black layer under the house foundation; d = foundation of the house; e = black culture layer (IV–I). a' = basis of a small ditch, b' = brown culture layer; e' = black culture layer; d' = foundation of the house; e' = black culture layer (IV–I).*

During the excavation seasons of 1996 to 2002 soil samples were taken for the investigation of fossil plant macro-remains from three areas of the settlement: from a trench which ran east of the central part of the hillfort, from a profile through the northern terrace scarp, and from deposits south of the canal and most probably east of the trench. A profile of the northern terrace scarp was prepared over a length of 12 m (Table 18.2a; Figure 18.5). Plough-marks are the oldest proof of human activity

No.	Lab. No.	Square	Layer	Height above ploughmarks	Description of the layer	Description of structures	Culture plant (charred)
R-n1	95/8	6/5?	-	-	plough	Profile II	-
	95/4	7/6?	-	-	plough	Profile I	-
R-n2	95/7	6/5?	-	-	brown?	Profile II	Hord.
	95/3	7/6?	-	-	brown?	Profile I	Hord.
	96/3	7	-	-	brown	above ploughmarks	Hord.
	96/4	7	-	-	brown	above ploughmarks	Hord.
	96/8	8	-	-	brown	above ploughmarks	Hord.
	96/11	8	-	-	brown	below house "A"	Hord.
	96/16	9	-	-	brown	above ploughmarks	Hord.
	96/28	10	-	-	brown	below house "B"	Hord.
	96/32	10	-	-	brown	below house "B"	Hord.
R-n3	96/10	8	-	-	mixed	lowest layer house "A"	Hord.
	96/23	10	-	-	black	below house "B"	Hord.
	96/24	10	-	-	black	below house "B"	Hord.
	96/25	10	-	-	-	basis of small ditch	Hord.
	96/27	10	-	-	black	below house "B"	Hord.
	96/31	10	-	-	black	below house "B"	Hord.
R-n4	95/6	6/5?	-	-	loam	Profile II	Hord.
	95/2	7/6?	-	-	black	Profile I	Hord.
	96/15	9	IV	0.64–0.54	black	-	Hord.
	96/36	10/11	IV	0.64–0.54	black/brown	-	Hord.
R-n5	96/2	7	III + IV	-	black	-	Hord., Tr.aest.
	96/7	8	IV	0.64–0.54	black	above house "A"	Hord., Sec., Tr.aest.
	96/6	8	III	0.74–0.65	black	above house "A"	Hord., Sec.
	96/14	9	III	0.74–0.65	black	-	Hord., Sec.
	96/35	11	III	0.74–0.65	black	-	Hord., Sec.
R-n6	95/5	6/5?	-	-	black	Profile II	Sec., Hord., Tr.aest.
	95/1	7/6?	-	-	black	Profile I	Sec., Hord.
	96/1	7	I + II	-	black	-	Sec., Hord.
	96/5	8	II	0.84–0.75	black	above house "A"	Sec., Hord.
	96/13	9	II	0.84–0.75	black	-	Sec., Hord., Tr.aest.
	96/34	11	II	0.84–0.75	black	-	Sec., Hord., Tr.aest.
R-n7	96/12	9	I	above 0.85	black	-	Sec., Tr.aest.
	96/17	10	I	above 0.85	black	above house "B"	Sec., Tr.aest.
	96/18	10	II	0.84–0.75	black	above house "B"	Sec.
	96/19	10	III	0.74–0.65	black	above house "B"	Sec.
	96/20	10	IV	0.64–0.54	black	above house "B"	Sec., Tr.aest.
	96/33	11	I	above 0.85	black	-	Sec.
R-n8	96/9	8	-	-	black	above house "A"	Sec., Hord., Tr.aest.
	96/21	10	-	-	-	above house "B"	Sec., Hord., Tr.aest.
	96/26	10	-	-	-	above house "B"	Sec., Hord., Tr.aest.
	96/29	10	-	-	black	above house "B"	Sec., Hord., Tr.aest.
	96/30	10	-	-	black	west of house "B"	Sec., Hord., Tr.aest.
	96/22	10	-	-	-	niveau of house "B"	Sec., Hord., Tr.aest.

Table 18.2a Ryurik Gorodishche, profile of the northern terrace scarp east of the trench. Information on samples. Plant macrofossils. Abbreviation of species according to Table 18.1.

No.	Square	Layer	Culture Plant (charred)	Culture Plant (water-logged)
R-d1	28	1	Sec., Tr.aest.	-
	29	3	Sec., Tr.aest.	-
	30	3	Sec., Tr.aest.	-
	31	1	Sec., Tr.aest.	-
	33	2	Sec., Tr.aest.	-
	33	3	Sec., Tr.aest.	-
	35	3	Sec., Tr.aest.	-
	40	2	Sec., Tr.aest.	-
	41	2	Sec., Tr.aest.	-
	41	3	Sec., Tr.aest.	-
	42	2	Sec.	-
R-d2	26	1	Cerealia	-
	26	2b	Hord.	-
	27	2	Hord.	-
	31	2	Hord.	-
	31	2b	Hord.	-
	39	2b	Hord., Sec.	-
	40	3	Cerealia	-
R-d3	28	6	Hord.	Pan., Tr.dic., Hum., Can., Lin.
	28	7	Hord.	Pan., Tr.dic., Hum., Can.
	28	8	Hord, Pan.	Tr.dic., Hum.
	29	6	Hord.	Pan., Tr.dic., Hum., Can., Lin.
	29	7	-	Pan., Tr.dic., Hum., Can.
	29	8	Hord.	Pan., Tr.dic., Hum., Can.
	30	6	-	Pan., Tr.dic., Hum., Can., Lin.
	30	7	-	Pan., Tr.dic., Hum., Can., Lin.
	30	8	Hord.	Pan., Tr.dic., Hum., Can.
	32	6	Hord.	Pan., Hum.
	32	7	Hord.	Pan., Hum.
	33	6	Hord., Pan.	Pan., Hum., Lin.
	33	7	Pan.	Pan., Hum., Lin.
	34	6	-	Pan., Hum., Can., Lin.
	34	7	-	Pan., Tr.dic., Tr.sp., Hum., Can., Lin.
	34	8	Hord.	Pan., S, Tr.dic., Hum., Can., Lin.
	35	6	Hord., Pan.	Pan., Hum., Can., Lin.
	35	7	Hord.	Pan., Tr.dic., Hum., Can., Lin.
	39	6	Hord.	Pan., Tr.dic., Hum., Can., Lin.
	40	6	Hord., Pan.	Pan., Hum., Can., Lin.
	40	7	Pan.	Pan., Hum., Can.
	40	8	Hord.	Pan., Tr.dic., Hum.
	41	6	Hord., Pan.	Tr.dic., Hum., Can., Lin.

abbreviations:
Cerealia = not identifiable cere

Table 18.2b *Ryurik Gorodishche, trench. Information on samples. Plant macrofossils. Abbreviation of species according to Table 18.1 (continued on the next page).*

					legend
	41	7	Hord., Pan.	Pan., Hum., Lin.	Hord. = barley
	42	6	-	Pan., Tr.dic., Hum., Can., Lin.	Sec. = rye
	42	7	-	Pan., Tr.dic., Hum., Lin.	Tr.aest. = bread wheat
	43	6	Hord.	Pan., Tr.dic., Hum., Can., Lin.	Tr. dic. = emmer wheat
					Pan. = millet
R-d4	30	12	-	Pan., Hum.	Hum. = hop
	35	13	-	Pan., Hum.	Can. = hemp
	42	13	-	Pan., Hum.	Lin. = linseed/flax
	43	12	-	Pan., Hum.	
	48	12	-	Pan., Hum.	*layer:*
	53	11	-	Pan., Hum.	1 = +20–0 cm
	54	9	-	Pan., Hum., Can.	2 = 0--20 cm
	55	9	-	Pan., Hum., Can.	2b = 0--40 cm
	58	11	-	Pan., Hum.	3 = -20--40 cm
	54a	10	-	Pan., Hum.	4 = -40--60 cm
	55a	10	Hord.	Pan., Hum.	5 = -60--80 cm
					6 = -80--100cm
R-d5	58	1	Hord.	Hum.	7 = -100--120 cm
	58	3	-	Hum.	8 = -120--140 cm
	58	4	-	Pan., Hum., Lin.	9 = -140--160 cm
	58	5	Hord.	Pan., Hum., Can., Lin.	10 = -160--180 cm
	59	3	-	Hum.	11 = -180--200 cm
	59	4	-	Pan., Hum., Lin.	12 = -200--220 cm
	59	5	Hord.	Pan., Hum.	13 = -220--240 cm

at the site (Figure 18.5a). This stratum is covered by brown deposits rich in organic material (Figure 18.5b, b'), which are dated into the 9th century AD. An upper black layer rich in charcoal has an average height of 40 cm and is dated into the 10th century (Figure 18.5c, e, e'). Sterile loam separates the early medieval layers from the later and mixed deposits. At two places soil colour changes indicate the former existence of two houses, both founded on the lowest levels of the black cultural layer (Figure 18.5d, d'). House B was sunken in a small depression. From the material of the plough-marks no macro plant fossils are recorded. The density of charred plant remains was very low, in the brown layer as well as in the lowest black layers: less than 10 charred cereal grains per 10-litre soil sample compared to more than 20 in the upper samples. Barley is the dominant crop in all layers below the two houses (Table 18.IIIa on CD: sample R-n1-4). In the level of the house floors a change in the crop assemblage is visible; barley loses in importance (sample R-n5; 8) and is finally displaced by rye (Figure 18.5R-n6, 7) in the highest deposits.

Soil samples for archaeobotanical analysis were taken from several squares of the trench at the northern scarp, to a depth of two and a half metres (Table 18.2b). Because of archaeobotanical similarities the samples were summarized in five groups: two from the upper of the central part (sample R-d1) and eastern border (sample R-d2) of the trench, and three from the lower of the central part (sample R-d3), the bottom of the south-western edge of the excavated site (sample R-d4), and the bottom of the north-western edge (sample R-d5). The material from the higher levels (up to -40 cm) of the central parts of the trench can be paralleled with that of the black

No.	Lab.No.	Square	Century AD	Description of the layer	Description of structures	Culture plant (charred)
R-s1	95/2	11	10th	black	next to pit "A"	Hord., Tr.aest.
	95/3	11	10th	black	next to pit "A"	Hord., Tr.aest.
	95/4	12	10th	black	next to pit "A"	Hord., Tr.aest., Sec.
	95/5	9	-	sand	below the big timber	-
	95/9	9	10th	black	small sample material from a small	-
	95/10	13	-	black	pot	-
	95/11	13	10th	black	between timber	Hord., Sec.
	95/12	13	10th	black	between timber	Hord., Sec.
	95/13	13	10th	black	between timber	Hord.
	95/14	15	10th	black	-	Hord.
	96/1	7	-	black	-	Hord.
	96/2	15	-	brown	-	Hord., Tr.dic.
R-s2	93/1	7	10th–	mixed	small hole west of site I	Hord., Sec., Tr.aest., Tr.dic.
	93/2	7	10th–	mixed	small hole west of site I	Hord., Sec., Tr.aest., Tr.dic.
	93/3	7	10th–	brown/mixed	small hole west of site I	Tr.dic., Hord.
	95/1	11–14	13th/14th	mixed	younger pit "A"	Hord., Sec., Tr.aest.

Table 18.2c Ryurik Gorodishche, south of Siversovov Canal. Information on samples. Plant macrofossils. Abbreviation of species according to Table 18.1.

layers at the northern bank. Rye and bread wheat were the dominant crops (Table 18.IIIb on CD: sample R-d1). At the eastern border of the trench, plough-marks were exposed at a depth of approximately -40 cm; and again, the earliest layers in this sequence correspond botanically very well to the brown deposits found elsewhere at the site. In all these deposits only charred fruits and seeds have been preserved. In contrast, the deeper layers of the ditch provided excellent preservation conditions for wood and other organic remains. The permanently wet and consequently anaerobic deposits stopped the decay of organic material; plant remains have been preserved sub-fossil or water-logged. This offered a good chance to find different species of a variety of plants, such as hemp, flax, hop, fruits and berries, including strawberries, raspberries, blueberries, apples and pears. On the other hand, these conditions reduce the occurrence of the fragile, thin coats of the grains of cereals and pulses. Up to a depth of -140 cm numerous sub-fossil plant remains were discovered, mostly glume bases of emmer wheat, glumes of millet and nutlets of hemp *Cannabis sativus* and hop *Humulus lupulus,* and the seeds of linseed/flax *Linum usitatissimum* (sample R-d3).

Indicators of barley seem to be under-represented because the few charred grains are dominated by the large quantity of sub-fossil glumes of millet. But when the different preservation conditions are considered, average values of barley (20%), emmer (35%) and millet (39%) can be calculated. The diet of the former inhabitants of Gorodishche had been enriched by many collected berries, apples, pears and nuts. However, by means of the sub-fossil remains it is not possible to distinguish between wild and cultivated apples and pear.

At the bottom of the trench only some single glumes of millet were encountered, mixed in a seed collection of a more or less natural vegetation of high perennials that occur naturally in ditches (sample R-d4). Species such as burdock *Arctium* spec., double tooth *Bidens*-species, poison hemlock *Conium maculatum*, meadow sweet *Filipendula ulmaria*, celery-leaved crowfort *Ranunculus scelerathus*, yellow meadow rue *Thalictrum flavum* or great nettle *Urtica dioica* prefer nutrient-rich, fresh soils at the borders of ditches or floodplain forests. Hops are climbing plants of the borders of wet woods and could have been a natural element of the vegetation of Gorodishche. The glands of the female flowers are bitter and can be used for medical purposes (sedatives, narcotic) and help against all kinds of intestinal diseases. In later periods of the medieval era, hops became an important agent in brewing beer, but nothing is known about such a use here. Hemp could have been used for two purposes. The female plant produces nutlets containing fatty components, whereas mainly male plants are used for the production of fibre. Fibre-processing techniques are as time-consuming as those of flax. The choice, either hemp or flax, was determined by the kind of fabric (rope and rough cloth or fine linen, respectively) which was to be produced. Hemp has a Nordic distribution and grows up to northern polar regions in Archangelsk. There are some early pollen grains of the hop/hemp-type in sediments dated to the Bronze Age of a bog near Radbelik on Poozerie (Königsson 2001). In the Baltic area, the earliest finds of nutlets of hemp are known from medieval sites. So it is not until the Viking Period that we have indicators of the cultivation of hemp for fibre production purposes (Dörfler 1990).

On the southern bank of the Siversovov Canal only some small areas have been excavated, which yielded charred botanical remains from clearly dated black layers of the 10th century and mixed material of the 10th to 13th century (Table 18.2c). The fossil material of the 10th century deposits (R-s1) can be paralleled to that of the earliest medieval deposits (R-n2-4; R-d2; 3) on the opposite side of the canal. On both banks barley and rye occur in similar proportions (Table 18.IIIc on CD). The later crop assemblage (R-s2) has no equivalent from the northern and central part of Gorodishche. With its balanced proportions of all main cereals, it resembles that of Georgii.

THE PLANT ECONOMY OF RYURIK GORODISHCHE AND ITS AGRARIAN HINTERLAND

Summing up the development of the plant economy at Ryurik Gorodishche, the investigation of fossil plant remains tells the following story (Figure 18.6).

- The first evidence of agriculture is plough-marks, but nothing is known about the cultivated crops on the associated fields;
- The plant economy of the first Slavonic settlers is reflected by the charred plant remains from the brown layers and from the water-logged remnants of the lower levels of the ditch (R-nb). Barley is far and away the most frequent cereal followed by emmer, millet, bread wheat and rye in similar portions;
- By the time the two houses were built, the picture of the crop assemblage had already changed: both barley and rye occur in portions of 40% and at least from that time onwards rye can be regarded as a crop in its own right (R-nm) that has found a regular position within daily food;
- Finally, barley lost its former importance in the plant-based economy, for in the uppermost black deposits of the early medieval period its grains occur in small numbers only. Artefacts of the material culture of Scandinavians are frequent in these layers of the 10th century, the period of the constitution of medieval Russia, meaning that Slavs and Scandinavians lived side by side. For this period we can postulate two different vegetarian diets in Gorodishche. Within food waste of people living in the central part of the hillfort, rye and bread wheat dominated the other cereals (R-na). Usually wheat belonged to the rare cereals in settlements; such bread was a luxury and was baked for special occasions. Probably, the high amount of wheat grains found in certain deposits could be explained by the existence of an oven within the hillfort. Millet and spelted wheats were of nearly no importance. Unlike in the central part of Gorodishche, people outside, i.e. the southern, outer area of the fortified hillfort ("Vorburg-Siedlung") processed and consumed a balanced mixture of crops, as they did at Georgii. Next to rye and bread wheat, we found emmer, spelt, barley, oats and millet (R-s2). This may indicate the existence of different diets within the population of Ryurik Gorodishche which may be due, at least to some extent, to people of different social groups and origin.

Because of the topographic situation, the amount of arable land was limited in the immediate neighbourhood of the hillfort of Ryurik Gorodishche. The existence and prosperity of the Prince's Court here – and Yaroslav Court within Novgorod itself – depended on the potential of the hinterland of Poozerie to produce agrarian surplus. The flow of goods towards the central place, which Ryurik Gorodishche undoubtedly was at this time, could be stimulated by trade to and from local markets or by taxation (tribute). Concerning these aspects, different crop assemblages from Georgii or Gorodishche's southern part versus the central part of Gorodishche, reflect two different 'communities': producer versus consumer. A high variety of crop species might have diminished the negative consequences of a bad harvest. An assemblage dominated by one or two main crops, i.e. rye and bread wheat, even though the local markets offered a wealth of other cereals, demonstrates that the people of Gorodishche selected from their food supply.

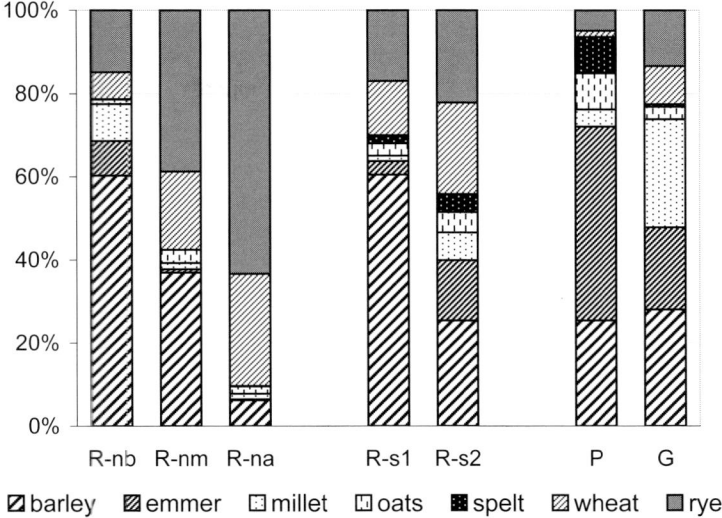

Figure 18.6 Novgorod hinterland. Proportions of crops in different sites and periods. Ryurik Gorodishche (R): R-nb = Northern terrace, lowest layer of 9th century; R-nm = Northern terrace, layer of the house foundations, 10th century; R-na = Northern terrace, upper black layers, 10th century; R-s1 = South of Siversovov Canal, 10th century; R-s2 = South of Siversovov Canal, 10th–13th century. P = Prost, 6th–9th century. G = Georgii, 9th/10th century.

ARCHAEOBOTANICAL INVESTIGATIONS IN THE REGION OF LAKE KUBENSKOYE

Exploitation of natural resources was the prevailing motor for establishing dwelling sites and rural settlements at the north-eastern margin of medieval Russia, some 650 km east of the region of Lake Ilmen. At the end of the first and the beginning of the second millennium AD Byeloozero became one of the nuclei of Russian colonisation in the outlands of the Vologda region (Figure 18.7). Since 1996 systematic excavations of two dwelling sites, Minino I and Minino VI, were carried out. Both sites were located at the western shore of Lake Kubenskoye separated from each other by the small river Dmitrovka. The habitation area of Minino I lay in a plain near the outflow of the river into Lake Kubenskoye at an elevation of not more than 2 m above the level of the lake. Minino VI lay a little more landwards on the opposite side and was protected against seasonal floods by a steep 6 m high bank (Makarov 2001). The ground slowly elevates towards the west and here suitable conditions for arable farming could be found. But even the low lands close to the lake had been under cultivation because plough marks, covered by medieval cultural layers, were found during the excavations at both Minino I and VI. Material culture dates the two dwelling sites to the 10th–13th century. At first, Minino I was settled in the second half of the 10th century and probably 100 years later people built dwelling houses on the opposite bank. Here,

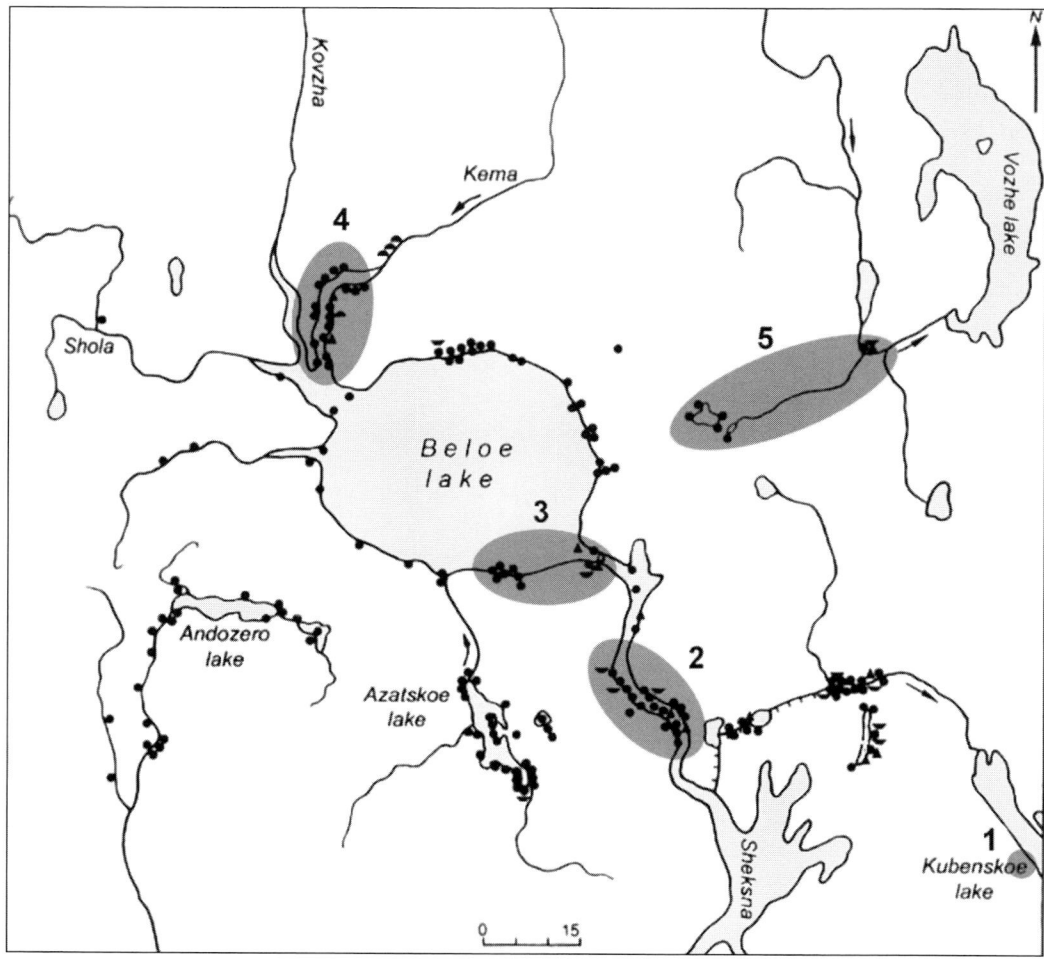

Figure 18.7 *Rural Russia in the North. The location of samples taken for analysis of macro plantfossils. 1 = Minino I and VI; 2 = Sheksna River region; 3 = southern Lake Byeloe region; 4 = lower Kema River region; 5 = sites Volok A, B and Pogostischtsche III, VI (Makarov 2000).*

traces of a longer lasting habitation were observed, but modern ploughing disturbed all archaeological structures except for medieval pits.

To study the plant economy of the people of Minino, soil samples were taken from undisturbed archaeological features, such as the medieval cultural layers in Minino I and pits in Minino VI. Kiryanova started the investigation of fossil plants and since 2002 these analyses were continued by the author. Detailed information about each analysed sample is given in Table 18.3. Samples with the Lab. No. k-1 to k-20 were analysed by Kiryanova, those with the Lab. No. a-1 to a-48 by Alsleben. The charred plant remains were washed out of the soil by simple flotation methods. The density of botanical findings was very low, only about 15 fragments of fruits or seeds per 10-litre substrat. Only one sample (k-15) yielded over 2000 grains of barley. The low density might be due to the fact that the medieval layers are covered by a very thin surface and so they were more or less exposed to destruction by erosion.

No.	Lab. No.	Year	Square/Feature	Layer	Volume (l)	Century AD
Minino I						
I	k-1	1996	М-33	3	50	XI
	k-3	1996	М-32	4	50	XI
	k-4	1997	М-35	2	50	XI–XII
	k-5	1997	К-34	2/3	55	XI–XII
	k-6	1997	М-34	3	50	XI–XII
	k-7	1997	М-35	3	15	XI–XII
	k-8	1997	П-11А	3	50	XI–XII
	k-9	1997	Р-11Г	3	-	XI–XII
II	k-10	1999	АА-28-В	-	25	2nd half XI–1st half XII
	a-1	2002	Ш-50-Б	3	50	2nd half XI–1st half XII
	a-2	2002	Э-0-Г	3	50	2nd half XI–1st half XII
	a-3	2002	Ы-50-Г	3	95	2nd half XI–1st half XII
	a-4	2002	Ц-0-Б	3	50	2nd half XI–1st half XII
	a-5	2002	Ы-50/51-Б/В	3	30	2nd half XI–1st half XII
	a-6	2002	Щ-50-Б	4	50	2nd half XI–1st half XII
	a-7	2002	Ы-51-АБ	4	-	2nd half XI–1st half XII
	a-8	2002	Щ-50-Г	4	50	2nd half XI–1st half XII
	a-9	2002	Ш-0-Г	4	200	2nd half XI–1st half XII
III	a-10	2002	Х-51-А	2	50	XII
	a-11	2002	Ы-50-В	2	60	XII
	a-12	2002	Э-50-Б	2	50	XII
	a-13	2002	Ц-51-Г	2	50	XII
IV	a-14	2002	Ч-50-В	2	50	XII–1st half XIII ?
	a-15	2002	Ы-51-Г	2	50	XII–1st half XIII ?
	a-16	2002	pit 3	5	100	XII–1st half XIII ?
V	k-11	1999	Ы-2-Г	2	25	2nd half XII–1st half XIII
	k-12	1999	Ш-2	2	25	2nd half XII–1st half XIII
	k-13	1999	Ы-1	-	25	2nd half XII–1st half XIII
	k-14	1999	Щ-1/2-Г/А	-	50	2nd half XII–1st half XIII
	k-15	1999	Ш-1-В	-	21	2nd half XII–1st half XIII
	k-16	1999	Ы-0/1-Г	3	32	2nd half XII–1st half XIII
	k-17	1999	Щ-0-Б/В	-	50	2nd half XII–1st half XIII
	k-18	1999	Ш-2	5	25	2nd half XII–1st half XIII
	k-19	1999	АА-28-Б/В	2	25	2nd half XII–1st half XIII

Table 18.3 Minino I, VI, II. Information on samples. Lab.No. (k-1 to k-20) analysed by N. A. Kiryanova; Lab.No. (a-1 to a-48) analysed by A. Alsleben (continued over the page).

	k-20	1999	Я-27/28-Б/В	3	30	2nd half XII–1st half XIII

Minino VI

	Lab.No.	Year	Square/Feature		Volume	Century AD
VI	a-20	2001	pit 21		49	XI ?
	a-21	2001	pit 24		50	XI ?
	a-22	2001	pit 25, АГ-47 – А/Г		50	XI–1st half XII
	a-23	2001	pit 53		50	XI–XII
	a-24	2001	pit 54		19	XI–XII
	a-25	2001	pit 55		50	XI–XII
	a-26	2003	pit 27, -112-113/-116		50	2nd half XI–1st half XII
	a-27	2003	pit 125, -100/-110	34		2nd half XI–1st half XII
	a-28	2003	pit 126, -112/-122	44		2nd half XI–XII
	a-29	2003	pit 148, -117/-127	15		2nd half XI–1st half XII
VII	a-30	2003	pit 135, -120/-135	51		XII
	a-31	2001	pit 29		50	XII ?
	a-32	2003	pit 145, -99/-120		48	2nd half XI–XIII
	a-33	2003	pit 130, -116/-133	45		2nd half XI–XIII
	a-34	2001	pit 12		76	XII–XIII
	a-35	2001	pit 12		54	XII–XIII

No.	Lab.No.	Year	Square/Feature		Volume (l)	Century AD
VII	a-36	2001	pit 43		50	XII–XIII
	a-37	2001	pit 17		70	2nd half XII–XIII
	a-38	2001	pit 23		50	2nd half XII–XIII
	a-39	2001	pit 32		66	2nd half XII–XIII
	a-40	2003	pit 129, -111/-122	30		2nd half XII–XIII
	a-41	2003	pit 146, -110/-111	36		2nd half XII–XIII

Minino II

	a-42	2003	pit 62		15	end X–XIII
	a-43	2003	pit 63		50	end X–XI
	a-44	2003	pit 48a		50	end X–XI
	a-45	2002	pit 2, Шурф 5		40	2nd half XII–XIV
	a-46	2002	pit 30		30	-
	a-47	2002	pit 31		30	-
	a-48	2002	pit 24		100	-

The results of the analysis of fossil plant remains are summarized in Table 18.IVa, b (on CD). Although the assemblages show slight differences, both sites give a similar picture of vegetarian food consumption. The remains of pulses usually occur in low numbers from archaeological contexts, so it may be suggested from even single finds of peas *Pisum sativum* and beans *Vicia faba* that these are definite proof for their cultivation at Minino. Climatic conditions in the Vologda region exclude the cultivation of lentils *Lens culinaris* but peas and beans cause no problems because their young plants are not sensitive to chilling temperatures. The chance of being charred is greater for parts of some of the other used plants (cultivated or collected), such as oil and fibre plants or fruits and nuts. That is why the latter group is less often preserved in the archaeological deposits of settlements on dry soils.

Among the cultivated plants, cereals are most often found, reaching values of 50% of the seed collections in Minino I and VI. Barley and rye were the main crops, nearly equal in numbers, which clearly indicates that rye was already a crop in its own right and no longer a tolerated weed in the crop fields. Both cereals appear regularly in all samples. Barley was most likely used to prepare all kinds of gruel or soups. Because of its high content of gluten, rye provides a suitable flour to bake bread that could have been eaten on its own or crumbled into soups. Oats are also found frequently, but in less numbers. Comparing the two sites, oats obviously were more often used in Minino I where oat grains seem to predominate in squares III / Щ / Ы -50/51 (sample: a-3, a-8, a-9). Probably part of a dwelling house with an oven covered these squares. Grains of bread wheat were rarely detected in either settlement.

As Table 18.IVa, b (on CD) shows, single samples are too poor in cereal grains to allow the determination of specific distribution patterns within the habitation area. Only one sample (k-15; square III-1-B) is exceptional because of its high concentration of grains. It can be regarded as a store place for barley, accidentally mixed with a portion of rye (16%) and modest amounts of oats and bread wheat. As well as grains, chaff was also sometimes encountered. It is mainly the rachis fragments of free-threshing rye which were very well preserved. In Minino I there is only one sample (a-10) which is rich in both chaff and the remains of wild species. This place (square X-51-A) is a little bit distant from the dwelling house and might have been a place for threshing, coarse sieving or winnowing. In Minino VI however, the proportion of rachis fragments of rye reaches a value of 6.8% of the cereals, and chaff remains were regularly dispersed in many of the pits. The sample from Minino I can be regarded as a trace of on-site activity, whereas the plant material from Minino VI reflects on-site deposition.

The medieval cemetery, Minino II, was located directly west of the settlement of Minino I. The graves were partly destroyed by several pits dated to the 10th to 11th, 13th or 14th century. All medieval structures in turn, cut into a mesolithic site. So, because of these mixed deposits, it is impossible to assign the fossil botanical material to a certain period. None of the pits contained remains of cultivated plants, but three of them (pit 2; 48a; 63) were rich in berries, partly or totally charred (Table 18.4). Except some specimens of strawberry *Fragaria vesca* and fragments of needles of spruce *Picea* spec., the botanical material was remarkable because of its concentration of fruit from raspberry *Rubus idaeus*. Raspberries are an element of the natural vegetation in this

	Minino I						Minino VI		Minino II
Sample group, No.	I	II	III	IV	V	k-15	VI	VII	VIII
Century AD.	XI–XII	XI–XII	XII	XII–XIII	XII–XIII		XI–XII	XI–XIII	X–XIV
Volume (1)	37	625	200	200	290	21	412	626	315
Number of samples	9	10	4	3	9	1	10	12	7
CEREALS	n%	n%	n%	n%	n%	n	n%	n%	n
Hordeum vulgare vulgare	75.8	34.0	34.9	33.6	66.0	2621	42.4	35.1	.
Hordeum vulgare, rf.	.	.	0.5	.	.	.	0.5	0.7	.
Secale cereale	17.0	26.1	21.9	45.5	28.6	519	23.2	24.7	.
Secale cereale, rf.	.	.	8.3	.	.	.	4.5	6.3	.
Avena spec.	4.4	22.1	13.5	.	2.5	12	3.0	6.5	1
Triticum aestivum s.l.	2.7	0.9	2.1	.	2.9	11	1.0	1.3	.
Triticum dicoccum	.	.	.	.	.	.	.	0.4	.
Cerealia indet.	.	16.9	18.8	20.9	.	.	25.3	25.1	1
Sum of cereals = 100%	364	456	192	110	920	3163	198	542	2
USED PLANTS	n	n	n	n	n	n	n	n	n
Pisum sativum	4	2	1	.	.	.	1	6	5
Vicia faba	.	.	.	2	.	.	.	1	.
Leguminosae sativae indet.	.	1	3	1	.	.	1	3	.
cf. Cannabis sativa	.	2	.	.	.	.	.	1	.
cf. Linum usitatissimum	1	.	1	.	.	.	.	2	.
Rubus idaeus	1	1	10	.	.	.	13	20	313
Fragaria vesca	6	2	.	.	.	.	3	4	4
Pyrus/Malus	.	.	.	.	.	.	.	.	22
Prunus spec.	.	.	.	.	.	.	1	.	.

Table 18.4 Minino. *Charred remains of cultivated plants. Absolute (n) and relative (n%) numbers of summarized groups of samples according to Table 18.3; rf. = rachis fragment; s.l. = sensu latu; cf. = confer.*

region; they grow on clearings or alongside edges of woods preferring fresh humus soils. It is possible, though unlikely, that fruits were thrown into the fire intentionally. In this case it would reflect a kind of funeral rite, but this could not be supported by findings of any other cultivated plants or those containing aromatic essences. It seems to be more likely that they accidentally burnt and then somehow were preserved in the pits.

THE PLANT ECONOMY OF MININO AND NORTHERN RURAL RUSSIA

In Table 18.4 results concerning crops, i.e. the cereals, are summarized in seven groups (No. I – VII) and ordered chronologically. Because the archaeological structures date from more than one century and are overlapping in time ranges, samples could only be divided into an older group (10th to 11th century) and a slightly younger group (11th/12th to 13th century). Therefore differences in the results do not reflect more than a general trend of agricultural development. Regarding crop proportions, the most obvious difference is seen between the material analysed by the two botanists. Whereas in the sample groups No. II–IV and VI and VII the main crops barley and rye appeared in more or less equal numbers, Kiryanova noticed a clear dominance of barley (No. I; V), even if the barley storage sample (k-15) is removed from the calculation. Even if not perfectly preserved, the identification of rye and barley is not problematic; therefore differences in the results are not artificial. That means, charred grains were not regularly dispersed within the dwelling site. The data base is too small to see any kind of intentional differentiation within the deposits which might explain why samples more rich in barley were found in an area closer to the river Dmitrovka. But also, in case the food waste had been deposited at random, this example shows that reliable results can only be obtained by sampling a bigger area of the dwelling sites.

Chronologically comparing the fossil material from Minino, there is no distinct change visible in arable farming, because the picture given by the archaeobotanical data is too diverse. Even on the assumption that Minino VI is generally younger than Minino I and people moved from the northern riverside to the southern bank, this did not go along with a break in arable farming. Traditional cultivation of barley was not replaced by rye in the medieval period which means that the first settlers appear not to have known the potential of domesticated rye, especially with regard to arable farming in these latitudes. We observe at most a tendency towards a slight increase in the use of rye; not at barley's expense, but at that of oats. Whereas the values for barley fluctuate over time, those of oats decline over time, starting with proportions of over 20% in the 11th–12th century and reaching a level of 2% in the 12th–13th century. That probably points to an impoverishment of the plant economy, which was eventually based on two crops only (namely barley and rye).

The archaeobotanical results from Minino show similarities to those of other

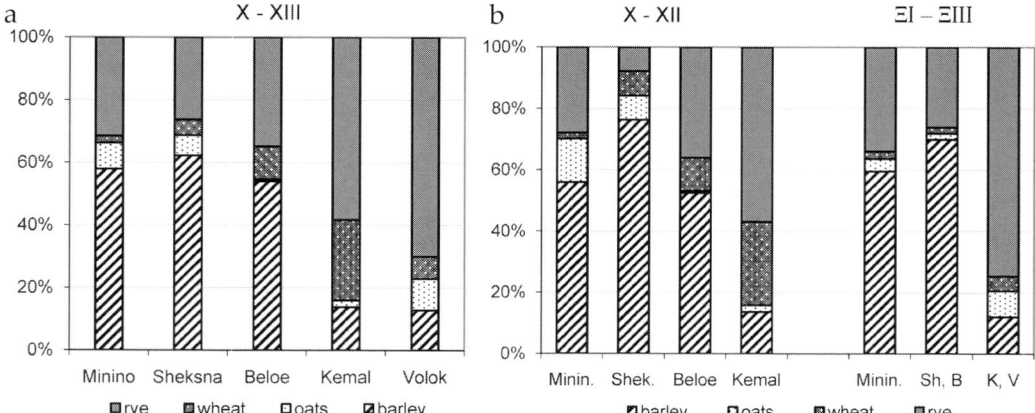

Figure 18.8 *Rural Russia in the North. Proportions of four main crops. Geographical (Figure 18.8a) and chronological (Figure 18.8b) grouping of 19 dwelling sites. Columns left to right. Figure 18.8a: Minino I and VI; Sheksna River region; Southern Lake Byeloe region; Lower Kema River region; sites Volok A, B and Pogostischtsche III, VI. Figure 18.8b: Minino I and VI; Sheksna River region; Southern Lake Byeloe region; Lower Kema River region; Minino I and VI; Sheksna River/Lake Byeloe region; Lower Kema River region/sites Volok A, B and Pogostischtsche III, VI.*

regions in the north of medieval Russia (Makarov *et al.* 1998). When considering the crop assemblages from medieval settlements located in the Sheksna river region, the southern Lake Byeloe region, the lower Kema region and Volok-Pogastishche, even this enlarged data base does not reflect any development in agriculture, i.e. a change from barley to rye dominance. But as illustrated in Figure 18.8a, the columns allow a geographical differentiation. On the one hand there is a distinct gradient between cultivation of barley in the south and of rye in the north, on the other hand the estimated proportions of bread wheat and oats indicate a gradient between central and peripheral places. It seems as if people in the Kubenskoye-Sheksna region and in Volok cultivated oats used for human consumption or as high-quality fodder for animals. In the central places of Lake Byeloe and on the lower Kema River the emphasis was on bread wheat reaching values above 10% (Lake Byeloe) and 25% (lower Kema River). A possible explanation for this result could be that, in general, bread wheat was a rare or even luxury commodity, because in these high latitudes in particular the longer (and colder) winter season resulted in a shorter growing period, and excluded the economic cultivation of the more thermophilic crops, such as millet and all the wheat species. But it might be possible that bread wheat was sold at local markets of central places, next to other agricultural products. In the end of first or beginning of the second millennium AD the process of agglomeration increased strongly in the areas of Lake Byeloe and the lower Kema River (Makarov 2000) and this surely was accompanied by the lively exchange of goods in these areas.

During the early stages of medieval farming practices, this picture is especially distinct (Figure 18.8b, left columns). But during the following period the variability in arable farming decreased in all parts of what may be termed the marginal lands of northern Russia. Only those crops were kept in cultivation which guaranteed agricultural success. Compared to wheat and oats, barley is less sensitive to temperature and is able to finish its growing period during the short northern Russian summer. Barley requires nutrient-rich and deeply grounded soils which are rare in an area of mainly damp and seasonally wet podsolic soils, whereas rye can grow even on the poorer sandy soils. The tolerance to predominantly climatic and edaphic conditions made barley and rye the most successful crops. The impoverishment of arable farming towards the end of this period of northern internal colonisation might be due to a change in agricultural or even economical structures. Possibly, the environmental resources could not support varied arable farming any longer, and therefore a shift to a subsistence-based economy was accompanied by a shift in land use: formerly agglomerated, large villages disappeared and in their place developed small hamlets dispersed within the same territory.

Arable farming

Remains of synanthropic species of flora (i.e. weeds that were brought into the settlement together with the harvest and ruderal plants also adapted to unstable habitats growing in or close by habitation areas) almost always dominate the wild plant assemblages in archaeobotanical material, especially when they originate from dry soils, which allow only charred preservation of fruits and seeds. Deposits under wet and anaerobic conditions reveal a rich natural flora comprising species which prefer damp habitats such as wetlands, bogs or ditches. This is seen by the species list from the excavation at Ryurik Gorodishche. To study former arable farming these synanthropic species are of special interest. Their successful growth in the countryside depends on their specific requirements in terms of climatic and edaphic conditions and their resistance to mechanical disturbance. On a local level the latter two factors have the main effect on distribution patterns. The fossil weed species from all northwest Russian sites studied in this paper, belong to very common wild plants widely spread in the synanthropic sphere (Table 18.5). Indigenious species growing on the water's edge such as *Chenopodium album*, *Polygonum persicaria*, *P. lapathifolium* or in riverine forests such as *Galium aparine* belong to the most successful weeds in the fields (based on high values of number and constancy). From their natural habitats they spread into nearby fields or settlement areas. *Polygonum convolvolus* is the only frequent species which is not a natural element of northern Russia and occurs only in places disturbed by man. Unfortunately a big part of the wild plant remains were not identifiable to species level. Among those, the grass family (Poaceae, *Bromus*, *Lolium*) and sedges (Cyperaceae, *Carex*, *Schoenoplectus*) reach a relatively big portion, and that means up to one third of all weeds were perennials. The occurrence of sedges is surely due to the close proximity of settlements and wetlands. But it also shows that

Site	Prost	Georgii	Ryurik G.	Ryurik G.	Minino	Novgorod later than 13th			Giekau	Starigard	Wandelwitz
Century AD.	6th-9th	9th/10th	9th	10th	11th/13th	rye	barley	oats	8th/9th	10th/11th	11th/12th
Main cereal	emmer barley	(-)	barley	rye	barley rye				barley	rye	bread wheat
RUDERAL PLANTS											
Chenopodium album	37.0	46.4	8.9	22.2	29.2	6.0	55.7	9.1	21.9	+	+
Polygonum convolvulus	1.7	2.8	+	0.9	2.4	0.9	15.0	4.4	2.3	+	+
Galium spurium / spec.	8.4	3.0	3.9	37.9	10.2	0.5	0.9	26.0	9.1	13.0	2.1
Polygonum lapathifolium	1.1	0.9	+	+	0.9	+	4.2	31.4	14.4	+	.
Silene spec.	11.9	7.9	+	+	5.7	+	6.2	.	.	r	.
Vicia-type	2.3	0.5	+	+	1.8	+	.	1.3	3.8	2.2	1.3
Polygonum persicaria-type	1.1	2.7	+	+	+	0.5	.	.	3	+	r
Poa annua	1.9	1.2	2.0	+	0.6	7.6	.	.	8.3	+	+
Polygonum aviculare	2.8	2.2	+	+	+	.	+	+	1.3	r	.
Brassica nigra / campestris	.	.	.	+	+	1.1	14.0	0.6	.	r	.
Neslia paniculata	.	.	.	.	.	.	+	.	+	r	.
Lolium temulentum	.	.	.	.	.	.	.	+	.	.	.
PLANTS IN FIELDS OF WINTER CROPS											
Apera spica-venti	.	.	.	.	.	65.8	.	.	.	.	.
Bromus secalinus /spec.	r	.	.	+	+	7.2	.	+	1	12.5	32.9
Lolium spec, small-seeded	+	.	.	.	0.6	1.7	+	0.7	1	.	0.5
Rhinanthus spec.	.	.	.	.	.	1.6	.	.	.	.	.
Lapsana communis	+	.	.	.	+	0.7	.	+	.	r	.
Poaceae	.	.	.	.	5.6	+	.	1.1	2.8	+	.
Spergula arvensis	0.9	+	+	+	+	2.2	+	3.1	1.3	r	.
Rumex acetosella	.	.	.	+	1.3	1.5	.	+	1.8	r	+
Agrostemma githago	.	.	.	.	.	+	+	+	8.8	68.0	56.8
Centaurea cyanua	.	.	.	.	.	.	.	r	.	+	.
Sherardia arvensis	.	.	.	.	.	.	.	.	.	r	.
Consolida regalis	.	.	.	.	.	.	.	.	.	+	.

XEROPHYLITIC PLANTS											
Echinochloa crus-galli	0.7	7.1	0.9	+	+	.	.	.	+	r	.
Solanum nigrum	0.9	1.5	+	+	.	.	.	.	.	r	.
Hyoscyamus niger	10.4	+	.	+	.	.	.	.	.	.	.
Setaria pumila	+	1.1	+	r	.	.	.	+	.	.	.
Setaria viridis /spec.	+	+	.	.	.	.	0.7	+	.	r	.
total sum of wild species	2817	2054	1270	4521	1415	3247	3269	1369	397	21603	1598

Table 18.5 Settlements of the early and later Slavonic period in Northwest Russia and Eastern Holstein, Germany. Selection of hemerophilic species in archaeobotanical assemblages. Relative numbers of the identified weeds: + = (0.5% > + < 0.1%); r = less than 0.1%. Starigard is published by H. Kroll and U. Willerding (2004); Wandelwitz by Alsleben (1998)

perennials could easily survive in the fields and this again might indicate that fields were still young and not deeply grounded by permanent tillage.

When comparing the weed flora of the two regions at least one difference is significant: the presence of xerophytic species, which indicate climatic conditions favourable for the cultivation of wheat and millet in the region of Lake Ilmen. In Minino, the growing season is too short: millet needs only 70 days from germination to maturity but has to be sown in warm soils; wheat requires 95 to 130 days. Soil temperatures (5–7°C) during the first 3–4 weeks in spring are decisive for the development of the vegetative plant parts and have positive effects on the yield. In the northern margins these temperatures are not reached before April or even May, too late for the economic cultivation of wheat. Contrary to west European settlements of the early medieval period, none of the specialist weeds sensitive to soil or the rhythm of ploughing were found in the Russian material. There were two species, corn-cockle *Agrostemma githago* and rye-brome *Bromus secalinus,* which contaminated the fields of the winter crops to a high extent as for example at Starigard/Oldenburg (Kroll and Willerding 2004) and Wandelwitz (Alsleben 1998), both settlements that date into the late Slavonic period in Eastern Holstein, Germany. In all the sites at Lake Ilmen and Lake Kubenskoye corn-cockle was not be identified, neither with rye nor with other cereals (Table 18.5). According to a compilation of Kiryanova (1992), this is also true for large grain stores of rye from most of the medieval settlements in the northwest Russian plain north of the main watershed (that is, north of the Volga). Southwest of it, corn-cockle occurred quite frequently together with rye. This means that corn-cockle is not an indicator of winter cultivation in the northern regions.

So, did Slavonic agriculture achieve a rotary-field-system with rye as the most suitable winter crop? Kiryanov (1959) studied large charred grain assemblages and found a significant difference in the set of weed species associated with rye, barley/oats, and wheat. He confirmed *Bromus secalinus, Apera spica-venti, Lapsana communis, Centaurea cyanus* to be specific to autumn-sown rye. The author's own analyses of samples from the Troitsky excavations in Novgorod show that fossil rye, barley, or oat staples differed in their associated weed species, with an emphasis on grass species in rye (Table 18.5). Interestingly, Linkola (1916) identified a similar set of plants when he studied the weed flora of the rye fields in the region north of Lake Ladoga. Here, they stood for a 10-to-15-year-rhythm of shifting-cultivation: a short phase of running was followed by long periods of wasteland grassland and reforestation. Hence, there are wild plants which can be used as an indicator of autumn-sown crops. But although some of these species appear in the botanical material of Prost, Georgii, Ryurik Gorodishche and Minino, they are not strongly associated to samples rich in rye. In consequence, plant macrofossils do not indicate winter-cultivation in early medieval Russia. That is striking, because climatic requirements of rye are low: it survives ice-scorching and heavy freezing in winter in cases where the seedlings are already well developed, but it is sensitive to night frosts in summer until its grains harden in July/August and it is severely threatened by snow moulds *Fusarium nivale*. As the snow melts, these fungi damage young plants, which often happens in regions with mild winters when snow covered unfrozen ground. High yields are expected when – in autumn – the period between germination and the development of minor shoots is long (about 150 days) and the following period of stalk growing – in spring – quite short (Brouwer 1972). Depending on the local climatic conditions, winter damages might be severe and all this made the cultivation of rye rather risk-prone. Summer cultivation of rye is less risky, but also less profitable.

Another consequence of persisting with traditional arable farming at the beginning of "Slavonic Landnahme" in northwestern Russia may have affected the whole economic system as it adjusted to the cultivation of summer crops. Livestock had to be kept away from the fields, hitherto only during the growing period in spring and summer. For the rest of the year the cattle could freely graze. But within a rotary-field-system, livestock had to be fenced in or at least kept under control. It might have been necessary to stable cattle over the winter and this consequently brought with it the need for providing fodder. Finally, a new agricultural system has implications that may lead to changes in communal organisation. Questions to do with land ownership and property rights may be affected when a closer rotation of crops reduces the availability of 'waste' or common land. All these related facts would help to explain why it took some time for people to learn how to handle the cultivation of winter crops and to reorganize their economic life accordingly. It was not until that moment that rye was able to achieve its position as a staple crop in both regions.

THE DEVELOPMENT OF AGRICULTURE IN NORTHERN RUSSIA

According to the Primary Russian Chronicle, the northern marginal territory was inhabited by the Ves (a Finno-Ugrian people) when the first Slavonic settlers penetrated the country in the early medieval period. The rich material culture of Finno-Ugrian design was found in the grave yards but the location of their dwelling sites are presently unknown to us. In the regions south of Lake Onega Finno-Ugrian culture lived on until the beginning of the 11th century: Finno-Ugrians and Slavs, both groups formed the population of Minino and other settlements in this region. Around Lake Ilmen, the assimilation of Finno-Ugrians happened earlier, in the second half of the first millennium AD, when Slavonic people settled first on the sandy moraines of the last Valdai glaciation. Their culture is characterized by long burial mounds and shifting cultivation, but again their dwelling sites are less well known. The following people of the *sopki*-culture (with their round and steep burial mounds) settled at the border of the moraines and alongside the high river terraces, as the discoveries of plough-marks of an one-shoed-ard demonstrate. These people established fortified settlements and were able to cultivate the more nutrient-rich and heavy soils of the plains. The first traces of permanent habitation are connected with the appearance of Slavonic agriculture-orientated tribes and from this period onwards

Period	Rom.Iron A.	Early Medieval			Medieval	appearance of the Slavs → constitution of Ancient Rus'			
Date / century	3rd - 5th	700-900 AD	1000 AD	9th-12th	1100-1300 AD	5th - 9th	5th - 9th	9th / 10th	10th - 13th
Author	*Aalto 1982*	*Onnela et al. 1996*	*Matiskainen 1984*	*Lempiäinen 1992*	*Lempiäinen 1995*	*Kirijanova 1992*	*Kirijanova 1992*	*Aalto et al. 1997*	*Kirijanova 1992*
Place / region	SW-Finland	SW-Finland	SW-Finland	S-Finland	Karelia (Rus')	NW-Russia	NW-Russia	NW-Russia	NW-Russia
Location	Katamajäki	Lieto	Karjaa	Varikkoniemi	Käkisalmi	-	Staraya Ladoga	Staraya Ladoga	-
Sum of cereals	235	8408	178	-	75	-	-	-	>1.000.000
CEREALS									
Barley	++	+++	+++	+++	++	+++	+	+++	++
Wheat	+	+	++	+	+	+++	++	-	++
Emmer	+	-	-	-	-	+++	+++	++	-
Rye	-	++	+	++	++	+	+	+	+++
Oats	+	+	+	+	++	+	+	++	+
Millet	-	-	-	-	++	++	+	++++	+
PULSES									
Bean	-	-	-	-	-	++	++	-	+
Pea	-	+	-	+	-	++	++	-	+++
Lens	-	-	-	-	-	-	-	-	+
Vetch	+	-	-	-	-	+	-	-	-
Pulses, not identified	+	-	-	-	-	-	-	-	-
USED PLANTS									
Hemp	-	-	-	+	+	+	+	+	++
Flax	+	-	-	-	++	+	-	+	+
Hop	-	-	+	+	+	-	-	+	-

Table 18.6 Northern Europe. Compilation of crop plants from dwelling sites in southern Finland and north-western Russia. Frequencies (++++ = very frequent to + = present) in relation to each group of cultivated plants.

the plant economy can be studied by means of macrofossil remains. To understand the agricultural background and its development we have to focus on localities in South-Finland, even though the archaeobotanical literature is not very rich (Table 18.6). Nevertheless, all these studies show that the range of crops was not large in southern Finland; it was mainly based on barley and small amounts of oats and wheat (bread wheat and emmer wheat are not always differentiated in the publications). It was not before the beginning of the second millennium AD that variability was brought into the plant diet. The studies of macrofossils were underlined by the results of pollen analyses in the northern shoreline of Lake Onega and in the South-Finnish boreal zone (Vuorela *et al.* 2001). Permanent habitation and the beginning of arable farming started not before the middle of the 13th century at Lake Onega and around 200 years later in the adjacent western forests.

Compared with the monotonous crop assemblages in Finland, agriculture was put on a broader base in north-west Russia (Table 18.6). A larger variety of cereals and pulses were at the people's disposal and next to barley, farmers cultivated mainly bread wheat and emmer wheat, beans and peas, but also oats, rye and millet. While evidence for the early use of millet and rye is rare, from the 10th century both species became important crops in Russian settlements. In Staraya Ladoga excellent preservation conditions provided large amounts of water-logged millet glumes, which were underrepresented in the charred plant material of other pre-urban centres. It was the slightly more continental climate which favoured especially the cultivation of millet in the Baltic part of Russia. Farming on permanent fields was introduced in the Vologda-District much earlier than in Karelia, Finland. Already in the 10th century noticeable human impact may be seen in the palynological results from sites on the western shore of Lake Kubenskoye (Spiridonova and Aleshinskaya, this volume). It seems that in the early medieval period the Vologda-Byeloozero region forms a connecting link between the Finno-Scandinavian north and the Slavonic south-west. The continuation of the cultivation of barley as a main crop can be regarded as continuity of traditional Finno-Ugrian farming. The introduction of rye as a new cultural plant represents the Slavonic element in the agriculture of northern rural Russia.

In pollen diagrams of the Novgorod region (Königsson *et al.* 1997; Spiridonova and Aleshinskaya, this volume) the pollen curves for cereals and for other species of the synanthropic flora became continuous by the 8th/9th century, indicating the opening of the landscape and different land-use processes. Whereas the region at Lake Ilmen benefits from a moderate continental climate facilitating the cultivation of many different crops, the cold, long winter limits agricultural possibilities in the north-east. Many crops such as millet, the wheats, and oats are reaching the north-eastern borders of their distribution. Nevertheless, an economy based on subsistence enabled people to live in the Lake Byeloe-Kubenskoye region. In contrast, environmental factors of the Lake Ilmen region allowed an advanced agricultural system, which made surplus production possible and became the basis for the development of a powerful centre at a strategic point on the river Volkhov.

Acknowledgements

This study was part of a 10-year project "Starigard/Oldenburg-Wolin-Novgorod" initiated by Prof. Michael Mueller-Wille and financed by the Academy of Science and Literature in Mainz, Germany. In 2001 Prof. Mark Brisbane invited the author to take part in the European INTAS Project 2000-154. During ten years of fieldwork in Russia I received help from many colleagues in both Novgorod and Minino. I want to thank in particular Prof. Evgenij Nosov and all the members of the Novgorod-Ryurik Gorodishche expedition and Dr. Nikolaj Makarov and colleagues from the Minino-expedition for many stimulating discussions and practical support in the field. Not least I enjoyed the scientific exchange of ideas with Michael Monk in Novgorod and Helmut Kroll in Kiel.

Note

1   Differences, concerning relative numbers of cereals from tables and column diagrams are due to the portion of unidentified cereals. In all sites up to 30% of the cereals could not be assigned to either rye *Secale cereale*, barley *Hordeum vulgare*, bread wheat *Triticum aestivum* or oats *Avena* spec. But it is assumed that within the "Cerealia indet." these four species are present in similar proportions to that seen in the identified assemblages.

FROM *ALCES* TO ZANDER: A SUMMARY OF THE ZOOARCHAEOLOGICAL EVIDENCE FROM NOVGOROD, GORODISHCHE AND MININO

M. Maltby

INTRODUCTION

History and nature of zooarchaeological studies in Novgorod

Animal bones survive exceptionally well in the anaerobic levels in Novgorod. However, the potential of the information obtainable from the millions of animal bones that have been excavated in various areas of the medieval town has largely been ignored. There has been no systematic retrieval of animal bones throughout the decades of archaeological investigation. Some bones were retained for analysis in the 1950s, forming part of a comparative survey of animal remains from various Russian towns by Tsalkin (1956). This work was typical of archaeological bone reports of that era, being largely concerned with zoological issues, particularly the sizes of the animals. It did, however, also provide some basic quantification of the relative abundance of mammalian species. A similar survey of the types of fish bones found was carried out by Sychevskaya (1965). This was based on the study of about 1,000 fish bones and scales from the Nerevsky site. However, this appears to have been the limit of zooarchaeological analysis prior to the early 1990s. Although bone and antler artefacts were retained and recorded, other animal bones were discarded. The absence of zooarchaeologists associated with the excavations and the major logistical problems regarding the storage of bones were the main reasons for this.

The INTAS collaboration provided funding to carry out an assessment of the potential of animal bones studies in Novgorod and sites in its hinterland and also provided resources to set up a reference collection and basic training in zooarchaeology for Russian colleagues. Although the project focussed on the potential of the resource, particularly in relation to the sampling and analysis of bones from the town itself, rather than attempting to provide definitive studies, substantial amounts of data were collected and analysed and it is a summary of these results that is presented here.

Assemblages

The bulk of material assessed from the town of Novgorod was derived from the Troitsky excavations that were carried out during the 1990s. In particular, we were able to obtain samples of hand-collected bones throughout a substantial part of the archaeological layers from properties on Site XI and the lowest spits of Site X together with some material from the lower spits of Site IX. This provided a sample of over 58,000 mammal bones, of which over 34,000 were identified to species and summarily recorded. In addition, about 4,200 bird and over 1,200 fish bones were examined. It was clear from our site visits that hand-retrieval was unlikely to be effective enough to provide an accurate reflection of the fish bone assemblage in particular and so a small wet-sieving experiment was carried out, producing a sample of over 6,100 fragments that were dominated by fish bones. A small amount of material was also obtained from the Fedorovsky site.

It was also possible to examine faunal samples from a number of recent excavations from sites in the immediate hinterland of Novgorod. Assemblages from 9th and 10th century deposits from Gorodishche included material collected by hand and from sieves. Combining material from all the assemblages studied, over 10,700 mammal bone fragments were recorded in full, including over 4,400 identified to species. In addition, over 600 bird and over 5,500 fish bones were retrieved. From other early medieval sites in the immediate hinterland, small assemblages were examined from Georgii, Prost and Vasilievskoye. At the edge of the Novgorod Lands, the excavations from Minino have produced a faunal sample also obtained from wet sieving as well as by hand. The mammalian assemblage from across the site has produced over 4,000 identified mammal bones. In addition, a sample of over 3,800 fish bones has been studied from a few selected features from the site.

The fish bones from all the sites have been identified and recorded by Sheila Hamilton-Dyer. She also recorded all the bird bones from Gorodishche and most of the bird bones from Novgorod. Ellen Hambleton and Mark Maltby also recorded some of the bird bones from Troitsky Site XI. The Minino mammal bones were analysed by Arkedy Savinetskii. The recording of the mammal bones from the Troitsky sites and Gorodishche, Georgii and Prost was carried out either directly by, or under the supervision of, Mark Maltby, Sheila Hamilton-Dyer and Ellen Hambleton. We were assisted at various times by a total of 13 Bournemouth students, Sheila's two daughters and two Russian colleagues, principally Natasha Efimova.

Aims

This paper aims to summarise some of the results arising from the above work. The analyses of the various assemblages are being published in detail in another volume in this series (Maltby in press) and it is there that the detailed data that support these brief conclusions reside, along with a much more comprehensive discussion of the evidence. However, it would be remiss not to include some of the conclusions in this volume, which aims to provide an integrated approach to the study of production and consumption in medieval Novgorod and its territory.

MEAT

One of the key questions that can be addressed by zooarchaeological studies is that of the evidence for meat production and consumption in the town and its satellite settlements. Beginning with the produce from domestic stock, this section will review the findings from the sites mentioned above.

Beef and veal

The percentages of domestic mammals from the various sites investigated during this project are given in Table 19.1. These are based on the numbers of individual specimens of bones and teeth (NISP). It can be seen that cattle elements form a very high proportion of all the assemblages from the Troitsky sites investigated in Novgorod, consistently forming 60–70% of the identified domestic mammal fragments. Although these high percentages are undoubtedly influenced by retrieval standards (they form only 46% of the domestic mammal elements in sieved samples), it would appear that beef was comfortably the most important type of meat consumed, particularly when one considers the larger size of their carcasses than pigs, sheep and goat. In the sequence from Troitsky XI, cattle elements tended to increase in relative abundance in the more recent levels. Although other factors could account for these variations, it remains a possibility that beef consumption increased slightly in the later phases.

Direct comparisons of the abundance of cattle in the Troitsky samples with those from the other sites are difficult because of the greater use of sieving in the latter. Therefore, the higher percentage of cattle in the Troitsky assemblages does not necessarily imply that there was a greater focus on beef consumption in the town. This is only going to be established once more extensive sieving strategies have been introduced.

At Gorodishche, although overall cattle elements form smaller proportions of the 9th–10th century assemblage, they are still the most commonly represented. This indicates that beef production was important in the area prior to the foundation of Novgorod. The area is well suited for cattle with abundant pasture available. It should be noted, however, that there are significant variations in cattle abundance in different samples (Table 19.1). Of particular interest is the high percentage of cattle elements from the southern area of the excavations. These include a fairly high proportion of foot bones and cranial elements including horn cores, which could indicate that this area was one where a greater proportion of primary processing waste was deposited (Maltby and Hamilton-Dyer 2001, 122). Although there are also some variations in the relative abundance of different types of cattle elements in the Troitsky samples, the presence of large amounts of both high and low quality meat bones on all the

Settlement	Area/Spit	Date	Cattle	Pig	S/G	Horse	Dog	Cat	To
Novgorod	Troitsky IX Lower	10-E12	2410	756	257	196	30	8	3(
Novgorod	Troitsky X Lower	10-E12	4761	1322	381	260	68	57	6(
Novgorod	Troitsky XI below S-13	10-E12	8160	2822	1394	373	83	389	13
Novgorod	Troitsky XI S-8 to S-13	M12-E13	3505	1090	376	137	84	49	5(
Novgorod	Troitsky XI S-1 S-7	M13-E15	3463	842	413	123	66	106	5(
Novgorod	Troitsky IX–X1 Total	10-E15	22299	6832	2821	1089	331	609	33
Novgorod	Troitsky IX–XI Sieved	10-M13	137	103	40	4	0	11	2
Gorodishche	1979	9-10	324	209	43	59	18	1	6
Gorodishche	Pre-1998 North	9-10	290	483	62	63	10	1	9
Gorodishche	Pre-1998 South	9-10	946	355	21	110	7	4	14
Gorodishche	Pre-1998 N/S	9-10	19	30	2	5	1	0	5
Gorodishche	1998	9-10	497	503	122	137	23	6	12
Gorodishche	Total	9-10	2076	1580	250	374	59	12	43
Georgii	Total	9-10	203	249	31	47	3	0	5(
Prost	Total	9-10	87	85	15	17	0	0	2
Minino	Early Phases	11-E12	87	46	106	38	3	0	2
Minino	Late Phases	L12-13	148	52	128	8	7	0	3
Minino	Unphased Medieval	11-13	82	33	112	14	4	0	2
Minino	Total Medieval	11-13	317	131	346	60	14	0	8

Settlement	Layers/Area	Date	Cattle	Pig	S/G	Horse	Dog	Cat	To
Novgorod	Troitsky IX Lower	10-E12	65.9	20.7	7.0	5.4	0.8	0.2	3(
Novgorod	Troitsky X Lower	10-E12	69.5	19.3	5.6	3.8	1.0	0.8	6(
Novgorod	Troitsky XI below S-13	10-E12	61.7	21.3	10.5	2.8	0.6	2.9	13
Novgorod	Troitsky XI S-8 to S-13	M12-E13	66.9	20.8	7.2	2.6	1.6	0.9	5(
Novgorod	Troitsky XI S-1 S-7	M13-E15	69.1	16.8	8.2	2.5	1.3	2.1	5(
Novgorod	Troitsky IX–XI Total	10-E15	65.6	20.1	8.3	3.2	1.0	1.8	33
Novgorod	Troitsky IX–XI Sieved	10-M13	46.4	34.9	13.6	1.4	0.0	3.7	2
Gorodishche	1979	9-10	49.5	32.0	6.6	9.0	2.8	0.2	6
Gorodishche	Pre-1998 North	9-10	31.9	53.1	6.8	6.9	1.1	0.1	9
Gorodishche	Pre-1998 South	9-10	65.6	24.6	1.5	7.6	0.5	0.3	14
Gorodishche	Pre-1998 N/S	9-10	33.3	52.6	3.5	8.8	1.8	0.0	5
Gorodishche	1998	9-10	38.6	39.1	9.5	10.6	1.8	0.5	12
Gorodishche	Total	9-10	47.7	36.3	5.7	8.6	1.4	0.3	43
Georgii	Total	9-10	38.1	46.7	5.8	8.8	0.6	0.0	5
Prost	Total	9-10	42.6	41.7	7.4	8.3	0.0	0.0	2
Minino	Early Phases	11-E12	31.1	16.4	37.9	13.6	1.1	0.0	2
Minino	Late Phases	L12-13	43.1	15.2	37.3	2.3	2.0	0.0	3
Minino	Unphased Medieval	11-13	33.5	13.5	45.7	5.7	1.6	0.0	2
Minino	Total Medieval	11-13	36.5	15.1	39.9	6.9	1.6	0.0	8

Counts are of number of individual specimens (NISP)

Table 19.1 *Domestic mammal fragment totals and percentages from recent excavations.*

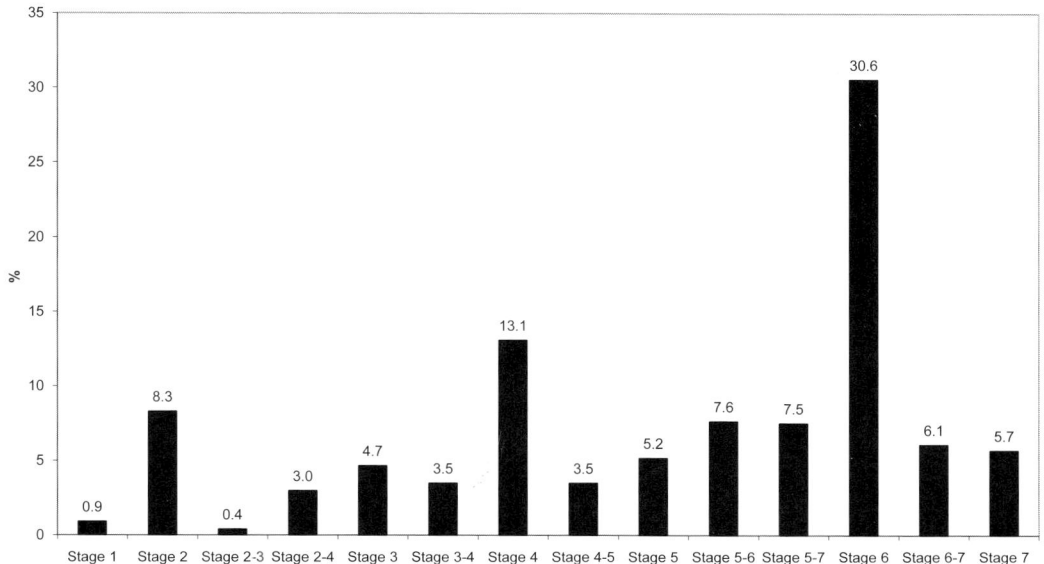

Figure 19.1 Novgorod Troitsky IX–XI: cattle mandibles age stages.

properties investigated suggests that much of the processing took place within these properties. This observation is supported by the presence of insects associated with carcass processing (Reilly this volume). However, detailed analysis of butchery marks from some spits in Troitsky XI (Maltby in press) indicates some consistency in processing methods, particularly regarding the segmentation of the trunk, which could indicate the activities of the specialist butchers of the town.

Ageing analysis has established the intensity of beef production. Results from the examination of 782 cattle mandibles from the Troitsky excavations (Table 19.2; Figure 19.1) show that a minimum of 42% of the mandibles recovered from sites IX–XI possess fully erupted cheek teeth (Stages 6–7) and belonged to adult cattle probably over 40 months of age (Higham 1967). This indicates that many cattle were old enough to have been exploited for other uses such as dairy production, traction and transport and that meat production was not particularly intensive. However, the most common age category is Stage 6, which indicates that many animals were slaughtered prior to very old age. This would suggest that many cattle were slaughtered between four and seven years of age. In addition, over half the cattle represented did not reach full dental maturity. Around 13% of the cattle mandibles are at Stage 4 of the tooth eruption sequence, indicating a significant cull of third year animals. These animals would have been too young for working and therefore represent cattle raised and slaughtered primarily for beef. It is interesting to note that this age group is represented by only a single specimen from a sample of 50 mandibles from Gorodishche, yet they are present in consistently higher proportions in the lower spits of all three of the Troitsky sites (Table 19.2). This could reflect a change in the exploitation of cattle during the

Stage	1	2	2–3	2–4	3	3–4	4	4–5	5	5–6	5–7	6	6–7	7	Total
Troitsky IX Lower	0.6	5.6		3.4	3.9	2.2	14.0	3.4	4.5	7.3	3.9	36.0	9.0	6.2	178
Troitsky X Lower	0.8	7.1	0.8	3.3	3.8	5.0	13.8	1.7	2.5	7.5	9.2	35.4	6.7	2.5	240
Troitsky XI below S-13	1.0	12.2	0.5	2.0	5.4	3.9	11.2	2.0	8.8	9.8	8.8	24.9	5.4	4.4	205
Troitsky XI S-8 to S-13		1.2		2.4	2.4	1.2	14.3	8.3	10.7	7.1	8.3	32.1	7.1	4.8	84
Troitsky XI S-1 S-7	2.7	16.0		5.3	9.3	2.7	10.7	8.0	1.3	8.0	4.3	25.3	2.7	2.7	75
Troitsky IX–XI	0.9	8.3	0.4	3.1	4.6	3.5	12.9	3.5	5.3	8.1	7.4	31.5	6.6	4.1	782
Gorodischche		16.0		2.0			2.0		6.0	12.0	2.0	50.0	8.0	2.0	50

Pig

Stage	1	2	2–3	2–4	3	3–4	4	4–5	5	5–6	5–7	6	6–7	7	Total
Troitsky IX Lower		6.3	2.1		9.8	2.1	3.5	3.5	13.3	18.2	4.9	8.4	4.9	23.1	143
Troitsky X Lower		4.0	2.3	1.7	13.1	0.6	2.3	1.7	25.6	8.5	5.1	8.0	6.3	21.0	176
Troitsky XI below S-13		9.1	0.9	0.5	15.6	1.4	3.2	1.8	22.8	11.9	5.9	14.2	5.0	7.8	219
Troitsky XI S-8 to S-13		2.7	1.3		1.3	1.3	2.7	1.3	20.0	21.3	2.7	17.3	8.0	20.0	75
Troitsky XI S-1 S-7		1.1	1.1		2.2			2.2	21.1	15.6	6.7	10.0	6.7	33.3	90
Troitsky IX–XI	0.0	5.5	1.6	0.6	10.5	1.1	2.6	2.1	21.1	13.8	5.3	11.2	5.8	18.8	703
Gorodischche	2.6	15.4	1.3		9.0	5.1	5.1	3.8	14.1	10.3	2.6	3.8	6.4	20.5	78
Georgii					27.8		11.0		16.7	11.1		27.8		5.6	18

Sheep/Goat

Stage	1	2	2–3	2–4	3	3–4	Sheep/Goat 4	4–5	5	5–6	5–7	6	6–7	7	Total
Troitsky IX Lower		11.0		1.6	19.0	7.9	25.4		11.1	3.2		17.5	1.5	1.6	63
Troitsky X Lower			2.0		19.6		29.4		15.7		2.0	29.4		2.0	51
Troitsky XI below S-13	1.0	3.8	6.7	1.9	19.0	5.7	21.9	4.8	12.4	1.9	1.0	12.4	1.9	5.7	105
Troitsky XI S-8 to S-13		20.0		4.0	4.0	12.0	12.0		4.0	4.0		36.0		4.0	25
Troitsky XI S-1 S-7			2.2		8.9	17.8	15.6	2.2	17.8	2.2	2.2	13.3	6.7	11.1	45
Troitsky IX–XI	0.3	5.5	3.1	1.4	16.3	7.6	22.1	2.1	12.8	2.1	1.0	18.7	2.1	4.8	289
Gorodischche		5.3		5.3	15.8		26.3		10.5		5.3	15.8	5.3	10.5	19

Stage 1 = 4th deciduous premolars (dp4) not in wear

Stage 2 = dp4 in wear; 1st molar (M1) not in wear

Stage 3 = M1 in wear; 2nd molar (M2) not in wear

Stage 4 = M2 in wear; 3rd molar (M3) and permanent premolars not in wear

Stage 5 = M3 in wear; 4th permanent premolar (P4) not in wear (Cattle)

Stage 5 = M3 in wear; M1 at Grant (1982) wear stage g (S/G)

Stage 5 = P4 in wear; M3 not in wear (Pig)

Stage 6 = P4 in wear; MWS <46 (Cattle)

Stage 6 = M1 at Grant wear stages h–m; M2 at Grant wear stage g (S/G)

Stage 6 = M3 at Grant wear stages a–b (Pig)

Stage 7 = MWS >45 (Cattle)

Stage 7 = M1 and M2 at Grant wear stages h–m (S/G)

Stage 7 = M3 at Grant wear stages c–g (Pig)

Table 19.2 Percentage of mandibles of major domestic mammals at different age stages.

11th–12th centuries with a greater emphasis on meat production. It could, of course, also be a phenomenon restricted mainly to the town. Here, it is unfortunate that we do not have comparable contemporary samples from sites in the adjacent hinterland.

Evidence for the consumption of veal and beef from cattle under 18 months of age is indicted by the numbers of Stage 1–3 mandibles (Table 19.2; Figure 19.1). These form over 14% of the sample from the Troitsky sites. Most are from calves of around 2–6 months old (Stage 2 and early part of Stage 3). Given the probability that such mandibles are under-represented because of retrieval and possibly survival biases, their presence does indicate that veal was fairly commonly consumed in the town. There is some fluctuation in their percentages. They are relatively uncommon in the 12th–13th century assemblage from Troitsky XI. However, they form 28% of the sample from the mid 13th to 15th century levels. This could indicate a significant increase in veal production during the later medieval period, although it would of course be useful to examine samples from other parts of the town, to see whether this was a widespread trend. Stage 2 mandibles are also represented in significant numbers at Gorodishche, indicating veal also formed a common component of the meat diet there in the 9th and 10th centuries.

Pork and bacon

Pig is the second most common species represented in the hand-collected assemblage from the Troitsky sites, forming 20% of the identified domestic mammal elements with relatively little variation overall between sites (Table 19.1). At Gorodishche, pigs are better represented overall (36%) and form more than half of the identified domestic mammal remains in some areas. They are better represented still at Prost and Georgii forming over 40% of the mammal elements recovered from these sites. However, at Minino, they form only 15% of the domestic mammal assemblage.

As discussed above, comparisons of species represented in these samples are handicapped by the varied methods of retrieval, as the sieving strategies employed in the later seasons at Gorodishche and at Minino were more favourable for the recovery of pig bones. However, comparisons can also be made between pig and sheep/goat counts only. Although there are still some methodological problems with such comparisons, retrieval bias between these species should be less than between cattle and pig, for example. Adapting NISP counts from Table 19.1, pig elements account for 71% of the total pig and sheep/goat recovered from the three Troitsky sites. Percentages vary between 67% and 78%. This is lower than in all three of the 9th–10th century samples from sites in the hinterland, where equivalent percentages of pig range between 85% (Prost) and 89% (Georgii). Therefore it would appear that the proportion of pork consumed (compared with sheep and goat meat at least) was slightly higher in those earlier settlements than in the Novgorod sites considered here. This may be linked with changes in habitat; with perhaps suitable woodland for pig pannage being decreased slightly and replaced by agricultural land around the time of the foundation of Novgorod (see Spiridonova and Aleshinskaya, this volume).

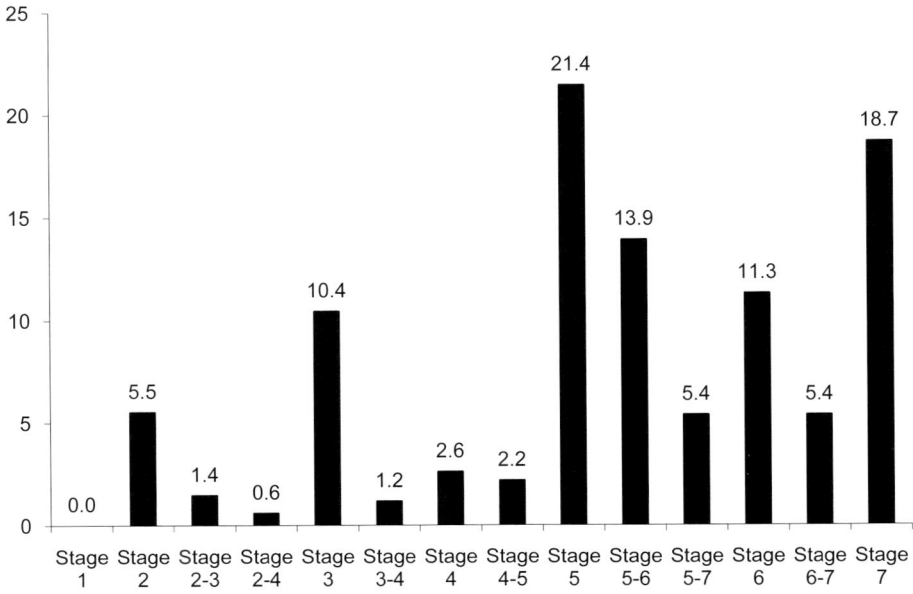

Figure 19.2 *Novgorod Troitsky IX–XI: pig mandibles age stages.*

The contrast with Minino is even more marked with pig elements contributing only 27% of the total pig and sheep/goat sample. The low proportion of pig remains at Minino is interesting given the high percentage of wild mammal species that favour woodland habitats present in that sample (Table 19.3). It is possible that the local climatic conditions were less favourable for pig keeping. The area has lower mean winter temperatures and longer and deeper coverings of snow (Spiridonova and Aleshinskaya, this volume). It has been shown that modern wild boar population densities decrease significantly in northern latitudes in relation to lower winter temperatures (Melis *et al.* 2006) and the need possibly to supply their domestic pigs with supplementary winter fodder may have limited the numbers kept by the inhabitants of Minino.

Ageing analysis from the Troitsky sites (Table 19.2; Figure 19.2) has confirmed initial observations (Maltby and Hamilton-Dyer 2001, 121) that there were a substantial number of mandibles of juvenile pigs (Stages 2 and 3) in the 10th–12th century deposits. This was witnessed in the assemblages from the lowest spits of all three sites, which include between at least 18% and 26% of pig mandibles at these stages. The Stage 3 specimens are likely to be mainly from pigs culled in the autumn and winter of their first year (Bull and Payne 1982). However, the proportion of young pigs drops significantly in the later deposits of Troitsky XI, where they form only around 5% of the mandible assemblage (Table 19.2), suggesting that pigs became less intensively exploited. Specimens at Stages 5 and 6 of the ageing sequence are common throughout the Troitsky deposits (Figure 19.2) and indicate a substantial slaughter of pigs from the latter part of their second year and possibly throughout their third year. The

Settlement	Area/Spit	Date	Dom Mam	Wild Mamm	Unid Mamm	Total Mamm	Id Bird	Unid Bird	Total Bird	Id Fish	Unid Fish	Total Fish	Total
Novgorod	Tr IX Lower	10-E12	3657	44	2587	6288	374	38	412	84	44	128	6828
Novgorod	Tr X Lower	10-E12	6272	27	4464	10763	445	58	503	68	22	90	11356
Novgorod*	Tr XI below S-13	10-E12	13221	112	9271	22604	1953	297	2250	590	176	766	25620
Novgorod	Tr XI S-8 to S-13	M12-E13	5241	61	4351	9653	717	76	793	102	47	149	10595
Novgorod	Tr XI S-1 S-7	M13-E15	5013	71	3759	8843	274	30	304	81	77	158	9305
Novgorod	Tr IX-X1 Total	10-E15	33404	315	24432	58151	3763	499	4262	925	366	1291	63704
Novgorod	%	10-E15	99.1	0.9		91.3	88.3	11.7	6.7	71.6	28.4	2.0	
Novgorod	Troitsky Sieved	10-M13	295	11	1005	1311	94	127	221	1496	3124	4620	6152
Novgorod	Troitsky Sieved %	10-M13	96.4	3.6		21.3	42.5	57.5	3.6	32.4	67.6	75.1	
Gorodishche	1979	9-10	654	8	171	833	17	1	18	0	0	0	851
Gorodishche	Pre-1998 North	9-10	909	14	2067	2990	228	83	311	1016	1143	2159	5460
Gorodishche	Pre-1998 South	9-10	1443	53	2005	3501	167	72	239	2002	1145	3147	6887
Gorodishche	Pre-1998 N/S	9-10	57	0	176	233	0	0	0	0	0	0	233
Gorodishche	1998	9-10	1288	17	1876	3181	58	18	76	192	53	245	3502
Gorodishche	Total	9-10	4351	92	6295	10738	470	174	644	3210	2341	5551	16933
Gorodishche	Total %	9-10	97.9	2.1		63.4	73.0	27.0	3.8	57.8	42.2	32.8	
Georgii	Total	9-10	533	25	187	745	9	3	12	30	41	71	828
Georgii	Total %	9-10	95.5	4.5		90.0	75.0	25.0	1.4	42.3	57.7	8.6	

peak at Stage 5 may again be related to autumn and winter culls. A substantial proportion of pigs survived to reach the latest stage (7) of the mandible sequence, indicating they were probably over three years old. However, many of these had only just reached this stage and very few specimens have heavy wear on the third molars, suggesting that the majority are from pigs of less than four years of age. This is supported by the epiphyseal fusion evidence, that shows that only 32 of the 307 latest-fusing limb bone epiphyses recovered from the Troitsky sites have fused (Maltby in press), indicating that only about 10% of these surviving elements were from pigs older than 3–3.5 years of age (Bull and Payne 1982).

The Gorodishche pig mortality profile has many of the characteristics of the 10th–12th century sample from the Troitsky sites with similar percentages belonging to adults (Table 19.2). There are two mandibles from neonatal pigs (Stage 1), which were not recorded in the hand-collected samples from the Troitsky sites. Their presence suggests that at least some of the pigs may have been reared and kept for at least part of the year in the vicinity of the settlement. The higher percentages of Stage 2 mandibles (15%) may also reflect this and also suggests that sieving increased the recovery rates of young piglet bones. The small sample from Georgii shows peaks at Stages 3, 5 and 6 but no Stage 1 or 2 specimens were recovered.

Site	Category	Phase											Total
Prost	Total	9-10	204	56	1681	1941	1	0	1	395	786	1181	3123
Prost	Total %	9-10	78.5	21.5		62.2	100.0	0.0	0.0	33.4	66.6	37.8	
Minino*	Early Phases	11-E12	280	741		1021							1021
Minino*	Late Phases	L12-13	343	476		819							819
Minino*	Unphased	11-13	245	366		611							611
Minino*	Total Medieval	11-13	868	1583		2451			641				3092
Minino*	%	11-13	35.4	64.6									

Table 19.3 Mammal, bird and fish elements from recent excavations (NISP).

* Fish counts from Troitsky XI below S-13 from selected spits only; fish counts from selected features from Minino not included

The possibility that there was a peak of slaughter of pigs in the autumn and winter months leads to a consideration of the likelihood that much of the meat of pigs (and indeed of other animals) was preserved in some form. References to salt have been deciphered on several birch-bark documents (Rybina 2001, 128) and salt was extracted and traded extensively in the Novgorod region in the medieval period (Smith and Christian 1984, 27). Other forms of meat preservation such as smoking and drying would also have been used. Over 45% of the pig elements from the Troitsky sites are cranial elements (Maltby in press), indicating that processing of pig carcasses probably took place commonly within the properties.

Goat meat, lamb and mutton

Both sheep and goats are present in the Troitsky assemblage. Unfortunately, due to frequent changes of personnel, positive identifications of the two species were not recorded consistently. However, 63% of the 62 mandibles with deciduous 4th premolars and 62% of 92 measured bones with positive species identifications belonged to sheep (Maltby in press), suggesting that sheep were present in greater quantities than goats but that goats were not uncommon within the ovicaprid assemblage. At Gorodishche, 57% of the 35 specifically identified elements of sheep and goat belonged to sheep. At Georgii only four definite sheep but no goat bones were recorded and at Prost only a single element of sheep was positively identified. At Minino, 90% of the 21 positively distinguished elements belonged to sheep. Variations in the relative abundance of the two species need further clarification but there does seem to be significant variations between sites. The high percentage of sheep at Minino could reflect their greater suitability to the local ecological conditions, where there is good pollen evidence for substantial development of more open conditions including dry pasture suitable for sheep during the medieval period (Spiridonova and Aleshinskaya, this volume). This may also be the case in Poozerie. Some goats may have been kept in Novgorod itself, which may explain their better representation in the Troitsky deposits.

Generally, however, sheep/goat elements are relatively poorly represented in the assemblages from Novgorod and its immediate hinterland, providing less than 10% of the domestic mammal elements in virtually all of the samples (Table 19.1). It would appear that lamb, mutton and goat-meat were much less commonly consumed than beef and pork. Much of the swamps and wet meadowland around the area would have been more suitable for cattle grazing and the substantial forests in the area would not have favoured keeping sheep in large numbers either. In stark contrast, at Minino sheep/goat formed the highest percentage (40%) of the domestic mammal elements overall, although their relative numbers declined slightly in the later phase. The development of agricultural land and the increase in dry pasture seems to have encouraged the keeping of more sheep.

Although there is relatively little change in the relative percentage of sheep/goat and pig within the Troitsky deposits, the very highest spits examined in this study (-1 to -4) on Troitsky XI, dating mainly to the 14th century, have some of the highest

Settlement	Area/Spit	Date	Bos	Elk	Rein	Roe	Hare	Boar	Bear	Squirrel	Beaver	Otter	Marten	Pole	Stoat	Fox	Lynx	Wolf	Badger	Total
Novgorod	Tr IX Lower	10-E12		9	2		14	1		1	18									44
Novgorod	Tr X Lower	10-E12		5			5		1	1	16									27
Novgorod	Tr XI below S-13	10-E12		16			26	1	2	2	64		1							112
Novgorod	Tr XI S-8 to S-13	M12-E13		34			20	1	4		2									61
Novgorod	Tr XI S-1 S-7 Tr IX-X1	M13-E15		16	1		49	2	2							1				71
Novgorod	Total	10-E15	0	80	3	0	114	4	9	3	100	0	1	0		1	0	0	0	315
Novgorod	Troitsky Sieved	10-M13	0	0	0	0	4	0	0	1	6	0	0	0	0	0	0	0	0	11
Gorodishche	1979	9-10					2				4							2		8
Gorodishche	Pre-1998 North	9-10					10				3				1					14
Gorodishche	Pre-1998 South	9-10		4			29			11	9									53
Gorodishche	Pre-1998 N/S	9-10																		0
Gorodishche	1998	9-10		3			3		1		7		1					2		17
Gorodishche	Total	9-10	0	7	0	0	44	0	1	11	23	0	1	0	1	0	0	4	0	92
Georgii	Total	9-10	0	18	0	0	1	0	1	1	3	0	0	0	0	0	1	0	0	25
Prost	Total	9-10	1	0	0	0	0	0	0	0	1	0	54	0	0	0	0	0	0	56
Minino	Early Phases	11-E12		31	7	2	6	2		214	423	4	45	2		5				741
Minino	Late Phases	L12-13		56	4	2	13	6	2	153	183	7	40	4		5			1	476
Minino	Unphased	11-13		20	2	2	5	7		56	252	1	19	1		1				366
Minino	Total Medieval	11-13	0	107	13	6	24	15	2	423	858	12	104	7	0	11	0	0	1	1583

Counts are of number of individual specimens (NISP)

Table 19.4 Wild mammal species totals from recent excavations (NISP).

sheep/goat to pig percentages (43%), compared with the average of 31% from the site overall (Maltby in press). This ties in quite nicely with the significant decrease in woodland and increase in agricultural land around Gorodishche by the end of the 13th century (Spiridonova and Aleshinskaya, this volume), making available more pasture suitable for sheep.

Analysis of sheep/goat mandibular ageing data (Table 19.2) must bear in mind that most of the older mandibles (and many of the younger ones) were not identified specifically to sheep or goat. The two species may have been exploited in different ways. However, immature lambs and kids are both represented on the Troitsky sites and there is a significant percentage of juvenile and immature sheep/goat killed under two years old (Stages 1–4). At least 59% of the sheep/goat mandibles lie within these stages in the 10th–12th century assemblages from the three sites. Such high percentages indicate that their exploitation was mainly focused on meat production at this time. Percentages of mandibles of immature animals decrease to 52% in the much smaller 12th–13th century sample from Troitsky XI and to 45% in the highest spits sampled, indicating that meat exploitation may have become gradually less intensive. In most of the samples the highest percentage of sheep and goats are represented by Stage 4 specimens, which mainly belonged to animals killed in their second year at a time their carcasses had reached nearly full size. A similar peak of second year mortalities was observed in the Gorodishche sample (Table 19.4).

Meat from other mammals

Horsemeat is not often considered to have been consumed by humans in many parts of medieval Europe because of Christian taboos. However, their bones form a small but fairly consistent percentage of the domestic mammal assemblage in the Troitsky samples ranging from 2.5% to 5.4% of the identified domestic mammal elements and their presence needs to be explained (Table 19.1). As discussed further below, there is good evidence that horses were stabled within properties on the Troitsky sites and presumably elsewhere in Novgorod. What happened to such horses after they died? This analysis has confirmed that substantial numbers of their carcasses were butchered. The scan revealed that over 16% of the horse bones bear processing marks. A few of these are skinning and bone-working marks but many others are dismemberment and filleting marks closely similar to those observed on cattle (Maltby in press). Although the relatively frequency of butchery marks was much lower than for cattle (28%) and their exploitation for meat less intensive, significant numbers of the horse carcasses were nonetheless butchered for meat. It could be argued that some of the meat was prepared for dogs rather than humans but there is no clear evidence to support this, although the incidence of gnawed horse bones (41%) is higher than for cattle (31%). In all probability, however, many residents of medieval Novgorod occasionally consumed horseflesh.

Horse remains form a much larger proportion of the Gorodishche assemblage, forming near 9% of the domestic mammal elements, although this total includes a substantial number of associated bone groups, the presence of which implies that many of their carcasses were not fully processed for food. However, 5% of the horse bones bear processing marks including marks made during dismemberment and filleting and these do appear to indicate some horsemeat consumption.

Similarly, meat from dogs and cats are rarely considered to have been consumed. There is much less evidence for such exploitation in any of the samples investigated. However, butchery marks were noted on 16 (5%) of the dog bones and several of these are clearly not simply skinning marks. Similarly, two cat bones bear types of butchery mark not usually associated with skinning. That the inhabitants of Novgorod sometimes resorted to eating cats and dogs is noted in a chronicle reference dated to 1230 when desperate measures were taken during a famine (Riha 1970, 39). There is no definite evidence that any of the dogs and cats represented at any of the other sites had been butchered apart from a split dog lumbar vertebra from Gorodishche.

In Novgorod and the early medieval settlements in its immediate hinterland there is little evidence that meat from wild mammals played a significant role in the diet. From counts of wild and domestic mammals species (Table 19.3), it can be seen that elements of wild species formed 1% or less of the total identified mammal remains recovered by hand from the Troitsky excavations. This figure rose to over 3% in the sieved samples, although this figure is inflated by the removal of some of the hand-collected bones of larger mammals prior to sieving. At Gorodishche, wild species contribute only 2% of the mammal sample. This figure rises to nearly 5% at Georgii and 21% at Prost. However, if the bones associated with marten skins at the latter (see below) are omitted, this percentage falls to 1%.

The assemblage from Minino is completely different from the others. Wild mammal elements provide 65% of the identified mammal remains, indicating significant exploitation of such species for meat as well as furs and skins. Although there is evidence for a decline in wild mammal elements in the later medieval phase (58%) compared with the 11th and early 12th century assemblage (73%), the inhabitants of Minino relied much less heavily on meat from domestic mammals than the residents of Novgorod and Gorodishche (Savinetskii in press).

Of the wild mammals likely to have provided meat in Novgorod, elk was probably the most important, although they only provide 0.2% of the identified mammal elements. Because of limitations of the reference collection, a few other possible elk remains noted during the scan were not recorded as positive identifications. These counts also omit antler, which was commonly used in artefact manufacture (see below). Butchery marks were observed on 33% of the elk elements. There is little evidence for bias in the parts of the skeleton represented. Good and poor meat bones are both present and it would seem that complete elk carcasses may have been brought to the town for processing.

Although numbers are small (<0.3% of the identified mammal elements), the types of beaver elements represented on the Troitsky sites clearly indicate that whole carcasses were sometimes brought to the town. Processing marks were observed on

33% of the elements recovered and many of these represent dismemberment and filleting rather than skinning. However, as discussed below, beaver meat disappeared even as an occasional resource in the later medieval period.

Despite their small size, hare elements are the most common of the wild species represented, although forming only 0.3% of the identified mammal assemblage. Butchery marks were noted on 9% of their bones. A few bones of wild boar were also recorded (Table 19.4), identifications being made on the exceptionally large size of the elements involved. Although it is likely that other wild boar remains were not detected amongst the domestic pig assemblage, it does not seem likely that wild boar was a common resource in Novgorod. Although antler of reindeer, red deer and roe deer has been identified amongst the worked assemblage, no bones of these species were catalogued in these deposits apart from three elements of reindeer from the Troitsky sites (Table 19.4).

There is butchery evidence that hare, beaver and elk were processed for meat at Gorodishche and possibly squirrel was also eaten occasionally, although no conclusive butchery evidence was recorded (Table 19.4). Elk and possibly beaver and hare also appear to have been consumed occasionally at Georgii. Indeed, elk provided over 3% of the identified mammal elements from this site and several of these were butchered. Prost is the only site in this survey to produce a bone (2nd phalanx) of a wild large bovid. This possibly belonged to an aurochs (*Bos primigenius*), a species that may not have become extinct in Russia until the 13th century (van Vuure 2005). Perhaps more likely is that it belonged to a bison (*Bison bonasus*), which can still be found in very small numbers in Eastern Europe.

Although the high incidence of beaver, squirrel and marten from Minino is undoubtedly linked with the acquisition of skins, the presence of all parts of the skeletons and butchery marks (Savinetskii in press) attest that beaver meat at least was eaten and possibly also the meat of the other fur-bearing species as well. Although represented by much fewer elements (Table 19.4), meat from elk probably made a greater contribution to the diet. Much less important sources of venison were reindeer and roe deer. Red deer may also have been exploited (seven possible specimens are not listed in Table 19.4). Hare and wild boar elements also formed a small component of the assemblage.

FISH

The importance of fish to the communities in and around medieval Novgorod is indicated in various forms of evidence. These include artefacts such as fishing rods, nets, floats, weights, fish-hooks (Rybina 2007, 124–130) and boats (Dubrovin 2007a, 260–261). More birch-bark documents refer to fish than any other food product, and some of the later ones refer to particular species (Rybina 2001; 2007, 124; Brisbane and Maltby 2002).

Unfortunately, standard excavation methods in Novgorod are not conducive to the

Table 19.5 Fish species totals from recent excavations (NISP).

Settlement	Area/Spit	Date	Whitefish	Sturgeon	Pike	Cyprinid	Wels	Zander	Perch	Ruffe	Eel	Total Id	Unid.	Total
Novgorod	Tr IX Lower	10-E12			16	26	8	25	9			84	44	128
Novgorod	Tr X Lower	10-E12			18	9	8	32	1			68	22	90
Novgorod*	Tr XI below S-13	10-E12		1	143	117	38	176	5			480	286	766
Novgorod	Tr XI S-8 to S-13	M12-E13 M13-E15		2	24	23	4	47	2			102	47	149
Novgorod	Tr XI S-1 S-7	E15		1	12	33		35				81	77	158
Novgorod	Tr IX-X1 Total	10-E15	0	4	213	208	58	315	17	0	0	815	476	1291
Novgorod	Tr IX-X1 %	10-E15	0.0	0.5	26.1	25.5	7.1	38.7	2.1	0.0	0.0	63.1	36.9	
Novgorod*	Troitsky Sieved	10-M13			238	900	2	262	89	2	3	1496	3124	4620
Novgorod	Troitsky Sieved %	10-M13	0.0	0.0	15.9	60.2	0.1	17.5	5.9	0.1	0.2	32.4	67.6	
Gorodishche	1979	9-10												0
Gorodishche	Pre-1998 North	9-10	1		314	298		371	32			1016	1143	2159
Gorodishche	Pre-1998 South	9-10	1		592	880	4	519	6			2002	1145	3147
Gorodishche	Pre-1998 N/S	9-10										0		0
Gorodishche	1998	9-10	1	1	68	68	1	52	1			192	53	245
Gorodishche	Total	9-10	3	1	974	1246	5	942	39			3210	2341	5551
Gorodishche	Total %	9-10	0.1	0.0	30.3	38.8	0.2	29.3	1.2	0.0	0.0	57.8	42.2	
Georgii	Total	9-10	0	0	4	17	0	6	3	0	0	30	41	71
Georgii	Total %	9-10	0.0	0.0	13.3	56.7	0.0	20.0	10.0	0.0	0.0	42.3	57.7	
Prost	Total	9-10	0	0	74	209	0	81	31	0	0	395	786	1181
Prost	Total %	9-10	0.0	0.0	18.7	52.9	0.0	20.5	7.8	0.0	0.0	33.4	66.6	
Minino*	Medieval	11-13	0	2	159	627	0	1	822	1	0	1612	2236	3848
Minino	Medieval %	11-13	0.0	0.1	9.9	38.9	0.0	0.1	51.0	0.1	0.0	41.9	58.1	

* selected pits/features only

recovery of fish bones. This has been clearly demonstrated by the sieving experiments (wet-sieving through a 2 mm mesh) that were carried out initially in 1993 and 1994 (Maltby and Hamilton-Dyer 2001, 119). The point is graphically illustrated in Table 19.3. Fish contribute only 2% of the total elements retrieved by hand from the Troitsky excavations. Even allowing for the fact that, because of time restraints, fish were only recorded from some of the lower spits from Troitsky XI (Maltby in press), this is a very small component of the assemblage. The contrast with the make-up of the sieved assemblages is stark. Fish elements contribute 75% of the total fragments. This percentage is inflated slightly by the fact that some of the hand-collected bones from the quadrants sampled were not incorporated into the counts. However, the fact that over three times as many fish bones were obtained in samples from a minute portion of the total excavated area than the total recovered by hand is testament to the severe problems faced. It is hardly surprising that the hand-collected sample is dominated by larger bones of large fish. For example, bones of large catfish (wels) account for 7% of the identified fish, whereas they form only 0.1% of the sieved remains (Table 19.5).

The fish species identified in the sieved samples from the Troitsky sites are dominated by Cyprinidae. Of those elements further identifiable, most belonged to bream but here, and at Gorodishche, bones of roach, dace, chub, ide and silver bream were also recorded. Several further cyprinid species were identified in the sample from the Nerevsky excavations (Sychevskaya 1965). Zander and pike of various sizes are also quite commonly represented. Bones of perch and occasionally ruffe were also found. All these freshwater species are available locally in Lake Ilmen and its rivers. Many would have been caught in nets from boats. However, despite the importance of local commercial fishing, only two birch-bark documents refer to these species by name; one mentions pike, another bream (Rybina 2001, 131). The documents are often concerned with tribute and hence they tend to refer to more unusual fish as a preferred tribute item. There is a reference to sturgeon in one document but finds of this species are rare (Table 19.5). Sturgeon is not present locally now, although it may have been found as far upriver as Novgorod in the past. This highly prized species was an important trade item and it would not be surprising to find that most of the sturgeons eaten in the town were traded from some distance. A similar explanation would account for the few bones of whitefish found in the Nerevsky excavations and at Gorodishche. No bones of other salmonids were recovered from these excavations, although salmon are referred to in a couple of birch-bark documents (Rybina 2007, 124). Many of the bones of catfish are also large. Although these could have been caught locally, there is a possibility that some could have been imported. The three bones of eel also probably represent the importation of preserved fish, possibly from the Baltic, as the area around Novgorod is at the edge of their distribution.

Extensive sieving at Gorodishche has confirmed that fish bones are likely to form an important part of any sieved assemblage from medieval sites in this area. Fish bones provide over 32% of all the bones recorded (Table 19.3). The species represented are largely the same as those recovered from Novgorod. However, cyprinid elements, although still the most common, are not as dominant because both zander and pike are better represented than in the Troitsky sample. Perch is poorly represented. The same species are represented at Georgii and Prost, with over half the identified elements from both sites belonging to cyprinids. Both sites produced higher percentages of perch than Gorodishche, although, as in the other samples, they are less abundant than zander and pike (Table 19.5). Zander, cyprinids and pike were also present in a small sample from another contemporary Poozerie settlement at Vasilievskoye (Maltby in press). The exploitation of local waters for fish was clearly established by the 9th century and the fish stocks continued to be an important resource thereafter. A few bones of whitefish, catfish and sturgeon were found at Gorodishche but were not recorded at the other sites. Although local catches cannot be ruled out, the presence of catfish and whitefish in particular may indicate that the acquisition through trade of prized fish may have begun prior to the foundation of Novgorod.

The analysis of fish bones from selected medieval contexts at Minino (Hamilton-Dyer in press) revealed that the remains were dominated by perch and cyprinids. Pike is moderately represented but only a single bone of zander was identified. Another difference to the assemblages from near Lake Ilmen is that, amongst the cyprinids, roach elements outnumber bream. Minino is situated next to Kubenskoye Lake, where zander has only recently been introduced and has failed to flourish (Bolotova *et al.* 2003) and therefore it may not have been locally available during the medieval period. Zander and sturgeon may have been acquired through trade fairly locally (for example from Byeloe Lake) or from further afield, as part of the long distance trading network. Concentrations of scales and other bones in pits show that quite large numbers of fish were sometimes processed at the same time, perhaps for preservation for winter consumption. The presence of fish deposited in some of the graves at Minino provides a further insight into the importance of fishing to the community (Hamilton-Dyer in press).

BIRDS

Although bird elements were found more frequently than those of fish amongst the hand-collected assemblages from Novgorod, results from the sieved samples from all the settlements investigated show that they are heavily outnumbered by both mammal and fish remains and never form more than 4% of the total assemblage (Table 19.3). Generally, it seems that birds provided only a supplementary addition to the diet.

Bones of mallard form the highest percentage of bird bones, forming up to 40% of the overall samples from Novgorod and Gorodishche (Table 19.6). Some of these may have been from domesticated birds but most are no larger than wild specimens. It is conceivable therefore that many of these were hunted along with other species of smaller duck, which also form a substantial proportion of the assemblage. Speciation

Settlement	Area/Spit	Date	Domestic		Other		Other		Raptors	Corvids	Passerines	Total Id	Unid.	Total
			Fowl	Mallard	Ducks	Geese	Waterfowl	Landfowl						
Novgorod	Tr IX Lower	10-E12	123	176	47	10	5	6	3	4		374	38	412
Novgorod	Tr X Lower	10-E12	99	245	49	26	6	15	4	1		445	58	503
Novgorod	Tr XI below S-13	10-E12	540	805	327	92	35	54	53	47		1953	297	2250
Novgorod	Tr XI S-8 to S-13	M12-E13	345	141	82	46	12	34	45	12		717	76	793
Novgorod	Tr XI S-1 S-7	M13-E15	142	46	37	20	1	9	17	2		274	30	304
Novgorod	Tr IX-X1 Total	10-E15	1249	1413	542	194	59	118	122	66	0	3763	499	4262
Novgorod	Tr IX-X1 %	10-E15	33.2	37.5	14.4	5.2	1.6	3.1	3.2	1.8	0.0	88.3	11.7	
Novgorod	Troitsky Sieved	10-M13	19	37	27	1	2				8	94	127	221
Novgorod	Troitsky Sieved %	10-M13	20.2	39.4	28.7	1.1	2.1	0.0	0.0	0.0	8.5	42.5	57.5	
Gorodishche	1979	9-10	11	1	1	3				1		17	1	18
Gorodishche	Pre-1998 North	9-10	62	94	46	20		2	2	2		228	83	311
Gorodishche	Pre-1998 South	9-10	28	84	41	10	2	2				167	72	239
Gorodishche	Pre-1998 N/S	9-10										0		0
Gorodishche	1998	9-10	17	10	16	4	2	3	4	2		58	18	76
Gorodishche	Total	9-10	118	189	104	37	4	7	6	5		470	174	644
Gorodishche	Total %	9-10	25.1	40.2	22.1	7.9	0.9	1.5	1.3	1.1	0.0	73.0	27.0	
Georgii	Total	9-10		2	1	6						9	3	12
Prost	Total	9-10			1							1		1

Table 19.6 Bird category totals from recent excavations (NISP).

of duck bones is difficult but the majority of the smaller duck bones are a good match for teal. However, several other small and medium-sized ducks, such as wigeon, pochard, goldeneye and garganey amongst others are also all probably represented. Apart from the resident mallard, all the duck species are summer visitors (Hamilton-Dyer 2002). Higher percentages of smaller ducks, particularly teal, were found in the sieved samples from the Troitsky sites (Table 19.6).

Bones of geese, apart from in the tiny sample from Georgii, are substantially less common than mallard but consistently present throughout the Troitsky spits (Table 19.6). They are mainly the size of greylag goose, which is a summer visitor, but some of them may have been domesticated birds. A few bones may be from smaller species such as the pink-footed or white-fronted geese. Chicken bones (domestic fowl) are present in significant numbers and it is likely that many were kept within Novgorod itself. Absent from Georgii, and substantially outnumbered by mallard at Gorodishche and in the lower levels on all three Troitsky sites, domestic fowl bones became the most commonly occurring bird species in the later medieval deposits on the Troitsky site (Table 19.6) and also on the Fedorovsky site (Hamilton-Dyer 2002), indicating a greater reliance on chickens probably from the middle of the 12th century onwards.

Other waterfowl are present in small numbers in the samples from Novgorod and Gorodishche. Species identified include swan, crane, stork, heron, great-crested grebe, coot, cormorant, gull, (cf.) woodcock and (cf.) snipe. Most of the other game bird bones are from capercaillie and black grouse, although sometimes it is difficult to distinguish between these species. The large size of capercaillie, in particular, meant that their bones were more likely to be retrieved. Hazel hen, partridge and woodpigeon were also identified. Butchery marks were found on bones of many of the species discussed above.

Various birds of prey, corvids and smaller passerines are present (see Appendix for full list) but there is no conclusive evidence that any of them were eaten. A wing of a white-tailed eagle from Novgorod had cuts on the humerus and the carpometacarpus, indicating that the wing had been detached and the feathers removed (Hamilton-Dyer 2002) but probably not further processed. It is likely that some of the birds of prey were used in falconry. Bones of goshawk and sparrowhawk are the most common and sometimes survived as associated groups. Hobby and kestrel were also identified and these may also have been trained. However these and many of the other raptors and corvids may have been birds resident in the settlements, exploiting the abundant food supply available within Novgorod in particular.

OTHER ANIMAL PRODUCTS

Dairy products

The presence of substantial numbers of calf mandibles in both the Troitsky and Gorodishche assemblages indicates that milk would have been readily available

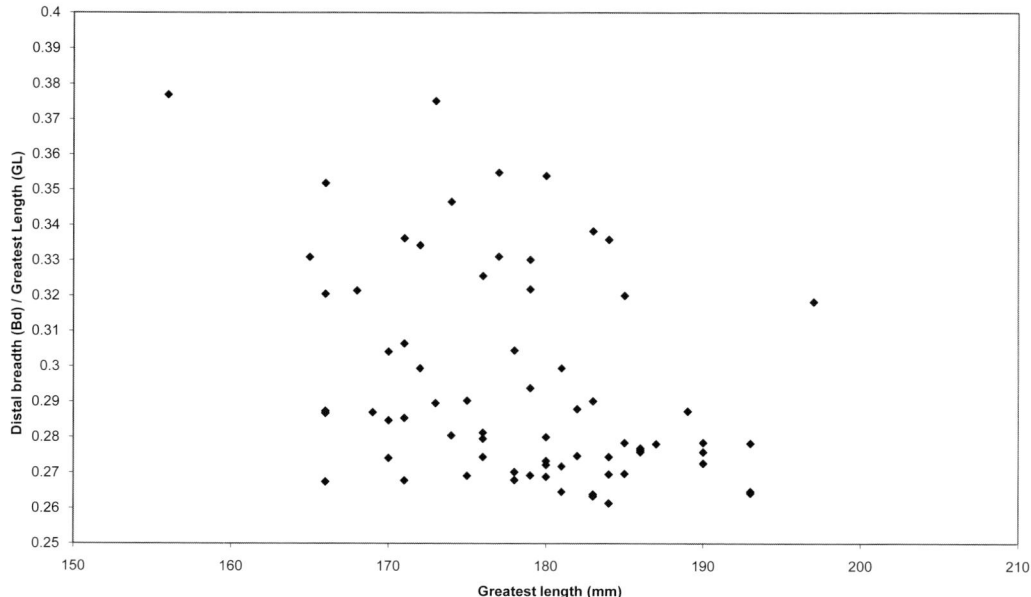

Figure 19.3 *Novgorod Troitsky IX–XI: cattle metacarpal greatest length and distal breadth measurements.*

for human consumption, as veal production is often closely linked with dairying. Metrical analysis of complete metacarpals (Figure 19.3) shows that the majority of fused specimens from the Troitsky sites (over 24–30 months of age) have dimensions sufficiently slender (Bd/GL <0.30) to be considered as females. It is more likely that immature bulls and steers would be slaughtered for meat. Adult cows would then act as both a source of milk and as breeding stock. However, as noted above, most of the cattle did not live to a very old age. A 13th century birch-bark document refers to a dry cow (Rybina 2001, 129). Similar results have been obtained from Gorodishche where the preliminary interpretation was that about two-thirds of the fused metacarpals belonged to females (Maltby and Hamilton-Dyer 2001). Milk production could also have been a factor in goat and sheep husbandry. Where distinction of Stage 2 mandibles was made in the Troitsky assemblage, equal numbers of sheep and goat were represented. These young lambs and kids may have been slaughtered prior to weaning, which again would release milk for human consumption.

The manufacture and trade of cheese and butter is mentioned in a few birch-bark documents (Rybina 2001, 130). Amongst other household objects that could be associated with butter- and cheese-making are perforated wooden moulds (Khoroshev 2007, 276).

Eggs

Deposits of medullary bone were noted within the shafts of a number of domestic fowl bones. Its presence indicates that the hens had recently been in lay and consequently this provides evidence for the production of eggs. In a sub-sample of 62 femora and tibiotarsi (bones in which the most medullary bone is deposited) from the lower levels of Troitsky XI, 21 showed evidence of medullary bone. Given that the sample will have included both males and females, this is quite a high proportion of laying hens. Interestingly, no records of medullary bone were observed in any of the duck or goose bones.

Hides, wool, furs and skins

The importance of Novgorod in the international fur trade is well known and a detailed synthesis of recent work is provided elsewhere (Makarov, Chapter 20, this volume). This section will therefore be restricted to a brief review of zooarchaeological results obtained during this project. As Makarov discusses, Savinetskii (in press) has shown that bones of fur-bearing mammals provide a substantial component of the assemblage from Minino (Table 19.4). As has been discussed above, there is evidence that the numbers of beaver caught by the inhabitants of Minino declined in the 13th century arguably through over-exploitation. It is interesting to note that the importance of beaver fur exploitation is not evident from the bone evidence from Novgorod itself, unsurprisingly in assemblages largely derived from meat processing. However, the virtual disappearance of beaver remains from the upper layers at Troitsky XI (Table 19.4) also reflects the decline in beaver exploitation at the same time as at Minino and supports other evidence for the decline in the trade of its fur at this time (Makarov, Chapter 20, this volume). Probably also significant is that none of the Novgorod birch-bark documents referring to beaver are dated later than the early 13th century Rybina 2007, 132).

Although the overall percentage of squirrel remains also declined slightly overall in the 13th century deposits at Minino, the exploitation of squirrels for their fur appears to have been sustained in the region into the later medieval period, as is reflected in other evidence (Makarov, Chapter 20, this volume), including fairly frequent references to squirrels in birch-bark documents (Rybina 2007, 132). Again, this trade is not reflected in the assemblages recovered by hand in the Troitsky excavations, from which only three squirrel bones were retrieved, all from lower layers, and only one squirrel bone was found in the sieved samples. Similarly only 11 squirrel bones were recovered from Gorodishche despite an extensive sieving programme (Table 19.4). Bones of pine marten are also common finds throughout the medieval deposits at Minino (Table 19.4). Their abundance has also been argued to reflect their exploitation for fur (Savinetskii in press). In contrast, only single specimens of marten were discovered at Troitsky and Gorodishche. However, undoubtedly the best evidence for the processing of skins comes from Prost, where there is a discrete accumulation of 54 marten foot bones from at least four individuals. Two of these bones bear skinning marks. The remains indicate that the pelts of several marten were processed.

None of the excavations produced positive identifications of sable bones. However, the presence of bones of bear, otter, fox, wolf, polecat, stoat, badger and lynx could all indicate that these species were also exploited for their pelts. Unsurprisingly the largest number of bones and greatest diversity of these species occur at Minino, indicating that a wide range of species was potentially exploited. However, it should also be noted that the relatively small sample from Georgii produced bones of beaver, lynx, squirrel and a bear metacarpal with clear skinning marks. If one adds the evidence for the martens at Prost, it would appear that inhabitants of settlements in Poozerie in the 9th and 10th centuries were involved in acquiring pelts, albeit on a smaller scale than that which developed in the Minino region. Several fur-bearing species were also recovered from Gorodishche (Table 19.4).

From the Troitsky sites all nine bear elements are third phalanges, two of which have fine knife cuts. Although it is feasible that these could have been amulets (one of the specimens is clearly worked), it is probable that they represent the presence of bear skins acquired by the inhabitants of the properties. Birch-bark documents indicate that bear skins were expensive to acquire (Rybina, this volume).

There is a diverse range of evidence from Novgorod regarding the exploitation of the hides and skins of domestic mammals. The superb survival of footwear, purses and other leather objects has allowed for the development of comprehensive typological sequences of some items (Izyumova 1959; 1967; Rybina 1992, 181–187; Kurbatov, this volume). Workshops associated with the production of shoes and other leather objects have been found on properties on the Nerevsky End (Izyumova 1967) and in excavations of the Nutny site (Slavensky End) as well as on several of the Troitsky sites (Rybina 1992, 183; Kublo 2007a). Some of the insect remains associated with leather offcuts on Troitsky Site XIII are indicative of the storage of hides for working (Reilly, this volume). Birch-bark documents include specific references to cured and uncured skins and hides of elk, sheep, goat and calf. The absence of horse and cattle hides from specific mention in the documents is interesting and it could be that cattle hides were too common a commodity to receive special attention in such records. Preliminary identification of 42 specimens of leather offcuts from the Troitsky and Kremlin sites revealed that half belonged to bovines (including several from calves). Eleven specimens were provisionally assigned to sheep/goat and two to deer. Several others remained unidentified but no pig skins were noted (Sully pers. comm.).

It would have been most unusual for the hides of the major meat-producing animals slaughtered in Novgorod not to have been utilised. Fine incisions, indicative of initial skinning, were commonly observed on the shafts of cattle first phalanges from the Troitsky sites (Maltby in press). This again supports the impression that much of the processing of cattle carcasses took place within individual properties. Similar marks were observed occasionally on horse phalanges. Probable skinning marks were also observed on several cattle cranial elements and also on skulls of a cat, a beaver and an elk.

Wool was a very important commodity throughout medieval Europe and evidence for its exploitation in Novgorod comes in a variety of forms. Although the birch-bark documents refer more commonly to linen, sheepskin is specifically alluded to in some documents (Rybina 2001; this volume). Racks for cleaning wool have been discovered on an 11th century property in earlier Troitsky excavations and looms, carding combs and other wooden objects associated with the industry are common finds in Novgorod (Kublo 2007b). Nakhlik (Thompson 1967, 96–98) produced a detailed analysis of textiles from the Nerevsky sites, where those made of wool clearly outnumbered those of linen and silk. He suggested, on the basis of fibre morphology, that most of the wool was derived locally but also discussed the probability that some wool and woven cloth was imported.

The growing importance of wool production may be evident in the sheep/goat mandible assemblage from the Troitsky sites. Although these include goats as well as sheep, relatively high proportions (at least 20% to as high as 40%) of adult animals over three years old (Stages 6–7) were found throughout the sequence (Table 19.2). In addition to their value as breeding stock and perhaps dairy producers, sheep of this age would have produced several fleeces of wool. The increase in the proportion of the oldest age category (at least 11% of mandibles are at Stage 7) in the upper spits of Troitsky XI may indicate that wool production was becoming more important from the middle of the 13th century. Further samples of this date are, however, required to confirm this trend. At Gorodishche, 31% of the 19 sheep/goat mandibles were at Stages 6–7, indicating perhaps a slightly higher proportion of adult animals were slaughtered there than in the earliest period of Novgorod. Again, these adult animals would have provided fleeces as well as being breeding stock.

Bone, antler, horn and ivory

A summary of the types and quantities of production waste from some properties on the Troitsky site and elsewhere in Novgorod has been provided by Smirnova (2001). It is abundantly clear that manufacture of items from these materials was an important occupation in some properties. Elk antlers were by far the most commonly used but worked antler from other species has also been found. There is some evidence that the working of bone increased in the later medieval period. As is common practice in excavations, worked objects were separated from the rest of the faunal material and treated as small finds. Therefore, it is not surprising that the amount of worked material in the bulk faunal assemblage from the Troitsky sites is low. Only a single piece of sawn elk antler (Troitsky XI, Spit 8, Property I) can be added to the totals supplied by Smirnova. No walrus ivory or antlers from reindeer, red deer or roe deer were present in our assemblage. An elk skull did show evidence that the antlers had been removed for working. A worked offcut of elk antler was also recorded at Gorodishche.

What the assessment did establish, however, is that the utilisation of horns for working was also common. Horn itself is one of the few organic materials that are generally not preserved in Novgorod but horn cores survive well. Over 100 (30%)

cattle horn cores in the Troitsky assemblages have butchery evidence that indicates that horns were commonly separated from the skulls at their base. Even allowing for the possibility that some of the horns were removed with the hides and not worked, the evidence suggests that horn-working was probably an industry that was more important than has previously been realised. Similarly, over 30% of the goat and sheep horn cores bear evidence of butchery associated with their separation from the skulls. Unfortunately it was not possible to determine whether there were any concentrations of horn cores within the individual properties that could indicate areas of horn-working similar to those on the Duboshin site in the Slavensky Quarter (Smirnova 2001, 83). Discrete concentrations of butchered cattle horn cores were recorded at Gorodishche, indicating that small-scale horn-working may have been taking place there (Maltby in press). A group of over 100 sawn cattle distal metatarsals discarded as offcuts was found on the Federovsky site in 1997, providing an example of the stockpiling of bones for working (Maltby in press).

Apart from Smirnova's (2005) comprehensive analysis of combs, there has been no detailed survey of worked bone and antler objects from Novgorod (Rybina 1992, 167). Worked bones were noted in small numbers in the Troitsky assemblage, although most had previously been removed and recorded as small finds. The most common finds consisted of pierced and sometimes decorated sheep/goat astragali. A number of skates made out of horse radii and metapodials were also collected and added to the many recovered from previous excavations in Novgorod.

COMMENSAL SPECIES

Dogs (and wolves)

Although there is evidence, that dog meat was occasionally eaten in Novgorod, the presence of several groups of associated bones shows that it was much more likely that their bodies were simply buried or dumped after death. The presence of dogs is mainly evident in the abundant evidence for gnawing damage on the bones. In the hand-collected Troitsky assemblage, over 10,000 of the elements of identified mammals scanned had gnawing damage recorded, representing 31% of the total. Given the rapidity of scanning, this should be regarded as very much a minimum figure. Dogs caused the vast majority of gnawing damage. They clearly had easy access to butchery and table waste deposited within these properties. The dogs themselves varied quite widely in size but few very small dogs are represented. Shoulder heights of dogs recovered from the Troitsky IX–XI sites range between 33 cm and 69 cm. The largest specimen is from an ulna, which along with an associated radius, is from an animal substantially larger than any of the others. They are very similar in size to wolf and perhaps are from a wild animal. Two skulls of wolves were found at Gorodishche but the only definite identifications of wolf at Minino are from Iron Age contexts (Savinetskii in press). Dogs would have had a wide range of uses including shepherding, guarding and hunting. One birch-bark document refers to a hound, presumably indicating its use in hunting (Rybina 2001, 129).

Cats

Domestic cats also appear to have been commonly kept in Novgorod. Their recovery is handicapped by their small size but in fact cat bones are nearly twice as common as dog in the Troitsky assemblages and they were recovered in relatively higher numbers in sieved samples (Table 19.1). Their remains include several groups of associated bones and, apart from the rare specimens that bear cut marks associated with skinning, butchery or bone-working, most cat carcasses were probably deposited unprocessed. The presence of substantial numbers of unfused bones (Maltby in press) indicates both that cats were resident in the town but that many failed to attain old age. Their tooth marks were observed on a number of bones, particular those of birds. The excavations at Gorodishche have also produced cat bones but they form a very small percentage of the assemblage and their bones have not been found on any of the other 9th to 10th century sites in the area, nor, perhaps more surprisingly, in medieval deposits at Minino (Table 19.1). Cats appear to have been better adapted to urban life and would have been useful in the control of vermin. A few bones of rat were recovered from the Troitsky excavations (Maltby in press).

Horse

The perhaps surprising frequency of evidence for the exploitation of horsemeat and horse hides has been discussed above. However, it is beyond argument that the value of horses for riding and as beasts of burden was far greater. The stabling of horses in various Novgorod properties has been confirmed by the plant macrofossil and insect analysis (Monk and Johnston this volume; Reilly this volume). Horses are mentioned in birch-bark documents on many more occasions than any other species (Rybina 2001, 129), indicative of their high value. Epiphyseal fusion evidence indicates that nearly all the limb bones found on the Troitsky sites are fused and the limited mandible evidence indicates that most horses could expect to live a relatively long life. Evidence for wooden elements associated with horses include harness parts, saddles, whips and sleigh runners (Dubrovin 2007b).

Macaque

Although it does not come from the assemblage examined in detail from Gorodishche, it would be remiss not to note the discovery of the skull of a macaque from later excavations of the site (Brisbane et al. 2007). First identified as being from the monkey family by Sheila Hamilton-Dyer in 2003, its identification as an adult, probably female, Barbary macaque was confirmed at the British Museum (Natural History). It has a calibrated radiocarbon date centred on AD1180. Macaques are known to have inhabited North Africa and parts of SW Europe at this time. Therefore this animal had been brought a long distance. Although the skull could have been brought back as a trophy or a curiosity, it is more likely that the live animal was brought to Gorodishche, perhaps as an exotic gift to the Prince.

SUMMARY AND CONCLUSIONS

The project has been able to demonstrate that zooarchaeological studies can have a significant part to play in the interpretation of the lives of medieval communities in the Novgorod region. Given a more consistent retrieval policy, the potential to further these preliminary results, in Novgorod in particular, is enormous. More detailed comparisons of faunal remains from within and between different properties and between different areas and periods are required but that will require much greater control of sampling and a significant increase in sieving.

However, it has already been established that there were significant variations in the exploitation of animals within the region and between different periods. For example, it can be postulated that the inhabitants of the later medieval properties of Troitsky IX–XI, whilst continuing to eat a lot of beef, consumed relatively more mutton, goat meat and chicken and perhaps less pork and duck than their forebears. They may have consumed more dairy produce but the occasional beaver ham was a thing of the past. However, they continued not to be averse to eating horsemeat. Exactly how important fish was in their diet will require further research but it is likely that the resources of Lake Ilmen and the local rivers were exploited at least as intensively as they were in the 10th century by the inhabitants of Georgii, Prost and Gorodishche. Occasionally, from at least the 10th century onwards, some of them acquired prized fish such as sturgeon, large wels, whitefish and smoked eels.

At the edge of the Novgorod Lands the inhabitants of Minino relied much more heavily on the meat of the wild mammals they were killing for their skins. Venison, beaver and probably even squirrel were staples of the meat diet rather than occasional supplements. They also fished the local lake but unlike the residents of Novgorod they rarely ate zander, because the species did not inhabit its waters. They often preserved perch and cyprinids. They did keep some domestic animals and consumed fair quantities of beef. They kept relatively more sheep than the farmers around Novgorod but the colder winters restricted pig keeping.

The international importance of the fur industry is reflected in the make-up of the zooarchaeological assemblage at Minino. However, this is not evident in the bones from Novgorod itself. Most processing took place elsewhere and, apart from the occasional bearskin, evidence for the importance of furs and skins of wild species is extremely limited beyond the documentary evidence. Interestingly, however, the decline in the importance of the trade in beaver pelts in the 13th century is reflected in several ways. Their numbers declined markedly in the Minino assemblage and they virtually disappeared in the Novgorod samples. References to beavers have not been found in contemporary birch-bark documents. Overexploitation, perhaps reflected in their mortality patterns at Minino, and the increasing clearance of woodland for agriculture and pasture are both likely to have been factors in their decline.

The project has also demonstrated that a holistic approach to the study of animal exploitation can produce great benefits, particularly when there are superb survival conditions. For example, our understanding of how horses were valued, stabled and exploited in Novgorod has utilised evidence not just from the bones themselves but has also used evidence from documents, insect remains, plant macrofossils, wooden objects, metal objects and building plans. To understand the complexity of life in the medieval period, we all need to look beyond our own individual sites and areas of specialist interest.

APPENDIX

SPECIES IDENTIFIED IN THE PROJECT

Domestic Mammals
Cattle (*Bos taurus*)
Pig (*Sus scrofa domesticus*)
Sheep (*Ovis aries*)
Goat (*Capra hircus*)
Horse (*Equus caballus*)
Cat (*Felis catus*)
Dog (*Canis familiaris*)

Wild Mammals
Aurochs (*Bos primigenius*)
Badger (*Meles meles*)
Bear (*Ursus arctos*)
Beaver (*Castor fiber*)
Bison (*Bison bonasus*)
Boar (*Sus scrofa*)
Elk (*Alces alces*)
Fox (*Vulpes* sp.)
Hare (*Lepus* sp.)
Lynx (*Lynx lynx*)
Macaque (*Macaca sylvanus*)
Marten (*Martes* sp.)
Otter (*Lutra lutra*)
Polecat (*Mustela putorius*)
Reindeer (*Rangifer tarandus*)
Roe deer (*Capreolus capreolus*)
Squirrel (*Scirius vulgaris*)
Stoat (*Mustela ermina*)
Wolf (*Canis lupus*)

Birds
Black grouse (*Tetrao tetrix*)
Buzzard (*Buteo buteo*)
Capercaillie (*Tetrao urogallus*)
cf. Garganey (*cf. Anas querquedula*)
cf. Goldeneye (*cf. Bucephala clangula*)
cf. Jay (*cf. Garrulus glandarius*)
cf. Pochard (*cf. Aythya ferina*)
cf. Snipe (*cf. Gallinago gallinago*)
cf. Wigeon (*cf. Anas penelope*)
cf. Woodcock (*cf. Scolopax rusticola*)

Coot (*Fulica atra*)
Cormorant (*Phalacrocorax carbo*)
Crane (*Grus grus*)
Domestic duck or Mallard (*Anas platyrhynchos*)
Domestic fowl (*Gallus gallus*)
Domestic or *cf.* greylag goose (*cf. Anser anser*)
Eagle *cf.* white-tailed (*cf. Haliaeetus albicilla*)
Goshawk (*Accipiter gentilis*)
Great-crested grebe (*Podiceps cristatus*)
Gull (*Larus* sp.)
Hazel hen (*Bonasa bonasia*)
Hen harrier (*Circus cyaneus*)
Heron (*Ardea cinerea*)
Hobby (*Falco subbuteo*)
Jackdaw (*Corvus monedula*)
Owl *cf.* tawny (*cf. Strix aluco*)
Partridge (*Perdix perdix*)
Raven (*Corvus corax*)
Rook/Crow (*Corvus frugilegus/corone*)
Sparrowhawk (*Accipiter nisus*)
Stork (*Ciconia* sp.)
Swan (*Cygnus* sp.)
Teal (*Anas crecca*)
Woodpigeon (*Columba palumbus*)

Fish
Common eel (*Anguilla anguilla*)
Cyprinidae (Bream family) including
    Bream (*Abramis brama*)
    Dace (*Leuciscus leuciscus*) and/or
    Chub (*Leuciscus cephalus*)
    Ide (*Leuciscus idus*)
    Roach (*Rutilus rutilus*)
    Silver bream (*Blicca bjoerkna*)
Perch (*Perca fluviatilis*)
Pike (*Esox luscus*)
Ruffe (*Gymnocephalus cernuus*)
Sturgeon (*Acipenser* sp.)
Wels (catfish) (*Siluris glanis*)
Whitefish (*Coregonus lavaretus*)
Zander (*Sander*) (*Stizostedion lucioperca*)

– 20 –

THE FUR TRADE IN THE ECONOMY OF THE NORTHERN BORDERLANDS OF MEDIEVAL RUSSIA

N. A. Makarov

INTRODUCTION

The subject of the fur trade as a source for the accumulation of wealth and economic growth in medieval Russia has once again become a topic for discussion. This has come about largely due to advances in the study of hoards of Arab silver coins of the 8th–10th centuries, which have helped to make it possible for scholars to chart geographical features and locations more precisely, to date the circulation of Kufic coins in Eastern Europe, and to determine quantitative data relating to the exchange of commodities (Noonan 1990; 1998; 2000; 2004). The calculations for the total volume of Kufic silver coins imported into Eastern Europe in that period made by Noonan inevitably led to consideration of the volume of fur obtained, which is regarded as the main commodity ensuring the influx of silver coins. According to Noonan's calculations, during the 10th century approximately 1,250,000 whole Samanid dirhams came into Eastern Europe from Central Asia every year, which when expressed in material terms was the equivalent of 500,000 ermine skins (Noonan 1990, 255–256; 2004, 295–296). These figures are similar to those for the volume of Russian fur exports via Archangel in the middle of the 17th century (approximately 500,000 skins), determined with the help of documentary sources (Khoroshkevich 1963, 116).

No less important a stimulus to re-examine the significance of the fur trade for medieval Russian society was provided by certain archaeological materials relating directly to the sphere of the fur trade and the transportation of valuable furs. The wooden cylinders with carved inscriptions found in Novgorod are among the most important categories of archaeological materials providing records of the trapping of fur-bearing animals, the transportation of furs, and commercial transactions involving furs. These objects were recognised by Yanin (1992, 78–82; 2001, 12–13; 2007) to be locks for sealing the sacks of fur brought to Novgorod, having been collected as tribute in the northern *volosts* (small administrative areas, pre-1917). What indicates the extreme importance of these deliveries for the prosperity of early Novgorod is the complex organization of the collection of furs involving the direct participation of the Novgorod *boyars* in this activity and the compulsory recording of fur quantities brought in from individual *volosts* liable for poll-tax.

In addition, it has been established by these seals that as early as the 11th century fur was being delivered to Novgorod from administrative areas in the regions of the Onega and Dvina rivers (Figure 20.1) (Yanin 1982; 2001).

A major step forward in the archaeological investigation of the fur trade was the identification of *tomar*s – arrowheads with a blunt end made from wood, horn or iron and designed to be used by hunters for fur. These have been found in the archaeological collections from Novgorod and medieval sites in the area of Byeloe Ozero (literally White Lake, hereafter referred to as Byeloe Lake, and the associated region as Byeloozero) (Makarov 1997, 159; Gaidukov and Makarov 1993, 179–188; Smirnova 1994, 143–155).

Finally, another important landmark was the identification within the Novgorod collection of a group of tally-sticks that were used for counting and recording the numbers of skins. These usually had 40 notches on them, divided into four blocks with ten in each (Kovalev 2002, 42–43, 48; 2003, 57–72; 2007). These finds, together with the new osteological collections obtained from various North-Russian settlements discussed below, have made possible a progression from general reconstructions of the structure and directions of commodity exchange to the study of the specific organization of the fur trade and its development and the location of the areas where fur-bearing animals were hunted. The materials collected during excavations at Minino make a considerable addition to the range of sources related to this aspect of the medieval economy and make it possible for us to move forward in our study of it.

MININO AND OTHER SITES IN THE NORTHERN BORDERLANDS OF MEDIEVAL RUSSIA

The excavations at Minino reveal a picture of a fur trade which lasted for a long time and was conducted on a wide scale: these activities were pursued by the inhabitants of the settlements around Kubenskoye Lake over the course of around 250 years. The main animals hunted for this purpose were beavers, squirrels and pine marten, whose total number of bones constitute more than 56% of all the faunal remains from the occupation levels of the medieval period (Savinetskii in press). In those levels of the Minino settlements nine blunt arrowheads were found (Figure 20.3) and another three came from burial complexes. Lightweight horn arrowheads were most probably used for hunting squirrels, and larger horn or iron arrowheads were likely to have been used for larger animals such as beavers. The presence of arrowheads with a blunt end in the grave goods of the earliest male burials in the burial-grounds at Minino and Vladyshnevo, and also in the Nefedievo burial ground on the Slavensky Volok[1] when grave goods accompanying male burials were generally meagre (Makarov 1997, 159), testifies to the fact that hunting fur-bearing animals was one of the main economic activities of medieval settlers, symbolic commemoration of which was required in the funerary rite. In addition, finds of a series of amulets made from the astragali of beavers possibly reflect the existence of some special symbolism associated with this animal as well as its significance to individual members of this community.

The significance of the beaver as one of the main animals hunted for fur in the forest zone of Eastern Europe in the 10th and 11th centuries has been well documented thanks to archaeological and palaeozoological evidence (Fekhner 1989, 71–78). It is usual for beaver bones to make up a substantial component of bone collections from a medieval settlement in the forest zone of Eastern Europe, in particular those from large villages and urban sites of the 10th–12th centuries – from the Smolensk Lands in the West (Sedov 1960, 76–77) to the Kamsko-Vyatskii region in the East (Bogatkina 1995, 143, 146–148; 2002, 292–297; Goldina 1985, 150). Among the sites near Byeloe Lake, which provide evidence of involvement in the beaver-fur trade, the best known is the settlement of Krutik. In its osteological collection, beaver bones account for 49% of the total (Andreyeva 1991, 182–186). Excavations of that settlement first revealed the importance of Byeloozero as an important trading area, the exploitation of which would ensure an influx of silver. Further excavations revealed the presence of beaver bones which made up between 7% and 17% in bone assemblages from a further five settlements of the 10th–12th centuries near Byeloe Lake and in the Srednyaya Sheksna area (Krivets, Nefedovo, Oktyabrskii Most, Lukovets, Nikolskoye VI on the Suda River; Figure 20.2). This contrasts with their absence or insignificant percentage in assemblages from occupation levels from sites dated to the second half of the 12th or the 13th century (Lukovets, Minino IV at Yug) and from the 12th–15th centuries (Minino II at Yug) (Kudryashov 2002; Bashenkin 1989, 13–14). This means that in the Byeloozero and Sheksna regions beaver hunting developed rapidly in the 10th century and continued to be practised in the 11th and 12th centuries. The zooarchaeological evidence indicates that beaver hunting declined markedly or disappeared altogether in subsequent periods.

Beaver, together with sable, black fox, pine marten and squirrel, is mentioned in Arab sources as one of the main categories of fur exported from medieval Russia to the lands of the East in the 9th–12th centuries (Novoseltsev 2000, 291–318; Mongait 1959, 172; Noonan 2004, 276–278). According to observations made by Khoroshkevich (1963, 63–4), by the 14th–15th centuries beaver furs were extremely rare amongst those exported from Novgorod to the West. This observation matches up with the data obtained from birch-bark documents: beaver furs are mentioned in the texts of five birch-bark documents beginning in the period from the early 12th century to the second half of the 13th century (Rybina 2001, 129) and, moreover, in one of those documents (No. 721/647/683) there is reference to furs being obtained in the Zavolochie region (Yanin and Zaliznyak 2000, 20–21). In the osteological collections from the occupation levels at Staraya Ladoga and Ryurik Gorodishche (near Novgorod), beaver bones are extremely rare, as indeed are bones of other fur-bearing animals (Maltby and Hamilton-Dyer 2001, 119–121; Kasparov 1997, 26–30). It has been noted in deposits from excavations at the Troitsky site in Novgorod that beaver bones occur in small numbers in lower levels, but are absent from later deposits (Maltby, in press).

Savinetskii considers that although the hunting pressure on the beaver population in the Minino hunting area increased in the late-12th and early-13th century, we have no direct evidence of the beaver population being in an endangered state at that time. Moreover, the impossibility of closely dating osteological assemblages, which might, at best, be dated to a range of several decades, makes it impossible to specify the precise date and circumstances of the drastic drop in the numbers of beavers found at Kubenskoye Lake. Economic documents from the Kirillo-Byelozersky Monastery in the 15th century, in which beavers are mentioned only once, indicate that at that time the beaver was no longer playing an important role in the economy of the Byeloe Lake region.

Squirrel bones, unlike those of the beaver, are rare finds in the osteological collections from these medieval settlements. One of the probable reasons for this is the nature of the bones themselves, which are small and inconspicuous for those sorting through the soil from the occupation levels. Another reason may be that beaver meat was probably more commonly eaten and therefore carcasses would have been brought back to the settlements. This is unlikely to be the case for squirrel which could have been skinned where caught, the meat fed to the dogs, if used at all.

During the excavation of the Krutik settlement only seven squirrel bones were found, which accounts for 0.2% of the total number of bones from wild animals (Andreyeva 1991, 183) and in the osteological collection from the medieval urban site of Idnakar in northern Udmurtia they only account for 2.5% of the total number of wild-animal bones (Bogatkina 1995, 143, 146). Excavations at the settlement of Minino I provided palaeozoological material that revealed, for the first time, wide scale squirrel hunting between the late-10th and early 13th centuries. At the same time Savinetskii (in press) notes the small number of squirrel bones at Minino in the levels of the Early Iron Age, which indicate that squirrel skins did not then possess economic significance (or, alternatively, were not brought back to the settlement). In the Medieval period, squirrel hunting for furs in the Minino micro-region remained at approximately the same level and even increased slightly in the late-12th and early-13th centuries in comparison with the preceding period, if the percentages in the faunal assemblages directly reflect this activity. This observation is perfectly compatible with a supposedly stable squirrel population, which was able to withstand the high level of pressure from hunting activity at this time. The relatively low price for squirrel fur was made up for by the fact that it was possible to obtain large numbers of pelts and the trade was a stable one.

DOCUMENTARY EVIDENCE

In addition, we know that squirrel fur in the 14th–15th centuries was exported by Hanseatic merchants in enormous quantities and comprised the bulk of all Novgorod exports (Lesnikov 1948, 61–93; Khoroshkevich 1964, 73–86; Martin 1986, 61–85). In the documentary sources there are no accounts that make it possible to calculate with precision the absolute volume of the export trade, but if we start with certain specific documents from the Hanseatic archive indicating the numbers of squirrel pelts on ships travelling from Reval (Tallinn, Estonia) in the last third of the 14th and the early-15th century (up to 230,000 items), it can be assumed that every year several hundred thousand squirrel skins were exported from Novgorod to Western Europe through the Baltic (Khoroshkevich 1963, 107–116). The hunting of squirrels, whose fur was then exported westwards from Novgorod, was carried out in various places: in the northern part of the Novgorod Lands, including the areas along the Dvina River beyond Lake Onega, and in the centre of the Novgorod Lands and beyond. The geographical spread of this hunting can in part be established with reference to the names for the various sorts of squirrel fur. For instance, "anigen" refers to squirrel fur from the Onega region and "klezemes" are from Klyazma squirrels (Khoroshkevich 1963, 78–81). In the birch-bark documents from Novgorod the words *vevereitsy*, *vekshi* and *bely* were used both to refer to squirrel fur and also to small units of money. In this respect it is interesting to note that there are also words such as *bel/belka* and *gornostal* which appear in 16th-century documents that refer to squirrel tax and ermine tax respectively.

As has been pointed out by Rybina, squirrel fur is mentioned more often in economic documents than other varieties of fur. The earliest of these documents dates from the 12th century (Rybina 2001, 129). In addition, an inscription on a Novgorod 12th-century cylindrical seal records the number of furs contained in a sack collected from the Pinega River region as 3,000: "pineze 3 tysyache" (Yanin 2001, 97; 1992, 78). This enables us to assume that the trading in squirrel fur in the eastern part of the basin of the Northern Dvina River began no later than the first quarter of the 12th century. It would appear that only squirrel pelts could be calculated in thousands. The use of the term "vevereitsy" in the birch-bark documents of the 11th and 12th century as a collective word to designate money (Nos. 105, 246, 335, 657, 722) (Yanin and Zaliznyak 2000, 21) testifies to the considerable economic importance of squirrel fur at this time.

The excavations at Minino have made it possible for the first time to trace the emergence of squirrel hunting in the northern part of Russia in the late-10th and 11th centuries and its stable continuation in the 12th and early-13th centuries. Martin (1986, 63–65) explains this with reference to the exceptional demand for squirrel fur on fashion items, which emerged in the countries of Western Europe in the 13th and 14th centuries – first in aristocratic circles and then gradually spreading to a wider strata of the urban population. In her opinion the English aristocracy at that time preferred squirrel fur to other sorts, such as sable. What probably explains the predominance of squirrel in the Novgorod fur market is first and foremost the nature of the actual natural resources available to the citizens of Novgorod in the 13th–15th centuries at a time when the size of beaver populations was falling and access to sable hunting-grounds involved additional logistical difficulties.

Arab writers, in particular Ibn Fadlan, Gardizi, Al-Istakhri and Ibn-Hauqal, make reference to the Russians' trade in sable and mention sable as one of the main categories of valuable fur exported from the northern regions of Eastern Europe (Kovalevskii 1956, 136–144; Novoseltsev 2000, 305, 316–17). Yet in the osteological collection from the large villages in the Minino area sable bones have not been identified (just as they have not been identified in the occupation levels of the medieval settlements near Byeloe Lake). All the mandible fragments from animals of the genus *Martes* (which includes both marten and sable) have been identified by Savinetskii (in press) as belonging to the pine marten. A different picture emerges when we study the osteological collections from medieval sites of Western Siberia, in particular, the urban site of Yendyrskoye, where all the mandibles from the *Martes* genus for which the species can be identified belong to sable (Zykov and Koksharov 2001, 254–55). At the medieval sites in the area of the Kama River and in North-western Siberia, amulets made of sable bones are widespread (Goldina and Kananin 1989, Figure 77.5; Zykov and Koksharov 2001, 119, Figure 38.11; Figure 41.14, 15, 20, 21). It can thus be seen how palaeozoological evidence regarding the trapping of sable indicates how the fur of this animal came from the Kama River region and Western Siberia soon after AD 1000.

Documentary materials relating to the northern parts of medieval Russia such as the Life (*Zhitie*) of Stefan of Perm record the existence of trade in sable fur and the fact that "state tribute" in the late 14th and 15th century was being paid in sable furs from the Perm Lands: i.e. from the region of the Rivers Vychegda, Vym, Udora and Sysola (*Zhitie svyatogo Stefana*, 1897, 47; *ASEI*, 1964, Vol. III, No. 291, 308–311). As regards the collection of sable furs to pay tribute to the Novgorod citizens at Yugra, there is a chronicle reference recounting the Novgorodians campaign into Yugra in 1193, which states "we collect silver and sable and other costly furs" [*PSRL* (Complete Collection of Russian Chronicles), Vol. III, 2000, 232]. Sable is only mentioned once in Novgorod birch-bark documents (Birch-bark document No. 722, late-12th/early-13th century) (Yanin and Zaliznyak 2000, 21). It can be assumed that the area within which sables were hunted at the beginning of the second millennium was bordered in the West by the region of the Kama River and the eastern part of the basin of the Severnaya Dvina and that the population of the northern borderlands of Russia – Byeloozero, Vologda and the western part of Zavolochie – did not engage in sable hunting and could only obtain it through trade and tribute-collecting expeditions to the North-east.

DISCUSSION

Where and how were the valuable furs exported from the region round Lake Kubenskoye? Archaeological materials do not provide a direct answer to this question, but if we consider the general range of imports and the cultural features of the sites from the Minino group, it can be assumed that there were two routes which met at Lake Kubenskoye, one of which led to the Volga, to the towns of the Rostov and Suzdal Lands and Volga Bulgaria, while the second led to Novgorod and the Baltic. It needs also to be taken into account that the intensity of the use of these trading routes varied from one period to another. The firm links between the area around Lake Kubenskoye and the Rostov-Suzdal principality were based on trade and economic links, on the export of fur to the South along the Sheksna and Volga Rivers rather than to the markets of Volga Bulgaria. To judge from the presence of Volga-Finnish jewellery, belt sets and purses of Volga Bulgarian origin in the grave goods of the earliest burials, the initial economic settlement of the lands around Lake Kubenskoye for hunting purposes must have been bound up with the functioning of the Volga route and the import of Arab silver coinage. The silver crisis in the East and the interruption of the import of Kufic coins into Volga Bulgaria at the end of the 10th century must have given rise to major changes in the system for commodity exchange, which had only just taken shape. Numerous finds of *denarii* at the sites of the Minino group would appear to reflect the re-orientation of trade links in the 11th century, principally the export of furs to Novgorod and from there to the Baltic, which in its turn ensured the influx of West-European silver coinage. This re-orientation did not mean the complete interruption of southern trade links, since silver was not the only commodity attracting Russian merchants to the markets of Volga Bulgaria.

Materials from the excavations at Minino go a long way towards changing stereotyped ideas about how the fur trade was organized and the extent to which the population of the remote forest-zone territories participated in its organization. What was unexpected was, first and foremost, the concentration of the trade within a comparatively large, permanent settlement. It emerges that hunting animals for fur in the area around Lake Kubenskoye required the concentration in one centre of population of a sizeable group of hunters catching beavers, pine martens and squirrels to sell. Archaeological traces of specialized temporary settlements – small hunters' camps, which to judge from ethnographic data were an essential element of the hunting infrastructure in many parts of the North – have not been found in the region round Lake Kubenskoye. However, it would be wrong to rule out the existence of a network of temporary hunters' settlements, which are difficult for archaeologists to locate, around the Minino cluster of permanent settlements. If we refer to archaeological materials, we can be confident that the majority of the activities linked with preparations for hunting and the primary processing of hunted produce took place in the central settlement.

It should be acknowledged that Minino, whose inhabitants obtained furs in considerable quantities, was not a centre specializing in one kind of economic activity. The range of activities its inhabitants engaged in was fairly wide: while acting as suppliers of furs, the people of Minino were utterly autonomous when it came to providing their own food and manufacturing some of the equipment needed both inside and outside their own immediate household. This means that we have evidence for the development of highly complex forms of economic organization in the borderlands of medieval Russia in the 10th–12th centuries, which were essential to support normal everyday life.

In historical writing the point of view has taken firm root according to which the main means of accumulating furs in the Novgorod fur market in the 13th–15th centuries was the collection of tribute undertaken by the *boyars* both from the northern borderlands, including areas inhabited by the Finno-Ugric population, for which hunting was a traditional occupation, and also from the peasant population of the central parts of the Novgorod Lands (Khoroshkevich 1963, 47–72). Indeed, 15th-century written sources contain numerous pieces of evidence concerning the payment by the population of the Novgorod *pyatins* (a *pyatin* was one of five areas into which the Novgorod region was divided) of part of their taxes in furs. Khoroshkevich (1963, 68–72) assumes that the participation by peasants in the fur trade only became noticeable at all in the last third of the 15th century when barter payments in fur were replaced by quit-rent paid in money. Cylindrical seals from the Novgorod excavations recording the collection of state taxes (tribute) in fur from the outlying administrative areas along the Onega River and in the basin of the Northern Dvina in the 11th and the first quarter of the 12th century (Yanin 2001, 48–57) leave us in no doubt that this practice had evolved during the earliest period of Novgorod's history and was crucially important for the economic prosperity of the Novgorod *boyars*.

However, the excavations at Minino shed light on completely different mechanisms underlying the collection of valuable furs. The archaeological materials collected in the vicinity of Lake Kubenskoye testify to the high level of prosperity enjoyed by groups involved directly with hunting fur-bearing animals and to the concentration of significant material resources at their disposal. They have shown that a large share of the imports being brought into medieval Russia in the 10th–12th centuries came to rest in the hands of people living in the borderlands. From this it follows that the furs made their way to markets not only as a result of the compulsory exaction of it in the form of tribute, but to a lesser degree as a result of a chain of commercial operations, in which the inhabitants of forest-zone settlements in the northern borderlands were direct participants. The exporters of fur were evidently not in a position to obtain the whole volume of valuable furs required by relying solely on the collection of fur for tribute. Participation in this trade and inclusion in a system of long-distance trading links determined to a large extent the culture and type of consumption to be found in the northern villages of the 10th–12th centuries.

It may be appropriate to apply the observations regarding the economic organization of rural settlements made on the basis of the materials from the Minino archaeological complex to an extensive territory incorporating Byeloozero, the Sheksna River and the Upper Volga (that is, from its source to Yaroslavl, see Figure 20.4). There are many common features to be observed in the appearance of rural settlements over the whole of this territory: first and foremost the relatively large size of the settlements; the large amounts of metal jewellery to be found in the occupation levels; the presence of glass beads and other articles reflecting a high level of consumption; the presence of the bones of fur-bearing animals in the occupation levels, especially beaver bones; the presence of blunt arrowheads; and agricultural tools which point to the fact that arable farming was being carried out by these communities, as well as the rearing of domestic animals. It may thus be assumed that the economy of these settlements was of a complex nature and was based on a combination of agriculture and forest pursuits, the produce from which would be sold. It is evident that throughout this territory, hunting for fur was a pursuit carried out by the inhabitants of these large villages and not by specialized hunters in separate settlements. Of course the way such hunting developed in different areas could have varied. We can assume that in the region of the Upper Volga fur-bearing animals were hunted almost to extinction earlier than along the Sheksna River or around Byeloe Lake, after which the main area for hunting gradually shifted towards the North and the North-east. This can be traced to some extent with the help of materials from the Minino archaeological complex. The inhabitants of Minino continued to hunt beaver in the 12th century at a time when in the adjacent western territories along the Sheksna River and near Byeloe Lake hunting was no longer practised or had at least been curtailed to a substantial extent.

Is it possible to regard the "Minino model" for the organization of hunting, which involved the organization of large, permanent settlements and intensive trading in areas where the furs were actually obtained, as a universal method for settling borderlands in the 10th–12th centuries and ensuring the local population's livelihood? Despite the incomplete nature of the archaeological data relating to the situation pertaining in various parts of the North, we have to answer this question in the negative. It is clear that in a large number of regions colonization and the establishment of trading involved setting up small settlements, from which there have survived only very meagre archaeological traces. Large settlements with rich assemblages of artefacts, similar to those found in the Upper Volga and Lake Kubenskoye regions, have not been found in the basins of the Onega and Northern Dvina Rivers, even in those places from which, to judge from inscriptions on cylindrical seals, furs were brought to Novgorod. The compact groups of archaeological sites of the 11th–13th centuries which are modest in size correspond to the "Zavolotsk toponyms" (Figure 20.1) inscribed on the Novgorod wooden cylinders (Ust Vaga, Tikhmega) and their occupation levels do not contain significant quantities of jewellery, household articles or tools (Makarov 2003, 149–163).

The most striking example of a fundamentally different way of organizing the fur trade is provided by the network of trading villages of the 10th–11th centuries round Lake Onega and beyond it in the region known as Zaonezhie. It is a system of small settlements with very meagre household remains, which functioned over a short period of time. According to Spiridonov (2001, 303–309), the emergence of such a network of settlements was linked with the hunting activity of the inhabitants of the south-eastern part of the region round Lake Ladoga, who used the Lake Onega region for the hunting of fur-bearing animals but were not interested in tilling the land there.

The "Zaonezhie model" was based on the setting up of small temporary settlements in the hunting zone without creating any long-term settlements and is the complete opposite of the "Minino model" (Figure 20.4). Unfortunately the occupation levels of the Vaga and Onega villages do not contain osteological remains, which deprives us of the chance of finding out the actual range of animals hunted.

Finally, we need to consider the presence of at least 100 blunt arrowheads from 10th–15th century levels at Novgorod and of the finds of these in 10th-century levels at nearby Ryurik Gorodishche (Smirnova 1994, 143–155). It is difficult to say how far from Novgorod were the hunting territories where these specialised arrowheads were used, but there is no doubt that the townsfolk themselves engaged in the hunting of fur-bearing animals. Furs reached Novgorod properties not only as a result of the collection of taxes or commodity exchange, but, albeit on a lesser scale, as a result of the hunting in which the townspeople themselves participated.

CONCLUSIONS

However much methods for settling different territories may have varied, these new excavations have provided reliable evidence for the influence of international trade on life within the various regions of Russia, where fur-bearing animals were hunted and caught. They have provided confirmation for the conclusion drawn by Noonan (2000) after analysis of materials from the Kama River area to the effect that wide-scale trading in fur is impossible without creating a fairly complex socio-economic infrastructure in those areas, from which fur was supplied. They also oblige us to reject the widespread view that the movement of commodities along major waterways had virtually no impact on the culture and economy of the rural population. The circulation of furs and silver made possible the enrichment not only of the élite, which conducted the trading operations in the towns and effected control of the waterways, but also a fairly wide stratum of the population, including the hunters who obtained the fur. The commodity exchange which took shape in the 11th and 12th centuries between Northern Russia and Western Europe stimulated the integration of the north-eastern borderlands into a long-distance trading system and created favourable conditions for the accumulation of wealth in the borderlands and for the development of more complex forms of culture and social organization.

Note

1   Editors' note: a *volok* was a portage, an area across which boats were dragged overland from one river to another.

LEATHER-WORKING IN NORTH-WEST RUSSIA

A. V. Kurbatov

INTRODUCTION

Novgorod the Great was a large centre of craft production in medieval Russia, which stood out from other towns on account of the high level of technology used and the organization of craft manufacturing. Novgorod enjoyed long established trade links with various regions both within Russia's borders and beyond. The emergence of this town on the Baltic-Volga trade route and its inclusion from the very beginning in the sphere of European trade within the Baltic region led to the rapid development of crafts on a par, from the technological point of view, with manufacturing in other regions of Northern Europe. The Western European demand for fur and other commodities passing through Novgorod led to a constantly expanding cultural and technical exchange. It can be assumed that many European innovations and inventions reached Novgorod almost as soon as they came into being.

There are many objective reasons for singling out the Novgorod Lands in connection with a study of leather-working. Firstly, the well-preserved organic materials in the occupation levels of most towns in North-western Russia make this region particularly promising for the study of medieval leather-working. By now archaeological materials have been studied from all the main urban centres in the Novgorod Lands, namely Staraya Ladoga, Oreshek, Novgorod, Pskov, Ivangorod, Yam, Gdov, and Ryurik Gorodishche. Leather articles from Late Medieval burials at the Antoniev Dymskii Monastery and certain burials in the Ishorsk Plateau have also been studied. The leather materials date from a variety of different historical periods right across the medieval period of Russia's history from the time when the Russian state was first coming into being in the 8th–10th centuries until the radical reforms introduced by Peter the Great in the first quarter of the 18th century. This makes it possible to elaborate a regional chronological scale of changes in craft techniques and the technology that was used, in the tools and equipment in workshops, and in the range of articles manufactured by craftsmen. On the basis of many years' excavation in the fortress of Ivangorod (1980–1991) for the first time a reference collection of leather articles produced in that region in the 16th–17th centuries has been assembled. It includes nearly 12,000 leather artefacts, including waste cuts from a cobbler's workshop dating from the first half of the 16th century. The excavations in Ivangorod also enabled scholars to devise methods for processing large amounts of leather materials both in the field and in laboratory conditions.

Secondly, the region included the extended territory of a single state formation, the Novgorod boyars' republic, in which one city, namely Novgorod, played the key role in state administration, trade and the development of various crafts during the whole of the medieval period. Novgorod's well-developed trade links with the cities of Western Europe, other regions of medieval Russia and the countries of the East helped it to assemble here many of the technical achievements of the period and adapt them so that they should be in keeping with local production capacities and meet the needs of the local market. It would seem that the experience of the Novgorod craftsmen was taken up in the rest of medieval Russia and first and foremost in the manufacturing centres in the outer margins of the Novgorod Lands. This makes it possible to examine questions relating to the political and economic interaction, between Novgorod and the outlying areas via an analysis of craft production. The influence of the centre on the outlying areas finds its clearest expression in the largest and most widespread groups of items, such as shoes and other leather articles.

Thirdly, Novgorod's broad network of trade links opens up possibilities for comparing medieval crafts in the Novgorod Lands with close neighbours and far-away trading partners in Western Europe and Asia respectively. It is precisely in Novgorod that initially isolated and comparatively rare items produced in Western Europe occur, and these differed markedly in quality and style from the numerous and standardized articles produced locally. For purposes of comparisons with the output of Novgorod's leather-workers, reference can be made to finds from towns in other parts of Russia and the states adjoining it, which the author has processed using one and the same method from Vyborg, Tallinn, Polotsk, Chernigov, Tver, Torzhok and also from the Late-Medieval towns beyond the Arctic Circle of Mangazeya and Pustozersk.

Fourthly, the north-western part of Russia during most of the medieval period was blessed with a comparatively large number of varied written sources. When it comes to the 11th–15th centuries, new research possibilities are opened up by the collection of birch-bark documents, as well as charters issued by princes, trading contracts, municipal and clerical registers, and inventories, while customs records and other documents provide important sources for the study of craft production in the 16th and 17th centuries.

RAW MATERIALS AND LEATHER GOODS

The development of the raw-material base and techniques for treating leather in Novgorod exerted considerable influence on the advance of techniques for leather-working, the range and quality of items produced, the dynamics of their distribution and the ways in which that was organized, both within Russian lands and beyond them. Leather was particularly important in that it could be produced anywhere from local materials and be processed using traditional methods, which had taken root in every region. The ubiquity of leather-working to some extent held back the expansion of the trade in leather goods, the introduction of new methods and techniques for processing the raw material and the appearances of new shapes and decorations for leather goods. Within the Novgorod Lands the influence of the centre was of crucial importance, as is borne out by archaeological finds, but for other regions it is quite difficult to maintain this.

The main sources of raw materials for the leather-working trade in the Novgorod Lands were the skins of the domestic animals bred in the region – cows, sheep and goats, and also horses. On the other hand, pig skins were used in leather-working only occasionally, although pigs played a considerable part in the peasant holdings of the period. In archaeological collections, oil-tanned and dressed pig skins are encountered very rarely (Kurbatov 1991, 131, 134). The high fat content in pig skin meant that its processing required an inordinate amount of time and physical effort. Pig skins also have a more open structure, i.e. the link between the collagens in the various layers of the hide is uneven, which tends to make the hides delaminate. The difficulties encountered in removing the fat from pig skin and therefore the impossibility of dressing it to a high standard account for the limited use of this raw material in the medieval period.

According to conclusions reached by palaeo-zoologists the bones which predominate among the faunal remains from Ryurik Gorodishche (excavations carried out in 1979 and 1993) are cattle bones. Materials from the Troitsky excavation in Novgorod made it possible to establish that no less than 25% of the animals had been slaughtered at the age of 2–4 (Maltby and Hamilton-Dyer 1995, 136, 139, 141–143).

Osteological materials from the town's medieval occupation levels show that the domestic animals kept in the forest zone of Russia were of small breeds and this continued into the 16th and 17th centuries (Tsalkin 1971, 172–179). Foreigners also commented on the small size of Russian livestock in their travel notes in the 16th and 17th centuries: Sigismund Gerbershtein in the first quarter of the 16th century (Gerbershtein 1988, 130) and, at the end of that century, Giles Fletcher, who wrote that the treating of elk and cow hides was an important branch of industry in Russia, noting that the elk hides were very fine and large, while those of cows and oxen were smaller (Fletcher 1906, 12–13). According to observations made by Aleppskii, the cows of Muscovy were very small, resembling calves in size. He assumed that this was because of the extreme cold and that they were only used to provide milk during winter and summer (Aleppskii 1898, 123). Johann Kielburger also wrote of the mediocre nature of the livestock in Russia in the mid-17th century (Kurts 1915, 100).

The small size of domestic animals in North-west Russia was one of the reasons why fairly thin hides of cattle and sheep/goat were used for the most part for making leather items. Another reason was the fairly high level of technology available for currying hides, particularly in the pre-Mongol period (Kurbatov 1997a, 369–372). In the damp climatic conditions of the North-West, it was evidently quite difficult to preserve raw leathers. The demand for raw leather was satisfied in part by the use of the skins of marine animals (walrus, seal) brought in from the northern parts of the Novgorod Lands (Kurbatov 2001a, 10–21). Seal skins are mentioned in birch-bark documents from Novgorod Nos. 133 and 622. It is quite difficult, however, to establish their commercial significance in the economy. It was not until the 16th century that seal skins and articles made from them figure constantly in various economic documents.

The skins of wild animals seldom come to the fore in the archaeological record. In Tartu reference is made to a bear-skin (Valk-Falk 1985, 65) and deer and seal skins have been noted among the finds from Pustozersk (Kurbatov 2003, 229). Skin from beaver tails is frequently encountered in towns (Tver, Novgorod), the appearance of which is reminiscent of fish scales. They were used to make holders for knives, swords and arrows. In the written sources "holders made of beaver skins" are mentioned in the Ipatiev Chronicle [SlRYa XI–XVII vv. (Dictionary of the Russian Language of the 11th–17th Centuries), 1, 75]. Elk and deer skins are mentioned in three birch-bark documents (Nos. 153, 266/275, and 384), but not everywhere as a commodity (Zaliznyak 1995, 274–275, 362; Rybina 1989, 78; 2001, 312, 323). There is a particular abundance of information for the 16th and 17th centuries. In the accounting ledgers of the Uspenskii Monastery of Tikhvin not only horse, sheep and goat hides are mentioned but those of elk as well (Serbina 1951, 163). In Vitebsk there worked a special craftsman who used to curry elk hides (Levko 1984, 98). There are references to elk and deer hides in many of the written documents relating to the north-west and the far north of Russia. For instance, among imported items registered by the Mangazeya customs authorities in 1633 and 1635 were deer and elk hides, specifically from shanks (Belov et al. 1981, Chapter 10).

It is possible to piece together a picture of the technology used for currying skins in the forest zone of medieval Russia with reference to artisans' methods used later on (Kurbatov 2004, 10–11). In Russia at the end of the 19th and beginning of the 20th century there was a whole range of possible methods used for this work, ranging from the extremely primitive to the highly sophisticated. A leather worker and specialist in such technology, G. Povarnin, has re-constituted an ancient method for currying leather formerly used by the Slavs and which probably survived in medieval Russian towns to the second half or end of the 13th century as follows: 1) the process was carried out not in vats, but in other containers (made of clay, wood or leather); 2) the skins were soaked in an ash and lime solution for two or three weeks; 3) the hides were briefly rinsed by being trodden in water, but there was no de-liming stage in the process; 4) the tanning phase was also short, in two or three stages, each lasting 1–1½ weeks and involving the use of macerated oak bark, but without first steeping the hides in a dilute acid solution; 5) the hides were not dyed and they did not have bitumen rubbed into them. Povarnin regards the introduction of the stage in the process involving the hides being soaked in an acid solution as an important stage in the development of leather-working technology. In his work to chart the territory within which the soaking in acid was a well developed technique, Povarnin refers to the towns of Torzhok, Tver, Yaroslavl, Kostroma, Rostov Velikii, Moscow and Bezhetskii Verkh. It is assumed that it was in the 13th century that this stage in the treatment of leather first appeared in Torzhok, from where it spread east, while in the 14th century it spread to other centres as well. The introduction of acid solutions marks the time when 'Russian leather' and sole leather first appeared.

It is necessary to distinguish the drenching of hides in acid from the process known as *zalichka* carried out with acid tanning juices, sometimes with the admixture of bread or fresh bark. The aim of this second process was to soften the hide before it was tanned and it appeared earlier than the use of acid solutions, perhaps as early as the 12th century, and spread quickly within the same region, evidently in the 13th–15th centuries. Soaking hides in an acid solution was linked with another operation, liming, and it was used as a high-quality method for removing ash and lime from hides. The spread of this use of acid solutions and other innovations in leather-working techniques led to major changes in the processes used for treating hides as a whole, in the use of various types of raw materials, and in the range of leathers produced. It became possible to treat thicker hides of adult cattle. The hides duly prepared were later divided into different categories: for the soles and uppers of footwear, for accessories and other leather goods.

Up until the 16th century there are few references in the written sources to technical details relating to the treatment of hides. In birch-bark documents from Novgorod there is only one reference to "treated" and "untreated" skins (Zaliznyak 1995, 448–449). In other medieval Russian sources various words are used to designate raw materials to be made into leather: *kozha* (the standard word for skin or leather), *cherevna, yazno, usma* or *khoz*. These terms, however, may well be interpreted in different ways. Sreznevskii considered *usma* to mean tawed leather, while Rybakov took the word *kozha* to be a designation for a raw, untreated hide and *usnie* as a designation for leather material ready for a cobbler to use. He saw these terms as accounting for the words *kozhemyak* and *usmoshvets* used for different kinds of leather-workers (Rybakov 1948, 400–401). When examining texts, doubts can arise with regard to rigid distinctions having existed between the meanings of the words *kozha* and *usma* in medieval Russia. Historians have come up with a variety of definitions for the term *khoz*. In the opinion of Fasmer the word *khoz* in medieval Russia was used simply to denote leather, but by the 16th century it had acquired a new, more narrow meaning, that of *saffian* or morocco leather (Fasmer 1996, Vol. IV, 253). Yet, in those cases when the term *khoz* was linked with certain breeds of animals, only horses were mentioned. This was confirmed later on as well in the 18th and 19th centuries when the toughest parts of skin from the back of a horse were known as a *khoz*. The "boots of green *khoz*" referred to in the Ipatiev Chronicle for 1247 should be regarded as footwear made of horse hide that had been tanned in alum like *saffian* (Levashov 1959, 49–50). This technique was not widespread in medieval Russia. Other leather-working terms for leather which should perhaps be mentioned are *yazno* and *kozha voobshche,* which can be traced back to the proto-Slavic language and meant "goat skin" and which ceased to be used in common parlance in the latter part of the medieval period (Fasmer 1996, Vol. IV, 550).

CRAFT TRADITIONS AND FASHION

The peak of technical achievement by leather-workers is represented by the most mass-produced item of this trade, namely footwear. Given that shoes and boots are worn everyday, feet need to be protected as well as possible in a variety of climates and weather conditions, to be comfortable in a variety of situations and also to comply with the aesthetic demands of current fashion. All this determines the requirements regarding the quality of workmanship with which skins are treated, sewn together and decorated.

Early Slavic footwear appears to have developed along the lines of the main trends for constructing it known in the northern half of Europe since the Bronze Age. Archaeological finds make it possible to determine that these primitive shoes were made of a single piece of leather and were all of a similar shape. Examples of these occur throughout much of the forest zone in Central and Eastern Europe, and also in Scandinavia. Despite the simplicity of the one-piece design, it is possible to single out local variations. Some typical elements of such "prehistoric" shoes were still in use in the early medieval period. Finds of the earliest examples of leather footwear in Central Europe and Jutland can be regarded as prototypes for the articles of footwear worn in a proto-Slavic and Slavic context (Swann 2001, 17–23; Kurbatov forthcoming).

The initial stage in the emergence of the medieval craft of the leather-worker and shoe-maker in the Novgorod Lands can be traced in the archaeological materials from the era of the Vikings from Staraya Ladoga and Ryurik Gorodishche (hereafter Gorodishche). In the West this period is represented better by finds in mainland Europe than in Scandinavia itself. In the opinion of Swann only one technical feature of footwear can be identified from the finds made in Scandinavia: the pointed and upturned heel as a separate piece of the sole. A feature of this kind appears for the first time in Late Roman footwear and is encountered in the 8th and 9th centuries in footwear made from one piece of leather in several settlements, such as Wedelspang for example. As a constant feature of this period long heels on soles are widely known in footwear with a separate sole, as, for example, in the shoes with a lace at the side from Staraya Ladoga in the 8th–9th century (Figure 21.1.21). They were also found among materials from Ribe (from the period c. 720–825), Elisenhof (second half of the 9th century), Haithabu (850–980) and Dublin (10th century). In England footwear of this kind has been found in London, Durham and York. Footwear of this kind

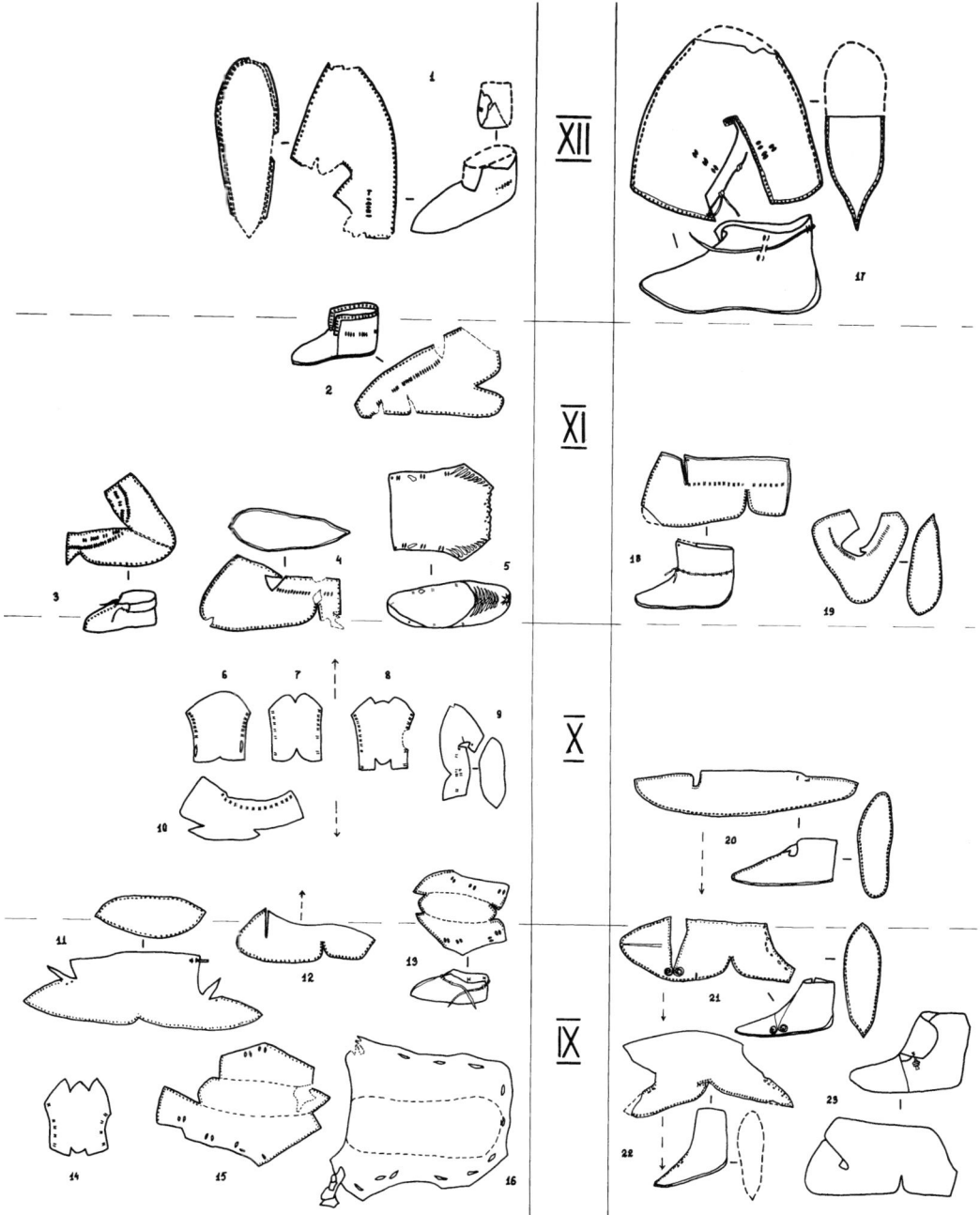

Figure 21.1 *A diagram to show the development of footwear shapes in the 9th–12th centuries in Northern Europe: 1) London; 2,3,4) Lund; 5, 18) Novgorod; 6, 8–10) Wedelspang Mose; 7) Lunden Mose; 11) Oseberg; 12) York; 13) Gniezno; 14) Lemdecksburg; 15, 16) Elisenhof; 17) Riga; 19) Oslo; 20–22) Staraya Ladoga; 23) Middelburg.*

found in a boat-burial from Oseberg produced a radiocarbon date of 834 (Bonde 1994, 138–144). A long heel is also found in footwear dating from between the late-9th and late-10th century from Winchester. In Scandinavia it was found in urban levels at Lund, Oslo and Trondheim as well as other settlements. In most of them it went on being used until the 12th century. In Bergen and Borgund, however, they were being used for most of the 12th century (Swann 2001, 40–44). Models of footwear with soles incorporating a long, pointed heel lasted significantly longer in medieval Russia than in their western parallels. They are encountered in levels of the late-12th and early-13th century in Polotsk, in levels of the last quarter of the 13th century and the first quarter of the 14th century in Tver and other towns of Russia's forest zone (Kurbatov 1997b, 100; Kurbatov 1999, 110–111).

However, it would be ill-advised to assign categorically this one technical feature to the Vikings, as it can be traced in many proto-urban settlements in the Baltic and North Sea regions linked to each other by trade. These trade contacts tended to reduce considerably the differences between individual areas, since they led to the spread and adoption of many cultural elements. It is no coincidence that we find many different footwear shapes and designs in such settlements. Among the most representative collections it is worth singling out Staraya Ladoga with eight types of footwear and Haithabu with ten types. Parallels for Ladoga footwear of the 8th–10th centuries have been found in a number of towns in Western Europe such as Dublin, York, Oseberg, Birka, Middelburg, Dorstad, Ribe, Elisenhof, Haithabu and Gross Raden (Figure 21.2).

The trend towards pronounced development of footwear styles and techniques used in leather-working in Northern Europe in the 8th–10th centuries reflects in the main the specific nature of the cultural processes at work in this particular region, where Late Roman influence had been less tangible than, for instance, in England. Echoes of it can be felt in long enduring features of footwear, such as the long strap not completely separated from the main piece of leather. Vestiges of this Late Roman influence had little influence, however, on the dominant trend of development with regard to footwear in countries where separate soles and uppers cut asymmetrically were to be found with a side seam at the back of the foot (first variant). This kind of pattern for footwear in Northern Europe in the first millennium AD embarked on its own independent course of development from the simplest coarsely cut pieces of leather "wrapping round" the foot to standardized, asymmetrical footwear patterns of the Late Medieval period. Refinements in the craftsmanship of leather-working production is bound up with the transformation of proto-urban settlements orientated towards trans-European trade into medieval towns with well-developed and organized systems of craft production, which was satisfying demand from both town-dwellers and those inhabiting rural areas (Kurbatov 1997c, 117–128).

Another direction found in footwear design (transitional models) is represented by the length-ways symmetrical pattern from one piece of leather and with slits for drawing in the shoe at the top edge and with points marked at the front and back

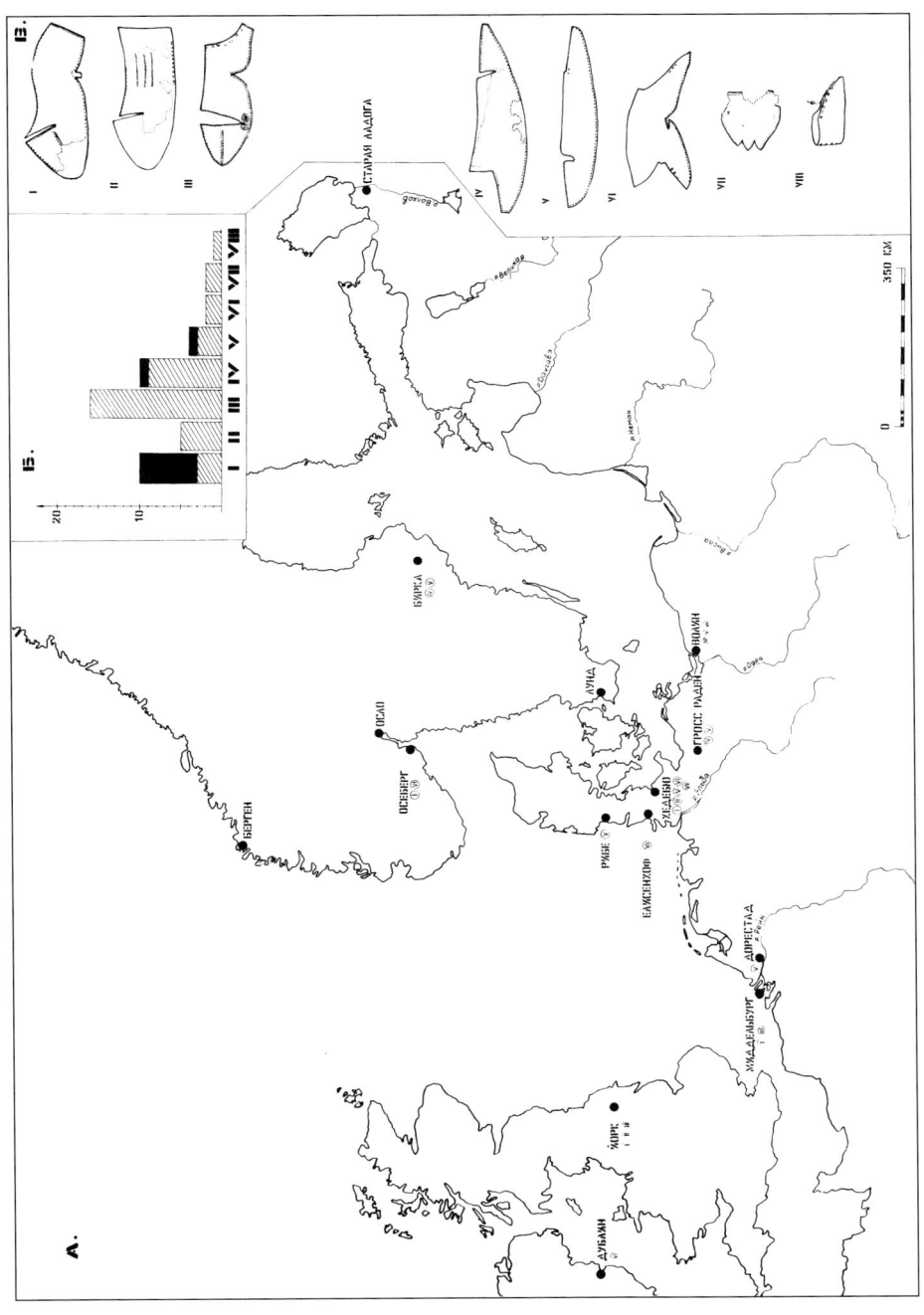

Figure 21.2 The distribution of footwear in Europe in the 8th–10th centuries similar to finds made in Staraya Ladoga: A) map of the sites where similar models have been found; B) the quantity of finds from Staraya Ladoga according to types of cut-out pattern (the bars with diagonal lines across them relate to materials included in the study undertaken by Oyateva and the solid areas represent new finds); C) types of footwear from Staraya Ladoga as presented by Oyateva.

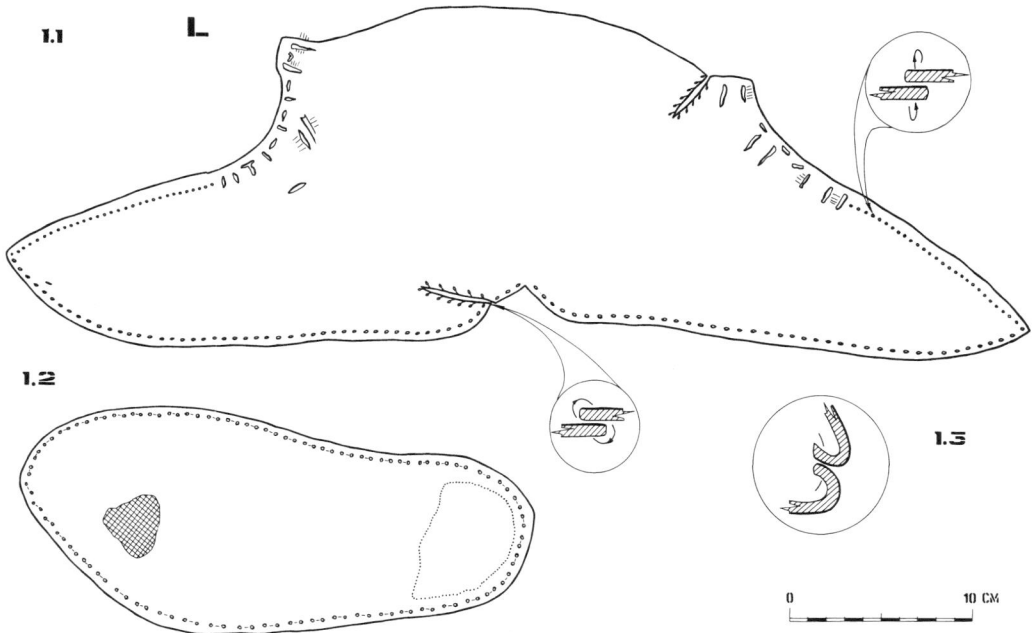

Figure 21.3 *Shoes from the 1994 excavation on the south bank of the Siversov Canal in Ryurik Gorodishche: 1.1) Upper; 1.2) Sole; 1.3) Section of the join between sole and upper.*

Figure 21.4 *Photograph of shoes from the 1994 excavation on the south bank of the Siversov Canal in Ryurik Gorodishche.*

of the sole where the leather needed to be trimmed. This pattern has been found in the following settlements: Wedelspang, Lemdeksburg, Lunden Mose, Elisenhof and Gross Raden and in the early levels of the following towns: Staraya Ladoga, Wolin and Gniezno. This kind of design can be regarded as the prototype for footwear with separate soles and uppers consisting of two halves sewn together along the lengthways axis all along the shoe from tip to heel (Wojtasik 1960, Figure 1a, b, Plate XI; Keiling 1988, 25–28, Figure 30). Variants of this symmetrical design are models with the halves of the upper joined at toe or heel, as for example in Oseberg, Middelburg, Staraya Ladoga and at Gorodishche (Figures 21.3, 21.4).

The third trend in footwear at the end of the first millennium AD involves a one-part design of irregular shape with unevenly arranged slits for drawing the shoe together, as found, for example, in shoes from Elisenhof (Grenander and Nyberg 1985, Plate 68, 2 and 3). While the first two trends were fairly complex with their elements of standardization, a series of evenly arranged holes for drawing the shoe together, and neat seams lending the footwear a decorative air, the third trend preserved a very simple structure satisfying purely utilitarian requirements. Models with a pattern of irregular shape had remained almost unchanged since the Bronze Age (Groenman van Waateringe 1988, 34–38, Figures 2–4), but during the Viking period they could be regarded as articles that had been treated within the household rather than by professionals. After noting this, it is important to bear in mind that in some proto-urban settlements there is little archaeological evidence for craft activity, as for example in Northern Holland (Besteman 1989, 21–22). In addition we know that in some regions of Europe, in Scandinavia for example, itinerant craftsmen who engaged in leather-working were to be found (Schia 1977, 149).

It can be assumed that making shoes in early urban centres, where the population was multi-ethnic and multi-cultural was bound to reflect diverse variants of design, sewing techniques and decoration. It is just such diversity which distinguishes the footwear assemblage in Staraya Ladoga, where in the levels from the late-8th, 9th and 10th century eight types of pattern have been found, including non-professional ones (Oyateva 1965, Figure 1). On the other hand in settlements like Wolin, as early as the 9th century a specific range of footwear designs had emerged, which later spread to most European towns (Kowalska 1999, 235–237; Wojtasik 1960, Figure 1). It is probable that near the very end of the first and beginning of the second millennium a series of unified footwear designs was emerging in a number of towns in both Eastern and Western Europe, as can be seen from the appearance of professional craftsmen. The basic feature of these designs was a pattern consisting of two parts with a one-layer sole and an asymmetrical upper.

The fundamental principles underlying the organization of the shoe-maker's trade in Staraya Ladoga, if we believe that the shoes found there had been made locally, could have been different from those found in such large trading centres of the 8th–9th century in the Baltic region as Wolin or Ribe. During excavation of those centres, enormous concentrations of standardized off-cuts resulting from the cutting out of shoes were found, which shows that commercial shoe production catering

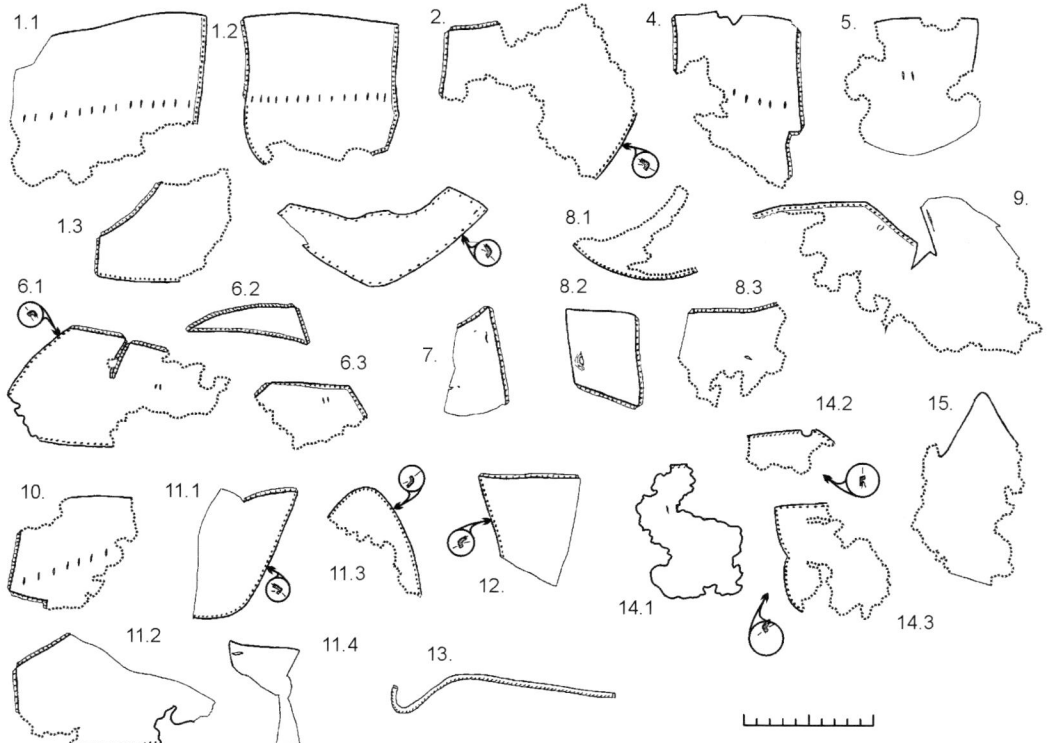

Figure 21.5 *Details of shoes and off-cuts from Ryurik Gorodishche. Excavations of 2000–2001.*

for a large population had existed over a long period (Jensen 1991, 28). One way or another leather articles of the 8th–10th century from the region of the Volkhov River area help us to determine when the craft of leather-working and shoe-making became established in the proto-urban settlements of urban Russia, a craft which clearly possessed the distinctive characteristics of a medieval urban craft. Features of both standardization and individuality become conspicuous here by the middle of the 10th century (Kurbatov 1997c, 126).

The qualitative 'leap' in the organization of leather-working as a craft in the Novgorod Lands and the transition from its Early Medieval form to that of the Late Medieval period can be traced with the help of finds made in 2000 to 2003 at Gorodishche. Among the leather articles found there were a number of variants for the design of soft low-cut footwear dating from the last quarter or end of the 11th century and the first quarter of the 12th (Kurbatov 2004b, 220–22). The **First Variant** for this design has an asymmetrical upper cut as a single piece, in which the front section is half cut off from the sides, which had a bent-over (or "turned-down") edge. The slits for drawing the shoe together came in pairs and on rare occasions, only twice, in sets of three. An additional part in the shape of an elongated triangle was sewn on

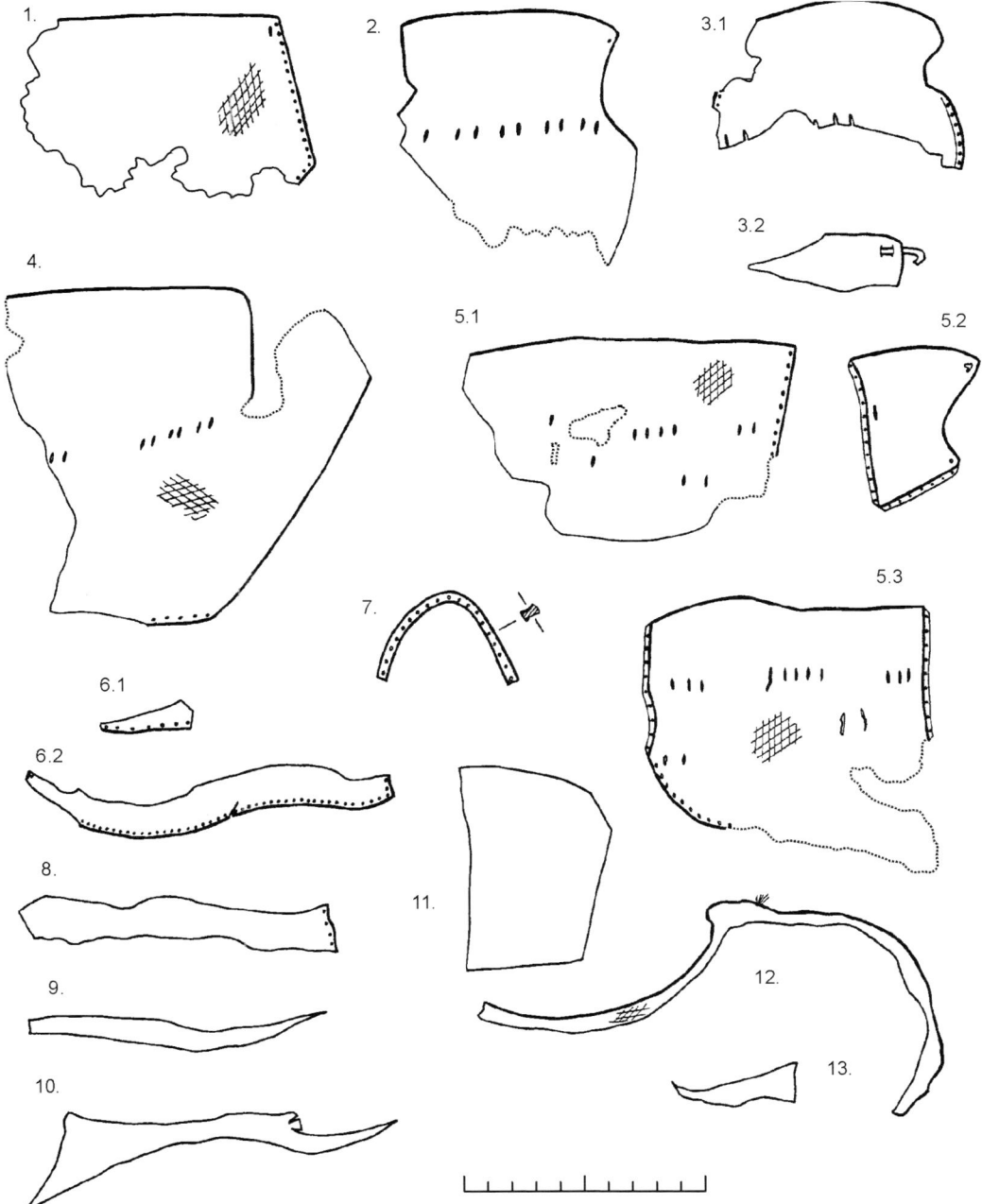

Figure 21.6 Details of shoes and off-cuts from Ryurik Gorodishche. Excavations of 2000 and 2001.

to the top edge of the overfold and there were stitches all round the edge to strengthen it (Figure 21.5). The **Second Variant** was distinguished by the symmetrical cut of its upper, found in the form of small fragments and a few details (Figure 21.6.2).

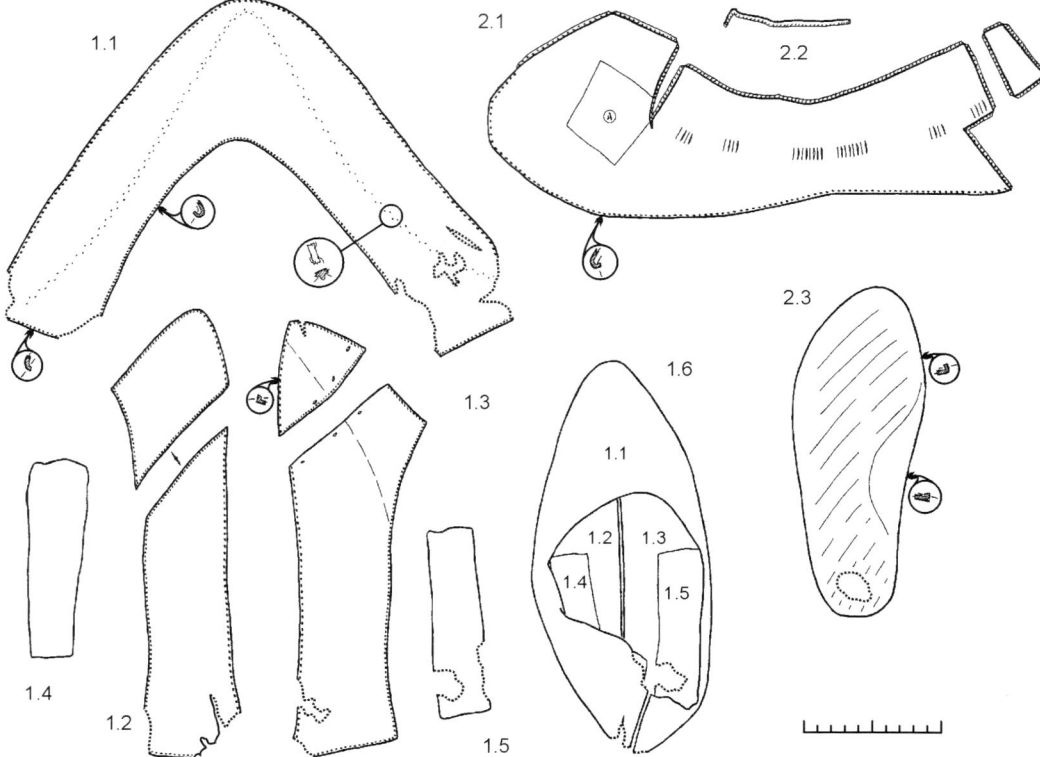

Figure 21.7 *Two models of shoes from Ryurik Gorodishche. Excavations of 2001.*

Of particular interest are two examples of low shoes, which have survived intact and were found all in one piece. The first was a soft low shoe for the left foot with a sole and upper which had been cut out separately (Figure 21.7.2). The second was a pattern for a low soft shoe cut as one piece and with its main seam along the lengthways axis of the sole side (Figure 21.7.1). Similar to this shoe in design was a pair of shoes found during recent excavations in Staraya Russa in levels from the second half of the 11th and the 12th century (Antropova and Toropova 2001, 245, 255). Both finds are distinguished by the use of fine leather and a number of internal details. The design approach for this model was distinctive and it has also been found in other medieval Russian towns. It was first singled out as a specific variant of shoe design in materials from Tver dating from the 13th and 14th centuries (Kurbatov 1997d, 136).

When characterizing the level of leather-working on the basis of finds from Gorodishche at the end of the 11th and beginning of the 12th century the most revealing features are, firstly, the range of off-cuts from the patterns used and, secondly, minor features of the way these shoes were cut out and put together. These details include the precise shape of the cut-out parts, the regularity and neatness of the holes for sewing and the use of various techniques for trimming edges. In addition there is another distinctive feature, namely the use of leather with an embossed surface

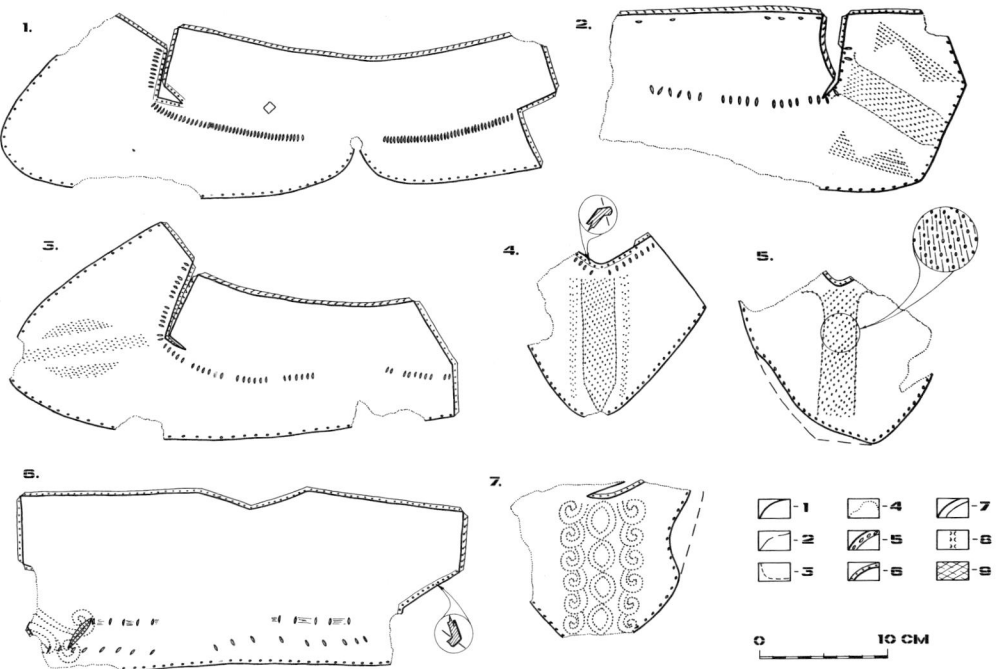

Figure 21.8 *Shoes of the first pattern variant from Polotsk. Second half of the 12th or 13th century.*

to create a "grid" pattern. It is possible to compare the materials used in different medieval towns in Russia and Western Europe, bearing in mind the whole range of structural and stylistic features. Conspicuous in this collection is the asymmetrical cut of the upper for the complete model and the advanced standardized shape of the pattern (Figure 21.7). A pattern of this sort became characteristic of medieval Russian and western models in the 16th century. This pattern when used for relatively thin leather, with wide-spaced slits for pulling the shoe tight (an unusual stylistic feature?) and sewn edges could well point to the late-11th or 12th century as the most likely time for such footwear to have been made. Among medieval Russian materials, finds from Byeloozero and Polotsk (Figures 21.8 and 21.9) should be regarded as the closest parallels, but they already date from the second half of the 12th century (Kurbatov 1999, 100ff). Other articles from the 11th and early-12th century which can be compared with the finds from Gorodishche originate from the towns of North-western Europe, for example from Lund (Blomquist 1937; 1939) and Trondheim (Marstein 1989, Figure 3b).

What can be regarded as the distinctive features of the footwear from Gorodishche are the use of thin leather and the style of the seams, which were sewn with short stitches and very fine thread. This method of sewing footwear indicates, on the one hand, a professional class of leather-workers and shoe-makers was coming into being

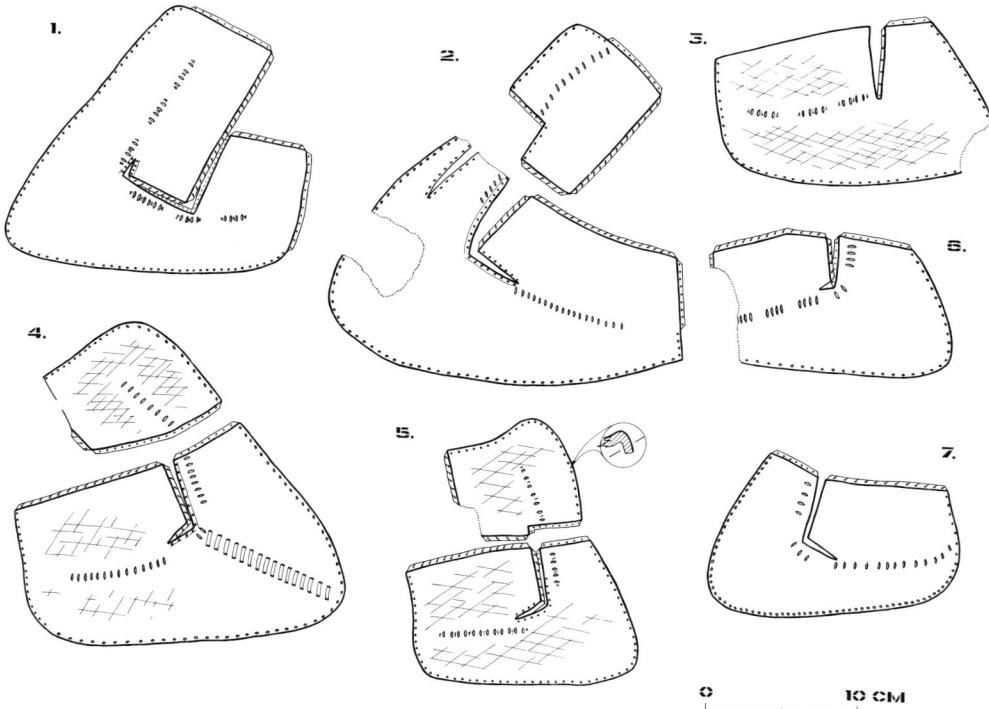

Figure 21.9 *Shoes of the second pattern variant from Polotsk. Second half of the 12th or 13th century.*

and that these craftsmen possessed a high level of technical skills. On the other hand, these features set the finds from Gorodishche apart from articles made in Novgorod, Pskov and other medieval Russian towns, where more practical techniques were to be found involving stitches 4–5 mm long and thicker thread. The practical character of the work carried out by medieval shoemakers has been confirmed by modern experimental data regarding the strength of seams depending upon the length of stitches used (Tsvetkov 1963, 140–143).

Leather articles from Gorodishche can be linked with the period when craft activity intensified in Novgorod in the last quarter of the 11th century (Nosov 1990, 150–151). The upper time limit for this can be regarded as the beginning of the fundamental changes in the organization of Novgorod crafts in the first half of the 12th century. Using Novgorod as an example, Kolchin and Yanin identified stages in the emergence and development of crafts in medieval Russian towns (Kolchin 1975, 53ff; Yanin and Kolchin 1978, 25, 27–28). Assessment of the technical organization of crafts, labour productivity, the volume of production and the marketability of wares produced by craftsmen in the Novgorod market made it possible to break down the history of craft manufacture into four periods. The collection of finds from Gorodishche relates to the first and second of these periods. The **First Period** (mid-10th to 1120s/1130s) is distinguished by comparatively advanced production techniques and it is then that all the main forms of specialized craft tools were created and the technological basis for production was established. The volume of production, however, was still fairly limited and the articles manufactured by craftsmen were still expensive. This was the period of patrimonial craft production involving work for commissions and only an insignificant market for the free sale of the goods produced. The dependence of craftsmen outside the realm of strictly economic considerations is reflected in one of the articles of *Russkaya Pravda*, where substantial compensation of 12 *grivnas* is allocated to any property-owner if one of his craftsmen suffers mutilation [*SIRYa XI–XVII vv.* (Dictionary of the Russian Language of the 11th–17th centuries), Vol. 22, 143].

The **Second Period** (1130s to 1270s/1280s) is distinguished from a technical point of view by a rapid expansion in the range of products, by a high level of specialization within different branches of the craft and by a considerable rationalization or simplification of the technical equipment used. There is a marked increase in the number of series of articles produced and in the degree of standardization used, particularly when it comes to metal-working and the manufacture of textiles. Extremely narrow professions appear as a result of the division of labour within the craft sphere. This was the time of conspicuous development in small-scale craft production, the output of which was designated for sales throughout the whole of the Novgorod Lands. Metallographic research into knives from the Polotsk Lands and from Novgorod confirms the rapid development of advanced technologies in the 12th century, such as the welding of steel on to a cutting edge (Rozanova 1997, 276, 279). By the middle of the 12th century similar changes were noted in Ryazan and Rostislavl Ryazanskii (Zavyalov 2002, 32).

Considerable changes have also been noted in connection with various crafts in Novgorod. In relation to bronze-casting they have been recorded in materials from certain categories of jewellery (Pokrovskaya 1995, 190; 2000, 147–48). In pottery production materials from the Troitsky XI excavation make it clear that the period of the mid- and late-12th century stands out as one of the four chronological cut-off points, when pottery shapes changed (Malygin *et al.* 2001, 96). The craft of bone-carving, using the Fedorovsky excavation as an example, also underwent a period of significant development in the first half of the 12th century or even from the end of the 11th (Smirnova 1998, 94ff). When it comes to house-building in Novgorod, the materials from the Troitsky excavation reveal that an element of standardization took place from the second half of the 12th century, when there was a marked drop in the share of five-walled log houses and an increase in the number of four-walled houses of medium size. Within the latter group some two-storied buildings were re-constructed, so that the upper floor was used for living quarters and the lower one for craft activities (Faradzheva 1998, 79).

These developments in craft production coincide with the general socio-economic picture of the emergence of the feudal republic of Novgorod with a prince at its head. In the period from the 1120s/1130s to the 1280s the main political structures of boyar power took shape. The links between land-ownership, trade, craft production and the political order become clearly visible in the events which took place in the late-11th century and early-12th century, when the transition from craft-producers carrying out commissions to production aimed at satisfying market demands required a dramatic increase in the volume of imported raw materials. Increased imports of these raw materials led to an increase in the territory of the state through expansion into the area known as Zavolochie, the main area for profitable hunting. Linked to these processes is the rapid consolidation of the power of the Novgorod boyars, who at precisely that time created the institutions which established the republic's statehood. It was also at this time that the first foreign merchants' enclaves appeared, while the leading merchants of Novgorod itself united to form a 'corporation' known as *Ivanskoe sto* (Yanin and Kolchin 1978, 34; Kolchin and Yanin 1982, 91, 122–124ff).

Shoe designs from the second half or end of the 12th century and the early-13th century have been found in large numbers in Novgorod, Pskov, Staraya Russa and Byeloozero. Their dating is based on materials from the excavations of Karger at Polotsk (Kurbatov 1999). Various kinds of soft footwear were found there: boots, shoes, *porshni* (sandals strapped to the feet) and what were known as "house (or "work") slippers". Shoes predominate in this collection, the designs for which (there were 3 variants) combined a one-layer sole consisting of a single piece and an upper consisting of one or two parts and lacking any additional inner linings. The **First Variant** (19 specimens) had an upper consisting of one piece and cut asymmetrically: the 'surplus' was drawn together round the foot and there was a seam on the inside (Figure 21.8). The side parts of the upper, which were either vertical or turned outwards, were 5–5.5 cm high and covered the anklebone and the lower part of the shin. The shoe was pulled tight on the leg using narrow leather straps threaded through a series of slits at the level of the ankle. The **Second Variant** (21 specimens) had an upper consisting of two parts cut symmetrically in relation to its lengthways axis and a seam at the heel (Figure 21.9). Shoes of medium and small sizes predominated. The **Third Variant** was represented by two models with a two-part upper cut asymmetrically.

A total of 76 parts of boots cut using two different patterns have been identified. One of these, which had a reversible (or 'stitched') seam for the main join, that of the sole and upper, also had a protruding tongue on the heel of the sole. The second variant was represented by a few boot parts with a vertical sheer seam at the main join. "House slippers" were represented by off-cuts from the sole part (28 specimens). These were made up of two main parts (the front and the back) with a seam in the sole along the axis of the foot, over which a lining was sewn-in, consisting of a strip of leather folded in two. Three parts of a *porshna* (sandal strapped to the foot) were also included in the collection.

Major changes occurred concerning the craft of leather-working in the second half and at the end of the 13th century in the Novgorod Lands. A stage known as drenching began to be introduced into the technique for treating leather, which served effectively to neutralize the hides and soften them before they were tanned (Kurbatov 1994, 191–192). At the same time as adopting this differentiated approach to the tanning of

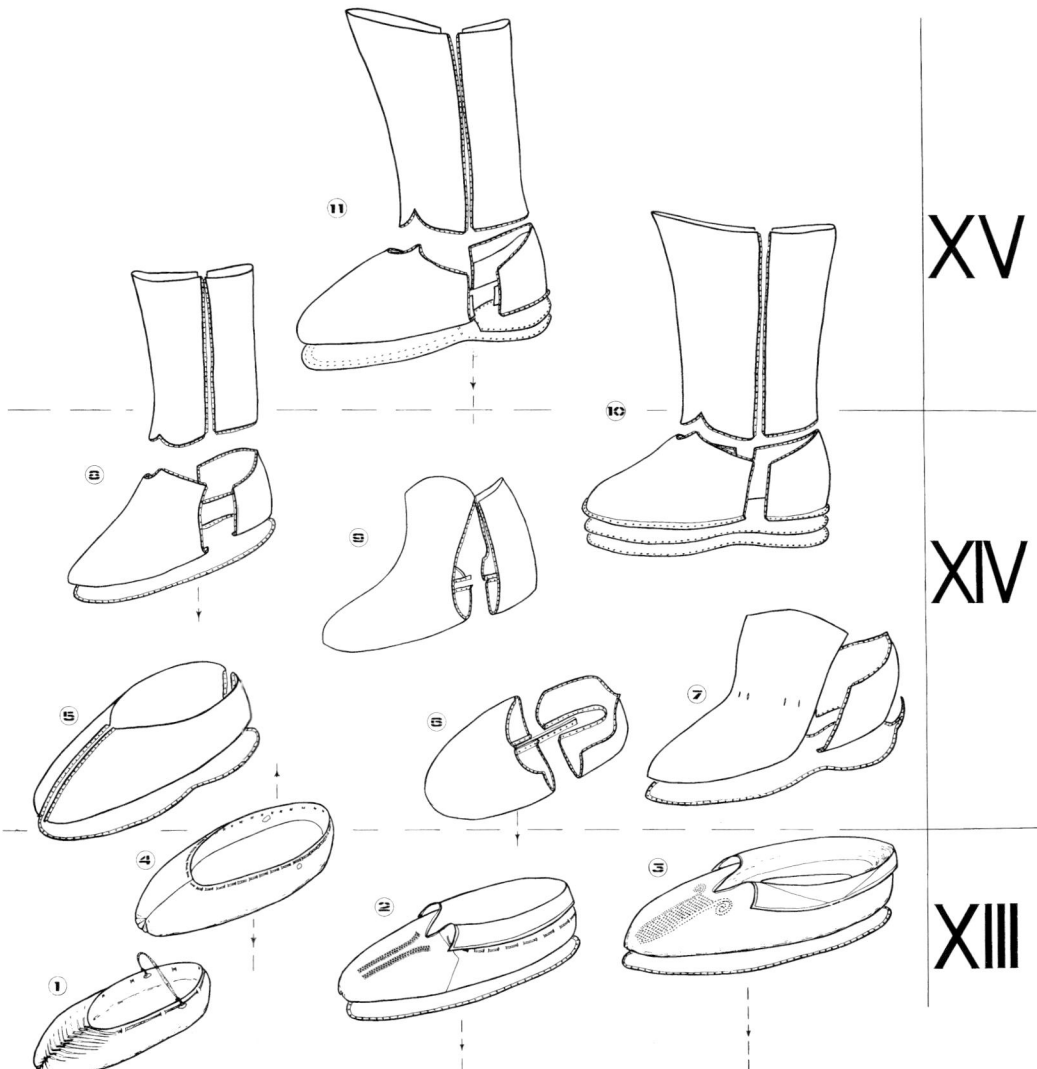

Figure 21.10 *Footwear shapes of the period from the last quarter of the 13th to the first half of the 15th century from the Tver kremlin.*

different sorts of skins and introducing changes into the methods used at each stage in the currying of the leather, the craftsmen began to produce a wider range of leathers of different qualities and for different purposes. They also began to make active use of thick hides from adult cattle. Clear distinctions were drawn between hides suitable for soles and those to be used for uppers, accessories or leather goods. As regards footwear, the 13th century was the heyday of low, embroidered shoes. Embroidery in coloured threads of wool or silk became highly varied in style and covered not only the front part of the shoe's upper but the side parts as well. There are grounds

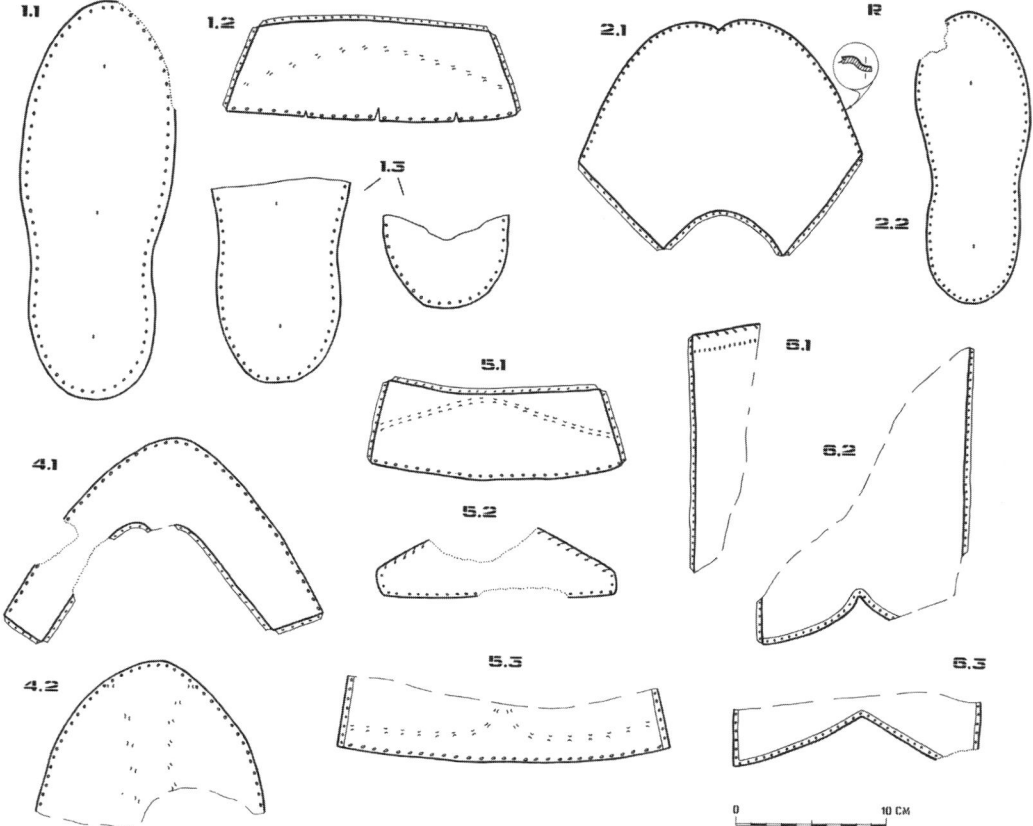

Figure 21.11 *Footwear parts found in the Oreshek fortress dating from the Novgorod period.*

for assuming that at this time there was also a 'fashion' for 'lattice-work' *porshni* (sandals strapped to the foot), as noted in Novgorod (Izyumova 1959, 210–14) and also in Berestie (medieval Brest, Belarus). In the important collection from Berestie that contains over 500 leather articles, mainly shoes, there are 43 *porshni* and of these eight are lattice-work specimens found in levels of the 13th and early-14th century (Lysenko 1985, 288; Lysenko 1989, 113, 114).

At the end of the 13th century shapes for high footwear began to predominate in Novgorod and other Russian towns. These boots later became an item of general use. In Tver (Figure 21.10) the predomination of boots was first noted in the second quarter of the 14th century (Kurbatov 2004, 72). The predominance of boots in Russian towns and also the growing popularity of high footwear (boots) in certain countries of Europe that started in the 13th century may be linked with the influence of steppe-dwellers (Kurbatov 2001b, 205–206; Wiklak 1969, 217–219).

The influence of the craft tradition of Novgorod on the surrounding area at that time can be traced through comparison of collections from the same period relating

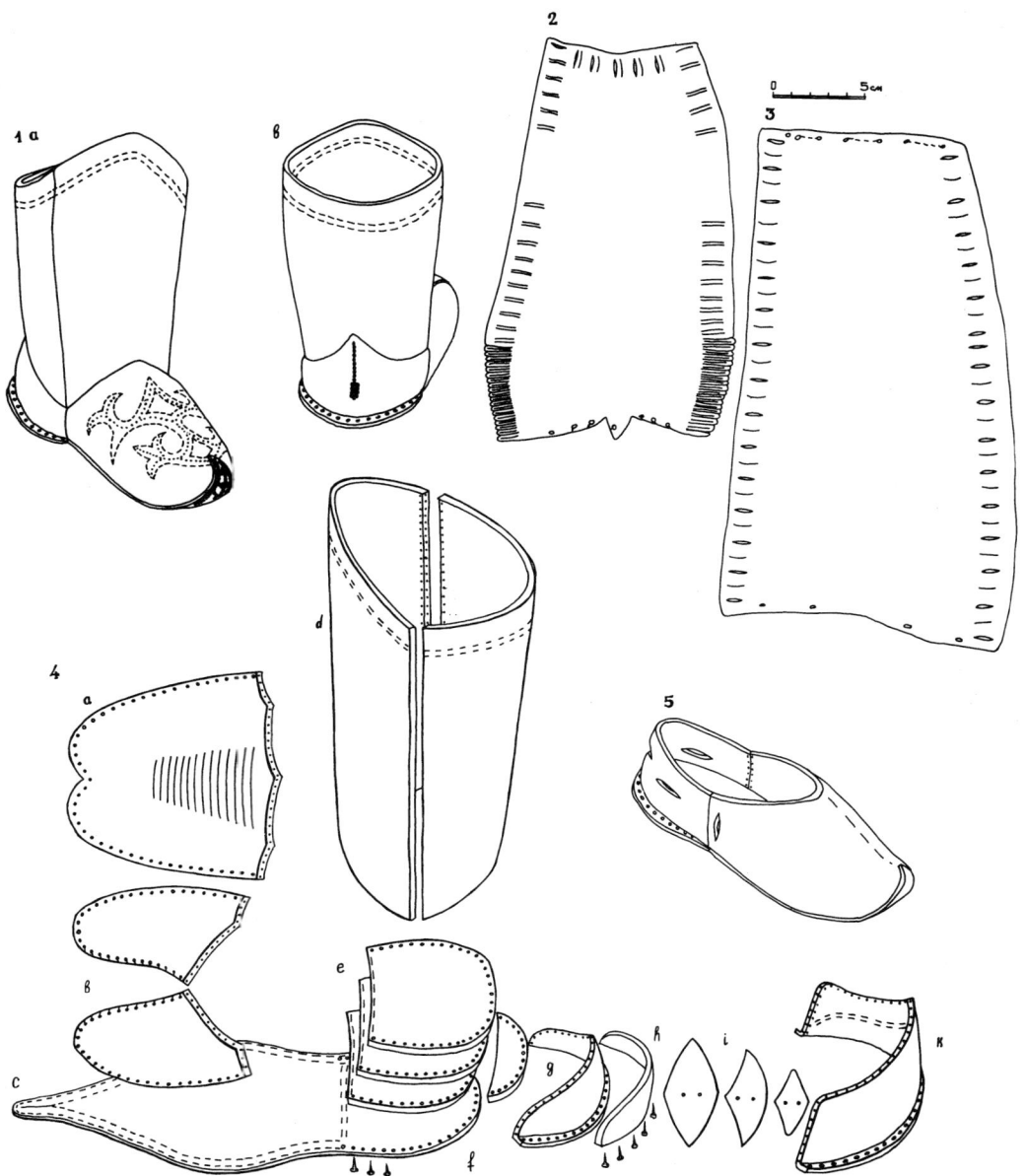

Figure 21.12 The shapes and structure used for boots and porshni (a type of slip-on footwear) found in Ivangorod dating from the late-15th and 16th centuries.

to the centre and to the towns at the periphery of the Novgorod Lands respectively. Today finds from Oreshek relating to the Novgorod period in the history of the fortress (Kildyushevskii and Kurbatov 1997, 273–276) can be regarded as the most objective materials available for such comparison. The footwear concerned representing the

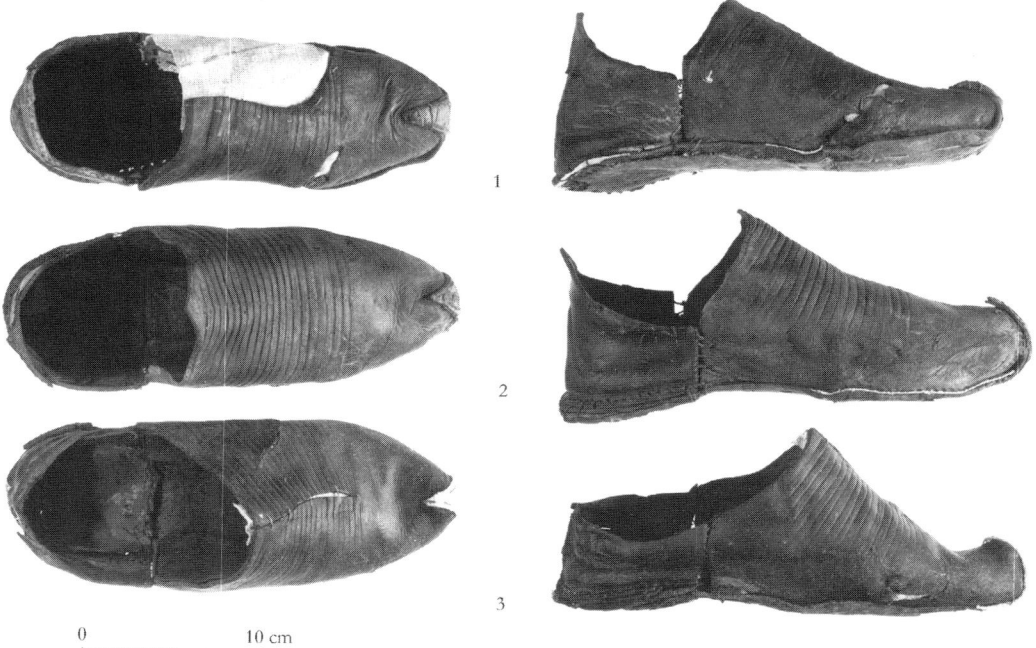

Figure 21.13 *Restored boots from the late-15th/16th century found during excavations at Ivangorod.*

whole of the period (1323–1478) preserves unchanged all the techniques used for making footwear (Figure 21.11). Apart from professionally made articles, the collection also includes footwear cut and sewn in a not very neat 'homely' style without attention being paid to any decorative finish (Kildyushevskii and Kurbatov 2001, 313).

In the 15th and 16th centuries the leather-workers and shoe-makers of Novgorod held on to their leading position in relation to other Russian towns and they perfected their techniques for dressing hides. Europeans' familiarity first and foremost with wares from Novgorod gave rise to the high reputation of "Russian leather" in Western Europe in the 16th century, which was valued as being hard-wearing and resistant to decay after having been tanned in extracts of oak and willow bark. As regards archaeological evidence it has proved possible to assemble data relating to leather-working in the 16th and 17th centuries using materials from Ivangorod, a fortress on the north-western border of Russia on the river Narova opposite the Narva Fortress (Figures 21.12–14). It is no coincidence that leather articles of the late-15th and early-16th century from Vyborg stylistically similar to finds made in the towns of Western and Northern Europe were evidently made from leather produced in the towns of North-western Russia (Figure 21.15).

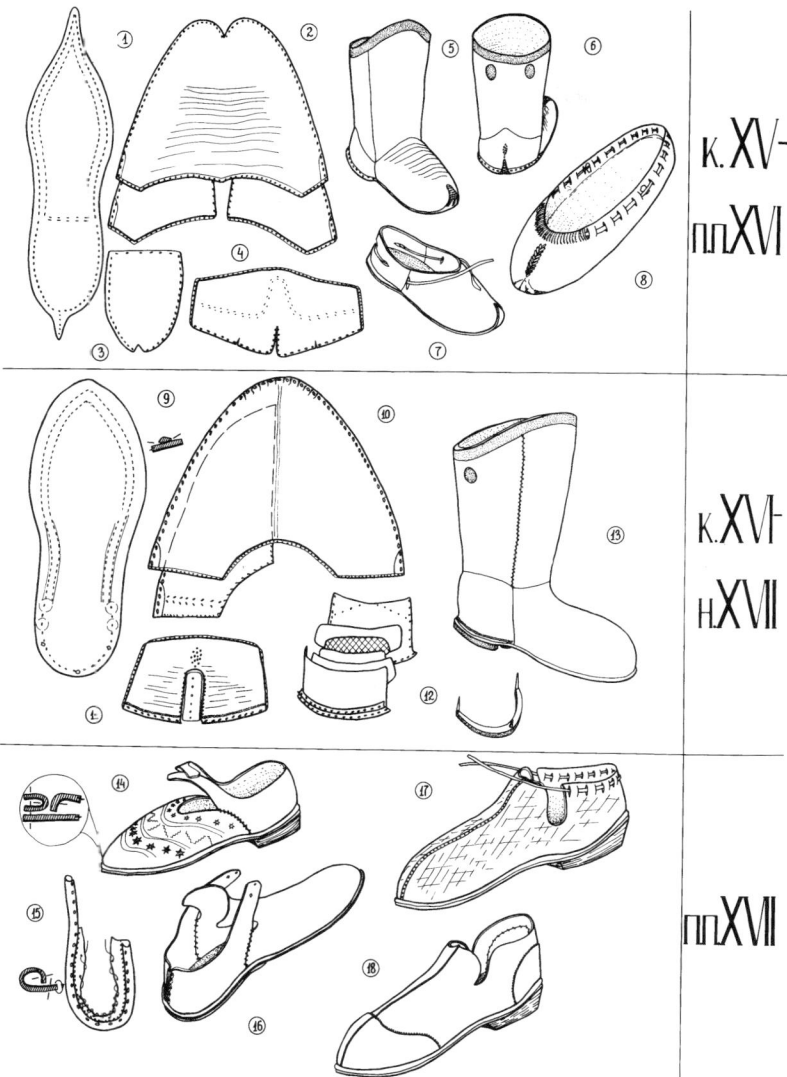

Figure 21.14 Changes in the shapes of leather footwear between the late 15th and early 17th century as illustrated by finds made at Ivangorod and Pskov.

SUMMARY: THE MAIN PERIODS OF LEATHER-WORKING

On the basis of the study of leather materials from the towns of the Novgorod Lands it has been possible to single out a number of stages in the development of this craft in the North-west of medieval Russia. These can be traced most clearly in the use of different sorts of leather, the techniques for cutting out and sewing footwear, and in the methods and styles for decorating various items.

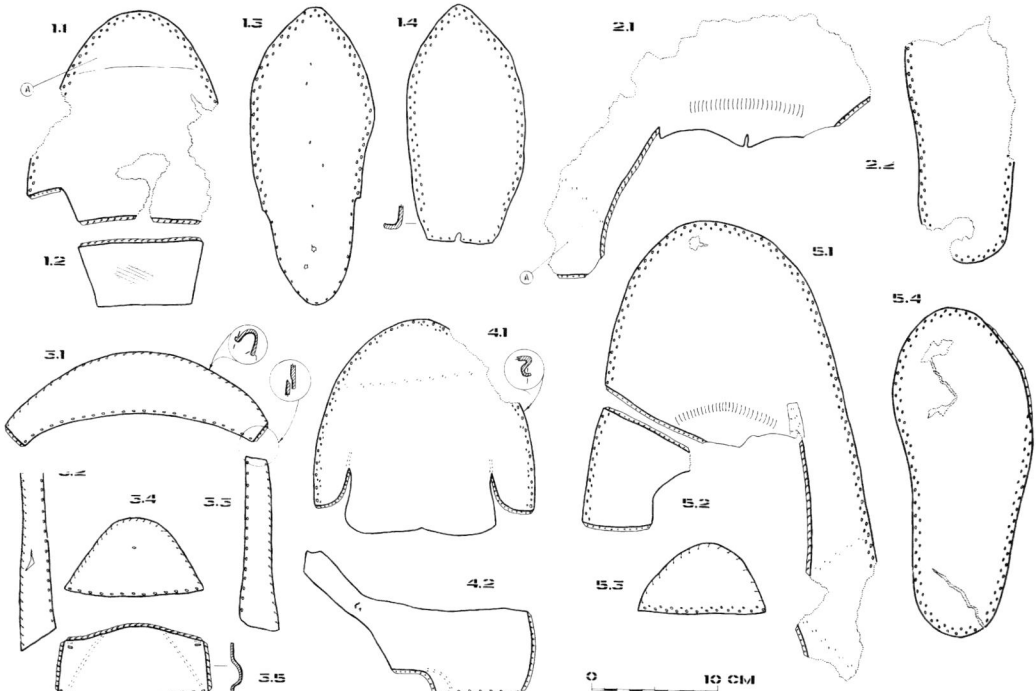

Figure 21.15 *Patterns for parts of leather footwear from the late-15th and early-16th century levels in Vyborg.*

(1) The 8th–10th centuries or the Early Medieval period. This is when the craft of leather-working came into being in emerging urban centres, when technical and design principles for this sphere of production were selected and elaborated, and when efficient techniques for cutting out and sewing items of footwear were selected. It was the time when the main varieties of medieval Russian footwear were emerging along with its models, shapes and types of decoration, when there was a consistency in the production of leather as well as in the types of leather articles produced. A common North-European tradition can be identified by this time, both with regard to the dressing of skins and also to the way leather articles were sewn together.

(2) The 11th–13th centuries or the Medieval Russian period. This is when the professional activity of leather-workers and shoe-makers became widespread, who by now were using universal techniques, which were developing along similar lines for most of the towns of Russia's forest zone. At this time the various trends in leather production were coming together in a unified version, while certain regional stylistic features were being retained. In the technology of production and the shapes of items a trend in the development of this craft, common to that found in the towns of Western Europe, can be traced, yet certain features peculiar only to production in medieval Russia may still be singled out. The influence of leading centres of craft production,

such as Novgorod, was still making itself felt in the small towns in the margins of the Novgorod Lands.

(3) The 14th–15th centuries or the more advanced medieval period, when rapid improvements in the technology for dressing hides were taking place and when the main shapes used in leather-working and footwear production were developing and changing. Under the influence of this craft in the lands of the East with regard to the techniques and equipment used, specific methods and shapes for articles of footwear were being developed, which were quite different from those found in Western Europe. The wide trade links enjoyed by Novgorod and Pskov facilitated the rapid spread of new technology in the towns and rural settlements of Russia. The closest, traditional links between the towns and their hinterland had survived especially when it came to the role of the latter as a source of raw materials and a market for the standardized output of shoe-makers. The highly professional techniques characterizing leather-work in the towns were widely adopted in rural areas.

(4) The 16th–17th centuries or the Late Medieval period, when the influence of West-European fashion and production techniques increased conspicuously. This development led to the wide introduction (starting at the end of the 16th century) of shapes for leather articles similar to those found throughout Europe, particularly in Scandinavia. Movements of population in the late 15th and 16th centuries led to a merging of techniques for currying hides and for sewing and decorating leather goods in the towns of the various regions of Russia.

– APPENDIX A –

LEATHER OBJECTS FROM TROITSKY XI, NOVGOROD

D. I. Solovyov

INTRODUCTION

This short paper examines the leather objects from the Troitsky XI excavation in Novgorod that were kept and stored in the archives of the Novgorod State Museum. A list of all the finds is provided in Table 21A.10 below.

Items of leather not only provide a rich source of information on the techniques of leather working and levels of the development of manufacturing technology, but they also provide a useful source for the study of the raw materials used by medieval craftsmen. Examination of a piece of leather makes it possible to determine the species of animal from which the skin came, the approximate age of the animal concerned, and also the place on the animal's hide from which the fragment under discussion was taken. The key to identification of the sort of leather used is the grain, the outer layer of any leather. The original follicles form a pattern, which can be characterized with reference to the angle at which these are arranged in relation to the grain, their diameter and their shape. These follicles also form a pattern, which varies according to the species of animal, its age and the position of the animal's hide from which it was taken. When attempting to identify the sort of hides from which articles extracted from excavations were made, including the finds from the collection pertaining to the Troitsky XI excavation, several difficulties arise. The fact is that articles obtained from excavation have been exposed to major physical impact: (a) while being used the articles were wearing out (the outer layer or grain is often rubbed away); articles lose their original shape (they might stretch or shrink); (b) when exposed to the external environment and through processes of decay, fragments of the original article are lost and layers of the leather may peel away; (c) the articles are distorted under the weight of deposits and finally (d) during conservation work prior to storage the leather dries out and its thickness can sometimes shrink by as much as 2 cm also bringing about change in the nature and pattern of the follicles.

At the present stage in the study of the raw-material base for leather-working in medieval Novgorod, it is possible to identify with almost 100% reliability leather from goat hides, the follicles of which form a distinctive pattern, which is identifiable even when the grain has been badly damaged. Hides from cattle can also usually be identified reliably, although sometimes it is not possible to distinguish them from horse hides.

	Goat skin	Cow hide	Indeterminate
Shoes with uppers consisting of more than one part	-	80	8

Table 21A.1 Shoes with uppers consisting of more than one piece (composite).

	Goat skin	Cow hide	Indeterminate
Shoes with undecorated uppers consisting of a single piece	24	9	6

Table 21A.2 Shoes with undecorated uppers consisting of a single piece (seamless).

	Goat skin	Cow hide	Indeterminate
Decorated shoes with uppers consisting of a single piece	54	8	3

Table 21A.3 Decorated shoes with uppers consisting of a single piece (seamless).

SHOES

Despite the simple design of medieval footwear, analysis of the raw materials used is not always straightforward and shoes are no exception to this. Shoes consisted of soles and uppers and the sole was always made from a single piece of leather, while the upper might be designed in several different ways. They might be seamless (made from a single piece of leather) or composite (consist of various pieces sewn together). As a rule the latter type consisted of three parts joined at the heel and on the inside of the foot. In the overwhelming majority of the shoes with composite uppers examined, the raw material used was from cow hides (Table 21A.1), while for undecorated seamless uppers the share made from goat hides markedly increased (Table 21A.2). For decorated shoes with seamless uppers, goat hide was the main raw material used (Table 21A.3).

This picture with regard to the different kinds of raw material used for shoes of different design is not coincidental. In medieval Novgorod seamless uppers were normally used when shoes were decorated, since extra seams would have spoilt the appearance of the items concerned. Decoration was applied, as a rule, using embroidery or interlacing and the material used for decoration had to be simultaneously durable, elastic and not very thick. Goat leather was most suitable in the light of these criteria. This can explain the somewhat lower share of goat hides in the manufacture of uppers made of a single piece but without decoration. The elasticity of the leather had to ensure that the shoe was hard-wearing especially in the heel section, where it had to be bent in the sharpest of curves. It would appear that some varieties of cow hide also possessed the necessary characteristics, possibly hides from young animals which had been particularly well dressed.

For shoes with composite uppers, elasticity and minimal thickness of the raw materials used were not essential from a functional point of view: the part of the shoe incorporating the sharpest curve (the heel section) was covered over by a seam. In the Novgorod habitation levels, no evidence for decorated shoes made with uppers consisting of more than one piece has been found to date. This probably explains why not a single upper consisting of more than one part made from goat hides was found (Table 21A.1).

	Goat skin	Cow hide	Indeterminate
Tops of boots and half-boots	8	27	2

Table 21A.4 *Tops of boots and half-boots.*

	Goat skin	Cow hide	Indeterminate
Vamps of boots	10	97	9

Table 21A.5 *Vamps of boots.*

	Goat skin	Cow hide	Indeterminate
Counters of boots and half-boots	8	44	4

Table 21A.6 *Counters of boots and half-boots.*

	Goat skin	Cow hide	Indeterminate
Small details in boots made no earlier than the 15th century	7	5	1

Table 21A.7 *Small details in boots made no earlier than the 15th century.*

No.	Name of Category	Amount	Goat skin	Cow hide	Indeterminate
1	Lining under vamp of boot	4	3	1	-
2	Lining under counter of boot	6	4	1	1
3	Insert for counter of boot	3	-	3	-

Table 21A.8 *Varieties of small parts in boots of the 'Moscow' period.*

No.	Name of Category	Amount	Goat skin	Cow hide	Indeterminate
1.	Bottom layer	7	-	7	-
2	Inner layer	4	2	2	-
3	Intermediate layers	3	1	2	-

Table 21A.9 *Varieties of soles for boots of the 'Moscow' period.*

BOOTS

Prior to the 15th century mainly cow hide was used for the manufacture of boots (Tables 21A.4–6). The simple design of the boots did not require more elastic or thinner skins than those obtained from cattle. Boots were made from a mere 3–5 parts: the nose, the vamp, the counter and the sole (sometimes the top was sewn together from two parts and in some cases the counter and the back section of the top consisted of a single part and also the vamp and the front section of the top accordingly).

From the 15th century onwards the technique used for manufacturing boots became much more complex compared to that from earlier periods. The later boots were distinguished by counters, vamps and soles consisting of more than one layer. The more complex manufacturing technique for boots made it necessary to use raw materials that were more durable, elastic and at the same time not particularly thick: as in the case of goat skins. At this stage in the development of the shoe-maker's craft we can already observe combinations of various types of raw material in the manufacture of a single item (Tables 21A.8–9). The instep linings for both the vamp and the counter were more often made of goat skins, while the inserts between counter and the lining of the counter would be made of cow hide, so as to make the structure of the counter stiffer and less supple.

In summary, the main raw materials for leather-working were cow hide and goat skins, while horse hide perhaps played a minor role as well. During the medieval period there already existed a differentiated approach to the selection of raw material for a specific item and from the 15th century onwards to the selection of various kinds of leather for different parts of one and the same item.

No.	Name of Category	Amount	Goat skin	Cow hide	Indeterminate
1	Decorated shoes with seamless upper	65	54	8	3
2	Shoes with seamless upper	39	24	9	6
3	Shoes with multi-piece upper	88	80	-	8
4	Shoes with unidentified upper pattern	1	-	1	-
5	Tops for boots and half-boots	37	8	27	2
6	Tops and counters of half-boots	5	1	4	-
7	Boot vamps	116	10	97	9
8	Counters of boots and half-boots	56	8	44	4
9	Soles of boots no earlier than 15th c.	14	See Table 9	See Table 9	See Table 9
10	Soles pre 15th c.	11	-	11	-
11	Small parts of boots no earlier than 15th c.	13	See Table 8	See Table 8	See Table 8
12	Loops for boot tops	2	1	-	1
13	Unidentified Items	48	7	36	5
14	Mittens	4	-	4	-
15	Sheaths	19	-	17	2
16	Balls	11	5	3	-
17	Straps	1	-	1	-
18	Cases	2	1	1	-
19	Fastener loops	7	5	1	-
20	Button fasteners	7	-	7	-
21	Appliqués	6	-	5	1
22	Patches	6	-	3	3
23	Masks	1	-	1	-

Table 21A.10 Leather items from the Troitsky XI excavation.

– APPENDIX B –

PRELIMINARY IDENTIFICATION OF LEATHER FRAGMENTS FROM NOVGOROD EXCAVATIONS (1991–2001)

D. Sully

INTRODUCTION

The intention of this preliminary identification was to assess the potential of excavated leather for animal species identification, using physical examination of skin morphology (hair follicle pattern on grain surface, cross section features and hair morphology).

Identification was carried out at the Institute of Archaeology, London with a binocular microscope 10–40 magnification, using an existing reference collection of commercially produced leather. The identifications (see Table) were reviewed with the assistance of Chris Calnan, The National Trust advisor on Conservation of Organic materials, former Director of the Leather Conservation Centre, Northampton, UK.

The majority of the samples showed a good level of preservation of diagnostic features. The general condition of the samples was good and was able to withstand handling and examination during the identification process.

The potential source of animals used in the manufacture of leather has included the suggestion of the use of wild animals from trapping. Initial examination suggests that a conventional range of skins from domesticated animals have been used in the manufacture of leather used in these artefacts. The potential exception to this is the presence of deer in the identified samples, further information on the likely species present and the acquisition of specific reference material will help to clarify the presence of such animals in the artefactual record.

IDENTIFICATION

The identification of animal type based on grain pattern (distribution, grouping, presence of primary and secondary hairs) is a straight forward process with modern leather samples. This is based on the identification of diagnostic features cross-referred to comparative leather samples. The reference collection used in this initial examination is based on modern commercially available leather samples. The majority of domestic species are likely to be satisfactorily identified by such comparisons.

The sequence of examination starts with an initial identification of major animal groups. The main types likely to be encountered are; bovine (calf, cattle, oxen), pig, sheep/goat, and unusual/exotic. The majority of leather assemblages can be expected to be catagorised into these groups.

Following separation of major animal groups, further identification can then focus on confirming diagnostic features for more detail identifications, enabling further distinctions to be made. This process seeks to increase the level confidence of identification of more unusual leather samples, to separate identification of goat/ sheep/ deer skins (especially to establish percentage presence of deer), to distinguish between adult and young skins, and to distinguish between domesticated and wild animal sources.

POTENTIAL FOR IDENTIFICATION USING THESE TECHNIQUES

Sheep and goat can be difficult to discriminate between on basis of grain pattern, due to the range of sheep skins from fine wool to course hair sheep, the later being similar to goat. Additional information from coarseness of fibres, presence of hairs and the tendency for sheep to delaminate is often required to make the identification. With suitable reference materials it is possible to distinguish deer skin from sheep/goat.

Level of detail of relevant reference collection

It is likely that leather manufacture is related to butchery in Novgorod and its hinterland therefore close reference to the animal bone identification would be important in order to build up a useful reference collection. Therefore it is suggested that a reference collection should be created from commercially available leather, which reflects the range of animals identified in the animal bone record (see Maltby, this volume).

In addition a reference collection of archaeological leather samples materials should be produced showing the range of preservation of diagnostic features for each identified animal type.

A photographic key will need to be developed from a range of sources, to supplement the reference collection of actual leather samples, potential sources such as the Natural History Museum (London), zoos in Russia and elsewhere, etc.

Obviously the greater the level of distinctions identified in the reference collection, the greater the potential to identify subtle difference in the leather assemblage.

Preservation of diagnostic features

Burial and post excavation changes have lead to an alteration of surface detail which can compound the identification of standard diagnostic details when related to information from non-archaeological leather samples. A sample of fresh (wet) leather samples should be examined to determine the benefits of performing identification prior to the drying of excavated leather.

Where abrasion of the surface has lead to loss of diagnostic features then horizontal sectioning may reveal hair distribution patterns and variations in leather fibre structure (for example this can help distinguish fine woolled sheep and hair of sheep/goat).

ADDITIONAL INFORMATION ABOUT THE LEATHER

It is assumed (due to the nature of preservation) that the material sampled is all vegetable tanned leather. Due to contamination in the archaeological deposits any identification of potential tanning agents would be unlikely to prove fruitful. The potential for SEM imaging needs to be investigated as a technique to detect the physical presence of tannate aggregates within collagen structure. This might also be used with "unusual" leather samples.

Use of standard condition assessment techniques, such as measurement of shrinkage temperature (hydrothermal shrinkage) are likely to be distorted by the presence of iron within the collagen structure. Therefore without further work standard comparisons with non-archaeological leather is unlikely to be valid. Comparisons between different leather from Novgorod excavations might provide useful information using this technique.

Preliminary identification of 42 leather fragments from excavations at Novgorod; Troitsky and Kremlin excavations (1991–2001). Sample numbers refer to list accompanying samples delivered to Institute of Archaeology, London in July 2002.

Sample number	animal type	detail
1	bovine,	calf (possibly deer)
2	sheep/goat	goat (hair present, no scale pattern identified)
3	sheep/goat	possibly sheep
4	bovine	calf (unusual pattern possibly representing wild bovine, alternatively horse is a possibility)
5	bovine	calf (unusual pattern possibly representing wild bovine, alternatively horse is a possibility)
6	unusual	(not sheep/goat/ deer, bovine)
7	sheep/goat	possibly sheep
8	sheep/goat	possibly sheep (diagnostic features abraded, delamination suggests possibly sheep)
9	bovine	possibly calf
10	possibly deer	
11	sheep/goat	possibly goat

Sample number	animal type	detail
12	bovine	
13	bovine	
14	sheep/goat	possibly goat
15	bovine	possibly calf
16	no diagnostic features	
17	possibly deer	
18	no diagnostic features	
19	sheep/goat	possibly sheep
20	bovine	possibly calf
21	bovine	possibly calf
22	sheep/goat	possibly goat
23	no diagnostic features	
24	bovine	
25	bovine	(unusual pattern possibly representing wild bovine, alternatively horse is a possibility)
26	no diagnostic features	
27	bovine	possibly calf
28	bovine	
29	no diagnostic features	
30	sheep/goat	possibly goat
31	bovine	
32	bovine	
33	sheep/goat	possibly sheep
34	bovine	
35	no diagnostic features	
36	bovine	
37	bovine	
38	bovine	
39	bovine	
40	sheep/goat	possibly sheep
41	sheep/goat	possibly sheep
42	bovine	

Summary table *of major animal groups identified*

	bovine	sheep/goat	deer	unknown	Pig
Sample numbers	1,4,5,9,12,13,15,20,21, 24,25,27,28,31,32,34,36,37,38,39,42	2,3,7,8,11,14,19 22,30,40,41	10,17	6,16,18,23, 26,29,35	-

– 22 –

POTTERY PRODUCTION IN THE NOVGOROD REGION: LOCAL TRADITIONS AND FOREIGN INFLUENCES

T. Brorsson

INTRODUCTION

During the course of 20th-century excavations at Ryurik Gorodishche (hereafter Gorodishche) and Novgorod enormous amounts of pottery sherds were found. The sherds bear witness to concentrated activities on the settlement and later the city during several hundred years. Many of these vessels were made by hand out of suitable local clays and tempers for vessel-building. The conservative technology behind these pots was most likely practised over a long period of time, adopted from one generation of potters to another. However, at times ideas and innovations in technology were imported from the southern Baltic area. This article will examine these circumstances.

The pottery from Novgorod and it predecessor Gorodishche have been previously studied from several different aspects. A main goal has been to present what forms the material takes and how it was made. Furthermore, it has been used as an indicator of contacts between what are now Russia, Sweden, Poland and Germany during the Viking age and early medieval period. The material has been connected with Vikings as well as with the Hanseatic League. The common thread is these pots have been discussed in combination with aspects of trade and exchange (Brorsson 2001; Gaimster 2006).

Gorodishche was founded in the late 8th or early 9th century, was in use through the whole Viking age, and became one of the most important sites in Northern Europe (Nosov 1992). The Vikings, the Varangians, visited the place and settled there in the middle of the 9th century. Furthermore, according to the chronicle of Nestor, the Varangians played an important role in the foundation of Gorodishche and the Russian state. The Vikings' name for the place was Holmgård. Gorodishche was in use until around AD 1000, when many of the settlement's activities moved a few kilometres down the River Volkhov, where Novgorod had been established around a hundred years earlier. The earliest finds of pottery in Novgorod date to around AD 930 (Malygin *et al.* 2006). Novgorod became even more important than its predecessor and many traces in the city bear witness to contacts with several areas in Western Europe and the East.

Since the pottery is both well preserved and normally found in large amounts (Orton 2006, 117), it is an important source, telling us about contacts and development of Gorodishche and Novgorod from the Viking age to the end of the medieval period. This article discusses how the pots were made during the Viking age (800–1000) and the first part of the medieval period (1000–1400) and how the shape and decoration of the vessels changed during this time. When and most of all, why, did the pottery change during these periods?

POTTERY TECHNOLOGY DURING THE VIKING AGE: THE 9TH AND 10TH CENTURIES

Ladoga vessels were the dominating vessel type during the Viking age and were used by the East Slavs, especially in the Novgorod region. This type has also been found in great amounts on other trading sites such as Staraya Ladoga close to Lake Ladoga. It was strongly influenced by the West-Slavonic type, Menkendorf, which can be mainly dated to the 9th and 10th centuries (Nosov 1992, 55) and the dating of the Ladoga ceramics can mainly be placed in the 9th to the 11th centuries. Studies have shown that this kind of pottery appeared at Helgö (Rydh 1936, 45) and Birka (Brorsson 2004, 363) in Sweden from the 9th to the 10th century.

This kind of pottery was made by coiling and the coils were fastened to each others by the so called N-technique (Figure 22.1). It means that the clay of the coils was in turns pulled upwards on one side and downwards on the other side. This was a method which was common in Northern Europe from the beginning of the Neolithic until the end of early medieval period. The Ladoga vessels from Gorodishche were made by hand without any use of turntable or potters-wheel, and without any decoration. Furthermore, it is characterized by an out-turned rim and a distinct sharp shoulder. The base was flat. The ware of this kind of pottery was coarse and consisted most often of a fine clay, tempered with crushed granite in proportions between 15% and 20% (Brorsson 2001, Table 1). Unpublished analyses of Ladoga pottery from Staraya Ladoga and from Prost and Vasilievskoye close to Novgorod have provided similar results.

Figure 22.1 Coiling. Most of the Viking age pottery at Ryurik Gorodishche was made by coiling. The coils where fasten to each other by the so called N-technique (Andersen 1975, 56f). Drawing by A. Jeppsson.

The imported vessel types during the Viking age at Gorodishche mainly consist of Scandinavian-type vessels. These are most likely the result of trade and other types of exchange between present day Russia and central Sweden. The Scandinavian-type pots were made by the same methods as the Ladoga pots, but the shape of the body and rim differs. The Scandinavian-type pot had an in-turned rim and the vessel profile looks more or less like a barrel. Analyses of a sample of Scandinavian-type pots from Gorodishche have shown beyond doubt that some of these pots were made within the region of Gorodishche itself (Brorsson 2001, 56). Local diatoms in the clay were used as clear evidence for this statement. This result clearly shows that imported as well as locally made Scandinavian pots where found at the trading site.

It is important to bear in mind that Ladoga vessels were the most common vessel type at Gorodishche and the foreign Scandinavian pots only comprise a maximum of 1% of the total pottery assemblage. The pots were most likely used individually by the two different cultural groups living there (i.e. the Slavs and the Scandinavians). Furthermore, although the vessel building technique was the same, there seems not to have been any influence from one vessel type to the other.

From the second half of the 10th century decorated black earthenware can be found at Troitsky VIII and X in Novgorod (Hulthén and Brorsson, 2008, 604; Goryunova 2006, 47). The context for these sherds has been dated by dendrochronology to between 950 and 970. These vessels were most likely made by means of coiling and shaped on a turntable (Figure 22.2). This type of pottery may be classified as Baltic ware. The same pottery occurs at Gorodishche, dated to after the middle of the 10th century. These pots were shaped on turntables (Goryunova 2006, 44).

Baltic ware is a quite different vessel type compared to Ladoga ware. The most distinct difference is the presence of decoration, of which wavy-lines and linear decoration are the most common (Rud 2006, 127). The Baltic ware in Novgorod has more or less the same shapes as the Ladoga vessels, of which the out-turned rim and the distinct shoulder are visible in both types (Figure 22.3). However, the way of shaping and decorating the vessels differs. The Baltic ware was also made by coiling, but it was shaped and decorated on a slow-wheel,

Figure 22.2 *The use of a turntable probably first appeared in the Novgorod region in the middle of the 10th century. Drawing by A. Jeppsson.*

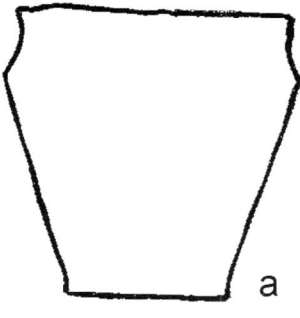 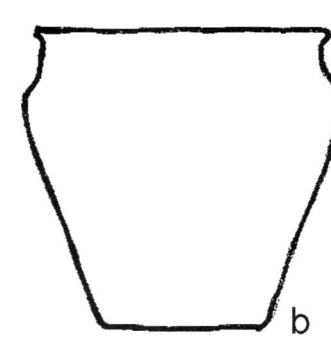

a

b

Figure 22.3 Shape. The dominating vessel types at Ryurik Gorodishche and Novgorod from the 9th to the 15th century. The Ladoga vessels (a) and the early wheel turned vessels were further developed into Baltic ware (b).

which the potter used his hands to rotate while shaping and subsequently decorating the pot.

The differences between pots shaped on turntables and pots made on the potter's-wheel are mainly seen in two important aspects of the pottery (Brorsson 2005). The first concerns the temper, it is difficult to use large and angular grains in the clay used for wheel-throwing. The grains could hurt the potter's hand as well as causing an uneven surface finish. The second aspect concerns the presence of the horizontal lines on the inside of the vessels. Horizontal lines appear on wheel-thrown pots on the whole inside, from the base to the rim. On pots shaped on a turntable lines occur only on the upper part. The constructions of the potter's-wheel and the turntable are quite similar, but differ in one important aspect. The potter's-wheel is rotated by foot or by stick, whereas the turntable is rotated by hand. The rotation speed is much higher on a potter's-wheel than on a turntable. Practical experiments have shown that the rotation speed must be higher than 0.7 m/sec. Otherwise the vessel wall will collapse and make the wheel-throwing impossible (Hulthén 1974, 69). The wheel-thrown pots are built up by hand and with the aid of centrifugal force. Vessels shaped on turntables are normally made by coiling and given a final shape when rotated on the turntable.

The Baltic ware was still made of a fine clay which was tempered with crushed rocks but the grains were smaller than before. The ware was finer and the sherd thickness was thinner than on the Ladoga vessels. However, the early Baltic ware at Troitsky VIII seems to have been made out of rather coarse wares.

Baltic ware was the result of a combination of East and West Slavonic vessels within the region. The vessel shape belonged to the East-Slavs, meanwhile the ware, vessel building technique, and decoration were West-Slavonic (Hulthén and Brorsson, 2008, 608). A similar pattern may be discerned in Sweden, where typical Viking age pottery can be seen in the local and later Baltic ware (Brorsson 2004, 346ff). The fact that the vessels shape and especially the shape of the base and rim did not change may indicate that there was little or no change in the way of cooking or storing food. It was simply a change in how the pottery was made and how it was decorated.

POTTERY TECHNOLOGY DURING THE 11TH AND 12TH CENTURIES

Hand made pottery was still in use in the earliest layers of the 11th century in Novgorod (Malygin *et al.* 2006, Table 4.3). This was the same type of ware that was earlier found at Gorodishche. However, Baltic ware dominated the pottery inventory in Novgorod through the whole of the early medieval period, i.e. during the 11th and 12th centuries. Unpublished analyses of Baltic ware from this period clearly shows that the pots still were made out of fine clays, tempered with crushed granite, just like the Viking age pots.

The Baltic ware in Novgorod was of a local type and consisted of vessels with out-turned rims. It was normally decorated with wavy-lines, horizontal lines and small impressions. Malygin and Orton have discovered that lids came into use in the 12th century. The lid could represent a new function for the vessels, possibly as a container for liquids, or may be associated with new cooking practices (Malygin and Orton 2001, 64).

During this period another type of vessel appeared in Novgorod, namely amphora. These vessels did not affect the local pottery making technique, but bear witness to trade links with the south, all the way down to Byzantium. The amphorae were shipped through Kiev on the River Dnieper (Rybina 1992, 193). The trade existed mainly during the 11th and 12th century. However, amphorae in Novgorod may be found already during the 10th century and appeared in small amounts in the 13th century. Four different main groups of amphorae from the Black Sea region have been identified within the Novgorod assemblage (Volkov 2006).

From the very end of the 12th century Novgorod's trade with the Germans increased. German merchants founded a quarter complete with a Church dedicated to St. Peter at that time and they played an important part in several different aspects of the development of the city (Rybina 1992, 198). The Hanseatic League became established in the city in 1191, which may of course have been a most important event for Novgorod. However, a Gotlander's Court, or Gotenhof, was founded in the early 12th century (Gaimster 2006, 135). The connections with the Germans are very clear and visible in the ceramics, but connections with Gotland and its Court are more or less invisible in the archaeological record of 12th and 13th century Novgorod.

By the end of the 12th century a new type of pottery occurred in Novgorod. It was the hard grey ware (*Harte Grauware*). It was originally produced in western Germany and became an important trade good during the 13th century. However, production of this type of pottery was already established in the middle of the 12th century in several German cities such as Lübeck (Gläser 1987). The dating of the first finds in Novgorod is uncertain.

This type of pottery was made from a different type of clay than that used before and it was wheel-thrown and fired in kilns. New vessel types included jugs and tripod vessels. It therefore represented a completely different craft technology. This significant change in the way of making pots has been connected with the establishment of special pottery workshops in Germany at this time. However, when potters' workshops were established in the city of Novgorod is still an unsolved problem.

From the end of the 12th century and for several hundred years onwards, different types of faiences and majolica from the Near and Middle East can be found in Novgorod (Koval 2006). But the amount of these sherds is extremely low and appears not to have affected local pottery technology in Novgorod itself.

The change in the pottery inventory did not only involve technological aspects. New vessel types occurred at the same time. The change in vessel type, from a big open vessel during the early medieval period to jugs and tripod vessels must have been a most important change in North-European kitchens. The shape of the vessel may have been the result of a change in the way of cooking or storing as well as serving food and drink.

Figure 22.4 The potter's wheel most likely came into use in Novgorod from the later part of the 13th century. Drawing by A. Jeppsson.

POTTERY IN NOVGOROD DURING THE 13TH AND 14TH CENTURIES

The first finds of red earthenware in Novgorod can be dated to the turn of the 12th and 13th centuries. For example, from the Duboshin site situated on the market side of the city, sherds of a lead-glazed, red earthenware were found in layers which were dated by dendrochronology from 1213 to 1280 (Gaimster 2001, 72). Red earthenware was originally produced in the Netherlands but quickly became an important product in several of the North-German cities, where they also produced grey ware. The assembly at Duboshin Street in the 13th century compares well with contemporaneously imported groups found on other Hanseatic mercantile sites in the north-eastern Baltic region (Gaimster 2006, 141).

This Novgorodian red ware was made with lead glaze on the outer surface and the vessel was fired in an oxidising atmosphere, both of which were major local innovations. The earlier black ware, e.g. Ladoga and Baltic wares, were fired in a reduced atmosphere. Furthermore, the red ware was made with a naturally coarse, sandy clay, which was possible to throw on a potter's wheel. Just like the hard grey ware, the red ware represents a completely different craft technology from what preceded it.

At Duboshin Street, excavations produced evidence for a locally made, lead-glazed red earthenware found. The contexts for these shards have been dated by dendrochronology from 1265 to 1280. Technological analyses have shown that the pots were most likely made in Novgorod (Hulthén and Brorsson, 2008, 609). But the vessels were made out of clays which were tempered with crushed granite and grog. It appears to have been a mixture between the old and the new craft techniques. However, unpublished analyses from Troitsky XI have shown that a change in local wares occurred at the end of the 13th century. The presence of local lead glazed pottery and a medieval ware consisting of a naturally tempered clay, indicates that the first real potters' workshops in Novgorod were created at this time.

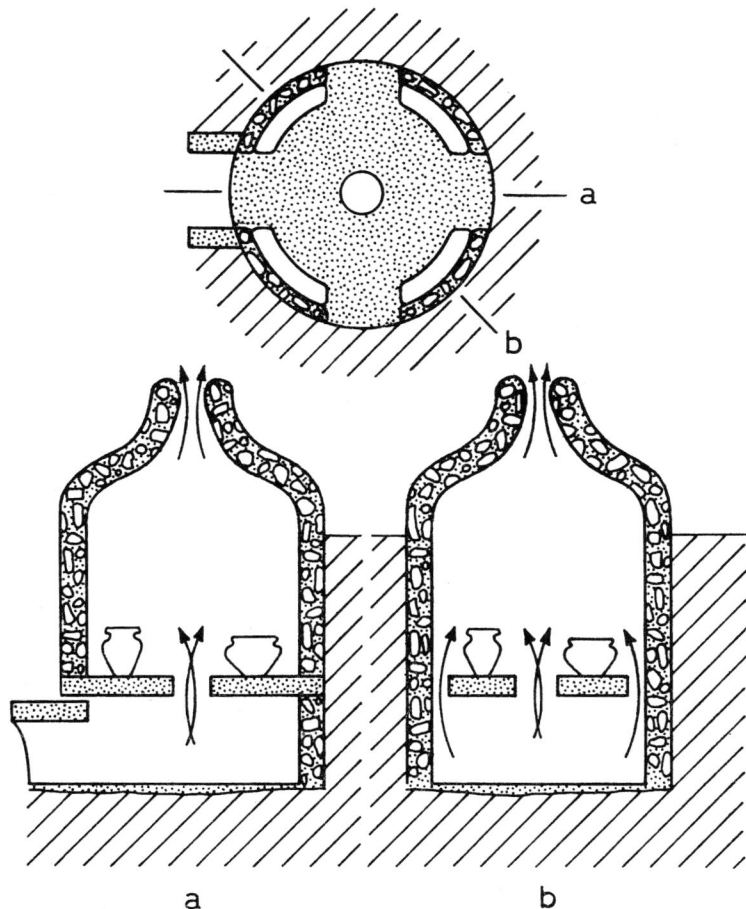

Figure 22.5 Kiln. From the late 13th century onwards the medieval pottery of Novgorod was most likely fired in kilns, perhaps similar to the one shown here which has two chambers, one for the fire, and another for the pots (After Knorr 1970, Abb. 32).

During the 14th century a completely new type of pottery appeared in Novgorod, namely proto-stoneware. Most of this ceramic was made in the middle of Germany and shipped through different harbours along the southern Baltic and North Sea coasts to the towns of Northern Europe. The major difference between the proto-stoneware and the earlier pottery was the clay. Proto-stoneware was made from a clay that could be fired to about 1300–1400°C, without losing its shape. The earlier pots were made out of clays that could only be fired to a maximum of around 1000°C, at which point they would start to sinter and melt and then totally lose their shape. The reason why the stoneware production sites were situated in Germany was of course due to the presence of suitable stoneware clays in the region.

Jugs were more or less the only vessel type that was produced by proto-stoneware. It out-competed the red earthenware jugs rather quickly – there are few finds of red ware jugs found during the 15th century. During the following centuries, developed stoneware and red ware with glaze on its inner surface were the dominating pottery types in Northern Europe.

LOCAL TRADITIONS AND FOREIGN INFLUENCES

During the Viking age the pottery craft in Novgorod region could be classified as a typical 'prehistoric' craft. The vessels were made by methods that were several thousand years old, and most of these pots were most likely made in the homes where they were used.

Vessels finished on a slow wheel start to appear in Gorodishche and in Novgorod towards the end of the Viking age. These pots were made with the same type of raw material as the older pots, but the craft did change, and a minor technological improvement is visible. The use of a turntable was most likely the result of contacts with what is now Poland and northern Germany. During this period the decoration also changed with Slavonic wavy-lines occurring in abundance.

Aside from small amounts of imported vessels like amphorae, no changes in the pottery inventory in Novgorod is visible during the 11th and 12th centuries. The craft is more or less homogenous and based on local production. This production was not located in every household, as the pots were more likely to have been bought in a local market within the city. Studies of pottery from this period in Sweden have shown that it was most likely slaves that made vessels for a limited market (Jönsson and Brorsson 2003, 178). But, from this point, we can start to talk about specialist workshops making pottery for the marketplace. The workshops may have been the property of free potters working on their own.

Technological analyses have shown that the pottery during the second half of the 13th and 14th centuries was made by new methods. Analyses of pottery from Troitsky XI show that the pottery at this time was made out of clays tempered with sand. These changes may have been connected with the introduction of the potter's wheel in Novgorod. However, analyses of the red earthenware sherds with lead glaze from the Duboshin site reveal that certain of the old methods, e.g. the choice of clay and temper, were still in use during the second half of the 13th century.

Kilns may have been connected with the introduction of the potter's wheel, lead glaze and new types of clay. No kilns from this time have been found in Novgorod, but there may have been several small kilns within the city as have been found elsewhere (e.g. Greifswald in Mecklenburg (Brandt 2000), where four separate kilns were found within the city wall, but in the outer parts of the town). Cooking pots as well as jugs were made out of red or black earthenware.

Besides the technological aspect of the pottery craft, another major change appeared in the beginning of the 13th century. It was the introduction of new vessel types, and jugs as well as tripod cooking vessels may be found from this period. This was most likely the result of contacts with Germany and the Hanseatic League.

The pottery craft in Germany was of major importance, not only for its own region but for the whole Baltic area. For instance, in the documents of the Hanseatic towns of Rostock and Wismar, potters were mentioned as being present by the middle of the 13th century (Mangelsdorf 1990, 269). The same is true for other towns of this period, e.g. Stralsund and Greifswald (Mangelsdorf 1990, 271–277). During the 12th and 13th centuries, the mode of pottery production changed from a household to a specialised and professional craft activity, connected with pottery workshops. The old Slavonic pottery was replaced by the hard grey ware made on the potter's wheel and fired in kilns. This change occurred around 1200 in the region around Lübeck and a minor, later change took place to the east, in Poland (Kempke 2001, 249–256). This minor change consisted of the production of a finer ware and new vessel types. The beginning of the 13th century seems to have been a very important time for developments in vessel production in Northern Europe.

Stoneware was another type of pottery that does not appear to have affected local vessel production. The reason for this was the absence of suitable stoneware clays in the region, and it was therefore not possible to make this kind of pottery in Novgorod. However, the potters made their own type of white pottery in Novgorod, which was a white earthenware that goes back to the 13th century (Malygin and Orton 2001, 64). This type of pottery was made out of naturally tempered, coarse clays.

It is most likely that the Ladoga vessels and the later Baltic ware were locally made, but with the lead glazed red earthenware in the beginning of the 13th century and the wheel-thrown hard grey ware, the local pottery tradition was declined. A question that should be raised is why the local ceramic production increased again in Novgorod in the 13th century. It was then a medieval pottery craft, consisting of wheel-thrown, lead glazed pottery, fired in kilns. This pottery was most likely made in professional workshops and sold in the local markets of Novgorod. However, for more than 75 years this type of pottery was based upon imports from present day Germany, traded by the Hanseatic League for local goods in Novgorod. Perhaps this started as the manufacture by German potters in Novgorod itself who found suitable clays and established workshops. On the other hand, the coarse sherds with lead glaze from Duboshin Street may indicate that local potters tried to make their own type of pots, but with glaze. It may be that German potters took an important role in the ceramic production in Novgorod, but there were also Russian potters working in the city. In any event, these new pots were similar to the pots from Germany and the Russian shapes were abandoned.

The same pattern may be visible in the early Baltic ware, dated to the middle of the 10th century. The introduction of the use of the slow-wheel may have been connected with foreign potters. The potters at Gorodishche and Novgorod could have been from present day Poland, where similar pots have been found. Furthermore, this may indicate that Poland and the Novgorod region had some level of contact, where potters moved to Novgorod from that area. These potters made the Baltic ware look like the earlier Ladoga pots. The same patterns can be seen in Sweden and Denmark (Jönsson and Brorsson 2003, 178).

SUMMARY

The pottery from Gorodishche and Novgorod shows how the craft changed from a handicraft which was connected to the household to a professional craft connected to workshops. The development of the craft was the result of foreign merchants and perhaps also foreign potters visiting the Novgorod region. The changes in making the pots and how to use them was initially influenced by the West-Slavs and later by the Germans, which were connected to the Hanseatic League. The appearance of special cooking pots and table wares were most likely partly the result of new types of food preparation and serving. The pottery can be linked to social as well as economical changes through time. However, the change from the Viking-age Ladoga vessel to the Baltic ware was not affected by the change of preparing and cooking food. The different vessel types were very similar, including the shaping, decoration and the coarseness of the ware. The Scandinavian influence, especially in the 9th and 10th centuries, does not appear to have affected local pottery technology, nor did it affect how the pots were used.

INDICATORS OF CRAFT SPECIALISATION IN MEDIEVAL CERAMICS FROM NORTH-WEST RUSSIA

C. Orton

INTRODUCTION

In discussing craft specialisation, we are looking for evidence for the organisation of the production of pottery in a social context, and for ways in which this may have changed over time. A model or typology for the organisation of production was provided by van der Leeuw (1977), in the form of five stages (or 'modes of production') of increasing scale and intensity: household production, individual industry, household industry, village industry and large-scale industry. This was modified by Peacock (1982) for the study of Roman pottery, by the addition of a second dimension, representing the degree of official or élite participation, in the form of military/official production and estate production. Costin (1991, 8–9) and Costin and Hagstrum (1995, 620) developed this second dimension further by the idea of 'attached' and 'independent' types of specialists, each of which could operate at a range of scales. She also used the concept of the degree of specialisation (the ratio of producers to consumers), and four aspects which can be used to characterise production – context, concentration, scale or constitution, and intensity. These were important in breaking the link between scale and intensity of production, a model which has been criticised by others (e.g. Feinman (1999, 96) who challenged the original model as too 'monolithic' by giving examples of high-intensity craft production at a domestic scale).

Costin's aspects of production (1991, 11–18) are worth considering in more detail, because they ask questions of the archaeological record, the answers to which can shed light on the organisation of production. Under *context*, she contrasts the 'command' production of attached specialists, sponsored and managed by élite or governmental institutions or patrons, with independent specialists producing for a general market of potential customers. Her term *concentration* refers to the spatial organisation of production – for example, are specialists distributed throughout a community, do they each serve a particular community, or are they nucleated to the extent that one centre may serve several communities? *Scale* describes the size of the production unit, which is commonly determined by considerations of efficiency. Increasing size can bring economies of scale, but can also incur administrative overheads, thus limiting the optimum size of a unit. Finally, Costin's *intensity* reflects the amount of time producers spend on their craft. The choice of full- or part-time production depends on many factors, such as the scope for alternative activities (e.g. agriculture), the efficiency of a particular strategy, the possibility of scheduling potting activities throughout the year, and the need for and availability of capital investment.

These general issues can be translated into questions specific to the circumstances of medieval Novgorod. Although 'independent producers' is the obvious model, there could be attached specialists if a boyar family employed potters to produce specifically for their estates, rural as well as urban. If their products were also made available on the market, this could be seen as hybrid attached/independent specialisation. The topic of concentration raises questions of the locations of potters in the town or region; do they have a rural or urban location, and are they nucleated or dispersed? The size of a production unit should be reflected in the space devoted to potting activities, and the extent of specialised sub-areas for specific tasks. Intensity can perhaps best be inferred from evidence for other activities that are undertaken at the same location as potting, whether purely domestic activities or those relating to other productive processes.

There is considerable interest in identifying changes in modes of production, both within a region and over time, as well as in characterising them. In some respects, this is an easier task, because the measures used to indicate specialisation are relative rather than absolute (Costin 1991, 35). In other words, it is easier to say that one assemblage has more evidence of specialisation than another (through, for example, its level of standardisation), than it is to specify the absolute strength of that evidence. Advances in craft specialisation are often associated in the archaeological literature with the emergence of élites (Peregrine 1991), but this relates to prestige goods and 'attached' specialists.

Over the period we are considering (10th to 15th century), changes can be expected to occur, but not necessarily in a linear progression; waves or cycles may be observed (Orton 1985). Also, changes may not take place simultaneously across a region, and different modes may co-exist.

ARCHAEOLOGICAL EVIDENCE

The archaeological record can only provide indirect evidence for answering such questions, and as many different sorts of evidence as possible must be sought, to try to build a coherent picture. Four broad sources of evidence may be looked for:

1. Structural evidence, e.g. kilns, workshops, ancillary structures such as clay preparation pits. Production waste.
2. Technical evidence from the pottery itself – clay and inclusions, methods of construction, decorative techniques, firing temperature and methods.

3.   Standardisation/diversity of the product: variation of form and type within and between assemblages across sites, towns and regions.
4.   The scale of production – how many pots were being made?

Structural evidence

Permanent kilns (*gorns*) and ancillary structures are one of the clearest forms of evidence for production beyond the household level, but none have yet been found, in Novgorod (Gaidukov, pers. comm.), in Pskov (Kildyushevskii 2006, 85), or in Torzhok (Malygin, pers. comm.). This is not a purely regional phenomenon; large medieval settlements elsewhere have also failed to reveal evidence of pottery production within the settlement, for example southern England (e.g. Winchester, Southampton, Chichester, Salisbury) in the medieval period, or Vijayanagara in south India (Sinopoli 1999, 119). The general view in north-west Russia is that kilns would have been located outside towns, for reasons of the fire hazard that they represent, and for access to resources (clay, fuel, water). Certainly, there are abundant resources of good potting clay in the immediate vicinity of Novgorod and at Ryurik Gorodishche, where potting may also have taken place (Plokhov 2006, 13).

The possibility of firing pots in a domestic stove (*pech*) has also been suggested (Kildyushevskii 2006, 86), though this could only be on a small scale and would indicate household production. It is thought that such stoves could achieve a temperature of 600–700°C, probably below the firing temperature of most of the 'grey' or 'brown' pottery (700–800°C, see Kildyuskevskii 2006, 86) and certainly below that of the 'white' pottery (950°C).

However the pottery was fired, production centres should be characterised by large quantities of production waste, in the form of broken, distorted or over-fired pottery (*wasters*), as well as ash and possibly fragments of firing structures. No large deposits of such material have been found in either Novgorod or Pskov (Kildyuskevskii 2006, 85), although debris from the production of tiles has been found at Pskov. Small quantities of potential waster sherds have been found throughout the material from Troitsky XI, but it has proved extremely difficult to distinguish between genuine wasters and sherds derived from pots that had been destroyed in a house fire. It is also possible that waster sherds in bulk may have had a value in their own right, and may have been moved from their source for such a purpose. Such a practice has been observed by the author at an 18th-century site in Mitcham, London, where large quantities of kiln waste had been moved several kilometres, for use as hard core when the floor level of a building was raised.

Possible production sites should be sought in the immediate hinterland of towns, though admittedly this could be like looking for a needle in a haystack. They are likely to be located above the level of spring floods, and could perhaps be found by field-walking for concentrations of sherds, or by magnetometer survey. However, in the short term we must look for other sources of evidence, including documentary and place-name evidence. With the latter in mind, one of the so-called 'ends' or quarters of medieval Novgorod is referred to as Goncharski (potters') End, first mentioned in 1360, although better known by its earlier name of Lyudin (people's) End (Khoroshev, unpub.).

Technology

This is the most common source of evidence, being present in some way on every sherd found. It can be sub-divided into: the clay and inclusions, evidence for forming and finishing, decorative techniques and glaze, and firing.

The pottery generally has substantial additions of filler – up to 20 or 30% (Brorsson, pers. comm.), although some has inclusions that are naturally present, and a small minority has no inclusions at all. The most common inclusions are crushed granite (*gruss*) and various grades of sand; grog is also sometimes used. There appear to be chronological trends in the use of different fillers: Kildyushevskii (2006, 83) notes that at Pskov, fine, medium and coarse sand predominate in the 12th and 13th centuries, with little gruss; in the 14th and 15th centuries there is more gruss and fine sand, but less medium and coarse sand, while in the 16th and 17th centuries fine and medium sand predominate. In contrast, Brorsson (pers. comm.) notes a trend away from added gruss towards the use of naturally-occurring sand from the 13th century. Analysis of Orton and Wilson's data suggests that the proportion of sand-tempered pottery at Novgorod did not exceed 10% in the 13th century, and was about 40% in both the 14th and 15th centuries. Brorsson (this volume) makes the point that clay with gruss inclusions could not have been thrown on a wheel, while clay with sand could have been, and so they see the change from one to the other as reflecting a change to fully wheel-thrown pottery. However, as gruss continued to be used right to the end of the period (see above), the change may have been very gradual.

It is generally agreed that there are three broad stages of development in the forming of pottery: entirely handmade, wheel-finished (usually referred to as wheel-turned in the Russian literature), and fully wheel-thrown. Bobrinskii's seven stages (Bobrinskii 1978; see Goryunova 2006, 32) seem more elaborate than is needed for our purposes here. In the first two stages, pots are built up from wide flat coils of clay (Kildyushevskii 2003, 84; Plokhov 2006, 14). Direct evidence for throwing is best seen in the form of marks on the inside of pots, especially on the lower parts, which are however not always retained from excavations. Russian authors tend to see the step from handmade to wheel-finished as fundamental, while Brorsson sees it as a minor change within a conservative tradition, and puts more emphasis on the introduction of wheel-throwing, which he places in the later part of 13th century (Brorsson this volume). Kildyuskevskii (2006, 84) sees the main advances (wheel-throwing, improved firing techniques, glazing and other finishing techniques) as coming later, in the late 15th or 16th and 17th centuries. This period is poorly represented at Novgorod.

An interesting technical aspect is the use of glaze, whether functional (to seal the surface of a pot) or decorative. Evidence from Pskov (Kildyushevskii 2006, 85) shows that glaze was introduced for decorative purposes in the 16th and 17th centuries, linked to the introduction of a range of 'table ware' forms. The timing is probably similar at Novgorod, but this period has been little studied there. Novgorod, however, shows an earlier attempt to introduce glazing (on the inner surface, and therefore presumably functional), in the form of a small group of late-13th-century glazed wasters from the Duboshin site. Although made of local clays (Gaimster 2006, 141), they are similar in style and technique to Baltic ware, and ultimately to the redwares of the Low Countries. While this appears to be a failed experiment (in that production did not continue), it is perhaps the best evidence of that date for craft potters who have the resources to attempt to innovate (even if their innovation was not taken up by the consumer). Failed attempts at ceramic innovation are known from other medieval towns, for example from Canterbury (Cotter 1997) and possibly from Exeter (Allan 1984, 27–30) in England. By way of explanation, Gaimster (2006, 141) links this attempt to the proximity of Duboshin to the German and Gotland quarters, where more advanced 'western' pottery (stoneware and glazed redwares) was being used by foreign merchants.

Standardisation and diversity

The more concentrated and centralised the production of pottery, the more 'standard' (or less diverse) the product should be. Diversity should therefore be capable of indicating the level of industrial and/or craft pottery as against domestic potting (with the domestic being the more diverse). The problems with this approach are the level at which diversity is to be measured, and how it is to be measured. Ideally, diversity can be measured by the number of different types (cf. species) in an assemblage, or by their relative proportions. This approach gives rise to both theoretical and practical problems (Orton 2000, 171–6), but a specific one here is the meaning of 'type' (compare, for example, Blackman et al. 1993, 61). Russian authors generally use a four-level type system, for example class-series-group-type (Koval 2006, 162–4) or group-type-subtype-variant (e.g. Malygin et al. 2006, 58), and it is far from obvious which of these levels (if any) is appropriate. The top (Malygin's 'group') level is too high, as it often represents different functional groupings, and the production of a wide range of functional groups is more likely to indicate industrial or craft production. The 'variant' level is likely to be too low, as it represents minor variations which are designated for typological convenience (Malygin, pers. comm.). In fact, the whole typological system is geared towards chronological or functional variation, and is not suited to questions about diversity, which it was never intended to answer.

Decoration might be a more fruitful approach (Hagstrum 1985, 68), since it is less related to function, and might hypothetically be used to differentiate different producers of the same functional type. At both Novgorod and Pskov, the chronological trend is towards simplicity of decoration, with (a) fewer pots being decorated, (b) a smaller area of each pot being decorated, and (c) fewer decorative styles ('combinations') being used together (Kildyushevskii 2006, 110; Rud 2006, 128). This might reflect an increased scale of production and market orientation (Kildyushevskii 2006, 111), but there could be other social or ethnic reasons (e.g. less need to assert individuality?).

Whether one looks at form or decoration (or both), the question can also be asked within or between assemblages. For example, diversity could be expressed by the presence of a wide range of types within an individual site or location, or by differences between different parts of a town or region. The latter might give some idea of the local scale of production, in the sense of the area supplied by a particular producer. However, far more sites will have to be investigated before this approach becomes even remotely possible, and care will have to be taken to distinguish different ethnic groups, for example in the German or Gotlander quarters.

Because of the difficulties of choosing an appropriate level of definition of form type or decoration for studying diversity (see above), alternative variables are sometimes sought. Measurement variables (e.g. height or rim diameter of pots; weight) are attractive because they can be easily defined and reliably recorded. Variability can be measured statistically by use of the standard deviation (*sd*) or, better, the coefficient of variation (*cv*). The cv is the sd divided by the mean, and is preferred because it scales variability to the size of the variable (Costin and Hagstrum 1995, 631). For example, a sd of 1 cm on a diameter of 10 cm expresses greater variability (cv = 1/10 = 10%) than it does on a diameter of 20 cm (cv = 1/20 = 5%). Eerkens and Bettinger (2001, 495) have suggested a theoretical lower limit to the cv of 1.7% as the best that can be achieved in craft processes, due to the limitations of human perception.

The data on rim diameters collected from the ceramic sample of the Troitsky XI excavation, Sector B can be used to test this approach. It has already been established that average rim diameters vary both between forms and over time (Orton 2006, 125), so variability must be measured for contemporaneous groups of the same form, which can then be compared with other forms of the same date, or the same forms at other dates. For each of the spits that had been catalogued in detail, the means, sds and cvs of the rim diameters were calculated for each form that was well represented in that spit. The cvs were universally large: all were greater than 10%, typical values were between 15% and 20%, and a few were greater, ranging up to 26%. The only exception is a group of lids that has a cv of only 5%. However, because of the difficulty of distinguishing between the rims of lids and bowls, not too much should be made of this difference. There are no chronological trends in the cvs, and no consistent differences between the cvs of hand-made and wheel-turned types. The scale of the variability strongly suggests that, at any one time, each form was being made in a range of sizes. This observation supports the view of Kildyushevskii (pers. comm.), and may in fact be indirect evidence for specialised production, since manufacture of the same form in a range of sizes suggests production for a number of consumers, while manufacture aimed at just one size may be more typical of domestic production.

Scale of production

This brings us to the last of our indicators. The actual numbers of pots being produced may give us an idea of how they are produced, with industrial production more prolific than craft production, which in turn is more prolific than domestic production.

Normally, such figures would be unobtainable, but the particular circumstances of Novgorod may make it possible to obtain estimates, which although not precise, may suggest the order of magnitude. It is thought (Sorokin, pers. comm.) that rubbish was generally disposed of inside the town, and that pottery in particular is concentrated in and around buildings. This being so, it should be possible to estimate the numbers of pots present per unit area or volume, and hence the total 'throughput' of pottery, which can be equated to local production, since imported wares are insignificant in quantity. However, it does not tell us about the numbers of pots in use at any time, because we have no information on use-lives. Once again, we really need a series of samples from across the town to achieve reliable estimates, and so far only one sample area – Sector B of the Troitsky XI excavation – has been recorded in sufficient detail. This area may of course not be representative of density of occupation across the town (in fact, there is evidence that it may not be, see below), but it at least gives a starting point.

The argument proceeds in a series of steps of increasing complexity:

Step 1

Troitsky XI: 167,000 sherds from 320m^2 ≅ 520 sherds/m^2 or about 100 sherds/m^3 (based on a depth of 26 spits = 5.2 m). This pottery density is likely to be too high because the average 'property building density' (i.e. the proportion of each property occupied by buildings) is about 0.25 (Khoroshev *et al.* 2001, 26), but the plan of Troitsky XI (Alexandrovskaya *et al.* 2001, 18) shows that its property building density is considerably greater than this.

Troitsky X: 247,000 sherds from 775 m^2 ≅ 320 sherds/m^2 or about 60 sherds/m^3

Nerevsky XV–XXXII: 900,000 sherds from (say) 4000 m^2 ≅ 200 sherds/m^2 or 40 sherds/m^3 (depth of excavated deposits = 5 m, Rybina and Khoroshev 2002, 111).

Take a weighted average of about 50 sherds/ m^3 or 250 sherds/m^2.; a figure of 80 sherds/pot (Orton 2006, 117) would suggest about 0.6 pots/m^3 or 3 pots/m^2.

Taking the area of the medieval town to be about 400 ha, and reducing it by 15% to allow for non-domestic areas (e.g. roads and churches) (Kolchin 1985, 65), would lead to a total of 10.2 million pots, or about 18,000 p.a. This is only a 'point' estimate, and must be subject to a considerable margin of error. There are two main sources of error: error in the estimate of the number of sherds per m^3 (point estimate of 50 sherds/m^3), and error in the estimate of the number of sherds per pot (point estimate of 80 sherds/pot). Statistical arguments suggest that reasonable 'interval' estimates for these factors would be from 30 to 80 and from 60 to 100 respectively. These can be combined (Orton 2002) to give an overall interval estimate of the total number of pots of between 6.0 million and 17.5 million pots (10,000 and 30,000 p.a.).

Step 2

The first attempt is too high, as it assumes that the cultural layer has the same depth across the town as it does at Troitsky and Nerevsky (about 5 m), which is not the case.

Calculations based on a map (Rybina and Khoroshev 2002) that divides Novgorod into 'zones', and the median thicknesses of the cultural layer in sites in each zone, suggest an average depth across Novgorod of about 2.0 m, leading to a revised estimate of about 4.8 million pots overall, or about 8,400 p.a. Similar arguments to those used in Step 1 lead to an interval estimate of the total number of pots of between 2.4 million and 7.2 million pots (4300 and 12700 p.a.).

Step 3

These calculations are still too simple, as they assume a constant density of pottery (in terms of pots per m³ of deposits) throughout the period. Data collected from Troitsky XI (Table 23.1) shows that this is not the case. In this table, the numbers of rim sherds per spit have been converted to numbers per century, and then to numbers of pots per century, using figures of rim sherds per pot derived from the more detailed cataloguing of the pottery from Sector B. The table shows a relatively low density of pots in the 10th to 12th centuries, followed by a higher density in the 13th and 14th centuries (a more detailed analysis shows that this increase started in the second half of the 12th century). A relative decline in the 15th century may be due, at least in part, to disturbance of the 15th-century spits (Malygin *et al.* 2006, 74).

Considerations from Step 1 suggest that these figures should be halved to be representative of Novgorod as a whole (since the pottery density on Troitsky XI seems to be about twice the notional 'average'). If the depth of deposits can be related to the length of occupation, then the zonal map of deposit thickness can be used to plot the approximate extent of the occupied area within the town on a century-by-century basis. The density of pottery in Table 23.1 can be applied to these areas to give a revised estimate of the total number of pots, which on this basis comes to about 6.9 million, or 12,000 p.a. on average, varying from around 4000 p.a. in the 11th century to almost 20,000 p.a. in the 13th and 14th centuries. There is insufficient evidence to permit the calculation of interval estimates for these quantities, but they are likely to be of the same order as those for the previous steps.

Kolchin, in a discussion of medieval Russian towns, explains that the average 'ordinary' property or estate had an area of about 400 m², and a population of six occupants (Kolchin 1985, 64–5). The 'boyar' properties would typically have been

| | Centuries | | | | | | |
	10th	11th	12th	13th	14th	15th	total
Rim sherds	2342	3114	4389	5482	5848	4286	25461
Rim sherds per year	33	31	44	55	58	43	
Percentage	13	12	17	21	22	16	100
Rim sherds per pot	11.8	11.5	11.5	10.7	11.3	11.3	
Total pots	198.5	270.8	381.6	512.3	517.5	379.3	
Pots per m²	0.62	0.85	1.19	1.60	1.62	1.19	

Table 23.1 Density of pottery per century in Troitsky XI.

from 2.5 to four times this size, with a proportionally greater population. This meant that the population density of the urban area occupied by properties would have been about 120–150 per hectare, only about one-third to one-half of that estimated for West European towns at that date, according to Kolchin. From this he concludes that the population of Novgorod in the 13th century (before the Tatar invasion) was unlikely to have exceeded 30 or 35,000.

These figures can be compared with the estimates of numbers of pots to give some idea of the intensity of use. The ratio of pots to people in the 13th century seems to be about 0.6, i.e. the production of pottery was about 0.6 pots per person per annum. This does not tell us about the number in use at any particular time, as that would depend on the life-span of the pots, for which we have no information. The ratio is markedly lower in the earlier centuries, increasing gradually from around 0.25 in the 10th century, and seems to be static later, perhaps falling off in the 15th century.

These figures, even allowing for reasonable errors, seem well within the capabilities of domestic production. On the other hand, the production of some 20,000 pots per annum (13th century) would require the resources of several production units (on the basis of 100 pots per firing, one firing every three days for five months of the year – which is optimistic – would imply the regular use of four kilns of say 1.5m diameter and 1.0m height).

VIEWS ON SPECIALISATION

As we have seen in the Technology section, different writers emphasise different aspects of the development of pottery production throughout this period, and thus come to different conclusions about the emergence of specialist craft potters.

Plokhov (2006, 13) comments that "Observations by ethnographers show that among the peoples of Eastern Europe hand-made pottery was produced in the home or by craftsmen and was used mainly within the confines of the settlement in which it was made".

Kildyushevskii (2006, 85) refers to the craft nature of production in Pskov in the 12th to 17th centuries, citing as evidence "the large series of identical vessels, the very small number of stamps on the bases of vessels and the use of fairly advanced techniques". He does not refer to the earlier material (9th to 12th centuries), as that had already been published elsewhere. He also links the decrease in both the quantity and complexity of decoration throughout this period with an increasingly 'mass production' nature of the pottery (Kildyushevskii 2006, 114).

Malygin *et al.* say little directly about the context of pottery production, but they see the hand-made tradition ending at the close of the 10th or the beginning of the 11th century (2006, 76), followed by a fundamental change within the wheel-turned tradition in the middle and 2nd half of the 12th century (Spits 12–11). At that date, many news forms appear, and rims with ledges for lids appear for the first time. They also note the use of finer temper from the late 13th or early 14th century, and the use of white-firing clay at the end of the 15th century (Malygin *et al.* 2006, 55). Both of these changes might be linked to increasing specialisation; the former because it is a precondition for wheel-throwing, and the latter because it requires a higher firing temperature.

Brorsson (this volume) stresses the importance of the introduction of wheel-throwing (in contrast to wheel-turning) as an indicator of the change from household handicraft to professional workshop production. He links this to the switch from gruss to sand temper, which starts in the 13th century (see above), and notes that this seems to be contemporary with the Duboshin glazed wasters. He raises the possibility of the acquisition of a package of technological advances (glazing, wheel-throwing, finer temper) from alien pottery in the nearby Gotland or German quarters (pers. comm.). However, he also notes that the glazed sherds themselves are gruss-tempered, and therefore presumably not from wheel-thrown vessels.

DISCUSSION

In the context of the medieval ceramics of north-west Russia, some potential indicators of craft specialisation have proved to be more useful than others. Virtually no evidence has been found of centres of production, leaving open such questions as the use of purpose-built kilns (in contrast to bonfires, temporary kilns or the use of domestic stoves), their possible nucleation, and their location in rural or urban areas.

The standardisation approach has been of limited use; reliance on a typology devised for chronological purposes means that diversity cannot be expressed through counts of types, while the variability of measured dimensions (e.g. rim diameter) shows no patterning either between types or through time. Indeed, there are reasons to suggest that craft production here might be expected to show greater diversity in this respect, reversing the usual argument. Only decoration seems to hold some promise; there are significant trends in the proportion of pots being decorated, the extent of decoration on each pot, and the number of decorative styles in use at the same time, at both Novgorod and Pskov. Calculations of the overall scale of production are of necessity speculative, and in many circumstances would not be possible at all – only the particular circumstances of Novgorod make this approach even remotely realistic. Some idea of the reliability of such estimates can be obtained by calculating their margins of error, which are typically and expectedly large. Nevertheless, they are adequate to show that the consumption of pottery in Novgorod seems low relative to the population, despite the apparently large quantities retrieved in excavations. This is perhaps only to be expected in a culture in which wood is the predominant raw material, and in which wooden vessels and containers are abundant. The most useful indicator here is that of the potting technology, in which evidence of clay preparation, forming, decorating, and firing can all contribute to an understanding of the organisation of production.

The general type of clay used (the so-called 'grey-brown' clay (Kildyushevskii

2006, 82) seems consistent over the region and throughout the period, although there was much variation between and even within local sources (Brorsson, pers. comm.). Clay from more restricted sources (the 'red' and 'white' clays (Kildyushevskii 2006, 82) start to appear at the end of the period (late 15th century), perhaps reflecting the growing dominance of Moscow over the region at that time. The grey-brown clay (unlike the red and the white) requires considerable temper (either natural or deliberately added) to make it workable (Kildyushevskii 2006, 83). The same materials (various grades of sand, and gruss) are used at both Novgorod and Pskov, but there are important chronological differences in their relative importance at the two towns – gruss dominates the early production at Novgorod, with sand becoming important only from the 13th century, while at Pskov the position is almost reversed. This shows one extent to which local variation is possible within the regional tradition. As for forming, pots that are completely hand-made are known in Novgorod only in the 10th century (pots of this date from Pskov are not reported on in Kildyushevskii 2006), while wheel-throwing is clearly evident at Pskov from the 16th century onwards and Novgorod is presumed to be similar. Wheel-turning is the norm throughout most of the period at both Novgorod and Pskov. The timing of the introduction of full wheel-throwing is debatable; it may be reflected in the use of sand rather than gruss for tempering, but the reverse trend at Pskov seems to make this less likely, and the wheel-turning of coil-built pots is thought to continue there until the late 15th century (Kildyushevskii 2006, 84). More direct evidence for wheel-throwing is difficult to obtain because of selective collection policies. Glazing, which is a strong indicator of specialist potters, does not occur until the 16th century. Trends in form types are less likely to reflect production techniques than functional requirements, such as the introduction of lid-bearing rims at Novgorod in the second half of the 12th century, or the trend from tall cooking pots with conical bodies to squatter ones with rounded bodies noted at Pskov (the better to fit into the newer style of oven, see Kildyushevskii 2006, 114). The trends in decoration are towards simplicity and ease of application, both suggestive of increasing intensity of production and decreasing 'personalisation' of the pottery. The discovery of associations between two specific rim forms and rouletting and wavy line decoration respectively (Orton 2006, 124) suggests the possibility of a more decoration-based definition of types, which might be related to different production centres, and may open up new directions of analysis. Finally, there are two episodes of technological (in contrast to functional or stylistic) innovation: the apparently short-lived experiment with glazed wares at the Duboshin site in the later 13th century, and the period of use of naturally sand-tempered white-firing clay at Novgorod in the 13th and particularly the early 14th century (Malygin and Orton 2001, 60). The former appears to have no direct effect on subsequent production (unless as part of a package which includes the introduction of wheel-throwing), while the latter gives rise to new rim forms (the 'folded' rims) and a decorative technique (a combination of horizontal grooves and 'stabbing'), which continue until the end of the period, although the use of this fabric does not.

What does all this evidence imply for the social organisation of the production of medieval pottery in the region? The beginning and end of the transition from domestic to specialised production are easy to pin down. The hand-made, highly decorated and individually distinctive pottery that dies out in the 10th century has all the signs of domestic production, while the combination of wheel-throwing, fine white-firing clay, and glazing in the 16th and 17th century clearly indicate fully specialised production. The question is whether the progression through the period was gradual or took place in one or more distinct steps. Key to this is the date of the introduction of wheel-throwing. The evidence for the introduction of the fast wheel at Novgorod is indirect, depending on the introduction of sand-tempered pottery in the late 13th century. But, because the absence of *gruss* is a precondition for wheel-throwing, it does not mean that wheel-throwing actually took place at this time. Also, since the use of *gruss* in Novgorod continued alongside sand until the end of the 15th century, wheel-throwing (if it took place) must have been practised in parallel with the earlier coiling method for some two centuries. The quantity of *gruss*-tempered pottery appears to peak in the 13th century, but it is still substantial in the 14th and 15th centuries. This might seem to rule out the contemporary use of wheel-throwing, but the parallel production of similar forms in coiled and wheel-thrown fabrics, both by specialist potters, is known elsewhere, for example in the production of BB1 and BB2 pottery in Roman Britain (Tyers 1996, 182–7). However, the contemporary trend from sand to *gruss* at Pskov makes this parallel usage less likely at Novgorod, and strengthens the argument that full wheel-throwing did not develop there until the late 15th or 16th century.

A more likely starting date for specialised craft potting is in the mid-12th century, with the emergence of a distinct local style at Pskov and a new range of simply-decorated forms at Novgorod. It could have developed through increasing intensity of production in certain households, gradually deriving more of their income from potting and less from other activities. Certainly, there is enough confidence by the late 13th century for attempts at innovation to take place, even if only partly successfully. Despite the reference to a Goncharski (potters') End within Novgorod, the location of these potters is still unknown; their presence in the towns cannot yet be ruled out, but rural locations become increasingly likely as successive excavations fail to find structural evidence for potting. The existence of itinerant potters, exploiting local resources on a cyclical basis, is another possibility. The quantities of pottery being produced from the mid-12th century onwards would require the operation of more than one kiln even if worked intensively, but whether they were nucleated into a potting quarter or village, or dispersed throughout settlements or their hinterlands, remains unknown.

IMPLICATIONS FOR THEORY

This study has revealed two major weaknesses in the theory that was used to underpin it. In both cases, the concept of diversity or standardisation has proved to be something of a broken reed. First, no general or chronological typology of pottery forms can be expected to establish the level of diversity in an urban assemblage, even on a relative basis. To achieve a typology that reflects the intentions of an individual potter would of itself be extremely difficult; add to this the need to encompass the products of several producers over a period of time, and the need to work from mainly fragmentary material, and it becomes virtually impossible. Second, the use of measured dimensions as an indicator of standardisation can actually be misleading, since there are circumstances in which the products of specialist potters could show greater variability than those of domestic producers. This could occur, for example, if specialist potters were producing pots of a particular form in a range of sizes. There is a technique for the detection of the basic units of measurement of which such sizes would be multiples (the cosine quantogram, see Baxter 2003, 232), but its use here would be complicated by the natural variation in the material and the problem of obtaining precise estimates of measurement such as rim diameters, from sherds that are only a fraction of a rim. It would, however, be an interesting line of future research.

Suggestions for future work

A large-scale search for centres of production is probably not a practical proposition, and we will have to continue to hope for chance discoveries. Further microscopic work would probably be premature at this stage; the main fabrics have now been characterised and can be recognised macroscopically. More detailed study of detailed technological characteristics, such as the methods of attaching different parts of vessels, can be expected to help distinguish between the products of different centres, and perhaps even between potters. This could be greatly assisted by the further development of a system for describing decoration, taking account of the different techniques used, the way in which they are combined, and their location and extent on a pot. Both studies would require more comprehensive retention of material; for example, bases often reveal important technological information. Questions of the scale of use, and trends in it, can be answered through the construction of quantified sequences based on standardised and reproducible typologies of fabric, form and decoration. Such sequences could be compared, both within and between settlements, to examine the distribution of the products of particular sources. The extent to which this will be possible will depend on the choice of sites for future excavations, a choice that is however not likely to be driven by ceramic concerns. The aim must therefore be to draw up an agenda of research questions and tasks, which can be implemented as and when the opportunity arises.

– 24 –

EVIDENCE CONCERNING CRAFT PRODUCTION IN THE BIRCH-BARK DOCUMENTS OF NOVGOROD

E. A. Rybina

Birch-bark documents (henceforth BBDs in this paper) have long been recognised as a valued written source of information on many aspects of medieval life: the structure of society, trade, family relations and so on. These documents on birch-bark are also invaluable for the study of money-lending, the money system and land ownership in Novgorod in the 10th to 15th centuries. As for craft production, its development is well documented through diverse archaeological finds and the remains of buildings, but there are very few references to craft activity to be found within the BBDs themselves.

Among the BBDs found in Novgorod so far (962 in total as of June 2008), there are only a few examples that provide direct evidence concerning the crafts of jewellery production and weaving, although there are occasional indirect references to the existence of other crafts in the city. This paper will briefly examine this evidence.

JEWELLERY PRODUCTION

The most informative document with regard to jewellery production is BBD 644 found in a level dated to the first quarter of the 12th century. It is a splendidly preserved and complete letter from Nezhka to her brothers (Zaliznyak 2004, 267). It is addressed to one of the brothers with a reproach to the effect that her order for gold *koltki* (temple rings worn by women) had not been completed. It is also pointed out in the letter that Nezhka had given her brothers two gold rings to provide material for their manufacture. To judge from the archaeological and historical context, the Nezhata brothers, Zavid to whom it had been addressed and the other brother mentioned in it, were not themselves jewellers. They were owners of properties, within the grounds of which there lived craftsmen dependent on them for their livelihood as was normal in Novgorod at this time. BBD 664 is, without doubt, a reliable piece of evidence with regard to the manufacture of expensive gold jewellery within Novgorod itself.

Gold *koltki* are mentioned on another occasion as well, in BBD 335 (dated to the 1160s or 1170s). The beginning and end of this letter have been lost, but in the surviving text there is a request for four gold *koltki* (each of which cost half a *grivna*) to be exchanged but we don't know what for (Zaliznyak 2004, 372). It is evident that in this case as well reference is being made to expensive pieces of jewellery made by local craftsmen.

The author of BBD 723 (dated to 1140–1180) in a letter which has survived in its entirety informs his addressee that he had left for Kuchkov (the earliest name given to Moscow) and intended, after delivering an *obruch* (bracelet) to Fedka, to collect something of his own (Zaliznyak 2004, 335). Unfortunately, despite the fact that the text of this letter is complete, it is not possible to glean from it information on the specific circumstances relating to this transaction. What is important for us here is the mention of the bracelet as an expensive piece of jewellery. It is unlikely that the author of the letter would have shown concern regarding a cheap item of jewellery made from copper alloy, for instance.

As regards mention of some specific pieces of jewellery, there is mention of such in a two-sided document BBD 809 (dated to 1160–1180): "instruct someone to make pearl ornaments resembling arrows" (Zaliznyak 2004, 371).

Indirect evidence pertaining to the development of metal casting and jewellery production in Novgorod is provided in BBD 439 (late-12th/early-13th century) referring to trade in non-ferrous metals (Zaliznyak 2004, 436). The author informs his addressee that he has already sold the tin, lead and all the forged items and asks for more tin and copper to be delivered. The document concerned is without doubt part of a correspondence between Novgorod merchants and warehouse-owners, who traded with merchants from other lands. In exchange for non-ferrous metals, which were brought to Novgorod from Western Europe, the merchants of Novgorod sold them wax. It is worth pointing out that the property in which BBD 439 was found belonged very likely to a merchant, as can be seen from the texts of the seven other BBDs found there and various imported artefacts including amber in enormous quantities (more than 1,000 pieces of varying sizes) and numerous slate distaffs made from pink slate that would have made their way to Novgorod from the South near Kiev. It is also worthy of note that within this same property various pieces of evidence for the existence of metal casting and jewellery production have come to light thanks to finds of raw materials (wire and off-cuts of non-ferrous metals), production equipment (a casting mould and fragments of crucibles) and jeweller's scales. Analysis of the artefacts found within this particular property make it possible to conclude that its owner was a wealthy merchant who was not only engaged in various trading activities but also in the organization of jewellery production. It is likely that his trading activities were to some extent dictated by his interests in jewellery production (Rybina 2001b, 271).

WEAVING AND TEXTILES

There is a direct reference to the manufacture of textiles, specifically to the production of linen, in BBD 21 (dated to the first quarter of the 15th century). The text of this letter (apart from the opening) has survived intact: it is addressed to a weaver (female) who was supposed to have woven some linen and sent it to a client who had ordered it (Zaliznyak 2004, 650). There is reference to the fact that the linen duly prepared required additional work (to whiten it). This letter confirms that there were several stages involved in the manufacture of linen cloth.

In BBD 536 (dated to the second half of the 14th century) after a list of various sorts of cloth, it is stated that the cloth concerned needs additional work on it so as to achieve the quality as in the sample which the author of the letter is sending to his addressee. The words actually used are "soaked and clipped" (Zaliznyak 2004, 629). In addition the author would appear to have links with shoe-making, since he asks his correspondent to send him some shoe nails.

Indirect evidence in connection with weaving, not only in Novgorod but also in the Novgorod Lands, is to be found in a number of BBDs containing lists of different forms of tribute (taxes) including various textiles which were obviously of local production. For instance, in BBD 718 (late-12th/early-13th century) in the list of forms of *pogorodie* (tribute levied from towns) alongside money, produce and animals there is mention of *kletchatina* which is a term used for coarse, home-made linen made from flax or hemp (Zaliznyak 2004, 468–9). Moreover, this term was used to imply pieces of bleached linen of a particular size, which was evidently included in the list of taxes to be levied. Another list of home-woven textiles, which the citizens of Novgorod collected as tribute or bought from Karelians, is to be found in BBD 130 (last quarter of the 14th century) (Zaliznyak 2004, 597).

Complete BBDs 609 and 722 (dated to the end of the 12th century or beginning of the 13th) are inventories of property, which include among other things home-woven cloth (Zaliznyak 2004, 426).

TAILORING

Information on this craft is to be gleaned from BBD 638 (second half of the 12th century). The surviving text, despite its fragmentary nature, tells us that the author of the letter had made a cloak (or *korzno*) to order and that he was planning to dye it dark blue (Zaliznyak 2004, 386–87). The author of BBD 765 (mid-13th century), which is emotional in style and content, turns to his brother with a request that he should send a reddish-brown cloak and he promises to return some cloth to him (Zaliznyak 2004, 480). BBD 129 (dated to the second half of the 14th century) also contains a correspondence between brothers engaged in joint trading. Its author Yesif, apart from the advice he offers on how to conduct trade, asks his brother Foma to send him various wares including some good sheepskin from which coats could be made for them both: "Be so good as to send wax and soap and sheepskin, from which each of us could have a coat made…." (Zaliznyak 2004, 643).

FURRIERY

We are able to conclude that this craft existed thanks to the names for skins of both domestic and wild animals, which have survived in various BBDs. There are several mentions of deer and bear skins, two mentions of sheepskin and one of an elk skin. To judge from the contexts where the BBDs were found, animal skins were highly valued and were not cheap.

The author of BBD 681 (dated to the second half of the 12th century) requests (or advises) that a deer-skin be sold and the burial of a monk be arranged (Zaliznyak 2004, 386). The person to whom BBD 275/266 (dated to the second half of the 14th century) was addressed is given instructions to look after the belongings of the letter's author, among other things "to give the deer skins, which are in the downstairs store-room to the sexton" (Zaliznyak 2004, 603).

To judge from BBD 722 (dated to the first decade of the 12th century) which contains a list of belongings including the prices of the items, bear-skins in the 12th century cost 2 *grivnas*, which was the equivalent of 400 grammes of silver. In two other cases, authors of letters (BBD 65 dated to the early-14th century and BBD 354 dated to the second half of the 14th century) asked for bear skins to be sent to them. It is worth noting in this connection that the individuals involved in both correspondences were people well-known to us from the chronicles: BBD 65 was addressed to the boyar Yesif Davydovich and the long letter of BBD 354 was written by the renowned governor and introducer of reforms known as Ontsifor Lukinich (Zaliznyak 2004, 536, 550).

The author of BBD 153 (dated to the late-12th/early-13th century) asks that an elk skin be purchased for him and he even mentions a potential vendor by the name of Fyodor and indicates his address: "he lives in Slavno…look [him] out [there] (Zaliznyak 2004, 434). It is possible that Fyodor was a furrier who cured animal skins.

As for skins of domestic animals, sheep-skin is mentioned twice in BBDs. Apart from the above-cited BBD 129, the other document of interest is BBD 500 (dated to the first third of the 14th century), which consists of a long and extremely varied list of belongings, including "five sheep skins" (Zaliznyak 2004, 543).

LEATHER-WORKING AND SHOE-MAKING

The existence of these crafts is made clear by infrequent mentions in the BBD of both dressed and undressed cured skins and also ready-made leather items. In addition, we find in BBD 355 (dated to the first quarter of the 14th century) a list of debtors including a leather worker from Dorofei Street (Zaliznyak 2004, 566).

In BBD 500 quoted above, as well as coats, sheep skins and other items of property the list includes "cured skins, two uncured skins, and five *telyan*" (i.e. calf skins) (Zaliznyak 2004, 543). In BBD 445 (dated to the first half of the 14th century) the list of items which the author of the letter asks to be sent includes "three skins" (Zaliznyak 2004, 542). The extracts cited make it clear that there obviously existed some kind of standard size for skins or pieces thereof, since these are referred to on more than one occasion in the texts. In BBDs 261–264 (dated to the second half of the 14th century), as well as the general concept of a "skin" constituting a specific range of items, saffian (known as *tim* in Russian), i.e. dressed goat skin, figures prominently in a list of wedding gifts (Zaliznyak 2004, 609).

Finally, in BBD 438 (dated to the end of the 12th century), which contains a list of wares complete with their prices, completed articles fashioned by Novgorod shoe-makers are listed: soles and vamps (the front parts of boots) (Zaliznyak 2004, 435).

BLACK-SMITHING

A good testimony for the existence of the blacksmith's craft in Novgorod is the two-sided BBD 750 (dated to the beginning of the 14th century), which has survived in its entirety. To judge from the context, its author Stepan, although his profession is not specifically mentioned in this BBD, was evidently a craftsman who fashioned armour and other iron articles including knives (Zaliznyak 2004, 531).

The profession of blacksmith is named, meanwhile, in two other BBDs, which have survived in their entirety. One of these, BBD 630 (second quarter of the 12th century), contains a long list of debtors, among whom the blacksmith Mestok is mentioned by name (Zaliznyak 2004, 295). In the complete BBD 318 (dated to the mid-14th century) reference is made to the purchase of villages, the names of which are listed in the text. This list of sales is headed by a blacksmith by the name of Adreyan (Zaliznyak 2004, 611–12).

Of course, the actual articles fashioned by Novgorod blacksmiths are constantly being encountered during the excavation of the city. Some of these are occasionally mentioned in BBDs and sometimes even with their price. In BBD 438 cited above and listing various wares, reference is made to 50 knives with the total price of half a *grivna*. Knives are also found in lists of objects in BBD 384 (dated to the second half of the 12th century) and 660 (dated to the end of the 12th or beginning of the 13th century). In BBD 138 (dated to the first quarter of the 14th century), which has survived in its entirety, armour (*broni*) worth two *grivnas* of silver is mentioned together with sums of money and other possessions bequeathed by the author. Military equipment is also mentioned in BBD 332 (dated to the second half of the 12th century), whose author asks for a helmet, armour, a shield and a spear to be sent to him (Zaliznyak 2004, 431). Mention is also made of other articles made by blacksmiths: chains (BBD 725: dated to the end of the 12th or beginning of the 13th century), frying-pans (BBDs 586, 500), a cooking-pot, a forged bridle, a chain for a cooking pot (BBD 500), trivets and a *korakul* (iron tool) referred to in BBD 354, and a lock (BBD 358).

POTTERY PRODUCTION

Despite the enormous quantity of pottery sherds found during excavations every year, information on the craft of pottery production is virtually absent from the BBDs. In the existing BBDs from Novgorod, there are only two pieces of evidence that may relate to pottery production. In the already cited BBD 445, a potter is mentioned by the author of the letter as owing him money (Zaliznyak 2004, 542). In BBD 379 (dated to the second half of the 12th century) a request to the author's correspondent has survived, namely "to straighten my *korchaga*" (Zaliznyak 2004, 453). In this context the verb 'to straighten' (*vypravi*) could be translated as 'manufacture' (or 'make') a *korchaga*, that is a round, two-handled pottery vessel normally used for holding grain or oil, similar to an amphora.

LISTS OF ITEMS

More than ten of the BBDs contain various lists of articles including a good number of craft items, which without doubt were produced locally: a wooden vessel (BBD 500), combs (BBD 438), a pot (BBD 220), items of jewellery (BBDs 429, 500, 660) and all manner of garments (BBDs 429, 586, 659/648, 141). A list of craft items (two spoons, two knives, a whetstone, reins made of cloth and deerskin) is also to be found in BBD 384 (dated to the second half of the 12th century) (Zaliznyak 2004, 358).

ICON-PAINTING

When excavation work was going on in the Lyudin End of Novgorod at the Troitsky excavation in 1977–1983 in late-12th century levels, the first ever workshop of an artist and icon-painter was excavated (Kolchin *et al.* 1981). His name was Olisei Grechin, a fact discovered only from the BBDs. Two complete BBDs (549 and 558) were found in the grounds of the artist's house and workshop, which had been written by priests approaching Grechin with requests that he should paint icons for them. In BBD 549 the request was expressed as follows: "…paint for me two six-winged angels in two small icons above the Deësis". The icons being ordered were obviously destined for an iconostasis, presumably of the church where the author of the letter served as a priest. In addition to these letters, 15 other BBDs were found containing lists of names. These BBDs are none other than orders for icons or small icons for the home. In one of them, BBD 553, the names are arranged in a definite order indicating the icon compositions which had been ordered. In the centre was the figure of Christ, to each side of whom would be positioned patron saints, i.e. the patrons of the painter's client and members of the client's family. It is worth pointing out that within this particular property some examples of small wooden icon cases were found, which bore the inscription: *svyatoi Nikolai* (Saint Nicholas). The discovery of this icon-painter's workshop caused quite a sensation, since the BBDs had, for the first time in the history of Russian medieval art, revealed to us the name of an artist who had been living and working in the 12th century. This meant that, in part at least, the anonymity of Russian medieval art had been breached.

The absence of any significant information about craft production in the Novgorod BBDs would appear to be more than a coincidence. It reflects the system underlying the Novgorod economy and the main concerns of the city's inhabitants, namely land ownership and trade, the specific nature of which required an extensive correspondence. As for craft production, the archaeological evidence reflects beyond any doubt the high level and the professional specialization attained. Yet the organization of craft production in medieval Novgorod was such that the craftsmen involved presumably did not experience a need for correspondence with each other or their customers. The craftsmen's workshops were mainly located within the confines of the boyars' properties and the boyars supplied the craftsmen with the necessary raw materials for making whatever articles might be needed. During the investigations of medieval Novgorod and its history, which have been going on over the last 75 years, not one property belonging to an independent craftsman has so far been definitely recorded.

LIST OF ABBREVIATIONS

AV   *Arkheologicheskie vesti* (Archaeological News), Institute for the History of Material Culture, Russian Academy of Sciences. St Petersburg.

ChOIDR   *Chteniya v Obshchestve lyubitelei istorii i drevnosti rossiiskikh* (Lectures for the Society of Enthusiasts for the History and Antiquities of Russia).

NNZIA   *Novgorod I Novgorodskaya zemlya* (Novgorod and the Novgorod Lands), Novgorod.

RA   Rossiikaia arkheologiia (Russian Archaeology). From 1994 onwards. Moscow.

SA   *Sovietskaya Arkheologiya* (Soviet Archaeology), Replaced by RA in 1994. Moscow.

SlRYa XI-XVII vv.   *Slovar Russkogo Yazyka XI–XVIIvv.* (Dictionary of the Russian Language of the 11th–17th centuries), Moscow.

TAS   *Tverskoi arkheologicheskii sbornik* (Collection of Articles on the Archaeology of Tver). Tver.

REFERENCES

Aalto, M. (1982) 'Archaeobotanical studies at Katajamäki, Isokylä, Salo, South-West Finland'. PACT 7 (Second Nordic conference on the application of scientific methods in archaeology), 137–147. Helsingør, Aug. 1981. Strasbourg.

Aalto, M. and Heinäjoki-Majander, H. (1997) 'Archaeobotany and Palaeoenvironment of the Viking Age Town of Staraja Ladoga, Russia', PACT 52, *Birka Studies 4* I.1, 13–30.

Aleksandrovskaya, E. L., Aleksandrovsky, A. L., Gaidukov, P. G. and Krenke, N. A. (2001) 'Woodland, meadow, field and town layout: the evidence from analyses of the earliest cultural deposits and buried soil in Novgorod', in Brisbane, M. A. and Gaimster, D. (eds) *Novgorod: the Archaeology of a Russian Medieval City and its Hinterland*, 15–22. British Museum Occasional Paper Number 141. London

Aleppskii, P. (1898) 'The Journey of Patriarch Makarius to Russia in the third quarter of the 17th century described by his son Arch-Deacon Pavel Aleppskii', *ChOIDR* (Lectures to the Society of Enthusiasts for the History and Antiquities of Russia) Book V, Chapter XIII. Moscow.

Alexander, K. N. A. (2002) 'The Invertebrates of Living and Decaying timber in Britain and Ireland: a provisional annotated checklist', *English Nature Research Reports* No. 467. Peterborough.

Allan, J. P. (1984) *Medieval and Post-medieval Finds from Exeter, 1971–1980*. Exeter Archaeological Reports 3. Exeter.

Alsleben, A. (1995) 'Nutzpflanzen aus dem mittlelalterlichen Wolin Zwei ausgewahlte Gruppen: Getreide und Lein', *Offa* 52, 185–217.

Alsleben, A., (1997) 'Zemledelie novgorodskoj okrugi v IX–X vv. Archeobotanickie metody i ich primenenie na gorodischtsche Georgij' [Agriculture in the hinterland of Novgorod in the 9th/10th century. Archaeobotanical methods and results of the excavation in Georgii] in Kirpichnikov, A. N. and Nosov, E. N. (eds) *Drevnosti Povolchov'ja*, 191–204. St Petersburg.

Alsleben, A. (1998) 'Ein jungslawischer Vorratsfund in Ostholstein. Saatweizen *Triticum aestivum* s.l.', in Wesse, A. (ed.) *Studien zur Archäologie des Ostseeraumes. Von der Eisenzeit zum Mittelalter*, 187–194. Neumünster.

Alsleben, A. (2001a) 'Angebot und Nachfrage. Frühmittelalterliche Nahrungswirtschaft im Umland von Novgorod', in Müller-Wille, M., Janin, V. L., Nosov E. N. and Rybina, E. A. (eds) *Novgorod. Das mittelalterliche Zentrum und sein Umland im Norden Rußlands*, 359–368. Neumünster.

Alsleben, A. (2001b) 'Early Medieval Agriculture in the Hinterland of Novgorod', in Brisbane, M. A. and D. Gaimster (eds) *Novgorod: the Archaeology of a Russian Medieval City and its Hinterland*, British Museum Occasional Paper Number 141, 107–112. London.

Alsleben, A. (2007) 'Food consumption in the Hanseatic towns of Germany'. In Karg, S. (ed.) *Medieval Food Traditions in Northern Europe*, National Museum Studies in Archaeology and History Vol. 12, 13 – 31. Copenhagen.

Alsleben, A., Janssson, I., Hammer, T., Konigsson, L.-K., Kroll, H., Müller-Wille, M. and Nosov, E. (1993) 'Palaeobotanical studies on the Novgorod Land c. 400–1200 AD', *Archäologisches Korrespondenzblatt*, 23 (1993) HEFT 4, 527–535.

Ambrosiani, B., Gaidukov, P. G., Nosov, E. N. and Jansson, I. (1994) 'The First Find of a Scandinavian Equal-armed Fibula of the Valst Type in Russia', *Arkheologicheskie Vesti* (Archaeological News) No. 3, 110–120. St Petersburg.

REFERENCES

Andersen, S. H. (1974) 'Ringkloster, en jysk inlandsboplats med Ertebøllekultur', *KUML* 1973–1974. Årbog for Jysk Arkæologisk Selskab, 11–108. Aarhus.

Andreyeva, E. G. (1991) 'Fauna at the Krutik settlement (based on osteological materials from archaeological excavations' in Golubeva L. A. and Kochurkina S. I. (eds) *Belozerskaya ves [po materialam poseleniya Krutik 9th–10th centuries]* (The Beloozerskaya Ves (based on materials from the Krutik settlement dating from the 9th and 10th centuries). Petrozavodsk.

Ankudinov, I. Y. (1999) 'An historical-geographical commentary on Novgorod Birch-bark Document No. 390', *Ocherki feodalnoi Rossii* (Essays on Feudal Russia) Issue 4. Moscow.

Ankudinov, I. Y. (2003) 'Novgorod Birchbark documents as a source on the history of assarting new land', in Yanin, V. L. (ed.), *50 years since their discovery, 50 years of their study*. Materials from an International Conference Sept 24–27, 2003. Novgorod.

Antropov, Y. V. and Toporova, E. V. (2001) 'Medieval Leather Footwear from Staraya Russa: first results from the research', *NNZIA* (Novgorod and the Novgorod Lands, History and Archaeology) Issue 15, 245–257. Novgorod.

Anufriev, G. I. (1925) 'Short Account of the vegetation in the flood-plain of Lake Ilmen and the lower reaches of the Rivers of the Ilmen Basin', *Materialy po issledovaniyu reki Volkhova i ego basseina* (Materials on the Investigation of the River Volkhov and its Basin) Issue IV, 1–41.

Arbman, H. (1940) *Birka I. Plates*. Uppsala.

Arbman, H. (1943) *Birka I. Text*. Stockholm.

Arbman, H. (1962) *Vikingarna*. Stockholm.

Artsikhovskii, A. V. and Bokovskii, V. I. (1955) *Novgorodskie gramoty na bereste iz raskopok 1953–1954 goda* (Novgorod Birch-bark Documents from the excavations of 1953–1954). USSR Academy of Sciences. Moscow.

ASEI (1958) (Documents relating to the social and economic history of North-eastern Russia) Vol. II. Moscow.

Atlas Novgorodoskoi Oblasti (Atlas of the Novgorod Region) 1982. Moscow.

Atlas Vologodskoi Oblasti (Atlas of the Vologda Region) 1965. Moscow.

Aun, M. (1975) 'The Settlement of Kivivare in the Valga District', *Izvestiya Akademii nauk Estonskoi SSR*, (Bulletins of the Academy of Sciences of the Estonian SSR), Social Sciences series No. 1, 81–83. Tallinn.

Ayers, B. and Murphy, P. (1983) 'A Waterfront Excavation at Whitefriars Street Car Park, Norwich, 1979', *East Anglian Archaeology* Report No. 17. Norfolk.

Bachmann, H. G. (1982) *The Identification of Slags from Archaeological Sites*. Institute of Archaeology Occasional Publications 6. London.

Bain, A. (2001) *Archaeo-entomological and Archaeo-parasitological Reconstructions at Îlot Hunt (CeEt-110), Quebec City, Canada: New perspectives in historical archaeology, 1850–1900*. British Archaeological Reports International Series 973. Oxford.

Baranov, D. A., Baranova, O. G., Madelevskaya, E. L., Sosnina, N. N., Fishman, O. M. and Shangina, I. I. (1999) *The Russian Peasant House, Illustratated Encyclopaedia of the Internal Space of a Peasant House, Furniture and Decoration: Household Utensils and Work Implements*. Iskusstvo (Art-SPB). St Petersburg.

Barclay, M. V. L. (2005) *Priobium carpini* (Herbst) (Coleoptera: Anobiidae), a European woodworm established in Britain. *Entomologist's Monthly Magazine* 141, 43–47.

Barrett, J., Hall, A., Johnstone, C., Kenward, H., O'Connor, T. and Ashby, S. (2004) 'Plant and animal remains from Viking Age deposits at Kaupang, Norway', Reports from the Centre for Human Palaeoecology, University of York, Report 2004/10. Centre for Human Palaeoecology, Department of Archaeology, University of York.

Barrett, J., Hall, A., Johnstone, C., Kenward, H, O'Connor, T. and Ashby, S. (2007) 'Interpreting the plant and anmal remains from Viking-age Kaupang', in Skre, D. (ed.) *Kaupang in Skiringssal*. Kaupang Excavation Project Publication Series, Vol. 1, Norske Oldfunn XXII, 283–319. Aarhus University Press.

457

REFERENCES

Barysheva, A. A. (1966) 'On the Influence of Lake Ilmen on the temperature regime in the adjacent territories', *Uchonye zapiski NGPI* (Scholarly Notes from the Novgorod State Pedagogical Institute) Vol. IV. Novgorod.

Bashenkin, A. N. (1995) 'The Cultural-Historical Processes at work in the Mologa-Sheksna Interfluve at the end of the first millennium BC and beginning of the first millennium AD', in *Problemy istorii Severo-Zapada Rusi. Slavyano-russkie drevnosti* (Questions regarding the History of the North-West of Rus. Slavonic and Russian Antiquities) Issue 3, 3–28. St Petersburg.

Baxter, M. (2003) *Statistics in Archaeology*. London. Hodder Arnold.

Bayley, J. (1992) 'Anglo-Scandinavian Non-Ferrous Metalworking from 16–22 Coppergate', *The Archaeology of York, Vol. 17, The Small Finds*, 747–67. CBA. London.

Behre, K.-E. (1983) *Ernährung und Umwelt der wikingerzeitlichen Siedlung Haithabu, Die Ergebnisse der Untersuchungen der Pflanzenreste*. Neumünster. Karl Wachholtz Verlag.

Behre, K.-E. (1984) 'Zur Geschichte der Bierwűrzen nach Fruchtfunden und schriftlichen Quellen – Aspects of the history of beer flavouring agents based on fruit finds and written sources', in van Zeist, W. and Casparie, W. A. (eds) *Plants and Ancient Man, Studies in palaeoethnobotany*, 115–122. Proceedings of the Sixth Symposium of the International Work Group for Palaeoethnobotany, Groningen, 1983, Rotterdam. A. A. Balkema.

Behre, K.-E. (1992) 'The history of rye cultivation in Europe', *Vegetation History and Archaeobotany* 1, 141–156.

Belov, M. I., Ovsyannikov, O. V. and Starkov, V. F. (1981) 'Mangazeya', Part II, *Materialnaya kultura russkikh polyarnykh morekhodov i zemleprokhodtsev XVI–XVII vv.* (The Material Culture of Russian Arctic Seafarers and Explorers, 16th–17th centuries). Moscow.

Beneš, J., Kaštovský, J., Kocárová, R., Kocár, P., Kubecková, K., Pokorný, P and Starec, P. (2002) 'Archaeobotany of the Old Prague Town defence system, Czech Republic: archaeology, macro-remains, pollen and diatoms'. *Vegetation History and Archaeobotany* 11, 107–119.

Besteman, J. C. (1989) 'The pre-urban development of Medemblik: from an early medieval trading centre to a medieval town', *Medemblik and Monnikendam. Aspects of medieval urbanization in northern Holland*, Cingula, 11, 1–30. Amsterdam.

Bielenin, K. (1976) 'Eingetiefte Rennöfen der frühgeschichtlichen Eisenverhüttung in Europa', *Archaeologica Austriaca* Beiheft 14, 13–27.

Bitterauf, T. (1967) *Die Traditionen des Hochstifts Freising. Quellan und Erorterungen zur bayerischen und deutschen Geschichte, N.F. 4, A.D. 744–926*. Aalen.

Blackman, M. J., Stein, G. J. and Vandiver, P. B. (1993) 'The standardization hypothesis and ceramic mass production: technological, compositional, and metric indexes of craft specialization at Tell Leilan', *American Antiquity* 58 (1), 60–80.

Bleasdale, A. (undated manuscript) *The History, Distribution and Ecology of the Rye crop and its associated Weed Flora on the Aran Islands, Co. Galway*. Results of Fieldwork Carried out on the Aran Islands from 1989–1994.

Blomqvist, R. (1937) 'Medeltida svard, dolkar och slidor funna i Lund', *Kulturens Arsbok*, 134–169.

Blomqvist, R. (1939) 'Medeltida skor i Lund', Fynden fron Kvarteret Apotekaren 5, *Kulturens Arsbok*, 189–219.

Bobrinskii, A. A. (1978) *Goncharstvo Vostochnoi Evropy: Istochniki i metody izucheniya* (Pottery-making in Eastern Europe: sources and research methods). Moscow.

Bobrov, E. G. (1978) *Lesoobrazuyushchie khvoinye SSSR* (Forest-forming conifers in the USSR). Leningrad.

Bogatkina, O. G. (1995) 'Archaeological investigations of materials from the city-site of Idnakar' in *Materialy issledovanii gorodishcha Idnakar IX–XIII vv.*(Materials from the investigations at the city-site of Indakar in the 9th–13th centuries). Izhevsk.

Bolotova, N. L., Konovalov, A. F. and Dumnich, N. V. (2003) 'Introduction of Zander (Stizostedion lucioperca L.) in a shallow Kubenskoe Lake in 1936 and its consequences', in *The Proceedings of Percis III*, The Third International Percid Fish Symposium, Madison. University of Wisconsin.

REFERENCES

Bonde, N. (1994) 'De norske vikingeskibgraves alder', *Nationalmuseets Arbejdsmark*, 128–146. Copenhagen.

Borisenkov, E. P. and Pasetskii, V. M. (1983) *Ekstremalnye prirodnye yavleniya v russkikh letopisyakh* (Extreme Natural Phenomena in Russian Chronicles). 'Gidrometeoizdat' publishers. Leningrad.

Brandenburg, N. E. (1884) 'Bulletin I (Issue 1) on Chemical-technical Research into Ancient Bronzes from the northern part of Russia, undertaken by mining engineer D. A. Sabaneyev', *RAO* (Russian Archaeological Society) Vol. 10. St Petersburg.

Brandt, D. (2000) 'Ein mittelalterlicher Töpfereinachweis in der Langen Straße der Hansestadt Greifswald', in Müller, I. U. (ed.) *Greifswalder Mitteilunger 4*, 115–129. Frankfurt am Main. Peter Lang.

Brich Madsen, H. (1984) 'Metal-casting. Techniques, Production and Workshops', *Ribe Excavations 1970–1976*, Vol. 2. Esbjerg.

Brisbane, M. A. (2001) *Proposed Work Programme: INTAS-00–154*. Bournemouth University.

Brisbane, M. A., Hambleton, E., Maltby, M. and Nosov, E. N. (2007) 'A monkey's tale: the skull of a macaque found at Ryurik Gorodishche during excavations in 2003', *Medieval Archaeology* 51, 185–191.

Brisbane, M. A. and Hather, J. (eds) (2007) *Wood Use in Medieval Novgorod*, The Archaeology of Medieval Novgorod Series. Oxford. Oxbow.

Brisbane, M. A. and Maltby, M. (2002) 'Love letters to bare bones: a comparison of two types of evidence for the use of animals in medieval Novgorod', *Archaeological Review from Cambridge* 18, 99–119.

British Leather Manufacturers' Research Association (1957) *Hides, Skins and Leather under the Microscope*. The British Leather Manufacturers Research Association. Egham.

Brorsson, T. (2001) 'Behind the Pottery: Signs of Contacts across the Baltic Sea', in Brisbane, M. A. and Gaimster, D. (eds) *Novgorod: the archaeology of a Russian Medieval City and its Hinterland*. The British Museum. Occasional Paper Number 141, 51–58. London.

Brorsson, T. (2003) 'Keramiken på en centralplats', in Söderberg, B. (ed.) *Järrestad. Huvdgård I centralbygd*. Riksantikvarieämbetet Arkeologiska undersökningar Skrifter No. 51, 341–372. Lund.

Brorsson, T. (2004) 'Pottery from Early Viking age graves in the Baltic Region: Towards the interpretation of a society', *Bodendenkmalpflege in Mecklenburg. Jahrbuch 2003*, 361–374. Lübstorf.

Brouwer, W., (1972) *Handbuch des speziellen Pflanzenbaus 1. Weizen, Roggen, Gerste, Hafer, Mais*. Berlin and Hamburg.

Buchwald, V.F. and Wivel, H. (1998) 'Slag analysis as a method for the characterization and provenancing of ancient iron objects'. *Materials Characterization* Vol. 40, 73–96.

Buckland P. I. and Buckland P. C. (2006) *Bugs Coleopteran Ecology Package* (Versions: BugsCEP v7.61; Bugsdata v7.09; BugsMCR v2.0; BugStats v1.2) [Downloaded/CDROM: June 2007] www. bugscep.com.

Buckland, P. C., McGovern, T. H., Sadler, J. P. and Skidmore, P. (1994) 'Twig layers, floors and middens: Recent palaeoecological research in the Western Settlement, Greenland', in Ambrosiani, B. and Clarke, H. (eds) *Developments around the Baltic and North Sea in the Viking Age*. Birka Studies 3 (The Twelfth Viking Congress, Stockholm), 132–143.

Buckland, P. C., Holdsworth, P. and Monk, M. (1976) 'The interpretation of a group of Saxon pits in Southampton'. *Journal of Archaeological Science* 3, 61–69.

Bull, G. and Payne, S. (1982) 'Tooth eruption and epiphyseal fusion in pigs and wild boar', in Wilson, B., Grigson, C. and Payne, S. (eds), *Ageing and Sexing of Animal Bones from Archaeological Sites*, British Archaeological Reports (British Series) 109, 55–71. Oxford.

Bullock, J. A. (1993) Host plants of British beetles: A list of recorded associations. *Amateur Entomologist* 11a, 1–24.

Buzhilova, A. P. (2009) 'Medieval population from Minino: analysis of the anthropological data'

459

REFERENCES

in Makarov, N. A. (ed.) *Arkheologiya severnorusskoi derevni X–XIII vv. Srednevekovye poseleniya i mogilniki na Kubenskom ozere. Tom 3.* (The Archaeology of the Rural Areas of Northern Rus AD 900–1300. Medieval Settlements and Burial-grounds in the Kubenskoye lake region. Vol. 3), 30–54 (Russian), 218–220 (English summary). Nauka. Moscow.

CalCurve Comparison, (2004) *A comparison of INTCAL98 / CALPAL 1998 / CALPAL2001 / CALPAL2003 / CalPal2004_Jan / CalPal-Online.* Updated January 2004

Callmer, J. (1989) 'Gegossene Schmuckanhänger mit nordischer Ornamentik', *Birka II: 3. Systematische Analysen der Gräberfunde,* 19–42. Stockholm.

Calnan, C. and Haines, B. (eds) (1991) *Leather: Its composition and changes with time.* Northampton: The Leather Conservation Centre. 1991.

Carrot, J. and Kenward, H. K. (2001) 'Species associations among insect remains from urban archaeological deposits and their significance in reconstructing the past human environment'. *Journal of Archaeological Science* 28, 887–905.

Caseldine, C., Gearey, B., Hatton, J., Reilly, E., Stuijts, I. and Casparie, W. (2001) 'From the wet to the dry: Palaeoecological studies at Derryville, Co. Tipperary, Ireland, Lisheen Archaeological Project', in Raftery, B. and Hickey, J. (eds) *Recent Developments in Wetland Research.* Seandálaíocht: Monograph 2, Department of Archaeology, UCD and WARP Occ. Paper 14, 99–115.

Catalogue (1992) *From Viking to Crusader. The Scandinavians and Europe 800–1200.* Uddevalla. Sweden.

Chernosvitov, P. Y. (1991) *Osvoenie Krainego Severa* (The Settlement of the Extreme North). Moscow.

Chernykh, N. B. (1958) 'Novgorod Textiles from the Nerevsky excavation', *Vestnik Moskovskogo universiteta* (Bulletin of Moscow University), 4.

Chernykh, N. B. (1996) *Dendrokhronologiya i arkheologiya* (Dendro-chronology and archaeology). Moscow.

Choroshkevich, A. L. (1963) *Novgorod's trade in the 14th–15th centuries.* Moscow.

Clapham, A. R., Tutin, T. G. and Warburg, E. F. (1962) *Flora of the British Isles.* Cambridge University Press. Cambridge.

Cockayne, O. (1864) *Leechdoms, Wortcunning and Starcraft of Early England* (Rerum Britannicarum Medii Aevi Scriptores, XXI). Longmans. London.

Costin, C. L. (1991) 'Craft specialization: issues in defining, documenting, and explaining the organisation of production' in Schiffer, M. B. (ed.) *Archaeological Method and Theory* 3, 1–56.

Costin, C. L. and Hagstrum, M. B. (1995) 'Standardization, labor investment, skill, and the organization of ceramic production in Late Prehispanic Highland Peru', *American Antiquity* 60 (4), 619–639.

Cotter, J. P. (1997) *A Twelfth-century pottery kiln at Pound Lane, Canterbury: Evidence for an immigrant potter in the late Norman period,* Canterbury Archaeological Trust Occasional Paper 1. Canterbury.

Crabtree, P. J. (1996) 'Production and Consumption in an early complex society: Animal use in Middle Saxon East Anglia'. *World Archaeology* Vol. 28, 58–75.

Daiga, J. (1962) 'Krasaino metalu kimiskais sastavs Latvija', 6–13, Gs. *Arheologija un Etnografija* IV. Riga.

Dajoz, R. (2000) *Insects and Forests.* Paris. Intercept Ltd.

Davidan, O. I. (1980) 'Bronze-casting in Ladoga', Arkheologicheskii sbornik Gosudarstvennogo Ermitazha (Collection of Archaeological Articles from the State Hermitage Museum) No. 21, 59–67.

Davidson, A. (1999) *The Oxford Companion to Food.* Oxford. Oxford University Press.

Domrachov, P. F. (1923) *Ocherk nauchno-promyslovykh issledovanii oz. Ilmenya i r. Volkhova* (Account of the Scientific and Commercial Research that has been undertaken regarding Lake Ilmen and the River Volkhov). Novgorod.

Domrachov, P. F. (1925) 'Preliminary Results of Hydrological Research carried out at Lake Ilmen in

REFERENCES

1923–1924', *Izvestiya Rossiiskogo Gidrologicheskogo Instituta* (Bulletin of the Russian Hydrological Institute) Issue 13, 53–63. Leningrad.

Domrachov, P. F. (1926) 'A Hydrological Account of Lake Ilmen', *Materialy po issledovaniyu reki Volkhova i ego basseina* (Materials on the Investigation of the River Volkhov and its Basin) Issue X, 343–428. Leningrad.

Dörfler, W., (1990) 'Die Geschichte des Hanfanbaus in Mitteleuropa aufgrund palynologischer Untersuchungen und von Großresten', in *Praehist. Zeitschr.* 65, 218–244.

Doughty, P. S. (ed.) (1973) 'Excavated shoes to 1600', *Transactions of the Museum Assistants Group* 12.

Dovzhenyuk, V. I., Goncharov, V. K. and Yura, R. O. (1966) *Drevnoruske misto Voïn* (Medieval Russian Battle Sites). Kiev.

Dubrovin, G. E. (2007a) 'Water transport', in Brisbane, M. A. and Hather, J. (eds), *Wood Use in Medieval Novgorod*, The Archaeology of Medieval Novgorod Series, 229–262. Oxford. Oxbow.

Dubrovin, G. E. (2007b) 'Land transport', in Brisbane, M. A. and Hather, J. (eds), *Wood Use in Medieval Novgorod*, The Archaeology of Medieval Novgorod Series, 209–228. Oxford. Oxbow.

Dungworth, D. (2000) 'A note on analysis of crucibles and moulds', *Historical Metallurgy* Vol. 34, part 2, 175–92.

Edwards, G. and Mould, Q. (1995) *Guidelines for the care of waterlogged archaeological leather*. English Heritage Scientific & Technical Publications, Guideline No. 4. English Heritage & Archaeological Leather Group. London.

Eerkens, J. W. and Bettinger, R. L. (2001) 'Techniques for assessing standardization in artefact assemblages: can we scale material variability?', *American Antiquity* 66 (3), 493–504.

Egorkov, A. N. and Shchetenko, A. Y. (1999) 'The Composition of Metal used in the Late Bronze-Age Settlement of Tekkem-depe (Southern Turkmenistan)', Arkheometriya ta okhorona storiko-kulturnoi spadshchini (Archaeometry and Protection of the Historical-Cultural Heritage) No. 3. Kiev.

Eikhvald, E. I. (1856) 'An Extract from the Comments made by D.S.S., Merited Professor and Academician Eikhvald during his journey across Lake Ilmen and in the Environs of Staraya Russa'. Novgorod.

Ekosistema ozera Ilmen i ego poimy (The Ecosystem of Lake Ilmen and its Flood-plain) (1997). Nauka. Novgorod.

Eniosova, N. V. (1998) 'Casting Moulds from Gnezdovo', *Istoricheskaya arkheologiya. Traditsii i perspektivy* (Historical Archaeology. Traditions and Prospects), 67–81. Moscow.

Eniosova, N. V. (1999) *Yuvelirnoye proizvodstvo Gnezdova po materialam kurganov i poseleniya* (Jewellery production at Gnezdovo based on materials from burial-mounds and the settlement), Dissertation for a Candidate's degree. Moscow State University.

Eniosova, N. V. and Mitoyan, R. A. (1999) 'Crucibles from the Settlement of Gnezdovo', Arkheologicheskii sbornik. Trudy GIM (Collection of archaeological articles. Proceedings of the State Historical Museum) Issue III, 54–63. Moscow.

Eniosova, N. V., Mitoyan, R. A. and Sarachova, T. G. (2000) 'Brasses of Medieval Novgorod', Novgorod i Novgorodskaya zemlya. Istorya i arkheologiya (Novgorod and the Novgorod Lands. History and Archaeology series). Novgorod.

Eniosova, N. V., Mitoyan, R. A. and Sarachova, T. G. (2003) 'Features of Bronze Alloys from North-western Rus', Arkheologiya i istoriya Pskova i pskovskoi zemli (The Archaeology and History of Pskov and the Pskov Lands). Pskov.

Faradzheva, N. N. (1998) 'Five-walled Log Structures in Medieval Novgorod. Questions as to their Emergence and Evolution based on materials from the Troitsky Excavation', *NNZIA* (Novgorod and the Novgorod Lands. History and Archaeology) Issue 12, 70–82. Novgorod.

Faradzheva, N. N. (1999) 'The Earliest Buildings in the Troitsky XI Excavation', *Novgorod i Novgorodskaya zemlya* (Novgorod and the Novgorod Lands), History and Archaeology series. Issue 13. Novgorod.

REFERENCES

Feinman, G. M. (1999) 'Rethinking our assumptions: economic specialization at the household scale in ancient Ejutla, Oaxaca, Mexico', in Skibo, J. M. and Feinman, G. M. (eds) *Pottery and People: a dynamic interaction*, 81–98. Salt Lake City. University of Utah Press.

Fekhner, M. V. (1959) 'On the question of economic links between villages in medieval Russia' in *Ocherki po istorii russkoi derevni X–XIII vv.* (Studies of the History of Russian Villages in the 10th–13th centuries) in *Trudy GIM* (Proceedings of the State Historical Museum) Issue 33. Moscow.

Fekhner, M. V. (1967) 'Conclusion. Villages of north-eastern and north-western medieval Russia in the 10th–13th centuries according to Archaeological Data" in: *Ocherki po istorii russkoi derevne X–Xiii vv.* (Studies of the History of Russian Villages in the 10th–13th centuries) in *Trudy GIM* (Proceedings of the Russian State Historical Museum) Issue 43. Moscow.

Figes, O. (2002) *Natasha's Dance: A cultural history of Russia.* London. Penguin Books.

Fisher, R. A., Corbet, A. S. and Williams, C. B. (1943) 'The relation between number of species and the number of individuals in a random sample of an animal population', *Journal of Animal Ecology* 12, **42**–58.

Fitter, R., Fitter, A, and Blamey, M. (1993) *Wild Flowers of Britain and Northern Europe*. London. Harper Collins.

Fletcher, G. (1906) *O gosudarstve russkom* (On the Russian State), 3rd ed. A. S. Suvorin. St Petersburg.

Fonyakov, D. I. (1989) 'Shoes and other Leather Items from the excavations at Toropets', *KSIA* (Short Reports from the Institute of Archaeology of the Academy of Sciences of the USSR) Issue 195. Moscow.

Fredskild, B. (1971) 'Makroskopiske planterester fra det aeldste Arhus', *Jysk Arkaeologisk Selskabs Skrifter 9*, 307–318. København.

Friendship Taylor, D. E. (ed.) (1987) *Recent advances in archaeological footwear.* Association of Archaeological Illustrators in association with The Archaeological Leather Group. London.

Frolov, A. A., Mesnyankin, S. V. and Toropov, S. E. (1995) 'Some Findings from archaeological research in the vicinity of the villages of Zaruchevie and Bor, Okulovka District', *Novgorod i Novgorodskaya zemlya* (Novgorod and the Novgorod Lands. History and Archaeology Series) Issue 9, 71–82. Novgorod.

Gaidukov, P. G. (1992) 'A Bibliography for the Archaeology of Novgorod', in Brisbane, M.A. (ed.) *The Archaeology of Novgorod, Russia*, Society for Medieval Archaeology Monograph Series No. 13, 225–234. Lincoln.

Gaidukov, P. G. (1997) 'Topography, stratigraphy and chronology of the Duboshin excavation in Novgorod', in *The Slavic Medieval Town*, Works of the VIth International Congress of Slavic Archaeology, Vol. 2, 59–67. Moscow.

Gaidukov, P. G. (2006) 'Pottery from the Settlements in the Northern Part of the Ilmen Region (8th–10th centuries) and from Medieval Novgorod (10th–15th centuries): Bibliographical Index 1937–2001', in Orton, C. R. (ed.) *The Pottery from Medieval Novgorod and its Region*, 193–203. Oxford. Oxbow.

Gaidukov, P. G. (2007) 'A Bibliography of Novgorod Wood Published between 1933 and 2000', in Brisbane, M. A. and Hather, J. (eds) *Wood Use in Medieval Novgorod*, 418–448. Oxford. Oxbow.

Gaidukov, P. G. and Makarov, N. A. (1993) 'New archaeological materials on the fur trade in medieval Russia' in *Novgorod i Novgorodskaya zemlya. Istoriya i arkheologiya* (Novgorod and the Novgorod Lands. History and Archaeology) Issue 7, 179–188. Novgorod.

Gaimster, D. R. (2001) 'Pelts, Pitch and Pottery: the Archaeology of Hanseatic Trade in Medieval Novgorod', in Brisbane, M. A. and Gaimster, D. (eds) *Novgorod: the archaeology of a Russian Medieval City and its Hinterland.* The British Museum. Occasional Paper Number 141, 67–78. London.

Gaimster, D. R. (2006) 'Pottery imported from the West: Reception and Resistance', in Orton, C. (ed.) *The Pottery from Medieval Novgorod and its Region.* The Archaeology of Medieval Novgorod Series, 135–143. London.

Galibin, V. A., Osvyannikov, O. V. and Ryabinin, E. A. (1986) 'The Nature of Alloys in Bronze Artefacts from the Medieval Finno-Ugrian Regions in the northern parts of Eastern Europe', Finno-ugry i slavyane [Problemy istoriko-kulturnykh kontaktov] (Finno-Ugrians and Slavs [Questions of Historical and Cultural Contacts]). Syktyvkar.

Ganzelewski, M. (2000) 'Archäometallurgische Untersuchungen zur frühen Verhüttung von Raseneisenerzen am Kammberg bei Joldelund, Kreis Nordfriesland', in Haffner, A., Jöns, H. and Reichstein, J. (eds) Frühe Eisengewinnung in Joldelund, Kr. Nordfriesland, Teil 2: Naturwissenschaftliche Untersuchungen zur Metallurgie- und Vegetationsgeschichte, 3–100. Universitätsforschungen zur prähistorischen Archäologie 59.

Geijer, A. (1938) Birka III. Die Textilfunde aus den Gräbern. Uppsala.

Gelfer, A. A. (1927) 'Lake Ilmen and its Flood-plain (A Short Account regarding Physical Geography to accompany the series of Maps)', in Materialy po issledovaniyu reki Volkhova i ego basseina (Materials on the Investigation of the River Volkhov and its Basin). Leningrad.

Gembel, A. V. et al. (1963) Priroda Novgorodskoi oblasti (Nature in the Novgorod Region). Novgorod.

Geraghty, S. (1996) Viking Dublin: Botanical Evidence from Fishamble Street. Medieval Dublin Excavations 1962–1981, Section C, Vol. 2. Dublin. Royal Irish Academy.

Gerbershtein, S. (1988) Zapiski o Moskovii (Notes on Muscovy). Novgorod.

Gläser, M. (1987) 'Keramikchronologie des 12 und 13 Jahrhunderts in Lübeck', Archäologisches Korrespondenzblatt 17, 387–399. Mainz. Von Zabern.

Godwin, G. (1975) History of the British Flora, A Factual Basis for Phytogeography. Cambridge. Cambridge University Press.

Goldina, R. D. (1985) Lomovatovskaya kultura v Verkhnem Prikamie (The Lomovatovskaya Culture in the upper reaches of the Kama River). Irkutsk.

Goldina, R. D. and Kananin, V. A. (1989) Srednevekovye pamyatniki verkhoviev Kamy (Medieval sites in the upper reaches of the Kama River). Sverdlovsk.

Golubeva, L. A. (1973) Ves i slavyane na Belom ozere: X–XIII vv. (The Ves and the Slavs in the Byeloe Ozero Region: 10th–13th centuries). Moscow.

Golubeva, L. A. and Kochkurkina, S. I. (1991) Belozerskaya ves [po materialam poseleniya Krutik: IX–X vv.] (The Ves from the Byeloye Ozero region [based on materials from the Krutik settlement: 9th–10th centuries]. Petrozavodsk.

Gonyanyi, M. I., Katz, M. Y. and Naumov, A. N. (2003) 'Medieval Russian Archaeological Sites of the late 12th century and the third quarter of the 14th century in the region of the mouth of the Nepryadva River at Kulikovo Field', Rus v XIII veke: Drevnosti temnogo vremeni (Russia in the 13th century: Antiquities of a dark period). Moscow.

Goryunova, V. M. (1974) 'New Developments in Research into the Settlement of 'Gorodok' on the River Lovat', KSIA (Short Reports from the Institute of Archaeology) Issue 139, 74–80. Leningrad.

Goryunova, V. M. (1978) 'A Craftsman's Settlement on the River Lovat', Problemy arkheologii (Questions of Archaeology) Issue 2, 140–148. Leningrad.

Goryunova, V. M. (1985) 'Non-ferrous Metal in Gorodok on the River Lovat of the 10th–12th centuries', Novoye v arkheologii Severo-Zapada SSSR (New Research in Archaeology in the North-west of the USSR). Leningrad.

Goryunova, V. M. (1988) 'Craft complexes (10th and early 11th centuries)' in Trudy V Mezhdunarodnogo Kongressa Arkheologov-slavistov (Proceedings of the Vth International Congress of Slavonic Archaeologists) Vol. 2, 51. Kiev.

Goryunova, V. M. (1994) 'Some aspects of the Jeweller's Craft in Early Urban Centres of Northern Rus (crucibles)', Novye istochniki po arkheologii Severo-Zapada (New Sources for the Archaeology of the North-West), 60–73. St Petersburg.

Goryunova, V. M. (2006) 'Early wheel-turned pottery from Ryurik Gorodishche (10th century) and certain questions connected with its synchronisation with the pottery of Novgorod and Staraya

Ladoga', in Orton, C. (ed.) *The Pottery from Medieval Novgorod and its Region*. The Archaeology of Medieval Novgorod Series, 31–51. Oxford. Oxbow Books.

Goubitz, O. (1984) 'The Drawing and Registration of Archaeological Footwear'. *Studies in Conservation* 29, 187–196.

Graham-Campbell, J. (1980) *Viking Artefacts: A Select Catalogue*. London. British Museum.

Grant, A. (1982) 'The use of tooth wear as a guide to the age of domestic ungulates', in Wilson, B., Grigson, C. and Payne, S. (eds), *Ageing and Sexing of Animal Bones from Archaeological Sites*, British Archaeological Reports British Series 109, 91–108. Oxford.

Grenander-Nyberg, G. (1985) 'Die Lederfunde aus der frühgeschichtlichen Wurt Elisenhof', *Studien zur Küstenarchäologie Schleswig-Holsteins* Series A, Elisenhof, Vol. 5. Frankfurt am Main.

Grew, F. and De Neergaard, M. (1988) *Medieval Finds from Excavations in London 2: Shoes and Pattens*. London. Museum of London.

Grichuk, V. P. (1950) *Pyltsevoi analiz* (Pollen Analysis). Nauka. Moscow.

Griffin, K. (1988) 'The plant remains', in Shia, E. (ed.), *De Arkeologiske Utgravninger i Gamlebyen, Oslo, 5 'Mindets Tomt', Sondre Felt*, 15–108. Øvre Ervik. Alvheim and Eide.

Griffin, K. and Sandvik, P. U. (1991) 'Plant remains from medieval Trondheim, Norway', in Hajnalová, E. (ed.), *Palaeoethnobotany and archaeology*, 111–12. Nitra. Acta Interdisciplinaria Archaeologica.

Groenman-van Waateringe, W. (1988) 'Een prehistorische schoen uit Klazienaveen', *Varia bio-archaeologica* 74. Groningen.

Groenman-van Waateringe, W. (1994) 'The menu of Medieval Dutch society', in Hall, A. R. and Kenward, H. K. (eds) *Urban-Rural Connexions: Perspectives from Environmental Archaeology, Symposia of the Association for Environmental Archaeology No. 12*, 147–169. Oxbow Monograph 47. Oxford. Oxbow Books.

Hagstrum, M. B. (1985) 'Measuring prehistoric ceramic craft specialization: a test case in the American Southwest', *Journal of Field Archaeology* 12, 65–75.

Hall, A. R. and Kenward, H. K. (1990) 'Environmental evidence from the Colonia'. *The Archaeology of York*, 14/6. London. CBA.

Hall, A. R. and Kenward, H. K. (1998) 'Disentangling Dung: Pathways to Stable Manure', *Environmental Archaeology* 1, 123–126.

Hall, A. R. and Kenward, H. K. (2003) 'Can we identify biological indicator groups for craft, industry and other activities?', in Murphy, P. and Wiltshire, P. E. J. (eds) *The Environmental Archaeology of Industry*, 114–130. Symposia of the Association for Environmental Archaeology 20. Oxford. Oxbow Books.

Hall, A. R., Kenward, H. K., Williams, D and Greig, J. R. A. (1983) *Environment and Living Conditions at Two Anglo-Scandinavian Sites*, The Archaeology of York, The Past Environment of York 14/4. London. CBA.

Halperin, C. J. (1999) 'Novgorod and the "Novgorodian Land"', in *Cahiers du Monde russe* 40/3, 345–364.

Hamilton-Dyer, S. (2002) 'The Bird Resources of Medieval Novgorod, Russia', in Bochenski, Z. M., Bochenski, Z. and Stewart, J. (eds), Proceedings of the 4th Meeting of the ICAZ Bird Working Group, Krakow, Poland, September, 2001. *Acta zoologica cracoviensia* 45 (special issue), 99–107.

Hamilton-Dyer, S. (in press) 'The fish remains from Minino', in Maltby, M. (ed.), *Animals and Archaeology in Northern Medieval Russia*. The Archaeology of Medieval Novgorod Series. Oxford. Oxbow.

Hansson, A-M. and Dickson, J. H. (1997) 'Plant Remains in Sediment from the Björkö Strait Outside the Black Earth at the Viking Age Town of Birka, Eastern Central Sweden', Pact 52 *Birka Sudies* 4, III.3, 205–215.

Haslam, S. M. (1978) *River Plants, the Macrophytic Vegetation of Water Courses*. Cambridge. Cambridge University Press.

Hellqvist, M. and Lemdahl, G. (1999) 'Local environment at Viking Age and Medieval Novgorod, Russia, reconstructed from insect assemblages', in Hellqvist, M. (ed.) *Urban and rural environments from Iron Age to medieval time in Northern Europe. Evidence from insect remains from South-Eastern Sweden and Novgorod, Russia*, 1–20. Acta Universitatis Upsaliensis. Uppsala.

Hellqvist, M. and Lemdahl, G. (1996) 'Insect Assemblages and Local Environment in the Mediaeval Town of Uppsala', Sweden. *Journal of Archaeological Science* 23, 873–881.

Hellwig, M. (1990) *Paläoethnobotanische Untersuchungen an mittelalterlichen und frühneuzeitlichen Pflanzenresten aus Braunschweig*. Dissertationes Botanicae 156. Stuttgart.

Hickin, N. E. (1968) *The Insect Factor in Wood Decay: An account of wood-boring insects with particular reference to timber indoor*. London. Hutchinson.

Higham, C. F. W. (1967) 'Stock rearing as a cultural factor in prehistoric Europe', *Proceedings of the Prehistoric Society* 33, 84–106.

Hjelmqvist, H. (1983) 'Bröd. Botanisk analys av förhistoriska brödfynd från Löngbro socken, Närke', in Hansson, P. (ed.) *Jägerbacken. Ett gravfält från yngre järnålder*, 17. Örebro.

Hjelmqvist, H. (1984) 'Botanishe Analyse einiger Brote', in *Birka II:I*, 263–290. Systematische Analysen der Gräberfunde, Kungl. Vitterhets Historie och Antikvitets Akademien. Stockholm.

Hjelmqvist, H. (1991) 'Några Tädgårdsväter från Lunds Medeltid' (Some garden plants from Medieval Lund), *Svensk Bot. Tidskr* 85, 225–248.

Hulthén, B. (1974) 'On Documentation of Pottery', *Acta Archaeologica Lundensia Series* in 8° Minore: No. 3. Lund.

Hulthén, B. and Brorsson, T. (2008) 'Viking Age and Early Medieval Pottery in Western Russia', *Archäologisches Korrespondenzblatt*. Jahrgang 37, 2007, Heft 4, 597–610. Römisch-Germanischen Zentralmuseum. Mainz.

Hyvarinen, E., Kouki, J. and Martikainen, P. (2006) 'Fire and green-tree retention in conservation of Red-Listed and rare deadwood-dependent beetles in Finnish boreal forests'. *Conservation Biology* 20, No. 6, 1711–1719.

Ignashina, E. V. (2003) *Drevnerusskoye litsevoye i ornamentalnoye shityo v sobranii Novgorodskogo muzeya* (Medieval Russian Ornamental Embroidery in the collection of the Novgorod State Museum), Catalogue. Novgorod.

Ivanova, M. G. (1998) *Indakar. Drevneudmurtskoye gorodishche IX–XIV vv.* (A medieval Udmurtian city-site. 9th–14th centuries). Izhevsk.

Izyumova, S. A. (1959) 'On the History of the Crafts of Leather-working and Shoe-making in Novgorod the Great', *MIA* (Materials and Research on Archaeology), Vol. II, Issue 65, 199–222. Moscow.

Izyumova, S. A. (1967) 'Leather-working and shoemaking', in Thompson, M. W. (compiler), *Novgorod the Great: Excavations at the Medieval City 1951–1962 directed by A. V. Artsikhovsky and B. A. Kolchin*, 82–84. London. Eyelyn, Adams and MacKay.

Jansson, I. (1984) 'Kleine Rundspangen', *Birka II: 1. Systematische Analysen der Gräberfunde*, 58–74. Stockholm.

Jansson, I. (1999) 'Scandinavian Finds of the 9th and 10th centuries from Ryurik Gorodishche', *Velikii Novgorod v istorii srednevekovoi Evropy* (Novgorod the Great in the History of Medieval Europe), 18–38. Moscow.

Jensen, H. A. (1985) *Catalogue of late and postglacial macrofossils of Spermatophyta from Denmark, Schleswig, Scania, Halland and Blekinge dated 13,000 BP to 1536 AD*. Danm. Geol. Undersog., Ser, A:6.

Jensen, H. A. (1986) 'Seeds and other diasporas in soil samples from Danish town and monastery excavations, dated 700–1536 AD'. *K. Danske Vidensk . Selskab, Biol. Skr. 26.*

Jensen, H. A. (1991) 'The Nordic Countries', in van Zeist., W., Wasylikowa, K. and Behre, K.-E. (eds), *Progress in Old World Palaeoethbotany*, 335–346. Rotterdam.

Jensen, S. (1991) *The Vikings of Ribe*. Ribe.

Johnston, P. and Monk, M. (1998) 'Plant Remains from Troitsky XI, Novgorod: the results from 1998', unpublished interim report for INTAS.

Jones, G., Straker, V. and Davis, A. (1991) 'Early Medieval Plant Use and Ecology', in Vince, A.

G. (ed.) *Aspects of Saxon and Norman London 2: Finds and Environmental Evidence*, London and Middlesex Archaeological Society Special Paper 12, 347–385.

Jönsson, L. and Brorsson, T. (2003) 'Oxie I sydvästra Skåne', in Anglert, M. and Thomasson, J. (eds) *Landskapsarkeologi och tidig medeltid.* Uppåkrastudier 8. 145–224. Lund.

Joosten, I. (2004) *Technology of Early Historical Iron Production in the Netherlands*. Geoarchaeological and Bioarchaeological Studies 2. Amsterdam.

Kadieva, E. K. (1996) 'Wheel-turned pottery from the central areas of the Rostov-Suzdal Lands between the late-10th and early-14th century', Summary of a thesis for Candidate's Degree in Historical Sciences. Moscow.

Kadieva, E. K. (2003) 'Pottery from a Property in the Vladimir End in the late-12th and 13th century (based on materials excavated in 1993–1998 in Section 22)' in *Rus v XIII veke: Drevnosti temnogo vremeni* (Russia in the 13th century: Antiquities from a Dark Age). Moscow.

Kamentskii, I. S., Marshak, B. I. and Sher, Y. A. (1975) *Analiz arkheologicheskikh istochnikov* (Analysis of Archaeological Sources). Moscow.

Kasparov, A. K. (1997) 'Faunal Remains from the city-site of Staraya Ladoga (preliminary conclusions)' in A. N. Kirpichnikov and E. N. Nosov (eds), *Drevnosti Povolkhovya* (Antiquities from the River Volkhov area), 26–31. St Petersburg.

Keiling, H. (1988) *Archäologisches Freilichtmuseum Gross Raden*. Schwerin.

Keiling, H. (1994) 'Forschungsergebnisse von der slawischen Marktsiedlung Parchim (Löddigsee)', in Budesheim, W. (ed.) *Zur slawischen Besiedlung zwischen Elbe und Oder. Beiträge für Wissenschaft und Kultur 1*, 84–99. Neumünster.

Kempke, T. (2001) 'Slawische Keramik', in Lüdtke, H. and Schietzel, K. (eds) *Handbuch zur mittelalterlichen Keramik in Norddeutschland. Band 1: Text*, 209–256. Neumünster. Wachholtz Verlag.

Kenward, H. K. (1975) 'Pitfalls in the environmental interpretation of insect death assemblages'. *Journal of Archaeological Science* 2, 85–94.

Kenward, H. K. (1978) 'The analysis of archaeological insect assemblages: A new approach', in Addyman, P. V. (ed.) *The Archaeology of York: Principles and Methods* 19, 1–61. York. York Archaeological Trust.

Kenward, H. K. (1980) A tested set of techniques for the extraction of plant and animal macrofossils from waterlogged archaeological deposits. *Science and Archaeology* 22, 3–15.

Kenward, H. K. (2005) 'Insects and other invertebrate remains', in Iversen, M., Robinson, D., Hjermind, J. and Christensen, C. (eds) *Viborg Søndersø 1018–1030*, 215–37. Jysk Arkæologisk Selskabs skrifter Vol. 52. Denmark. Århus University Press.

Kenward, H. K. and Allison, E. (1994) 'A preliminary vew of the insect assemblages form the early Chritian rath site at Deer Park Farms, Northern Ireland', in Rackham, D. J. (ed.) *Environment and Economy in Anglo-Saxon England*, 89–107. York. CBA.

Kenward, H. K. and Hall, A. R. (1995) 'Biological evidence from 16–22 Coppergate, York'. *The Archaeology of York: The Environment* 14/7. York. York Archaeological Trust.

Kenward, H. K. and Hall, A. R. (1997) 'Enhancing bioarchaeological interpretation using indicator groups: stable manure as a paradigm', *Journal of Archaeological Science* 24, 663–73.

Kenward, H. K., Engleman, C., Robertson, A., and Large, F. (1986) 'Rapid scanning of urban archaeological deposits for insect remains'. *Circaea* 3, 163–172.

Khoroshev. A. S. (unpub. ms. dated 1998) 'Excavations at Lyudin Quarter, Novgorod: Archaeology corrects an historical tradition'. Novgorod.

Khoroshev, A. S. (2007) 'Household objects', in Brisbane, M. A. and Hather, J. (eds), *Wood Use in Medieval Novgorod*, The Archaeology of Medieval Novgorod Series, 263–277. Oxford. Oxbow.

Khoroshev, A. S. and Sorokin, A. N. (1992) 'Buildings and properties from the Lyudin end of Novgorod', in Brisbane, M. A. (ed.) *The Archaeology of Novgorod, Russia*, 107–159. Lincoln.

Khoroshev, A. S., Sorokin, A. N. and Petrov, M. I. (2001) 'Property layout in medieval Novgorod in the 10th to 15th centuries' in Brisbane, M. A. and Gaimster, D. (eds) *Novgorod: the Archaeology of a Russian Medieval City and its Hinterland*. British Museum Occasional Papers 141, 67–78. London.

Khoroshkevich, A. L. (1963) *Torgovlya Velikogo Novgoroda s Pribaltikoi i Zapadnoi Evropyiv XIV–XV vv.* (Novgorod the Great's Trade with the Baltic Region and Western Europe in the 14th–15th Centuries). Moscow.

Kildyushevskii, V. I. (2006) 'Pskov pottery in the 12th to 16th centuries' in Orton, C. R. (ed.) *The Pottery from Medieval Novgorod and its Region*, 79–115. London. UCL Press.

Kildyushevskii, V. I. and Kurbatov, A. V. (2001) 'Tradition in the Material Culture of the Russian Provinces in the Late Medieval period', *TAS* (Tver Archaeological Collection of articles) Issue 4, Vol. II, 307–315.

Kildyushevskii, V. I. and Kurbatov, A. V. (2002) 'Leather Items from Medieval Oreshek', *Pamyatniki stariny. Kontseptsii. Otkrytiya. Versii* (Monuments of the Past. Conceptions. Discoveries. Interpretations) Vol. 1, 270–280. St Petersburg and Pskov.

Kirpichnikov, A. N. and Eniosova, N. V. (2004) 'Casting Moulds for the Production of Ingots found in Staraya Ladoga', *Vostochnaya Evropa v Srednevekovie* (Eastern Europe in the Medieval Period), 290–296. Moscow.

Kirpichnikov, A. N. and Sarabyanov, V. D. (2003) *Staraya Ladoga: Drevnyaya stolitsa Rusi* (Staraya Ladoga: Medieval Capital of Russia). St Petersburg.

Kiryanov, A. V. (1959) 'A history of Novgorod agriculture from the tenth to the fifteenth centuries', in Artsikhovsky, A. and Kolchin, B. A. (eds), *Reports from the Novgorod Archaeological Expedition*, Vol. 2, MRA, 65, 306–362. Moscow.

Kiryanov, A. V. (1967) 'Agriculture in the Novgorod Province from the tenth to fifteenth centuries', in Thompson, M. V. (compiler) *Novgorod the Great, Excavations at the Medieval City 1951–62*, 87–92. London.

Kiryanova, N. A. (1979) 'On the assortment of the cultivated plants in the Ancient Russia of the 10th to 15th centuries, *Soviet Archaeology* No. 4, 72–85.

Kiryanova, N. A. (1992) *Selskochosjaistwennye kultury i sistemy semledelija w lesnoi sone Ruci XI–XV vv.* Moscow.

Klimanov, V. A., Khotinskii, N. A. and Blagoveshchenskaya, N. V. (1995) 'Climatic Fluctuations over a Historical Period in the centre of the Russian Plain', *Izvestiya RAN* (Bulletins of the Russian Academy of Sciences), Geography series, No. 1.

Knorr, H. A. (1970) Handwerk und Gewerbe, in Herrmann, J. (ed.) *Die Slawen in Deutschland. Ein Handbuch*. Berlin.

Koch, K. (1989) *Die Käfer Mitteleuropas*. Ökologie 1–3. Krefeld. Goecke & Evers.

Kochkurkina, S. I. and Spiridonov, A. M. (1988) 'Settlements of the Medieval Period' in *Poseleniya drevnei Karelii* (Settlements in medieval Karelia). Petrozavodsk.

Kolchin, B. A. (1953) 'Ferrous Metallurgy and Iron-working in Medieval Russia (pre-Mongol period)' *MIA* (Materials and Research on Archaeology), No. 32. Moscow.

Kolchin, B. A. (1959) Zhelezoobrabatyva'uschee remeslo Novgoroda velikovo. *Materiali I Iccledovaniya po Archeologii SSSR*, Vol. 65, 7–119. Moscow.

Kolchin, B. A. (1968) *Arkheologiya SSSR. Svod arkheologicheskikh istochnikov* (Archaeology of the USSR. Summary of Archaeological Sources), Issue E1–55; "Wooden Artefacts" *Novgorodskie drevnosti* (Novgorod Antiquities). Moscow.

Kolchin, B. A. (1975) 'The Emergence of Crafts in Medieval Novgorod', *Doklady na III Kongresse slavyanskoi arkheologii* (Papers delivered at the III Congress of Slavonic Archaeology), 3–137. Moscow.

Kolchin, B. A. (1985a) *Drevnyaya Rus: gorod, zamok, selo* (Medieval Russia: towns, castles and rural settlement), in Rybakov, B. A. (general ed.) The Archaeology of the USSR, Vol. 15. Moscow. Nauka.

Kolchin, B. A. (1985b) 'Handicraft', *Old Russia: Town, Castle, Village*. Archaeology of USSR, 243–97. Moscow.

REFERENCES

Kolchin, B. A., Khoroshev, A. S. and Yanin, V. L. (1981) *Usadba novgorodskogo khudozhnika XII v.* (The Property of a 12th-century Novgorod Artist). Moscow.

Kolchin, B. A. and Yanin, V. L. (1982) 'Fifty Years of Archaeology in Novgorod', *Novgorodskii sbornik: 50 let raskopok* (Novgorod Collection. Fifty Years of Excavations), 53–58. Moscow.

Konetskii, V. Y. (no date) 'Reports for 1985–1988', *Arkhiv IA RAN* (Archive of the Institute of Archaeology of the Russian Academy of Sciences). Leningrad.

Konetskii, V. Y. (1979) 'Report on work carried out within the Novgorod Region', *Arkhiv IA RAN* (Archive of the Institute of Archaeology of the Russian Academy of Sciences), Part 1, No. 7895.

Konetskii, V. Y. (1980) 'Report on research carried out by the Novgorod Museum' *Arkhiv IA RAN* (Archive of the USSR Academy of Sciences), Part 1, No. 8573.

Konetskii, V. Y. (1981) 'Report on research carried out by the Novgorod Museum', *Arkhiv IA RAN* (Archive of the Institute of Archaeology of the Russian Academy of Sciences), Part 1, No. 8514.

Konetskii, V. Y. (1982) 'Report on research carried out by the Novgorod Museum in 1982', *Arkhiv IA Ran* (Archive of the Institute of Archaeology of the Russian Academy of Sciences), Part 1, No. 9067.

Konetskii, V. Y. (1984) 'The Medieval Flat-grave Burial-ground near the village of Dervyanitsy near Novgorod', *Novogorodskii istoricheskii sbornik* (Collection of Novgorod Historical Papers), 2 (12), 39–61. Leningrad. Nauka.

Konetskii, V. Y. (1995) 'Questions and Prospects for Micro-regional Historical-Archaeological Research (taking as an example the lower reaches of the River Kholova)', *Proshloye Novgoroda i Novgorodskoi zemli* (The Past of Novgorod and the Novgorod Lands), 7–9. Novgorod.

Konetskii, V. Y. (2003) 'Novgorod Birch-Bark documents as a source on the history of land-cultivation' in Yanin, V. L. (ed.), *50 years since their discovery, 50 years of their study*. Materials from an International Conference, September 2001. Novgorod.

Konetskii, V. Y. and Nosov, E. N. (1995) 'On the Question of the Formation of Administrative Centres at the end of the Ist millennium in eastern parts of the Novgorod Lands' in *Problemy istorii Severno-Zapada Rusi.. Slavyano-russkie drevnosti* (Questions regarding the History of North-Western Russia, Slavonic and Russian Antiquities) Issue 3, 28–54. St Petersburg.

Königsson L.-K. *et al.* (1997) Economical and cultural changes in the landscape development at Novgorod, Russia. *Tor* 29, 353–382.

Konovalov, A. A. (1969) 'A Study of the Chemical Composition of Copper Alloys from Novgorod', *SA* (Soviet Archaeology) No. 3.

Konovalov, A. A. (1974) 'Tsvetnoi metall (med i eyo splavy) v izdeliyakh Novgoroda X–XV vv', (Non-ferrous Metals [copper and its alloys] in artefacts from Novgorod in the 10th–15th centuries), Resumé of a dissertation for a Candidate's degree.

Konovalov, A. A. (2008) 'Non-ferrous alloys in the Novgorod metalworking of the 10th–15th centuries', in *Non-ferrous and precious metals and their alloys in Medieval Eastern Europe*. Nauka. Moscow.

Körber-Grohne, U. (1964) *Bestimmungsschlüssel für subfossile Juncus-Samen und Gramineen-Früchte. Probleme der Küstenforachung im südlichen Nord-seegebiet* 7. Hildesheim.

Korolyova, E. V. (1996) 'Results of the Spectral Analysis of Jewellery Items from Medieval Pskov', Arkheologicheskoye izuchenie Pskova (The Archaeological Study of Pskov) Issue 3. Pskov.

Korolyova, E. V. (1997) 'The Jeweller's Craft in Medieval Pskov', Trudy VI Mezhdunarodnogo kongressa slavyanskoi arkheologii (Proceedings of the VI International Congress on Slavonic Archaeology) Vol. 2. Moscow.

Korzukhina, G. F. (1965) 'A Find from Ryurik Gorodishche near Novgorod', *KSIA* (Short Reports from the Institute of Archaeology) Issue 104, 45–46. Moscow.

Koval, V. Y. (2006) 'Eastern pottery from the excavations at Novgorod', in Orton, C. (ed.) *The Pottery from Medieval Novgorod and its Region*. The Archaeology of Medieval Novgorod Series, 161–192. Oxford. Oxbow.

Kovalev, R. K. (2002) 'Novgorod Wooden Tallies: general observations' in *Rossiiskaya arkheologiya* (Russian Archaeology) No. 1, 38–51.

Kovalev, R. K. (2003) 'On the question of the origin of the Sorochok counting system based on materials gleaned from Birch-bark Documents' in *Berestyanye gramoty: 50 let otkrytiya i izucheniya* (Birch-bark Documents: 50 Years of Discovery and Study), Materials for an International Conference. Moscow.

Kovalev, R. K. (2007) 'Accounting, Tag and Credit Tallies' in Brisbane, M. A. and Hather, J. (eds) *Wood Use in Medieval Novgorod*, 189–202. Oxford. Oxbow.

Kovalevskii, A. P. (1956) *Kniga Akhmeda Ibn-Fadlana o ego puteshestvii na Volgu v 921–922gg.* (The Book about Akhmed Ibn-Fadlan and his journey down the Volga in 921–922). Kharkov.

Kowalska, A. B. (1999) 'Wczesnosredniowieczne obuwie skorzane z Wolina', *Materialy Zachodniopomorskie*, Vol. XLV, 219–257. Szczecin.

Kroll, H. and Willerding, U. (2004) 'Die Pflanzenfunde von Starigard/Oldenburg', in *Starigard/ Oldenburg. Hauptburg der Slawen in Wagrien 5*. Naturwiss. Beiträge. Offa-Bücher 82, 135–184. Neumünster.

Krzywinski, K., Fjelldal, S. and Soltvedt, E.-C. (1983) 'Recent palaeoethnobotanical work at the medieval excavations at Bryggen, Bergen, Norway', in Proudfoot, B. (ed.), *Site, Environment and Economy*, 145–168. British Archaeological Reports International Series 173. Oxford.

Kublo, E. K. (2007a) 'Footwear production', in Brisbane, M. A. and Hather, J. (eds), *Wood Use in Medieval Novgorod*, The Archaeology of Medieval Novgorod Series, 158–164. Oxford. Oxbow.

Kublo, E. K. (2007b) 'Spinning and weaving', in Brisbane, M. A. and Hather, J. (eds), *Wood Use in Medieval Novgorod*, The Archaeology of Medieval Novgorod Series, 136–158. Oxford. Oxbow.

Kuchkin, A. V. (1984) *Formirovanie gosudarstvennoi territorii Severo-Vostochnoi Rusi v X–XIV vv.* (The Formation of the State Territory of North-Eastern Rus in the 10th–14th centuries). Nauka. Moscow.

Kudryashov, A. V. (1996) 'The Settlement and Burial-ground at Krivets on the Lower Suda River', Drevnosti Russkogo Severa (Antiquities of the Russian North), Issue I. Vologda.

Kudryashov, A. V. (2000) 'The Medieval Settlement of Oktyabrskii Most on the Sheksna River', RA (Russian Archaeology) No. 4.

Kudryashov, A. V. (2002) 'Archaeological sites in the middle reaches of the Sheksna River in the 10th–13th centuries' – Résumé of a Dissertation for a doctorate in Historical Sciences, Moscow.

Kudryashov, A. V. (2003) 'The Settlement and Burial-ground near the Village of Teleshovo on the River Sogozha', *Arkheologiya: istoriya i perspektivy* (Archaeology: History and Prospects), First Inter-regional Conference. A collection of articles. Yaroslavl.

Kurbatov, A. V. (1991) 'Methodological Aspects of the Historical and Archaeological Analysis of Medieval Leather Production', *Problemy khronologii i periodizatsii v arkheologii. Arkheologicheskie izyskaniya* (Questions of Chronology and Periods in Archaeology. Archaeological Investigations) Issue 3, 130–140. Leningrad.

Kurbatov, A. V. (1994) 'A Collection of Leather Items from the 1985 Excavations in the Tver Kremlin for analysis in connection with Advances in Craft Technology in Russian Medieval Towns', *TAS* (Tver Archaeological Collection of articles) Issue I, 189–195.

Kurbatov, A. V. (1997a) 'Ethnographic data used in the reconstruction of Russian medieval leather production', *Pamyatniki stariny. Kontseptsii. Otkrytiya. Versii.* (Monuments of the Past. Conceptions, Discoveries. Interpretations), Vol. 1, 367–373. St Petersburg and Pskov.

Kurbatov, A. V. (1997b) 'Leather production in the towns of the North-west of Russia in the 15th–17th century', Dissertation for a doctorate in History. St Petersburg.

Kurbatov, A. V. (1997c) 'Early Medieval Footwear in the region of the River Volkhov and Questions connected with the Emergence of Russian crafts', *Drevnosti Povolkhovya* (Antiquities of the Volkhov Region), 117–128. St Petersburg.

Kurbatov, A. V. (1997d) 'Leather production in Tver in the 13th, 14th and early-15th century based on evidence from the excavations of the Tver Kremlin in 1993–1996', *Mihkail Tverskoi: lichnost, epokha, nasledie* (Mikhail Tverskoi: the man, his times and his legacy), 127–147. Tver.

Kurbatov, A. V. (1999) 'The Legacy of M. K. Karger: a collection of leather articles from the 1957 excavations in the Upper Castle at Polotsk', *Rannesrednevekovye drevnosti Severnoi Rusi i eyo sosedei* (Early Medieval Antiquities from Northern Rus and its neighbours), 100–117. St Petersburg.

Kurbatov, A. V. (2001a) 'Leather Production in the vocabulary of the Birch-bark Documents', *Staroladozhskii sbornik* (Collection of Staraya Ladoga articles) Issue 4, 10–21. St Petersburg and Staraya Ladoga.

Kurbatov, A. V. (2001b) 'Cultural Influences from the East in the leather industry of Medieval Russia', *Kultury evraziiskikh stepei vtoroi poloviny I tysyacheletiya AD (iz istorii kostyuma)* [The Cultures of the Eurasian Steppes in the second half of the I millennium AD (from the history of costume)], Vol. 2, 197–210. Samara.

Kurbatov, A. V. (2003) 'Leather Articles from Pustozersk', in Yasinski, M. E. and Osvyannikov, O. V. (eds) *Pustozersk. Russkii gorod v* Arktike (Pustozersk. A Russian Town in the Arctic), 225–243. St Petersburg.

Kurbatov, A. V. (2004a) *Kozhevennoye proizvodstvo Tveri XIII–XVvv. (po materialam raskopok Tverskogo Kremlya 1993–1997gg.)* [Leather Production in Tver in the 13th–15th centuries (based on materials from the excavation of the Tver Kremlin 1993–1997)]. St Petersburg.

Kurbatov, A. V. (2004b) 'Leather Articles from the Excavations at Ryurik Gorodishche in 2001–2002', *AV* (Archaeological News) Issue 11, 218–225. St Petersburg.

Kurbatov, A. V. (in press) *Predystoriya russkogo kozhevennogo remesla* (The Prelude to Russian Craft-Production in Leather). Stratum.

Kurts, B. G. (1915) *Sochinenie Kilburgera o russkoi torgovle v tsarstvovanie Alexeya Mikhailovskogo* (The Work by Kilburger on Russian Trade during the reign of Alexei Mikhailovich). Kiev.

Küster, H. (1991) 'Phytosociology and Archaeobotany', in Harris, D. R. and Thomas, K. D. (eds) *Modelling Ecological Change, Perspectives from Neoecology, Palaeoecology and Environmental Archaeology*, 17–26. Papers from the Tenth Anniversary Conference of the Association for Environmental Archaeology held at the Institute of Archaeology, UCL, July 1989. London. Institute of Archaeology, University College London.

Kuza, A. V. (1975) 'The Novgorod Lands', *Drevnerusskie knyazhestva X–XIII* (Medieval Russian Princedoms of the 10th–13th centuries), 144–201. Moscow.

Kuza, *Gorod, Zamok, Selo* (Medieval Russia. Towns, Castles and Villages) in *Arkheologiya SSSR* (Archaeology of the USSR). Moscow.

Labutina, I. K. and Kostyuchuk, L. Y. (1981) 'Birch-bark Documents Nos. 3 and 4 from Pskov', *SA* (Soviet Archaeology) No. 1, 66–78.

Lapshin, V. A. (1989) 'The Archaeological Complex at the village of Gnezdilovo near Suzdal' in *KSIA* (Short Reports from the Institute of Archaeology) Issue 195. Moscow.

Lavrentiev Chronicle (1997) in *Polnoye sobranie russkikh letopisei* (Complete Collection of Russian Chronicles) Vol. 1. Moscow.

Leather Conservation Centre (1982) *The Fibre Structure of Leather*. The Leather Conservation Centre. London.

Lebedeva, E. Y. (2005) 'Cultivated plants of Rostislavl: archaeobotanical materials from d'yakovskoe fort-site and old russian town', in Chernykh, E. N. and Zavyalov, V. I. (eds) *Archaeology and Methods of Natural Sciences*, 159–180. Moscow.

Lekander, B., Bejer-Petersen, B., Kangas, E. and Bakke, A. (1977) 'The distribution of bark beetles in the Nordic Countries'. *Acta Entomologica Fennica* 32, 1–115.

Lempiäinen, T. (1992) *Pflanzliche Makroreste von der wikingerzeitlichen-frühmittelalterlichen Siedlung Varikkoniemi in Hämeenlinna, S. Finnland*. Suomen Museo 99. Helsinki.

Lempiäinen, T. (1995) 'Medieval plant remains from the fortress of Käkisalmi, Karelia, Russia', in *Fennoscandia archaeologica* XII, 83–94.

REFERENCES

Leontiev, A. E. (1996) *Arkheologiya meri. K predystorii Severo-Vostochnoi Rusi* (The Archaeology of the Merya Tribe. Towards a Pre-history of North-Eastern Rus). Moscow.

Leontiev, A. E. (1998) 'Rostov in the Era of Yaroslav the Wise (based on materials from archaeological excavations)' in *Istoricheskaya arkheologiya: traditsii i perspektivy* (Historical Archaeology: traditions and prospects). Moscow.

Lesman, Y. M. (1984) 'Burial Sites in the Novgorod Lands and Novgorod (the question of synchronization)' in *Arkheologicheskie issledovaniya Novgorodskoi Zemli* (Archaeological Research in the Novgorod Lands). Leningrad.

Lesnikov, M. P. (1948) 'Hanseatic trade in fur at the beginning of the 15th century' in *Uchonye zapiski MGPI im. V. P. Potemkina. Kafedra istorii srednikh vekov* (Scholarly Notes from Moscow's Potemkin State Education Institute. Department of Medieval History) Issue 1, Vol. XIII, 61–93. Moscow.

Levashova, V. P. (1959) 'The Processing of Leather, Fur and Other Types of Animal Products', in *Ocherki po istorii russkoi derevni* (Essays on the History of Russian Rural Life), *Trudy GIM* (Proceedings of the State Historical Museum) Issue 33. Moscow.

Levashova, V. P (1966) 'On the attire of the rural population in medieval Russia', *Trudy GIM* (Proceedings of the State Historical Museum) Issue 40, 112–119. Moscow.

Levillain, L. (1900) 'Les Statuts d'Adalhard', *Le Moyen Age*, XIII, 17–386.

Levko, O. N. (1984) *Vitebsk XIV–XVIII vv.* (Vitebsk in the 14th–18th centuries). Minsk.

Likhter, Y. A. and Shchapova, Y. L. (1991) *Gnezdovskie busy. Po materialam raskopok kurganov i poseleniya. Smolensk i Gnezdovo [k istorii drevnerusskogo goroda]* (Beads from Gnezdovo. Based on materials from excavations of burial-mounds and the settlement. Smolensk and Gnezdovo [Towards a History of Medieval Russian Towns]). Moscow.

Linkola, K. (1916) 'Studien über den Einfluβ der Kultur auf die Flora in den Gegenden nördlich vom Ladogasee'. *Acta Societatis pro Fuana et Flora* 45, Nos. 1, 216–221 & 2, 110–118.

Lohmeyer, W., Matuszkiewicz, A., Matuszkiewicz, W., Merker, H., Moore, J. J., Müller, Th., Oberdorfer, E., Poli, E., Seibert, P., Sukopp, H., Trautmann, W., Tüxen, J., Tüxen, R. and Westhoff, V. (1962) 'Contribution à l'unification du système phytosociologique pour l'Europe moyenne et nord-cccidentale', *Melhoramento* 15, 137–51.

Lucht, W. H. (1987) *Die Käfer Mitteleuropas, Katalog*. Krefeld. Goecke & Evers.

Lvova, Z. A. (1968) 'Glass Beads from Staraya Ladoga. Part I' in: *ASGE* (Archaeological Collection [of articles] from the State Hermitage) Issue 10. Leningrad.

Lvova, Z. A. (1970) 'Glass Beads from Staraya Ladoga. Part II' in: *ASGE* (Archaeological Collection [of articles] from the State Hermitage) Issue 12. Leningrad.

Lvova, Z. A. (1977) 'On explanations for the appearance of glass beads in the 10th or early-11th century in the northern regions of Eastern Europe' in *ASGE* (Archaeological Articles from the State Hermitage) Issue 18. Leningrad.

Lvova, Z. A. (2003) 'Glass Beads from Staraya Ladoga' in *Staraya Ladoga: drevnyaya stolitsa Rusi* (Staraya Ladoga: ancient capital of Russia). St Petersburg.

Lynch, A and Paap, N. (1982) 'Untersuchungen an Botanischen Funden aus der Lübecker Innenstadt (ein Vorbericht)', *Lübecker Schriften zur Archäologie und Kulturgeschichte (LSAK)* Bd. 6, 339–360. Bonn.

Lysenko, P. F. (1985) *Otkrytie Berestya* (The Discovery of Birchbark Documents). Minsk.

Makarov, N. A. (1983) 'Bowl-shaped Vessels from Medieval Sites in the Volga-Sheksna area', *KSIA* (Short Reports from the Institute of Archaeology) Issue 175, 18–25.

Makarov, N. A. (1985) 'Decoration of Byeloozero Pottery in the 10th and 11th centuries', *SA* (Soviet Archaeology) No. 2, 79–100.

Makarov, N. A. (1989a) 'Hand-made Pottery from the area east of Lake Onega in the 10th–12th centuries', *KSIA* (Short Reports from the Institute of Archaeology) Issue 199, 83–93.

Makarov, N. A. (1989b) 'Colonization by Novgorod and Rostov-Suzdal in the basins of the Byeloe and Lacha Lakes based on Archaeological Data', *SA* (Soviet Archaeology) No. 4, 86–102.

REFERENCES

Makarov, N. A. (1990) *Naselenie Russkogo Severa v XI–XIII vv.* (The Population of the Russian North in the 11th–13th centuries). Moscow.

Makarov, N. A. (1991) 'Hand-made Pottery from the Krutik Settlement', in Golubeva, L. A. and Kochurkina, S. I. (eds), *Byelozerskaya Ves po materialam poseleniya Krutik IX–X vv.* (The Ves from the Byeloozero Region based on materials from the Krutik settlement in the 9th–10th centuries), 129–165. Petrozavodsk.

Makarov, N. A. (1996) 'The Colonization of the North in the 10th–13th centuries and Certain General Questions concerning Relations between the Centre and Outlying Regions in the History of Medieval Russia', Drevnnosti Russkogo Severa (Antiquities from the Russian North) Issue 1. Vologda.

Makarov, N. A. (1997) *Kolonizatsiya severnykh okrain Drevnei Rusi v XI–XIII vv. Po materialam arkheologicheskikh pamyatnikov na volokakh Byelozeriya I Poonezhya* (The colonization of the northern margins of medieval Russia in the 11th–13th centuries. Based on materials from archaeological sites on the portages of Byeloozero and the Onega River valley). Moscow.

Makarov, N. A. (ed.) (1998) 'Paleobotanitscheskie materaly is beloserja: k istorii stanowlenija semledelija na sewernych okrainach drewnei ruci' in *Rocciiskaja archeologija*. Russian Academy of Science Vol. 1, 175–186.

Makarov, N. A. (2000) 'Medieval rural settlements in norther Russia: Nucleated villages and hamlets in the Beloozero-Kubenskoe region between 900 and 1250 AD' in *Ruralia III* (Conference Ruralia III, Maynooth, Sept. 1999/Památki archejlogické, Suppl. 14), 202–216. Prague.

Makarov, N. A. (ed.) (2001) *Kubenskoye ozero: vzglyad skvoz tysyacheletiya. Shest lyet raskopok Mininskogo arkheologicheskogo kompleksa* (Lake Kubenskoye: a view through the centuries. Six years of excavations at the Minino Archaeological Complex). Vologda.

Makarov, N. A. (2003) 'Putting toponyms from the region beyond the River Volok found in Novgorod birch-bark documents and wooden cylindrical seals on the archaeological map' in *Novgorodskie berestyanye gramoty: 50 let otkrytiya i izucheniya* (Novgorod Birch-bark Documents: 50 years of their Discovery and Study), 149–163. Moscow.

Makarov, N. A. (ed.) (2007) *Arkheologiya severnorusskoi derevni X–XIII vv. Srednevekovye poseleniya i mogilniki na Kubenskom ozere* (The Archaeology of North Russian villages in the 10th–13th centuries. Medieval Settlements and Burial-grounds at Lake Kubenskoye), *Tom 1, Poseleniya i mogilniki* (Vol. 1 Settlements and Burial-grounds). Moscow.

Makarov, N. A. (ed.) (2009) *Arkheologiya severnorusskoi derevni X–XIII vv. Srednevekovye poseleniya i mogilniki na Kubenskom ozere* (The Archaeology of the Rural Areas of Northern Rus AD 900–1300. Medieval Settlements and Burial-grounds in the Kubenskoye lake region), *Tom 3, Paleozkologisheskye uslovya, obshetvo i kultura* (Vol. 3 Environment, society and cultural pattern). Moscow.

Makarov, N. A., Leontiev, A. E., and Shpolyanskii, S. V. (2005) 'Rural Settlements in the central part of the Suzdal Lands at the end of the first millennium and in the first half of the second millennium AD – new materials', in Makarov, N. A. and Chernetsov, A. N. (eds), *Rus v IX–XIV vekakh. Vzaimodeistvie Severa i Yuga* (Russia in the 9th–14th centuries. The Interaction of the North and the South), 196–215. Moscow.

Makarov, N. A. and Zaitseva, I. E. (2003) 'Medieval Burial-grounds in the North of Medieval Russia: new research at Lake Kubenskoye', *Arkheologiya, etnografiya i antropologiya Evrazii* (No. 2, 14), 106–121.

Makarov, N. A. and Zakharov, S. D. (2000) 'The Archaeological study of the villages of North Russia: first findings from excavations at Minino, Kubenskoye Lake: Slavs, Finno-Ugrians, Scandinavians, and Volga Bulgarians' in *Doklady mezhdunarodnogo nauchnogo simpoziuma po voprosam arkheologii i istorii 11–14 maya 1999 g.* (Papers delivered at the International Academic Symposium on Questions of Archaeology and History: May, 1999), 145–161. St Petersburg.

Makarov, N. A. and Zakharov, S. D. (2003) 'On the Eve of Change: rural settlements around Lake

Kubenskoye in the 12th and early-13th centuries', *Rus v XIII veke: drevnosti tyomnogo vremeni* (Russia in the 13th Century: Antiquities of a Dark Age), 131–150. Moscow.

Makarov, N. A., Zakharov, S. D., and Buzhilova, A. P. (2001) *Srednevekovoye rasselenie na Byelom ozere* (Medieval Settlement around Byeloe Ozero). Moscow.

Malygin, P. D., Gaidukov, P. G. and Stepanov, A. M. (2001) 'The Typology and Chronology of Novgorod Pottery in the 10th–15th centuries based on materials from the Troitsky Excavation', *NNZIA* (Novgorod and the Novgorod Lands. History and Archaeology), Issue 15, 82–97. Novgorod.

Maltby, M. (ed.) (in press) *Animals and Archaeology in Northern Medieval Russia*. The Archaeology of Medieval Novgorod Series. Oxford. Oxbow.

Maltby, M. and Hamilton-Dyer, S. (1995) 'Animal Bones from Excavations in Novgorod and its Environs', *NNZIA* (Novgorod and the Novgorod Lands. History and Archaeology) Issue 9, 129–156. Novgorod.

Maltby, M. and Hamilton-Dyer, S. (2001) 'Animal bone studies in Novgorod and its hinterland', in Brisbane, M. A. and Gaimster, D. (eds), *Novgorod: the Archaeology of a Russian Medieval City and its Hinterland*, British Museum Occasional Papers 141, 119–26. London.

Malygin, P. D., Gaidukov, P. G. and Stepanov, A. M. (2006) 'Typology and chronology of Novgorod pottery of the 10th to 15th centuries (based on material from the Troitsky XI excavation)' in Orton, C. R. (ed.) *The Pottery from Medieval Novgorod and its Region*. The Archaeology of Medieval Novgorod Series, 53–77. London.

Malygin, P. D. and Orton, C. (2001) 'Approaches to a Large, Relatively Uniform Assembly of Ceramics', in Brisbane, M. A. and Gaimster, D. (eds) *Novgorod: the archaeology of a Russian Medieval City and its Hinterland*. The British Museum. Occasional Paper Number 141, 59–66. London.

Mandelshtam, M. Y. and Popovichev, B. G. (2000) 'Annotated list of Bark-Beetles (Coleoptera: Scolytidae) of Lennigrad Province'. *Entomological Review* 80 (8), 200–216.

Mangelsdorf, G. (1990) 'Töpfer und Töpferhandwerk an der mecklenburgisch-vorpommerschen Ostseeküste im Spiegel historischer und archäologischer Quellen des späten Mittelalters', *Zeitschrift für Archäologie 24*, 269–277. Berlin. Deutscher Verlag der Wissenschaften.

Marstein, O. (1989) 'Sko og andre gjenstander i laer', *Meddelelser* No. 23. Trondheim.

Maslov, S. P. and Antipina, E. E. (1992) 'On the question of the role of hunting in the economic activities of the population of medieval Russia' in *Ekologicheskie aspekty paleoantropologicheskikh I arkheologicheskikh rekonstruktsii* (Ecological Aspects of Palaeo-anthropological and Archaeological Reconstructions), 179–191. Moscow.

Matiskainen, H. (1984) 'Getreidekörner aus der späteiszeitlichen Siedlungskammer Domargård I in Karjaa, Südfinnland', in *Fennoscandia Archaeologica* I, 43–50.

McClatchie, M. (2003) 'The plant remains', in Cleary, R. M. and Hurley, M. F. (eds), *Cork City Excavations 1984–2000*, 391–413. Cork.

Melin, C., Szafranska, P. A., Bogumila, J. and Barton, K. (2006) 'Biogeographical variation in the population density of wild boar (Sus scrofa) in western Eurasia', Journal of Biogeography 33, 803–811.

Milkov, V. V. (1980) 'Report on the conduct of Archaeological Work in the Novgorod Region by a team from the Novgorod Museum', *Arkhiv IA RAN* (Archive of the Institute of Archaeology of the Russian Academy of Sciences), Part 1, No. 7741.

Milkov, V. V. (1986) 'Report on the conduct of Archaeological Work in the Novgorod Region by a team from the Novgorod Museum', *Arkhiv IA RAN* (Archive of the Institute of Archaeology of the Russian Academy of Sciences), Part 1, No. 11561.

Milkov, V. V. (1988) 'Report on the conduct of the Excavation of Sites near the village of Pleso-Poterpelitsa in the Borovichi District and Reconnaissance in the Novgorod Region', *Arkhiv IA RAN* (Archive of the Institute of Archaeology of the Russian Academy of Sciences), Part 1, No. 14142. Leningrad.

Milkov, V. V. (1989) 'Report on the Conduct of the Excavation of the Archaeological Complex near the village Pleso-Poterpelitsa in the Borovichi District, the burial-ground near the village of Kaplino in the Moshenskii District, the Bor-Zaruchevie complex consisting of burial-mounds, a burial-ground in the Okulovka District and archaeological reconnaissance in the Lyubytinskii, Moshenskii and Khvoininskii Districts', *Arkhiv IA RAN* (Archive of the Institute of Archaeology of the Russian Academy of Sciences), Part 1, No. 13742. Leningrad.

Milkov, V. V. (1990) 'Report on the conduct of Excavations of the destroyed burial-mounds and settlement not yet fully investigated near the village of Zaruchevie in the Okulovka District and of the destroyed burial-mounds near the village of Dregli in the Lyubytinskii District and on the reconnaissance work carried out in the Khvoininskii and Borovichi Districts of the Novgorod Region', *Arkhiv IA RAN* (Archive of the Institute of Archaeology of the Russian Academy of Sciences), Part 1, No. 15069.

Milkov, V. V. (1991) 'Report on the conduct of Archaeological work in 1991 (excavation of the burial-ground near the village of Zaruchevie in the Okulovka District , *sopki* near the villages of Brod-Luchki in the Valdai District, the burial-ground near the village of Dregli in the Lyubytinskii District and reconnaissance work in the Khvoininskii, Borovichi and Kholmskii Districts', *Arkhiv IA RAN* (Archive of the Institute of Archaeology of the Russian Academy of Sciences), Part 1, No. 16655.

Milkov, V. V. (1992) 'Report on the conduct of Excavations of the Burial-ground near the village of Zaruchevie in the Okulovka District and on reconnaissance work in the Borovichi, Khvoininskii and Valdai Distri cts in 1992', *Arkhiv IA RAN* (Archive of the Institute of Archaeology of the Russian Academy of Sciences) Part 1, No. 17667.

Minasyan, R. S. (1994) 'Methods for Manufacturing Ingots for Payment', *Peterburgskii arkheologicheskii vestnik* (Petersburg Archaeological Bulletin) No. 9, 168–172. Saint Petersburg.

Minasyan, R. S. (2002) 'Methods for casting Original and Mass-produced Objects in the territory of Eastern Europe in the Medieval Period', *Ladoga i Severnaya Evraziya ot Baikala do La-Mansha.* (Ladoga and Northern Eurasia from Lake Baikal to the English Channel), 117–123. Saint Petersburg.

Minyaev, N. A. (1965) 'Arctic and Arctic-alpine Elements in the Flora of the North-West of the European part of the USSR', *Arealy rastenii flory SSSR* (Distribution Areas of the Flora of the USSR). Moscow.

Mitchell, G. F. (1987) *Archaeology and Environment in Early Dublin, National Museum of Ireland, Medieval Dublin Excavations 1962–81* Series C, Vol. 1. Dublin. Royal Irish Academy.

Mitchell, G. F. and Dickson, C. A. (1985) 'Plant remains and other items from medieval Drogheda', *Circaea*, 3, 31–37.

Molchanovskii, F. N. (1934) 'Metal-working in the Ukraine in the 12th and 13th centuries based on materials from the fortified settlement of Raikovetsk', *PIDO* No. 4, 86.

Mongait, A. L. (1959) 'Abu Hamid al Garnati and his journey to the Russian Lands in 1150–1153' in *Istoriya SSSR* (History of the USSR) No. 1, 169–181.

Monk, M. A. (1996) 'Preliminary report on samples of plant remains from the 1995 excavations of Troitsky XI', *Novgorod and Novgorod Land: History and Archaeology* 10, 104–110.

Monk, M. A. and Johnston, P. (1999) Plant remains from from Troitsky XI, Novgorod: results from the 1998 season, *Novgorod and Novgorod Land: History and Archaeology* 13, 57–71.

Monk, M. A. and Johnston, P. (2001) 'Plants, people and environment: a report on the macro-plant remains within the deposits from Troitsky Site XI in medieval Novgorod', in Brisbane, M. A. and Gaimster, D. (eds) *Novgorod: the Archaeology of a Russian Medieval City and its Hinterland*, 113–119. London. British Museum Occasional Paper Number 141.

Moskalenko, A. N. (1965) *Gorodishche Titchikha* (The Titchikha City-site), Voronezh.

Müller-Wille, M. (1977) 'Der frühmittelalterliche Schmied im Spiegel skandinavischer Grabfunde', *Frühmittelalterliche Studien* 11, 127–201, Berlin.

Müller-Wille, M., Janin, V. L., Nosov, E. N. and Rybina, E. A. (eds) (2001) *Novgorod; Das mittelalterliche Zentrum und sein Umland im Norden Rußlands*. Neumünster. Wachholtz Verlag.

REFERENCES

Muravyov, N. N. (1828) *Istoricheskie issledovaniya o drevnostyakh Novgoroda* (Historical Research into the Antiquities of Novgorod). St Petersburg.

Nakhlik, A. (1963) 'The Textiles of Novgorod. Attempt at a Technological Analysis', in *Zhilishcha drevnego Novgoroda. Trudy Novgorodskoi arkheologicheskoi ekspeditsii* (The Dwellings of Medieval Novgorod. Proceedings of the Novgorod Archaeological Expedition), Vol. 4, *MIA* (Materials and Research on Archaeology), No. 123, 228–313. Moscow.

Nasonov, A. N. (1951) '"*Russkaya zemlya*" i obrazovanie territorii Drevnerusskogo gosudarstva' ('Rus Lands' and the Formation of the territory of the Medieval Rus State). Moscow.

Naumov, D. V. (1965) 'Results of the Semi-quantitative Spectral Analysis of Bronze Objects in the 10th–14th centuries found in the territory of Latvia', in Mugurevich, E. S. (ed.) *Vostochnaya Latviya i sosednie zemli v X–XIII vv.* (Eastern Latvia and Neighbouring Lands in the 10th–13th centuries). Riga.

Navolokskii istoriko-etnograficheskii muzei (Historical and Ethnographic Museum of Navoloki), (1990) Brochure with catalogue. Novgorod.

Noonan, T. S. (2004) 'The Trade of Volga Bulgaria with Central Asia under the Samanids in the 10th Century' in *Arkheologiya, istoriya, numizmatika, etnografiya Vostochnoi Evropy* (The Archaeology, History, Numismatics and Ethnography of Eastern Europe), 256–313. St Petersburg.

Nørbach, L.C. (ed.) (2003) *Prehistoric and Medieval Direct Iron Smelting in Scandinavia and Europe. Aspects of Technology and Science*. Aarhus. Aarhus University Press.

Nosov, E. N. (1990) *Novgorodskoye (Ryurikovo) Gorodishche* (Ryurik Gorodishche, precursor to Novgorod), Nauka. Leningrad.

Nosov, E. N. (1991) 'Archaeological Sites in the Upper Reaches of the Volkhov and in the Poozerie area near Lake Ilmen at the end of the first millennium AD (list of sites)' in *Materialy po arkheoloogii Novgorodskoi zemli* (Conference proceedings on the Archaeology of the Novgorod Lands in 1990), 5–37. Moscow.

Nosov, E. N. (1992a) *Novgorodskaya zemlya IX–XI vv.* [istoriko-arkheologicheskie ocherki] (The Novgorod Lands in the 9th–11th centuries [Historical and Archaeological Accounts]), Résumé of a dissertation for a doctorate in historical sciences. St Petersburg.

Nosov, E. N. (1992b) 'Rurik Gorodishche and the Settlements to the north of Lake Ilmen' in Brisbane, M. A. (ed.) *The Archaeology of Novgorod, Russia. Recent results from the town and its hinterland*, 5–66. Lincoln.

Nosov, E.N. (2001) 'Ein Herrschaftsgebiet entsteht. Die Vorgeschichte der nördlichen Rus' und Novgorods', in Müller-Wille, M., Janin, V. L, Nosov, E. N. and Rybina, E. A. (eds), *Novgorod. Das mittelalterliche Zentrum und sein Umland im Norden Rußlands*, 13–74. Neumünster.

Nosov, E. N. and Plokhov, A.V. (2002) 'New Research in the Poozerie region near Lake Ilmen', *Ladoga i yeyo sosedi v epokhu srednevekovya* (Ladoga and its neighbours in the Medieval Period), 159–180. St Petersburg.

Nosov, E. N., Goryunova, V. M., and Plokhov, A. V. (2005) *Gorodishche pod Novgorodom i poseleniya Severnogo Priilmenya* (Gorodishche near Novgorod and the Settlements to the North of Lake Ilmen). St Petersburg.

Nosov, E. N. and Musin, A. E. (eds) (2007) *The Origins of the Russian State: To the 30th anniversary of the archaeological studies of Novgorod Ryurik Gorodishche and the Novgorod Oblast Archaeological Expedition*, Proceedings of an international scientific conference, October 2005. St Petersburg.

Novoseltsev, A. P. (2000) 'Eastern Sources on the Eastern Slavs in Medieval Russia in the 6th–9th Centuries' in *Drevneishie gosudarstva Vostochnoi Evropy* (The Earliest States of Eastern Europe), Annual Bulletin for 1998, 264–323. Moscow.

O'Connor, T. P. (2004) 'Animal bones from Anglo-Scandinavian York', in Hall, R. A., Rollason, D. W., Blackburn, M., Parsons, D. N., Fellows-Jensen, G., Hall, A. R., Kenward, H. K., O'Connor, T. P., Tweddle, D., Mainman, A. J. and Rogers, N. S. H. (eds) *Aspects of Anglo-Scandinavian York*, Archaeology of York 8/4, 427–45. CBA.

475

REFERENCES

Onnela, J., Lempiäinen, T. and Luoto, J. (1996) 'Viking Age cereal cultivation in SW Finland: a study of charred grain from Pahamäki in Pahka, Lieto', in *Ann. Bot. Fennici* 33, 237–255.

Orlov, R. S. (1988) 'On the Jewellery Tradition of the Rural Population in the Chernigov Lands in the 10th–12th centuries', *Druga Chernigivska oblasna naukova konferentsiya z istorichnogo kraeznavstva* (Second Chernigov Regional Scientific Conference on Local History), Abstracts. Issue II. Chernigov-Nizhin.

Orlov, S. N. (no date) 'Log-book for 1960', *OPI NGOMZ* (Novgorod State Museum and Historical Reserve), File 10, Inventory 1, Stored Item 47, 22–34. Leningrad.

Orlov, S. N. (no date) 'Inventory of archaeological finds from the rescue excavations in the Borovichi District, Novgorod Region near the village of Pochinnaya Sopka at Ludnik in 1976', *OPI NGOMZ* (Novgorod State Regional Museum and Historical Reserve), File 10, Inventory 1, Storage Unit 72, Kp 38136, 142–143.

Orlov, S. N. (1959) 'Report on Archaeological Reconnaissance and Excavations in the Novgorod Region', *Arkhiv IA RAN* (Archive of the Institute of Archaeology of the Russian Academy of Sciences), Part 1, No. 1864. Leningrad.

Orlov, S. N. (1970) 'Report on the Survey of Archaeological Sites within the territory of the Novgorod Region', *Arkhiv IA RAN* (Archive of the Institute of Archaeology of the Russian Academy of Sciences), Part 1, No. 4532, 19–20. Leningrad.

Orlov, S. N. (1971) 'Report on the 1971 Excavations in the Novgorod Region', *Arkhiv IA RAN* (Archive of the Institute of Archaeology of the Russian Academy of Sciences), Part 1, No. 4517. Leningrad.

Orlov, S. N. (1972) 'Report on Archaeological Excavations in the Territory of the Novgorod Region', *Arkhiv IA RAN* (Archive of the Institute of Archaeology of the Russian Academy of Sciences), Part 1, No. 4861. Leningrad.

Orlov, S. N. (1984) 'Archaeological Investigations within the territory of the Saint Antony Monastery in Novgorod', *Novgorodskii Krai* (Novgorod Region), 152–156.

Orlova, N. I. (1990) 'Diagram for the Floristic Zoning of the Vologda Region', *Botanicheskii zhurnal* (Botany Journal), Vol. 75, No. 9.

Orton, C. R. (1985) 'Diffusion or impedance: obstacles to innovation in medieval ceramics', *Medieval Ceramics* 9, 21–34.

Orton, C. R. (2002) 'Never under-estimate the power of a model', in Burenhult, G. (ed.) *Archaeological Informatics: Pushing the Envelope. CAA2001 Computer Applications and Quantitative Methods in Archaeology* BAR Int Ser 1016 (2002) 495–9.

Orton, C. R. (2006) 'Handling large urban assemblages and their statistics' in Orton, C. R. (ed.) *The Pottery from Medieval Novgorod and its Region*, 117–126. London.

Orton, C., Reynolds, A. and Hather, J. (1999) 'Medieval Novgorod: epitome of early urban life in northern Europe', *Archaeology International* 1998/99, 31–38. London.

Osborne, P. J. (1971) 'An insect fauna from the Roman site at Alcester, Warickshire'. *Britannia* 2, 156–165.

Oyateva, E. I. (1962) 'Footwear and other Leather Items from Medieval Pskov', *Arkheologicheskii sbornik Gosudarstvennogo Ermitazha* (Archaeological Articles from the State Hermitage Museum) Issue 4. Leningrad.

Oyateva, E. I. (1973) 'On Methods for the Study of Medieval Leather Footwear', *Arkheologicheskii sbornik Gosudarstvennogo Ermitazha* (Archaeological Articles from the State Hermitage Museum) Issue 15. Leningrad.

Oyateva, E. I. (1973a) 'Leather Footwear from Byeloozero' in Golubeva, L. A. (ed.), *Ves i slavyane na Byelom ozere* (The Wes and the Slavs at Byeloozero in the 10th–13th centuries). Moscow.

Ozeretskovskii, N. Y. (1812) *Puteshestvie akademika N. Ozeretskovskogo po ozeram Ladozhskomu, Onezhskomu i vokrug Ilmenya* (Journey undertaken by Academic N. Ozeretskovskii across Lake Ladoga, Lake Onega and round Lake Ilmen). St Petersburg.

Peacock, D. P. S. (1982) *Pottery in the Roman World: an Ethnoarchaeological Approach*. London. Longmans.

Péhaut, Y. (2000) 'The invasion of foreign foods', in Flandrin, J.-L., Montanari, M. and Sonnenfeld, A. (eds) *Food: A culinary history from Antiquity to the Present* (English edition), 457–470. London. Penguin Books.

Peregrine, P. (1991) 'Some political aspects of craft specialization', *World Archaeology* 23 (1), 1–11.

Petrova, L. I. (1999) 'On the Methods used for the Modelling of the Palaeo-relief of a historical territory: an attempt to construct a model for the palaeo-relief of Novgorod the Great', Novgorod i Novgorodskaya zemlya. Istoriya i arlkheologiya (Novgorod and the Novgorod Lands. History and Archaeology series) Issue 13. Novgorod.

Pistsovye knigi Russkogo Severa. Katalog pistsovykh knig Russkogo gosudarstva (Land Registers from the Russian North. Catalogue of the Land Registers of the Russian State) (2001). Moscow.

Platonova, N. I., Zheglova, T. A. and Lesman, Y. M. (2007) 'A Medieval Russian Proto-urban Centre in the Peredol Parish (*pogost*)', in *Northern Rus i narody Baltiki* (Northern Rus and the Peoples of the Baltic), 142–194. St Petersburg.

Pleiner, R. (2000) *Iron in Archaeology. The European Bloomery Smelters*. Archeologicky Ustav AVCR. Prague.

Plokhov, A. V. (2002) 'Hand-made Pottery from Ryurik Gorodishche and Novgorod', *Arkheologicheskiye Vesti* (Archaeological News) No. 9, 141–154.

Plokhov, A. V. (2003) 'Unknown Finds from the Excavations of 1940 in Staraya Ladoga', *Novgorod i Novgorodskaya zemlya* (Novgorod and the Novgorod Lands), History and Archaeology series, 292–304. Novgorod.

Plokhov, A. V. (2006) 'Hand-made pottery from Ryurik Gorodishche and Novgorod' in Orton, C. R. (ed.) *The Pottery from Medieval Novgorod and its Region*, 13–30. London. UCL Press.

Pokrovskaya, L. V. (1995) 'Pins with Heads of complex shape', *NNZIA* (Novgorod and the Novgorod Lands, History and Archaeology) Issue 9, 181–191. Novgorod.

Pokrovskaya, L. V. (2000) 'Finno-Ugric Jewellery in Urban Attire in Medieval Novgorod", *NNZIA* (Novgorod and the Novgorod Lands. History and Archaeology) Issue 14, 139–149.

Polcyn, M. (1994) 'Archaeobotanical Evidence for Food Plants in the Poland of the Piasts, 10th–13th Centuries AD', in Dickson, J. H. and Mill, R. R. (eds), Plants and People, Economic Botany in Northern Europe AD 800–1800, *Botanical Journal of Scotland* 46 (4), 533–537.

Poli, E and Tüxen, J. (1960) 'Über Bidenentalia Gesellschaften Europas', *Mitt. flor.-soz. ArbGemein.* NF8, 136–44.

Polonskaya, M. Y. (1991) 'Leather Footwear from Medieval Smolensk', in *Smolensk i Gnezdovo* (Smolensk and Gnezdovo). Moscow.

Polyakova, G. F. (1996) 'Articles made of Non-ferrous and Precious Metals', *Gorod Bolgar: Remeslo metallurgov, kuznetsov, liteishchikov* (The City of the Bulgars: the crafts of metal-workers, blacksmiths and metal-casters). Kazan.

Prasolov, L. I. (1925) 'The Soils of the Flood-meadows along the banks of the Volkhov river and the shore of Lake Ilmen', *Materialy po issledovaniyu reki Volkhova i ego basseina* (Materials on the Investigation of the River Volkhov and its Basin) Issue IV. Leningrad.

Prasolov, L. I. (1927) 'The Soils from the Flood-plains in the area where the River Volkhov and Lake Ilmen are located', *Materialy po issledovaniyu reki Volkhov i ego basseina* (Materials on the Investigation of the River Volkhov and its Basin) Issue XVI. Leningrad.

Prazdnikov, V. V. (1996) 'Excavations at the Vvedenskoye settlement in the Nekrasov District of the Yaroslavl Region' in *Arkheologicheskie otkrytiya 1995* (Archaeological Discoveries for 1995). Moscow.

Prazdnikov, V. V. (1997) 'Excavations at the Vvedenskoye Settlement in the Nekrasov District of the Yaroslavl Region' in *Arkheologicheskie otkrytiya 1996* (Archaeological Discoveries for 1996). Moscow.

REFERENCES

Prazdnikov, V. V. (1999) 'Excavations at the Vvedenskoye Settlement in the Yaroslavl Region' in *Arkheologicheskie otkrytiya 1997* (Archaeological Discoveries for 1997). Moscow.

Problemy stratigrafii chetvertichnykh otlozhenii i kraevye obrazovaniya Vologodskogo regiona (Severo-Zapad Rossii) [Questions pertaining to the stratigraphy of quaternary deposits and marginal formations of the Vologda region (North-West of Russia)] (2000). Moscow.

Prummel, W. (1983) *Excavations at Dorestad 2: Early Medieval Dorestad an Archaeozoological Study*. ROB. Amersfoort.

Rappoport, P. A. (1975) 'Ancient Russian Dwellings', *SAI* (Summary of Archaeological Sources) E1–32. Leningrad.

Ravdonikas, V. I. (1950) 'Staraya Ladoga', in *Sovetskaya Arkheologiya* XII, 1–40.

Razvitie i preobrazovanie geograficheskoi sredy. Po materialam Novgorodskoi oblasti (Development and Transformation of the Geographical Environment. Based on Materials relating to the Novgorod Region) (1975) Issue I.

Razvitie i preobrazovanie geograficheskoi sredy. Po materialam Novgorodskoi oblasti (Development and Transformation of the Geographical Environment. Based on Materials relating to the Novgorod Region) (1975a) Issue 2.

Redwood, J. (1989) *Russian Food of the Peoples of all the Republics*. London. Oldwick Press.

Reed, R. (1972) *Ancient Skins, Parchment and Leathers*. London. Academic Press.

Reilly, E. (1994) *A study of the insect remains from the Viking-Medieval Excavations at Peter St., Waterford*. Unpublished M.Sc. thesis. Sheffield University.

Reilly, E. (1996) 'Chapter 13: The insect fauna (Coleoptera) from the Neolithic Trackways Corlea 9 and 10: the environmental implications', in Raftery, B. (ed.) *Trackway Excavations in the Mountdillon Bogs, Co. Longford, 1985–91*, 403–411. Irish Archaeological Wetlands Unit Transactions 3. Dublin. UCD.

Reilly, E. (2003) 'The contribution of insect remains to an understanding of the environment of Viking-age and medieval Dublin', in Duffy, S. (ed.) *Medieval Dublin IV*, 40–63. Dublin. Four Courts Press.

Reilly, E. (2005) 'Chapter 8: Coleoptera', in Gowen, M., O'Neill, J. and Phillips, M. (eds) *The Lisheen Mine Archaeological Project 1996–8*, 187–209. Dublin. Wordwell Press Ltd.

Reilly, E. and Johnston, P. (2002) 'Methodological Issues: Sampling for seeds and insects at Novgorod, Russia', Paper given at a seminar of the Association for Environmental Archaeologists in University College Dublin.

Repnikov, N. I. (1948) *Staraya Ladoga*. Leningrad.

Resi, H. G. (1979) 'Die Specksteinfunde aus Haithabu', *Berichte über die Ausgrabungen in Haithabu*. Neumünster, Bericht (Report) 14.

Reynolds, A. and Sudds, B. (2001) 'Building construction in Medieval Novgorod: the results of excavations in Troitsky Site XI and XII, 1998', in Brisbane, M. A. and Gaimster, D. (eds) *Novgorod: the Archaeology of a Russian Medieval City and its Hinterland*, 31–46. London. British Museum Occasional Paper Number 141.

Riha, T. (1970) *Readings in Russian Civilization: Russia before Peter the Great 900–1700*. Chicago. University of Chicago Press.

Robinson, M. (1979) 'The biological evidence', in Lambrick, G. and Robinson, M. (eds), *Iron Age and riverside settlements at Farmoor, Oxfordshire*, Oxfordshire Archaeological Unit Report 2, CBA Research Report 32, 77–147.

Robinson, M. (1991) 'The Neolithic and Late Bronze Age insect assemblages', in Needham, S. (ed.) *Excavation and Salvage at Runnymede Bridge, 1978: A Late Bronze Age Waterfront Site*, 277–326. London. British Museum.

Robinson, D. (1987) 'Botanical Remains', in Holdsworth, P. (ed.), *Excavations in the Medieval Burgh of Perth 1979–1981*, Society of Antiquities of Scotland, Monograph Series number 5, 199–209. Edinburgh.

Robinson, D. (1994) 'Plants and Vikings: Everyday Life in Viking Age Denmark', in Dickson, J. H. and Mills, R. R. (eds), Plants and People, Economic Botany in Northern Europe AD 800–1800 Special Issue of Papers, Botanical Society of Scotland, *Botanical Journal of Scotland* 46 (4), 542–551.

Robinson, D. E., Kristensen, H. K and Boldsen, I. (1992) 'Botanical analysis from Viborg Søndersø: a waterlogged urban site from the Viking period'. *Acta Archaeologica* 62, 59–87.

Roesdahl, E. (1982) *Viking Age Denmark*. London. British Museum.

Roesdahl, E. and Nordquist, J. (1971) *De dode fra Fyrkat*, Nationalmuseets Arbejdsmark, 15–32.

Roslund, M. (2001) *Gäster i huset. Kulturell överföring mellan slaver och skandinaver 900 till 1300*. Lund. Vetenskapssocieteten i Lund.

Rozanova, L. S. (1990) 'Svoeobraziye tekhnologii kuznechnovo proizvostva Yuzhnoi i Severnoi Ruci v domongolskii period'. *Problemy Arkeologii Yuzhnoi Ruci.*

Rozanova, L. S. (1997) 'Paths of Development and the Emergence of Tradition in the Craft of the Blacksmith in Medieval Russia' in Terekhova, N. N., Rozanova, L. S., Zavyalov, V. I. and Tolmachova, M. M. (1997) *Ocherki po istorii drevnei zheleznoobrabotki v vostochnoi Evrope* (Essays on the History of Ancient Iron-working in Eastern Europe). Moscow.

Rozanova, L. S. and Zavyalov, V. I. (1990) 'K voprosu o proizvodctvennoi tekhnologii v drevnem Novgorode', *Materiali po Archeologii Novgoroda 1988*. Novgorodskii Archeologicheskaya Ekspeditsiya, 154–186. Moscow.

Rozanova, L. S., Zavyalov, V. I. and Tomacheva, M. M. (1997) *Ocherki ob istorii drevnei zhelezoobrabotki v Vostochnoi Evrope* (Essays on the History of Medieval Iron-working in Eastern Europe), 265–295. Moscow.

Rud, O. A. (2006) 'An attempt to classify the decoration of Novgorod Medieval pottery using material from Troitsky excavation XI (spits 22–10)' in Orton, C. R. (ed.) *The Pottery from Medieval Novgorod and its Region*. The Archaeology of Medieval Novgorod Series, 127–134. London.

Rudnitskii, V. E. and Glinka K. D. (1908) *Pochvenno-geologicheskii ocherk Krestyanskogo uezda* (Description of the Soils and Geology of the Krestyanskii District). Novgorod.

Ryabinin, E. A. (1980) 'A Scandinavian Production Complex of the 8th century in Staraya Ladoga', *Skandinavskii sbornik XXV* (Scandinavian Collection XXV), 161–177. Tallinn.

Ryabinin, E. A. (1985) 'New Discoveries in Staraya Ladoga (findings from the excavations at Zemlyanoye Gorodishche in 1973–1975)', *Srednevekovaya Ladoga. Novye arkheologicheskie otkrytiya i issledovaniya* (Medieval Ladoga. New Archaeological Discoveries and Research). Leningrad.

Ryabinin, E. A. (1997) *Finno-ugorskie plemena v sostave Drevnei Rusi* (Finno-Ugrian Tribes within Medieval Russia). St Petersburg.

Rybina, E. A. (1989) 'Information on Trade found in Birch-bark Documents', *Istoriya i kultura drevnerusskogo goroda* (The History and Culture of Medieval Russian Towns), 74–81. Moscow.

Rybina, E. A. (1992) 'Recent finds from excavations in Novgorod', in Brisbane, M. A. (ed.), *The Archaeology of Novgorod, Russia: recent Results from the Town and its Hinterland*, Society for Medieval Archaeology Monograph 13, 160–192. Lincoln.

Rybina, E. A. (1992) 'Trade Links of Novgorod established through Archaeological Data' in Brisbane, M. A. (ed.) *The Archaeology of Novgorod, Russia*. The Society for Medieval Archaeology. Monograph Series No. 13, 192–205. Lincoln.

Rybina, E. A. (1993) 'On the Contents of Birch-bark Documents containing Geographical Names" in Yanin, V. L. and Zaliznyak, A. A. (eds) *Novgorodskie gramoty na bereste iz raskopok. 1984–1989* (Novgorod Documents on Birch-bark found during Excavations. 1984–1989). Moscow.

Rybina, E. A. (2001a) 'The Birch-Bark Letters: the Domestic Economy of Medieval Novgorod', in Brisbane, M. A. Gamister, D. (eds), *Novgorod: the archaeology of a Russian medieval city and its hinterland*. British Museum Occasional Papers No. 141, 127–131. London.

Rybina, E. A. (2001b) *Torgovlya srednevekovogo Novgoroda. Istoriko-arkheologicheskie ocherki* (Trade in Medieval Novgorod. Historical and Archaeological Essays). Novgorod.

Rybina, E. A. (2007) 'Fishing and hunting', in Brisbane, M. A. and Hather, J (eds), *Wood Use in Medieval Novgorod*, The Archaeology of Medieval Novgorod Series, 124–135. Oxford. Oxbow.

REFERENCES

Rybina, E. A. and Khoroshev, A. S. (compilers and eds) (2002) *Archaeologists of Novgorod the Great: a biographical manual*. Novgorod State Museum and the Centre for the Organisation of Archaeological Research in Novgorod. Novgorod.

Rydh, H. (1936) *Förhistoriska undersökningar på Adelsö*. Vittehets Historie och Antikvitets Akademien. Stockholm.

Rykunov, A. N. and Rykunova, I. I. (1994) 'Excavations at Rybinsk' in *Arkheologicheskie otkrytiya 1993* (Archaeological Discoveries for 1993). Moscow.

Rykunov, A. N. and Rykunova, I. I. (1997) 'Research in the town of Rybinsk' in *Arkheologicheskie otkrytiya 1996* (Archaeological Discoveries for 1996). Moscow.

Ryndina, N. V. (1963) 'The Technology of Production achieved by Novgorod Jewellers in the 10th–15th Centuries', *Novye metody v arkheologii*. MIA (Materials and Research on Archaeology) No. 117, 200–268.

Safarova, I. A. (1998) 'Beads from the Izbrizhie Burial-ground' in *Tver, Tverskaya zemlya i sopredelnye territorii v epokhu srednevekovya* (Tver, the Tver Lands and adjacent territories in the Medieval Period) Issue 3. Tver.

Savinetskii, A. (in press) 'The exploitation of domestic and wild mammals at Minino', in Maltby M. (ed.), *Animals and Archaeology in Northern Medieval Russia*. The Archaeology of Medieval Novgorod Series. Oxford. Oxbow.

Schelvis, J. (2000) 'Remains of mites as indicators of human impact on past environments: dwelling mounds and marine incursions in the Netherlands', in Nicholson, R. and O'Connor, T. P. (eds) *People as Agents of Environment Change*: *Symposia of the Association for Environmental Archaeology No. 16*, 71–75. Oxford. Oxbow Books.

Schia, E. (1977) 'Skomoter og handverk pa lands bygda I middelalder, belyst ved funn I to stavkirker og en gravhaug', *Universitetets Oldsaksamling*. Arbok, 1975/1976. Oslo.

Schia, E. (1994) 'Urban Oslo and its Relation to Rural Production in the Hinterland: an archaeological view', in Hall A. R. and Kenward, H. K. (eds) *Urban-Rural Connexions: Perspectives from Environmental Archaeology, Symposia of the Association for Environmental Archaeology No. 12*, Oxbow Monograph 47. Oxford. Oxbow.

Sedov, V. V. (1960) 'Rural Settlements in the central areas of the Smolensk Lands' in *MIA* (Materials and Research on Archaeology) No. 92. Moscow.

Sedov, V. V. (2002) *Izborsk – protogorod* (Izborsk – a Prototown). Moscow.

Sedova, M. V. (1978) *Yaropolch Zalesskii* (The town of Yaropolch Zalesskii). Moscow.

Sedova, M. V. (1981) *Yuvelirnye izdeliya drevnego Novgoroda: X–XVvv.* (Jewellery items from Medieval Novgorod: 10th–15th centuries). Moscow.

Serbina, K. N. (1951) *Ocherki po sotsialno-ekonomicheskoi istorii russkogo goroda*: *Tikhvinskii posad* (Essays on the Socio-economic History of a Russian Town: Tikhvinskii posad). Moscow.

Serditov, S. N. (1957) 'Inland Waters', *Priroda Vologodskoi oblasti* (Nature of the Vologda Region). Vologda.

Shchapova, Y. L. (1956) 'Glass Beads from Medieval Novgorod' in *MIA* (Materials and Research on Archaeology) No. 55. Moscow.

Shcheglova, O. A. (2002) 'Tin-lead Jewellery of the 8th–10th centuries in the North-west of Eastern Europe', *Ladoga i yeyo sosedi v epokhu srednevekovya* (Ladoga and its neighbours in the Medieval Period), 134–150. St Petersburg.

Shimwell, D.W. (1971) *The Description and Classification of Vegetation*. London.

Shnore, E. D. (1961) 'The Asotskoye city-site' in *Materialy i issledovaniya po arkheologii Latviiskoi SSR* (Materials and Research on the Archaeology of the Latvian SSR). Riga.

Shpolyanskii, S. V. (2003) 'The study of rural settlements consisting of small holdings as exemplified by the 13th-century settlement excavated near the village of Oznobishino near Moscow', *Rus v XIII veke: Drevnosti temnogo vremeni* (Russia in the 13th century: Antiquities of a dark period). Moscow.

REFERENCES

Shver, T. A., Altykis, E. V. and Evteyeva, L. S. (1985) *Klimat Novgoroda* (The Climate of Novgorod). Leningrad.

Šikula, J. (1979) *Grasses: A Concise Guide in Colour*. London. Hamlyn.

Sinopoli, C. (1999) 'Levels of complexity: ceramic variability at Vijayanagara, South India', in Skibo, J. M. and Feinman, G. M. (eds) *Pottery and People: a dynamic interaction*, 115–136. Salt Lake City. University of Utah Press.

Sizov, V. D. (1902) 'The Burial-mounds in the Smolensk Province. The Gnezdovo Burial-mound near Smolensk', *MAP* (Materials on the Archaeology of Russia) No. 28.

Skre, D. (2007) *Kaupang in Skiringssal*, Vol. 1 Norske Oldfinn XXII, Aarhus University Press and the Kaupang Excavation Project, Museum of Cultural History, University of Oslo. Oslo.

Slovar russkogo yazyka XI–XVIIvv. (Dictionary of the Russian Language of the 11th–17th centuries). Moscow.

Smirnova, L. I. (1994) 'Once more on the subject of blunt arrows (On the question of the hunting trade in medieval Novgorod)' in *Novgorod i Novgorodskaya zemlya. Istoriya i arkheologiya* (Novgorod and the Novgorod Lands. History and Archaeology). Novgorod.

Smirnova, L. I. (1998) 'Stages in the Emergence of the craft of Bone-carving in Medieval Novgorod based on materials from the Fedorovsky Excavation in the Plotnitsky End', *NNZIA* Issue 12, 94–109. Novgorod.

Smirnova, L. I. (2001) 'The working of antler, bone and ivory in Novgorod: a study of a craft industry', in Brisbane, M. A. and Gaimster, D (eds), *Novgorod: the Archaeology of a Russian Medieval City and its Hinterland*, British Museum Occasional Papers 141, 79–84. London.

Smirnova, L. I. (2005) *Comb-Making in Medieval Novgorod (950–1450): an Industry in Transition*. British Archaeological Reports International Series 1369. Oxford. Archaeopress.

Smith, D. N., Osborne, P. J. and Barrett, J. (1997) 'Preliminary palaeo-entomological research at the Iron Age sites at Goldcliff, Gwent, Wales 1991–1993', in Asworth, A. C., Buckland, P. C. and Sadler, J. D. (eds) *Quaternary Proceedings* 5, 255–267. Chichester. Wiley.

Smith, R. E. F., and Christian, D. (1984) *Bread and Salt: A social and economic history of food and drink in Russia*. Cambridge. Cambridge University Press.

Sokolov, N. N. (1926) 'A Geo-morphological Description of the Area in which the River Volkhov and Lake Ilmen are situated. Relief, Deposits and Historical Development', *Materialy po issledovaniyu reki Volkhova i ego Basseina* (Materials on the Investigation of the River Volkhov and its Basin) Issue VII. Leningrad.

Spegalskii, Y. P (1972) *Zhilishche Severo-Zapadnoi Rusi IX–XIIIvv.* (Dwellings in North-western Russia in the 11th–13th centuries). Leningrad.

Spiridonov, A. M. (2001) 'Archaeological Cultures of the River Onega Region from the Neolithic to the Medieval Period' in A. S. Gerd and G. S. Lebedev (eds), *Ocherki istoricheskoi geografii. Severo-Zapad Rossii. Slavyane I Finny* (Essays on Historical Geography. North-Western Russia. The Slavs and the Finns). St Petersburg.

Spiridonova, E. A. (1983) 'Palynological description of the Middle Valdai mega-interstadial and its importance for re-establishing the history of the development of the flora and vegetation of the Russian Plain', *Byulleten Komissii po izucheniyu chetvertichnogo perioda* (Bulletin of the Commission for the Study of the Quaternary Period of the Academy of Sciences of the USSR) No. 52.

Stace, C. (1995) *New Flora of the British Isles*. Cambridge. Cambridge University Press.

Stalsberg, A. (2003) 'Links between Norway and Medieval Russia: archaeological finds', *Ladoga i istoki rossiiskoi gosudarstvennosti i kultury* (Ladoga and the Origins of Russian Statehood and Culture), 115–126. St Petersburg.

Steiner, G. M. and Kinzel, H., (1980) 'Unter-suchungen zum Mineralstoffwechsel und zur Okophysiologie von Chenopodium album L.', *Flora* 169, 424–42.

Stepanov, E. S. (1927) 'A Description of the Meadows in the Volkhov-Ilmen Basin from the economic point of view and General Comments about the Extent of the Inundation of the Flood-plain

REFERENCES

of the River Volkhov', *Materialy po issledovaniyu reki Volkhova i ego basseina* (Materials on the Investigation of the River Volkhov and its Basin) Issue XIX. Leningrad.

Stuiver, M., Grootes, P. M. and Braziunas, T. F. (1995) 'The GISP2 δ 18O climate records of the past 16,500 years and the role of the sun, ocean and volcanoes', *Quaternary Research* 44.

Swann, J. (2001) *History of Footwear in Norway, Sweden and Finland*. Stockholm.

Sychevskaya, E. K. (1965) 'Fish of medieval Novgorod', *Soviet Archaeology* 1, 236–256.

Tarabardina, O. A. (2001) 'Dendrochronology in Novgorod: its history and current programme of research', in Brisbane, M. A. and Gaimster, D. (eds), *Novgorod: The Archaeology of a Russian Medieval City and its Hinterland*, 47–50. British Museum Occasional Paper No. 141. London.

Tarabardina, O. A. (2007) 'Building timber in medieval Novgorod based on materials from Troitsky XI and XII excavations', in Brisbane, M. A. and Hather, J. (eds) *Wood Use in Medieval Novgorod*, 106–116. Oxford. Oxbow Books.

Terekhova, N. N., Rozanova, L. S., Zavyalov, V. I. and Tolmachova, M. M. (1997) *Ocherki po istorii drevnei zheleznoobrabotki v vostochnoi Evrope* (Essays on the History of Ancient Iron-working in Eastern Europe). Moscow.

Thompson, M. W. (compiler) (1965) *Novgorod the Great: Excavations at the Medieval City 1951–1962 directed by A. V. Artsikhovsky and B. A. Kolchin*. London.

Tierney, J. and Hannon, M. (1997) Section 22 'Plant Remains', in Hurley, M. F., Scully, O. M. B. and McClutcheon, S. (eds) *Late Viking Age and Medieval Waterford*, 854–893. Waterford.

Tikhonov, N. P. (1931) 'Work on medieval textiles using photo-analysis', *Soobshcheniya GAIMK* (Reports from the State Archive of the Institute for the History of Material Culture), 1.

Toropov, S. E. (no date) 'Report on the rescue-archaeology excavations near the village of Novoye Rydino in the Krestsy District of the Novgorod Region in 1999', *Arkhiv IA RAN* (Archive of the Institute of Archaeology of the Russian Academy of Sciences).

Toropov, S. E. (1997) 'Settlement of the Culture of Long Burial-mounds at Lake Kryukovo', *Proshloye Novgoroda i Novgorodskoi zemli* (The Past of Novgorod and the Novgorod Lands), 12– 15. Novgorod.

Toropov, S. E. and Toropova, E. V. (2000) 'Excavation of a Medieval Russian Settlement near the village of Novoye Rydino in 1999', *Novgorod i Novgorodskaya zemlya* (Novgorod and the Novgorod Lands), 54–56. Novgorod.

Toropova, E. V. (no date) 'Report on rescue-archaeology excavations near the village of Novoye Rydino in the Krestsy District of the Novgorod Region in 1998', *Arkhiv IA RAN* (Archive of the Institute of Archaeology of the Russian Academy of Sciences).

Trudy komissii po proizvodstvu khimiko-tekhnologicheskikh analisov drevnikh bronz (Proceedings of the Commission on the Conduct of Chemical and Technological Analyses of Ancient Bronzes), (1884) Bulletin No. 1, Issue 2. St Petersburg.

Tsalkin, V. I. (1956) 'Material concerning the history of animal husbandry and hunting in medieval Russia', *Materials and Investigations of Archaeology*, USSR 51. Moscow. Academy of Sciences.

Tsalkin, V. I. (1971) 'Some Findings in the Study of Faunal Remains from Excavations in Moscow', *Drevnosti Moskovskogo kremlya* (Antiquities of the Moscow Kremlin), 5–56. Moscow.

Tsinzerling, Y. D. (1932) *Geografiya rastitelnogo pokrova Severo-zapada Evropeiskoi chasti SSSR* (The Geography of the Vegetation Cover of the North-West of the European part of the USSR). Leningrad.

Tsvetkov, V. N. (1963) 'Durability Characteristics of Thread Fastenings for Parts made of Kidskin depending upon the closeness of Stitching', *Nauchnye trudy Moskovskogo Tekhnologicheskogo instituta legkoi promyshlennosti* (Scientific Proceedings of the Moscow Technology Institute for Light Industry) Issue 27, 140–143. Moscow.

Tuganaev, V. V. and Tuganaev, A. V. (2001) 'Gorodishche Idnakar IX–XIII vv. n. e.: Agroekologitscheskij obsor', in *Ischevsk: Udmurtskij institut istorii, jasyka u luteratury*, UrO RAN, 62.

Tutin, T. G., Heywood, V. H., Burges, N. A., Walters, S. M., Webb, D. A. and Moore, D. M. (eds) (1964–1983). *Flora Europaea*, Six Volumes. Cambridge. Cambridge University Press.

REFERENCES

Tüxen, R. (1950) 'Grundriss einer Systematik der nitrophilrn Unkrautgesellschaften in der eurosibirischen Region Europas', *Mitt. flor.-soz. ArbGemein*, NF2, 94–175.

Tyers, P. A. (1996) *Roman Pottery in Britain*. London. Batsford Ltd.

Urieva, A. F. (1991) 'The Stratigaphy and Chronology of Trench V on Sobolev Street, Smolensk' in *Smolensk i Gnezdilovo* (Smolensk and Gnezdilovo).

Uspenskaya, A.V. (1967) 'Pendants worn on the Chest and on Belts', *Ocherki po istorii russkoi derevni X–XIII vv.* (Essays on the History of Russian Villages in the 10th–13th centuries), in Trudy GIM (Proceedings of the State Historical Museum) Issue 43, 88–132.

Valk-Falk, E. (1985) 'Arheoloogilised nahaleiud Tartu vanalinnast', *Tartu: minevik, tanapaev*, 64–70. Tallinn.

Van der Leeuw, S. (1977) 'Towards a study of the economics of pottery making', in van Beek, B. L., Brandt, R. W. and Groenman-van Waateringe, W. (eds) *Ex Horreo*, 68–76. Institute of Pre- and Proto-History, University of Amsterdam, The Netherlands.

van Haaster, H. (1994) 'Plant Resources and Environment in Late Medieval Lübeck', in Hall A. R. and Kenward, H. K. (eds) *Urban-Rural Connexions: Perspectives from Environmental Archaeology, Symposia of the Association for Environmental Archaeology No. 12*, Oxbow Monograph 47, 79–84. Oxford. Oxbow.

van Vuure, C. T. (2005) *Retracing the Aurochs: History, Morphology and Ecology of an Extinct Wild Ox*. Sofia. Pensoft.

Varfolomeeva, T. S. (1993) 'Leather Sheaths of the 11th–15th centuries from excavations in Novgorod', in *Novgorod i Novogorodskaya zemlya* (Novgorod and the Novgorod Lands), History and Archaeological series No. 7, 162–167.

Vasilieva, E. S. (1986) 'The Characteristics of Copper Alloys from the City-sites of Tiversk and Paaso', in Kochkurkina, S. I. (ed.) *Drevnyaya Korela* (Ancient Korelia). Leningrad.

Vaughan, J. G. (1970) *The Structure and Utilization of Oil Seeds*. London. Chapman and Hall.

Veldhuijzen, H. A. (2003) 'Slag Fun' – a new tool for archaeometallurgy: development of an analytical (P)ED-XRF method for iron-rich materials, *Papers from the Institute of Archaeology (PIA)* 14, 102–118.

Vikhrov, V. E. (1959) *Diagnosticheskie priznaki drevesiny* (Diagnostic Features of Timber), *ANSSSR* (Publishing house of the USSR Academy of Sciences). Moscow.

Vittanen, H. and Pulkkinen, M. (1989) *The wood attacking insects in wooden houses of an old open-air museum, Southern Finland*. The International Research Group on Wood Preservation Doc. No. IRG/WP/1409.

Volkov, I. V. (2006) 'Amphorae from Novgorod the Great and comments on the wine trade between Byzantium and Medieval Russia' in Orton, C. (ed.) *The Pottery from Medieval Novgorod and its Region*. The Archaeology of Medieval Novgorod Series, 145–159. London.

Voskresenskii, A. V. and Tikhonov, N. P. (1932) 'The technological study of textiles from burials in burial-mounds at Noion-Ula', *IGAIMK* (Institute of the State Archive for the Institute for the History of Material Culture) XI, Issues 7–9.

Voznesenska, G. O., Nedopako, D. P. and Pankov, S. V. (1996) *Chorna Metalurgiya ta metaloobrovka naselennya skhidnoevropeiskogo lisostepu za dobi rannikh slovyan i Kiivskoi Rusi* (Ancient Metallurgy and Iron-working by the population of the East European wooded steppe in the time of the Early Slavs and Kievan Rus). Kiev.

Vuorela, I. *et al.* (2001) 'Stone Age to recent land-use history at Pegrema, northern Lake Onega, Russian Karelia' in *Vegetation History and Archaeobotany* 10 (3), 121–138.

Walter, H. (1974) 'Die Vegetation Osteuropas, Nord- und Zentralasiens', in *Vegetationsmonographien der einzelnen Großräume* VII, 452. Stuttgart. Fischer-Verlag.

Wasylikowa, K., Cârciumaru, M., Hajnalová, E., Hartyányi., B. P., Pashkevich, G. A. and Yanushevich.,Z. V. (1991) 'East-Central Europe', in van Zeist., W., Wasylikowa, K. and Behre, K-E. (eds) *Progress in Old World Palaeoethbotany, a retrospective view on the occasion of the 20 years of the International Work Group for Palaeoethnobotany*,207– 239. Rotterdam. Balkema.

REFERENCES

Whitehouse, N. J. (2006) 'The Holocene British and Irish ancient forest fossil beetle fauna: implications for forest history, biodiversity and faunal colonization'. *Quaternary Science Reviews* 25, 1755–1789.

Wieserowa, A. (1979) 'Plant Remains from the Early and Late Middle Ages found in the Settlement Layers of the Main Market Square in Cracow', *Acta Palaeobotanica* XX (2), 137–212.

Wigh, B. (2001) 'Animal Husbandry in the Viking Age Town of Birka and its Hinterland', *Birka Studies* Vol. 7, The Birka Project. Stockholm.

Wiklak, H. (1969) 'Polskie obuwie wczesnosredniowieczne z VIII–XIII w,. na podslawie wykopalisk', *Materialy Wczesnosredniowieczne*, Vol. VI. Wroclaw.

Wilson, D. G., and Conolly, A. P. (1978) 'Environmental Studies Part 1. Plant Remains including the evidence for hops', in Fenwick, V. (ed.) *The Graveney Boat: a Tenth-Century Find from Kent*, British Archaeological Reports Series 53, 133–150. Oxford.

Wojtasik, J. (1960) 'Wczesnosredniowieczne wyroby ze skory znalezione na stanowisku 4 w Wolinie', *Materialy Zachodnio- Pomorslie*, Vol. VI, 159–208. Szczecin.

Wyse Jackson, P. and Sheehy Skeffington, M. (1984) *Flora of Inner Dublin*. Dublin. Royal Dublin Society.

Yanin, V. L. (1966) 'Polish Lead from Novgorod', *Soviet Archaeology* 2, 322–28.

Yanin, V. L. (1982) 'An Archaeological Commentary on *Russkaya Pravda*' in *Novgorodskii sbornik. 50 let raskopok Novgoroda* (Novgorod Collection [of articles]. Fifty Years of Excavations at Novgorod), 138–157. Moscow.

Yanin, V. L. (1990) 'The Archaeology of Novgorod' in *Scientific American* Feb. 1990, 72–79.

Yanin, V. L. (1993) 'Novgorod Birch-bark Documents from the St Michael the Archangel Excavation' in *Arkheologicheskie Vesti* (Archaeological News), Issue 2, 114–119. St Petersburg.

Yanin, V. L. (2001) *U istokov novgorodskoi gosudarstvennosti* (The beginnings of Novgorod's Statehood). Novgorod.

Yanin, V. L. (2004) *Srednevekovyj Novgorod. Ocherki arkheologii i istorii* (Medieval Novgorod. Essays on its Archaeology and History). Moscow.

Yanin, V. L. (2007) 'The Wooden Seals of Tribute Collectors' in Brisbane, M. A. and Hather, J. (eds) *Wood Use in Medieval Novgorod*, 203–208. Oxford. Oxbow.

Yanin, V. L. and Kolchin, B. A. (1978) 'Conclusions and Future Prospects for Novgorod Archaeology', *Arkheologicheskoye izuchenie Novgoroda* (The Archaeological Study of Novgorod), 5–56. Moscow.

Yanin, V. L. and Zaliznyak, A. A. (1993) *Novgorodskie gramoty na bereste iz raskopok 1984–1989gg.* (Novgorod Birch-bark Documents from excavations from 1984 to 1989). Moscow.

Yanin, V. L. and Zaliznyak, A. A. (2000) *Novgorodskie gramoty na bereste (iz raskopok 1990–1996gg.)* [Novgorod Birch-bark Documents (from the excavations of 1990–1996)] Vol. X. Moscow.

Yershevskii, B. D. and Konetskii V. Y. (1985) 'About one of the Transit Points on an Ancient Trade Route', *Novoye v arkheologii Severo-Zapada SSSR* (New Developments in the Archaeology of the North West of the USSR). Leningrad.

Yuft (1982) ('Russian Leather' for Footwear Uppers. Technical Specifications). GOST (State Standard) 485–82, published by the State Standards Committee of the USSR.

Yuriev, M. M. (1927) 'Buried Peat Bogs in the Lower Reaches of the River Msta', in Prasolov, L. I., "Soils in the Flood-plains near the River Volkhov and Lake Ilmen" in the series *Materialy po issledovaniyu reki Volkhova i ego basseina* (Materials on the Investigation of the River Volkhov and its Basin) Issue XVI. Leningrad.

Zaitseva, I. E. (2003) 'Alloys of non-ferrous metals at rural sites in the north-eastern margins of medieval Russia' in *Rossiiskaya arkheologiya* (Russian Archaeology) No. 3. Moscow.

Zakharov, S. D. (2001) 'On the question of excavation methods used in medieval settlements' in *KSIA* (Short Reports from the Institute of Archaeology) No. 211.

Zakharov, S. D. (2004) *Drevnerusskii gorod Byeloozero* (The Medieval Russian Town of Byeloozero). Moscow.

REFERENCES

Zaliznyak, A. A. (1995, 1st ed.; 2004, 2nd ed.) *Drevnenovgorodskii dialect* (The Dialect of Medieval Novgorod). Moscow.

Zarina, A. (1988) *Lîbieđu apgerbs 10–13 gs.* (Clothing of the Livonians of the 10–13th centuries). Riga. Zinätne (Science Publications).

Zasurtzev, P. I. (1963) 'Properties and Buildings in Medieval Novgorod', *Materials and research on the archaeology of the USSR* Vol. 123, 5–165. Moscow.

Zavyalov, V. I. (1989) 'O regionalnikh razlichiyakh v vostochnoevropeiskom kuznechnom remesle', *KSIA* 195.

Zavyalov, V. I. (1995) *Drevnenogorodskii dialekt* (The Dialect of Medieval Novgorod). Moscow.

Zavyalov, V. I. (2002) 'The Black-smith's Craft in the Capital and outlying areas (Ryazan and Rostislavl Ryazanskii)', in *Rus v IX–XIV vekakh: vzaimodeistvie Severa i Yuga* (Medieval Russia in the 11th–14th centuries: interaction between North and South), Mat. NK., 32. Moscow.

Zavyalov, V. I., Rozanova, L. S. and Terekhova, N. N. (2001) 'Archaeometallography as a Historical Source (results obtained through the study of Blacksmithing in Russia in 1995–2000)', *KSIA* (Short Reports from the Institute of Archaeology) Issue 212, 3–7. Moscow.

Zharnov, Y. E. (1997) 'A Property from the first third of the 13th century in the Vetchanyi District of Vladimir-on-Klyazma' in Proceedings of the VI International Congress of Slavonic Archaeology (Vol. 2) *Slavyanskii srednevekovyi gorod* (Slavonic Medieval Towns). Moscow.

Zhekulin, V. S. and Nekhaichik, V. P. (1979) *Ozero Ilmen* (Lake Ilmen). Leningrad.

Zhitie svyatogo Stefana, episkopa Permskogo, napisannoye Epifaniem Premudrym (The Life of Saint Stefan, Bishop of Perm, written by Epifanii the Wise), 1987. St Petersburg.

Zykov, A. P. and Koksharov, S. F. (2001) *Drevnii Emder* (Ancient Emder – an historic city in the Urals). Ekaterinburg.

INDEX

Compiled by Sue Vaughan

Illustrations are indicated by page numbers in *italics* or by *illus* where figures are scattered throughout the text.

INDEX

INDEX